Prevention/Early Intervention Learning Community
Supporting educators committed to Wilson Fundations®

C0-BIK-937

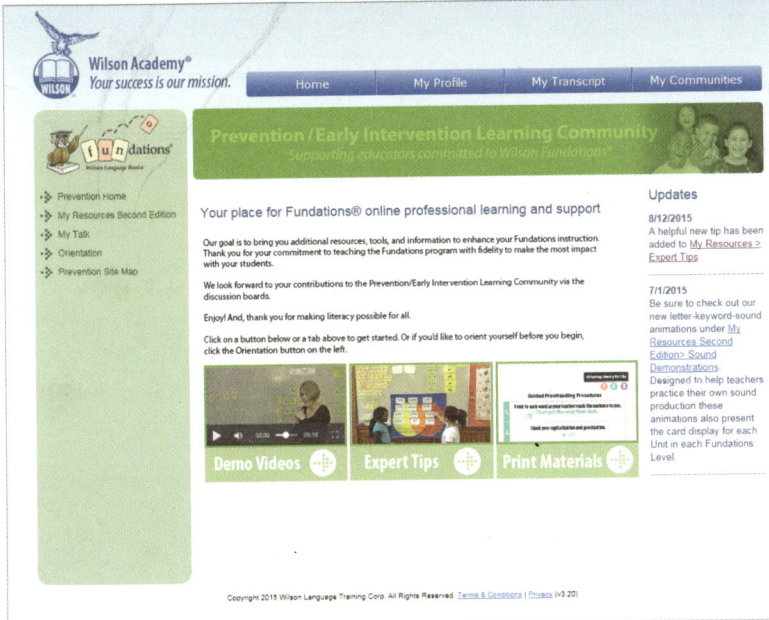

Your companion website and online community of resources and support for teaching Wilson Fundations®

The Prevention/Early Intervention Learning Community (PLC) on Wilson Academy® is a website dedicated to providing teachers with tools that will enhance their Fundations instruction. Teachers who enroll in the PLC will receive immediate support via numerous online resources such as video demonstrations, monthly expert tips and teaching ideas, learning plan templates, printable resources, and a discussion board that facilitates member communication and collaboration.

PLC Membership is included with the purchase of this Teacher's Manual and is renewable annually.

Just a few clicks away...

To begin your membership in the Prevention/Early Intervention Learning Community on Wilson Academy, please go to http://www.wilsonlanguage.com/register and enter this unique access code:

1Z2915T0P0

Teacher's Manual

Level K

SECOND EDITION

Wilson Language Training Corporation

www.wilsonlanguage.com

www.fundations.com

Fundations® Teacher's Manual Level K

Item #F2TMANK

ISBN 978-1-56778-524-1

SECOND EDITION

FUNDATIONS IS PUBLISHED BY:

Wilson Language Training Corporation
47 Old Webster Road
Oxford, MA 01540
United States of America

(800) 899-8454

www.wilsonlanguage.com

Copyright ©2002, 2012 Wilson Language Training Corporation.

All rights reserved. Limited permission is granted to the purchasing party to photocopy select content where such permission is indicated for use with his or her student during their Wilson program only. Otherwise, no part of this work may be reproduced or transmitted in any form or by any means, electronic or mechanical, including photocopying, recording, or by information storage and retrieval system or network, without the express permission in writing from Wilson Language Training Corporation.

Printed in the U.S.A.

September 2015

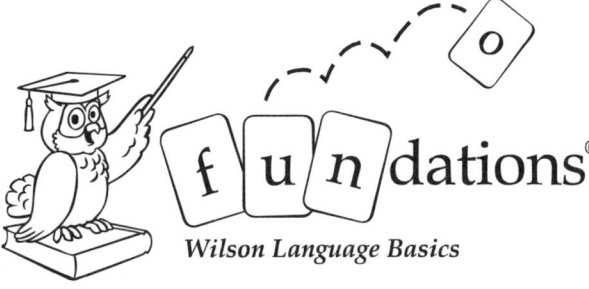

Contents

Author's Note v

Preface vi

Implementing Fundations 1

Fundations Companion Website and Learning Community 2

Skills Taught in Fundations 2

Principles of Instruction 8

Student Success 10

Introducing Fundations 13

References 16

Fundations Scope and Sequence 19

Learning Activity Overview 21

Orientation & Units 49

    Orientation 50

    Unit 1 60

    Unit 2 186

    Unit 3 232

    Unit 4 298

    Unit 5 344

Appendix 411

THIS PAGE IS INTENTIONALLY LEFT BLANK

Author's Note

Dear Friends,

For the past ten years, I have loved visiting Fundations® classrooms and watching all the wonderful **fun** teachers have as they teach their students the foundational skills of reading and writing. It is with great excitement that we at Wilson Language Training introduce *Fundations Second Edition*!

For those of you new to Fundations, it was first published in 2002. Fundations was based on reading research and the Wilson Reading System®- a highly structured and intensive program for challenged readers in grades 2-12 and beyond. Research was clear that all children could benefit from a program specifically designed for young students—with a similar but less intensive approach to decoding, reading, and spelling.

Fundations is now an established part of Wilson's three-tiered approach to successful reading and writing instruction: Fundations, for all K-3 students in the general classroom and as an intervention for those requiring a more targeted intervention; Just Words®, a word-level intervention program for older students; and the Wilson Reading System, an intensive program for our most challenged readers.

As with all of the Wilson® programs, our support for your teaching is central to our mission. This manual includes membership in the Prevention Learning Community (PLC) of Wilson Academy®. Our online support system will help you in the short run while you begin to master the program, and in the long run as you prepare your lessons and guide your students. You can find video demonstrations, monthly expert tips, discussion boards, printable materials, and lesson plan templates…all resources that will strengthen your skills and supplement your teaching.

One major impetus for creating *Fundations Second Edition* was in response to educators' requests for an easy-to-follow teacher manual. Each lesson now begins with that day's learning plan and required teacher and student materials, and includes a detailed description of that day's activities. In updating the manuals, we took the opportunity to add content, such as suggestions about differentiating instruction for advanced and struggling students.

Fundations Second Edition **thoroughly** teaches the Foundational Skills of the Common Core State Standards (CCSS). It also teaches or significantly supports other CCSS standards in reading, writing, speaking, listening, and language. Please refer to the PLC for a detailed "crosswalk."

I would like to express my gratitude to all those who contributed to *Fundations Second Edition*. This includes our talented staff at Wilson, particularly our Fidelity, Development, and Materials teams, as well as the many teachers and trainers who shared their experiences and ideas with us during the past decade. I would also like to acknowledge the many researchers, too numerous to mention, whose contributions to our scientific knowledge of how people learn to read and write have influenced our instruction of children throughout the years.

Our hopes and dreams are, as always, with the students who will benefit from your hard work, dedication and commitment to optimum outcomes through highly proficient instruction. We are here to assist you as we understand it is through our partnership that students will find success. Please contact us whenever you have questions or if you would like to arrange workshops and coaching in your district. For now, I wish you much success and encourage you to go have FUN!

Best wishes,

Barbara Wilson

Barbara A. Wilson, President and Co-Founder, Wilson Language Training

Preface

Building a foundation for reading and writing is key! It is also important to have fun while doing this - Fundations®.

Fundations provides a research-based program that includes instruction and assessments. It provides students with thorough practice and does everything possible to help them become completely proficient rather than just cover a standards-based curriculum. By teaching concepts fully and supporting student learning throughout, student mastery and success is inevitable. The instructional principles for teaching reading and writing have been identified by research and Fundations provides teachers with a program that incorporates these important principles:

- Fundations provides specific measurable student learning objectives which are aligned to the College and Career Ready Standards (Common Core State Standards CCSS).
- Fundations provides an integrated systematic word study, spelling, and handwriting curriculum.
- All parts of a Fundations lesson sequence relate to the Unit objective(s).
- Every lesson naturally builds upon student prior knowledge; and past concepts are reviewed and integrated within the learning activities.
- Every lesson is accessible to all students because the concepts are taught and practiced in multiple ways that target multiple learning styles.
- Fundations lessons provide students with multiple opportunities to meaningfully practice concepts, skills and strategies. Teachers provide both guidance and immediate feedback during practice so that the student's correct responses are reinforced.
- Within a Fundations lesson, teachers can provide challenges to students by differentiating interactions and questions posed to individuals.

The purpose of instruction is learning to both read and write for meaning, understanding and joy. The purpose of Fundations is to provide a truly strong and secure foundation for that reading success, with FUN!

Implementing Fundations

Fundations® can be implemented in one of three ways, depending upon a school district's comprehensive language-arts program.

1. Whole Class General Education Instruction with Targeted Instruction for Children with Difficulties

Fundations provides all students with a foundation for reading and spelling. It is part of the CORE language arts instruction, delivered to all students in general education classrooms 30-35 minutes per day as a supplemental program. Fundations instruction emphasizes phonemic awareness, phonics-word study, high frequency word study, fluency, vocabulary, handwriting, and spelling. Although it includes comprehension strategies, it must be combined with a core/literature-based language-arts program for an integrated and very comprehensive approach to reading and spelling.

In addition to the daily whole class lesson, the students who struggle in general education classrooms (in the lowest 30th percentile) should have additional intervention Fundations targeted instruction in a small group setting for 30 minutes 3-5 times per week.

2. Students In the Lowest 30th Percentile

In schools where Fundations is not used in the general classroom, it is appropriate to select Fundations as an intervention program for students in the lowest 30th percentile. Students should have the Fundations standard lesson (30 minutes daily) **plus** intervention lessons for an additional 30 minutes 3-5 times per week.

3. Students with a Language-Based Learning Disability

Students with a language-based learning disability require explicit, cumulative, and multisensory instruction. For kindergarten and first-grade students, Fundations can be combined with a literature-based program to provide this type of required instruction as an alternative to the district's core language-arts program. Lessons should be scheduled daily and students should receive:

- Fundations standard lessons in small-group settings (30 minutes daily).
- Fundations targeted, intervention lessons in small-group or 1:1 setting (additional 30 minutes daily).
- Literature-based comprehension instruction and other decodable text instruction (30 minutes - 1 hour daily).

For students in grades 2 and 3 who require more intensive instruction, the Wilson Reading System®, taught by a certified Wilson® Instructor, may be more appropriate.

Fundations®

Fundations Companion Website and Learning Community

Membership in the Prevention/Early Intervention Learning Community (PLC) is included with this manual. This companion website provides a multitude of resources to help you with your instruction. It includes documents to download, videos to watch, animations that will assist your understanding of word structure, and a discussion board connecting you to a community with other Fundations teachers across the country.

There are many resources to assist you and your students, including documents for your classroom or professional use. Since it is oftentimes challenging to reproduce a clear image of a page when copying from a book, you can download these resources from the companion website.

 Throughout the manual, you will see this icon indicating items that appear on the companion website.

To begin your membership in the Prevention/Early Intervention Learning Community, please go to http://www.wilsonlanguage.com/register and enter your unique access code that is provided in the front of this Manual. The learning community also provides a link to interactive white board content.

Skills Taught in Fundations

Fundations systematically and comprehensively instructs students in phonemic awareness and word study (both phonetic and high frequency sight words) and contributes greatly to fluency, vocabulary development and the applications of strategies for understanding text. All of these are necessary for the successful development of reading comprehension. Additionally, Fundations sets the foundation for writing with the direct teaching of handwriting, the study of English orthography for spelling, as well as the basic skills for capitalization and punctuation.

Phonological Awareness

Phonological awareness is a broad term. It is the understanding that spoken language consists of parts:

- A spoken sentence consists of separate words. (Word awareness)
- A word consists of separate syllables. (Syllable awareness)
- A syllable consists of separate sounds, or phonemes. (Phoneme awareness)

Phonological awareness can be taught and learned. In Fundations this is done both explicitly and sequentially, beginning with word awareness.

Appropriate explicit instruction benefits all children (Fielding-Barnsley, 1997) but is critical for many students who do not develop sufficient skill without it. This instruction should help children understand that words consist of a sequence of phonemes (Adams, 2001).

Phoneme awareness involves several sequential skills: isolating sounds, identifying sounds, categorizing sounds, blending sounds, segmenting sounds and manipulating them.

By the end of kindergarten, students will blend, segment and manipulate sounds in words containing up to 3 sounds. They will also have emerging skills in blending and segmenting the phonemes in longer words.

Phonemic Awareness and the Alphabetic Principle

English is an alphabetic language – that is – words are constructed in print with letters to represent sounds. In order for children to begin mastery of the written language, they must develop an understanding that words can be divided into smaller segments of sound. The word **map**, for example, has three sounds or phonemes: /m/ /a/ /p/. The coarticulation of phonemes in words makes speech fluent so that these phonemes blend together to form the word **map**. However, children must become aware of the phonemes as separate segments of sound so that they can begin mapping the letters to sounds and sounds to letters for both reading and spelling. This ability to notice, think about and manipulate the individual sounds in words is called phonemic awareness. The mapping of those sounds to the corresponding letters creates the ability to understand the alphabetic principle. To begin reading and writing, children must become aware of the individual phonemes in words and then understand the relationship of those sounds to letters. This development of phonemic awareness and the alphabetic principle is directly and explicitly

Skills Taught in Fundations

taught throughout Fundations®, beginning with the basic letter-sound correspondences (taught in Level K) and progressing to complex ones such as the letters **dge** to represent the sound /j/ (taught in a subsequent level).

Sound Mastery

A phoneme is the smallest unit of sound in our language. It cannot be broken down, or segmented. It takes practice to pronounce a phoneme individually, without adding a sound or distorting the sound. The sounds in a word are often influenced to some degree by the phonemes that precede or follow them. Speech is fluent because the pronunciation of sounds in a word overlap. This is called coarticulation of sounds. To help children learn the alphabetic principle, it is important to help them identify the individual phonemes and to minimize any addition or distortion of a sound. In segmenting the sounds in the word **mat**, the sound of the letter **m** /m/ should not be said /mu/ and the sound of the letter **t** /t/ should not be said /tu/. Thus, segment the sounds /m/ /a/ /t/, not /mu/ /a/ /tu/.

The phonemes /f/, /l/, /m/, /n/, /r/, /s/ and /z/ are all sounds that can be stretched out and they should not present any difficulty in isolating them without adding an extra vowel sound. Other phonemes are more difficult to pronounce without adding an extra vowel sound.

With sounds such as /b/, /d/, /g/, and especially /y/ and /w/ the consonant sound will be vocalized with some vowel sound, but the key will be to minimize this as much as possible.

Forming Key Linkages: Letter Name, Formation and Sound

"An extensive and evolving body of research shows that direct and explicit spelling and handwriting instruction is required if all students are to master the mechanics of reading and writing" (Gentry & Graham, 2010, p. 2). The Fundations program provides this carefully planned and explicit handwriting and spelling instruction. Students need to recognize and reproduce letters quickly and effortlessly. This, combined with the automatic association of the letter to its sound(s) for both reading and spelling will firmly set the foundation for all other literacy instruction. In Fundations, sound instruction is initially linked to letter formation. Students learn the letter name, its formation and its sound simultaneously. This creates an important link and uses motor memory learning to associate letters with their sounds.

This multisensory approach helps to form a tight association with the letter, its sound, and how it is formed. When a student learns how to write a letter, and simultaneously names the letter, and says the sound, it helps them to "bind the visual, motor, and phonological images of the letter together at once" (Adams, 1990, p. 355). These linkages are required for both reading and spelling.

In kindergarten, the sequence of letter and sound introduction is carefully considered based upon this integrated approach.

> It is preferable to teach the reading, spelling and writing of sounds and letters that reflect ease of learning, and frequency in English and similarities of strokes in writing. When planning the presentation of print letters, the following should be considered:
> - Ease of production of the letter
> - Continuity of stroke
> - Similarity of strokes to those letters previously taught
> - Ease of perception and production of the sound associated with the letter
>
> (Wolf, 2011, p. 191)

In Fundations, the sequence of letters presented is based upon these principles for an integrated and multisensory approach. The goal of instruction is to have children retrieve and produce letters automatically as well as link those letters to their associated sounds. This automatic letter production is key for all students, even those children who enter kindergarten with knowledge of the letters and sounds. The practice of consistent formations embeds the letter production into memory which then allows children to develop higher level written composition.

> Handwriting automaticity…is a strong predictor of the quality of composition in normally developing and disabled writers. If letter production is automatic, memory space is freed up for higher level composing processes, such as deciding what to write about, what to say and how to say it. (Berninger, 1999, pp. 20-21)

With both handwriting and spelling automaticity, students can then focus on higher level written communication.

Fundations®

Phonics

Sound mastery is a key component of phonics.

To remember a sound, students also learn a keyword. This word is used consistently. For example, for the letter **b**, the keyword is bat (**b-bat-/b/**). Be sure to say in this sequence so that the keyword helps students remember the sound and the sound is at the end. The / / marks represent the sound associated with the letter.

Another important aspect to sound mastery with Fundations is the teaching of sounds in two directions:

1 Letter to Sound

In this direction, students see the letter and identify the sound.

2 Sound to Letter

In this direction, students hear the sound and identify the corresponding letter(s).

Students do a daily drill of sounds, saying the letter-keywords and sounds. The daily 2-3 minute Sound Drill is the only "drill" aspect of Fundations. This is designed to create fast and efficient neurotransmitting pathways to access sounds. Students have lots of opportunities to practice the sounds with a variety of activities.

Phonics instruction, however, must go beyond this sound-symbol knowledge. In Fundations, students are explicitly taught how to blend sounds into words. This is systematically done following the six basic syllable patterns in English. (See Appendix.)

In Level K, students begin with blending CVC words that start with the continuous consonant sounds **f**, **m**, **n**, **l**, **r** and **s**. These are more easily blended since the consonant sound can be held into the vowel **/mmm/ /a/ /t/ - mat**.

In subsequent levels, students progress systematically from the CVC words to words with 4 then 5 sounds to words with more complex patterns including multisyllabic words and all vowel patterns.

Students learn how to blend words with the finger-tapping procedure used so successfully in the Wilson Reading System®. For example, to blend the sounds **/m/ /a/ /t/** into a word, students are taught how to say each sound as they tap a finger to their thumb. As they say **/m/** they tap their index finger to their thumb, as they say **/a/**, they tap their middle finger to their thumb and as they say **/t/** they tap their ring finger to their thumb. They then say the sounds as they drag their thumb across their fingers, starting with their **/m/**, index finger.

Say /m/ and tap index finger to thumb.

Say /a/ and tap middle finger to thumb.

Say /t/ and tap ring finger to thumb.

Students apply phonics skills to decode words, phrases, sentences and stories that contain the specific letter-sound relationships that they are learning. There are multiple opportunities within lessons for students to apply skills and read words and sentences.

Nonwords (called Nonsense Words in Fundations) help solidify the students' knowledge of word structure and will assist with your evaluation of the application of your students' skills. The nonwords in Fundations have no meaning but they conform to English spelling patterns and rules. To accurately read or spell a nonword that follows the rules of English orthography, a student must apply letter-sound correspondences to determine something that has not been memorized from exposure. You will challenge students with nonwords to help determine their decoding and spelling mastery. Difficulty with nonword repetition is a predictor of reading difficulties. Take note if a student is unable to accurately repeat nonsense words, as this may be an indicator of potential challenges with word level skills.

Vocabulary

In Level K, students develop vocabulary from hearing stories read aloud and classroom discussions. In subsequent levels, they also develop vocabulary from independent reading and explicit instruction, learning a "Word of the Day" selected to correspond with the word structure being studied. The Words of the Day were selected from resources such as Beimiller's list, so that they not only learn word structure, they learn the meaning of words with higher utility. Some multiple mean-

Skills Taught in Fundations

ing words are included. Words are used in sentences and are on flashcards to be reviewed frequently. Students enter the word and a sentence into a vocabulary dictionary, which is a section in their Student Notebooks.

In Level K, students begin dictionary skills by learning the following 4 quadrants of the alphabet:

1	a	b	c	d	e	f
2	g	h	i	j	k	l
3	m	n	o	p	q	r	s
4	t	u	v	w	x	y	z

Note that the letter arrangements on your Standard Sound Card Display and the students' Letter Boards reflect these four quadrants. Help students think of the letters in these quadrants to prepare for their subsequent dictionary work.

There is a strong relationship between a student's vocabulary knowledge and their ability to comprehend what they read. Since students come to school with a wide variance of word knowledge, it is essential that the classroom provides a rich oral language environment as well as access to the incidental and explicit word learning through exposure to many kinds of text. Throughout the primary grades, vocabulary growth can be enhanced by teacher read-alouds accompanied by talk about the text and vocabulary. During Storytime, be sure to stop and discuss the story and specific words as you help students visualize or make a movie. Do this at other times in the day, as this is an important part of your reading instruction.

Also, throughout your Fundations lessons, be sure you think about vocabulary and help with your students' word consciousness, or their awareness of and interest in words (Anderson & Nagy, 1992; Graves & Watts-Taffe, 2002).

Throughout every Fundations® lesson, it is important to weave vocabulary instruction and talk about word meanings. Do this at appropriate times within the Learning Activities. For example, when you make some words for students to decode, select some to discuss meaning. Also, have students use them in a sentence. Teach students how to expand sentences to better reflect the meaning of the selected words. Teachers can question to help expand and then resay the whole sentence. For example, for the word shed, a student might provide the sentence, "Dad likes his shed." Help them by expanding it to say, "Dad likes his shed because it is a good place to store his tools." Explain that the additional words help others know what the word shed means.

Also, introduce or challenge students, as appropriate, to provide multiple meanings. Thus, they might also say, "My dog sheds and now his fur is all over the couch."

High Frequency "Trick" Words

High frequency words are the words that appear most often in print. They are the very common everyday words of the English language (such as "they" and "what"). Some of these words are phonetically regular, but many are irregular, nonphonetic words which do not follow the "system" of the language. These high frequency words, whether phonetic or irregular, are used so commonly in English they need to be recognized and spelled quickly and easily even if their phonemic patterns have not yet been taught. Thus, these words are presented to be memorized.

In Fundations, the high frequency words are called trick words, and these words are not tapped out. The trick words were selected from common high frequency word lists such as Fry, and the American Heritage Word Frequency Book.

In kindergarten, students will learn 27 trick words for quick and automatic recognition. This, combined with their emerging phonetic knowledge, will provide mastery instruction for 25/25 of the most common words and 75% of the first 50 words on both the Fry and American Heritage word frequency lists (Fry & Kress, 2006; Caroll, Davies & Richmond, 1971).

Fluency

Fluent reading is an essential reading skill for comprehension. Automaticity is a term that refers to the quick and automatic recognition of words in isolation. It is necessary for fluency, but it is not sufficient. In addition to automaticity, students need to develop prosody (phrasing) and expression. In Fundations, students have multiple opportunities to develop quick and automatic word recognition. They also work to develop prosody and expression.

To develop fluency and speed of reading, students learn how to read in thought groups, or phrases that connect meaning. Students do both echo and

Fundations®

choral reading of stories to help develop fluency. During echo reading the teacher reads a sentence and students repeat. During choral reading the teacher and students read together. Teachers help students with phrasing by scooping sentences. "A focus on phrasing has substantial potential for delivering positive outcomes across a number of areas related to reading proficiency" (Rasinski, 2006, p.4).

One day, Echo sat on a branch, deep in the forest.

Comprehension

Although Fundations is not a comprehension program, it does provide instruction to help students learn how to think actively while reading and to self-monitor their understanding. This direct instruction includes the development of students' ability to form a visual image or construct a mental picture from words, the ability to imagine a scene and predict subsequent events, and to recall and explain what was in the written text. Mental images aid comprehension and memory by acting as mental pegs onto which the information can be hooked (Sadoski & Paivo, 2001).

Students must be able to hold onto information from one sentence to the next to create cohesion so that they understand and link the events in a story. You will help them do this by stopping and supporting their understanding of the words with gestures, mental imagery and drawing picture notes as needed. This scaffolding of understanding is called Comprehension S.O.S.™ in Wilson® Programs. This stands for Comprehension: Stop-Orient-Support/Scaffold. Comprehension S.O.S. is a teacher-led interactive discussion about written text.

Comprehension S.O.S activities always conclude with retelling. The ability to retell a story or information that has been read is an important skill that should be developed. Retelling confirms and solidifies understanding and helps with the learning of the information. It also helps develop a student's oral language skill.

Initially, students simply retell the sequence of events. As they progress in grades, they retell using paraphrasing and then linking content together to create a cohesive understanding of longer and longer passages. Eventually, beyond the elementary grades, students should retell information by summarizing complex passages emphasizing key points for a particular purpose. The comprehension work that you will do in Fundations will help to set the foundation for these ever-increasing levels of difficulty.

In Fundations, retelling begins in Kindergarten. Students follow gestures and picture notes to assist their oral retell of story events. Beginning in grade one, students also use mental imagery or visualization to help guide their words for retelling. You will also model and assist them with paraphrasing and the retelling of longer and longer segments of a passage or story.

In kindergarten, students begin this direct and explicit instruction to create mental images with listening comprehension. Students learn how to use their working memory to hold several words and sentences in mind and to process, understand and recall them. Oral stories are acted out with Echo and Baby Echo puppets. Students learn to re-tell the stories in their own words. The stories are read with both echo and choral reading.

Students learn how to read with prosody, in meaningful phrases and continue to develop their ability to re-tell stories in detail using their own words.

The understanding of text structures also aids comprehension. Students are introduced to the difference between narrative fiction and informational, non-fiction text. Discussion of narrative text includes:

- Setting and characters
- Major events: What happened first, next, etc.
- What happened in the end and how the characters felt

Students also learn that the key purpose of informational text is to teach or provide information about a specific topic.

Although Fundations includes the above aspects of comprehension, for a comprehensive program, combine Fundations with more formalized instruction and wide-reading experiences.

Handwriting, Spelling, and Punctuation: Foundations for Written Composition

Handwriting and spelling difficulties in later grades affect the composition quality and amount

Skills Taught in Fundations

that children write. As noted previously, research clearly indicates that handwriting and spelling skills are required for more advanced writing success (Gentry & Graham, 2010).

Automaticity of Handwriting

Automaticity and fluency in handwriting is a strong predictor of the quantity and quality of written composition. This is true for both typically developing writers and writers with disabilities (Blalock, 1985).

Fundations provides carefully planned and explicit handwriting instruction with the goal that all children will develop legible and fluent handwriting. This begins with automaticity of consistent letter formation which requires substantial repeated practice. To write a letter, a child must identify the letter by name, memorize the formation of it, and quickly retrieve this form from memory (Edwards, 2003). Fundations provides direct instruction so that teachers have the language and tools to instruct students in size, shape, spacing, slant and stroke for the formation of letters.

The Wilson Font provides a basic manuscript form of print. Often students come to kindergarten or Grade 1 with an ability to write uppercase letters of the alphabet. To begin reading and spelling instruction, however, lowercase letter knowledge is key. Rather than reinforce or teach the uppercase letters first, Fundations begins with lowercase. Lowercase letters are taught and mastered before the uppercase letters are introduced. First and foremost, the lowercase letters are necessary for students to begin reading words. Additionally, uppercase letters are used in only about 2% of writing. (While working with lowercase letters, you can teach individual students the capital letters needed for their names.)

Letters are practiced with sky writing. Gross motor memory helps students learn the letter formation. In kindergarten, sky writing and tracing are strongly emphasized throughout the first half of the year. Students master letter formation with verbal cues, repetition, sky writing, tracing and writing practice (all described in the learning activities).

In Fundations®, lines are given the following names:

Consistent verbalizations direct students' letter formation. For example, for the manuscript letter **l**, you will say "Point to the sky line. Go down to the grass line and stop." "Students appear to recall the sequence of movements of a letter better if the instructor verbalizes consistent, precise directions for writing each letter shape" (Wolf, 2011, p.192).

Students are provided **ample opportunity to practice** these skills with instruction embedded in various activities. When implemented with fidelity and as part of the Fundations program, students are practicing letter formation **daily** through explicit letter formation instruction and dictation activities. For those letters that have been directly taught, be sure to hold students accountable for proper letter formation during dictation and throughout the day.

It is also important to establish good writing habits. You will teach pencil grip and writing position. The students should write with their chairs pulled in and their feet on the floor. If a child can not reach the floor, you might put a box under the table for them. The student's elbow should be on the table with their "free" hand holding the paper in place.

 On the PLC, you will find the following page, called 1-2-3 Right / Let's Write. You can post this in the classroom to guide students.

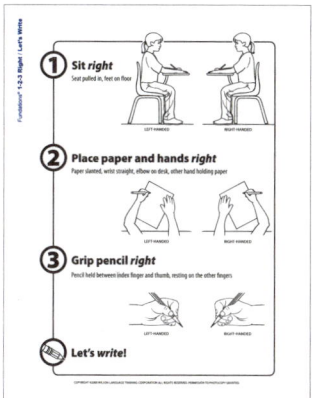

The question is often asked, "Why teach handwriting in this age of technology?" Handwriting is needed despite the increased reliance on digital text. First and foremost, it is an important com-

Fundations®

munication skill that reinforces both reading and spelling. Furthermore, fast legible handwriting improves note taking and test performance (Peverly et al., 2007), and illegible or poor handwriting can reduce the grade that teachers give students even when the content is the same (Graham & Weintraub, 1996). Most high-stakes tests include timed handwritten essays. Fluency and legibility of writing make a significant difference on this written performance. Lastly, students with fluent and legible handwriting are likely to be more confident about their academic ability overall and be more willing to improve the quantity and quality of their writing as they progress throughout the grades.

Spelling

The accurate visual representation of both letters and words is orthography. The ability to picture and store this visual representation provides the foundation for reading and spelling.

Students learn to segment and spell words in correspondence to decoding patterns. They learn to segment and associate letters with sounds rather than memorize these words. Spelling is generally more difficult than reading because with spelling, students have no visual cues and must determine the correct letters in sequence. Thus, although decoding and spelling instruction in Fundations will follow the same sequence, for some students, spelling skill may lag behind.

Punctuation and Capitalization

Students also systematically learn punctuation, capitalization and proofreading skills. This begins, along with print awareness in kindergarten and is reinforced throughout all levels.

You will teach students the beginning concepts of sentence structure. Manipulatives (Sentence Frames) are used to assist students with the understanding that words make up sentences. They will learn that sentences begin with a capital or uppercase letter and end with punctuation. In Level 1, students also learn that names of people and places as well as dates begin with uppercase letters. You will teach them the use of a period, a question mark and an exclamation mark for ending punctuation. Sentence Frames are used to represent this:

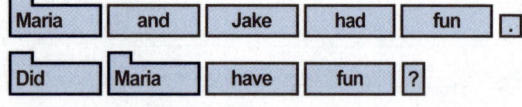

Principles of Instruction

The principles of instruction are key to the success of Fundations®. These principles, also basic to the Wilson Reading System®, are identified by research as effective teaching principles.

Explicit Instruction: Explaining Content Clearly

Instruction is visible and explicit. Unlike many programs where students work independently on phonics worksheets, all Fundations instruction is interactive.

The teacher directly teaches all skills to students through modeling and active learning. The owl puppets, named Echo and Baby Echo, are used to encourage students to model the teacher and repeat sounds and echo read sentences.

The teacher provides classroom demonstrations by using manipulatives to accompany explanation of word and sentence structure.

Systematic Instruction (Sequential and Cumulative)

Fundations presents all skills in a systematic and sequential manner in four levels: Level K, Level 1, Level 2 and Level 3. Due to the sequential aspect of the program, students ideally complete each Level. If Fundations is used with all students as part of the core/literature-based language arts program, Levels 1 and 2 can be presented without completing prior levels when just getting underway. Students must complete Level 2, however, in order to begin Level 3. Be sure to consult with Wilson Language Training for guidance.

Principles of Instruction

The four levels of Fundations will most often correspond to the students' grade level (e.g. Level 1 for grade 1 students). However, the program can also be used sequentially with struggling students in other grades. For example, if introducing Fundations to a second grade group of struggling students, they may need to begin in Level 1 if it was not previously completed.

 See the Intervention Placement Inventory on the PLC.

Each of the four levels presents skills in Units. These Units build on previously taught skills, presenting all new information explicitly. This is true for all areas of instruction. This direct and systematic instruction provides the greatest impact on children's reading and writing achievement.

All previously taught skills are brought forward in a cumulative way. Students have ample opportunity to apply these skills for reinforcement. Instruction continually spirals back to relate the new concepts with previously mastered ones. In this way, students are able to develop a deeper understanding of the structure of English words.

Engaging Multiple Learning Styles with Multi-Sensory Instruction

All lesson components involve active participation. This provides learning through various modalities and also helps maintain the students' focus.

Fundations instruction is highly interactive, often engaging several senses simultaneously. The Learning Activities are designed to incorporate visual, auditory, tactile, and kinesthetic modalities.

Much of the "doing" is in the form of motor-memory learning. Students use sky writing to learn letter formation and the challenging trick, or sight words. Gross motor memory is more memorable than fine motor memory. Students use a straight-arm and wrist when sky writing in order to maximize the gross-motor learning.

Students use their motor memory when tracing letters. A letter's corresponding sound is linked to the letter formation when tracing. This helps to facilitate the association between the letter, its sound and its formation.

Students use motor memory and tactile learning when they tap sounds to blend and spell words. This finger-tapping procedure has proven successful for over two decades in the Wilson Reading System. The tapping of fingers to thumb greatly enhances the students' blending ability. If students are unable to tap in this manner, have them tap their fingers to another surface, such as the desktop. The tapping procedure is fully described in each applicable Unit.

 See the Demonstrations on the PLC.

You will actively engage students as they study word and sentence structure. They manipulate sounds by moving magnetized letters to form words and they learn basic sentence structure by constructing magnetized sentence parts.

Repetition

Fundations provides a high frequency of skill presentations. Students have multiple opportunities to practice and reinforce all skills. The same information is presented in different ways and with varying activities.

Feedback

Throughout each lesson, students demonstrate their understanding and application of concepts through a variety of tasks such as building words from dictation. Students' correct responses are given immediate positive feedback. Students' errors are also corrected "on the spot" with guiding questions so that the students learn from mistakes. It is important to do this in a supportive way. You can then provide the student with an immediate opportunity to give a correct response to a similar item after a correction is made.

Fundations®

Student Success

Gradual Release Model

Optimal learning is facilitated by a gradual release of responsibility model. The Learning Activity sequence on a given day or within a week, moves students along toward independence following these steps:

1) "I Do It" → Teacher Demonstration

Teacher presents new material through a combination of verbal explanation and demonstration with manipulatives such as sound and syllable cards.

2) "We Do It" → Guided Instruction / Practice

Teacher guides students with questioning to use manipulatives or to demonstrate understanding of new concepts at the front of the class.

3) "You Do It Together" → Collaborative Learning

Students complete activities such as Dictation / Dry Erase in their working groups. Students can assist each other to successfully complete tasks.

4) "You Do It Alone" → Independent Success

Students demonstrate concept mastery on their own for check-up and unit tests. You can differentiate, providing structured support for students who have emerging skills.

Assessing Student Mastery

The Learning Activities are not assessments although they can be helpful as you will see some students needing more help than others. However, it is important to provide students with support for learning with guidance. During the Learning Activities, students may have help from teachers, aides or peers. Remember that gradual release of control approaches are effective. Formative assessment can be informal and is used during the learning process. Its purpose is to inform a teacher on how well the students are learning. "Show me" is a phrase that you will use with clear instructional objectives which require the learners to do both intellectual work and demonstrate their thinking with performance. You will then provide immediate feedback to students so that they know how they are doing and what they can do differently if they are struggling.

To assess student achievement of skills, knowledge, and application, be sure to look at student progress from multiple perspectives. This includes direct observation of daily work and independent application of skills throughout the day. See if students can explain their thinking when determining unknown words or when attempting to spell a word for their independent writing. Even if the word is not accurate, can they correct it with your guiding questions or do they know parts of the word that they have mastered and can they tell you about those parts? Watch to see if students are beginning to self-monitor their responses and use problem solving thinking to complete a decoding or spelling task. This might include looking at their Student Notebook for the spelling of a high frequency 'trick' word or referring to a poster to check a sound.

True assessments of student mastery will be with weekly check-up quizzes or Unit Tests. Students receiving an intervention of Fundations will also be assessed with the Fundations Progress Monitoring Tool.

 See Fundations® Progress Monitoring Tool on the PLC.

Engaging Students in Rigorous Work

Fundations engages students in metacognitive thinking as it is essential that they understand the underpinnings of word structure and can apply and generalize these concepts. You will teach students how to use their skills and have them become self-reliant, using tapping and scooping as well as reference materials (posters, Desk Strips and their Student Notebooks) to assist them with independent decoding and spelling throughout the day.

Use questions to reinforce their knowledge such as, "How can you check to be sure?" or "Show me how you know that." Also use questions to be sure they understand the importance and relevance of what they are learning such as, "How will knowing that the letter **q** always has **u** with it help you with spelling?" It is important to use questioning to guide higher order thinking. Metacognitive questions are built into instruction, however, be sure to add additional ones, as appropriate.

See the guidelines for Differentiation to help you challenge more advanced students as you systematically and thoroughly build their foundational knowledge of word structure. You will diagnostically plan lessons with all of your student groups in mind so that your questioning can both target student difficulties and challenge more advanced students.

Student Success

Differentiated Instruction

Whole group instruction is delivered to the entire class during the Fundations Standard Lesson. This provides high quality and consistent initial reading instruction. Explicit instruction in decoding benefits all children including those high in phonemic awareness and alphabetic knowledge (Fielding-Barnsley, 1997). Likewise, fluency instruction develops fluency skill with all students – normal, at-risk, low-achieving, ELL, and students with learning disabilities, and this may in turn increase overall reading comprehension achievement. In Fundations, you will conduct the Standard Learning Activities with students, scaffolding instruction by providing guiding, modeling and cueing of the students. This reduces the possibility of student error and is beneficial to all learners.

As you master the Fundations program, it will become easier to differentiate instruction for students who are lagging behind as well as for advanced students during the Standard Lesson. Suggestions are provided in: 1.) the Learning Activity section of this manual, 2.) the introduction for each Unit, and 3.) on the PLC.

Differentiated instruction is based on the assumptions that students differ in their learning styles, needs, strengths, and abilities. Fundations Learning Activities meet these differences. Fundations Learning Activities give students many ways to understand the content and assure that all students are able to participate. These activities involve all modalities of learning so that students who learn in a variety of ways can have access to the curriculum. Thus, you will differentiate via the process or the "how" of teaching as Fundations provides a variety of ways in which the students learn and make sense of the content.

Throughout the Standard Lesson, provide appropriate levels of challenge for all students. During desk activities, circulate around the room so that you can quietly interact with individual students. This can include using questions to guide struggling students to corrections as well as to challenge more advanced students by asking them extension questions (such as using a word in two different ways). You can differentiate *process* by engaging students in critical and creative thinking, and adding greater complexity or abstractness to the tasks for advanced students. Since this is a collaborative learning time, students who are English proficient and who are more readily developing English literacy can provide additional scaffolding for students who are lagging behind during the desk activities. Be sure to praise and acknowledge these students for their contributions, but also monitor that they do not "take over" and do the activity for their peers.

Many students in your classroom are likely to be English Language Learners (ELLs or ELs). If ELs can read in their native language, it will help them to also read in English. You will directly and systematically teach them how the English language works for both reading and spelling.

> Learning the English spelling system helps ELLs learn letter/sound correspondences, increase vocabulary, and develop greater fluency in reading and writing. Through the study of related words, students begin to see that English spelling, which is complex, is systematic and governed by rules. (Gentry & Graham, 2010, p. 6)

ELs often lack English vocabulary and background knowledge which is sometimes assumed. You can provide additional support by showing students pictures or using props and gestures. It is important to continually think of your ELs and create opportunities to practice new vocabulary and support their understanding.

Since the majority of ELs are Spanish speakers, in the Fundations Units, as appropriate, we provide specific information to help you understand differences between the English and Spanish sound and word structure. We will also post similar information for other common languages (Vietnamese, Arabic, Mandarin Chinese, and Mongolian) on the PLC. If ELs struggled to learn to read in their native language and show evidence of difficulty learning to read in English, it may be due to an underlying language learning disability in addition to the challenge of a second language. Further instruction and assessment can help to determine the student's needs.

ELs and students with a language learning disability (both primary English speakers and ELs) benefit from many of the principles of instruction built into the Fundations program. For example, during the initial teacher-led instruction, you will model using classroom demonstrations of concepts which can be particularly effective for these students (Janney & Snell, 2004). Classroom demonstrations occur when a teacher's verbal

Fundations®

explanation for concepts is enhanced by visual, physical, and kinesthetic involvement. Thus, the Fundations® multisensory instruction provides multiple examples of these demonstrations that can benefit these students, The interactive and "hands-on" activities help to reinforce the acquisition of language associated with reading and spelling as well as the literacy skills.

The following are key principles in Fundations that are critical for both ELs and students with a language learning disability:

- Integration of listening, speaking, reading and writing
- Explicitly modeled skill and strategy instruction
- Verbal explanation for concepts enhanced by visual, physical and kinesthetic involvement
- Opportunities for student interaction in supportive groups
- Procedures that ensure student engagement with hands-on activities
- Clear and consistent directions and cueing systems
- Ample opportunities to reinforce skills
- Scaffolded instruction
- Repetition of vocabulary, including the vocabulary of word structure (such as digraph, short vowel)
- Assessment of content knowledge that is performance rather than language-based

Furthermore, it is essential to foster a positive learning environment. Allowing students to respond when they are ready as well as allowing them time to acquire language and skill by listening and doing will show acceptance and ease with making mistakes. The more comfortable all students feel in your classroom, the more able they are to learn. ELs as well as students with language-based learning disabilities may have more difficulty retrieving the words to express concepts during the lesson. They may need to be given a choice of responses (such as "Is this a digraph or a blend?") instead of asking open-ended types of questions (such as "What is this called?"). This will allow them to recognize instead of having to retrieve the answer for a given concept or meaning of a word. It is important to note that while some ELs will also have a language learning disability, the majority of them will be very language-able and will quickly progress with direct instruction following the above principles.

In addition to the Fundations Standard Lesson, be sure to provide appropriate reading opportunities during the other parts of literacy instruction. Let advanced students select and read material that corresponds to their ability. For students who are just beginning word recognition, it is essential that you give them opportunity to practice and develop their skills with appropriate text.

> Appropriate texts for students to read at this stage contain the types of words they have learned to read. Material should be at the student's independent reading level. If a student is asked to read at his or her instructional level, there should be a teacher or parent to help with words that are more difficult and to listen as sentences with errors are re-read. Readers should not be expected to independently read materials at their frustrational level. Not only will this weaken their comprehension, but it also can produce negative feelings about reading. (Deshler & Gildroy, 2005, pp. 7-8)

For at-risk struggling students, the amount of fluency practice with controlled text will differ. Additional opportunity to practice skills must be provided in small group, Tier 2 instruction.

Students Who Are Struggling

For students who are identified as struggling or at-risk readers, instruction should include the Fundations® Standard lesson and an "Intervention" Lesson targeting areas of difficulty. Since the longer intervention for struggling readers is delayed, the greater the impact on a student's motivation to read, it is critical to help these at-risk readers as soon as possible (Snowling & Hulme, 2011).

 For intervention (Tier 2) Lesson guidance and specific recommendations, see the Intervention and Intervention Guidelines on the PLC.

Introducing Fundations®

Introducing Fundations

How to Proceed

Though it is essential that you take seriously the critical task of setting a foundation for lifelong literacy, it is just as important to remember to have FUN! Enjoy Fundations. Be sure you thoroughly read the previous sections to gain an overview of Fundations.

This manual, along with the corresponding Prevention Learning Community (PLC), provides guidance to successfully teach Fundations.

After reading this introduction, to begin instruction turn to the Orientation section which will direct you to prepare your material. Study the Learning Activities needed for the Orientation and Unit 1.

 Watch video demonstrations on the PLC.

Building a Learning Focused Classroom

Maximizing Instructional Time

To maximize instructional time, it is important to establish classroom routines. In the beginning of the year, spend time discussing and practicing materials management.

When you are underway with your lessons, be sure to establish efficient transitions from one activity to the next. (See PLC for varied recommendations on how to manage materials and establish instructional routines.) Some activities can be (and usually are) done on a classroom rug area, whereas others require a desktop. The activities vary from day to day, but usually begin on the rug and move to the desks. We recommend that you post the list of activities for each day, prepare students for the activity sequence, and describe the objective(s) of the day's lesson. You can print Fundations Activity Strips from the PLC, or simply write the daily list of activities on the board.

To maximize instructional time, you can also weave questions throughout the day. For example, when students are waiting in line you can have them finger write a trick word on the back of the student in front of them. Or you can ask students a question to "exit" from the rug.

Fundations Lessons: Learning Activities

Fundations provides a comprehensive weekly learning plan to support word study, spelling and handwriting. It is important to complete each standard lesson daily, otherwise, the goals of the curriculum can not be met. Fundations can be completed in 30 minutes. As you gain proficiency with each activity procedure and routines, you will be able to complete the lesson in the time frames. Take time to establish classroom routines. This will make all the difference in both the classroom climate and the pacing of your Fundations lessons.

Fundations Lessons are designed to keep students active. Learning Activities in Fundations incorporate the following steps to learning new concepts: modeling and explanation, guided practice and explanation, and independent practice and demonstration as skill is mastered.

Mastering the Fundations Learning Activity procedures will be key to your successful instruction of Fundations, as these procedures provide that gradual release of responsibility to students. The procedures also are designed so that you can both provide necessary guidance to your students and then see that the students are demonstrating and mastering the skills. Note the Learning Activity Overview section in this manual provides the procedures for all Fundations activities listed in alphabetical order. You will be directed to these activities as needed throughout the program. Activity Cue Cards are also provided to help you execute the procedures effectively. There is no need to read through all of these at this time. When directed, however, be sure to study and master the procedures as this is key to your students' success.

Using Questioning to Guide Student Learning and Mastery

Reflective awareness means to thoughtfully notice and consider information, including that which

Fundations®

you see, hear and touch. In Fundations, you will encourage students to be reflectively aware of word structure which will help them generalize, apply and transfer the principles to other learning contexts.

When you introduce a new concept, you will ask students to link it to previous knowledge and through questions, direct their attention to the word structure.

It is important to help students make connections with prior knowledge and bring that to the new learning. Likewise, it is essential that students become aware of patterns and relationships among bits of information so that they solidify their understanding of word structure.

Make sure that students understand the purpose of the Learning Activities. Take time to explain to students the kinds of thinking that is required during the lesson and how this thinking can be used as they read and write throughout the day. It is important to ask students what they have learned and how it will help them. At various and appropriate times throughout the day, be sure to ask students to explain or to describe how they determine a word's pronunciation or spelling.

Craftsmanship for Optimum Outcomes

People who value craftsmanship take time to review the models and criteria they are to use and re-work as needed. Craftsmanship requires effort, practice and attention to detail. It takes energy to produce exceptional results. "To be craftsman-like means knowing that one can continually perfect one's craft by working to attain the highest possible standards and by pursuing ongoing learning to bring laser-like focus of energies to accomplish a task" (Costa & Kallick, 2000, p. 28).

It takes time to develop craftsmanship with Fundations instruction. If available, coaching and mentoring from someone who has more experience can be very helpful. We also recommend that you share the learning with colleagues by gathering for monthly study group meetings to review activities, content and processes.

Also, use the PLC to network with teachers from school districts far and wide. A discussion board provides an interchange of ideas, energy and support as you continue to develop a higher degree of proficient teaching skill and student success.

 See the Study Group Guidelines and use the Discussion Boards on the PLC.

As you learn to teach your Fundations lesson, the following can assist you:

- Read through a daily lesson.
- Write out a plan (print from PLC).
- Review the activity procedures for the day's learning activities (practice with the cue cards will help you master these).
- Determine clear step-by-step instructions to guide students during transitions.
- Visualize your lesson and transitions between activities.

 Print out the Daily Plan from the PLC.

Throughout your Fundations® lesson, be metacognitive about what you are doing. That is, plan your lesson and a strategy to execute it, know why you are doing it, keep that in mind throughout the lesson, and then reflect upon the lesson to evaluate its effectiveness with your students. A key question to ask with each lesson is the following:

- What will students learn or reinforce today?

Questions to ask yourself as you prepare your lesson:

1	What do I want to accomplish in this lesson?	What concepts and principles do I want my students to learn?	What processes do I want my students to practice and develop for independence?
2	What will I do to make it happen?	What will I do to help them understand?	What will I do to help them develop the process(es)?
3	What will my students be doing if they are accomplishing it?	How will I know they understand the concepts?	How will I know that they are practicing and developing the process(es)?

Adapted from "Discovering and Exploring Habits of Mind" (p. 55), by Arthur L. Costa & Bena Kallick (ed.), Alexandria, VA: ASCD. © 2000 by ASCD. Reprinted with permission Learn more about ASCD at www.ascd.org.

Introducing Fundations®

Fundations®

References

Abbott, R., Berninger, V. W., & Fayol, M. (2010). Longitudinal relationships of levels of language in writing and between writing and reading in grades 1-7. *Journal of Educational Psychology, 102*(2), 281-298.

Adams, M. J. (1990). *Beginning to read: Thinking and learning about print.* Cambridge, MA: MIT Press.

Adams, M. J. (2001). Alphabetic anxiety and explicit, systematic phonics instruction: A cognitive science perspective. In S. B. Neuman & D. K. Dickinson (Eds.), *Handbook of early literacy research* (pp. 66-80). New York: Guilford Press.

Anderson, R. C., & Nagy, W. E. (1992). The vocabulary conundrum. *American Educator, 16*(4), 14-18, 44-47.

Beck, I. L., McKeown, M. G., & Kucan, L. (2002). *Bringing words to life: Robust vocabulary instruction.* New York, NY: Guilford Press.

Berninger, V. (1999). The "Write Stuff" for preventing and treating writing disabilities. *Perspectives on Language and Literacy, 25*(2), 20-22.

Berninger, V., Abbott, R. D., Abbott, S. P., Graham, S., & Richards, T. (2002). Writing and reading: Connections between language by hand and language by eye. *Journal of Learning Disabilities, 35*(1), 39-56.

Berninger, V., & Wolf, B. (2009). *Teaching students with dyslexia and dysgraphia: Lessons from teaching and science.* Baltimore, MD: Paul H. Brookes.

Biemiller, A. (2010). *Words worth teaching: Closing the vocabulary gap.* Columbus, OH: McGraw-Hill SRA.

Birsh, J. R. (Ed.). (2011). *Multisensory teaching of basic language skills* (3rd ed.). Baltimore, MD: Paul H. Brookes.

Blalock, J. W. (1985). *Oral language problems of learning-disabled adolescents and adults.* Paper presented at the 34th Annual Conference of the Orton Dyslexic Society, Chicago, IL.

Caroll, J. B., Davies, P., & Richman, B. (1971). *The American Heritage word frequency book.* Boston, MA: Houghton Mifflin.

Castles, A., & Coltheart, M. (2004). Is there a causal link from phonological awareness to success in learning to read? *Cognition, 91*(1), 77-111.

Costa, A. L. & Kallick, B. (Eds.). (2000). *Discovering and exploring habits of mind.* Alexandria, VA: Association for Supervision and Curriculum Development.

Deshler, D., & Gildroy, P. (2005). Reading development and suggestions for teaching reading to students with learning disabilities. *Insights on Learning Disabilities, 2*(2), 1-10.

Edwards, L. (2003). Writing instruction in kindergarten: Examining an emerging area of research for children with writing and reading difficulties. *Journal of Learning Disabilities, 36*(2), 136-148.

Fielding-Barnsley, R. (1997). Explicit instruction in decoding benefits children high in phonemic awareness and alphabetic knowledge. *Scientific Studies of Reading, 1*(1), 85-98.

Fletcher, J. M., Lyon, G. R., Fuchs, L. S., & Barnes, M. A. (2007). *Learning disabilities: From identification to intervention.* New York, NY: Guilford Press.

Fry, E., & Kress, J. E. (2006). *The reading teacher's book of lists* (5th ed.). Hoboken, NJ: John Wiley & Sons.

Gentry, J. R., & Graham, S. (2010). *Creating better readers and writers. The importance of direct, systematic spelling and handwriting instruction in improving academic performance* [White Paper]. Retrieved from http://www.sapersteinassociates.com/downloads/Color%20copy%20National_Whitepaper.pdf

Goswami, U. (2000). Phonological and lexical processes. In M. L. Kamil, P. B. Mosenthal, P. D. Pearson, & R. Barr (Eds.), *Handbook of reading research* (Vol. 3, pp. 251-268). Mahwah, NJ: Lawrence Erlbaum Associates.

Goswami, U. (2001). Early phonological development and the acquisition of literacy. In S. B. Neuman & D. K. Dickinson (Eds.), *Handbook of early literacy research* (pp. 111-125). New York: Guilford Press.

References

Graham, S. (2006). Strategy instruction and the teaching of writing: A meta-analysis. In C. MacArthur, S. Graham, & J. Fitzgerald (Eds.), *Handbook of writing research* (pp. 187-207). New York: Guilford Press.

Graham, S., Hebert, M. A., & Carnegie Corporation of New York. (2010). *Writing to read: Evidence for how writing can improve reading.* Washington, DC: Alliance for Excellent Education. Retrieved from: http://carnegie.org/fileadmin/Media/Publications/WritingToRead_01.pdf

Graham, S., & Weintraub, N. (1996). A review of handwriting research: Progress and prospects from 1980 to 1994. *Educational Psychology Review, 8*(1), 7-87.

Graves, M. F., & Watts-Taffe, S. (2002). The role of word consciousness in a research-based vocabulary program. In A. Farstrup & S. J. Samuels (Eds.), *What research has to say about reading instruction* (pp. 140-165). Newark, DE: International Reading Association.

Hanna, P. R., Hodges, R. E., & Hanna, J. S. (1971). *Spelling: Structure and strategies.* Boston, MA: Houghton Mifflin.

Henry, M. K. (1988). Beyond phonics: Integrated decoding and spelling instruction based on word origin and structure. *Annals of Dyslexia, 38,* 258-275.

Hernandez, D. J., & Annie E. Casey Foundation. (2011). *Double jeopardy: How third-grade reading skills and poverty influence high school graduation.* Baltimore, MD: The Annie E. Casey Foundation.

Hiebert, E. H., & Kamil, M. L. (2005). *Teaching and learning vocabulary: Bringing research to practice.* Mahwah, N.J: Lawrence Erlbaum Associates.

Hiebert, E. H., & Martin, L. A. (2009). Opportunity to read: A critical but neglected construct in reading instruction. In E. H. Hiebert (Ed.), *Reading more, reading better: Solving problems in the teaching of literacy* (pp. 3-29). New York: Guilford Press.

Janney, R., & Snell, M. E. (2004). *Teachers' guides to inclusive practices: Modifying schoolwork* (2nd ed.). Baltimore, MD: Paul H. Brookes.

Lehr, F., Osborn, J., Hiebert, E. H. (2004). *A focus on vocabulary.* Honolulu, HI: Regional Educational Laboratory at Pacific Resources for Education and Learning.

Lyon, G. R., & Weiser, B. (2009). Teacher knowledge, instructional expertise, and the development of reading proficiency. *Journal of Learning Disabilities, 42*(5), 475-480.

Mather, N., & Wendling, B. J. (2012). *Essentials of dyslexia assessment and intervention.* Hoboken, NJ: John Wiley & Sons.

McCardle, P., & Chhabra, V. (Eds.). (2004). *The voice of evidence in reading research.* Baltimore, MD: Paul H. Brookes.

McKeown, M. G., & Beck, I. L. (2003). Taking advantage of read-alouds to help children make sense of decontextualized language. In A. Van Kleeck, S. Stahl, & E. Bauer (Eds.), *On reading books to children* (pp. 159-176). Mahwah, NJ: Lawrence Erlbaum Associates.

Moats, L. C. (1995). *Spelling: Development, disability, and instruction.* Baltimore, MD: York Press.

Moats, L. C. (Winter 2005/06). How spelling supports reading: And why it is more regular and predictable than you may think. *American Educator, 29*(4), 12-22, 42-43.

National Governors Association Center for Best Practices and Council of Chief State School Officers. (2010). *Common Core State Standards: Standards for English language arts & literacy in history/social studies, science, and technical subjects.* Washington, DC: National Governors Association Center for Best Practices, Council of Chief State School Officers. Retrieved from http://www.corestandards.org/assets/CCSSI_ELA Standards.pdf

National Governors Association Center for Best Practices and Council of Chief State School Officers. (2010). *Common Core State Standards: Application to students with disabilities.* Washington, DC: National Governors Association Center for Best Practices, Council of Chief State School Officers. Retrieved from http://www.corestandards.org/assets/application-to-students-with-disabilities.pdf

National Reading Panel (U.S.), & National Institute of Child Health and Human Development (NICHD). (2000). *Report of the National Reading Panel: Teaching children to read: An evidence-based assessment of the scientific research literature on reading and its implications for reading instruction: Reports of the subgroups* (NIH Publication No. 00-4754). Washington, DC: U.S. Government Printing Office.

Fundations®

O'Connor, J. & Wilson, B. A. (1995). Effectiveness of the Wilson Reading System used in public school training. In C. W. McIntyre, & J. S. Pickering (Eds.), *Clinical studies of multisensory structured language education* (pp. 247-252). Salem, OR: International Multisensory Structured Language Education Council.

Paivio, A. (1979). *Imagery and verbal processes*. Hillsdale, NJ: Lawrence Erlbaum Associates.

Peverly, S. T., Ramaswamy, V., Brown, C., Sumowski, J., Alidoost, M., & Garner, J. (2007). What predicts skill in lecture note taking? *Journal of Educational Psychology, 99*(1), 167-180.

Rasinski, T. V. (2006). A brief history of reading fluency. In S. J. Samuels, & A. E. Farstrup (Eds.), *What research has to say about fluency instruction* (pp. 4-23). Newark, DE: International Reading Association.

Reed, D. K. (2012). *Why teach spelling?* Portsmouth, NH: RMC Research Corporation, Center on Instruction. Retrieved from http://www.centeroninstruction.org/files/Why%20Teach%20Spelling.pdf

Sadoski, M., & Paivio, A. (2001). Imagery and text: A dual coding theory of reading and writing. *Reading and Writing, 16*(3), 259-262. doi:10.1023/A:1022830720347

Schlagal, B. (2007). Best practices in spelling and handwriting. In S. Graham, C. A. MacArthur, & J. Fitzgerald (Eds.), *Best practices in writing instruction* (pp. 179-201). New York, NY: Guilford Press.

Shanahan, T. (2008). Relations among oral language, reading, and writing development. In C. A. MacArthur, S. Graham, & J. Fitzgerald (Eds.), *Handbook of Writing Research* (pp. 171-186). New York: Guilford Press.

Shankweiler, D., Liberman, I. Y., & Liberman, A. M. (1989). The alphabetic principle and learning to read. In D. Shankweiler & I. Y. Liberman (Eds.), *Phonology and reading disability: Solving the reading puzzle* (pp. 1-33). Ann Arbor, MI: University of Michigan.

Snow, C. E., Burns, M. S., Griffin, P., Committee on the Prevention of Reading Difficulties in Young Children, Commission on Behavioral and Social Sciences and Education & National Research Council. (Eds.). (1998). *Preventing reading difficulties in young children*. Washington, DC: National Academy Press.

Snowling, M. J., & Hulme, C. (2011). Interventions for children's language and literacy difficulties. *International Journal of Language and Communication Disorders, 47*(1), 27-34.

Stanovich, K. E. (1986). Matthew Effects in reading: Some consequences of individual differences in the acquisition of literacy. *Reading Research Quarterly, 21*(4), 360-407.

Uhry, J. K., & Shepherd, M. J. (1993). Segmentation/spelling instruction as part of a first-grade reading program: Effects on several measures of reading. *Reading Research Quarterly, 28*(3), 218–233.

Wagner, R. K., Muse, A. E., & Tannenbaum, K. R. (Eds.). (2006). *Vocabulary acquisition: Implications for reading comprehension*. New York, NY: Guilford Press.

Wanzek, J., & Vaughn, S. (2008). Response to varying amounts of time in reading intervention for students with low response to intervention. *Journal of Learning Disabilities, 41*(2), 126-142. doi:10.1177/0022219407313426

Weister, B. L., & Mathes, P. G. (2011). Using encoding instruction to improve the reading and spelling performances of elementary students at-risk for literacy difficulties: A best-evidence synthesis. *Review of Educational Research, 81*(2), 170-200. doi:10.3102/0034654310396719

Whitehurst, G. J., & Lonigan, C. J. (2001). Emergent literacy: Development from prereaders to readers. In Neuman, S. B, & Dickinson, D. K. (Eds.), *Handbook of early literacy research* (pp.11-29). New York, NY: Guilford Press.

Wilson, B. A. (1988). *Wilson Reading System*. Oxford, MA: Wilson Language Training.

Wolf, B. J. (2011). Teaching handwriting. In J. R. Birsh (Ed.). *Multisensory teaching of basic language skills* (3rd ed., pp. 179-206). Baltimore, MD: Paul H. Brookes.

Fundations® Scope and Sequence

Fundations Scope and Sequence

Level K of Fundations® will set a very strong foundation for reading and writing.

In addition to Fundations, provide your students with a wide variety of text experiences, and expose them to poetry, narrative and informational text.

By The End of Level K, Students Will Be Able To:

- Recognize and produce rhyming words
- Segment words in an oral sentence
- Segment words into syllables
- Segment and pronounce initial, medial and final phonemes in spoken CVC words
- Manipulate phonemes with additions or substitutions in one-syllable words
- Name all letters of the alphabet
- Write all manuscript letters in lowercase and uppercase
- Sequence letters of the alphabet
- Fluently produce sounds of consonants (primary) and short vowels when given the letter
- Fluently produce sounds for basic digraphs (**wh**, **sh**, **ch**, **th**, **ck**)
- Name and write corresponding letter(s) when given sounds for consonants, consonant digraphs, and short vowels
- Distinguish long and short vowel sounds within words.
- Read and spell approximately 200 CVC words
- Spell other words phonetically, drawing on knowledge of sound-letter relationships
- Identify 75% of first 100 high frequency words, including 25-30 irregular (trick words) such as **the**, **was**, **of**
- Identify and name correct punctuation at end of sentence
- Capitalize words at beginning of sentences and names of people
- Name the author and illustrator of a story and define their roles
- Explain narrative story structure including character, setting and main events
- Use a combination of drawing and dictating to narrate linked events to tell about a story in sequence
- Re-tell key details of narrative and informational text, using pictures or prompts as a guide
- Identify characters, setting and main events in a story, with pictures or other prompts
- Describe what happened in a story when given a specific illustration
- With prompts, compare and contrast the experiences of characters in two stories
- Explain difference between narrative and informational text
- Echo-read a passage with correct phrasing and expression
- Identify and explain new meanings for familiar words and newly taught words
- Produce and expand complete sentences in shared language activities

Fundations®

Unit 1 (12 weeks)
- Letter-Keyword-Sound for consonants
- Letter-Keyword-Sound for short vowels
- Letter Formation for lowercase letters (a-z)
- Sound recognition: consonants and short vowels
- Print and word awareness
- Rhyming
- Phonemic awareness: initial and final sounds
- Story retelling
- Beginning composition skills
- Fluency/phrasing with echo and choral reading

Unit 2 (4 weeks)
- Phonemic awareness skills: blending, segmenting, and manipulation of sounds
- Blending and reading three-sound short vowel words
- Story prediction
- Alphabetical Order
- Uppercase letter formation
- Sample words: **map**, **sad**, **rat**

Unit 3 (6 weeks)
- Phonemic awareness skills: blending, segmenting, and manipulation of sounds
- Blending sounds in nonsense CVC words
- Segmenting and spelling three-sound short vowel words
- Distinguish long and short vowel sounds
- Narrative story form: character, setting, main events

- Fluency and phrasing with echo and choral reading
- Beginning composition skills
- High frequency words (trick words)
- Sample words: **cut**, **tap**, **wet**
- Trick words: **the**, **a**, **and**, **are**, **to**, **is**, **his**, **as**, **has**, **was**

Unit 4 (4 weeks)
- Phoneme segmentation
- Concept of consonant digraph, keywords and sounds: **wh**, **ch**, **sh**, **th**, **ck**
- Decoding three-sound words with digraphs
- Spelling three-sound words with digraphs
- Spelling of **ck** at end of words
- Narrative story form: character, setting, main events
- Sample words: **bath**, **chop**, **thick**
- Trick words: **we**, **she**, **he**, **be**, **me**, **I**, **you**, **they**

Unit 5 (6 weeks)
- Sentence structure
- Sentence dictation
- Narrative fiction vs. informational books
- Trick words: **or**, **for**, **of**, **have**, **from**, **by**, **my**, **do**, **one**

Learning Activity Overview
Level K

The Fundations® Learning Activities are listed on the following pages in alphabetical order. Some Activities, (Word Play, Make It Fun and Storytime) are variable and are described on the last page of this section. These Activities provide the students with lots of repetition but in varied ways. The repetition is key to student mastery. The variation allows for learning with different modalities and also helps to maintain interest. You will need to master these activity procedures to help your lessons go smoothly. However, there is no need to learn them all at one time. Learning Activities will be gradually added as you progress through the Units.

How To Prepare For An Activity

- Read the Activity description (in this Overview section).
- Refer to the Activity Cue Cards for reference.
- View the corresponding teacher's video demonstrations on the Prevention/Early Intervention Learning Community (PLC).
- Practice the Activity.

Your mastery of the Learning Activities will take time. Since all activities require students to actively demonstrate their thinking, try visualizing the students in your class doing the activity and successfully completing it. Activity Cue Cards will provide you with guidance as you are learning the activity procedures. We recommend that you review/study the Activity Cue Cards that are designated for the next lesson that you will conduct. During the lesson have the cue cards handy for quick reference. Eventually, you will become automatic with the Learning Activity routines.

Learning Activity Overview

Alphabetical Order

In a Nutshell

- Students match the Letter Tiles to the letter squares on their Letter Boards.
- This is done in alphabetical order.
- You say the alphabet as students point to the Letter Tiles.

TEACHER MATERIALS
- Baby Echo
- Standard Sound Cards

STUDENT MATERIALS
- Fundations® Letter Board & Letter Tiles

VIEW THE PREVENTION/EARLY INTERVENTION LEARNING COMMUNITY

Learning Activity
- Alphabetical Order

ESTIMATED ACTIVITY TIME

10 MINUTES

SYNOPSIS

Students match the corresponding Letter Tile to the letter squares on their Letter Board. Students then practice naming the letters in alphabetical order. This activity helps students develop alphabetic knowledge, automatic letter naming and alphabetical order.

PROCEDURE

- Distribute the Letter Boards with the Letter Tiles randomly placed on the blank side of the Letter Board.
- Students match the Letter Tiles to the corresponding letter squares on their Letter Board in alphabetical order. They should match and place letters in order (**a** first, then **b**) rather than randomly.
- When students have their tiles placed, recite the alphabet all together. Use the Baby Echo pointer to point to your Standard Sound Card display and have students point to the Letter Tiles on their Letter Boards. Emphasize each row, pausing for a deep breath at the end of each one.

Say

a-b-c-d-e-f (breathe).

- Alternatively, you can also say a row and have students echo or you can have a student come up and use the Baby Echo pointer to do a row, and have others echo.

Differentiation

Assist at-risk or struggling students, or pair them with a student who is more proficient. You can also provide struggling students with a board that has the letters placed on the blank side of the board in alphabetical order rather than randomly placed. Remember to set these boards up ahead of time, then have students move the tiles to the squares without struggling to locate each letter. When reciting the alphabet in order, help students point to each letter as this is done.

Advanced students can be challenged by alphabetizing tiles on the blank side of their Letter Board. Be sure they still follow the four quadrants (a-f. etc.).

Learning Activity Overview

Alphabetical Order

Activity Cue Alphabetical Order

Teacher Does	Teacher Says	Response
Hand out the Letter Boards and Letter Tiles. Be sure the Letter Tiles are randomly placed on the blank side of the board.	We are going to match the letters to the correct square on your Letter Board in alphabetical order.	
Point to the first row: **a-b-c-d-e-f**	Which row do you set up first?	The top row.
	That's right. Set up the top row first. Start with the letter a and match the letters in order... a, then b, then c. Don't forget to say the names of the letters when you put them on the squares.	
Assist students as needed.		Students set up board, naming letters as they place them.
Once board is set, use Baby Echo pointer to say the alphabet together. The teacher should point to the Standard Sound Card Display as the alphabet is recited. Pause at end of each row. Variation: Student is the leader and uses Baby Echo pointer to do a row, then students echo.	a-b-c-d-e-f, breathe, g-h-i-j-k-l, breathe, m-n-o-p-q-r-s, breathe, t-u-v-w-x-y-z.	Students point to the letters on their own board and say the letter name while you (or a student) point to the Standard Sound Card Display.

Learning Activity Overview

Dictation/Sounds

In a Nutshell

- You dictate sounds, students write the corresponding letter.
- Students always repeat dictations of sounds.
- Students write on Dry Erase Writing Tablets.

TEACHER MATERIALS
- Echo the Owl
- Large Writing Grid
- Unit Resources (Echo Sounds List)

STUDENT MATERIALS
- Dry Erase Writing Tablet
- Desk Strip

VIEW THE PREVENTION/EARLY INTERVENTION LEARNING COMMUNITY

Learning Activity
- Dictation/Sounds

ESTIMATED ACTIVITY TIME

5-10 MINUTES

SYNOPSIS

Students write the letter(s) that correspond to a dictated sound. This activity supports the development of the alphabetic principle and helps students solidify both sound-symbol correspondence and letter formation.

This is a teaching time, not a testing time.

PROCEDURE

- Review correct sitting position and pencil grip.
- You dictate a sound (from Unit Resources).
- Students echo the sound when you hold up Echo.

Say

/m/ (hold up Echo and students echo /m/)

Write /m/.

- Then everybody writes the letter(s) that makes that sound. Have a student do it on the Large Writing Grid.
- Have the student at the board provide the letter name when you ask, "**What says /m/?**" (**m**)
- Have students check their work and correct it immediately.

Differentiation

Circulate the room so that you can provide assistance for students who struggle and show them how to use their resources such as posters, their Student Notebook, the Desk Strip, etc.

As you circulate, ask the advanced students quick, challenging questions such as, tell me what you know about that sound and how it is used (for **qu**, students might answer, "**q** is the buddy letter. It always has a **u** by its side").

Also, students can begin using the Dry Erase Writing Tablet with the smaller 3-line grid as they are ready.

Learning Activity Overview

Dictation/Sounds

Activity Cue Dictation/Sounds

Teacher Does	Teacher Says	Response
Select a sound from the Echo Sounds list in the Unit Resource.	/t/	
Hold up Echo the Owl.		/t/
	Write the letter that says /t/.	Students write the letter(s) on the Dry Erase Writing Tablet. Have one student do this on the Large Writing Grid.
	What says /t/ (student name or the class)?	Select the student at the classroom board to name the letters.
	Check your work.	On the Dry Erase Writing Tablets, students erase to fix any errors.

Learning Activity Overview

Dictation/Words

In a Nutshell

- You dictate words, students segment sounds and write the word.
- Students always repeat dictations of words.
- Students write the word.

TEACHER MATERIALS
- Echo the Owl
- Large Writing Grid
- Unit Resources (Review and Unit Words List)

STUDENT MATERIALS
- Dry Erase Writing Tablet
- Desk Strip (for reference as needed)

VIEW THE PREVENTION/EARLY INTERVENTION LEARNING COMMUNITY

Learning Activity
- Dictation/Words

ESTIMATED ACTIVITY TIME

5-10 MINUTES

SYNOPSIS

Students segment sounds and spell words. This activity helps students develop independent spelling and reinforces their understanding of word structure by marking up the word.

This is a teaching time, not a testing time.

PROCEDURE

- Review correct sitting position and pencil grip.
- You say a word (select from Unit Resources).
- Students echo the word when you hold up Echo.

Say

mat (hold up Echo and students echo **mat**)

- Direct students to tap the word (single syllable words only).

Say

Elbows up, let's tap it /m/ /a/ /t/.

- Rather then blend it again, keep the word segmented and have students name the letter(s) that correspond to each tap **m a t**.
- Select a student to write the word on the classroom board or Large Writing Grid and direct all students to write the word on their Dry Erase Writing Tablet. Then have all students spell the word chorally.

Say

Check your word and fix it if you need to.

- After review and current words are completed, have one student read back all the words and then direct the students to "mark up" their list of words (starting in Unit 4, underline the digraphs).

As students master spelling of Unit words, have them write the word before an individual names the letters or writes it for the whole class. Then have all students spell chorally.

Differentiation

Be aware of students' "trouble spots" such as the spelling of words with the letter **x**. Circulate the room when dictating these challenging Unit words. Provide additional assistance to struggling students by helping them tap or with questions that will guide them to determine the letter for a sound.

Advanced students could write the word more than once, focusing on excellent letter formation.

Also, students can begin using the Dry Erase Writing Tablet with the smaller 3-line grid as they are ready.

Learning Activity Overview

Dictation/Words

Activity Cue Dictation/Words

Teacher Does	Teacher Says	Response
Select a word from the Unit Resources Words.	**mat**	
Hold up Echo the Owl.		mat
	Elbows up. Let's tap it /m/ /a/ /t/.	Tap the word with the students and then have them re-tap, naming the letters that correspond to each tap.
	Who can spell mat?	Select a student to write the word on the Large Writing Grid and spell it orally. (See NOTE.)
	Write mat.	Students write the word.
	Now, let's all spell mat - m - a - t	All students spell the word chorally.
Check the word on the classroom board.	**Check your work.**	On the Dry Erase Writing Tablets, students erase to fix any errors.
Direct students to read all words.	**Read the words that you wrote today.**	Select a student or have all do chorally.
Direct students to "mark up" words (Begin in Unit 4).	**Example: Underline any digraph in your words.**	Students mark up words, as directed.

Note: *As students master spelling of Unit words, have them write the word before an individual is selected to model writing it for the whole class. Then have all spell chorally.*

Learning Activity Overview

Dictation/Sentences

In a Nutshell

- You dictate sentences, students write independently and proofread.
- Students always repeat dictations of sentences.

TEACHER MATERIALS
- Echo the Owl
- Sentence Frames
- Unit Resources (Sentence List)

STUDENT MATERIALS
- Dry Erase Writing Tablet
- Student Notebook

VIEW THE PREVENTION/EARLY INTERVENTION LEARNING COMMUNITY

Learning Activity
- Dictation/Sentences

ESTIMATED ACTIVITY TIME

5-10 MINUTES

SYNOPSIS

Students independently write a sentence from dictation. This helps them develop their auditory memory for words. They also develop their proofreading skills with guidance.

Teach students to leave a finger space between words. Every sentence must begin with a capital letter and end with a punctuation mark.

PROCEDURE

- Dictate the sentence (select from Unit Resources Sentences). Emphasize phrases by using a pause. Use somewhat of a sing-song voice to help students remember the sentence.
- Students echo the sentence when you hold up Echo.
- Select a student to place Sentence Frames for dictated sentence. Guide the student to circle any frame that has a trick word. Have a student tell you how to spell the trick words.
- Students independently write the sentence. Circulate among students and guide with questioning.
- You may have one student write the sentence on the Sentence Frames at the front of the class. Explain that high edged frames are for words with uppercase letters, small punctuation squares are for periods, and tall punctuation rectangles are for a question mark or exclamation point.
- Re-dictate the sentence as students point to the words on their Dry Erase Writing Tablets, making sure they have all the words. Ask if they have a capital letter at the beginning and punctuation mark at the end.
- Have students check the spelling of any trick words on the Trick Word page in their Student Notebooks.
- Have the students check the spelling of the other words by tapping. After students tap each word (not trick words), give them time to check their words.
- Have students fix any mistakes.
- Have them "mark up" the words, as directed.

Differentiation

Students should work independently when writing sentences. If struggling students need help, they can check their Student Notebooks for sounds, rules, or trick words. Give guidance, but have the students work toward correcting their own errors.

For advanced students, you can form a small group to do dictation of sounds, words and sentences on Composition Paper rather than on the Dry Erase Writing Tablets, providing more challenging words and additional sentences.

 Print Composition Paper from the PLC.

Learning Activity Overview

Dictation/Sentences

Activity Cue Dictation/Sentences

Teacher Does	Teacher Says	Response
Select a sentence from the Sentences list in the Unit Resources. Be sure to say it in phrases with expression.	The cat is on the bed.	
Hold up Echo the Owl.		The cat is on the bed.
Select a student to place Sentence Frames on board.		
Either you or a student circle any Sentence Frame with a trick word.		
Have students find the Trick Word page in their Student Notebooks. Select a student to tell you how to spell trick words and you write them on Sentence Frames.		Students look up the spelling of any trick words in the sentence. Have them spell it orally to you as you write it on the Sentence Frame.
Dictate the sentence again, directing students to write it. Circulate and guide students with questioning. Repeat the sentence as needed to individual students.	**Write the sentence, the cat is on the bed.**	Students write the sentence on Dry Erase Tablets. Have a student write the sentence on the Sentence Frames. If a student forgets the sentence, the teacher should repeat the sentence quietly (whisper) to that student.
Repeat the sentence for proofreading.	**The cat is on the bed.**	Students point to the words they wrote and add words if needed.
	Do you have a capital letter at the beginning? **Do you have punctuation?**	Students check.
Direct students to check any trick word spelling.	**Proofread your trick words, (word) and (word).** **Do not tap trick words.**	Students check spelling in their Student Notebooks.
Direct students to tap and check other words.	**Look at your other words.** **Tap out (each word).**	Teacher and students tap each word. Students correct their work.
Check the sentence on the Sentence Frames. Be sure it is right.	**Check your work.**	Have the students check their sentence with the one on the Sentence Frames and make corrections.

Learning Activity Overview

Drill Sounds/Warm-Up

In a Nutshell

- Students practice sounds, saying Letter-Keyword-Sound.

Vowels
- Always do vowels: **a-apple-/ă/**

Other Sounds
- Be selective (include new sounds, "trouble sounds," and rotate others for review).

TEACHER MATERIALS
- Baby Echo (on a pointer or ruler)
- Large Sound Cards
- Standard Sound Cards (magnetized for use on classroom board)
- Unit Resources (Drill Sounds/Warm-Up)
- Vowel Extension Poster

VIEW THE PREVENTION/EARLY INTERVENTION LEARNING COMMUNITY

Learning Activity
- Drill Sounds/Warm-Up

ESTIMATED ACTIVITY TIME
2-5 MINUTES

SYNOPSIS

Every lesson starts with a quick, warm-up sound drill. This activity helps students master the alphabetic principle of letter-sound associations. Eventually, students should be able to say the letter name, keyword and sound when the sound card is presented without modeling.

PROCEDURE

As a new sound is taught, the Standard Sound Card is added to your card display to be drilled at each lesson.

Large Sound Card Drill

All new sounds should be introduced with the Large Sound Cards. First discuss and practice some sounds with the Large Sound Cards including new and challenging sounds. You always model these sounds and have the students echo.

The Large Sound Cards are used to demonstrate, so be sure you do these cards.

Standard Sound Card Drill

Next, point to the Standard Sound Cards with the Baby Echo pointer. Students say the letter-keyword-sound.

Always include vowels. As students get to know their consonants, be selective. Do the new consonants and include any other new or difficult sounds. Be sure to say the letter, the keyword and then the sound (**m-man-/m/**). End with the sound, using the keyword to help them remember the sound. (See Note.)

Teacher as Drill Leader with Standard Cards

Initially, you should model the sounds and have the students repeat. Say letter-keyword-sound as you point to the card and have the students echo.

Student as Drill Leader with Standard Cards

Once students are familiar and comfortable with the format for drilling sounds, a student can lead the drill. The "**drill leader**" can change daily allowing each student a turn. The drill leader says the letter-keyword-sound (**m-man-/m/**) and the class repeats. This allows you an opportunity to assess a student's level of mastery.

Direct the student to select all vowels and any new sound. In addition, you can have her or him select 4-5 of their choice or with your direction. If there are troublesome consonants or any you want to assess for accuracy, you can identify them by placing a small sticky dot on the card. Also, you can select them by category (all sky line letters, all digraphs, etc.).

Differentiation

When you select a struggling student as drill leader, you can model and then have the student repeat *before* the whole class says the drill. Also, help the students refer to posters or Desk Strips to help them recall keywords.

When an advanced student is drill leader, select the more challenging sounds. Ask the student to tell you about selected sound (e.g.: **q** never goes in a word without **u**).

Learning Activity Overview

Drill Sounds/Warm-Up

Activity Cue Drill Sounds/Warm-Up

Teacher Does	Teacher Says	Response
As directed, discuss and practice sounds with Large Sound Cards. Include new and challenging sounds. Show students a Large Sound Card.	**Say** letter-keyword-sound (for example, **t - top - /t/**)	t - top - /t/
Point with Baby Echo to Standard Sound Cards on your magnetic display. Model letter-keyword-sound (see Note).	t - top - /t/	t - top - /t/
Variation: Students can be drill leader with Standard Sound Cards when they become more proficient.		
As directed, or periodically, you (or a student) point to the Vowel Extension Poster, and trace the line for each vowel. Stretch out the initial sounds and finish saying the keyword when you get to the picture.	a - /ăăă.....................pple/ - /ă/	
Have a student trace the line while everyone extends the vowel sound.		a - /ăăă.....................pple/ - /ă/

Note: *Discuss sounds as appropriate (e.g. Can you name the vowels? Name three plane line round letters? Can you name the digraphs?). Keywords for <u>mastered consonants</u> can be dropped from the drill. Thus students say **m-/m/** rather than **m-man-/m/**. However, in Kindergarten - do <u>not</u> drop any consonant keywords until Unit 4. Keywords for vowels, even though these sounds have been mastered, should <u>never</u> be dropped.*

Learning Activity Overview

Echo/Find Letters

In a Nutshell

- You dictate new sounds, review some previously taught sounds, and target "trouble sounds."
- Frequently include vowel sounds.

TEACHER MATERIALS

- Standard Sound Cards (magnetized for use on magnetic board display)
- Echo the Owl
- Unit Resources (Echo Sounds)

STUDENT MATERIALS

- Fundations® Letter Board & Letter Tiles (only taught sounds)

VIEW THE PREVENTION/EARLY INTERVENTION LEARNING COMMUNITY

Learning Activity

- Echo/Find Letters

ESTIMATED ACTIVITY TIME

2-3 MINUTES

SYNOPSIS

Students reinforce the skill of matching a letter with a given sound. This activity helps to solidify sound-symbol correspondence, and sets the foundation for spelling.

PROCEDURE

- Say a sound and hold up Echo. This is the students' cue to echo the sound. For example:

Say

/t/ (hold up Echo and students echo /t/)

Point to /t/.

Students then point to the Letter Tile that has the letter(s) representing the sound (**t**).

What says /t/?

Call on a student to answer ("t") by naming the letter that makes that sound.

- Students can also make the letter(s) with their index fingers on their Letter Board or desks to add tactile-kinesthetic reinforcement.
- Call on individual students to come to the front of the class to find and point to letter(s) on the Standard Sound Card display.
- Be sure they repeat the sound before answering. This "**echoing**" of the sound helps you know the students have heard it correctly, and helps them to better process the sound.
- Students need to name the letter, not just point to it.
- Be sure students give all responses that have been taught to each question. See the Unit Resources for the appropriate response. For example:

Say

What says /k/?

Students find **c**, **k**, and **ck**.

Differentiation

Be sure all students echo sound and match (or in later Units, point to) tiles.

For struggling students, direct students to use their resources, such as their Student Notebook and posters, referring to keywords to help them make associations.

For advanced students, you can extend the activity by asking a student to name a word that starts with, ends with or contains the sound. Then ask a student to use that word in a sentence.

Learning Activity Overview

Echo/Find Letters

Activity Cue Echo/Find Letters

Teacher Does	Teacher Says	Response
Have a student come up to the classroom board.	/t/	
Hold up Echo.		/t/
	Point to /t/.	Students find and point to the letter on their Letter Boards. The student at the Standard Sound Card display selects the letter.
	What says /t/, (student name)?	Have the student at the front say the letter name or call on another student.
Say another sound, and repeat procedure. Do all vowels and approximately 3-5 other sounds.		

Note: For Unit 1 in kindergarten, begin the activity with letters that have been introduced on the blank side of their Letter Boards. After students repeat the sound, point to the correct letter tile and name the letter, say "Match It" and have them place it onto the corresponding letter square. A selected student can repeat the sound, name the letter, and point to it on the Standard Sound Card Display. After all sounds are matched, dictate selected sounds, and have students repeat the sound and point to the letter.

Learning Activity Overview

Echo/Find Words

In a Nutshell

- You dictate words, students tap and spell with tiles.
- Practice 2-3 current words and 2-3 review words.

TEACHER MATERIALS
- Echo the Owl or Baby Echo
- Standard Sound Cards (magnetized for use on magnetic board/card display)
- Unit Resources (Review and Unit Word List)

STUDENT MATERIALS
- Magnetic Letter Tiles
- Fundations® Letter Board

VIEW THE PREVENTION/EARLY INTERVENTION LEARNING COMMUNITY

Learning Activity
- Echo/Find Words

ESTIMATED ACTIVITY TIME

5-7 MINUTES

SYNOPSIS

Students must segment sounds and identify the letter(s) that go with each segmented sound. The segmenting is done with finger tapping.

PROCEDURE

- Dictate the word, and hold up Echo. This is the students' cue to echo the word. For example:

Say

Elbows up-tap (the word).

- Tap the word with the students.

Make the word.

- Students then find the Magnetic Letter Tiles to make the word on their Letter Board.

- One student can come to the front of the class to find the letters at the Standard Sound Card display.

- When students have formed the word with their tiles, ask someone to spell it orally, and have a student provide a sentence with the word. Then say, **"Clear the deck"** or **"Spell away."** Students return the Letter Tiles to their squares while orally spelling the word again ("spell away"), in preparation for a new word. Be sure the students return tiles in the correct order of the spelling.

- Remember to **weave vocabulary** questions throughout.

Differentiation

For struggling students, be aware of students' "trouble spots" such as the spelling of words with the letter **x**. Circulate the room when dictating these challenging Unit words. Provide additional assistance to struggling students by helping them repeat and tap the word again or with questions that will guide them to determine the letter for a sound including asking them to look at the Basic Keywords Poster or Desk Strip to find a keyword that starts with or contains that sound.

For advanced students, as you circulate the room, you can also ask individuals questions that challenge them. For example, you might ask an individual who correctly spelled the word **mop** to tell you verbally how he/she would change it to make it **map**.

Learning Activity Overview

Echo/Find Words

Activity Cue Echo/Find Words

Teacher Does	Teacher Says	Response
Select a word from the Unit Resource List.	mad	
Hold up Echo.		mad
	Elbows up. Let's tap it /m/ /a/ /d/.	Tap the word with the students.
	Find mad.	Students find Magnetic Letter Tiles and spell word on their Letter Board.
	Who can spell mad?	
Select a student to spell the word orally.		m - a - d
Make word with Standard Sound Cards (or call on a student to form the word on the card display board).	**Yes, m - a - d. Check your word.** **Who can use that word in a sentence?**	
	Clear the deck or **Spell away.**	Students return Magnetic Letter Tiles to their letter squares, orally spelling the word again ("spell away"): **m - a - d**.
Dictate 3-5 words.		

© 2002, 2012 WILSON LANGUAGE TRAINING CORPORATION

Learning Activity Overview

Echo/Letter Formation

In a Nutshell

- You dictate sounds, students write the corresponding letter.

TEACHER MATERIALS

- Echo the Owl
- Letter Formation Guide
- Letter Formation Poster
- Large Writing Grid
- Pencil Grip Picture (See PLC)
- Unit Resources (Echo Sounds)

STUDENT MATERIALS

- Dry Erase Writing Tablet, Markers and Erasers

Dry erase markers and erasers are not provided with Fundations® since many classrooms are already equipped with them. Old socks can be used for erasers!

VIEW THE PREVENTION/EARLY INTERVENTION LEARNING COMMUNITY

Learning Activity

- Echo/Letter Formation

ESTIMATED ACTIVITY TIME

5 MINUTES

SYNOPSIS

Students develop correct pencil grip and letter formation procedures with guidance. This activity also reinforces sound-symbol correspondence.

Students need proper "pencil grip," so when you give them markers, show them how to pinch it (with pointer and thumb) and rest it (on their other 3 fingers) and place it on the table.

PROCEDURE

- Use the Large Writing Grid.
- As students show they are ready to write (chairs pulled in, feet on floor, arms on table), pass out Dry Erase Writing Tablets and dry erase markers.
- Use the Pencil Grip Picture as a cue to consistently reinforce proper pencil grip. Assist individual students throughout the day to help them with this pencil grip. It is important to establish this grip (see Orientation).

Say

Get your markers ready. Pinch it, and rest it on the "table."

- Dictate a sound and hold up Echo. This is the students' cue to echo the sound. For example:

Say

/t/ (hold up Echo and students echo /t/)

What says /t/?

- Call on a student to answer ("t") by naming the letter that makes that sound.
- Point to the letter on the Letter Formation Poster and discuss formation.
- Next have that student make the letter on the Large Writing Grid, as you guide them with the verbalization from the Letter Formation Guide.
- Then have all students write the answer on the their Dry Erase Writing Tablets and have them say the verbalization with you.
- Do several sounds. See the Echo Sounds Resource List in each Unit to select sounds.
- Have students say letter-keyword-sound.

Differentiation

For struggling students, have them do lots of practice with gross motor letter formation, tracing and copying the letter on the Large Writing Grid and then doing it on their Dry Erase Writing Tablets.

For advanced students who already know letter formation, be sure they follow your verbalizations to make the letter. Then, they can practice independently, making several letters on their Letter Boards. Have them circle the letter that they think is their best one. It is essential, however, that they follow the verbalization and proper formations. These students can also guide others as appropriate.

Learning Activity Overview

Echo/Letter Formation

Activity Cue Echo/Letter Formation

Teacher Does	Teacher Says	Response
Cue students to get into proper writing position (chairs pushed in, feet on floor, arms on table). Show students proper pencil grip. Display the Pencil Grip Picture.	**Get your markers ready. Pinch it, and rest it on the "table."**	Have students hold marker. (They pinch it between index finger and thumb and rest it on the other 3 fingers - the "table.")
Dictate a sound.	/t/	
Hold up Baby Echo.		/t/
	What says /t/?	Students answer, **t**.
If a new letter, demonstrate the letter on the Large Writing Grid while you say the verbalization. If review, select a student. (Point out the kind of letter it is on the Letter Formation Poster.)	Say the verbalization (see the Letter Formation Guide) for the targeted letter.	If review and student is making the letter: a student makes the letter on the Large Writing Grid, saying the verbalization.
	Okay. Let's make a t. Use the verbalization for the letter. Be sure to be consistent.	Students make the letter on their Dry Erase Writing Tablets while saying the verbalization.
Say letter-keyword-sound and have students echo.	**t - top - /t/**	t - top - /t/
	Erase your board.	Students erase.
Dictate another letter.		

Learning Activity Overview

Letter-Keyword-Sound

In a Nutshell

- Teach letter-keyword-sound.
- Students echo.

TEACHER MATERIALS
- Echo the Owl
- Large Sound Cards
- Standard Sound Cards

VIEW THE PREVENTION/EARLY INTERVENTION LEARNING COMMUNITY

Learning Activity
- Letter-Keyword-Sound

ESTIMATED ACTIVITY TIME

2-3 MINUTES / PER NEW SOUND

Note
This activity teaches new letter and sound association(s). The same procedures are used in Drill Sounds to practice letters that have been previously introduced.

SYNOPSIS

This activity introduces students to the letter name and sound association with the help of a "keyword" picture.

PROCEDURE

Large Sound Card

- Hold up the Large Sound Card with the letter you are introducing.

Ask

Does anyone know the name of this letter? (Name the letter.)

What is this picture? (Name the keyword.)

- As you say the word, emphasize the sound at the beginning of the word. Tell the students that the word in the picture begins with that sound.
- Explain that the picture is there to help them remember that the letter makes that sound and **say the sound**.
- Tell them that Echo wants them to echo so that they can learn all about this new letter and the sound it makes.
- Say the letter-keyword-sound, hold up Echo and then have the students echo.

Standard Sound Card

- Next show students the letter on the Standard Sound Card. Tell them that the letter on this card is the same letter, but it doesn't have a picture.
- If appropriate, point out the difference from how it looks on the Large Sound Card. For example, explain that **a** is the way this letter sometimes looks in books but the students will write an **a** similar to the one on the Large Sound Card.
- Tell the students that Echo wants them to practice this letter with both the Large Sound Card with a picture on it, and the Standard Sound Card.
- Hold up the Standard Sound Card and say the letter-keyword-sound, hold up Echo and then have the students echo.

Ask

Tell me the name of this letter. (t)

What is the word that will help us remember the sound /t/? (top)

What is the sound that it makes? (/t/)

Say

t-top-/t/ (hold up Echo and students echo **t-top-/t/**)

Differentiation

Since this activity introduces the letter-keyword and sound for the first time, it is standard for all students.

Learning Activity Overview

Letter-Keyword-Sound

Activity Cue Letter-Keyword-Sound

Teacher Does	Teacher Says	Response
Hold up a Large Sound Card (for example for the letter **t**).	**Who knows the name of this letter?**	Select a student to answer. **t**
	What is this picture?	Select a student to answer. **top**
	Say picture name, emphasizing the initial sound. Tell students the word in the picture begins with the sound made by the letter **t** and the picture helps us remember the sound: **/t/, /t/, /t/, top** Say that Echo wants them to learn the sound by echoing it: **t - top - /t/**	
Hold up Echo.		t - top - /t/
Hold up a Standard Sound Card (for example the letter **t**). Hold up Echo.	**Tell the students that Echo wants them to practice the letter with the Standard Sound Cards without the picture.** **t - top - /t/. Echo.**	t - top - /t/
Add Standard Sound Card to your card display board and point to it.	**What is the name of this letter?**	t
	What is the word to help us learn the sound?	top
	What is the sound?	/t/
	t - top - /t/	
Hold up Echo.		t - top - /t/

© 2002, 2012 WILSON LANGUAGE TRAINING CORPORATION

Learning Activity Overview

Sky Write/Letter Formation

In a Nutshell

- Write letter on Large Writing Grid.
- Students follow your verbalization to sky write a letter.

TEACHER MATERIALS

- Letter Formation Guide
- Large Writing Grid

VIEW THE PREVENTION/EARLY INTERVENTION LEARNING COMMUNITY

Learning Activity

- Sky Write/Letter Formation

ESTIMATED ACTIVITY TIME

3-5 MINUTES / PER LETTER

SYNOPSIS

Students use gross-motor memory to learn letter formation following your verbalization. This activity also helps students make a multisensory association between the auditory sound of a letter, the grapheme or its visual representation, and the kinesthetic memory of its letter formation.

PROCEDURE

- Use the Large Writing Grid.

- Have the students stand. Always start this activity by shaking out arms and body and stretching. Tell the students to point their arm out "**straight as a pencil.**" Tell them to point with 2 fingers. (Two fingers creates a stronger muscle pull, and thus is felt more. A straight arm is necessary for gross motor memory.)

Say

Let's warm up.

Point to the sky line.

Point to the plane line.

Point to the grass line.

Point to the worm line. (also, mix order)

- Students put their arms down. **Write the letter on the grid** and say what kind of letter (e.g. "**t is a sky line letter**"). Ask students where it will begin (on the sky line). Next demonstrate how to sky write the letter you are going to practice. Be sure to face the board and say the verbalization. After you demonstrate, have students put their arms out "**straight as a pencil**" and point with 2 fingers.

- Make the letter again and have the students make it with you, saying the verbalization themselves. Do it together several times. **After making the letter, say the letter-keyword-sound** (t-top-/t/). This helps to make an association between the formation and the sound. You can have students shake out their arms before teaching or practicing a new letter.

Differentiation

Since this activity introduces letter formation, it is standard for all students.

40 FUNDATIONS® LEVEL K © 2002, 2012 WILSON LANGUAGE TRAINING CORPORATION

Learning Activity Overview

Sky Write/Letter Formation

Activity Cue Sky Write/Letter Formation

Teacher Does	Teacher Says	Response
Instruct students to stand and shake out arms and body.		Students shake out arms and body, and stretch.
Face the Writing Grid. Extend your arm straight out, pointing with two fingers. Point to each line.	**Point to the sky line.** **Point to the plane line.** **Point to the grass line.** **Point to the worm line.** (Also, mix the order.)	Students point to each line with their arm out "straight as a pencil."
Write the letter on the grid, and tell students what kind of letter (e.g.: write **t**).	**t is a sky line letter. Where does it start?**	**On the sky line.**
Demonstrate how to sky write the letter, facing the Writing Grid, using your straight arm, pointing with two fingers.	Using the wording on the Letter Formation Guide, verbalize the letter formation as you make it. Be sure to use verbalization provided for that letter. Be consistent! e.g. for the letter **t**: **Point to the sky line.** **Go down to the grass line.** **Cross it on the plane line.**	Students face Writing Grid. Using a straight arm with two fingers pointed, they echo your verbalization and form the letter.
Say letter-keyword-sound. Practice several times.	**t - top - /t/**	Students make letter and say letter-keyword-sound. **t - top - /t/**

© 2002, 2012 WILSON LANGUAGE TRAINING CORPORATION

Learning Activity Overview

Student Notebook

In a Nutshell

- Students trace letter and say letter-keyword-sound.

TEACHER MATERIALS

- Letter Formation Guide
- Student Notebook

STUDENT MATERIALS

- Student Notebook

VIEW THE PREVENTION/EARLY INTERVENTION LEARNING COMMUNITY

Learning Activity

- Student Notebook

ESTIMATED ACTIVITY TIME

5 MINUTES / PER NEW LETTER

1-2 MINUTES / PER REVIEW LETTER

SYNOPSIS

Students use tactile and motor-memory to practice letter-keyword-sounds and letter formation in their Student Notebooks. This activity helps to solidify the link between a letter, its sound, and its formation. It supports handwriting and spelling.

PROCEDURE

Introduce New Letter

- Direct the students to find the letter that you are working on in their Student Notebooks. When students find the letter,

Ask

What is the name of this letter?

What is the picture to help us remember the sound?

What is the sound that this letter makes?

- Say the letter-keyword-sound and have students echo.
- Next, hold up your copy of the Student Notebook and show them how to trace the letter with their finger, using the verbalization from the Letter Formation Guide.
- Have students say the letter formation verbalization with you while they trace the letter with their finger. Say the letter-keyword-sound after the letter is traced.
- Next, have students retrace the letter saying verbalization and letter, keyword, and sound each time. Do it with them to model.
- After you do this with a new sound, the students can then color the keyword picture.

Practice Letters

- Students practice previously learned letters. To do this, students should trace the letter with their finger while naming the letter-keyword-sound. As more letters are introduced, you can do this by category (example: practice all sky line letters).
- Sometimes do this together as a group as you direct students with verbalization. Other times, students can do this independently as you circulate around the room to assist them.

Differentiation

Any student having difficulty should do additional practice of letters every day. Begin by having the student trace and then copy the letter from the model on the Large Writing Grid.

Advanced students can draw additional pictures that begin with the letter on the Student Notebook page (e.g. on the Bb page, students can draw a banana, boat, boy etc.).

Learning Activity Overview

Student Notebook

Activity Cue Student Notebook

Teacher Does	Teacher Says	Response
Hold up the Student Notebook opened to the current page. Walk around and assist students.	**Find the letter in your Student Notebook.**	Students find correct letter in their Student Notebooks.
Point to the letter on the page in your sample Student Notebook.	**What is the name of this letter?**	Select a student or have them answer in unison. **t**
Point to the picture.	**What picture helps us remember the sound?**	Select a student or have them answer in unison. **top**
	What sound does the letter make?	Select a student or have them answer in unison. **/t/**
	t - top - /t/. Echo.	Select a student or have them answer in unison. **t - top - /t/**
Trace the letter in the Student Notebook sample with your finger, holding it up for students to see.	**Now, let's practice.** **Get your tracing finger ready.** Following the Letter Formation Guide, say verbalization of letter formation while you trace letter.	Have students trace letter with their finger, saying your verbalization.
After the letter is traced say letter-keyword-sound.	**t - top - /t/**	t - top - /t/
	Let's practice the letter one more time. Repeat the verbalization. **t - top - /t/. Echo.**	Students trace again, saying the verbalization. **t - top - /t/** Students color keyword picture for letter.
For practice: Direct students to retrace previously learned letters using verbalizations, and naming the letter-keyword-sound after tracing the letter. Sometimes do as a group, other times students can do independently.	**Say letter verbalization for each letter you practice and say the letter-keyword-sound.**	Students practice the letters as directed.

Learning Activity Overview

Teach Trick Words

In a Nutshell

- Teach trick words using sentences from the Unit Resources.
- Students identify the new trick word in the sentence.

TEACHER MATERIALS

- Baby Echo
- Sentence Frames
- Trick Word Flashcards

VIEW THE PREVENTION/EARLY INTERVENTION LEARNING COMMUNITY

Learning Activity

- Teach Trick Words

ESTIMATED ACTIVITY TIME

5 MINUTES PER NEW TRICK WORD

SYNOPSIS

Students are introduced to trick words. This activity helps students learn high frequency words for reading. It also develops their word awareness and reinforces capitalization and punctuation.

PROCEDURE

Trick words must be presented to students as words that cannot be tapped out. To teach trick words, follow these steps.

- Dictate the sentence provided. Hold up Baby Echo and have students repeat the sentence.
- Ask a student to find and arrange the appropriate Sentence Frames for the sentence on the board.
- Say the sentence again, writing each word on a Sentence Frame as you say it. Then, circle the new trick word in the sentence.
- Slowly read the sentence, pointing to each word. Be sure to pause and emphasize the new trick word in the sentence. Ask the students to tell you the new trick word.
- Show students the corresponding Trick Word Flashcard. Explain that the word is called a trick word because it is tricky. It cannot be tapped out like some other words, so they will have to remember it.
- Present Trick Word Flashcards packet for students to read.

Differentiation

Students can make individualized flash card packets to practice automatic reading of trick words that have been introduced.

For struggling students, limit the number of words in their packet, adding more as they are ready.

For advanced students, eliminate words from their packet if clearly mastered.

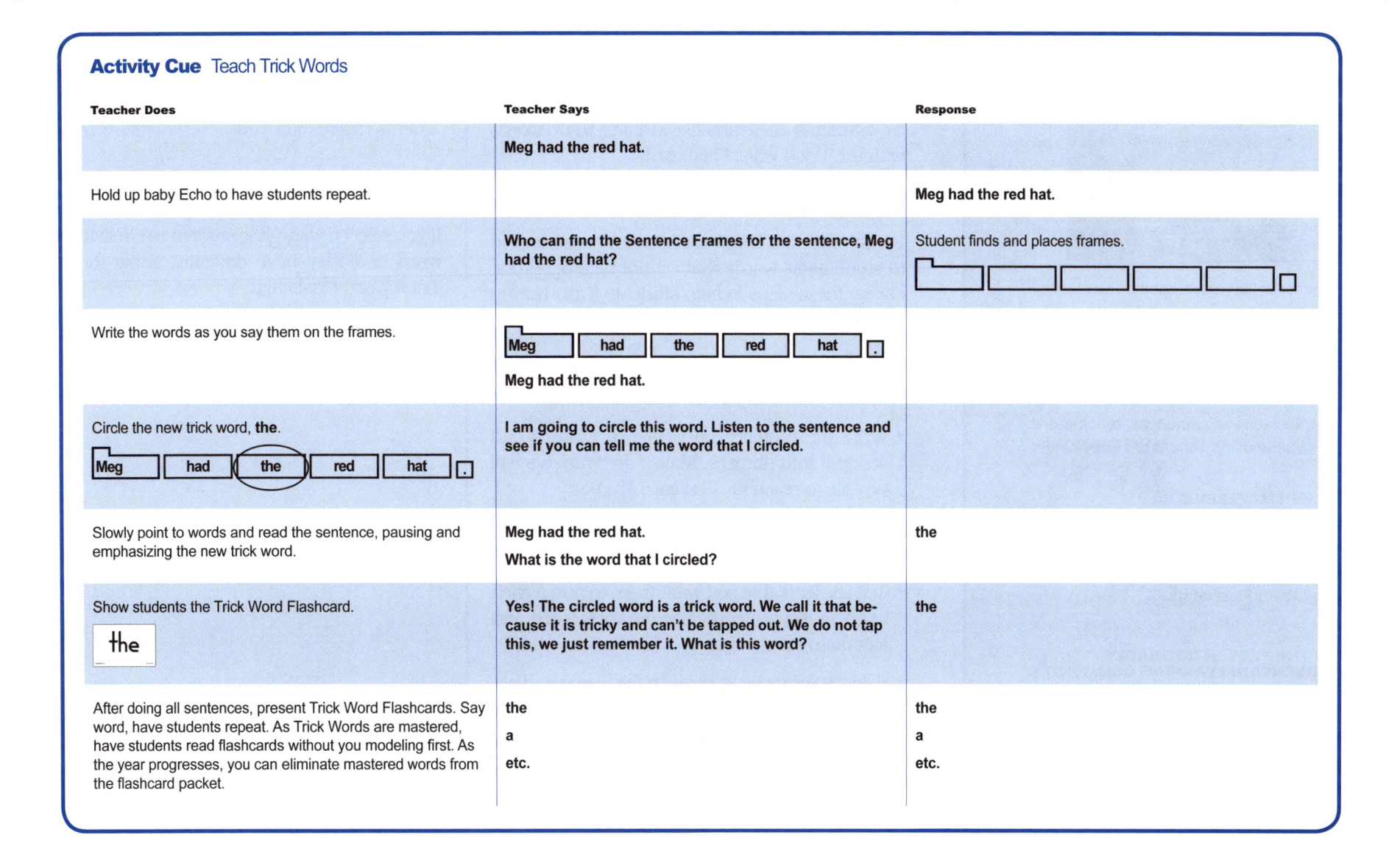

Learning Activity Overview

Teach Trick Words

Activity Cue Teach Trick Words

Teacher Does	Teacher Says	Response
	Meg had the red hat.	
Hold up baby Echo to have students repeat.		**Meg had the red hat.**
	Who can find the Sentence Frames for the sentence, Meg had the red hat?	Student finds and places frames.
Write the words as you say them on the frames.	Meg | had | the | red | hat | . **Meg had the red hat.**	
Circle the new trick word, **the**. Meg | had | (the) | red | hat | .	**I am going to circle this word. Listen to the sentence and see if you can tell me the word that I circled.**	
Slowly point to words and read the sentence, pausing and emphasizing the new trick word.	**Meg had the red hat.** **What is the word that I circled?**	the
Show students the Trick Word Flashcard. the	**Yes! The circled word is a trick word. We call it that because it is tricky and can't be tapped out. We do not tap this, we just remember it. What is this word?**	the
After doing all sentences, present Trick Word Flashcards. Say word, have students repeat. As Trick Words are mastered, have students read flashcards without you modeling first. As the year progresses, you can eliminate mastered words from the flashcard packet.	the a etc.	the a etc.

© 2002, 2012 WILSON LANGUAGE TRAINING CORPORATION

Learning Activity Overview

Trick Word Practice

In a Nutshell

- Teacher writes a sentence on Sentence Frames.
- Student circles trick word in sentence and class determines if the word is correctly identified.
- After dictating all sentences, teacher drills trick words using Trick Word Flashcards.

TEACHER MATERIALS

- Baby Echo
- Sentence Frames
- Trick Word Flashcards

VIEW THE PREVENTION/EARLY INTERVENTION LEARNING COMMUNITY

Learning Activity

- Trick Word Practice

ESTIMATED ACTIVITY TIME

5 MINUTES PER NEW TRICK WORD

SYNOPSIS

Students identify trick words by listening to and repeating the words as they are used in sentences. Students then practice drilling trick words with the Trick Word Flashcards.

PROCEDURE

Remember that trick words must be presented to students as words that cannot be tapped out. Follow these steps to help students learn how to identify trick words.

- Dictate the sentence provided for practice. Hold up Baby Echo and have students repeat.
- Write the sentence on Sentence Frames and scoop it into phrases. Make sure students will be able to reach the Sentence Frames.
- Read the sentence with prosody, and have students repeat.
- Tell students that you want them to find a trick word in the sentence. Say the trick word and ask them to repeat it.
- Select a volunteer to come to the board and circle the trick word. Slowly repeat the sentence while pointing to words so the student can find it.
- Show the class the corresponding Trick Word Flashcard. Ask them if the student found the correct word.
- Erase and dictate the other sentences from the Unit Resources.
- After repeating the exercise with all the sentences in the Unit Resources, present the Trick Word Flashcards. Say each word and have students repeat after you.

Differentiation

If you select a struggling student to circle the trick word and they have difficulty, show them the Trick Word Flashcard.

If you select an advanced student to circle the trick word, you can then erase it and have them spell it aloud and write it back on the frame themselves.

Learning Activity Overview

Trick Word Practice

Activity Cue Trick Word Practice

Teacher Does	Teacher Says	Response
Say the sentence provided for practice.	**Sid is the best dog.**	
Hold up baby Echo to have students repeat.		Sid is the best dog.
Write the sentence on Sentence Frames and scoop it into phrases. Read it with phrasing, and have students repeat. **Sid** | **is** | **the** | **best** | **dog** | .	**Sid is the best dog.**	Sid is the best dog.
Say a trick word and have students repeat.	**The trick word that I want you to find in this sentence is the. What is the trick word?**	the
Select a student to come to the board and circle the trick word. Slowly, repeat the sentence while pointing to the words so the student can find it.	**Sid is the best dog.**	**Sid** | **is** | **(the)** | **best** | **dog** | .
Show students the corresponding Trick Word Flashcard. [the]	**Did he/she find the?** **This word is the, what is it?**	Yes / the
Erase frames and the circle to dictate each new sentence.		
After doing all sentences, present Trick Word Flashcards. Say word, have students repeat. As Trick Words are mastered, have students read flashcards without you modeling first. As the year progresses, you can eliminate mastered words from the flashcard packet.	the / a / etc.	the / a / etc.

Learning Activity Overview

Variable Activities

Make It Fun

SYNOPSIS
Make It Fun Activities are designed to reinforce the Unit concepts or review previously taught concepts with a game activity.

PROCEDURE
Suggestions for various reinforcing activities are provided in each Unit.

Materials needed for this activity vary and are therefore listed in each Unit.

Storytime

SYNOPSIS
Storytime involves listening, reading and writing activities designed to help develop the students' awareness of print visualization, understanding of story structure, verbal memory and comprehension.

PROCEDURE
Activities for Storytime will be described in each Unit.

Materials needed for this activity vary and are therefore listed in each Unit.

Word Play

SYNOPSIS
Word Play activities teach or reinforce the development of print awareness, phonological awareness, and beginning decoding and spelling skills.

Students will also learn key elements of basic sentence structure, including capitalization and punctuation.

PROCEDURE
In the beginning of the year, the emphasis is on the understanding that sentences have separate words, and words have separate syllables.

In the second half of the year, the students learn that words or syllables have separate sounds. Activities for Word Play will be described in each Unit.

Materials needed for this activity vary and are therefore listed in each Unit.

Orientation & Units

Level K

Orientation Level K

In a Nutshell

NEW CONCEPTS

Echoing (Echo the Owl and Baby Echo)

The Large Writing Grid with the line names

Following verbalizations in making lines

Pencil grip and writing posture

The meaning of the word 'trace'

Letter-Keyword-Sound and Letter Formation for the letter t

TIME IN ORIENTATION

3-4 DAYS

Days 1-2 lessons will take approximately five-ten minutes.

Days 3 and 4 will take approximately ten minutes.

You can also accelerate the Orientation by combining Days 1 and 2.

Introduction

Take time first to get "oriented" and to prepare both yourself and your students for your year ahead with Fundations®.

THE LARGE WRITING GRID

The Large Writing Grid is designed to guide students in proper letter formation. It consists of four lines that correspond to specific letter placement. The lines are named and the pictures will assist students in identifying the lines.

```
_____ (SKY LINE)
- - - - - - - - - - - - - (PLANE LINE)
_____ (GRASS LINE)
_____ (WORM LINE)
```

The bold line (or the "dark" line) helps locate the top of the grid, especially on pages with multiple grids. This bold line is also the starting point for all uppercase letters.

Lowercase letters start on this bold line or on the (dashed) plane line just beneath it. You will stress this so that students do not form letters from the bottom up.

THE WILSON FONT

The Wilson Font provides a basic manuscript form of print. Often students come to Kindergarten or Grade 1 with an ability to write uppercase letters of the alphabet. To begin reading and spelling instruction, lowercase letter knowledge is key. Rather than reinforce or teach the uppercase letters first, Fundations starts with the lowercase letters.

In Fundations, letter formation is closely connected with sound instruction. Students learn the letter name, its formation and its sound simultaneously. This creates an important link and uses motor memory learning to associate letters with their sounds. Students will succeed with consistent verbal cues, repetition, sky writing, tracing and writing practice (all described in the Learning Activities).

Your Orientation Lessons are very brief. Beginning in Unit 1, the standard lesson will be 25-35 minutes in length.

LARGE WRITING GRID

You will need the Large Writing Grid. Be sure to secure it in a place that can be reached by students.

Orientation

LETTER FORMATION GUIDES

These laminated cards provide step-by-step verbalizations for letter formation on the Wilson grid.

STUDENT NOTEBOOK / DESK STRIPS

Write the students' names on the front of their Student Notebooks and Desk Strips. Use a thin black permanent marker. Be sure to print the name clearly using the Wilson Font letters. Do this for each student to provide them with a model to copy.

Put a Desk Strip on each student's desk. This can be removed at the end of the year.

BABY ECHO

To facilitate pointing with Baby Echo place it on a pointer or ruler.

PRINT FROM THE PLC: 1-2-3 RIGHT / LET'S WRITE PICTURE AND THE PENCIL GRIP PICTURE

Copy the 1-2-3 Right / Let's Write and the Pencil Grip Pictures. Tape the pictures in a place that can be seen by all students. These will serve as a reminder on how to sit for writing and properly hold a pencil or marker.

Print pictures from the PLC.

1-2-3 RIGHT / LET'S WRITE

1. **Sit** *right*
   Seat pulled in, feet on floor
2. **Place paper and hands** *right*
   Paper slanted, wrist straight, elbow to desk, other hand holding paper
3. **Grip pencil** *right*
   Pencil held between index finger and thumb, resting on the other fingers

Let's *write!*

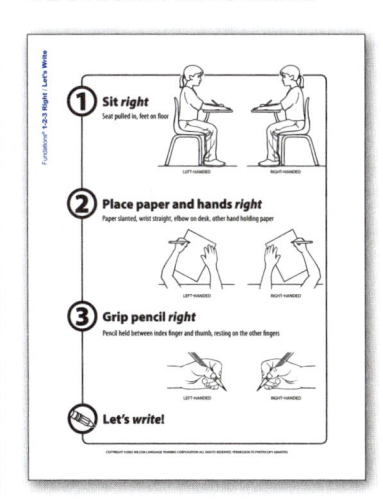

PENCIL GRIP PICTURES

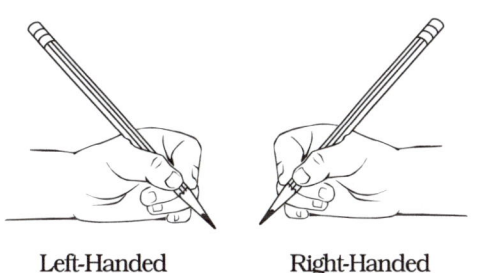

Left-Handed   Right-Handed

Getting Ready

MATERIAL PREPARATIONS

Teacher Materials

- Echo the Owl, Baby Echo the Owl
- Pencil Grip Picture
- Letter Formation Guide
- Large Writing Grid on Classroom Board
- Large Sound Card and Standard Sound Card for the letter t.

Student Materials

- Student Notebook
- Dry Erase Writing Tablet
- Dry Erase Markers and Erasers

Dry erase markers and erasers are not provided with Fundations® since many classrooms are already equipped with them. Old socks can be used for erasers!

HOME SUPPORT

Copy and send home the Orientation Letter and activities.

STUDY THE LEARNING ACTIVITIES

Study the following activities:

- Letter-Keyword-Sound
- Drill Sounds/Warm-Up
- Student Notebook
- Sky Write/Letter Formation
- Echo/Letter Formation

tip

Review the Learning Activity and Unit videos on the PLC.

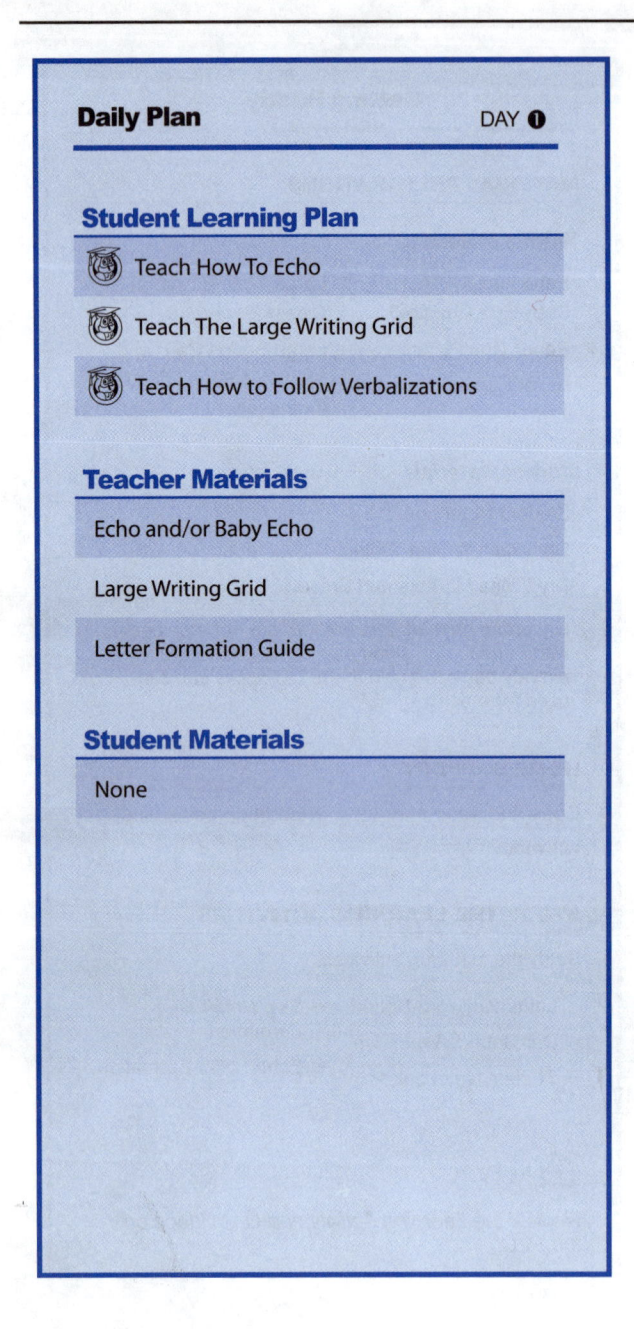

Orientation

Day 1

Daily Plan — DAY 1

Student Learning Plan
- Teach How To Echo
- Teach The Large Writing Grid
- Teach How to Follow Verbalizations

Teacher Materials
- Echo and/or Baby Echo
- Large Writing Grid
- Letter Formation Guide

Student Materials
- None

Teach How To Echo

Hold up the large white owl and ask the students to name the kind of bird. Explain that owls have very good eyesight and hearing.

Next, tell the students its name, Echo. Ask if anyone knows what the word echo means. Explain that Echo the Owl is going to help them learn their letters and sounds and that she wants the students to "echo" her whenever you hold her up.

Say the word, "hello" and hold up Echo. The students should say "hello." Say several words or phrases to practice echoing.

You can also introduce Baby Echo and say that he is just like big Echo. He wants to help the students learn their letters and sounds and so he has them echo too.

Teach The Large Writing Grid

In order to learn the letters, students will need to follow basic directions. Prepare them by teaching them the names of the lines on the Large Writing Grid.

Show Students The Large Writing Grid On Your Classroom Board

Explain that all the lines have names. Point to the cloud and ask what it is. Point to the sun and ask what it is.

Ask

Where do you find the sun and clouds? (In the sky).

Tell students the top line is called the sky line. Do the same for the other lines. Tell them that these lines will help them make their letters.

Show them that the plane flies along the plane line, tracing your finger from left to right. It reminds us to make our letters and words in that direction.

Have Students Point To The Grid Lines

Next have the students stand up and tell them to point their arms out "straight as a pencil." Don't let them bend their elbows. Tell them to point with two fingers.

Face the Large Writing Grid and point with the students to model.

Orientation

Day 1

Say

> Point to the sky line.
>
> Point to the plane line.
>
> Point to the grass line.
>
> Point to the worm line.

Next ask for line names randomly:

Say

> Listen carefully, I'll try to trick you.
>
> Point to the grass line.
>
> Point to the sky line.
>
> Point to the plane line.
>
> Point to the worm line.

Repeat until students can easily point to each line.

Teach How to Follow Verbalizations

Have students shake out their hands. Demonstrate wiggling and shaking body and arms. Have them stretch (stand on toes and stretch hands up to the ceiling).

Next, tell them you are going to do something a little different. First show them and then have them do it with you. Say the verbalization each time in order to direct them.

Say

> Point to the sky line – go down to the grass line. Stop!
>
> Point to the plane line, go down to the grass line. Stop!
>
> Point to the plane line, go all the way to the worm line. Stop!
>
> Shake out your hand.

Orientation

Day 2

Daily Plan — DAY 2

Student Learning Plan
- Review Grid Lines
- Teach Pencil Grip and Tracing

Teacher Materials
- Large Writing Grid

Student Materials
- Dry Erase Writing Tablet

Review Grid Lines

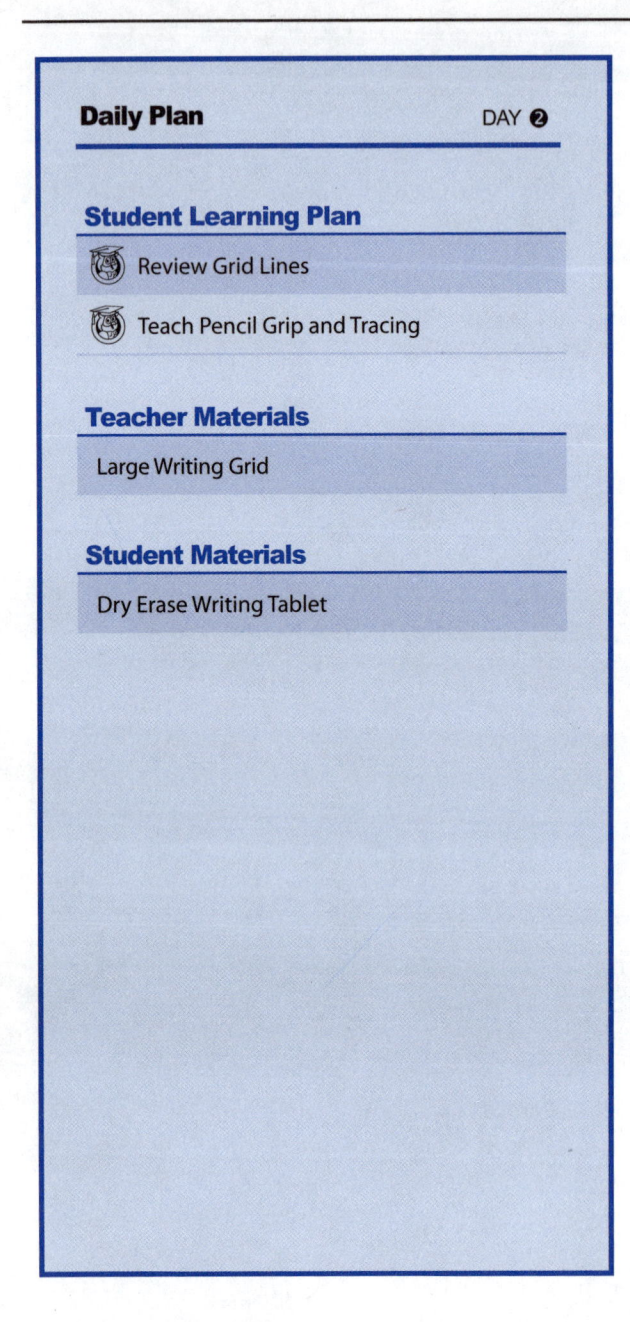

Have students stand up. Start this activity by shaking out arms and body and stretching. Tell them to point their arm out "straight as a pencil." Tell them to face the Large Writing Grid and point with 2 fingers.

Say
> Let's warm up.
>
> Point to the sky line.
>
> Point to the plane line.
>
> Point to the grass line.
>
> Point to the worm line.

Teach Pencil Grip and Tracing

Teach the students how to hold their markers and sit for writing. Have them follow your verbalizations to make lines. Lastly, teach students how to trace. You will need to reinforce these concepts daily throughout Unit 1.

Before you give out the Dry Erase Writing Tablets, explain to the students that you will help them do what they need to do in order to get a tablet.

Say
> First, all children need to pull in their seats and put their feet on the floor. Now put your hands on the desk.
>
> This is your writing position. Whenever we write, you need to sit like this.
>
> Maria is ready for her tablet.

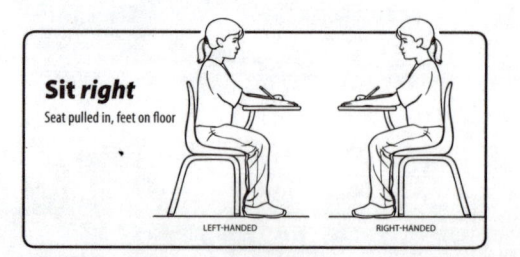

Sit right
Seat pulled in, feet on floor

LEFT-HANDED   RIGHT-HANDED

As students show readiness, give out the Dry Erase Writing Tablets, (but not the markers).

Say
> Next, let me show you how you will hold the markers.

Orientation

Day 2

> The first thing you do is pinch the marker between your thumb and pointer finger.
>
> Then put your three other fingers together to make a "table." Now, rest your marker on the "table."

Help students with their pencil grip as you give them the markers.

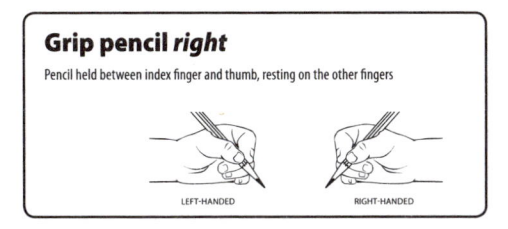

Grip pencil *right*
Pencil held between index finger and thumb, resting on the other fingers

LEFT-HANDED   RIGHT-HANDED

When all the markers are dispersed have the students do the following all together:

Say

> Pinch your marker between your thumb and your pointer finger.
>
> Put your other fingers together to make a "table." Now, rest your marker on the "table."
>
> Now I think you are ready to use the special tablets.

Have students practice following your direction, simply making lines.

Say

> Point your marker to the sky line. Go down to the grass line and stop.

Hold up your Dry Erase Writing Tablet and model and then do it again with them (say the same verbalization each time). After making each line, have students check to see if their line looks like your line and then erase.

Say

> Point your marker to the plane line. Go to the grass line. Stop!
>
> Point your marker to the plane line. Go to the worm line and stop!
>
> Now let's do one more thing. This is tricky.

Make a line from the sky line to the grass line and then explain what "trace" means, tracing the line back up to the sky line. Have them trace as you verbalize the directions:

Say

> Point to the plane line. Go to the grass line. Now trace back up to the plane line and stop.

Do other variations, directing students with your verbalizations.

Example

> Point to the sky line. Go to the grass line. Now trace back up to the plane line and stop.

tip
Use both the 1-2-3 Right / Let's Write and the Pencil Grip Pictures to remind students about proper writing readiness. Refer to these frequently throughout the day.

Orientation

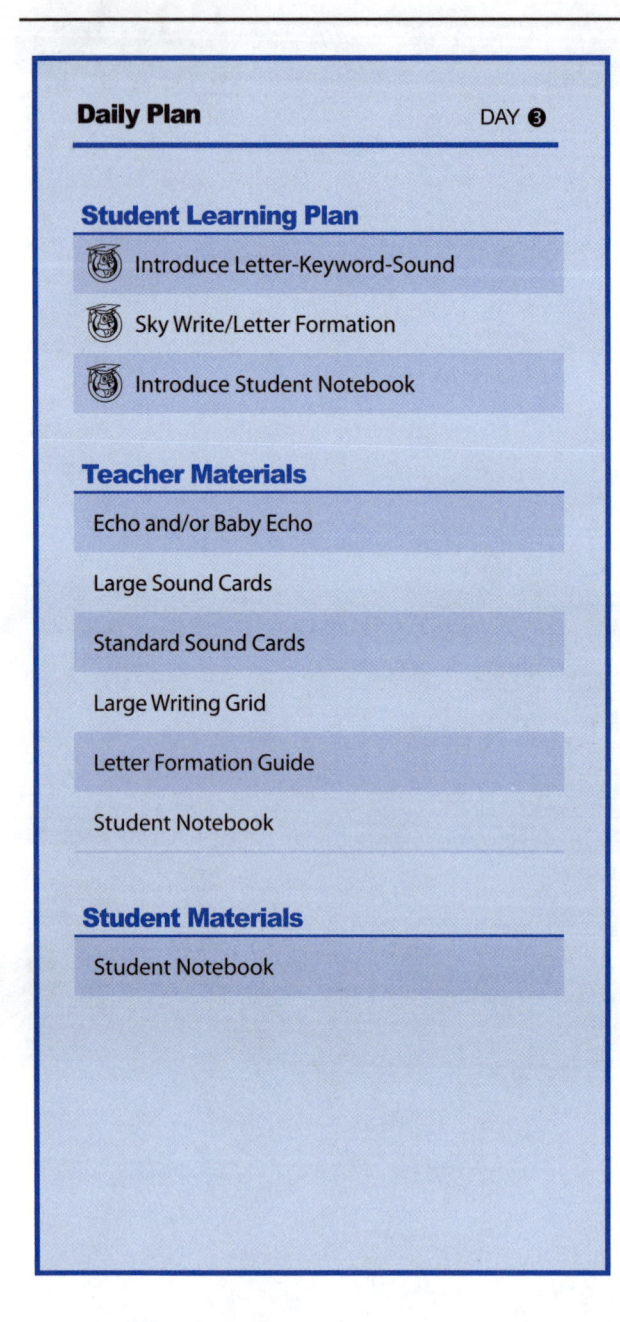

Day 3

Daily Plan — DAY 3

Student Learning Plan
- Introduce Letter-Keyword-Sound
- Sky Write/Letter Formation
- Introduce Student Notebook

Teacher Materials
- Echo and/or Baby Echo
- Large Sound Cards
- Standard Sound Cards
- Large Writing Grid
- Letter Formation Guide
- Student Notebook

Student Materials
- Student Notebook

Introduce Letter-Keyword-Sound

Hold up the Large Sound Card with the letter **t**.

Ask
> Does anyone know the name of this letter?

Tell students the letter name.

Ask
> What is this picture?

Say the word, **top**, and emphasize the /t/ sound at the beginning of the word. Tell the students that the word begins with the sound /t/.

Explain that the picture is there to help them remember that the letter makes a special sound and say the sound.

Tell them that Echo the Owl wants them to echo so that they can learn all about this new letter and the sound it makes.

Say
> t-top-/t/

Hold up Echo and have students repeat.

Next show the students the letter on the Standard Sound Card. [Tell them that the letter on this card is also the same letter, but it doesn't have a picture. Tell them that Echo the Owl wants them to practice this letter with both the big card with a picture on it and the small card without the picture.]

Hold up the Standard Sound Card and say, the letter name-keyword-sound.

Say
> t-top-/t/

Have the students echo.

Ask
> Tell me the name of this letter. (t)
>
> What is the sound that it makes? (/t/)
>
> What is the word that will help us remember the sound /t/? (top)

Say
> t-top-/t/

Have the students echo. Be sure that you do not add /ŭ/ to the sound of consonants. The sound of **t** is /t/ not /tŭ/.

Orientation

Day 3

Sky Write/Letter Formation

Warm Up

Have students stand up. Start this activity by shaking out arms and body and stretching. Tell them to point their arm out "straight as a pencil." Tell them to point with 2 fingers.

Say

>Let's warm up.
>
>Point to the sky line.
>
>Point to the plane line.
>
>Point to the grass line.
>
>Point to the worm line.

Students put their arms down. Next, demonstrate how to make the letter **t**. Write the letter on the Large Writing Grid and say the verbalization. After you demonstrate, have students put their arms out "straight as a pencil" and point with 2 fingers. Do the letter again and have the students do it with you, following the verbalization. Do it together several times.

Letter Formation for *t*

Use the following verbalization to direct students in proper letter formation.

>**t is a sky line letter.**
>
>**It starts on the** (sky line).

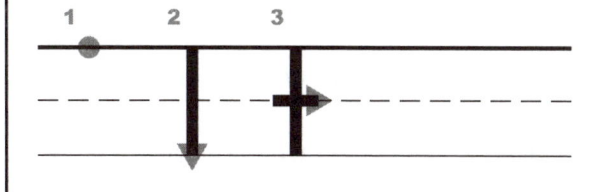

1. **Point to the sky line.**
2. **Go down to the grass line.**
3. **Cross it on the plane line.**
4. **Say t - top - /t/, have students repeat.**

Introduce Student Notebook

Give each student their Student Notebook and explain that they will be learning and practicing lowercase letters with this book.

Tell them that the lowercase letters are very important to learn for reading and writing. Direct the students to find the letter **t**.

Ask

>What is the name of this letter? (t)
>
>What is the picture to help us remember the sound? (top)
>
>What is the sound that this letter makes? (/t/)

Say the letter-keyword-sound and have the students echo.

Next, hold up your Student Notebook and show them how to trace the letter with their finger. Use the verbalization for the letter formation to direct the students while they trace it with their finger. Hold up your notebook to model. Next, have them trace it again, saying the letter-keyword-sound. Do it with them to model. After you do this, the students can then color the picture of the top.

Orientation

Days 4 and 5

Daily Plan — DAYS 4 & 5

Student Learning Plan
- Drill Sounds/Warm-Up
- Sky Write/Letter Formation
- Echo/Letter Formation

Teacher Materials
- Echo and/or Baby Echo
- Large Sound Cards
- Standard Sound Cards
- Large Writing Grid
- Letter Formation Guide

Student Materials
- Dry Erase Writing Tablet

Drill Sounds/Warm-Up

Say **t-top-/t/**, as you hold up the Large Sound Card. Hold up Echo and have students repeat. Point to the Standard Sound Card, and say **t-top-/t/** and have students repeat.

Sky Write/Letter Formation

Practice sky writing the letter **t**. Follow the sky writing directions from Day 3.

Echo/Letter Formation

Prepare The Students

Pass out Dry Erase Writing Tablets and dry erase markers as students show they are ready to write: chairs pulled in, feet on floor, and hands on table.

When you give the marker to each child, help them pinch it (with pointer and thumb) and rest it (on three other fingers) and place it on the table.

Say
> Get your markers ready. Pinch it, rest it, and put it on the table.

You can make a reminder poster using the Pencil Grip Picture (see PLC).

Use this cue consistently to reinforce the pencil grip throughout the year. Assist individual students to help them with this pencil grip. It is important to firmly establish this grip.

First have students follow your directions to make lines.

Say
> Point to the sky line. Go down to the grass line. Stop.
>
> Point to the plane line. Go down to the worm line. Trace back up to the plane line. Stop.

Dictate The Sounds

Say
> /t/

Hold up Echo and have students repeat.

Say
> What says /t/?

Have a student give you the answer, naming the letter **t**. Next have that student come up to the classroom board to make the letter on the Large Writing Grid.

Then have all students write the answer on their Dry Erase Writing Tablet as you direct them with the letter formation verbalization.

Orientation

Unit 1 Level K

In a Nutshell

NEW CONCEPTS

Letter-Keyword-Sound for consonants

Letter-Keyword-Sound for short vowels

Letter Formation for lowercase letters (a-z)

Sound recognition: consonants and short vowels

Print and word awareness

Rhyming

Phonemic awareness: initial and final sounds

Story retelling

Beginning composition Skills

Fluency/phrasing with echo and choral reading

PLANNED TIME IN UNIT

12 WEEKS

LETTER / SOUND / FORMATION

Week	Letters	Week	Letters
1	t b f	7	e r
2	n m	8	p j
3	i u	9	l h k
4	c o	10	v w
5	a g	11	y x
6	d s	12	z q

Introduction

You are ready to begin your "routine" for letter introduction. Each week you will introduce 2 or 3 new letters, teaching the letter name-keyword-sound as well as the lowercase formation for each of the new letters. You will practice these letters all week, reviewing previous letters as well as the new letters.

You will also begin phonemic awareness instruction with rhyming and initial and final sound awareness in one-syllable words.

You will use Sentence Frames to teach word awareness so that students learn to discern the separate words in a dictated sentence. You will introduce the concepts of capitalization and punctuation and have students identify telling and asking sentences.

Lastly, you will help students use pictures and visualization to retell the sequence of events from a story.

Differentiation

Unit 1 spans 12 weeks of instruction and sets a critical foundation for both reading and writing. It is important that this Unit is not omitted or rushed.

Follow the instructions on each Learning Activity to differentiate for struggling and advanced students.

Unit 1

PREPARING YOUR MATERIALS

Arrange your Standard Sound Card display in the following manner

As letters are introduced, the Standard Sound Cards (a-z) are placed on display. If your classroom board is magnetic, use a magnetic strip on the back of each Standard Sound Card to adhere it to the board. If your board is not magnetic, you can use a pocket chart or masking tape to display the cards. The letter cards should be added gradually during the weeks in Unit 1. Alternatively, you can place all cards on your board and use a sticky note to cover them. Progressively disclose cards by removing the sticky note as a letter is introduced.

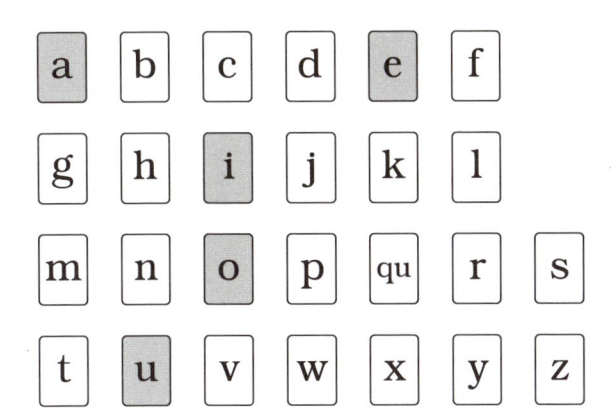

a	b	c	d	e	f
g	h	i	j	k	l
m	n	o	p	qu	r	s
t	u	v	w	x	y	z

Note How The Cards Are Arranged In Four Rows

This arrangement is designed to help the students learn the alphabet in four quadrants. These four quadrants are used for beginning dictionary skills.

DISPLAY POSTERS AND ALPHABET WALL STRIP

Display posters and the Alphabet Wall Strip in the classroom.

LETTER FORMATION GUIDE / LEARNING ACTIVITY CUE CARDS

Put the Letter Formation Guide ring on a hook in your classroom that makes it easily accessible.

Also, have your Learning Activity Cue Cards accessible to you during your Fundations® Lesson.

LEARNING PLANS AND RESOURCES

Print daily Learning Plans from PLC.

STUDENT MATERIALS

You will distribute student Magnetic Letter Tiles gradually as the letters are introduced. It may be helpful to remove the letter tiles from the Letter Boards and store them in individual sealed baggies.

Review the Learning Activity and Unit videos on the PLC.

Getting Ready

MATERIAL PREPARATIONS

Teacher Materials

- Echo and Baby Echo
- Large Sound Cards (a-z, as introduced)
- Standard Sound Cards, magnetized (a-z, as introduced)
- Large Writing Grid
- Vowel Extension Poster
- Letter Formation Guide
- Activity Cue Cards
- Sentence and Syllable Frames
- Student Notebook

Student Materials

- Student Notebook
- Letter Board with Magnetic Tiles (letters added as introduced)
- Dry Erase Writing Tablet

The Keyword Puzzles can be placed in the classroom to be used by students independently.

HOME SUPPORT

Copy and send home the Welcome Letter and Unit 1 Letter. Each week, send home the activities that correspond with the week.

STUDY THE LEARNING ACTIVITIES

Focus on learning the standard procedures for these six activities:

- Letter Keyword Sound
- Drill Sounds/Warm-Up
- Echo/Find Letters (Unit 1)
- Sky Write/Letter Formation
- Student Notebook
- Echo/Letter Formation

Unit 1

Student Learning Plan

THE LEARNING ACTIVITY SCHEDULE

Each week there is an outline of the Daily Schedule.

For example, on Day 1, you will do the following activities: Letter-Keyword-Sound, Sky Write/Letter Formation, Student Notebook.

Student Learning Plan
- Letter-Keyword-Sound
- Sky Write/Letter Formation
- Student Notebook

It is very important to follow the schedule in the sequence presented.

Learning Activity Procedures (in General)

There are standard procedures for each Learning Activity. This means that each time you do the activity, you will be following a standard procedure: teacher says, teacher does, students do/respond.

To smoothly execute these activities, refer to the Learning Activity Overview section of this manual. The Learning Activities are listed in alphabetical order for your quick reference.

Use the Learning Activity Cue Cards as a handy reference tool while you are conducting the lesson.

Over time, these lesson procedures will become second nature!

Unit 1 is 12 weeks and rotates the following activities. Focus on learning the standard procedures of these six activities first.

Letter Keyword Sound	Student Notebook
Sky Write/Letter Formation	Drill Sounds/Warm-Up
Echo/Letter Formation	Echo/Find Letters

Unit 1 also includes Make it Fun, Word Play and Storytime Activities; however these activities do not have standard procedures to learn. The activity details are provided in the Unit.

Learning Activity Information (Specific to the Unit)

In each week you will also find specific information for Learning Activities as it relates to what is taught in that week. For example, see Unit 1, Week 2, Day 1. When you do the Letter-Keyword-Sound activity, you will teach **m** and **n**.

The standard procedures along with the specific content provided in the Unit will give you what you need to present your lessons.

Unit 1

Student Learning Plan

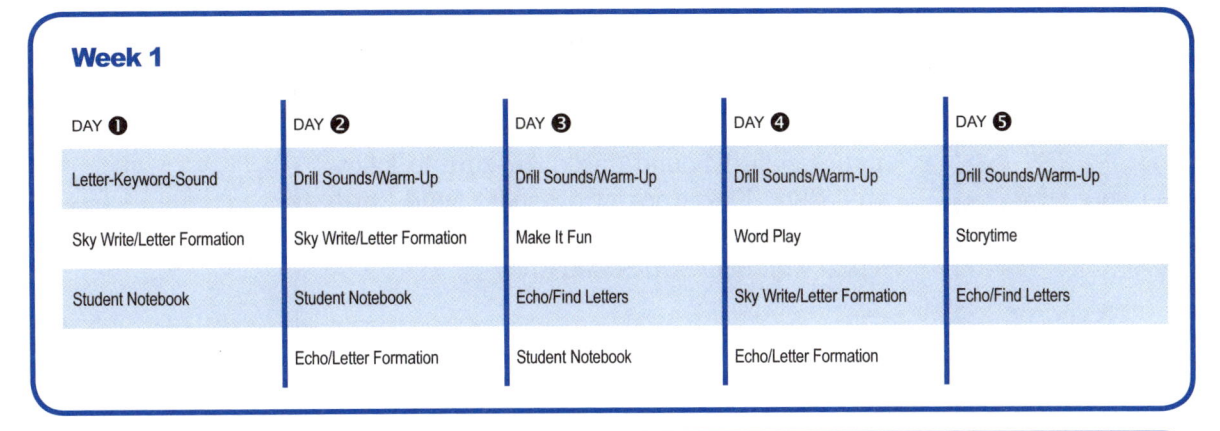

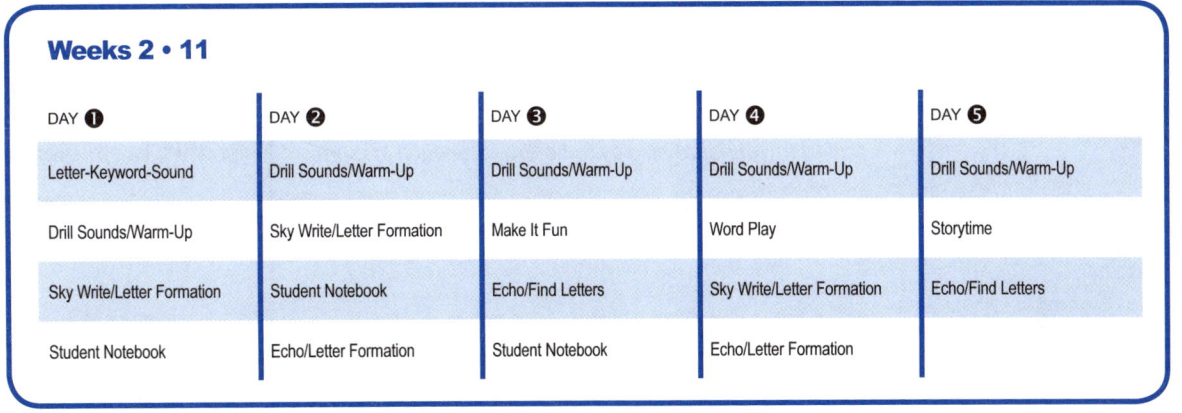

Week 1

DAY 1	DAY 2	DAY 3	DAY 4	DAY 5
Letter-Keyword-Sound	Drill Sounds/Warm-Up	Drill Sounds/Warm-Up	Drill Sounds/Warm-Up	Drill Sounds/Warm-Up
Sky Write/Letter Formation	Sky Write/Letter Formation	Make It Fun	Word Play	Storytime
Student Notebook	Student Notebook	Echo/Find Letters	Sky Write/Letter Formation	Echo/Find Letters
	Echo/Letter Formation	Student Notebook	Echo/Letter Formation	

Weeks 2 • 11

DAY 1	DAY 2	DAY 3	DAY 4	DAY 5
Letter-Keyword-Sound	Drill Sounds/Warm-Up	Drill Sounds/Warm-Up	Drill Sounds/Warm-Up	Drill Sounds/Warm-Up
Drill Sounds/Warm-Up	Sky Write/Letter Formation	Make It Fun	Word Play	Storytime
Sky Write/Letter Formation	Student Notebook	Echo/Find Letters	Sky Write/Letter Formation	Echo/Find Letters
Student Notebook	Echo/Letter Formation	Student Notebook	Echo/Letter Formation	

Week 12

DAY 1	DAY 2	DAY 3	DAY 4	DAY 5
Letter-Keyword-Sound	Drill Sounds/Warm-Up	Drill Sounds/Warm-Up	Drill Sounds/Warm-Up	Drill Sounds/Warm-Up
Drill Sounds/Warm-Up	Sky Write/Letter Formation	Make It Fun	Word Play	Storytime
Sky Write/Letter Formation	Student Notebook	Echo/Find Letters	Sky Write/Letter Formation	
Student Notebook	Echo/Letter Formation	Student Notebook	Echo/Letter Formation	

© 2002, 2012 WILSON LANGUAGE TRAINING CORPORATION

Unit 1 | Week 1

Day 1

Daily Plan — DAY 1

Student Learning Plan
- Letter-Keyword-Sound
- Sky Write/Letter Formation
- Student Notebook

Teacher Materials
- Echo and/or Baby Echo
- Large Sound Cards
- Standard Sound Cards
- Large Writing Grid
- Letter Formation Guide
- Student Notebook

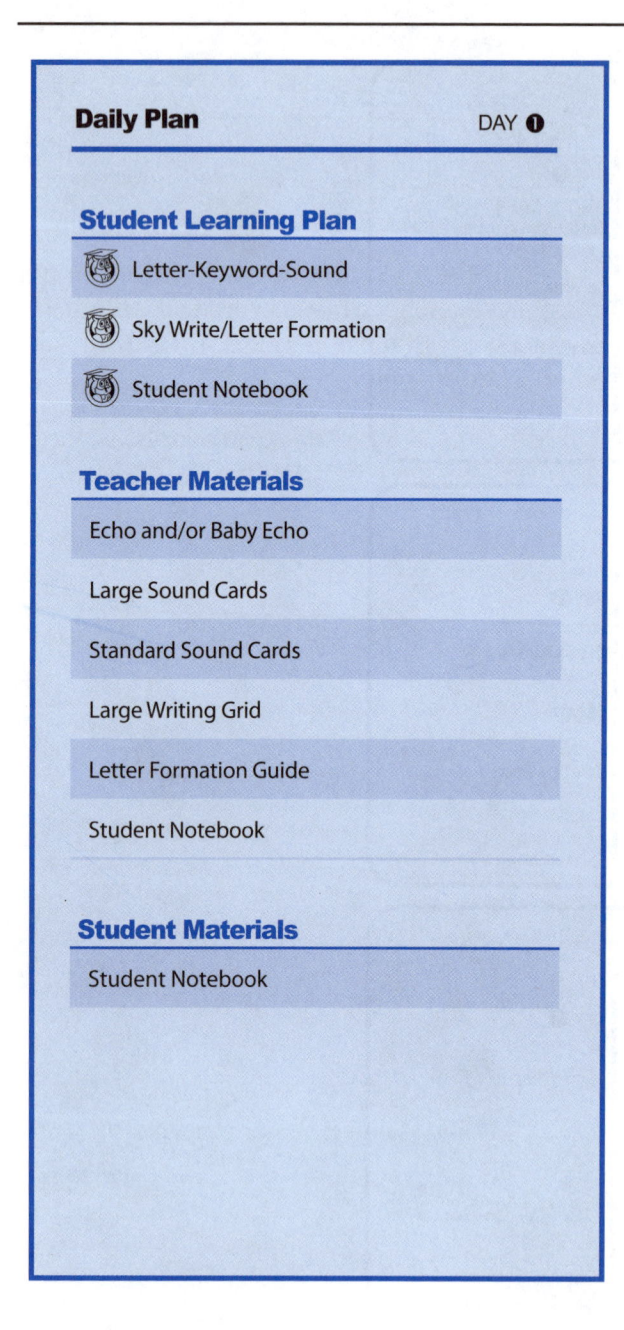

Student Materials
- Student Notebook

Letter-Keyword-Sound

Introduce Letter-Keyword-Sound with Large and Standard Sound Cards. Be sure to follow procedure. First teach with Large Sound Card. Have students echo letter-keyword-sound. Then repeat with Standard Sound Card.

[b] - b - bat - /b/

[f] - f - fun - /f/

Note

As a new letter is taught, its Standard Sound Card is added to your card display to be drilled at each lesson.

Sky Write/Letter Formation

Review Letter Formation

Review the letter formation for the letter **t** which was introduced in the orientation. Use the verbalization to direct students to sky write.

Teach Letter Formation

Teach **b** and **f** formation, linking formation with letter name, keyword and sound.

Follow activity procedure and have students sky write letters.

Emphasize that these letters are sky line letters, so they begin on the sky line.

Unit 1 | Week 1

Day 1

Letter Formation for b

Use the following verbalization to direct students in proper letter formation.

Say

b is a sky line letter.

It starts on the (sky line).

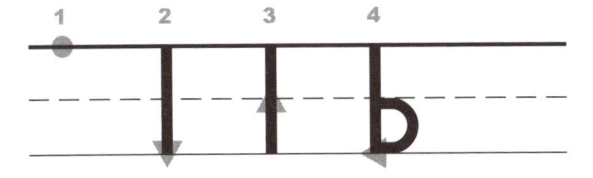

1. Point to the sky line.
2. Go down to the grass line.
3. Trace up to the plane line,
4. and around to the grass line.
5. Say b - bat - /b/, have students repeat.

Letter Formation for f

Use the following verbalization to direct students in proper letter formation.

Say

f is a sky line letter.

It starts on the (sky line).

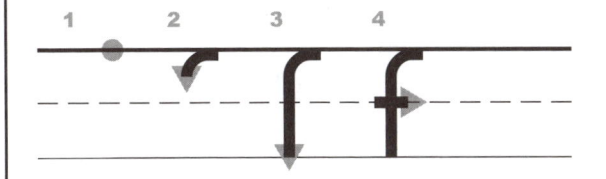

1. Point to the sky line.
2. Trace back on the sky line,
3. and then way down to the grass line.
4. Cross it on the plane line.
5. Say f - fun - /f/, have students repeat.

Student Notebook

Direct the students to find the newly introduced letters.

Use the verbalization for the letter formation to direct the students while they trace it with their finger. Do it with them to model. Have them say letter-keyword-sound.

After students trace following verbalizations, they can then color the keyword picture for the letter **b**.

Unit 1 | Week 1

Day 2

Daily Plan — DAY 2

Student Learning Plan
- Drill Sounds/Warm-Up
- Sky Write/Letter Formation
- Student Notebook
- Echo/Letter Formation

Teacher Materials
- Echo and/or Baby Echo
- Large Sound Cards
- Standard Sound Cards
- Large Writing Grid
- Letter Formation Guide
- Student Notebook

Student Materials
- Student Notebook
- Dry Erase Writing Tablet

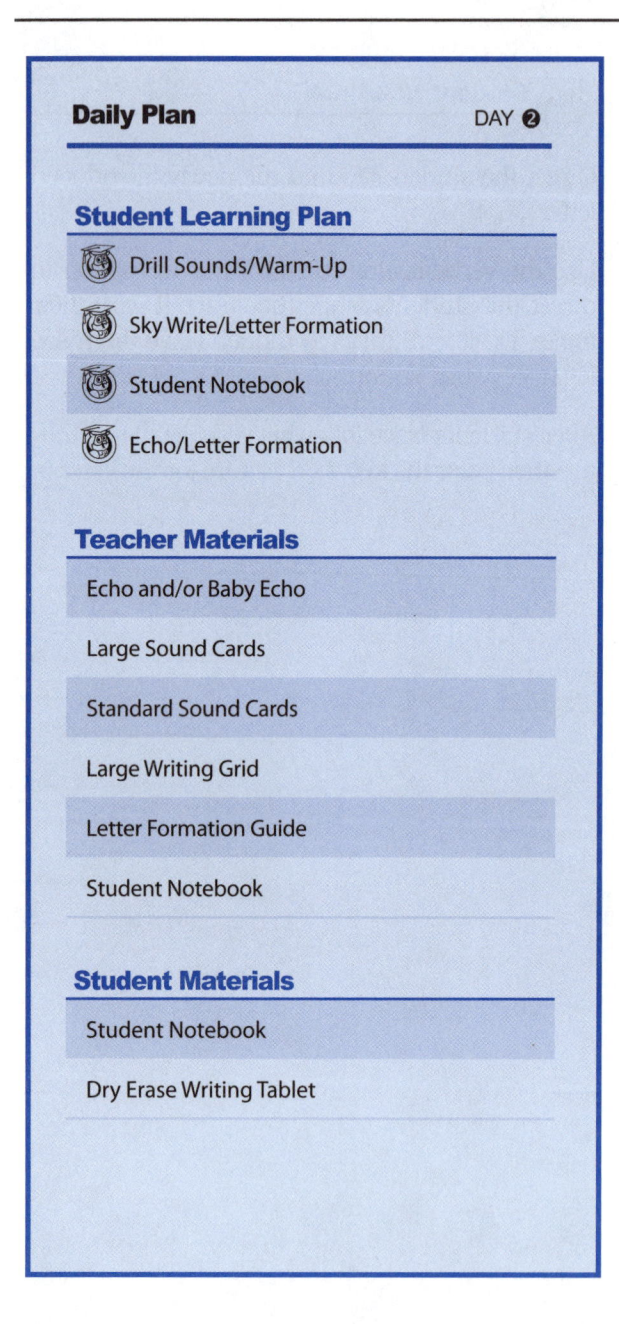

Drill Sounds/Warm-Up

DO ALL THE INTRODUCED SOUNDS EACH DAY

Large Sound Cards

Practice sounds with the Large Sound Cards. Model these, saying the letter-keyword-sound and have the students echo.

Standard Sound Cards

Next, point to the Standard Sound Cards (in card display) with the Baby Echo pointer. You say the letter-keyword-sound and hold up Baby Echo to have the students repeat.

Sky Write/Letter Formation

Review **b** and **f** formation, linking formation with letter name, keyword and sound.

Follow activity procedure and have students sky write letters.

Emphasize that these letters are sky line letters, so they begin on the sky line.

tip

Point to the Letter Formation Poster to show students where to look to remind them where to begin these letters.

Unit 1 | Week 1

Day 2

Student Notebook

Direct the students to find the newly introduced letters.

Use the verbalization for the letter formation to direct the students while they trace it with their finger. Do it with them to model. Have them say letter-keyword-sound.

After students trace following verbalizations, they can then color the keyword picture for the letter **f**.

Echo/Letter Formation

Remind students of proper pencil grip and sitting position, and give them their Dry Erase Writing Tablets.

Sounds appear between / /. Dictate the review sound **/t/** and **new** sounds. You select and say the sound. Students echo the sound and say the letter.

Next have a student come up to the classroom board to make the letter on the Large Writing Grid. Direct the student with the letter formation verbalization.

Then have all students write the answer on their Dry Erase Writing Tablets as you direct them with the letter formation verbalization. Circulate to reinforce pencil grip and assist students, as needed.

Sounds

/t/ - t   /b/ - b   /f/ - f

---

tip

Left-handed students can cross their letters from left to right as opposed to right to left. You will need to show this to them and work with students individually.

Unit 1 | Week 1

Day 3

Daily Plan — DAY 3

Student Learning Plan
- Drill Sounds/Warm-Up
- Make It Fun
- Echo/Find Letters
- Student Notebook

Teacher Materials
- Echo and/or Baby Echo
- Large Sound Cards
- Standard Sound Cards
- Student Notebook

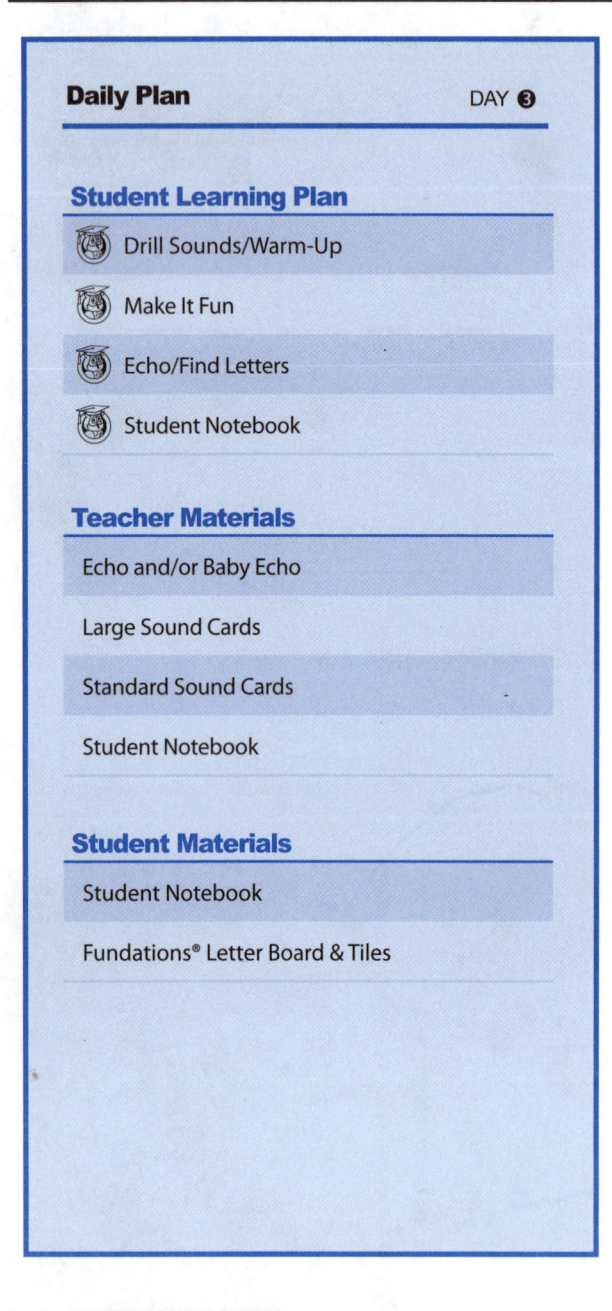

Student Materials
- Student Notebook
- Fundations® Letter Board & Tiles

Drill Sounds/Warm-Up

DO ALL THE INTRODUCED SOUNDS EACH DAY

Large Sound Cards

Practice sounds with the Large Sound Cards. Model these, saying the letter-keyword-sound and have the students echo.

Standard Sound Cards

Next, point to the Standard Sound Cards (in card display) with the Baby Echo pointer. You say the letter-keyword-sound and hold up Baby Echo to have the students repeat.

Tip: Make sure to clip sounds to avoid adding a schwa: /t/ not /tuh/

Make It Fun

Challenge students to think of words that start with the current sounds. Repeat any answer and respond appropriately.

Say

I'm thinking of someone whose name starts with /t/ (/b/, /f/).

Yes, Tom starts with /t/.

Or if incorrect,

Mary starts with /m/. I want /t/.

Say

Let's name other words that start with /t/.

Let's name other words that start with /b/.

Let's name other words that start with /f/.

Unit 1 | Week 1

Day 3

Echo/Find Letters

Students match Magnetic Letter Tiles to the letter(s) on their Letter Boards. Distribute Letter Boards and the Letter Tiles **t**, **b** and **f** to each student. Start with tiles on the blank side of the board. Dictate sounds. Students echo sound and match the tiles. After all sounds are matched, dictate the sounds and have students repeat the sound and point to the corresponding letter.

Sounds

/t/ - t /b/ - b /f/ - f

Student Notebook

Practice Letters

Students trace previously taught letters while naming letter-keyword-sound. Do as a group saying verbalization, or circulate around the room as students do independently.

Unit 1 | Week 1

Day 4

Daily Plan — DAY 4

Student Learning Plan
- Drill Sounds/Warm-Up
- Word Play
- Sky Write/Letter Formation
- Echo/Letter Formation

Teacher Materials
- Echo and/or Baby Echo
- Large Sound Cards
- Standard Sound Cards
- Large Writing Grid
- Letter Formation Guide
- Sentence Frames

Student Materials
- Student Notebook
- Dry Erase Writing Tablet

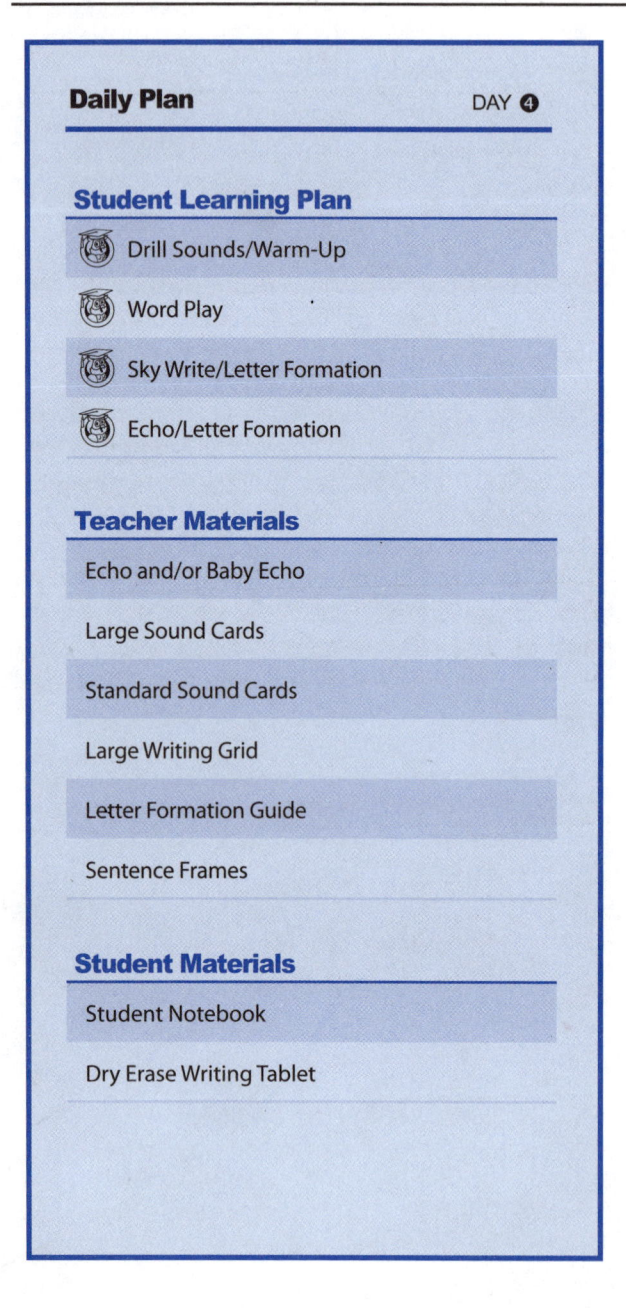

Drill Sounds/Warm-Up

DO ALL THE INTRODUCED SOUNDS EACH DAY

Large Sound Cards

Practice sounds with the Large Sound Cards. Model these, saying the letter-keyword-sound and have the students echo.

Standard Sound Cards

Next, point to the Standard Sound Cards (in card display) with the Baby Echo pointer. You say the letter-keyword-sound and hold up Baby Echo to have the students repeat.

Word Play

Teacher Materials
- Sentence Frames
- Baby Echo

WORD AWARENESS

You will teach the students that sentences are made up of words. Do this by writing the words on the Sentence Frames and adding a punctuation mark at the end. Be sure to use the high-cut frame for the first word in the sentence. Explain to them that this is for a capital or uppercase letter, which always starts a sentence.

Simply write sentences on the Sentence Frames. Use students' names and ask questions to help them generate sentences. Ask questions and then erase and change the words to answer the question.

Ask

Who is here today?

Write

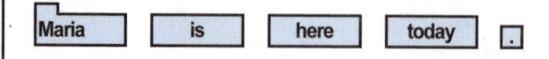

| Maria | is | here | today | . |

Explain that this is a sentence.

Say

Every sentence puts together words to say something.

Unit 1 | Week 1

Day 4

When we write sentences, we always start the first word with an uppercase or capital letter.

We also end sentences with a period.

Tell students that Baby Echo will help them read the sentence. Point to each word and read it. Then use Baby Echo to point again and have the students repeat.

Ask the students, "**Who else is here today?**" Erase the first student name and put another name. Read again pointing to each word. Each time, be sure to have students echo to read the sentence. Be sure to discuss capital letter and period.

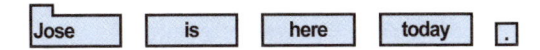

| Jose | is | here | today | . |

After doing several examples, ask:

Who was here yesterday?

Erase and write the answer:

| Manny | was | here | yesterday | . |

Sky Write/Letter Formation

Review **b** and **f** formation, linking formation with letter name, keyword and sound.

Follow activity procedure and have students sky write letters.

Emphasize that these letters are sky line letters, so they begin on the sky line.

Echo/Letter Formation

Remind students of proper pencil grip and sitting position, and give them their Dry Erase Writing Tablets.

Sounds appear between / /. Dictate the review sound /t/ and new sounds. You select and say the sound. Students echo the sound and say the letter.

Next have a student come up to the classroom board to make the letter on the Large Writing Grid. Direct the student with the letter formation verbalization.

Then have all students write the answer on their Dry Erase Writing Tablets as you direct them with the letter formation verbalization. Circulate to reinforce pencil grip and assist students, as needed.

Sounds

/t/ - t   /b/ - b   /f/ - f

Unit 1 | Week 1

Day 5

Daily Plan — DAY 5

Student Learning Plan
- Drill Sounds/Warm-Up
- Storytime
- Echo/Find Letters

Teacher Materials
- Echo and/or Baby Echo
- Large Sound Cards
- Standard Sound Cards

Student Materials
- Student Notebook
- Fundations® Letter Board & Tiles

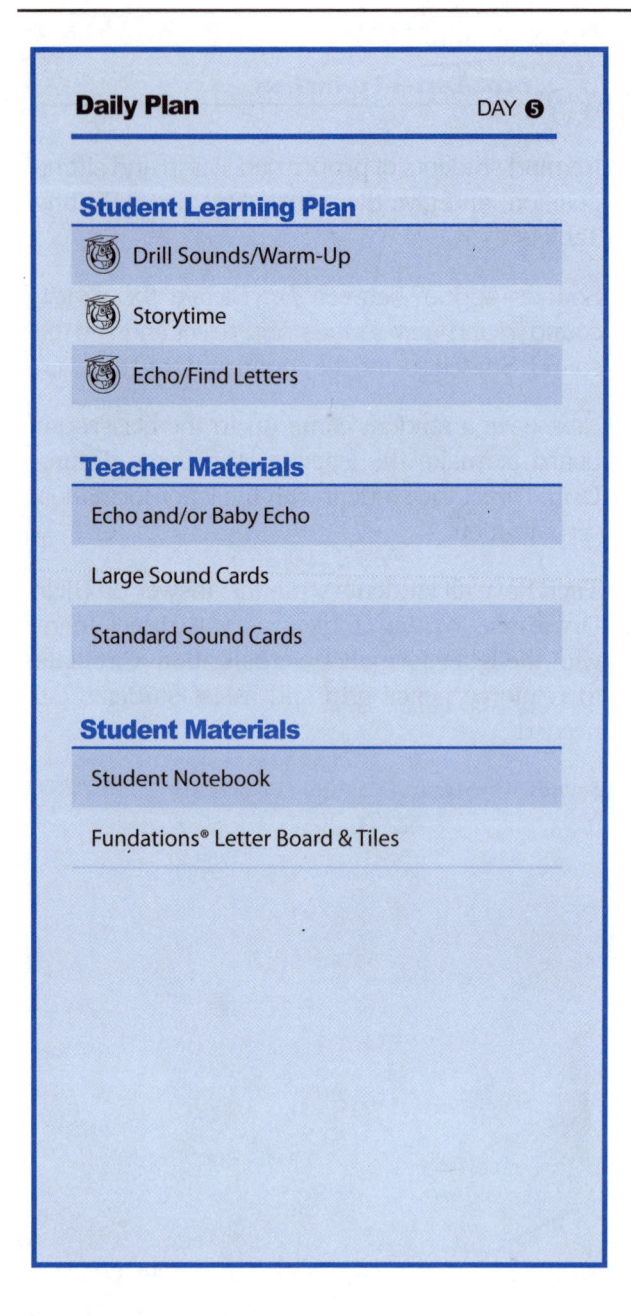

Drill Sounds/Warm-Up

DO ALL THE INTRODUCED SOUNDS EACH DAY

Large Sound Cards

Practice sounds with the Large Sound Cards. Model these, saying the letter-keyword-sound and have the students echo.

Standard Sound Cards

Next, point to the Standard Sound Cards (in card display) with the Baby Echo pointer. You say the letter-keyword-sound and hold up Baby Echo to have the students repeat.

Storytime

Teacher Materials
- Echo the Owl

Prior to the lesson with your students read through and practice the story.

ECHO FINDS DINNER I

Perform the Story

One day Echo was deep in the forest. She sat on a branch of a very tall tree.

Extend your arm out and sit Echo on it.

Echo had a problem. She was very hungry!

Rub Echo's stomach with her wing.

Echo had to find food so she searched and searched, looking all around the forest.

Have Echo look down and all around.

Echo saw something move! It was a mouse.

Have Echo pause and look in one spot.

Echo was fast. She flew down and scooped it up.

Fly Echo down and back to her branch... your arm!

Echo ate the mouse and was happy.

Move her wings.

Ask the Following Questions

Who was in this story?

Where did it take place?

Unit 1 | Week 2

Day 1

Sky Write/Letter Formation

Teach **n** and **m** formation, linking formation with letter name, keyword and sound.

Follow activity procedure and have students sky write letters.

Emphasize that these letters are plane line letters, so they begin on the plane line.

Letter Formation for n

Use the following verbalization to direct students in proper letter formation.

Say

n is a plane line letter.

It starts on the (plane line).

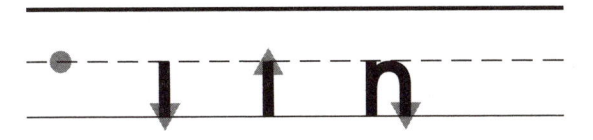

1. Point to the plane line.
2. Go down to the grass line.
3. Trace back up to the plane line,
4. and make a hump.
5. Say n - nut - /n/, have students repeat.

Letter Formation for m

Use the following verbalization to direct students in proper letter formation.

Say

m is a plane line letter.

It starts on the (plane line).

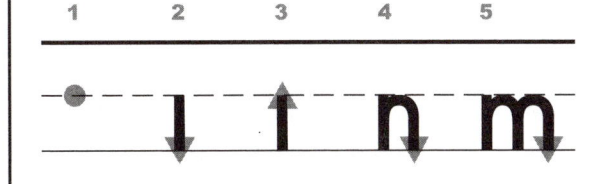

1. Point to the plane line.
2. Go down to the grass line.
3. Trace back up to the plane line,
4. and make a hump,
5. and then back up to the plane line and make another hump.
6. Say m - man - /m/, have students repeat.

Student Notebook

Direct the students to find the newly introduced letters.

Use the verbalization for the letter formation to direct the students while they trace it with their finger. Do it with them to model. Have them say letter-keyword-sound.

After students trace following verbalizations, they can then color the keyword picture for the letter **n**.

© 2002, 2012 WILSON LANGUAGE TRAINING CORPORATION

TEACHER'S MANUAL 75

Unit 1 | Week 2

Day 2

Daily Plan — DAY 2

Student Learning Plan
- Drill Sounds/Warm-Up
- Sky Write/Letter Formation
- Student Notebook
- Echo/Letter Formation

Teacher Materials
- Echo and/or Baby Echo
- Large Sound Cards
- Standard Sound Cards
- Large Writing Grid
- Letter Formation Guide
- Student Notebook

Student Materials
- Student Notebook
- Dry Erase Writing Tablet

Drill Sounds/Warm-Up

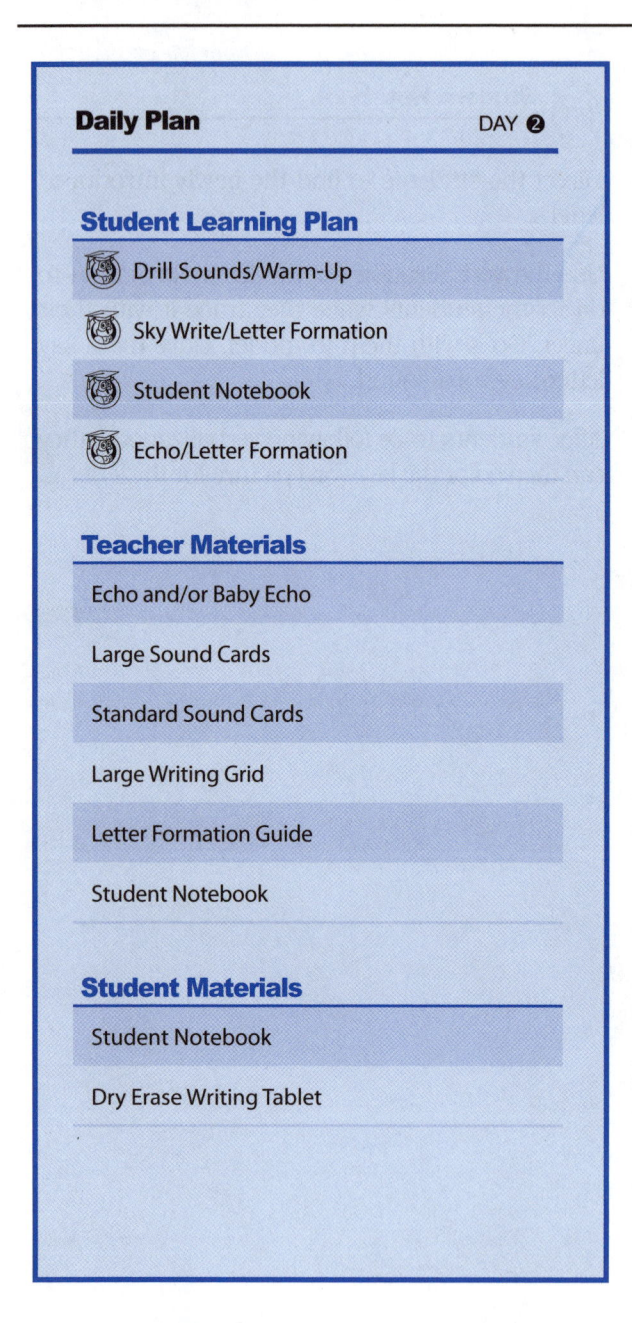

DO ALL THE INTRODUCED SOUNDS EACH DAY

Large Sound Cards

Practice sounds with the Large Sound Cards. Model these, saying the letter-keyword-sound and have the students echo.

Standard Sound Cards

Next, point to the Standard Sound Cards (in card display) with the Baby Echo pointer. You say the letter-keyword-sound and hold up Baby Echo to have the students repeat.

Sky Write/Letter Formation

Review **n** and **m** formation, linking formation with letter name, keyword and sound.

Follow activity procedure and have students sky write letters.

Emphasize that these letters are plane line letters, so they begin on the plane line.

76 FUNDATIONS® LEVEL K © 2002, 2012 WILSON LANGUAGE TRAINING CORPORATION

Day 5

What was Echo's problem?

What did she do about it?

How did things turn out? What happened in the end?

How did Echo feel at the beginning of the story?

How did Echo feel at the end of the story?

Echo/Find Letters

Students match Magnetic Letter Tiles to the letter(s) on their Letter Boards. Start with tiles off the board. Dictate sounds. Students echo sound and match the tiles. After all sounds are matched, dictate the sounds and have students repeat the sound and point to the corresponding letter.

Sounds

/t/ - t   /b/ - b   /f/ - f

Unit 1 | Week 2

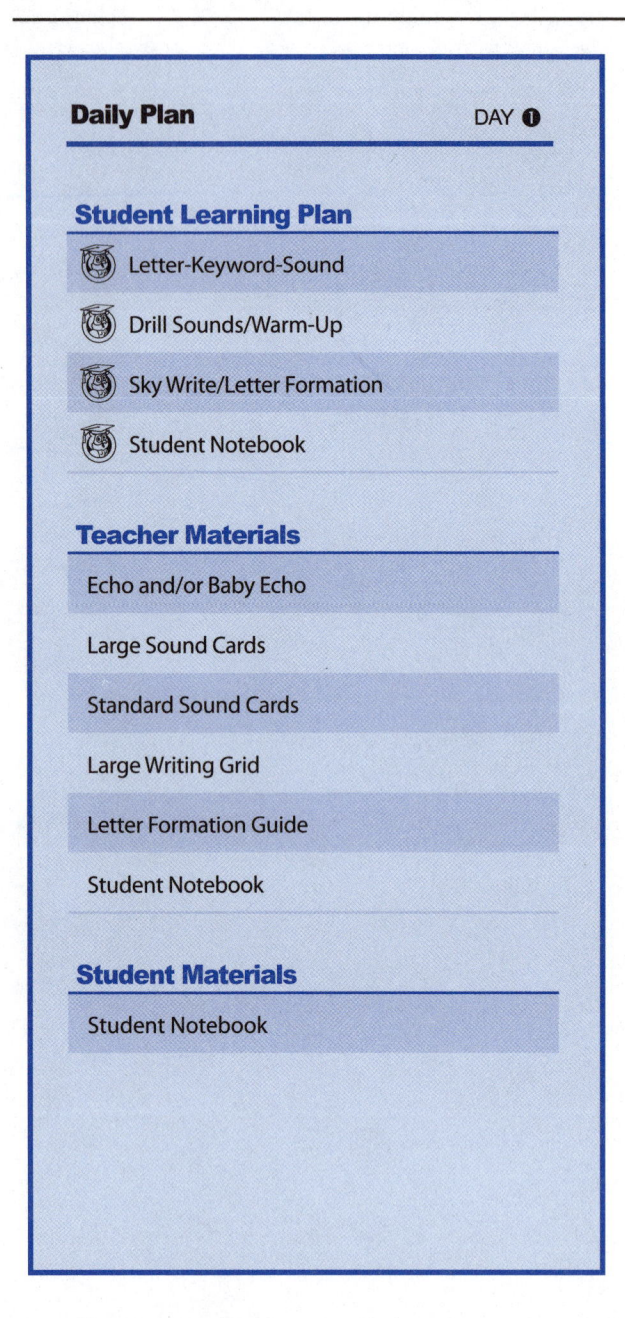

Day 1

Daily Plan — DAY 1

Student Learning Plan
- Letter-Keyword-Sound
- Drill Sounds/Warm-Up
- Sky Write/Letter Formation
- Student Notebook

Teacher Materials
- Echo and/or Baby Echo
- Large Sound Cards
- Standard Sound Cards
- Large Writing Grid
- Letter Formation Guide
- Student Notebook

Student Materials
- Student Notebook

Letter-Keyword-Sound

Introduce Letter-Keyword-Sound with Large and Standard Sound Cards. Be sure to follow procedure. First teach with Large Sound Card. Have students echo letter-keyword-sound. Then repeat with Standard Sound Card.

| n | - n - nut - /n/

| m | - m - man - /m/

Have the students look at your mouth position when saying /m/ and /n/. They sound similar but your mouth is closed when you say /m/.

Note

As a new letter is taught, its Standard Sound Card is added to your card display to be drilled at each lesson.

Drill Sounds/Warm-Up

DO ALL THE INTRODUCED SOUNDS EACH DAY

Large Sound Cards

Practice sounds with the Large Sound Cards. Model these, saying the letter-keyword-sound and have the students echo.

Standard Sound Cards

Next, point to the Standard Sound Cards (in card display) with the Baby Echo pointer. You say the letter-keyword-sound and hold up Baby Echo to have the students repeat.

Unit 1 | Week 2

Day 2

Student Notebook

Trace and say the letter-keyword-sound for all the previous letters introduced.

Direct the students to find the newly introduced letters.

Use the verbalization for the letter formation to direct the students while they trace it with their finger. Do it with them to model. Have them say letter-keyword-sound.

After students trace following verbalizations, they can then color the keyword picture for the letter **m**.

Echo/Letter Formation

Remind students of proper pencil grip and sitting position, and give them their Dry Erase Writing Tablets.

Sounds appear between //. Dictate **new** sounds and a selection of previously taught sounds. You select and say the sound. Students echo the sound and say the letter.

Next have a student come up to the classroom board to make the letter on the Large Writing Grid. Direct the student with the letter formation verbalization.

Then have all students write the answer on their Dry Erase Writing Tablets as you direct them with the letter formation verbalization. Circulate to reinforce pencil grip and assist students, as needed.

Sounds

/t/ - t   /b/ - b   /f/ - f

/n/ - n   /m/ - m

Unit 1 | Week 2

Day 3

Daily Plan — DAY 3

Student Learning Plan
- Drill Sounds/Warm-Up
- Make It Fun
- Echo/Find Letters
- Student Notebook

Teacher Materials
- Echo and/or Baby Echo
- Large Sound Cards
- Standard Sound Cards
- Large Writing Grid
- Letter Formation Guide
- Student Notebook

Student Materials
- Student Notebook
- Fundations® Letter Board & Tiles

Drill Sounds/Warm-Up

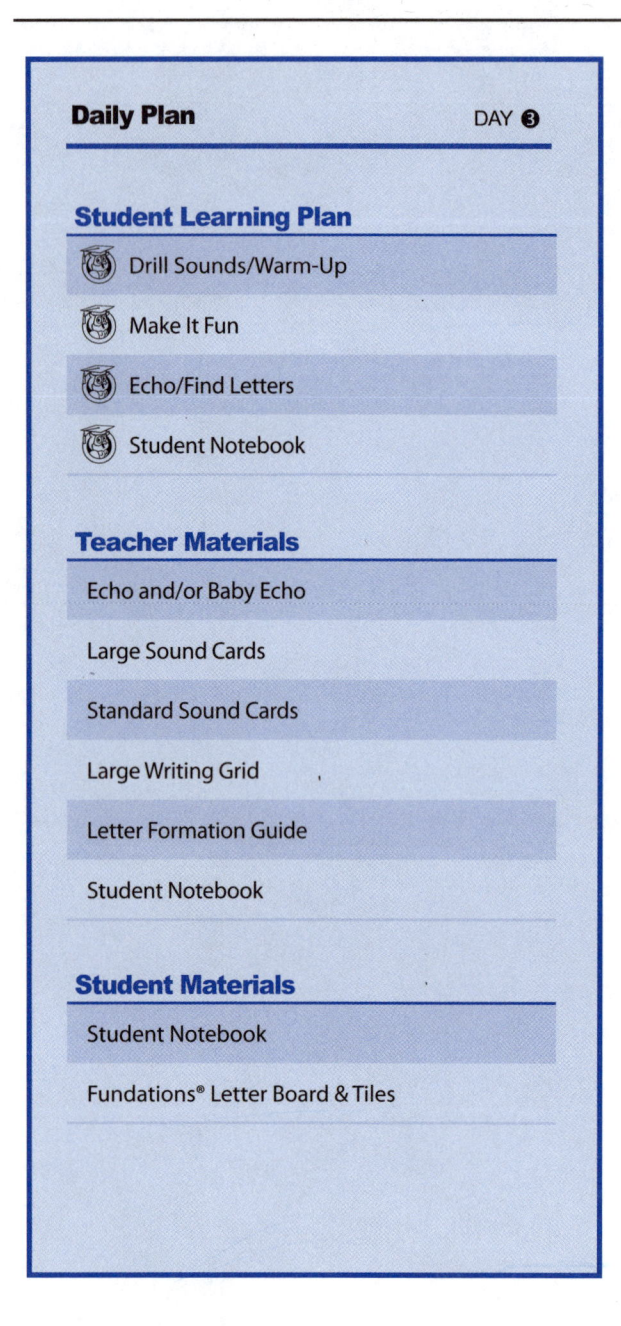

DO ALL THE INTRODUCED SOUNDS EACH DAY

Large Sound Cards

Practice sounds with the Large Sound Cards. Model these, saying the letter-keyword-sound and have the students echo.

Standard Sound Cards

Next, point to the Standard Sound Cards (in card display) with the Baby Echo pointer. You say the letter-keyword-sound and hold up Baby Echo to have the students repeat.

Make It Fun

Teacher Materials
- Standard Sound Cards
- Echo the Owl

Pass out the Standard Sound Cards (only those taught thus far). Have one student at a time come up and hold up their card and say the letter-keyword-sound. You hold up Echo so the other students repeat. Then ask:

> When you make this letter, where does it start?

Then provide the verbalization of the letter formation as the student sky writes it. You can redistribute cards and ask different questions.

Select a student by saying:

> Who is holding the card that says /t/?

or

> Who is holding a card that is a sky line letter?

or

> Who is holding a card that makes the sound at the beginning of the word boat?

or to challenge a student

> Who has a card with a keyword that rhymes with fan?

78 FUNDATIONS® LEVEL K

Unit 1 | Week 2

Day 3

Echo/Find Letters

Students match Magnetic Letter Tiles to the letter(s) on their Letter Boards. Distribute Letter Boards and the Letter Tiles **n** and **m** to each student. Start with tiles on the blank side of the board. Dictate sounds. Students echo sound and match the tiles. Include previous sounds and new sounds. After all sounds are matched, dictate 2-3 sounds and have students repeat the sound and point to the corresponding letter.

Sounds

/t/ - t   /b/ - b   /f/ - f

/n/ - n   /m/ - m

Student Notebook

Practice Letters

Students trace previously taught letters while naming letter-keyword-sound. Do as a group saying verbalization, or circulate around the room as students do independently.

Unit 1 | Week 2

Day 4

Daily Plan — DAY 4

Student Learning Plan
- Drill Sounds/Warm-Up
- Word Play
- Sky Write/Letter Formation
- Echo/Letter Formation

Teacher Materials
- Echo and/or Baby Echo
- Large Sound Cards
- Standard Sound Cards
- Large Writing Grid
- Letter Formation Guide
- Sentence Frames

Student Materials
- Student Notebook
- Dry Erase Writing Tablet

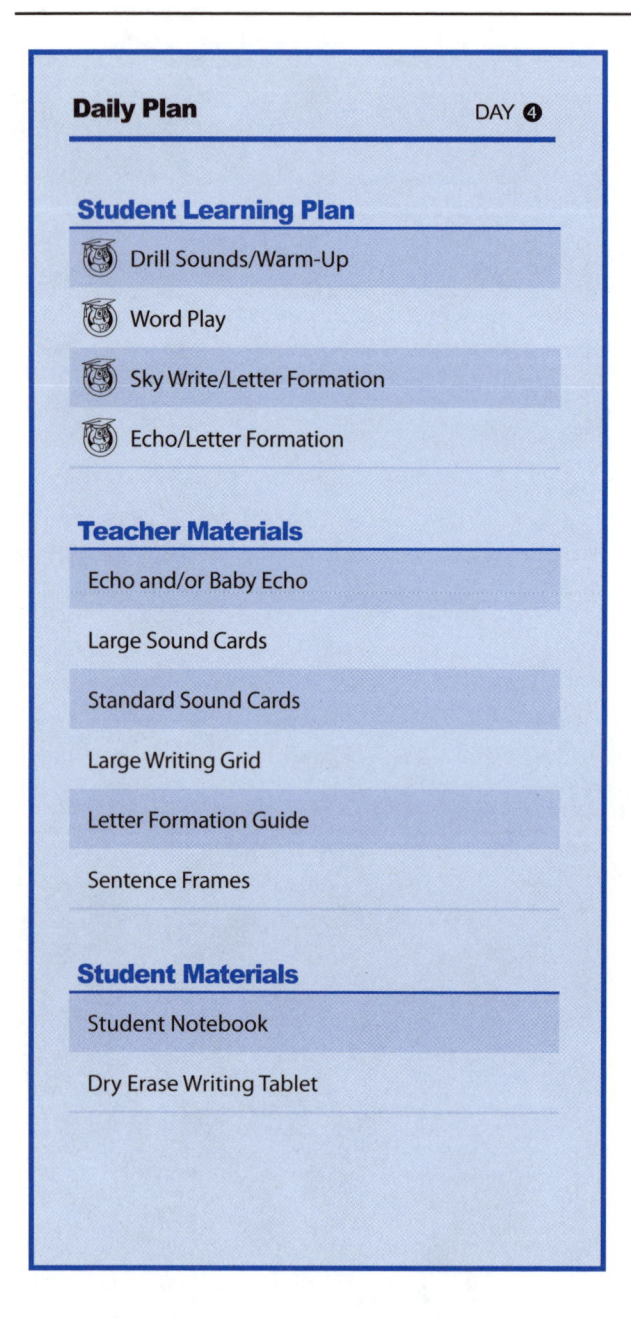

Drill Sounds/Warm-Up

DO ALL THE INTRODUCED SOUNDS EACH DAY

Large Sound Cards

Practice sounds with the Large Sound Cards. Model these, saying the letter-keyword-sound and have the students echo.

Standard Sound Cards

Next, point to the Standard Sound Cards (in card display) with the Baby Echo pointer. You say the letter-keyword-sound and hold up Baby Echo to have the students repeat.

Word Play

Teacher Materials
- Sentence Frames
- Baby Echo

WORD AWARENESS

Use the frames to write sentences. Discuss capital (uppercase) letter at the beginning of the sentence and the period at the end. Use Baby Echo to point to each word to read. Have the students echo and read the sentence as you point to the words again.

Ask

What does Peter like?

Write the answer on the Sentence Frames.

| Peter | likes | candy | . |

Ask several students this question. Each time, erase the words and replace with the new words. Read the sentence, pointing with Baby Echo and have the students read with you as you point to the words again.

Next ask, **"What do you dislike?"** Write the answer on the frames and follow the procedure above.

| Joey | dislikes | peas | . |

Unit 1 | Week 2

Day 4

Sky Write/Letter Formation

Review **n** and **m** formation, linking formation with letter name, keyword and sound.

Follow activity procedure and have students sky write letters.

Emphasize that these letters are plane line letters, so they begin on the plane line.

Echo/Letter Formation

Remind students of proper pencil grip and sitting position, and give them their Dry Erase Writing Tablets.

Sounds appear between / /. Dictate **new** sounds and a selection of previously taught sounds. You select and say the sound. Students echo the sound and say the letter.

Next have a student come up to the classroom board to make the letter on the Large Writing Grid. Direct the student with the letter formation verbalization.

Then have all students write the answer on their Dry Erase Writing Tablets as you direct them with the letter formation verbalization. Circulate to reinforce pencil grip and assist students, as needed.

Sounds

| /t/ - t | /b/ - b | /f/ - f |
| /n/ - n | /m/ - m | |

Unit 1 | Week 2

Day 5

Daily Plan — DAY 5

Student Learning Plan
- Drill Sounds/Warm-Up
- Storytime
- Echo/Find Letters

Teacher Materials
- Echo and/or Baby Echo
- Large Sound Cards
- Standard Sound Cards

Student Materials
- Student Notebook
- Fundations® Letter Board & Tiles

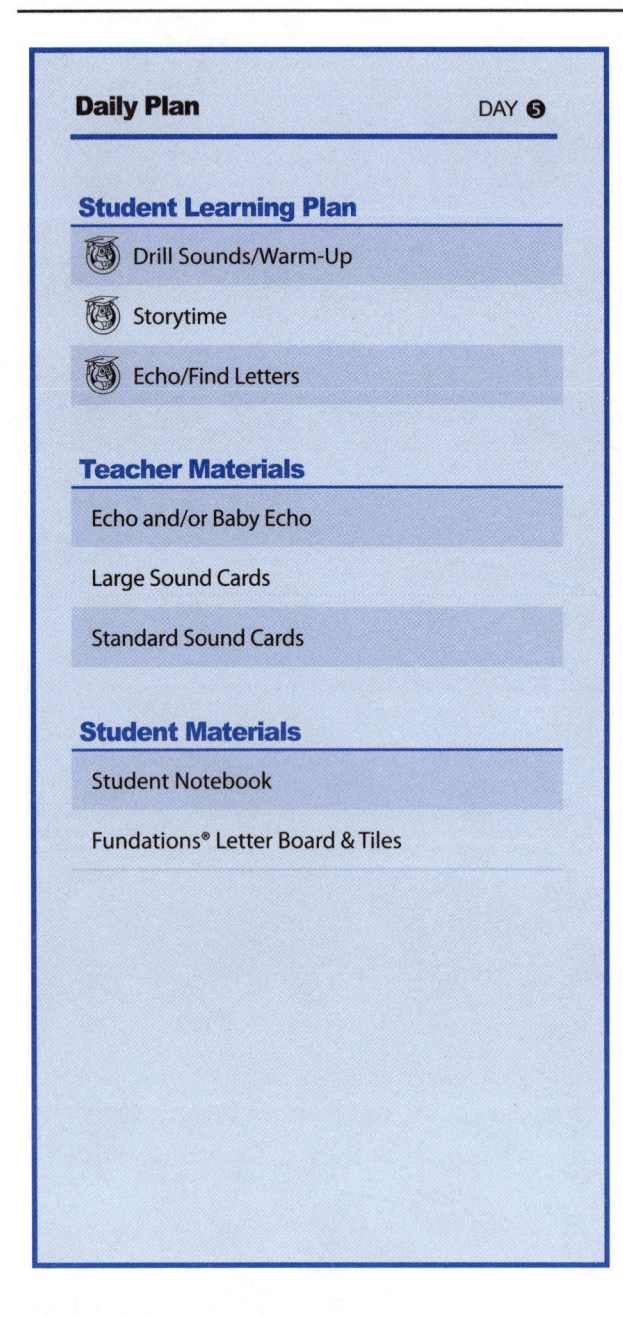

Drill Sounds/Warm-Up

DO ALL THE INTRODUCED SOUNDS EACH DAY

Large Sound Cards

Practice sounds with the Large Sound Cards. Model these, saying the letter-keyword-sound and have the students echo.

Standard Sound Cards

Next, point to the Standard Sound Cards (in card display) with the Baby Echo pointer. You say the letter-keyword-sound and hold up Baby Echo to have the students repeat.

Storytime

Teacher Materials
- Echo the Owl

ECHO FINDS DINNER II

This week you will say and act out the same story, "Echo Finds Dinner." Then you will perform it again, without words, and have the students retell the story as you "play it out."

Re-perform the Story

Tell and act out "Echo Finds Dinner." (See Week 1, Day 5.)

Perform the Story Without Words

Perform the story again, without words, (see below) and have students tell you what happened.

After a student tells you in his/her own words, restate the words from the story to clarify as needed.

Be sure to provide students positive feedback for retelling in their own words.

Extend your arm out and sit Echo on it.

> One day Echo was deep in the forest. She sat on a branch of a very tall tree.

Rub Echo's stomach with her wing.

> Echo had a problem. She was very hungry!

Have Echo look down and all around.

Unit 1 | Week 2

Day 5

Echo had to find food so she searched and searched, looking all around the forest.

Have Echo pause and look in one spot.

Echo saw something move! It was a mouse.

Fly Echo down and back to her branch... your arm!

Echo was fast. She flew down and scooped it up.

Move her wings.

Echo ate the mouse and was happy.

Echo/Find Letters

Students match Magnetic Letter Tiles to the letter(s) on their Letter Boards. Start with tiles off the board. Dictate sounds. Students echo sound and match the tiles. Include previous sounds and new sounds. After all sounds are matched, dictate 2-3 sounds and have students repeat the sound and point to the corresponding letter.

Sounds

/t/ - t　　　/b/ - b　　　/f/ - f

/n/ - n　　　/m/ - m

Make sure to clip sounds to avoid adding a schwa: /t/ not /tuh/

Unit 1 | Week 3

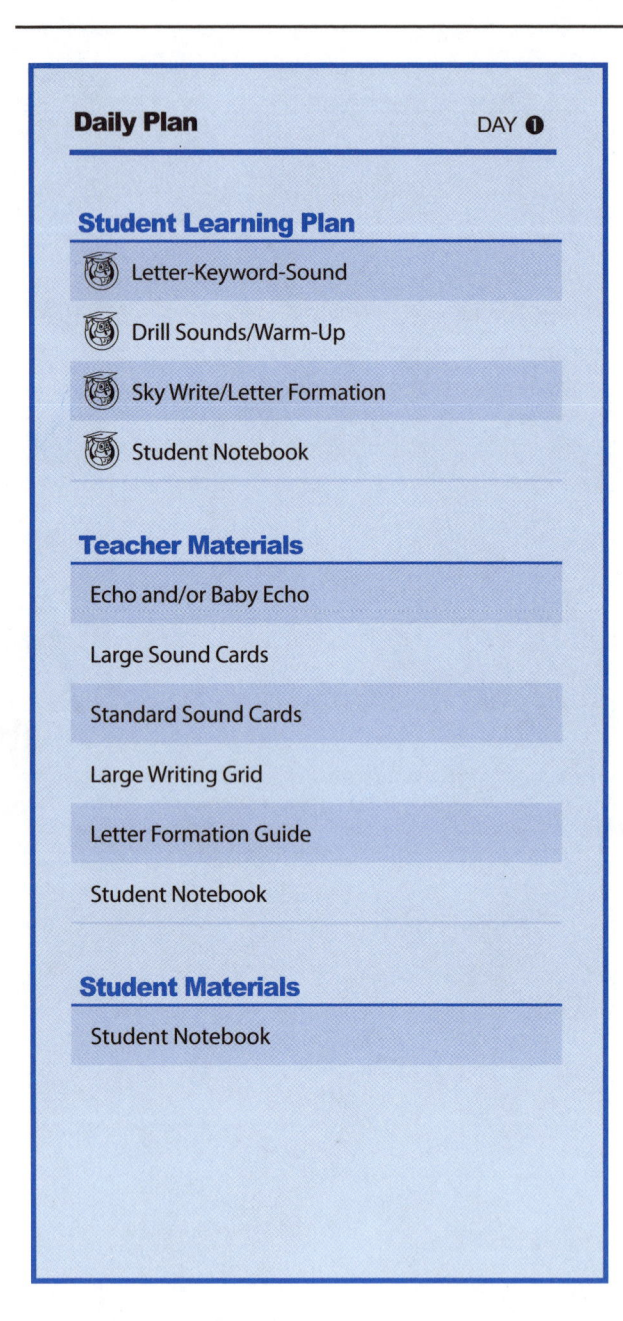

Day 1

Daily Plan — DAY 1

Student Learning Plan
- Letter-Keyword-Sound
- Drill Sounds/Warm-Up
- Sky Write/Letter Formation
- Student Notebook

Teacher Materials
- Echo and/or Baby Echo
- Large Sound Cards
- Standard Sound Cards
- Large Writing Grid
- Letter Formation Guide
- Student Notebook

Student Materials
- Student Notebook

Letter-Keyword-Sound

Tell students that they will learn two very important letters today. These letters are vowels. Explain that every word must have at least one vowel in it. Show them that the vowels are a different color than the other letters which are called consonants. Vowels will be on the salmon-colored cards.

Introduce Letter-Keyword-Sound with Large and Standard Sound Cards. Be sure to follow procedure. First teach with Large Sound Card. Have students echo letter-keyword-sound. Then repeat with Standard Sound Card.

i - i - itch - /ĭ/

u - u - up - /ŭ/

Note
As a new letter is taught, its Standard Sound Card is added to your card display to be drilled at each lesson.

Support for Spanish Speaking ELs: All short vowels are pronounced differently in Spanish. The letter-keyword-sound are very important to master the English pronunciations.

Drill Sounds/Warm-Up

DO ALL THE INTRODUCED SOUNDS EACH DAY

Large Sound Cards

Practice sounds with the Large Sound Cards. Model these, saying the letter-keyword-sound and have the students echo.

Standard Sound Cards

Next, point to the Standard Sound Cards (in card display) with the Baby Echo pointer. You say the letter-keyword-sound and hold up Baby Echo to have the students repeat.

Unit 1 | Week 3

Day 1

Sky Write/Letter Formation

Teach **i** and **u** formation, linking formation with letter name, keyword and sound.

Follow activity procedure and have students sky write letters.

Emphasize that these letters are plane line letters, so they begin on the plane line.

Letter Formation for i

Use the following verbalization to direct students in proper letter formation.

Say

i is a plane line letter.

It starts on the (plane line).

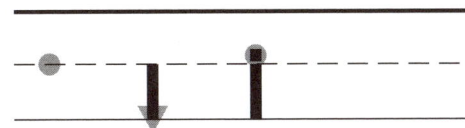

1. Point to the plane line.
2. Go down to the grass line.
3. Add a dot.
4. Say i - itch - /ĭ/, have students repeat.

Letter Formation for u

Use the following verbalization to direct students in proper letter formation.

Say

u is a plane line letter.

It starts on the (plane line).

1. Point to the plane line.
2. Go down to the grass line.
3. Curve up to the plane line,
4. and trace straight down to the grass line.
5. Say u - up - /ŭ/, have students repeat.

Student Notebook

Direct the students to find the newly introduced letters.

Use the verbalization for the letter formation to direct the students while they trace it with their finger. Do it with them to model. Have them say letter-keyword-sound.

After students trace following verbalizations, they can then color the keyword picture for the letter **i**.

Unit 1 | Week 3

Day 2

Daily Plan — DAY 2

Student Learning Plan
- Drill Sounds/Warm-Up
- Sky Write/Letter Formation
- Student Notebook
- Echo/Letter Formation

Teacher Materials
- Echo and/or Baby Echo
- Large Sound Cards
- Standard Sound Cards
- Large Writing Grid
- Letter Formation Guide
- Vowel Extension Poster
- Student Notebook

Student Materials
- Student Notebook
- Dry Erase Writing Tablet

Drill Sounds/Warm-Up

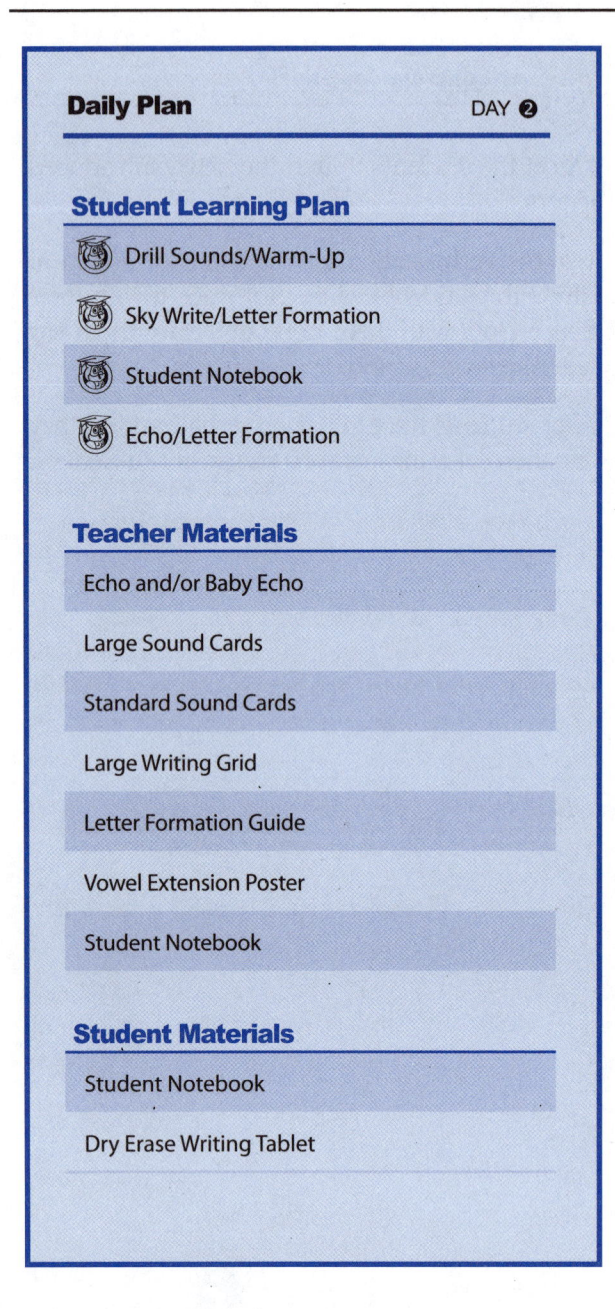

DO ALL THE INTRODUCED SOUNDS EACH DAY

Large Sound Cards

Practice sounds with the Large Sound Cards. Model these, saying the letter-keyword-sound and have the students echo.

Standard Sound Cards

Next, point to the Standard Sound Cards (in card display) with the Baby Echo pointer. You say the letter-keyword-sound and hold up Baby Echo to have the students repeat.

Vowel Extension

Display your Vowel Extension Poster in the classroom so students can reach it. Alternatively, cut the poster along the dotted lines and display each vowel when introduced.

Do the Vowel Extension activity with **i** and **u** vowels. Explain that this helps them stretch out the vowel sounds. Demonstrate how to hold the vowel sounds until you run out of breath.

Model extending the vowel sounds (example: **i-/ĭ/...tch-/ĭ/** and **u-/ŭ/...p-/ŭ/**). Extend the /ĭ/ and /ŭ/ sounds while you trace the line and finish the word when you get to the picture.

Have a student come trace the line while everyone extends the /ĭ/ and /ŭ/ sound.

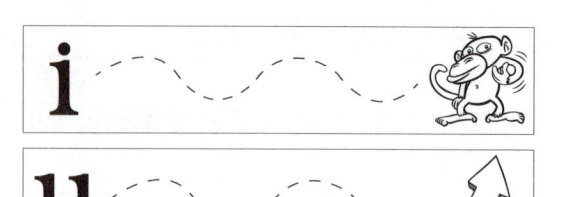

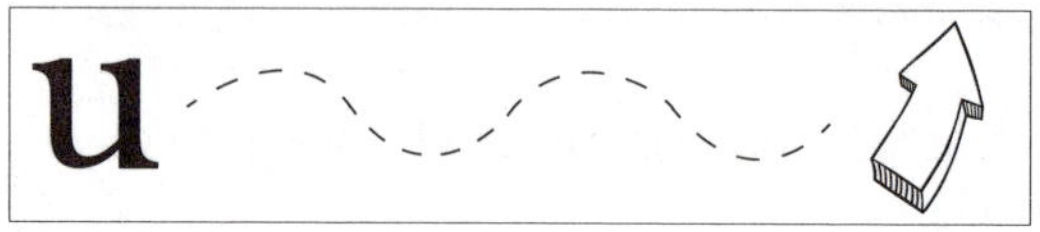

Unit 1 | Week 3

Day 2

Sky Write/Letter Formation

Review **i** and **u** formation, linking formation with letter name, keyword and sound.

Follow activity procedure and have students sky write letters.

Emphasize that these letters are plane line letters, so they begin on the plane line.

Student Notebook

Trace and say the letter-keyword-sound for all the previous letters introduced.

Direct the students to find the newly introduced letters.

Use the verbalization for the letter formation to direct the students while they trace it with their finger. Do it with them to model. Have them say letter-keyword-sound.

After students trace following verbalizations, they can then color the keyword picture for the letter **u**.

Echo/Letter Formation

Remind students of proper pencil grip and sitting position, and give them their Dry Erase Writing Tablets.

Sounds appear between / /. Dictate **new** sounds and a selection of previously taught sounds. You select and say the sound. Students echo the sound and say the letter.

Next have a student come up to the classroom board to make the letter on the Large Writing Grid. Direct the student with the letter formation verbalization.

Then have all students write the answer on their Dry Erase Writing Tablets as you direct them with the letter formation verbalization. Circulate to reinforce pencil grip and assist students, as needed.

Sounds

/t/ - t	/b/ - b	/f/ - f
/n/ - n	/m/ - m	/ĭ/ - i
/ŭ/ - u		

Unit 1 | Week 3

Day 3

Daily Plan — DAY 3

Student Learning Plan
- Drill Sounds/Warm-Up
- Make It Fun
- Echo/Find Letters
- Student Notebook

Teacher Materials
- Echo and/or Baby Echo
- Large Sound Cards
- Standard Sound Cards
- Letter Formation Guide
- Vowel Extension Poster
- Student Notebook

Student Materials
- Student Notebook
- Fundations® Letter Board & Tiles

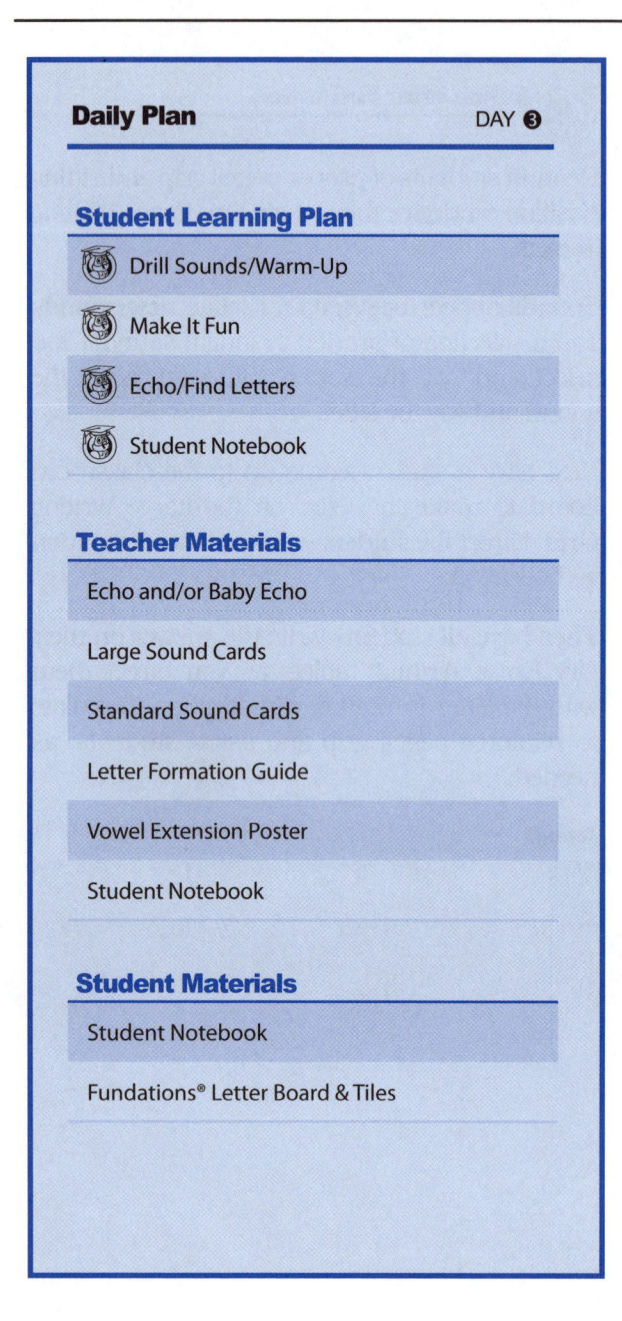

Drill Sounds/Warm-Up

DO ALL THE INTRODUCED SOUNDS EACH DAY

Large Sound Cards

Practice sounds with the Large Sound Cards. Model these, saying the letter-keyword-sound and have the students echo.

Standard Sound Cards

Next, point to the Standard Sound Cards (in card display) with the Baby Echo pointer. You say the letter-keyword-sound and hold up Baby Echo to have the students repeat.

Vowel Extension

Model extending the vowel sounds (example: **i-/ĭ/...tch-/ĭ/** and **u-/ŭ/...p-/ŭ/**). Extend the /ĭ/ and /ŭ/ sounds while you trace the line and finish the word when you get to the picture.

Have a student come trace the line while everyone extends the /ĭ/ and /ŭ/ sound.

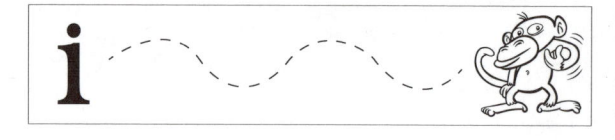

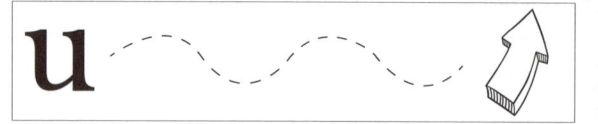

Make It Fun

Teacher Materials
- Standard Sound Cards
- Echo the Owl

Say the sound /t/ and have students repeat. Call on a student to come get the Standard Sound Card from your card display.

Ask

Who can come find /t/?

When they find it, have them say the letter-keyword-sound.

Hold up Echo the Owl so all the students can repeat. Then ask:

When you make this letter, where does it start?

Then provide the verbalization of the letter formation as the student sky writes it. Have the student sit down with the card.

When all cards are taken, tell the students with the cards to hand their card to someone who doesn't have a card. Next, have the students bring back each card.

Ask

I'm looking for /b/. Who has /b/?

Unit 1 | Week 3

Day 3

Echo/Find Letters

Students match Magnetic Letter Tiles to the letter(s) on their Letter Boards. Distribute Letter Boards and the Letter Tiles **i** and **u** to each student. Start with tiles on the blank side of the board. Dictate sounds. Students echo sound and match the tiles. Include previous sounds and new sounds. After all sounds are matched, dictate 2-3 sounds and have students repeat the sound and point to the corresponding letter.

Sounds

/t/ - t   /b/ - b   /f/ - f

/n/ - n   /m/ - m   /ĭ/ - **i**

/ŭ/ - **u**

Student Notebook

Practice Letters

Students trace previously taught letters while naming letter-keyword-sound. Do as a group saying verbalization, or circulate around the room as students do independently.

Unit 1 | Week 3

Day 4

Daily Plan — DAY 4

Student Learning Plan
- Drill Sounds/Warm-Up
- Word Play
- Sky Write/Letter Formation
- Echo/Letter Formation

Teacher Materials
- Echo and/or Baby Echo
- Large Sound Cards
- Standard Sound Cards
- Large Writing Grid
- Letter Formation Guide
- Vowel Extension Poster
- Sentence Frames

Student Materials
- Student Notebook
- Dry Erase Writing Tablet

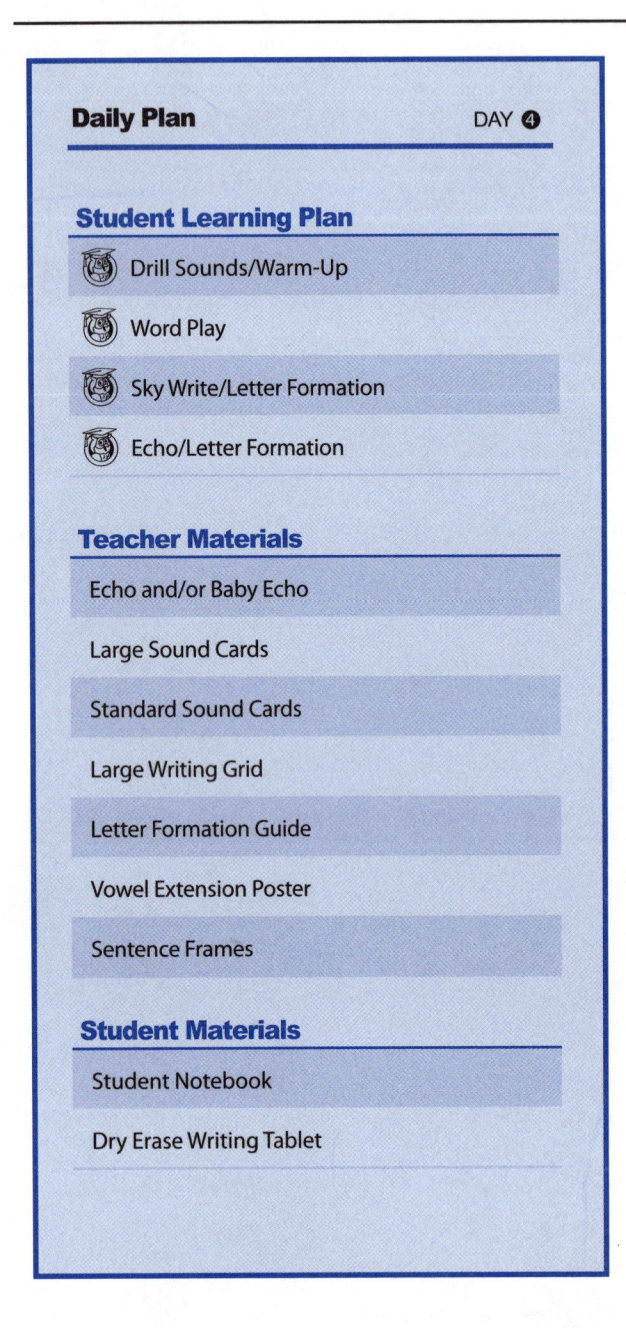

Drill Sounds/Warm-Up

DO ALL THE INTRODUCED SOUNDS EACH DAY

Large Sound Cards

Practice sounds with the Large Sound Cards. Model these, saying the letter-keyword-sound and have the students echo.

Standard Sound Cards

Next, point to the Standard Sound Cards (in card display) with the Baby Echo pointer. You say the letter-keyword-sound and hold up Baby Echo to have the students repeat.

Vowel Extension

Model extending the vowel sounds (example: **i-/ĭ/...tch-/ĭ/** and **u-/ŭ/...p-/ŭ/**). Extend the /ĭ/ and /ŭ/ sounds while you trace the line and finish the word when you get to the picture.

Have a student come trace the line while everyone extends the /ĭ/ and /ŭ/ sound.

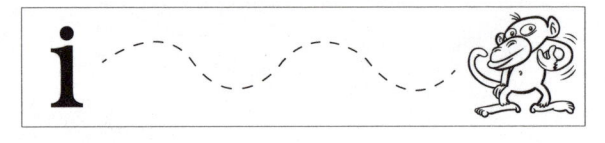

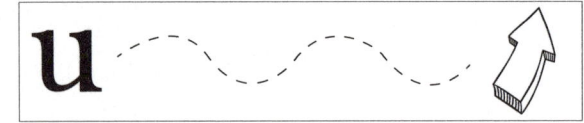

Word Play

Teacher Materials
- Sentence Frames
- Baby Echo

WORD AWARENESS

Use the following idea for a sentence:

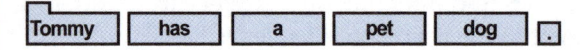

| Tommy | has | a | pet | dog | . |

Ask

Why did I use this frame to begin the sentence?

Point to the tall frame.

What does this tell me?

Point to the period.

Explain to the students that this time you are going to do the word game a little different to make it trickier!

Ask

Who else has a pet dog?

This time, rather than you erase the words to write the replacement words, ask for a student's help.

Say

Today I am going to have someone be my helper to erase the words we need to change.

We don't want to erase all the words, just the ones that change.

Day 4

Point to cards and say the new sentence. Then ask, pointing to each word:

Does this word change?

If it does, let the student erase it and you write the new word. When the sentence is done, let the student use Baby Echo and point to words while everyone reads the new sentence.

Next select another student who has a pet. Say the sentence, such as:

Mike has a pet hamster.

Have the student erase the words to be changed with your guidance.

Sky Write/Letter Formation

Review **i** and **u** formation, linking formation with letter name, keyword and sound.

Follow activity procedure and have students sky write letters.

Emphasize that these letters are plane line letters, so they begin on the plane line.

Echo/Letter Formation

Remind students of proper pencil grip and sitting position, and give them their Dry Erase Writing Tablets.

Sounds appear between / /. Dictate **new** sounds and a selection of previously taught sounds. You select and say the sound. Students echo the sound and say the letter.

Next have a student come up to the classroom board to make the letter on the Large Writing Grid. Direct the student with the letter formation verbalization.

Then have all students write the answer on their Dry Erase Writing Tablets as you direct them with the letter formation verbalization. Circulate to reinforce pencil grip and assist students, as needed.

Sounds

/t/ - t /b/ - b /f/ - f

/n/ - n /m/ - m /ĭ/ - i

/ŭ/ - u

Unit 1 | Week 3

Day 5

Daily Plan — DAY 5

Student Learning Plan
- Drill Sounds/Warm-Up
- Storytime
- Echo/Find Letters

Teacher Materials
- Echo and/or Baby Echo
- Large Sound Cards
- Standard Sound Cards
- Vowel Extension Poster
- 4 Sheets of large chart paper

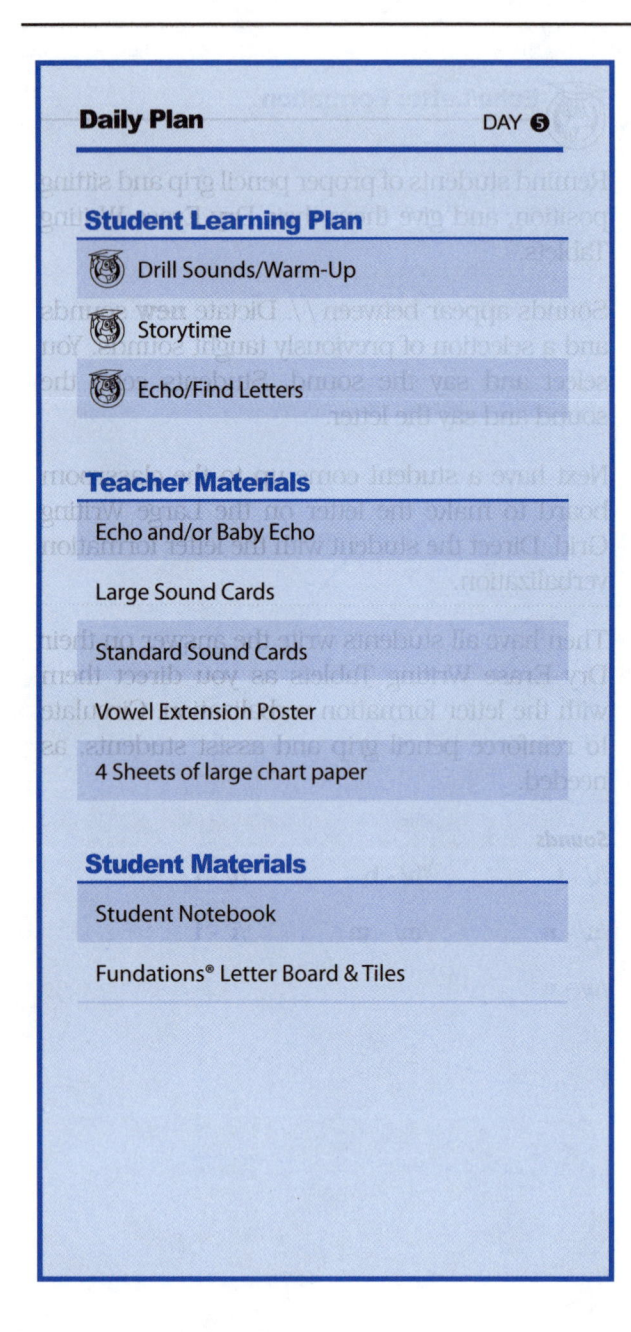

Student Materials
- Student Notebook
- Fundations® Letter Board & Tiles

Drill Sounds/Warm-Up

DO ALL THE INTRODUCED SOUNDS EACH DAY

Large Sound Cards

Practice sounds with the Large Sound Cards. Model these, saying the letter-keyword-sound and have the students echo.

Standard Sound Cards

Next, point to the Standard Sound Cards (in card display) with the Baby Echo pointer. You say the letter-keyword-sound and hold up Baby Echo to have the students repeat.

Vowel Extension

Model extending the vowel sounds (example: **i-/ĭ/...tch-/ĭ/** and **u-/ŭ/...p-/ŭ/**). Extend the /ĭ/ and /ŭ/ sounds while you trace the line and finish the word when you get to the picture.

Have a student come trace the line while everyone extends the /ĭ/ and /ŭ/ sound.

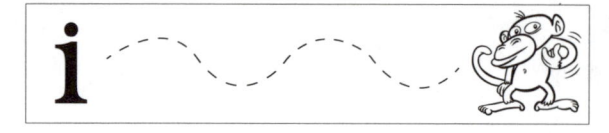

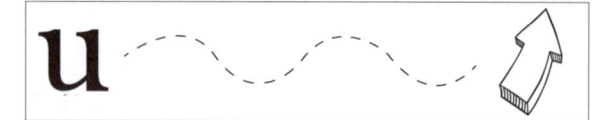

Storytime

Teacher Materials
- Echo the Owl
- 4 Sheets of large chart paper

ECHO FINDS DINNER III

This week you will say and act out the same story, "Echo Finds Dinner." Then, as the students retell the story, you will illustrate the story with four simple pictures. Leave space at the bottom of each page. You will need this space next week to write the words of the story. Keep these illustrations for next week's lesson. Remember that these illustrations can be simple. Do not worry about your artistic ability.

Perform the Story

Tell and act out "Echo Finds Dinner." (See Week 1, Day 5.)

Draw the Story

Next have students retell it to you as you draw it on chart paper. To assist them in retelling the story, ask:

Who was in the story? Where did the story begin?

1. Draw Echo on a branch.

What was Echo's problem?

2. Draw Echo looking down.

Unit 1 | Week 3

Day 5

What did she do to solve the problem?

3. Draw Echo flying.

How did it end?

4. Draw Echo smiling or rubbing stomach.

After the pictures are drawn, model retelling the story. It is very important to do this in your own words. Then select a student to come tell the story, pointing to the pictures. (You can have several students do this or have them do it at another time during the day or throughout the week.)

Note

Remember to save the illustrations. You will need it for Storytime next week.

Echo/Find Letters

Students match Magnetic Letter Tiles to the letter(s) on their Letter Boards. Start with tiles off the board. Dictate sounds. Students echo sound and match the tiles. Include previous sounds and new sounds. After all sounds are matched, dictate 2-3 sounds and have students repeat the sound and point to the corresponding letter.

Sounds

/t/ - t   /b/ - b   /f/ - f

/n/ - n   /m/ - m   /ĭ/ - i

/ŭ/ - u

Reminder!

Each student has a My Fundations Journal. This can be used anytime during the day as it is not part of the standard lesson time. At the beginning of the year, you can simply have students make pictures in it, adding words as the year progresses.

Students should draw and/or write in their My Fundations Journal several times a week. You can have them draw pictures of Echo Finds Dinner.

Unit 1 | Week 4

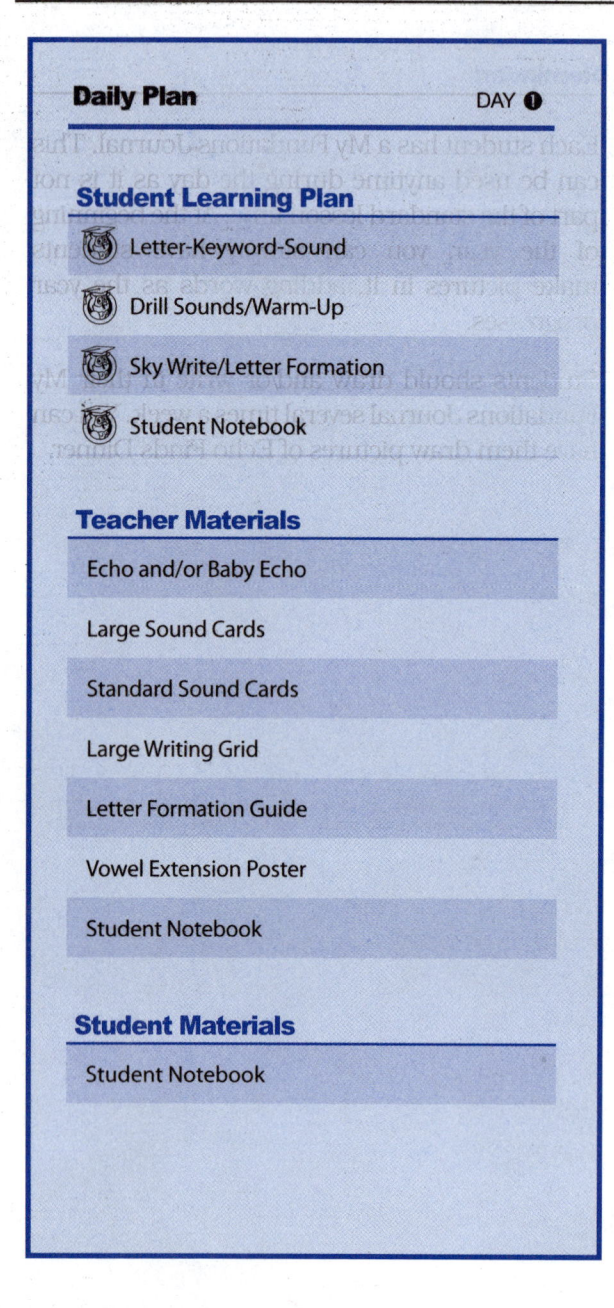

Day 1

Daily Plan — DAY 1

Student Learning Plan
- Letter-Keyword-Sound
- Drill Sounds/Warm-Up
- Sky Write/Letter Formation
- Student Notebook

Teacher Materials
- Echo and/or Baby Echo
- Large Sound Cards
- Standard Sound Cards
- Large Writing Grid
- Letter Formation Guide
- Vowel Extension Poster
- Student Notebook

Student Materials
- Student Notebook

Letter-Keyword-Sound

Introduce Letter-Keyword-Sound with Large and Standard Sound Cards. Be sure to follow procedure. First teach with Large Sound Card. Have students echo letter-keyword-sound. Then repeat with Standard Sound Card. Be sure to discuss that the letter **o** is a vowel letter and the letter **c** is a consonant.

c - c - cat - /k/

o - o - octopus - /ŏ/

Vowel Extension

Do the Vowel Extension activity with **o**. Explain that this helps them stretch out vowel sounds. Demonstrate how to hold the vowel sounds until you run out of breath.

Model 'reading' the keyword picture (example: /ŏ/...ctopus). Extend the /ŏ/ sound while you trace the line and finish the word when you get to the picture. Have a student come trace the line while everyone extends the /ŏ/ sound.

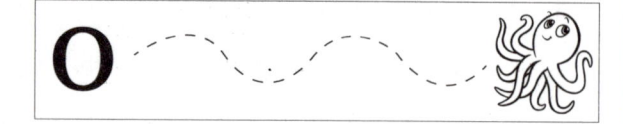

Note
As a new letter is taught, its Standard Sound Card is added to your card display to be drilled at each lesson.

Drill Sounds/Warm-Up

DO ALL THE INTRODUCED SOUNDS EACH DAY

Large Sound Cards
Practice sounds with the Large Sound Cards. Model these, saying the letter-keyword-sound and have the students echo.

Standard Sound Cards
Next, point to the Standard Sound Cards (in card display) with the Baby Echo pointer. You say the letter-keyword-sound and hold up Baby Echo to have the students repeat.

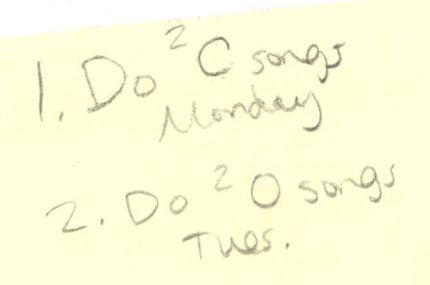

[Handwritten sticky note:]
1. Do 2 C songs Monday
2. Do 2 O songs Tues.

Unit 1 | Week 4

Day 1

Sky Write/Letter Formation

Teach **c** and **o** formation, linking formation with letter name, keyword and sound.

Follow activity procedure and have students sky write letters.

Emphasize that these letters are plane line round letters, so they begin on the plane line.

Letter Formation for C

Use the following verbalization to direct students in proper letter formation.

Say

c is a plane line round letter.

It starts on the (plane line).

1. Point to the plane line.
2. Start to fly backwards,
3. and go down and around to the grass line.
4. Say c - cat - /k/, have students repeat.

Letter Formation for O

Use the following verbalization to direct students in proper letter formation.

Say

o is a plane line round letter.

It starts on the (plane line) just like a c.

1. Point to the plane line.
2. Trace back, then down to the grass line,
3. and around back up to the plane line.
4. Say o - octopus - /ŏ/, have students repeat.

Student Notebook

Direct the students to find the newly introduced letters.

Use the verbalization for the letter formation to direct the students while they trace it with their finger. Do it with them to model. Have them say letter-keyword-sound.

After students trace following verbalizations, they can then color the keyword picture for the letter **c**.

Unit 1 | Week 4

Day 2

Daily Plan — DAY 2

Student Learning Plan
- Drill Sounds/Warm-Up
- Sky Write/Letter Formation
- Student Notebook
- Echo/Letter Formation

Teacher Materials
- Echo and/or Baby Echo
- Large Sound Cards
- Standard Sound Cards
- Large Writing Grid
- Letter Formation Guide
- Vowel Extension Poster
- Student Notebook

Student Materials
- Student Notebook
- Dry Erase Writing Tablet

Drill Sounds/Warm-Up

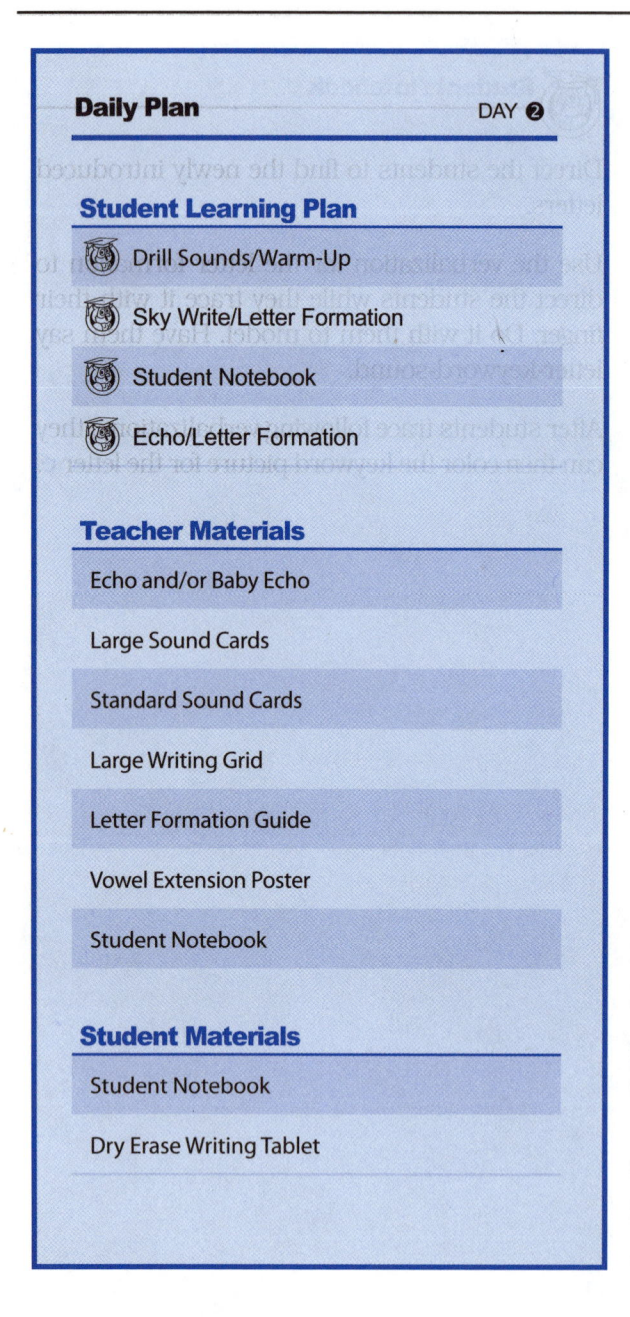

DO ALL THE INTRODUCED SOUNDS EACH DAY

Large Sound Cards

Practice sounds with the Large Sound Cards. Model these, saying the letter-keyword-sound and have the students echo.

Standard Sound Cards

Next, point to the Standard Sound Cards (in card display) with the Baby Echo pointer. You say the letter-keyword-sound and hold up Baby Echo to have the students repeat.

Vowel Extension

Model extending the vowel sounds (example: **o-/ŏ/...ctopus-/ŏ/**). Extend the sound while you trace the line and finish the word when you get to the picture.

Have a student come trace the line for other vowels previously taught. *i, u, o*

Sky Write/Letter Formation

Review **c** and **o** formation, linking formation with letter name, keyword and sound.

Follow activity procedure and have students sky write letters.

Emphasize that these letters are plane line round letters, so they begin on the plane line.

96 FUNDATIONS® LEVEL K

Unit 1 | Week 4

Day 2

Student Notebook

Trace and say the letter-keyword-sound for all the previous letters introduced.

Direct the students to find the newly introduced letters.

Use the verbalization for the letter formation to direct the students while they trace it with their finger. Do it with them to model. Have them say letter-keyword-sound.

After students trace following verbalizations, they can then color the keyword picture for the letter **o**.

Echo/Letter Formation

Remind students of proper pencil grip and sitting position, and give them their Dry Erase Writing Tablets.

Sounds appear between / /. Dictate **new** sounds and a selection of previously taught sounds. You select and say the sound. Students echo the sound and say the letter.

Next have a student come up to the classroom board to make the letter on the Large Writing Grid. Direct the student with the letter formation verbalization.

Then have all students write the answer on their Dry Erase Writing Tablets as you direct them with the letter formation verbalization. Circulate to reinforce pencil grip and assist students, as needed.

Sounds

/t/ - t	/b/ - b	/f/ - f
/n/ - n	/m/ - m	/ĭ/ - i
/ŭ/ - u	/c/ - c	/ŏ/ - o

Unit 1 | Week 4

Day 3

Daily Plan — DAY 3

Student Learning Plan
- Drill Sounds/Warm-Up
- Make It Fun
- Echo/Find Letters
- Student Notebook

Teacher Materials
- Echo and/or Baby Echo
- Large Sound Cards
- Standard Sound Cards
- Letter Formation Guide
- Vowel Extension Poster
- Student Notebook

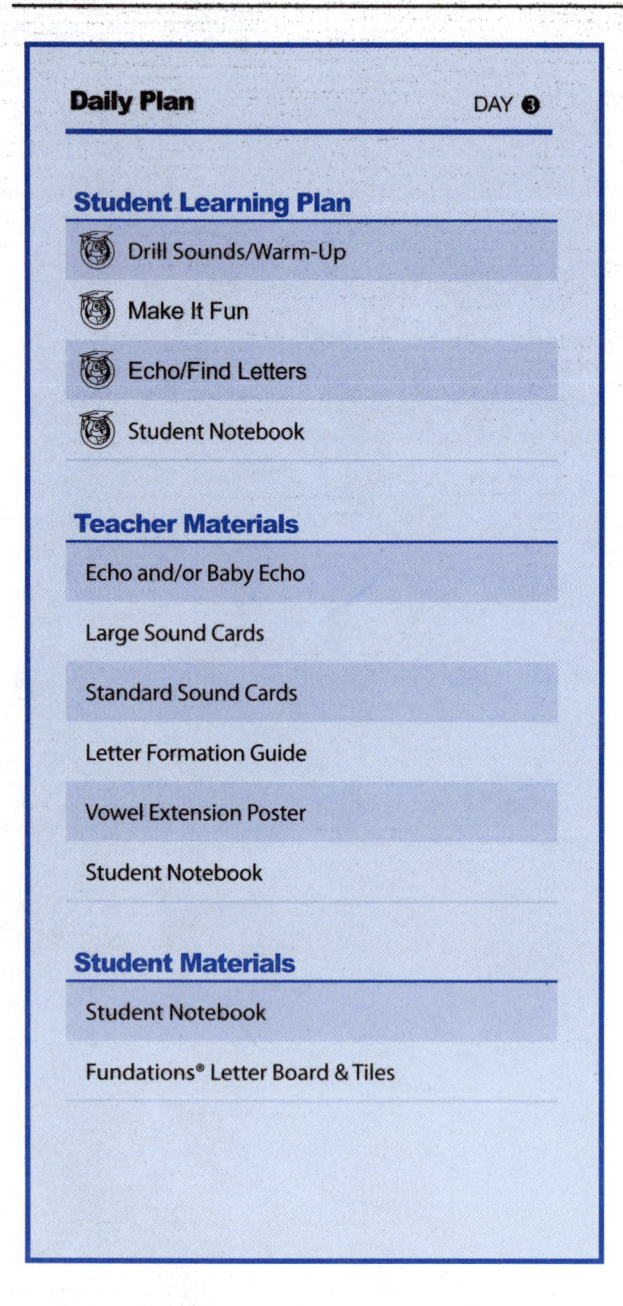

Student Materials
- Student Notebook
- Fundations® Letter Board & Tiles

Drill Sounds/Warm-Up

DO ALL THE INTRODUCED SOUNDS EACH DAY

Large Sound Cards

Practice sounds with the Large Sound Cards. Model these, saying the letter-keyword-sound and have the students echo.

Standard Sound Cards

Next, point to the Standard Sound Cards (in card display) with the Baby Echo pointer. You say the letter-keyword-sound and hold up Baby Echo to have the students repeat.

Vowel Extension

Model extending the vowel sounds (example: o-/ŏ/…ctopus-/ŏ/). Extend the sound while you trace the line and finish the word when you get to the picture.

Have a student come trace the line for other vowels previously taught.

Make It Fun

Collect objects that start with the letters taught so far. Put them in a big shopping bag. Call on a student to pick something out of the bag. Ask what it is (**truck**) and then have the student find the letter which starts the word (**t**).

They should then say the letter-keyword-sound. Hold up Echo to have the other students repeat. Then ask:

When you make this letter, where does it start?

Then provide the verbalization of the letter formation as the student sky writes it.

Unit 1 | Week 4

Day 3

Echo/Find Letters

Students match Magnetic Letter Tiles to the letter(s) on their Letter Boards. Distribute Letter Boards and the Letter Tiles **c** and **o** to each student. Start with tiles on the blank side of the board. Dictate sounds. Students echo sound and match the tiles. Include previous sounds and new sounds. After all sounds are matched, dictate 2-3 sounds and have students repeat the sound and point to the corresponding letter.

Sounds

/t/ - t	/b/ - b	/f/ - f
/n/ - n	/m/ - m	/ĭ/ - i
/ŭ/ - u	/c/ - c	/ŏ/ - o

Student Notebook

Practice Letters

Students trace previously taught letters while naming letter-keyword-sound. Do as a group saying verbalization, or circulate around the room as students do independently.

Unit 1 | Week 4

Day 4

Daily Plan — DAY 4

Student Learning Plan
- Drill Sounds/Warm-Up
- Word Play
- Sky Write/Letter Formation
- Echo/Letter Formation

Teacher Materials
- Echo and/or Baby Echo
- Large Sound Cards
- Standard Sound Cards
- Large Writing Grid
- Letter Formation Guide
- Vowel Extension Poster
- Sentence and Syllable Frames

Student Materials
- Student Notebook
- Dry Erase Writing Tablet

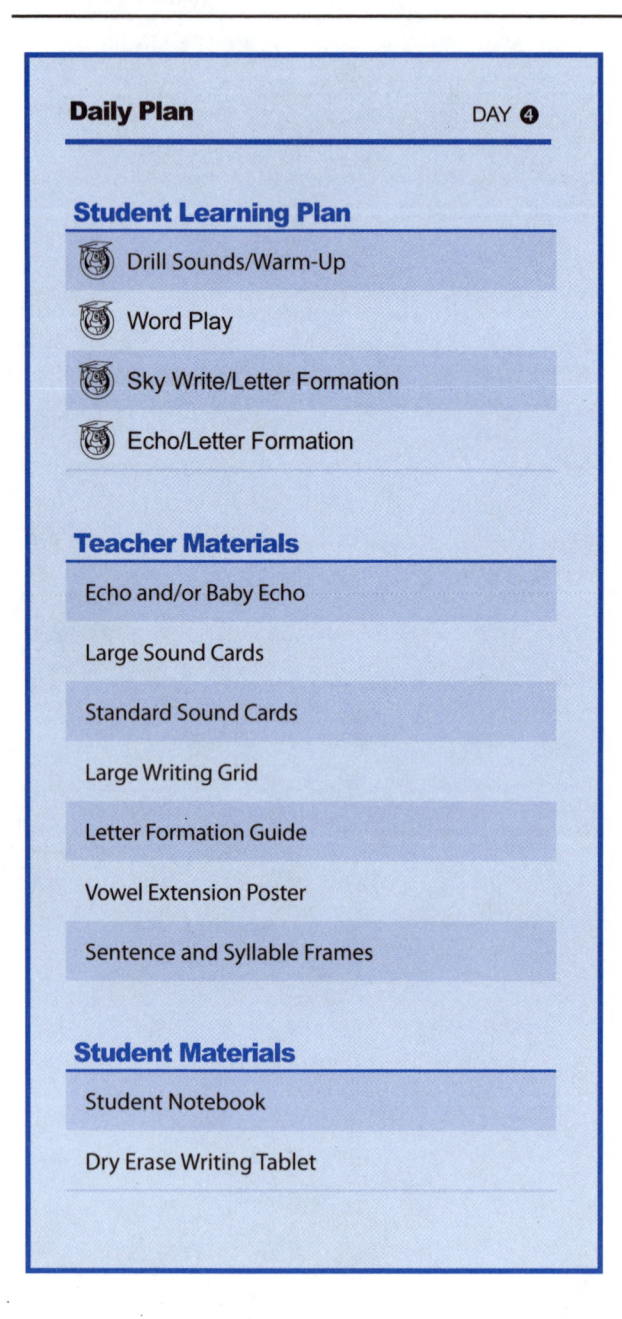

Drill Sounds/Warm-Up

DO ALL THE INTRODUCED SOUNDS EACH DAY

Large Sound Cards

Practice sounds with the Large Sound Cards. Model these, saying the letter-keyword-sound and have the students echo.

Standard Sound Cards

Next, point to the Standard Sound Cards (in card display) with the Baby Echo pointer. You say the letter-keyword-sound and hold up Baby Echo to have the students repeat.

Vowel Extension

Model extending the vowel sounds (example: **o-/ŏ/...ctopus-/ŏ/**). Extend the sound while you trace the line and finish the word when you get to the picture.

Have a student come trace the line for other vowels previously taught.

Word Play

Teacher Materials
- Sentence Frames
- Baby Echo

WORD AWARENESS

Again this week, students will help you erase the words for you to then write the replacement words.

Write the sentence:

| Amelia | is | a | girl | . |

Call on someone in the class and orally change the sentence, using that student's name. Change the name and gender as appropriate.

Have that student be your helper to erase the word(s) that need to change. Have the student erase the words to be changed with your guidance.

SYLLABLE COUNT

Preparation
- White Syllable Frames

This activity will help students segment words into syllables.

Instruct Students

Say a word (see Resources). Have students echo the word. Have them put their hands under their chin to "feel" the syllables. Then have

Unit 1 | Week 4

Day 4

them clap out the syllables. Ask them, how many syllables in the word? After they answer, write the word on the Syllable Frames, one-syllable per frame. Read the word, pointing to each syllable. Count the frames and tell the students whether or not their count was correct.

base	ball

Word Resources

Use students' names interwoven with a selection of words below.

baseball   basketball   book

jelly   dog   gingerbread

Sky Write/Letter Formation

Review **c** and **o** formation, linking formation with letter name, keyword and sound.

Follow activity procedure and have students sky write letters.

Emphasize that these letters are plane line round letters, so they begin on the plane line. Point to the poster to show students where to look to remind them where to begin the these letters.

Echo/Letter Formation

Remind students of proper pencil grip and sitting position, and give them their Dry Erase Writing Tablets.

Sounds appear between / /. Dictate **new** sounds and a selection of previously taught sounds. You select and say the sound. Students echo the sound and say the letter.

Next have a student come up to the classroom board to make the letter on the Large Writing Grid. Direct the student with the letter formation verbalization.

Then have all students write the answer on their Dry Erase Writing Tablets as you direct them with the letter formation verbalization. Circulate to reinforce pencil grip and assist students, as needed.

Sounds

/t/ - t	/b/ - b	/f/ - f
/n/ - n	/m/ - m	/ĭ/ - i
/ŭ/ - u	/c/ - c	/ŏ/ - o

Unit 1 | Week 4

Day 5

Daily Plan — DAY 5

Student Learning Plan
- Drill Sounds/Warm-Up
- Storytime
- Echo/Find Letters

Teacher Materials
- Echo and/or Baby Echo
- Large Sound Cards
- Standard Sound Cards
- Vowel Extension Poster
- Echo Story Illustrations on large chart paper
- Phrased story on large chart paper

Student Materials
- Student Notebook
- Fundations® Letter Board & Tiles

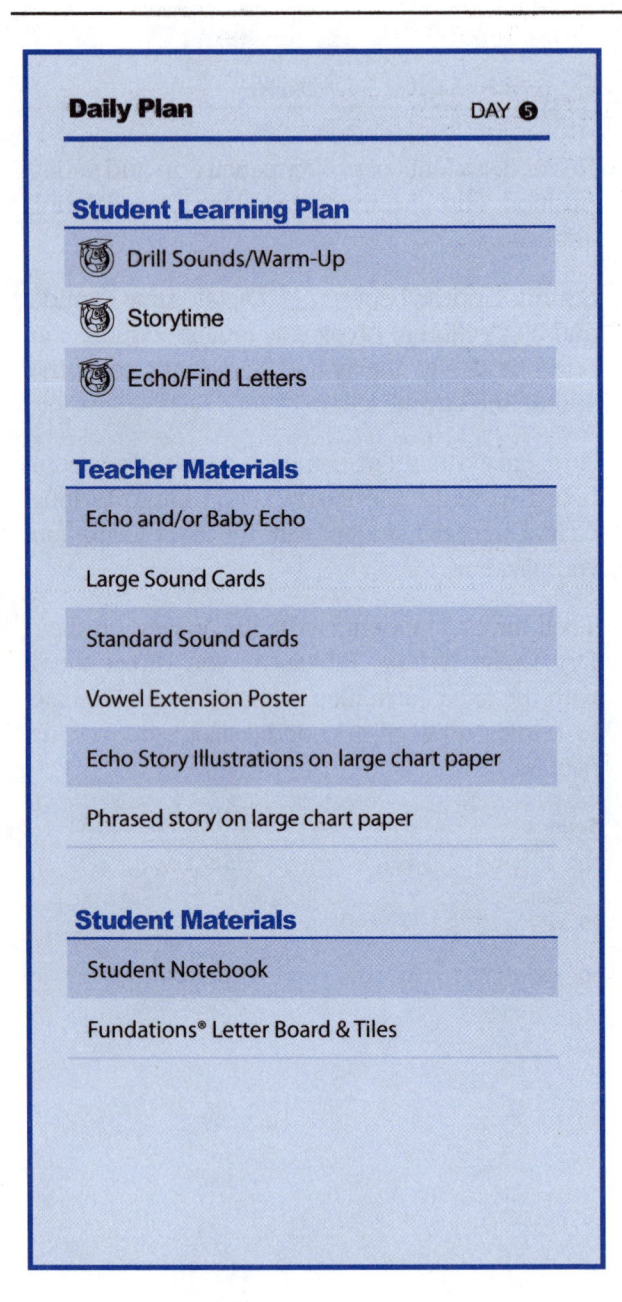

Drill Sounds/Warm-Up

DO ALL THE INTRODUCED SOUNDS EACH DAY

Large Sound Cards

Practice sounds with the Large Sound Cards. Model these, saying the letter-keyword-sound and have the students echo.

Standard Sound Cards

Next, point to the Standard Sound Cards (in card display) with the Baby Echo pointer. You say the letter-keyword-sound and hold up Baby Echo to have the students repeat.

Vowel Extension

Model extending the vowel sounds (example: ŏ-/ŏ/...ctopus-/ŏ/). Extend the sound while you trace the line and finish the word when you get to the picture.

Have a student come trace the line for other vowels previously taught.

Storytime

Teacher Materials
- Echo Story Illustrations on large chart paper (from Story III)
- Phrased story on large chart paper or projected to class

ECHO FINDS DINNER IV

This week, use your pictures on the chart paper from "Echo Finds Dinner III" (Week 3, Day 5). Have the students retell the story.

Use the Baby Echo pointer to read the story one sentence at a time and have the students echo. Be sure to scoop and read sentences in phrases.

Next, use both your pictures and the phrased story together. Look at a picture and then read the corresponding words on the phrased story chart.

Lastly, reread a sentence and ask a student to come find one of the key words in that sentence and circle it. Do several words such as: **tree, hungry, forest, mouse, happy**

tip

The phrased story is provided on the PLC.

Unit 1 | Week 4

Day 5

Echo Finds Dinner

One day Echo was deep in the forest. She sat on a branch of a very tall tree. Echo had a problem. She was very hungry! Echo had to find food so she searched and searched, looking all around the forest. Echo saw something move! It was a mouse. Echo was fast. She flew down and scooped it up. Echo ate the mouse and was happy.

Echo/Find Letters

Students match Magnetic Letter Tiles to the letter(s) on their Letter Boards. Start with tiles off the board. Dictate sounds. Students echo sound and match the tiles. Include previous sounds and new sounds. After all sounds are matched, dictate 2-3 sounds and have students repeat the sound and point to the corresponding letter.

Sounds

/t/ - t	/b/ - b	/f/ - f
/n/ - n	/m/ - m	/ĭ/ - i
/ŭ/ - u	/c/ - c	/ŏ/ - o

tip

Be sure to write the story with enough room so that you can scoop phrases. Use a different color marker to scoop the sentence into phrases.

© 2002, 2012 WILSON LANGUAGE TRAINING CORPORATION

TEACHER'S MANUAL 103

Unit 1 | Week 5

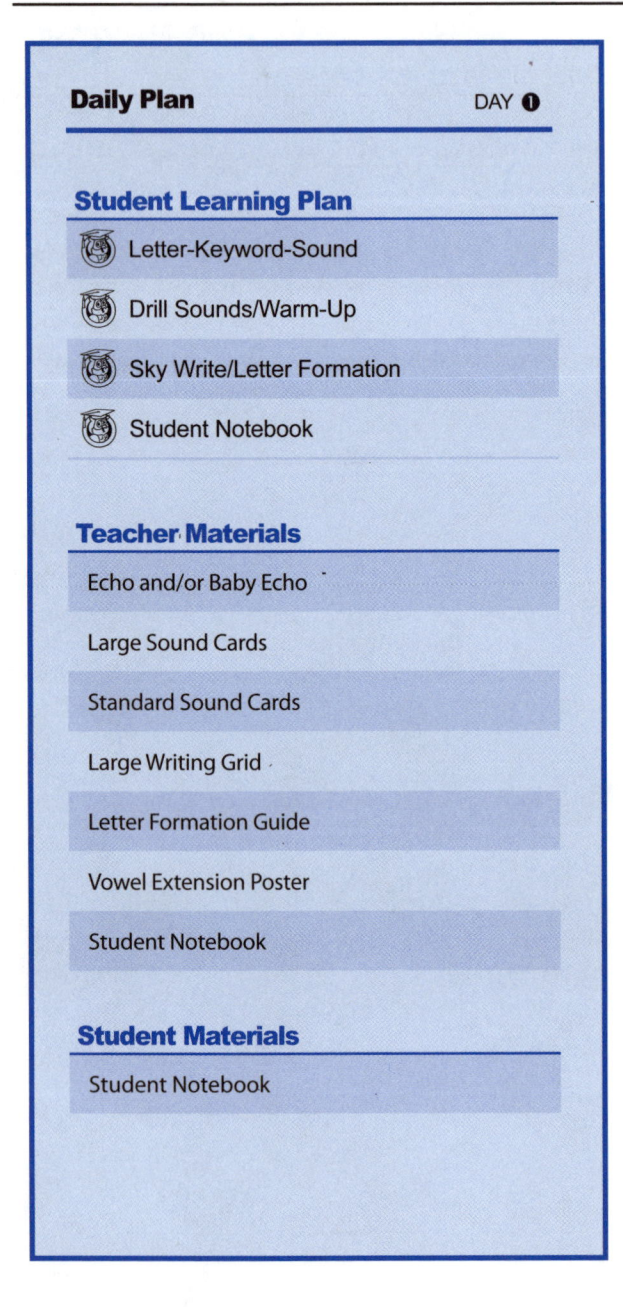

Day 1

Daily Plan — DAY 1

Student Learning Plan
- Letter-Keyword-Sound
- Drill Sounds/Warm-Up
- Sky Write/Letter Formation
- Student Notebook

Teacher Materials
- Echo and/or Baby Echo
- Large Sound Cards
- Standard Sound Cards
- Large Writing Grid
- Letter Formation Guide
- Vowel Extension Poster
- Student Notebook

Student Materials
- Student Notebook

Letter-Keyword-Sound

Introduce Letter-Keyword-Sound with Large and Standard Sound Cards. Be sure to follow procedure. First teach with Large Sound Card. Have students echo letter-keyword-sound. Then repeat with Standard Sound Card.

| a | - a - apple - /ă/ |
| g | - g - game - /g/ |

*[handwritten: * 2 ways to write a a — say to]*

Explain that **a** is a vowel and retell the students that the vowels will be on the salmon-colored cards. Demonstrate how to hold the vowel sound /ă/ until you run out of breath. Also show the students that the letter **a** on the Standard Sound Card looks different, similar to the way it looks in books. Tell them that they do not need to write it that way, but that they can write it like the one on the Large Sound Card.

Vowel Extension

Do the Vowel Extension activity with **a**. Explain that this helps them stretch out vowel sounds. Demonstrate how to hold the vowel sounds until you run out of breath.

Model 'reading' the keyword picture (example: /ă/...pple). Extend the /ă/ sound while you trace the line and finish the word when you get to the picture. Have a student come trace the line while everyone extends the /ă/ sound.

Show students that the letter **g** also looks different on the Standard Sound Card, similar to the way it looks in books.

Note *[handwritten: a d g look different than normal]*

As a new letter is taught, its Standard Sound Card is added to your card display to be drilled at each lesson.

Drill Sounds/Warm-Up

DO ALL THE INTRODUCED SOUNDS EACH DAY

Large Sound Cards

Practice sounds with the Large Sound Cards. Model these, saying the letter-keyword-sound and have the students echo.

Standard Sound Cards

Next, point to the Standard Sound Cards (in card display) with the Baby Echo pointer. You say the letter-keyword-sound and hold up Baby Echo to have the students repeat.

104 FUNDATIONS® LEVEL K © 2002, 2012 WILSON LANGUAGE TRAINING CORPORATION

Unit 1 | Week 5

Day 1

Sky Write/Letter Formation

Teach **a** and **g** formation, linking formation with letter name, keyword and sound.

Follow activity procedure and have students sky write letters.

Emphasize that these letters are plane line round letters, so they begin on the plane line.

Letter Formation for **a**

Use the following verbalization to direct students in proper letter formation.

Say

> a is a plane line round letter.
>
> It starts on the (plane line).

1. **Point to the plane line.**
2. **Go back on the plane line then down and around on the grass line,**
3. **and up to the plane line.**
4. **Trace back down to the grass line.**
5. **Say a - apple - /ă/, have students repeat.**

Letter Formation for **g**

Use the following verbalization to direct students in proper letter formation.

Say

> g is a plane line round letter.
>
> It starts on the (plane line) just like a c.

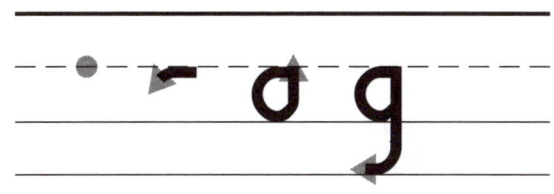

1. **Point to the plane line.**
2. **Trace back on the plane line,**
3. **down and around all the way back to the plane line.**
4. **Trace back down all the way to the worm line and make a curve.**
5. **Say g - game - /g/, have students repeat.**

Student Notebook

Direct the students to find the newly introduced letters.

Use the verbalization for the letter formation to direct the students while they trace it with their finger. Do it with them to model. Have them say letter-keyword-sound.

After students trace following verbalizations, they can then color the keyword picture for the letter **a**.

Unit 1 | Week 5

Day 2

Daily Plan — DAY 2

Student Learning Plan
- Drill Sounds/Warm-Up
- Sky Write/Letter Formation
- Student Notebook
- Echo/Letter Formation

Teacher Materials
- Echo and/or Baby Echo
- Large Sound Cards
- Standard Sound Cards
- Large Writing Grid
- Letter Formation Guide
- Vowel Extension Poster
- Student Notebook

Student Materials
- Student Notebook
- Dry Erase Writing Tablet

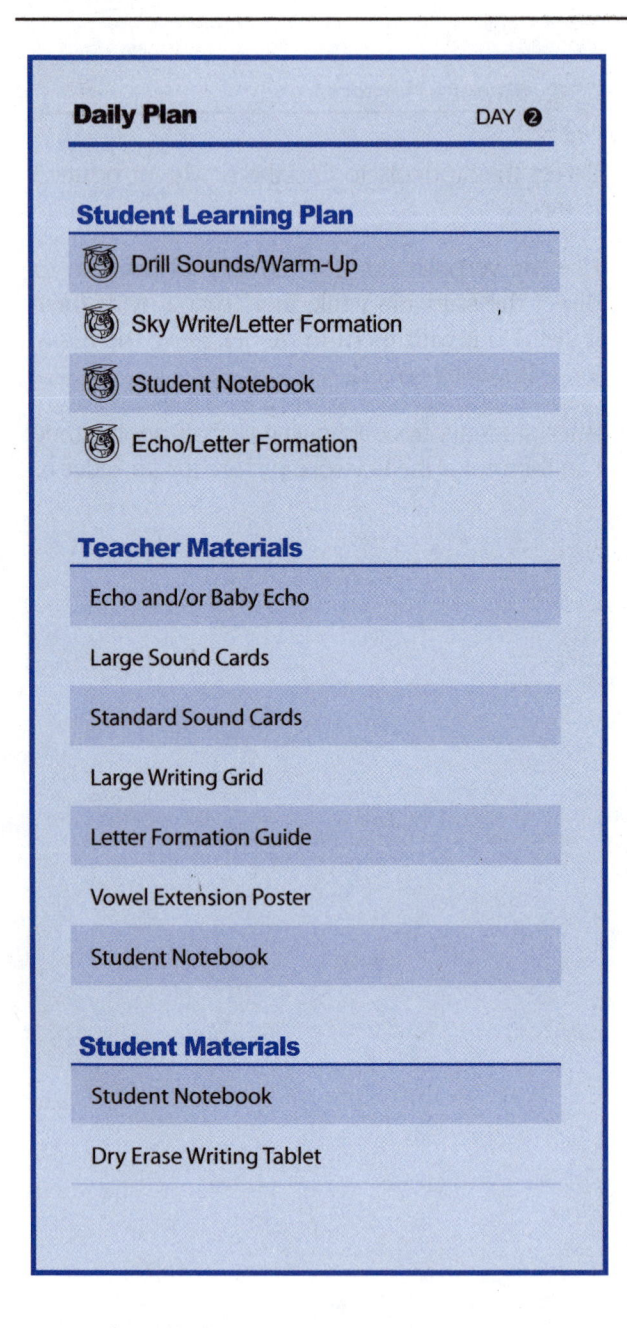

Drill Sounds/Warm-Up

DO ALL THE INTRODUCED SOUNDS EACH DAY

Large Sound Cards

Practice sounds with the Large Sound Cards. Model these, saying the letter-keyword-sound and have the students echo.

Standard Sound Cards

Next, point to the Standard Sound Cards (in card display) with the Baby Echo pointer. You say the letter-keyword-sound and hold up Baby Echo to have the students repeat.

Vowel Extension

Model 'reading' the keyword picture (example: /ă/...**pple**). Extend the /ă/ sound while you trace the line and finish the word when you get to the picture.

Have a student come trace the line for other vowels previously taught.

Sky Write/Letter Formation

Review **a** and **g** formation, linking formation with letter name, keyword and sound.

Follow activity procedure and have students sky write letters.

Emphasize that these letters are plane line round letters, so they begin on the plane line.

Unit 1 | Week 5

Day 2

Student Notebook

Trace and say the letter-keyword-sound for all the previous letters introduced.

Direct the students to find the newly introduced letters.

Use the verbalization for the letter formation to direct the students while they trace it with their finger. Do it with them to model. Have them say letter-keyword-sound.

After students trace following verbalizations, they can then color the keyword picture for the letter **g**.

Echo/Letter Formation

Remind students of proper pencil grip and sitting position, and give them their Dry Erase Writing Tablets.

Sounds appear between / /. Dictate **new** sounds and a selection of previously taught sounds. You select and say the sound. Students echo the sound and say the letter.

Next have a student come up to the classroom board to make the letter on the Large Writing Grid. Direct the student with the letter formation verbalization.

Then have all students write the answer on their Dry Erase Writing Tablets as you direct them with the letter formation verbalization. Circulate to reinforce pencil grip and assist students, as needed.

Sounds

/t/ - t	/b/ - b	/f/ - f
/n/ - n	/m/ - m	/ĭ/ - i
/ŭ/ - u	/c/ - c	/ŏ/ - o
/ă/ - a	/g/ - g	

Establish a routine for management and distribution of materials. See PLC Expert Tips.

Unit 1 | Week 5

Day 3

Daily Plan — DAY 3

Student Learning Plan
- Drill Sounds/Warm-Up
- Make It Fun
- Echo/Find Letters
- Student Notebook

Teacher Materials
- Echo and/or Baby Echo
- Large Sound Cards
- Standard Sound Cards
- Vowel Extension Poster
- Student Notebook

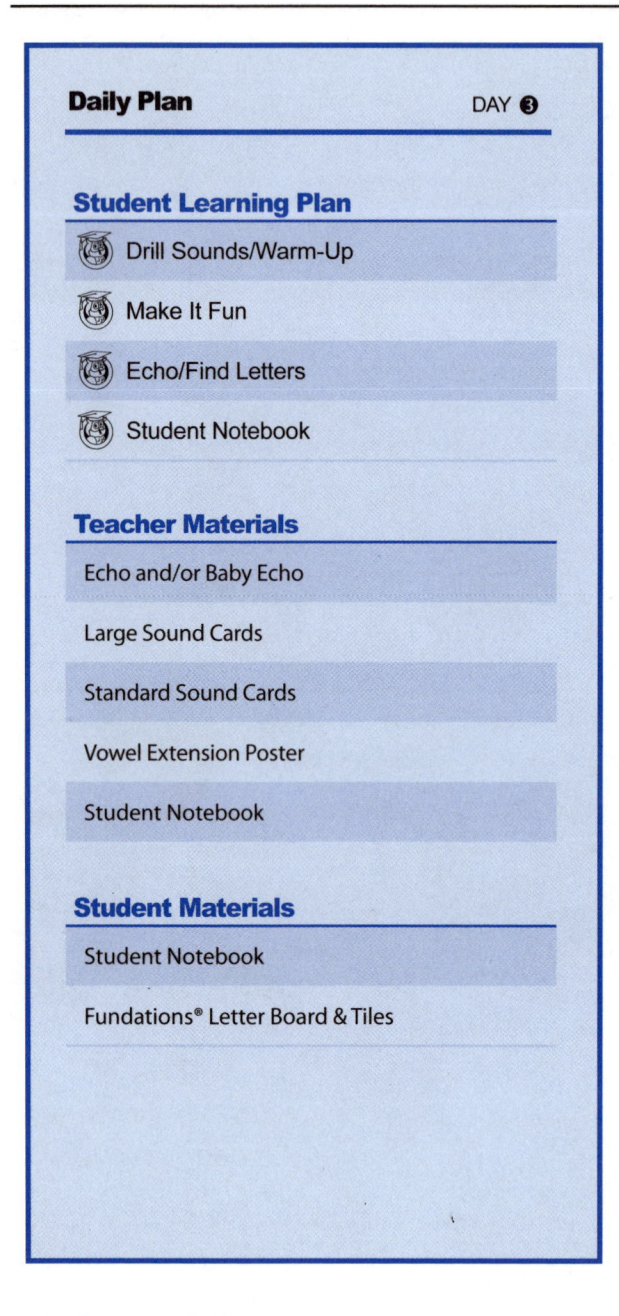

Student Materials
- Student Notebook
- Fundations® Letter Board & Tiles

Drill Sounds/Warm-Up

DO ALL THE INTRODUCED SOUNDS EACH DAY

Large Sound Cards
Practice sounds with the Large Sound Cards. Model these, saying the letter-keyword-sound and have the students echo.

Standard Sound Cards
Next, point to the Standard Sound Cards (in card display) with the Baby Echo pointer. You say the letter-keyword-sound and hold up Baby Echo to have the students repeat.

Vowel Extension
Model 'reading' the keyword picture (example: /ă/...pple). Extend the /ă/ sound while you trace the line and finish the word when you get to the picture.

Have a student come trace the line for other vowels previously taught.

Make It Fun

LETTER FUN
Pass out the Standard Sound Cards. Have one student at a time come up and hold up their card and say the letter-keyword-sound.

You hold up Echo so the other students repeat. Then ask:

When you make this letter, where does it start?

Then provide the verbalization of the letter formation as the student sky writes it. Select a student by saying:

Who is holding the card that says /t/?

RHYME TIME
Tell students that the next fun thing they will do is to help you rhyme words. Say three words that rhyme and have students name another word. They can also name a silly or nonsense word.

bat, cat, mat _____

bake, take, fake _____

snow, crow, mow _____

sit, spit, knit _____

tan, fan, ban _____

mop, slop, chop _____

Unit 1 | Week 5

Day 3

Echo/Find Letters

Students match Magnetic Letter Tiles to the letter(s) on their Letter Boards. Distribute Letter Boards and the Letter Tiles **a** and **g** to each student. Start with tiles on the blank side of the board. Dictate sounds. Students echo sound and match the tiles. Include previous sounds and new sounds. After all sounds are matched, dictate 2-3 sounds and have students repeat the sound and point to the corresponding letter.

Sounds

/t/ - t	/b/ - b	/f/ - f
/n/ - n	/m/ - m	/ĭ/ - i
/ŭ/ - u	/c/ - c	/ŏ/ - o
/ă/ - a	**/g/ - g**	

Student Notebook

Practice Letters

Students trace previously taught letters while naming letter-keyword-sound. Do as a group saying verbalization, or circulate around the room as students do independently.

Unit 1 | Week 5

Day 4

Daily Plan — DAY 4

Student Learning Plan
- Drill Sounds/Warm-Up
- Word Play
- Sky Write/Letter Formation
- Echo/Letter Formation

Teacher Materials
- Echo and/or Baby Echo
- Large Sound Cards
- Standard Sound Cards
- Large Writing Grid
- Letter Formation Guide
- Vowel Extension Poster
- Sentence and Syllable Frames

Student Materials
- Student Notebook
- Dry Erase Writing Tablet

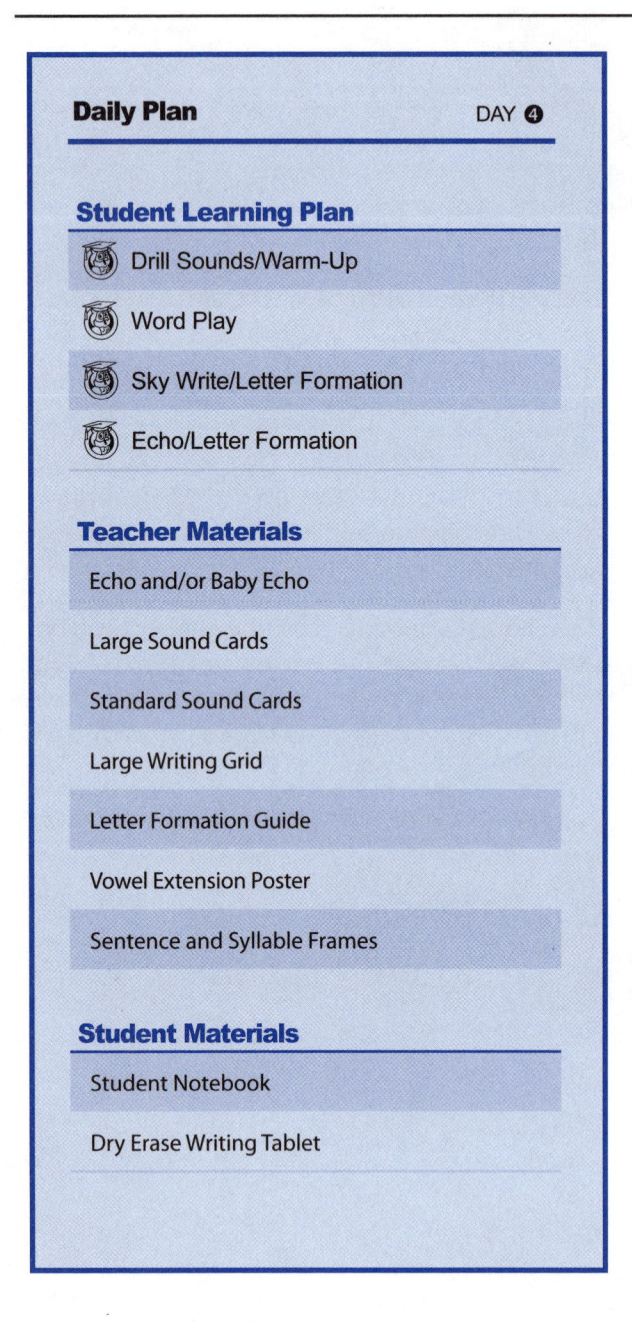

Drill Sounds/Warm-Up

DO ALL THE INTRODUCED SOUNDS EACH DAY

Large Sound Cards

Practice sounds with the Large Sound Cards. Model these, saying the letter-keyword-sound and have the students echo.

Standard Sound Cards

Next, point to the Standard Sound Cards (in card display) with the Baby Echo pointer. You say the letter-keyword-sound and hold up Baby Echo to have the students repeat.

Vowel Extension

Model 'reading' the keyword picture (example: /ă/...**pple**). Extend the /ă/ sound while you trace the line and finish the word when you get to the picture.

Have a student come trace the line for other vowels previously taught.

Word Play

Teacher Materials
- Sentence and Syllable Frames
- Baby Echo

WORD AWARENESS

Use the following idea for a sentence:

| Pedro | has | a | bike | . |

Erase the sentence.

Ask

> Who else has a bike?

Get the other tall word frame in order to write the sentence:

| Pedro | and | Carrie | have | bikes | . |

Point to the words with Baby Echo, read the sentence and have the students echo. Explain that a person's name always starts with a capital (uppercase) letter so you need to write it on a tall word frame.

Do several sentences with two names.

Examples

Fernando and Tony have brown hair.

Cathy and Maria have blonde hair.

Unit 1 | Week 5

Day 4

Each time, ask why you selected the tall frame. Ask this for both the first word in the sentence and for the student's name. Be sure to echo read each sentence.

SYLLABLE PLAY

Say a word and have students repeat. Have students clap out, and write the word on the Syllable Frames.

Instruct Students

base	ball

Point to each syllable as you say it.

Ask

What would it be if I took away ball?

Remove the | ball | *frame. After students answer, put it back.*

Ask

The word is baseball. What would it be if I took away base?

Again, point to each syllable as you say it. Remove the | base | *frame. After students answer, erase the frames.*

Word Resources

Use students' names interwoven with a selection of words below.

| picnic | candy | spotlight |
| hat | cupcake | kitten |

Sky Write/Letter Formation

Review **a** and **g** formation, linking formation with letter name, keyword and sound.

Follow activity procedure and have students sky write letters.

Emphasize that these letters are plane line round letters, so they begin on the plane line.

Ask a student to come point to all the plane line round letters that have been taught so far. Sky write other plane line round letters.

Echo/Letter Formation

Remind students of proper pencil grip and sitting position, and give them their Dry Erase Writing Tablets.

Sounds appear between / /. Dictate **new** sounds and a selection of previously taught sounds. You select and say the sound. Students echo the sound and say the letter.

Next have a student come up to the classroom board to make the letter on the Large Writing Grid. Direct the student with the letter formation verbalization.

Then have all students write the answer on their Dry Erase Writing Tablets as you direct them with the letter formation verbalization. Circulate to reinforce pencil grip and assist students, as needed.

Sounds

/t/ - t	/b/ - b	/f/ - f
/n/ - n	/m/ - m	/ĭ/ - i
/ŭ/ - u	/c/ - c	/ŏ/ - o
/ă/ - a	/g/ - g	

Unit 1 | Week 5

Day 5

Daily Plan — DAY 5

Student Learning Plan
- Drill Sounds/Warm-Up
- Storytime
- Echo/Find Letters

Teacher Materials
- Echo and/or Baby Echo
- Large Sound Cards
- Standard Sound Cards
- Vowel Extension Poster
- Large chart paper

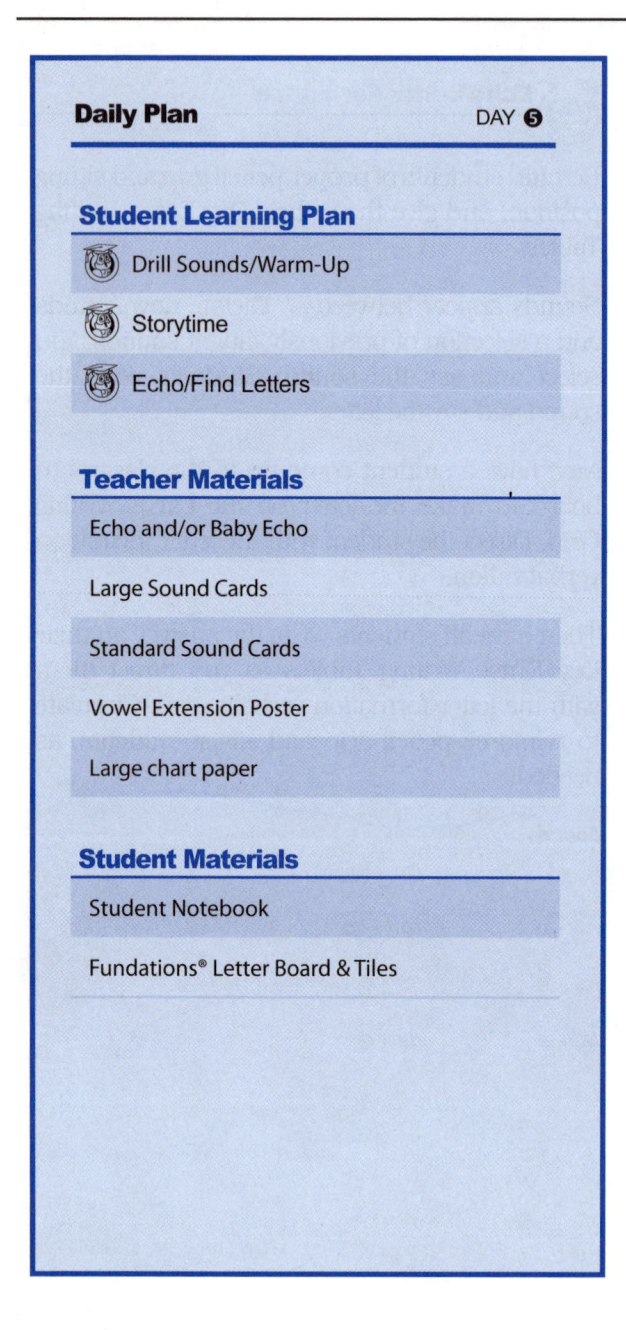

Student Materials
- Student Notebook
- Fundations® Letter Board & Tiles

Drill Sounds/Warm-Up

DO ALL THE INTRODUCED SOUNDS EACH DAY

Large Sound Cards

Practice sounds with the Large Sound Cards. Model these, saying the letter-keyword-sound and have the students echo.

Standard Sound Cards

Next, point to the Standard Sound Cards (in card display) with the Baby Echo pointer. You say the letter-keyword-sound and hold up Baby Echo to have the students repeat.

Vowel Extension

Model 'reading' the keyword picture (example: /ă/...pple). Extend the /ă/ sound while you trace the line and finish the word when you get to the picture.

Have a student come trace the line for other vowels previously taught.

Storytime

Teacher Materials
- Rhyming books
- Large chart paper

Preparation

During Storytime select a rhyming picture book to read to your students. Be sure that the story has no more than 4-5 sentences per page. It should have predictable rhyming patterns. The following list provides some suggestions.

Domanska, J. 1974. *What Do You See?* New York: Macmillan.

Galdone, P. 1986. *Three Little Kittens*. New York: Clarion.

Guarino, D. 1989. *Is Your Mama a Llama?* New York: Scholastic.

Hawkins, C., and J. Hawkins. 1987. *I Know an Old Lady Who Swallowed a Fly*. New York: Putnam.

Hayes, S. 1986. *This Is the Bear.* Philadelphia, PA: Lippincott.

Prater, J. 1991. *No! Said Joe.* Cambridge, MA: Candlewick.

Shaw, N. 1989. *Sheep On a Ship.* Boston: Houghton Mifflin.

Weiss, N. 1992. *On a Hot, Hot Day.* New York: G. P. Putnam's Sons.

Instruct Students

Before reading, look at the front and back cover of the book with your students. Discuss the title, author and illustrator, explaining each of those terms.

Unit 1 | Week 5

Day 5

Read the book once moving your finger under the words and emphasizing the rhymes. Pause 2-3 times and ask students to predict what will happen.

Say

> Now let's do it again but this time you can help me read.

Read the book again, moving your finger under the words. This time, do not say the rhyming words and let the students say it for you. You can also provide the onset **/m/** and have students say the rime **/at/** (for the word **mat**).

Lastly, write the rhyming words from the story on chart paper or the board. Put rhyming words on the same line.

Example

bat   cat   sat

down   clown

Tell the students that these are the words they read in the story. Explain that they rhyme. Read a set of rhyming words with Baby Echo and have the students repeat. Ask them to think of other words that rhyme with each set. Add them to the list and read.

Echo/Find Letters

Students match Magnetic Letter Tiles to the letter(s) on their Letter Boards. Start with tiles off the board. Dictate sounds. Students echo sound and match the tiles. Include previous sounds and new sounds. After all sounds are matched, dictate 2-3 sounds and have students repeat the sound and point to the corresponding letter.

Sounds

/t/ - t	/b/ - b	/f/ - f
/n/ - n	/m/ - m	/ĭ/ - i
/ŭ/ - u	/c/ - c	/ŏ/ - o
/ă/ - a	**/g/ - g**	

Unit 1 | Week 6

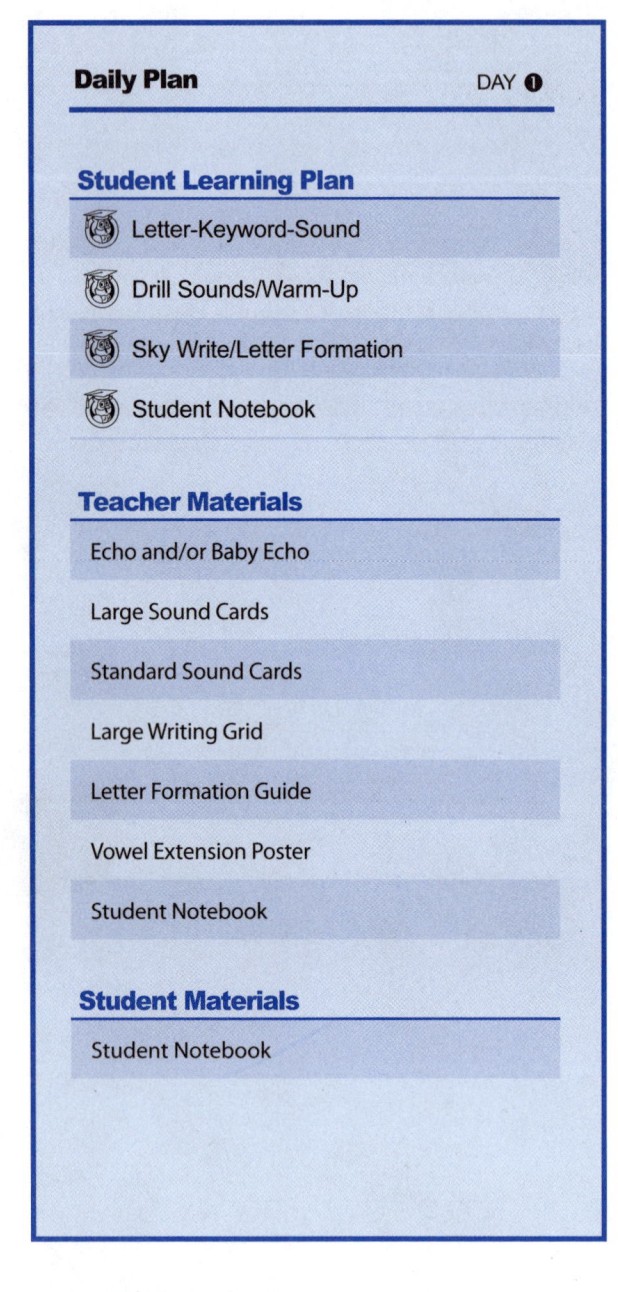

Day 1

Daily Plan — DAY 1

Student Learning Plan
- Letter-Keyword-Sound
- Drill Sounds/Warm-Up
- Sky Write/Letter Formation
- Student Notebook

Teacher Materials
- Echo and/or Baby Echo
- Large Sound Cards
- Standard Sound Cards
- Large Writing Grid
- Letter Formation Guide
- Vowel Extension Poster
- Student Notebook

Student Materials
- Student Notebook

Letter-Keyword-Sound

Introduce Letter-Keyword-Sound with Large and Standard Sound Cards. Be sure to follow procedure. First teach with Large Sound Card. Have students echo letter-keyword-sound. Then repeat with Standard Sound Card.

| d | - d - dog - /d/ |

| s | - s - snake - /s/ |

Vowel Extension

Model 'reading' the keyword pictures for the vowels previously taught. Extend the sound while you trace the line and finish the word when you get to the picture.

Have a student come trace the line while everyone extends the sound.

a
i
o
u

Note
As a new letter is taught, its Standard Sound Card is added to your card display to be drilled at each lesson.

Drill Sounds/Warm-Up

Do new sounds and vowel sounds each day. Selectively review 4-5 other consonants.

Large Sound Cards

Practice sounds with the Large Sound Cards. Model these, saying the letter-keyword-sound and have the students echo.

Standard Sound Cards

Next, point to the Standard Sound Cards (in card display) with the Baby Echo pointer. You say the letter-keyword-sound and hold up Baby Echo to have the students repeat.

Unit 1 | Week 6

Day 1

Sky Write/Letter Formation

Teach **d** and **s** formation, linking formation with letter name, keyword and sound.

Follow activity procedure and have students sky write letters.

Emphasize that these letters are plane line round letters, so they begin on the plane line.

Letter Formation for d

Use the following verbalization to direct students in proper letter formation.

Say

d is a plane line round letter.

It starts on the (plane line) just like a c.

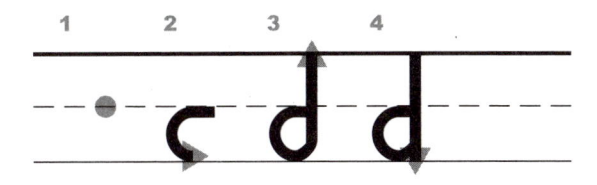

1. Point to the plane line.
2. Go back, down and around to the grass line,
3. all the way back up to the sky line.
4. Trace back down to the grass line.
5. Say d - dog - /d/, have students repeat

Letter Formation for s

Use the following verbalization to direct students in proper letter formation.

Say

s is a plane line round letter.

It starts on the (plane line) just like a c.

1. Point to the plane line.
2. Trace back and it curves in,
3. and goes back again and lands on the grass line.
4. Say s - snake - /s/, have students repeat.

Student Notebook

Direct the students to find the newly introduced letters.

Use the verbalization for the letter formation to direct the students while they trace it with their finger. Do it with them to model. Have them say letter-keyword-sound.

After students trace following verbalizations, they can then color the keyword picture for the letter **d**.

© 2002, 2012 WILSON LANGUAGE TRAINING CORPORATION

Unit 1 | Week 6

Day 2

Daily Plan — DAY 2

Student Learning Plan
- Drill Sounds/Warm-Up
- Sky Write/Letter Formation
- Student Notebook
- Echo/Letter Formation

Teacher Materials
- Echo and/or Baby Echo
- Large Sound Cards
- Standard Sound Cards
- Large Writing Grid
- Letter Formation Guide
- Vowel Extension Poster
- Student Notebook

Student Materials
- Student Notebook
- Dry Erase Writing Tablet

Drill Sounds/Warm-Up

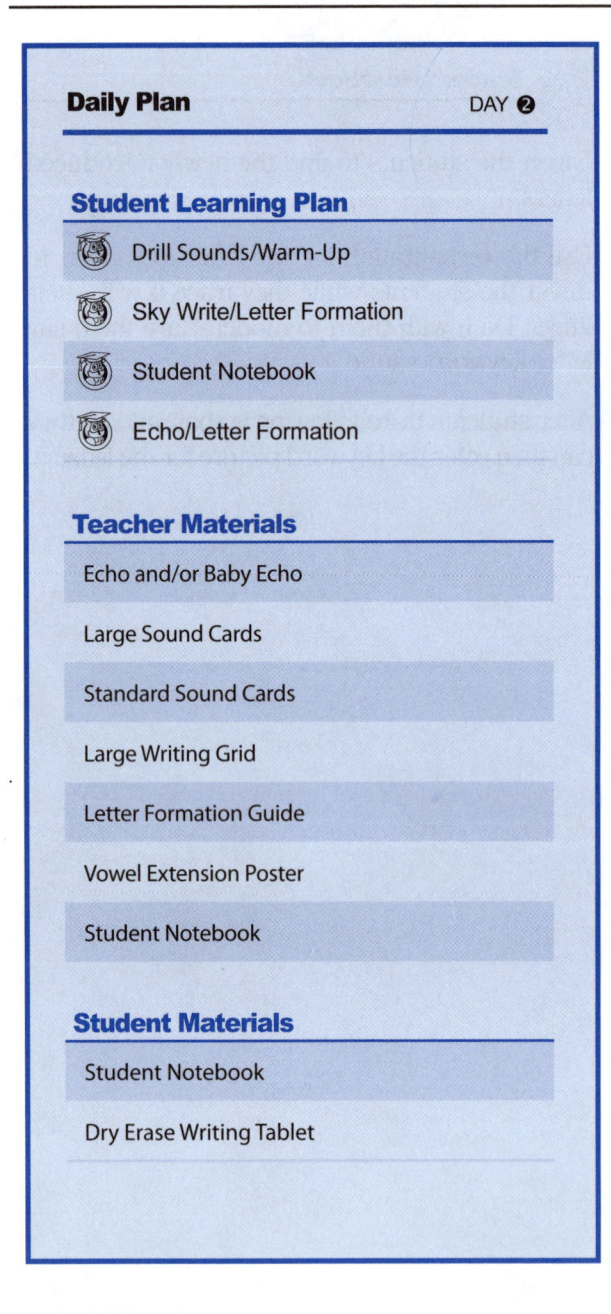

Do new sounds and vowel sounds each day. Selectively review 4-5 other consonants.

Large Sound Cards

Practice sounds with the Large Sound Cards. Model these, saying the letter-keyword-sound and have the students echo.

Standard Sound Cards

Next, point to the Standard Sound Cards (in card display) with the Baby Echo pointer. You say the letter-keyword-sound and hold up Baby Echo to have the students repeat.

Vowel Extension

Model 'reading' the keyword pictures for the vowels previously taught. Extend the sound while you trace the line and finish the word when you get to the picture.

Have a student come trace the line while everyone extends the sound.

Sky Write/Letter Formation

Review **d** and **s** formation, linking formation with letter name, keyword and sound.

Follow activity procedure and have students sky write letters.

Emphasize that these letters are plane line round letters, so they begin on the plane line.

116 FUNDATIONS® LEVEL K

Unit 1 | Week 6

Day 2

Student Notebook

Trace and say the letter-keyword-sound for all the previous letters introduced.

Direct the students to find the newly introduced letters.

Use the verbalization for the letter formation to direct the students while they trace it with their finger. Do it with them to model. Have them say letter-keyword-sound.

After students trace following verbalizations, they can then color the keyword picture for the letter **s**.

Echo/Letter Formation

Remind students of proper pencil grip and sitting position, and give them their Dry Erase Writing Tablets.

Sounds appear between / /. Dictate **new** sounds and a selection of previously taught sounds. You select and say the sound. Students echo the sound and say the letter.

Next have a student come up to the classroom board to make the letter on the Large Writing Grid. Direct the student with the letter formation verbalization.

Then have all students write the answer on their Dry Erase Writing Tablets as you direct them with the letter formation verbalization. Circulate to reinforce pencil grip and assist students, as needed.

Sounds

/t/ - t	/b/ - b	/f/ - f
/n/ - n	/m/ - m	/ĭ/ - i
/ŭ/ - u	/c/ - c	/ŏ/ - o
/ă/ - a	/g/ - g	/d/ - d
/s/ - s		

Unit 1 | Week 6

Day 3

Daily Plan — DAY 3

Student Learning Plan
- Drill Sounds/Warm-Up
- Make It Fun
- Echo/Find Letters
- Student Notebook

Teacher Materials
- Echo and/or Baby Echo
- Large Sound Cards
- Standard Sound Cards
- Vowel Extension Poster
- Keyword Puzzle
- Student Notebook

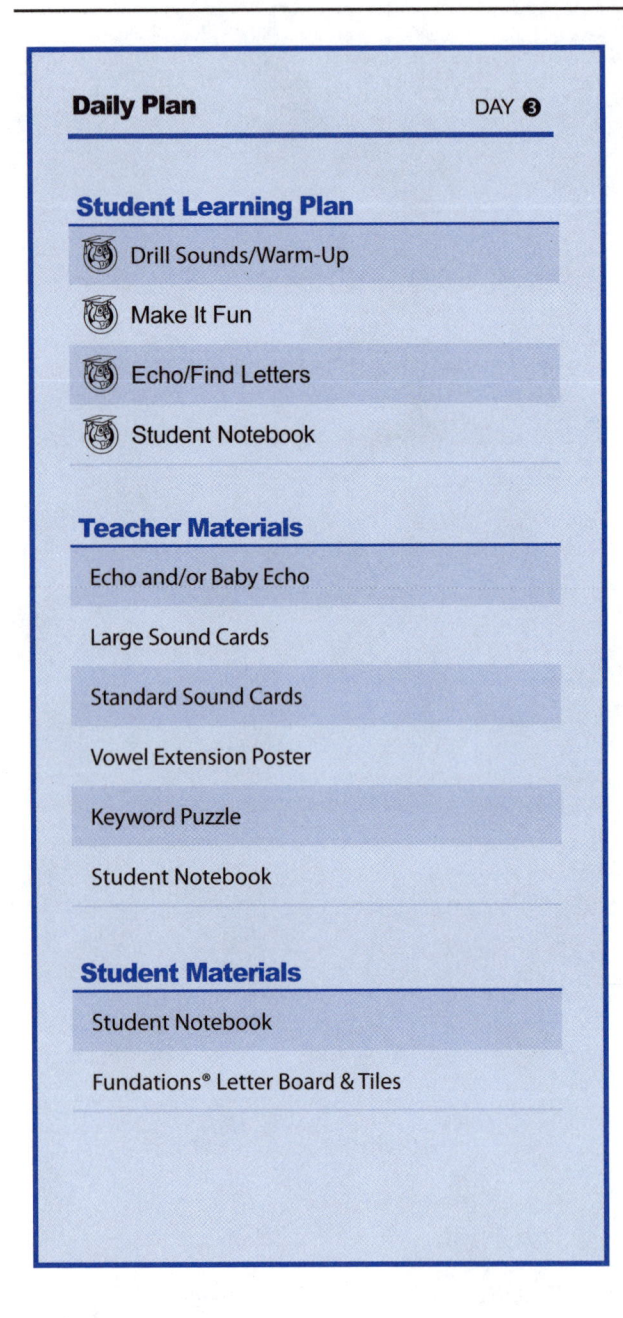

Student Materials
- Student Notebook
- Fundations® Letter Board & Tiles

Drill Sounds/Warm-Up

Do new sounds and vowel sounds each day. Selectively review 4-5 other consonants.

Large Sound Cards
Practice sounds with the Large Sound Cards. Model these, saying the letter-keyword-sound and have the students echo.

Standard Sound Cards
Next, point to the Standard Sound Cards (in card display) with the Baby Echo pointer. You say the letter-keyword-sound and hold up Baby Echo to have the students repeat.

Vowel Extension
Model 'reading' the keyword pictures for the vowels previously taught. Extend the sound while you trace the line and finish the word when you get to the picture.

Have a student come trace the line while everyone extends the sound.

Make It Fun

Materials
- Keyword Puzzle

Use the puzzle pieces for the letters taught thus far. Pass out the letters (one per child) and the pictures (one per child) until they are all disseminated. Then direct the students:

Stand up if you have the letter b. Stand up if you have the picture that goes with b.

Make a match!

or

Say

Stand up if you have a picture that rhymes with cut (nut). Stand up if you have the letter that begins the word nut.

Make a match!

Have the students come up front and put the puzzle pieces together, then have everyone say the letter-keyword-sound.

b-bat-/b/

Unit 1 | Week 6

Day 3

Echo/Find Letters

Students match Magnetic Letter Tiles to the letter(s) on their Letter Boards. Distribute Letter Boards and the Letter Tiles **d** and **s** to each student. Start with tiles on the blank side of the board. Dictate sounds. Students echo sound and match the tiles. Include previous sounds and new sounds. After all sounds are matched, dictate 2-3 sounds and have students repeat the sound and point to the corresponding letter.

Sounds

/t/ - t	/b/ - b	/f/ - f
/n/ - n	/m/ - m	/ĭ/ - i
/ŭ/ - u	/c/ - c	/ŏ/ - o
/ă/ - a	/g/ - g	**/d/ - d**
/s/ - s		

Student Notebook

Practice Letters

Students trace previously taught letters while naming letter-keyword-sound. Do as a group saying verbalization, or circulate around the room as students do independently.

tip

You can select a category of letters to find and practice, such as all the sky line letters or all the vowels taught thus far.

Unit 1 | Week 6

Day 4

Daily Plan — DAY 4

Student Learning Plan
- Drill Sounds/Warm-Up
- Word Play
- Sky Write/Letter Formation
- Echo/Letter Formation

Teacher Materials
- Echo and/or Baby Echo
- Large Sound Cards
- Standard Sound Cards
- Large Writing Grid
- Letter Formation Guide
- Vowel Extension Poster
- Sentence and Syllable Frames

Student Materials
- Student Notebook
- Dry Erase Writing Tablet

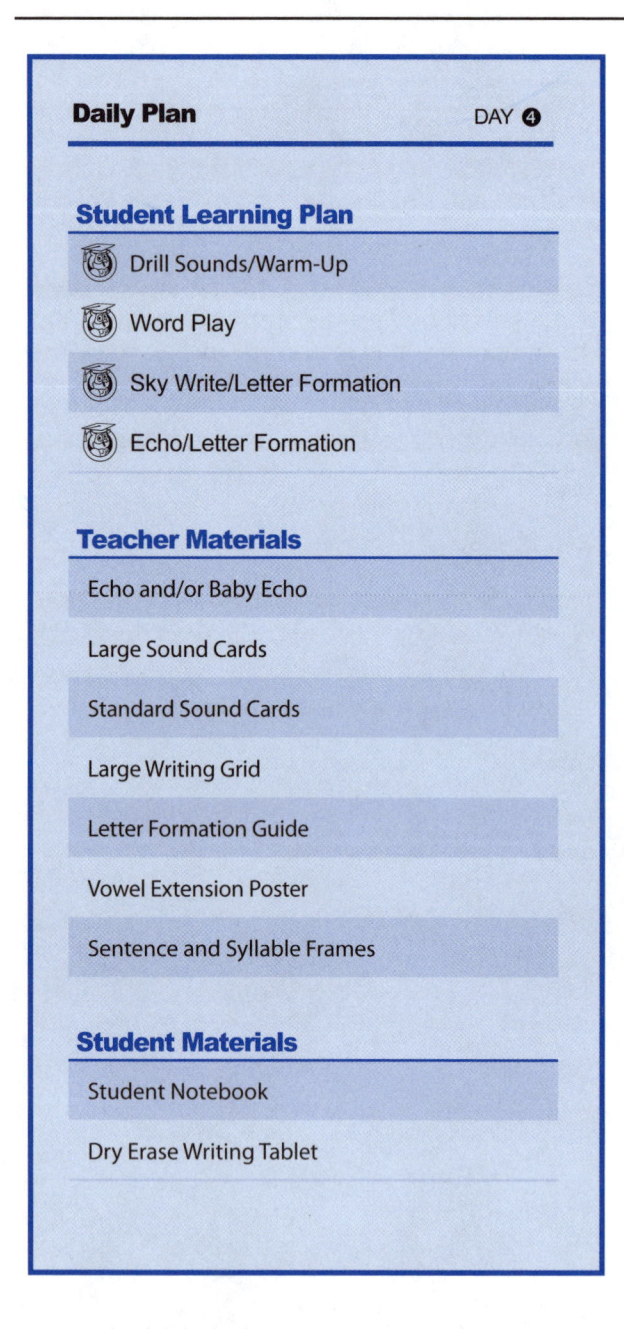

Drill Sounds/Warm-Up

Do new sounds and vowel sounds each day. Selectively review 4-5 other consonants.

Large Sound Cards

Practice sounds with the Large Sound Cards. Model these, saying the letter-keyword-sound and have the students echo.

Standard Sound Cards

Next, point to the Standard Sound Cards (in card display) with the Baby Echo pointer. You say the letter-keyword-sound and hold up Baby Echo to have the students repeat.

Vowel Extension

Model 'reading' the keyword pictures for the vowels previously taught. Extend the sound while you trace the line and finish the word when you get to the picture.

Have a student come trace the line while everyone extends the sound.

Word Play

Teacher Materials
- Sentence and Syllable Frames
- Baby Echo

WORD AWARENESS

Reinforce the capitalization of names, following the same procedures from Week 5.

Write sentences with two names.

Examples:

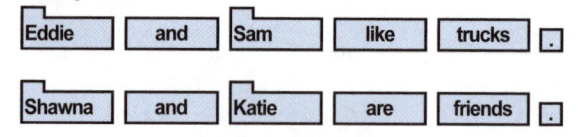

| Eddie | and | Sam | like | trucks | . |

| Shawna | and | Katie | are | friends | . |

Each time, ask why you selected the tall frames. Ask this for both the first word in the sentence and for the student's name. Be sure to echo read each sentence.

SYLLABLE PLAY

Say a word and have students repeat. Have students clap out, and write the word on the Syllable Frames.

Instruct Students

| base | ball |

Point to each syllable as you say it.

Ask

What would it be if I took away ball?

Unit 1 | Week 6

Day 4

Remove the [ball] frame. After students answer, put it back.

Ask

The word is baseball. What would it be if I took away base?

Again, point to each syllable as you say it. Remove the [base] frame. After students answer, erase the frames.

Word Resources

Use students' names interwoven with a selection of words below.

cobweb	remind	cupcake
disrupt	invent	airplane

Sky Write/Letter Formation

Review **d** and **s** formation, linking formation with letter name, keyword and sound.

Follow activity procedure and have students sky write letters.

Emphasize that these letters are plane line round letters, so they begin on the plane line.

Echo/Letter Formation

Remind students of proper pencil grip and sitting position, and give them their Dry Erase Writing Tablets.

Sounds appear between / /. Dictate **new** sounds and a selection of previously taught sounds. You select and say the sound. Students echo the sound and say the letter.

Next have a student come up to the classroom board to make the letter on the Large Writing Grid. Direct the student with the letter formation verbalization.

Then have all students write the answer on their Dry Erase Writing Tablets as you direct them with the letter formation verbalization. Circulate to reinforce pencil grip and assist students, as needed.

Sounds

/t/ - t	/b/ - b	/f/ - f
/n/ - n	/m/ - m	/ĭ/ - i
/ŭ/ - u	/c/ - c	/ŏ/ - o
/ă/ - a	/g/ - g	/d/ - d
/s/ - s		

Unit 1 | Week 6

Day 5

Daily Plan — DAY 5

Student Learning Plan
- Drill Sounds/Warm-Up
- Storytime
- Echo/Find Letters

Teacher Materials
- Echo and/or Baby Echo
- Large Sound Cards
- Standard Sound Cards
- Vowel Extension Poster
- Large chart paper

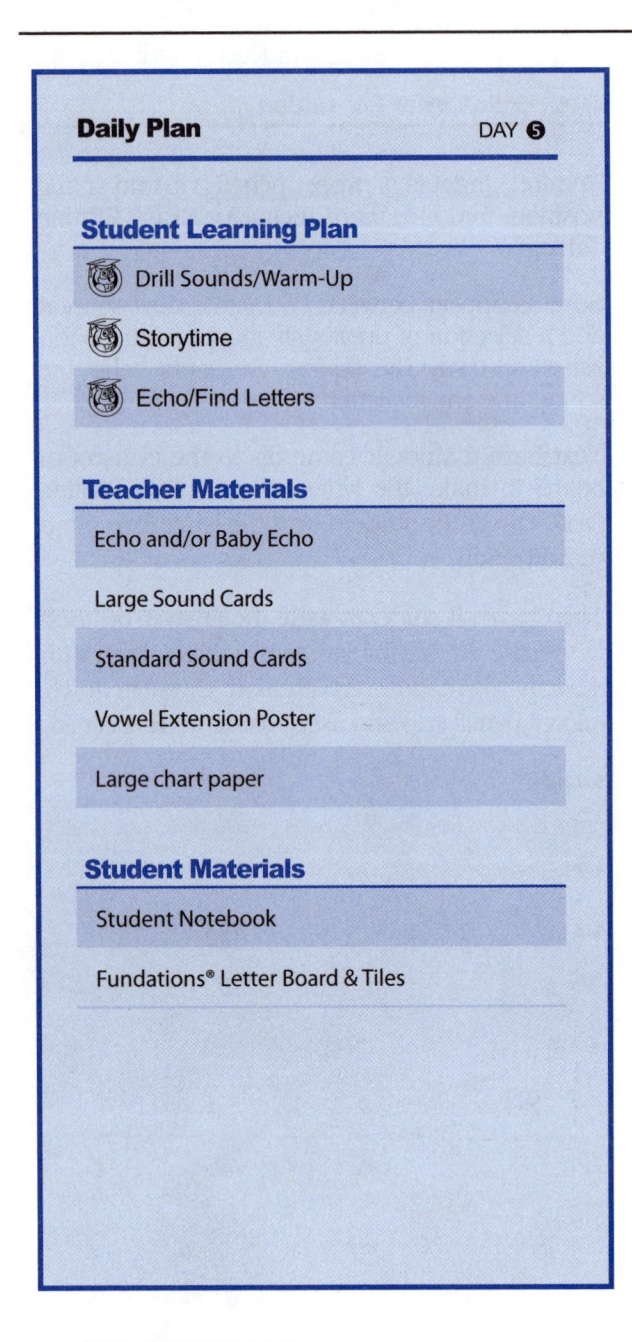

Student Materials
- Student Notebook
- Fundations® Letter Board & Tiles

Drill Sounds/Warm-Up

Do new sounds and vowel sounds each day. Selectively review 4-5 other consonants.

Large Sound Cards

Practice sounds with the Large Sound Cards. Model these, saying the letter-keyword-sound and have the students echo.

Standard Sound Cards

Next, point to the Standard Sound Cards (in card display) with the Baby Echo pointer. You say the letter-keyword-sound and hold up Baby Echo to have the students repeat.

Vowel Extension

Model 'reading' the keyword pictures for the vowels previously taught. Extend the sound while you trace the line and finish the word when you get to the picture.

Have a student come trace the line while everyone extends the sound.

Storytime

Teacher Materials
- Rhyming books
- Large chart paper

Preparation

During Storytime select a rhyming picture book to read to your students. Be sure that the story has no more than 4-5 sentences per page. It should have predictable rhyming patterns. The following list provides some suggestions.

> Domanska, J. 1974. **What Do You See?** New York: Macmillan.
>
> Galdone, P. 1986. **Three Little Kittens**. New York: Clarion.
>
> Guarino, D. 1989. **Is Your Mama a Llama?** New York: Scholastic.
>
> Hawkins, C., and J. Hawkins. 1987. **I Know an Old Lady Who Swallowed a Fly.** New York: Putnam.
>
> Hayes, S. 1986. **This Is the Bear.** Philadelphia, PA: Lippincott.
>
> Prater, J. 1991. **No! Said Joe.** Cambridge, MA: Candlewick.
>
> Shaw, N. 1989. **Sheep On a Ship.** Boston: Houghton Mifflin.
>
> Weiss, N. 1992. **On a Hot, Hot Day.** New York: G. P. Putnam's Sons.

Instruct Students

Before reading, look at the front and back cover of the book with your students. Discuss the title, author and illustrator, explaining each of those terms.

Unit 1 | Week 6

Day 5

Read the book once moving your finger under the words and emphasizing the rhymes. Pause 2-3 times and ask students to predict what will happen.

Say

> Now let's do it again but this time you can help me read.

Read the book again, moving your finger under the words. This time, do not say the rhyming words and let the students say it for you. You can also provide the onset **/m/** and have students say the rime **/at/** (for the word **mat**).

Lastly, write the rhyming words from the story on chart paper or the board. Put rhyming words on the same line.

Example

bat   cat   sat

down   clown

Tell the students that these are the words they read in the story. Explain that they rhyme. Read a set of rhyming words with Baby Echo and have the students repeat. Ask them to think of other words that rhyme with each set. Add them to the list and read.

Echo/Find Letters

Students match Magnetic Letter Tiles to the letter(s) on their Letter Boards. Start with tiles off the board. Dictate sounds. Students echo sound and match the tiles. Include previous sounds and new sounds. After all sounds are matched, dictate 2-3 sounds and have students repeat the sound and point to the corresponding letter.

Sounds

/t/ - t	/b/ - b	/f/ - f
/n/ - n	/m/ - m	/ĭ/ - i
/ŭ/ - u	/c/ - c	/ŏ/ - o
/ā/ - a	/g/ - g	**/d/ - d**
/s/ - s		

Mid-Unit Check

It is important to determine if any students need small group intervention instruction. If you do Benchmark assessments, such as AIMS-WEBB or DIBELS, use the Beginning of the Year scores to determine at-risk students. Also, you can use classroom performance in Fundations and do a Mid-Unit Check to determine any students who are struggling with the letter/sound associations or letter formations taught thus far.

Print Mid-Unit Check from the PLC.

Follow the guidelines for Intervention to help these students achieve success.

See Intervention Guidelines on the PLC.

Unit 1 | Week 7

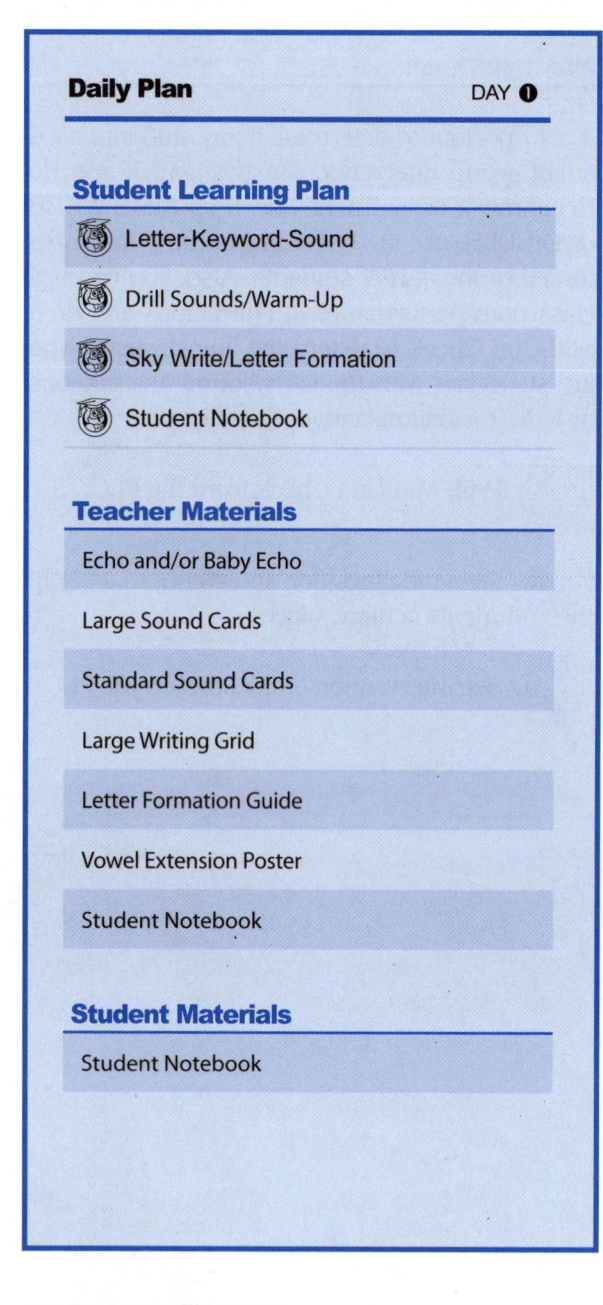

Day 1

Daily Plan — DAY 1

Student Learning Plan
- Letter-Keyword-Sound
- Drill Sounds/Warm-Up
- Sky Write/Letter Formation
- Student Notebook

Teacher Materials
- Echo and/or Baby Echo
- Large Sound Cards
- Standard Sound Cards
- Large Writing Grid
- Letter Formation Guide
- Vowel Extension Poster
- Student Notebook

Student Materials
- Student Notebook

Letter-Keyword-Sound

Introduce Letter-Keyword-Sound with Large and Standard Sound Cards. Be sure to follow procedure. First teach with Large Sound Card. Have students echo letter-keyword-sound. Then repeat with Standard Sound Card.

| e | - e - Ed - /ĕ/

| r | - r - rat - /r/

The letter **e** is the last vowel that we will learn. It is a plane line round letter that is different because it starts between the plane line and the grass line.

Vowel Extension

Model 'reading' the keyword picture (example: /ĕ/...d). Extend the /ĕ/ sound while you trace the line and finish the word when you get to the picture.

Have a student come trace the line while everyone extends the /ĕ/ sound.

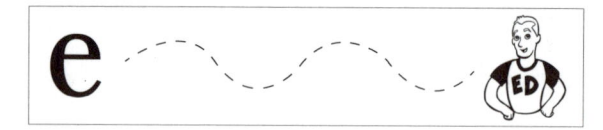

Do the Vowel Extension activity with all the vowels.

Note
As a new letter is taught, its Standard Sound Card is added to your card display to be drilled at each lesson.

Drill Sounds/Warm-Up

Do new sounds and vowel sounds each day. Selectively review 4-5 other consonants.

Large Sound Cards

Practice sounds with the Large Sound Cards. Model these, saying the letter-keyword-sound and have the students echo.

Standard Sound Cards

Next, point to the Standard Sound Cards (in card display) with the Baby Echo pointer. You say the letter-keyword-sound and hold up Baby Echo to have the students repeat. Discuss vowels and consonants as you select letters.

Unit 1 | Week 7

Day 1

Sky Write/Letter Formation

Teach **e** and **r** formation, linking formation with letter name, keyword and sound.

Follow activity procedure and have students sky write letters.

Letter Formation for e

Use the following verbalization to direct students in proper letter formation.

Say

e is a plane line round letter, but it is special.
e starts below the plane line.

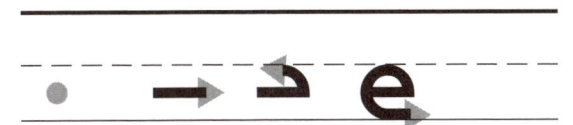

1. **Point between the plane line and the grass line.**
2. **Fly under the plane line.**
3. **Then go up to the plane line,**
4. **and around to the grass line.**
5. **Say e - Ed - /ĕ/, have students repeat.**

Letter Formation for r

Use the following verbalization to direct students in proper letter formation.

Say

r is a plane line letter.

It starts on the (plane line).

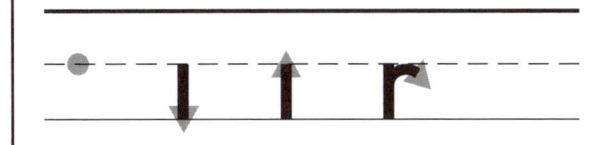

1. **Point to the plane line.**
2. **Go down to the grass line.**
3. **Trace back up to the plane line,**
4. **and make a little curve.**
5. **Say r - rat - /r/, have students repeat.**

Student Notebook

Direct the students to find the newly introduced letters.

Use the verbalization for the letter formation to direct the students while they trace it with their finger. Do it with them to model. Have them say letter-keyword-sound.

After students trace following verbalizations, they can then color the keyword picture for the letter **e**.

© 2002, 2012 WILSON LANGUAGE TRAINING CORPORATION

TEACHER'S MANUAL 125

Unit 1 | Week 7

Day 2

Daily Plan — DAY 2

Student Learning Plan
- Drill Sounds/Warm-Up
- Sky Write/Letter Formation
- Student Notebook
- Echo/Letter Formation

Teacher Materials
- Echo and/or Baby Echo
- Large Sound Cards
- Standard Sound Cards
- Large Writing Grid
- Letter Formation Guide
- Vowel Extension Poster
- Student Notebook

Student Materials
- Student Notebook
- Dry Erase Writing Tablet

Drill Sounds/Warm-Up

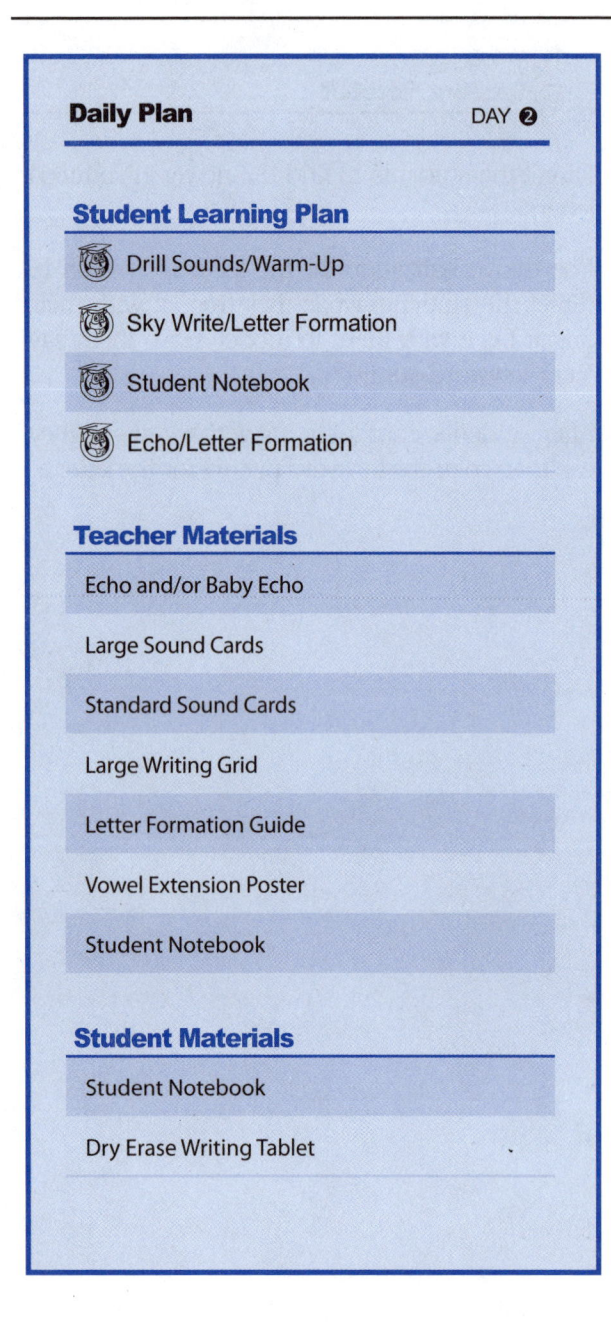

Do new sounds and vowel sounds each day. Selectively review 4-5 other consonants.

Large Sound Cards
Practice sounds with the Large Sound Cards. Model these, saying the letter-keyword-sound and have the students echo.

Standard Sound Cards
Next, point to the Standard Sound Cards (in card display) with the Baby Echo pointer. You say the letter-keyword-sound and hold up Baby Echo to have the students repeat. Discuss vowels and consonants as you select letters.

Vowel Extension
Model extending the vowel sounds (example: **a-/ă/...apple-/ă/**). Have a student come trace the line for each of the vowels.

Sky Write/Letter Formation

Review **e** and **r** formation, linking formation with letter name, keyword and sound.

Follow activity procedure and have students sky write letters.

Remind students that **e** is a very tricky letter to form. It is the only letter that starts between the plane line and grass line.

126 FUNDATIONS® LEVEL K

© 2002, 2012 WILSON LANGUAGE TRAINING CORPORATION

Unit 1 | Week 7

Day 2

Student Notebook

Trace and say the letter-keyword-sound for all the previous letters introduced.

Direct the students to find the newly introduced letters.

Use the verbalization for the letter formation to direct the students while they trace it with their finger. Do it with them to model. Have them say letter-keyword-sound.

After students trace following verbalizations, they can then color the keyword picture for the letter **r**.

Echo/Letter Formation

Remind students of proper pencil grip and sitting position, and give them their Dry Erase Writing Tablets.

Sounds appear between / /. Dictate **new** sounds and a selection of previously taught sounds. You select and say the sound. Students echo the sound and say the letter.

Next have a student come up to the classroom board to make the letter on the Large Writing Grid. Direct the student with the letter formation verbalization.

Then have all students write the answer on their Dry Erase Writing Tablets as you direct them with the letter formation verbalization. Circulate to reinforce pencil grip and assist students, as needed.

Sounds

/t/ - t	/b/ - b	/f/ - f
/n/ - n	/m/ - m	/ĭ/ - i
/ŭ/ - u	/c/ - c	/ŏ/ - o
/ă/ - a	/g/ - g	/d/ - d
/s/ - s	/ĕ/ - e	/r/ - r

Unit 1 | Week 7

Day 3

Daily Plan — DAY 3

Student Learning Plan
- Drill Sounds/Warm-Up
- Make It Fun
- Echo/Find Letters
- Student Notebook

Teacher Materials
- Echo and/or Baby Echo
- Large Sound Cards
- Standard Sound Cards
- Vowel Extension Poster
- Student Notebook

Student Materials
- Student Notebook
- Fundations® Letter Board & Tiles

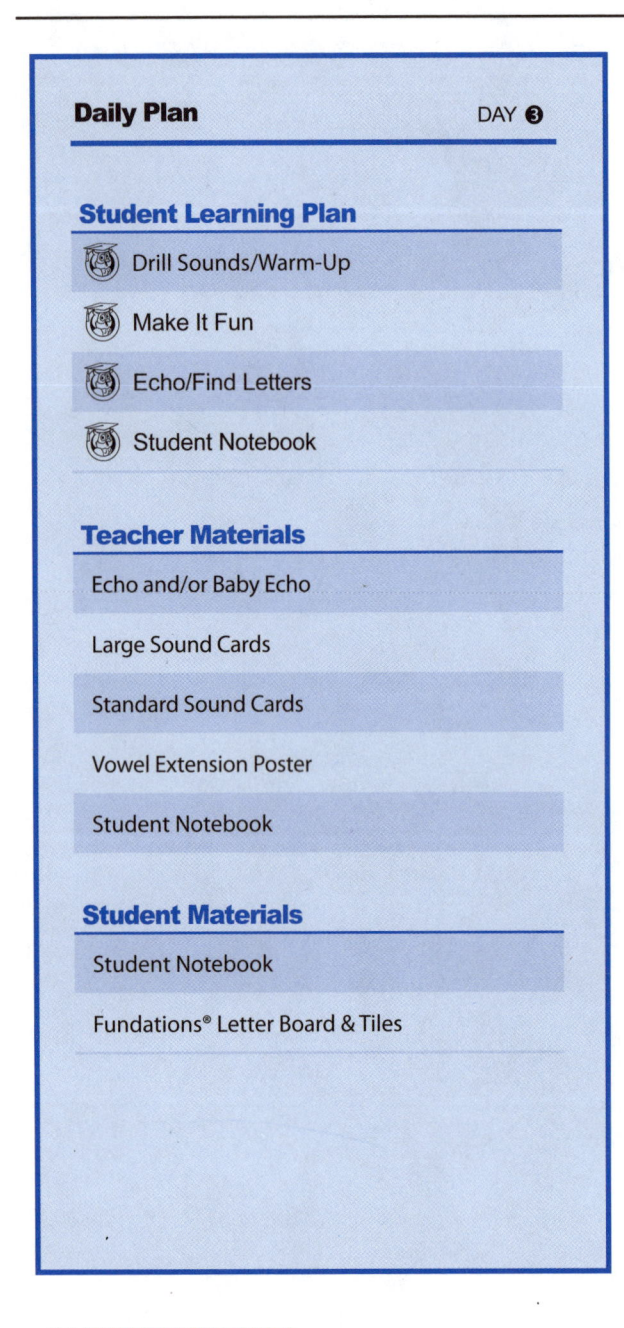

Drill Sounds/Warm-Up

Do **new** sounds and **vowel** sounds each day. Selectively review 4-5 other consonants.

Large Sound Cards
Practice sounds with the Large Sound Cards. Model these, saying the letter-keyword-sound and have the students echo.

Standard Sound Cards
Next, point to the Standard Sound Cards (in card display) with the Baby Echo pointer. You say the letter-keyword-sound and hold up Baby Echo to have the students repeat. Discuss vowels and consonants as you select letters.

Vowel Extension
Model extending the vowel sounds (example: a-/ă/...apple-/ă/). Have a student come trace the line for each of the vowels.

a
e
i
o
u

Make It Fun

Teacher Materials
- Standard Sound Cards
- Baby Echo (on a pointer or ruler)

Call a student to the front of the room. Have the student close his (her) eyes and point to a letter with the Baby Echo pointer. Then have the student open eyes and see the selected letter.

Ask
What is the name of the letter?

What is the sound of the letter?

When you make this letter, where do you start it?

Name three words that start with /__/.

Pick one of the words that the student gives and ask if anyone can think of a word that rhymes with it. Also, have a student think of a sentence with that word in it. Use questions to guide the students so that they come up with a complete sentence. Model for them as needed.

Other students can help. Then allow the student to select the next student to come up and do the same.

Unit 1 | Week 7

Day 3

Echo/Find Letters

Students match Magnetic Letter Tiles to the letter(s) on their Letter Boards. Distribute Letter Boards and the Letter Tiles **e** and **r** to each student. Start with tiles on the blank side of the board. Dictate sounds. Students echo sound and match the tiles. Include previous sounds and new sounds. After all sounds are matched, dictate 2-3 sounds and have students repeat the sound and point to the corresponding letter.

Sounds

/t/ - t	/b/ - b	/f/ - f
/n/ - n	/m/ - m	/ĭ/ - i
/ŭ/ - u	/c/ - c	/ŏ/ - o
/ă/ - a	/g/ - g	/d/ - d
/s/ - s	/ĕ/ - e	/r/ - r

Student Notebook

Practice Letters

Students trace previously taught letters while naming letter-keyword-sound. Do as a group saying verbalization, or circulate around the room as students do independently.

You can select a category of letters to find and practice, such as all the sky line letters or all the vowels taught thus far.

Unit 1 | Week 7

Day 4

Daily Plan — DAY 4

Student Learning Plan
- Drill Sounds/Warm-Up
- Word Play
- Sky Write/Letter Formation
- Echo/Letter Formation

Teacher Materials
- Echo and/or Baby Echo
- Large Sound Cards
- Standard Sound Cards
- Large Writing Grid
- Letter Formation Guide
- Vowel Extension Poster
- Sentence Frames

Student Materials
- Student Notebook
- Dry Erase Writing Tablet

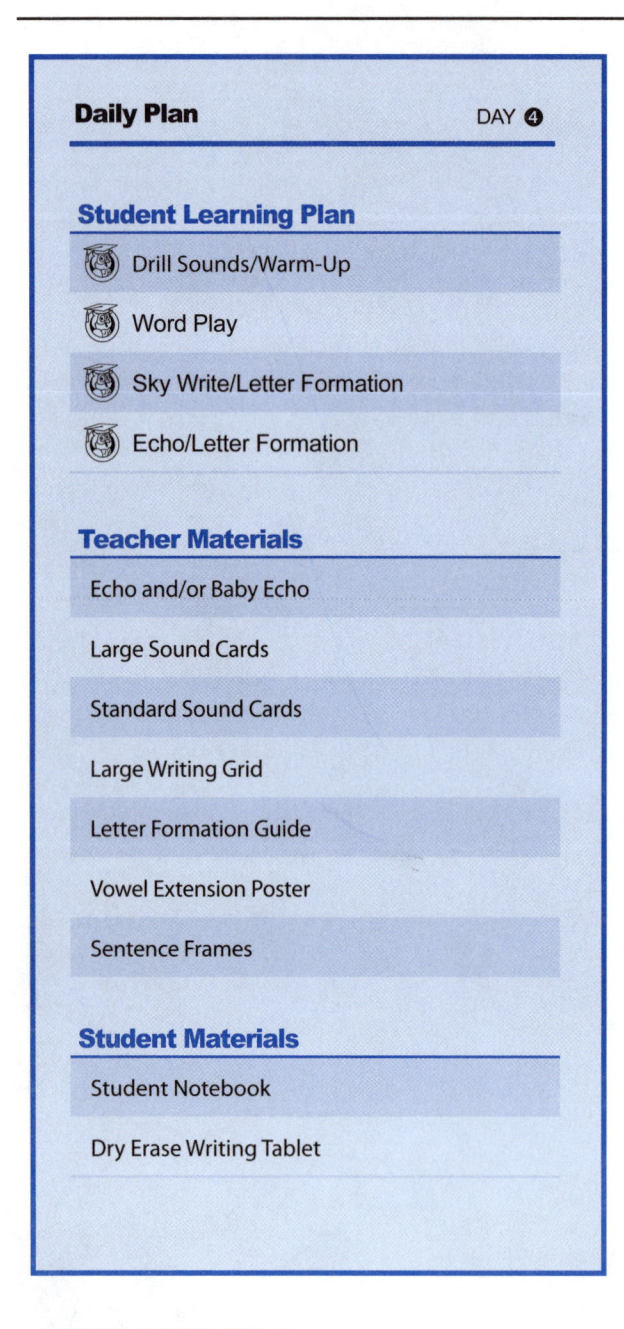

Drill Sounds/Warm-Up

Do **new** sounds and **vowel** sounds each day. Selectively review 4-5 other consonants.

Large Sound Cards

Practice sounds with the Large Sound Cards. Model these, saying the letter-keyword-sound and have the students echo.

Standard Sound Cards

Next, point to the Standard Sound Cards (in card display) with the Baby Echo pointer. You say the letter-keyword-sound and hold up Baby Echo to have the students repeat. Discuss vowels and consonants as you select letters.

Vowel Extension

Model extending the vowel sounds (example: **a**-/ă/...**apple**-/ă/). Have a student come trace the line for each of the vowels.

Word Play

Teacher Materials
- Sentence Frames
- Baby Echo

WORD AWARENESS

During word play, you will further develop the students' word awareness by adding a new step.

The students will now have to get you the frames needed so that you can write the sentence.

Display Sentence Frames in a Column

Display the Sentence Frames and period frame in a column rather than across the board. Tell the students that you are going to have them help you get the pieces you need to write your sentence.

Demonstrate

Say a sentence orally such as:

   Maria is here today.

Tell them that you need the high-cut frame first because every sentence must start with a capital letter.

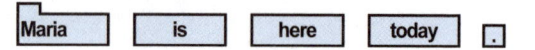

| Maria | is | here | today | . |

Say the words as you place the frames. Then tell them that at the end you need to put a period because all sentences today end with a period because they tell something.

130 FUNDATIONS® LEVEL K

© 2002, 2012 WILSON LANGUAGE TRAINING CORPORATION

Unit 1 | Week 7

Day 4

Write the words on the frames and read it again, pointing to each word.

Erase and put the frames back in a column and ask for a student volunteer. Give them the same sentence, but replace "Maria" with the student's name.

Ask them to put the pieces in order for you to write the sentence. Remind them,

> **Don't forget which one you need to begin the sentence.**

Say the sentence with them as they place the pieces. Be sure they add the period.

> **Let's see if Wanda** (the student's name) **is correct.**

Write the sentence and ask the students,

> **Did Wanda get all the pieces I needed?**

Do several sentences. Each time, erase frames and put them in a column for students to select from.

Example Sentences

It is raining (or sunny) outside today.

(your name) likes to teach Fundations.

See the Word Play Advanced video on the PLC.

Sky Write/Letter Formation

Review **e** and **r** formation, linking formation with letter name, keyword and sound.

Follow activity procedure and have students sky write letters.

tip

Select 1-2 review letters and sky write them, pointing out where they start on the Letter Formation Poster K·1.

Echo/Letter Formation

Remind students of proper pencil grip and sitting position, and give them their Dry Erase Writing Tablets.

Sounds appear between / /. Dictate **new** sounds and a selection of previously taught sounds. You select and say the sound. Students echo the sound and say the letter.

Next have a student come up to the classroom board to make the letter on the Large Writing Grid. Direct the student with the letter formation verbalization.

Then have all students write the answer on their Dry Erase Writing Tablets as you direct them with the letter formation verbalization. Circulate to reinforce pencil grip and assist students, as needed.

Sounds

/t/ - t	/b/ - b	/f/ - f
/n/ - n	/m/ - m	/i/ - i
/ŭ/ - u	/c/ - c	/ŏ/ - o
/ă/ - a	/g/ - g	/d/ - d
/s/ - s	/ĕ/ - e	/r/ - r

Unit 1 | Week 7

Day 5

Daily Plan — DAY 5

Student Learning Plan
- Drill Sounds/Warm-Up
- Storytime
- Echo/Find Letters

Teacher Materials
- Echo and/or Baby Echo
- Large Sound Cards
- Standard Sound Cards
- Vowel Extension Poster
- Large chart paper

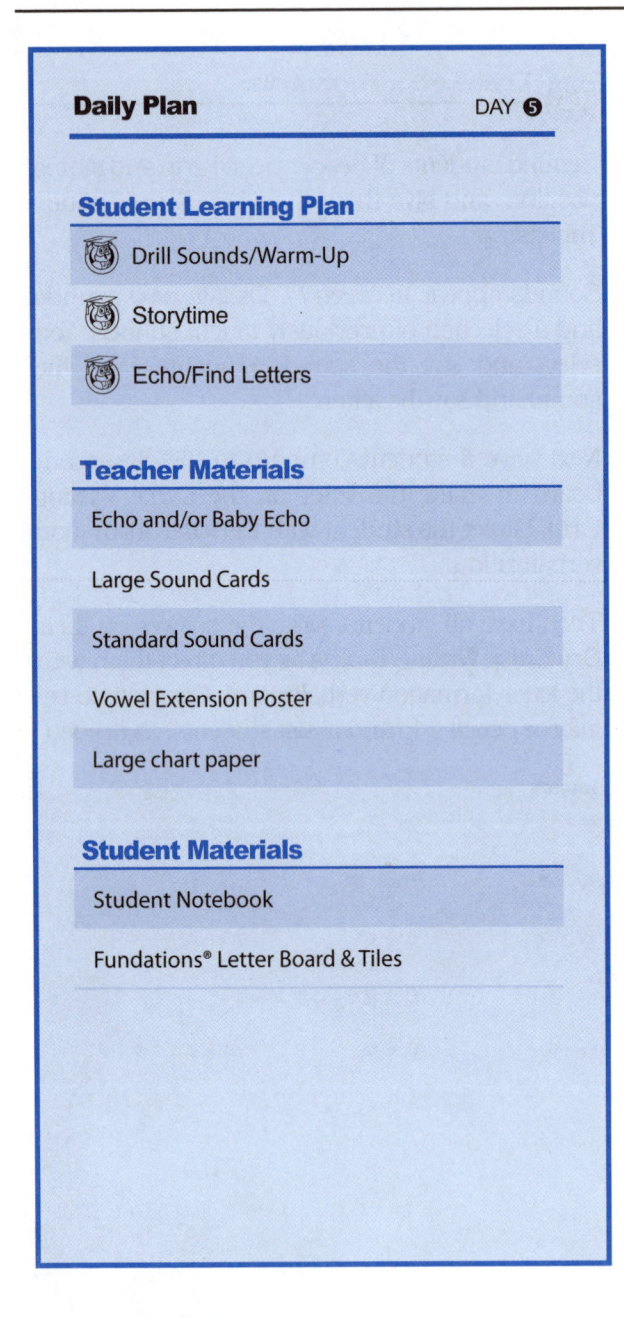

Student Materials
- Student Notebook
- Fundations® Letter Board & Tiles

Drill Sounds/Warm-Up

Do **new** sounds and **vowel** sounds each day. Selectively review 4-5 other consonants.

Large Sound Cards

Practice sounds with the Large Sound Cards. Model these, saying the letter-keyword-sound and have the students echo.

Standard Sound Cards

Next, point to the Standard Sound Cards (in card display) with the Baby Echo pointer. You say the letter-keyword-sound and hold up Baby Echo to have the students repeat. Discuss vowels and consonants as you select letters.

Vowel Extension

Model extending the vowel sounds (example: **a-/ă/...apple-/ă/**). Have a student come trace the line for each of the vowels.

Storytime

Teacher Materials
- Alliteration picture book
- Large chart paper

Preparation

During Storytime select an alliteration picture book to read to your students. The following list provides some suggestions.

Heck, E. 2010. **Many Marvelous Monsters**. New York: Price Stern Sloan.

Duncan Edwards, P. 1995. **Four Famished Foxes and Fosdyke**. New York: Harper Collins

Fleming, D. 2007. **Beetle Bop**. Orlando: Harcourt

Mosel, A., 2007. **Tikki Tikki Tembo**. New York: Square Fish

Root, P. 1986. **Soup for Supper**. New York: Harper Collins.

Instruct Students

Before reading, look at the front and back cover of the book with your students. Discuss the title, author and illustrator, explaining each of those terms.

Read the book once moving your finger under the words and emphasizing the alliteration. Pause 2-3 times and ask students to predict what will happen.

Lastly, write some of the alliteration words from the story on chart paper or the board.

Unit 1 | Week 7

Day 5

Example

many	marvelous	monsters
sip	soup	supper

Tell the students that these are the words they read in the story. Explain that they begin with the same sound. Read a set of words with Baby Echo and have the students repeat. Ask them to think of other words that begin with the same sound for each set. Add them to the list and read, emphasizing the first sound.

Lastly, help students to use some of the words in a sentence. Guide them with questions so that they provide a complete and grammatically correct sentence.

Echo/Find Letters

Students match Magnetic Letter Tiles to the letter(s) on their Letter Boards. Start with tiles off the board. Dictate sounds. Students echo sound and match the tiles. Include previous sounds and new sounds. After all sounds are matched, dictate 2-3 sounds and have students repeat the sound and point to the corresponding letter.

Sounds

/t/ - t	/b/ - b	/f/ - f
/n/ - n	/m/ - m	/ĭ/ - i
/ŭ/ - u	/c/ - c	/ŏ/ - o
/ă/ - a	/g/ - g	/d/ - d
/s/ - s	/ĕ/ - e	/r/ - r

Unit 1 | Week 8

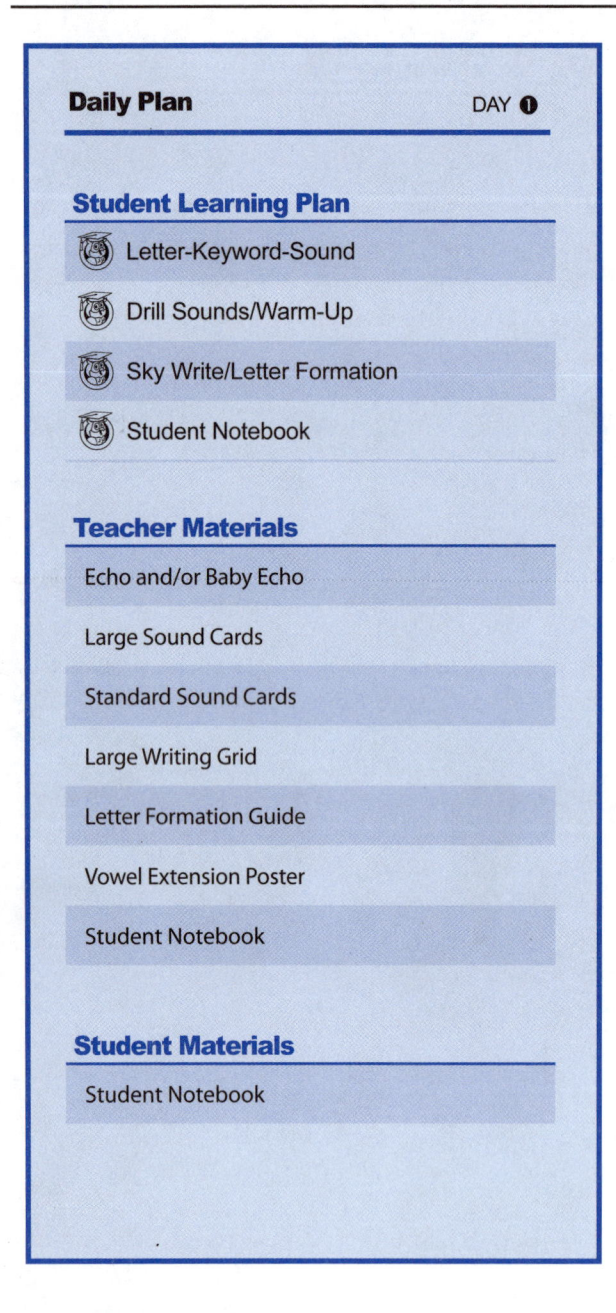

Day 1

Daily Plan — DAY 1

Student Learning Plan
- Letter-Keyword-Sound
- Drill Sounds/Warm-Up
- Sky Write/Letter Formation
- Student Notebook

Teacher Materials
- Echo and/or Baby Echo
- Large Sound Cards
- Standard Sound Cards
- Large Writing Grid
- Letter Formation Guide
- Vowel Extension Poster
- Student Notebook

Student Materials
- Student Notebook

Letter-Keyword-Sound

Introduce Letter-Keyword-Sound with Large and Standard Sound Cards. Be sure to follow procedure. First teach with Large Sound Card. Have students echo letter-keyword-sound. Then repeat with Standard Sound Card.

p - p - pan - /p/

j - j - jug - /j/

Note
As a new letter is taught, its Standard Sound Card is added to your card display to be drilled at each lesson.

Support for Spanish Speaking ELs: The letter **j** makes the **/h/** sound in Spanish. Therefore, Spanish speaking children may make the **/h/** sound when they see **j**. Provide additional practice with the keyword to master the sound.

tip: Make sure to clip sounds to avoid adding a schwa: **/j/** not **/juh/**

Drill Sounds/Warm-Up

Do **new** sounds and **vowel** sounds each day. Selectively review 4-5 other consonants.

Large Sound Cards

Practice sounds with the Large Sound Cards. Model these, saying the letter-keyword-sound and have the students echo.

Standard Sound Cards

Next, point to the Standard Sound Cards (in card display) with the Baby Echo pointer. You say the letter-keyword-sound and hold up Baby Echo to have the students repeat. Discuss vowels and consonants as you select letters.

Vowel Extension

Model extending the vowel sounds (example: **a-/ă/...apple-/ă/**). Have a student come trace the line for each of the vowels.

Unit 1 | Week 8

Day 1

Sky Write/Letter Formation

Teach **p** and **j** formation, linking formation with letter name, keyword and sound.

Follow activity procedure and have students sky write letters.

Emphasize that these letters are plane line letters, that go all the way down to the worm line.

Letter Formation for p

Use the following verbalization to direct students in proper letter formation.

Say

p is a plane line letter.

It starts on the (plane line).

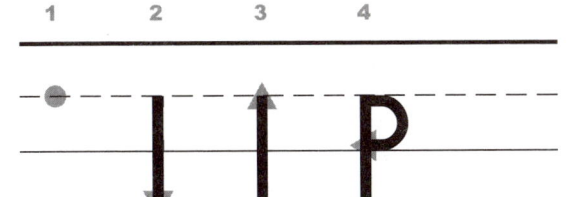

1. Point to the plane line.
2. Go down to the worm line.
3. Trace back up to the plane line,
4. and curve all the way around to the grass line.
5. Say p - pan - /p/, have students repeat.

Letter Formation for j

Use the following verbalization to direct students in proper letter formation.

Say

j is a plane line letter.

It starts on the (plane line).

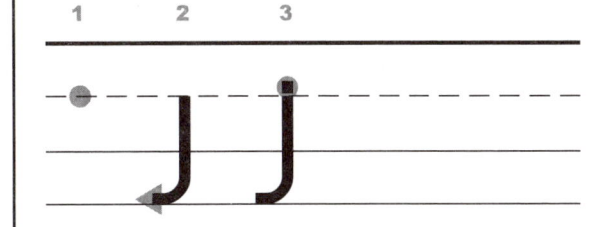

1. Point to the plane line.
2. Go all the way down to the worm line, and make a curve.
3. Add a dot.
4. Say j - jug - /j/, have students repeat.

Student Notebook

Direct the students to find the newly introduced letters.

Use the verbalization for the letter formation to direct the students while they trace it with their finger. Do it with them to model. Have them say letter-keyword-sound.

After students trace following verbalizations, they can then color the keyword picture for the letter **p**.

Unit 1 | Week 8

Day 2

Daily Plan — DAY 2

Student Learning Plan
- Drill Sounds/Warm-Up
- Sky Write/Letter Formation
- Student Notebook
- Echo/Letter Formation

Teacher Materials
- Echo and/or Baby Echo
- Large Sound Cards
- Standard Sound Cards
- Large Writing Grid
- Letter Formation Guide
- Vowel Extension Poster
- Student Notebook

Student Materials
- Student Notebook
- Dry Erase Writing Tablet

Drill Sounds/Warm-Up

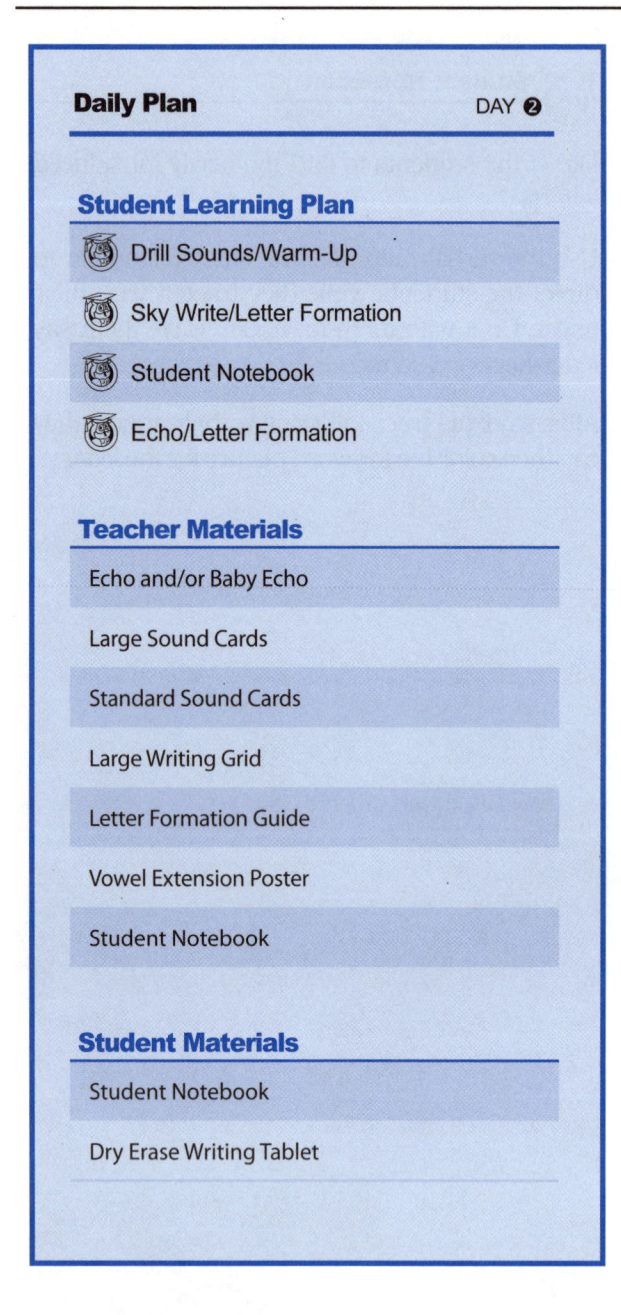

Do **new** sounds and **vowel** sounds each day. Selectively review 4-5 other consonants.

Large Sound Cards

Practice sounds with the Large Sound Cards. Model these, saying the letter-keyword-sound and have the students echo.

Standard Sound Cards

Next, point to the Standard Sound Cards (in card display) with the Baby Echo pointer. You say the letter-keyword-sound and hold up Baby Echo to have the students repeat. Discuss vowels and consonants as you select letters.

Vowel Extension

Model extending the vowel sounds (example: **a-/ă/...apple-/ă/**). Have a student come trace the line for each of the vowels.

Sky Write/Letter Formation

Review **p** and **j** formation, linking formation with letter name, keyword and sound.

Follow activity procedure and have students sky write letters.

Emphasize that these letters are plane line letters, that go all the way down to the worm line.

Select 1-2 review letters and sky write them, pointing out where they start on the Letter Formation Poster K·1.

Unit 1 | Week 8

Day 2

Student Notebook

Trace and say the letter-keyword-sound for all the previous letters introduced.

Direct the students to find the newly introduced letters.

Use the verbalization for the letter formation to direct the students while they trace it with their finger. Do it with them to model. Have them say letter-keyword-sound.

After students trace following verbalizations, they can then color the keyword picture for the letter **j**.

Echo/Letter Formation

Remind students of proper pencil grip and sitting position, and give them their Dry Erase Writing Tablets.

Sounds appear between / /. Dictate **new** sounds and a selection of previously taught sounds. You select and say the sound. Students echo the sound and say the letter.

Next have a student come up to the classroom board to make the letter on the Large Writing Grid. Direct the student with the letter formation verbalization.

Then have all students write the answer on their Dry Erase Writing Tablets as you direct them with the letter formation verbalization. Circulate to reinforce pencil grip and assist students, as needed.

Sounds

/t/ - t	/b/ - b	/f/ - f
/n/ - n	/m/ - m	/ĭ/ - i
/ŭ/ - u	/c/ - c	/ŏ/ - o
/ă/ - a	/g/ - g	/d/ - d
/s/ - s	/ĕ/ - e	/r/ - r
/p/ - p	**/j/ - j**	

Unit 1 | Week 8

Day 3

Daily Plan — DAY 3

Student Learning Plan
- Drill Sounds/Warm-Up
- Make It Fun
- Echo/Find Letters
- Student Notebook

Teacher Materials
- Echo and/or Baby Echo
- Large Sound Cards
- Standard Sound Cards
- Large Writing Grid
- Vowel Extension Poster
- Student Notebook

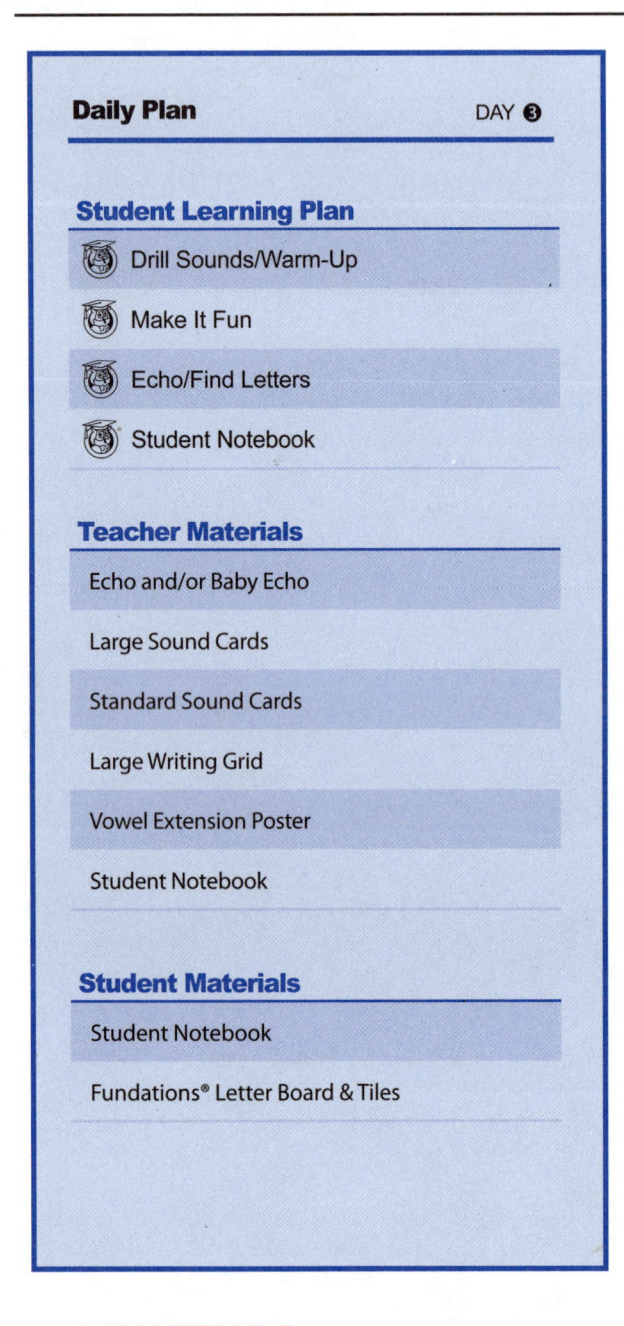

Student Materials
- Student Notebook
- Fundations® Letter Board & Tiles

Drill Sounds/Warm-Up

Do **new** sounds and **vowel** sounds each day. Selectively review 4-5 other consonants.

Large Sound Cards
Practice sounds with the Large Sound Cards. Model these, saying the letter-keyword-sound and have the students echo.

Standard Sound Cards
Next, point to the Standard Sound Cards (in card display) with the Baby Echo pointer. You say the letter-keyword-sound and hold up Baby Echo to have the students repeat. Discuss vowels and consonants as you select letters.

Vowel Extension
Model extending the vowel sounds (example: **a-/ă/...apple-/ă/**). Have a student come trace the line for each of the vowels.

Make It Fun

Teacher Materials
- Large Writing Grid

Have a student come up to the front of the room. Whisper a letter name to him/her. Next have the student form the letter with their finger (not write it) on the Large Writing Grid.

The other students need to watch and decide which letter was formed. When they guess, they should say the letter-keyword-sound (**p-pan-/p/**, etc). Whoever guesses correctly gets to do the next one.

Unit 1 | Week 8

Day 3

Echo/Find Letters

Students match Magnetic Letter Tiles to the letter(s) on their Letter Boards. Distribute Letter Boards and the Letter Tiles **p** and **j** to each student. Start with tiles on the blank side of the board. Dictate sounds. Students echo sound and match the tiles. Include previous sounds and new sounds. After all sounds are matched, dictate 2-3 sounds and have students repeat the sound and point to the corresponding letter.

Sounds

/t/ - t	/b/ - b	/f/ - f
/n/ - n	/m/ - m	/ĭ/ - i
/ŭ/ - u	/c/ - c	/ŏ/ - o
/ă/ - a	/g/ - g	/d/ - d
/s/ - s	/ĕ/ - e	/r/ - r
/p/ - p	**/j/ - j**	

Student Notebook

Practice Letters

Students trace previously taught letters while naming letter-keyword-sound. Do as a group saying verbalization, or circulate around the room as students do independently.

You can select a category of letters to find and practice, such as all the sky line letters or all the vowels taught thus far.

Unit 1 | Week 8

Day 4

Daily Plan — DAY 4

Student Learning Plan
- Drill Sounds/Warm-Up
- Word Play
- Sky Write/Letter Formation
- Echo/Letter Formation

Teacher Materials
- Echo and/or Baby Echo
- Large Sound Cards
- Standard Sound Cards
- Large Writing Grid
- Letter Formation Guide
- Vowel Extension Poster
- Sentence Frames

Student Materials
- Student Notebook
- Dry Erase Writing Tablet

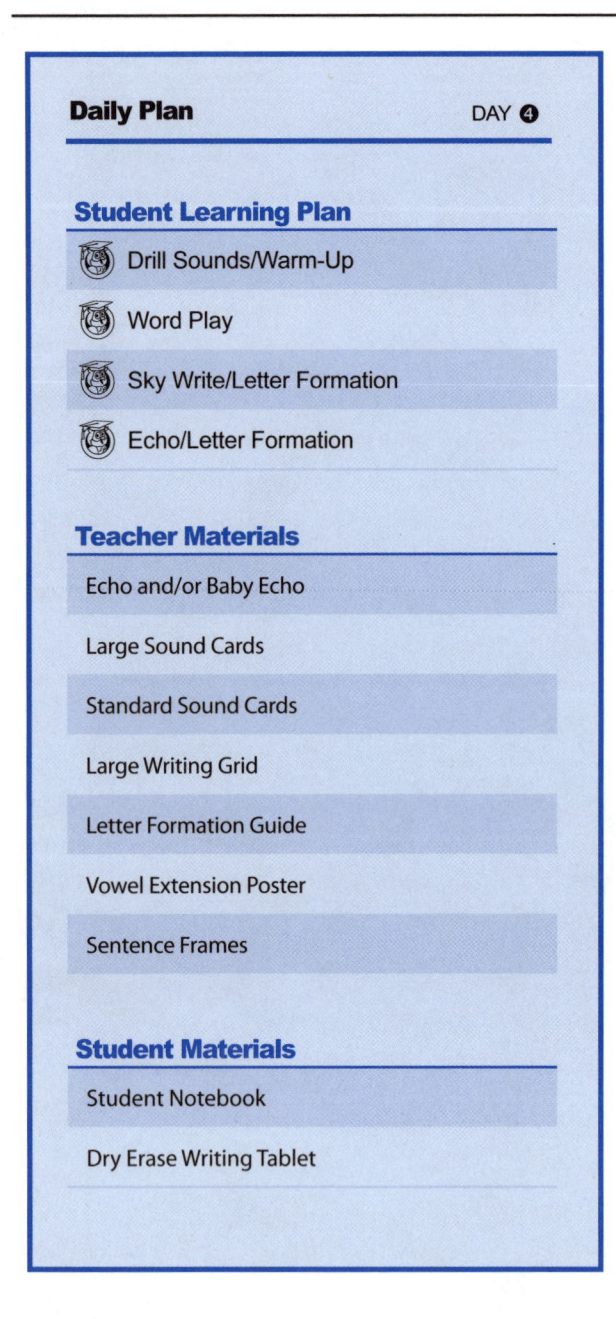

Drill Sounds/Warm-Up

Do **new** sounds and **vowel** sounds each day. Selectively review 4-5 other consonants.

Large Sound Cards

Practice sounds with the Large Sound Cards. Model these, saying the letter-keyword-sound and have the students echo.

Standard Sound Cards

Next, point to the Standard Sound Cards (in card display) with the Baby Echo pointer. You say the letter-keyword-sound and hold up Baby Echo to have the students repeat. Discuss vowels and consonants as you select letters.

Vowel Extension

Model extending the vowel sounds (example: a-/ă/...apple-/ă/). Have a student come trace the line for each of the vowels.

Word Play

Teacher Materials
- Sentence Frames
- Baby Echo

WORD AWARENESS

Display Sentence Frames in a Column

Display the Sentence Frames and period frame in a column rather than across the board. Tell the students that you are going to have them help you get the pieces you need to write your sentence.

Do Several Sentences

Ask a student to put the Sentence Frames in order for you to write the sentence. Say the sentence with them as they place the pieces.

Write the sentence (saying each word as you write it). Next, have the student use Baby Echo to read the sentence. Have the other students echo.

Include some sentences with two names so that the student will need to get two tall frames in constructing the sentence. Review capitalization of people's names.

Example Sentences

Maya has brown hair.

Jose and Maria have black hair.

Maria found a little puppy.

Unit 1 | Week 8

Day 4

Sky Write/Letter Formation

Review **p** and **j** formation, linking formation with letter name, keyword and sound.

Follow activity procedure and have students sky write letters.

Emphasize that these letters are plane line letters, that go all the way down to the worm line.

Select 1-2 review letters and sky write them, pointing out where they start on the Letter Formation Poster K·1.

Echo/Letter Formation

Remind students of proper pencil grip and sitting position, and give them their Dry Erase Writing Tablets.

Sounds appear between / /. Dictate **new** sounds and a selection of previously taught sounds. You select and say the sound. Students echo the sound and say the letter.

Next have a student come up to the classroom board to make the letter on the Large Writing Grid. Direct the student with the letter formation verbalization.

Then have all students write the answer on their Dry Erase Writing Tablets as you direct them with the letter formation verbalization. Circulate to reinforce pencil grip and assist students, as needed.

Sounds

/t/ - t	/b/ - b	/f/ - f
/n/ - n	/m/ - m	/ĭ/ - i
/ŭ/ - u	/c/ - c	/ŏ/ - o
/ă/ - a	/g/ - g	/d/ - d
/s/ - s	/ĕ/ - e	/r/ - r
/p/ - p	**/j/ - j**	

Unit 1 | Week 8

Day 5

Daily Plan — DAY 5

Student Learning Plan
- Drill Sounds/Warm-Up
- Storytime
- Echo/Find Letters

Teacher Materials
- Echo and/or Baby Echo
- Large Sound Cards
- Standard Sound Cards
- Vowel Extension Poster

Student Materials
- Student Notebook
- Fundations® Letter Board & Tiles

Drill Sounds/Warm-Up

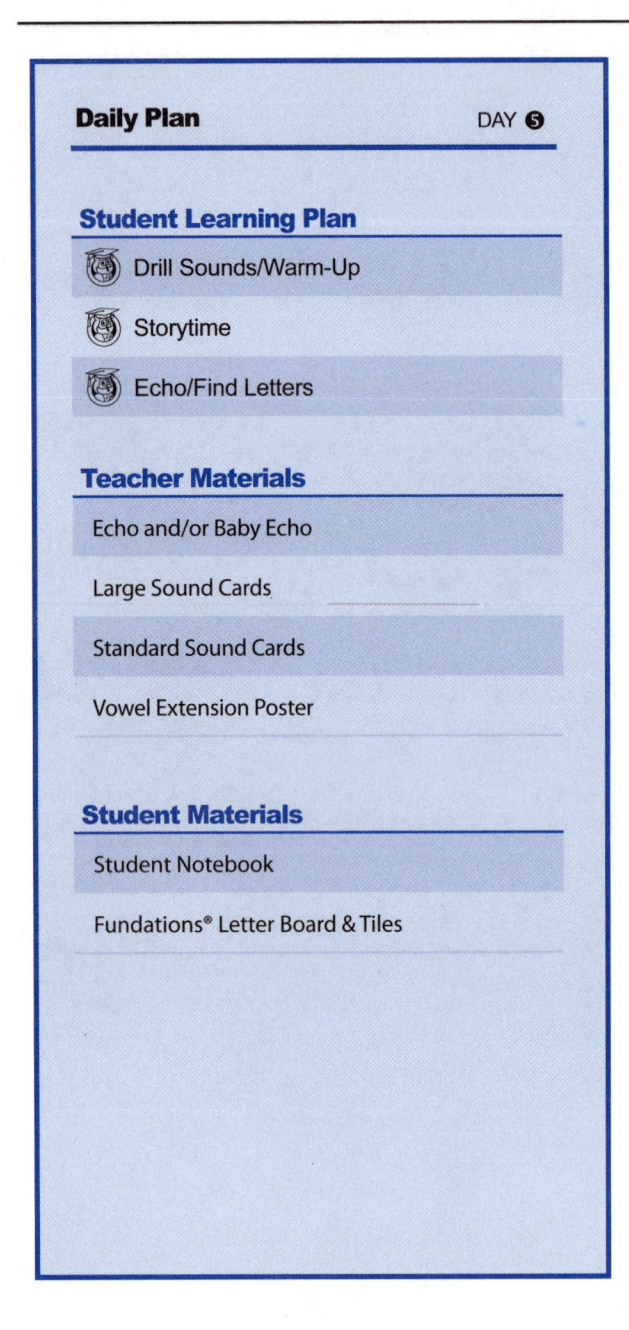

Do **new** sounds and **vowel** sounds each day. Selectively review 4-5 other consonants.

Large Sound Cards

Practice sounds with the Large Sound Cards. Model these, saying the letter-keyword-sound and have the students echo.

Standard Sound Cards

Next, point to the Standard Sound Cards (in card display) with the Baby Echo pointer. You say the letter-keyword-sound and hold up Baby Echo to have the students repeat. Discuss vowels and consonants as you select letters.

Vowel Extension

Model extending the vowel sounds (example: a-/ă/...apple-/ă/). Have a student come trace the line for each of the vowels.

Storytime

Teacher Materials
- Echo the Owl and Baby Echo

Prior to the lesson with your students read through and practice the story.

BABY ECHO FLIES I
Perform the Story

Baby Echo sat on a branch snuggled in the shelter of his mother's wings.

Put Baby Echo on your finger and tuck him into Echo's wings.

It was warm and safe there. Baby Echo was happy. Then Echo looked down at Baby Echo and said, "It is time for you to fly."

Move Echo's head to look at Baby Echo.

Baby Echo snuggled closer to his mother and said, "But I don't know how to fly!"

Move Baby Echo closer to Echo.

Echo said, "Watch me, I will teach you," and she flapped her wings.

Fly Echo to the floor.

Baby Echo was brave. He followed his mother and landed next to her.

Fly Baby Echo to the floor.

"I did it!" cried Baby Echo. "Yes you did and I am proud," said Echo. "Hooray for you."

Unit 1 | Week 8

Day 5

Ask the Following Questions

Who was in this story?

Where did it take place?

What was Baby Echo's problem?

What did he do about it?

How did things turn out? What happened in the end?

How did Baby Echo feel at the beginning of the story?

How did Baby Echo feel at the end of the story?

Echo/Find Letters

Students match Magnetic Letter Tiles to the letter(s) on their Letter Boards. Start with tiles off the board. Dictate sounds. Students echo sound and match the tiles. Include previous sounds and new sounds. After all sounds are matched, dictate 2-3 sounds and have students repeat the sound and point to the corresponding letter.

Sounds

/t/ - t	/b/ - b	/f/ - f
/n/ - n	/m/ - m	/ĭ/ - i
/ŭ/ - u	/c/ - c	/ŏ/ - o
/ă/ - a	/g/ - g	/d/ - d
/s/ - s	/ĕ/ - e	/r/ - r
/p/ - p	/j/ - j	

Tip: Read a story aloud to students with the similar theme of trying something new, such as the **Little Engine That Could**. Help students to compare and contrast it to Baby Echo's attempt to fly.

Unit 1 | Week 9

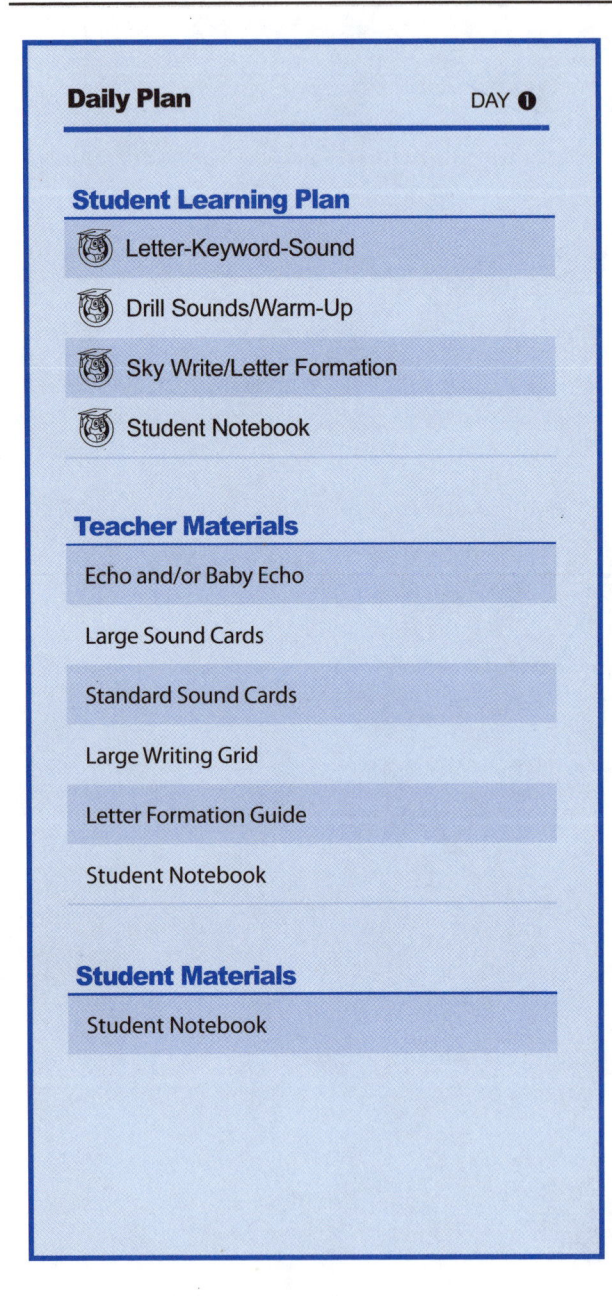

Day 1

Daily Plan — DAY 1

Student Learning Plan
- Letter-Keyword-Sound
- Drill Sounds/Warm-Up
- Sky Write/Letter Formation
- Student Notebook

Teacher Materials
- Echo and/or Baby Echo
- Large Sound Cards
- Standard Sound Cards
- Large Writing Grid
- Letter Formation Guide
- Student Notebook

Student Materials
- Student Notebook

Letter-Keyword-Sound

Introduce Letter-Keyword-Sound with Large and Standard Sound Cards. Be sure to follow procedure. First teach with Large Sound Card. Have students echo letter-keyword-sound. Then repeat with Standard Sound Card.

l	- l - lamp - /l/
h	- h - hat - /h/
k	- k - kite - /k/

Support for Spanish Speaking ELs: In Spanish, **h** is a silent letter. Be sure to reinforce the sound with your Spanish speaking students.

Drill Sounds/Warm-Up

Do **new** sounds and **vowel** sounds each day. Selectively review 4-5 other consonants.

Large Sound Cards
Practice sounds with the Large Sound Cards. Model these, saying the letter-keyword-sound and have the students echo.

Standard Sound Cards
Next, point to the Standard Sound Cards (in card display) with the Baby Echo pointer. You say the letter-keyword-sound and hold up Baby Echo to have the students repeat. Discuss vowels and consonants as you select letters.

Sky Write/Letter Formation

Teach **l**, **h** and **k** formation, linking formation with letter name, keyword and sound.

Follow activity procedure and have students sky write letters. Emphasize that these letters are sky line letters, so they begin on the sky line.

Letter Formation for *l*

Use the following verbalization to direct students in proper letter formation.

Say

l is a sky line letter.

It starts on the (sky line).

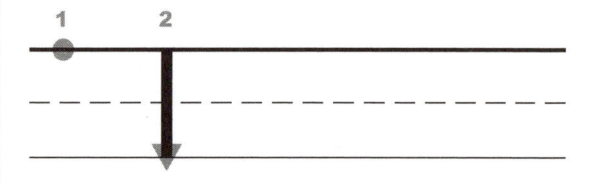

1. **Point to the sky line.**
2. **Go down to the grass line and stop.**
3. **Say l – lamp - /l/, have students repeat.**

144 FUNDATIONS® LEVEL K

Unit 1 | Week 9

Day 1

Letter Formation for h

Use the following verbalization to direct students in proper letter formation.

Say

h is a sky line letter.

It starts on the (sky line).

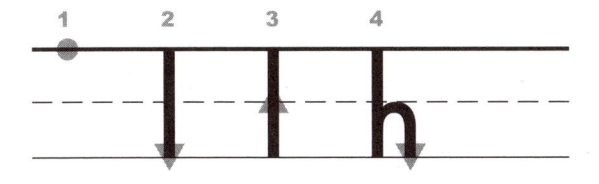

1. Point to the sky line.
2. Go down to the grass line.
3. Trace back up to the plane line,
4. and make a hump.
5. Say h - hat - /h/, have students repeat.

Letter Formation for k

Use the following verbalization to direct students in proper letter formation.

Say

k is a sky line letter.

It starts on the (sky line).

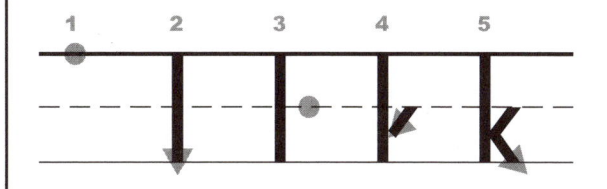

1. Point to the sky line.
2. Go all the way down to the grass line.
3. Point to the plane line and leave a space.
4. Slide over and touch your tall line,
5. and slide back to the grass line.
6. Say k - kite - /k/, have students repeat.

Student Notebook

Direct the students to find the newly introduced letters.

Use the verbalization for the letter formation to direct the students while they trace it with their finger. Do it with them to model. Have them say letter-keyword-sound.

After students trace following verbalizations, they can then color the keyword pictures for the letters l and h.

Unit 1 | Week 9

Day 2

Daily Plan — DAY 2

Student Learning Plan
- Drill Sounds/Warm-Up
- Sky Write/Letter Formation
- Student Notebook
- Echo/Letter Formation

Teacher Materials
- Echo and/or Baby Echo
- Large Sound Cards
- Standard Sound Cards
- Large Writing Grid
- Letter Formation Guide
- Vowel Extension Poster
- Student Notebook

Student Materials
- Student Notebook
- Dry Erase Writing Tablet

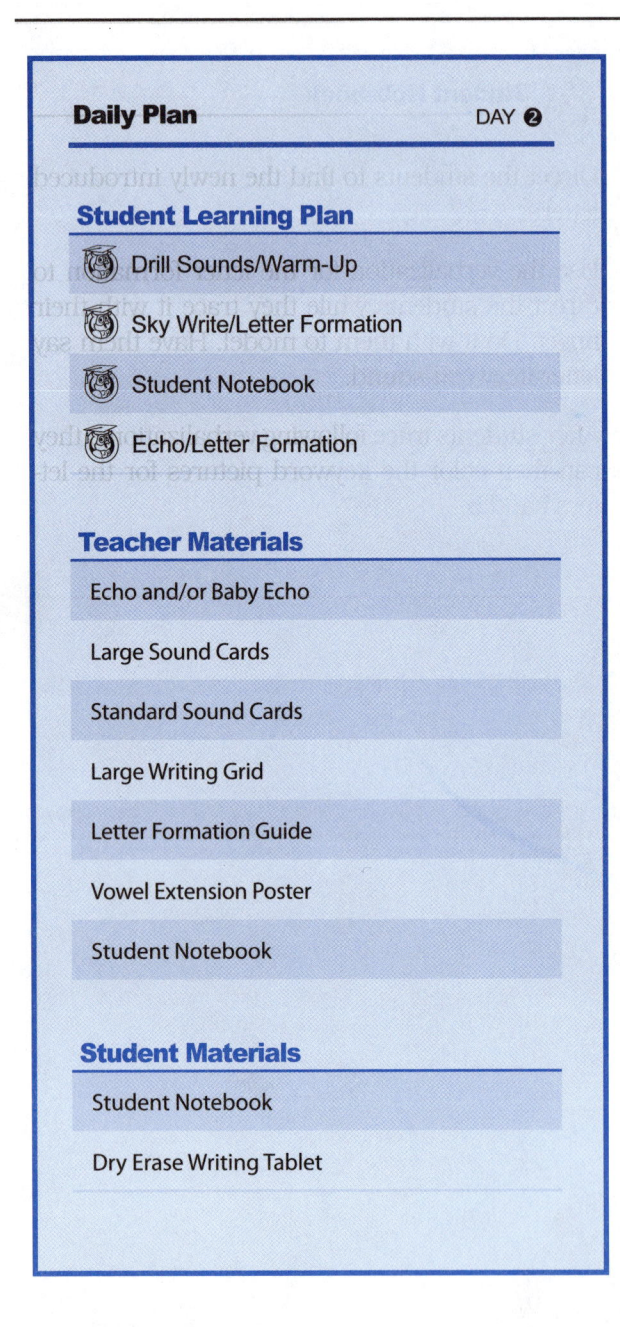

Drill Sounds/Warm-Up

Do **new** sounds and **vowel** sounds each day. Selectively review 4-5 other consonants.

Large Sound Cards

Practice sounds with the Large Sound Cards. Model these, saying the letter-keyword-sound and have the students echo.

Standard Sound Cards

Next, point to the Standard Sound Cards (in card display) with the Baby Echo pointer. You say the letter-keyword-sound and hold up Baby Echo to have the students repeat. Discuss vowels and consonants as you select letters.

Vowel Extension

Model extending the vowel sounds (example: **a-/ă/...apple-/ă/**). Have a student come trace the line for each of the vowels.

Sky Write/Letter Formation

Review **l**, **h** and **k** formation, linking formation with letter name, keyword and sound.

Follow activity procedure and have students sky write letters.

Emphasize that these letters are sky line letters, so they begin on the sky line.

Select 1-2 review letters and sky write them, pointing out where they start on the Letter Formation Poster K·1.

Unit 1 | Week 9

Day 2

Student Notebook

Trace and say the letter-keyword-sound for all the previous letters introduced.

Direct the students to find the newly introduced letters.

Use the verbalization for the letter formation to direct the students while they trace it with their finger. Do it with them to model. Have them say letter-keyword-sound.

After students trace following verbalizations, they can then color the keyword picture for the letter **k**.

Also, have students find the letter-keyword Fun Match page. Explain that they have to draw a line to match the letter with its keyword picture. After students complete the matches, select someone to say the letter-keyword-sound and have students check their answers.

Echo/Letter Formation

Remind students of proper pencil grip and sitting position, and give them their Dry Erase Writing Tablets.

Sounds appear between / /. Dictate **new** sounds and a selection of previously taught sounds. You select and say the sound. Students echo the sound and say the letter.

Next have a student come up to the classroom board to make the letter on the Large Writing Grid. Direct the student with the letter formation verbalization.

Then have all students write the answer on their Dry Erase Writing Tablets as you direct them with the letter formation verbalization. Circulate to reinforce pencil grip and assist students, as needed.

Sounds

/t/ - t	/b/ - b	/f/ - f
/n/ - n	/m/ - m	/ĭ/ - i
/ŭ/ - u	/c/ - c	/ŏ/ - o
/ă/ - a	/g/ - g	/d/ - d
/s/ - s	/ĕ/ - e	/r/ - r
/p/ - p	/j/ - j	/l/ - l
/h/ - h	/k/ - k, c	

Note

If you dictate /k/, students need to make both **c** and **k**.

Unit 1 | Week 9

Day 3

Daily Plan — DAY 3

Student Learning Plan
- Drill Sounds/Warm-Up
- Make It Fun
- Echo/Find Letters
- Student Notebook

Teacher Materials
- Echo and/or Baby Echo
- Large Sound Cards
- Standard Sound Cards
- Letter Formation Guide
- Vowel Extension Poster
- Student Notebook

Student Materials
- Student Notebook
- Fundations® Letter Board & Tiles

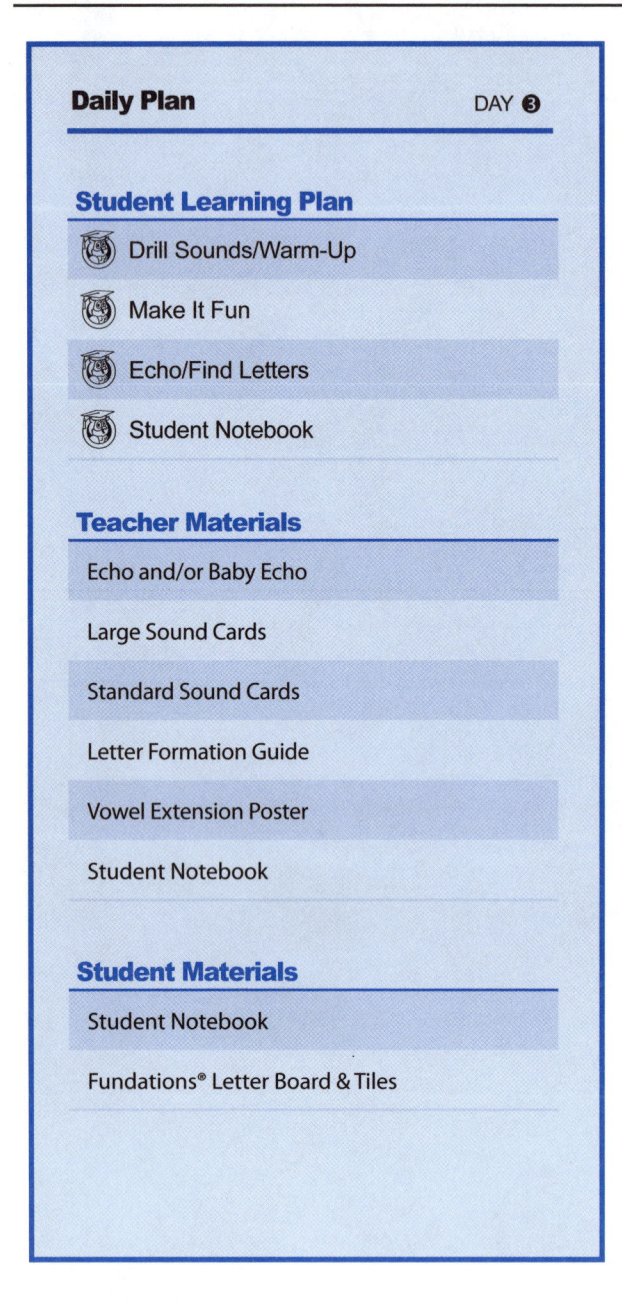

Drill Sounds/Warm-Up

Do **new** sounds and **vowel** sounds each day. Selectively review 4-5 other consonants.

Large Sound Cards

Practice sounds with the Large Sound Cards. Model these, saying the letter-keyword-sound and have the students echo.

Standard Sound Cards

Next, point to the Standard Sound Cards (in card display) with the Baby Echo pointer. You say the letter-keyword-sound and hold up Baby Echo to have the students repeat. Discuss vowels and consonants as you select letters.

Vowel Extension

Model extending the vowel sounds (example: a-/ă/...apple-/ă/). Have a student come trace the line for each of the vowels.

Make It Fun

Teacher Materials
- Standard Sound Cards
- Echo the Owl

Ask the students to listen to the end of a word. Emphasize the last sound when you say the word. For example, with /p/ emphasized, say:

map

Select a student to come get the Standard Sound Card that *ends* with the last sound in the word. If they select the wrong letter, say:

map

/p/ ends the word map.

Find me the letter that says /p/.

Help them locate the correct letter. If they select the correct letter, have them say letter-keyword-sound and have students repeat. Then ask:

When you make this letter, where does it start?

Then provide the verbalization of the letter formation as the student sky writes it. Have a student take a card and sit down.

Do several words. Then have the students with cards give their card to a student without a card. Say other words and have the students return cards with the correct final sound.

Unit 1 | Week 9

Day 3

Echo/Find Letters

Students match Magnetic Letter Tiles to the letter(s) on their Letter Boards. Distribute Letter Boards and the Letter Tiles **l**, **h** and **k** to each student. Start with tiles on the blank side of the board. Dictate sounds. Students echo sound and match the tiles. Include previous sounds and new sounds. After all sounds are matched, dictate 2-3 sounds and have students repeat the sound and point to the corresponding letter.

Sounds

/t/ - t	/b/ - b	/f/ - f
/n/ - n	/m/ - m	/ĭ/ - i
/ŭ/ - u	/c/ - c	/ŏ/ - o
/ă/ - a	/g/ - g	/d/ - d
/s/ - s	/ĕ/ - e	/r/ - r
/p/ - p	/j/ - j	**/l/ - l**
/h/ - h	**/k/ - k, c**	

Note

If you dictate /k/, students need to make both **c** and **k**.

Student Notebook

Practice Letters

Students trace previously taught letters while naming letter-keyword-sound. Do as a group saying verbalization, or circulate around the room as students do independently.

You can select a category of letters to find and practice, such as all the sky line letters or all the vowels taught thus far.

Unit 1 | Week 9

Day 4

Daily Plan — DAY 4

Student Learning Plan
- Drill Sounds/Warm-Up
- Word Play
- Sky Write/Letter Formation
- Echo/Letter Formation

Teacher Materials
- Echo and/or Baby Echo
- Large Sound Cards
- Standard Sound Cards
- Large Writing Grid
- Letter Formation Guide
- Vowel Extension Poster
- Sentence Frames

Student Materials
- Student Notebook
- Dry Erase Writing Tablet

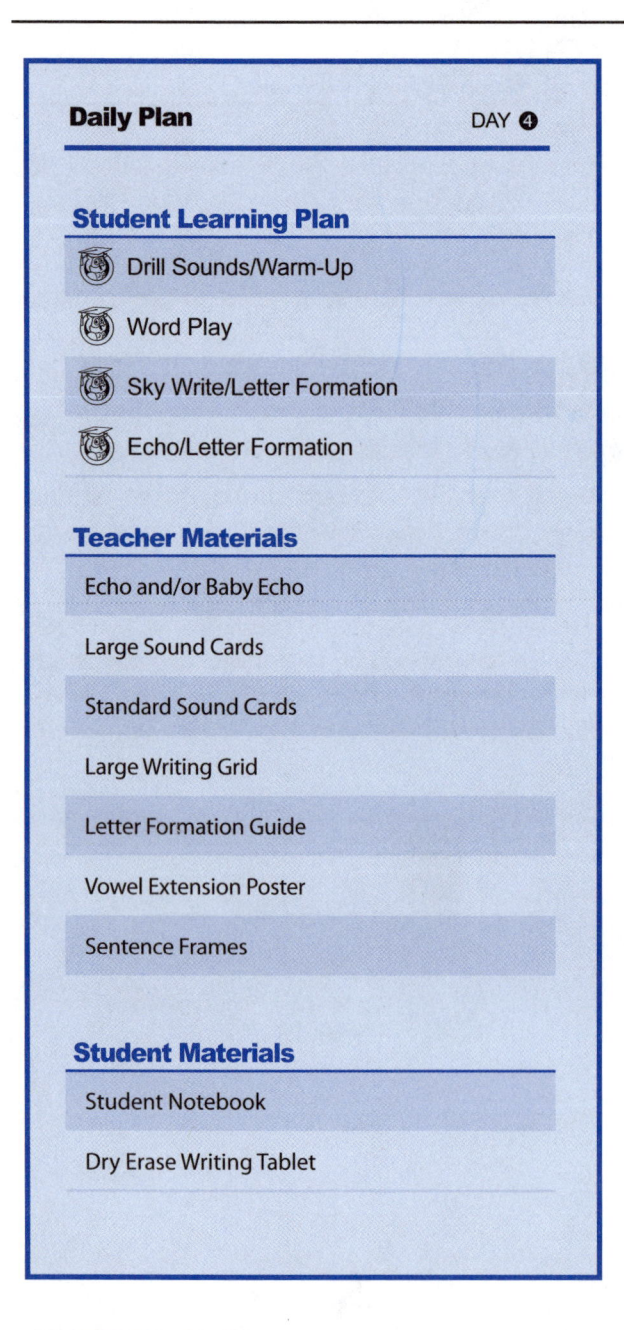

Drill Sounds/Warm-Up

Do **new** sounds and **vowel** sounds each day. Selectively review 4-5 other consonants.

Large Sound Cards

Practice sounds with the Large Sound Cards. Model these, saying the letter-keyword-sound and have the students echo.

Standard Sound Cards

Next, point to the Standard Sound Cards (in card display) with the Baby Echo pointer. You say the letter-keyword-sound and hold up Baby Echo to have the students repeat. Discuss vowels and consonants as you select letters.

Vowel Extension

Model extending the vowel sounds (example: a-/ă/...apple-/ă/). Have a student come trace the line for each of the vowels.

Word Play

Teacher Materials
- Sentence Frames
- Baby Echo

WORD AWARENESS

Say

> I'm going to ask you a question.
>
> Does Tyler have a bike?

Write the sentence on the Sentence Frames. Show the students how to write a question mark. Make one on the tall punctuation frame and add it to the sentence.

| Does | Tyler | have | a | bike | ? |

Explain that the question mark shows that this is a question. It asks something. Model reading this (be sure to raise your voice for a question). Have students echo.

> The period is used when we tell something.
>
> The question mark is used when we ask something.

Read and have students echo. Make other question sentences.

Each time, read with proper expression, emphasizing the question with your voice. Have students echo, pointing to the words. Erase the frames, and write an answer to the question.

Unit 1 | Week 9

Day 4

Have students echo read the answer and discuss the period.

For vocabulary development, remember to extend the students' word awareness and knowledge. For example, when you do the sentence about color, if a student says red, discuss scarlet, or blue - turquoise, etc.

Example Sentences

What is your name?

What is your favorite color?

I like to swim.

Did Jake go fishing?

Sky Write/Letter Formation

Review **l**, **h** and **k** formation, linking formation with letter name, keyword and sound.

Follow activity procedure and have students sky write letters.

Emphasize that these letters are sky line letters, so they begin on the sky line.

Select 1-2 review letters and sky write them, pointing out where they start on the Letter Formation Poster K·1.

Echo/Letter Formation

Remind students of proper pencil grip and sitting position, and give them their Dry Erase Writing Tablets.

Sounds appear between / /. Dictate **new** sounds and a selection of previously taught sounds. You select and say the sound. Students echo the sound and say the letter.

Next have a student come up to the classroom board to make the letter on the Large Writing Grid. Direct the student with the letter formation verbalization.

Then have all students write the answer on their Dry Erase Writing Tablets as you direct them with the letter formation verbalization. Circulate to reinforce pencil grip and assist students, as needed.

Sounds

/t/ - t	/b/ - b	/f/ - f
/n/ - n	/m/ - m	/ĭ/ - i
/ŭ/ - u	/c/ - c	/ŏ/ - o
/ă/ - a	/g/ - g	/d/ - d
/s/ - s	/ĕ/ - e	/r/ - r
/p/ - p	/j/ - j	/l/ - l
/h/ - h	/k/ - k, c	

Unit 1 | Week 9

Day 5

Daily Plan — DAY 5

Student Learning Plan
- Drill Sounds/Warm-Up
- Storytime
- Echo/Find Letters

Teacher Materials
- Echo and/or Baby Echo
- Large Sound Cards
- Standard Sound Cards
- Vowel Extension Poster

Student Materials
- Student Notebook
- Fundations® Letter Board & Tiles

Drill Sounds/Warm-Up

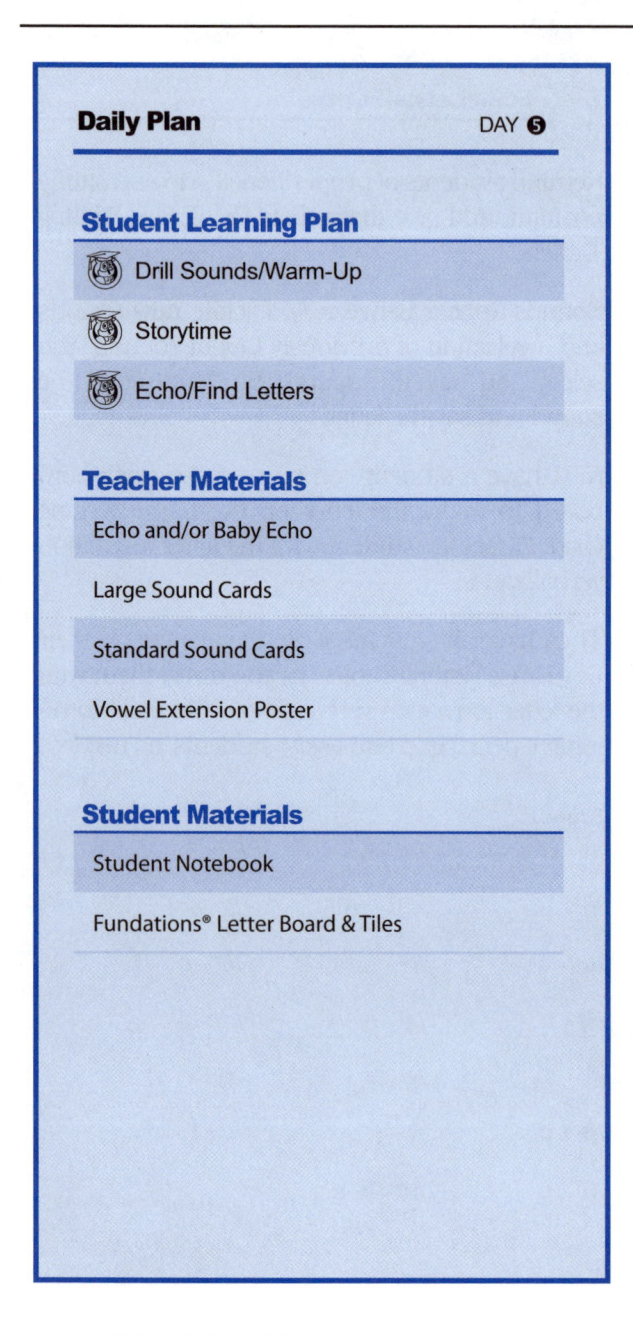

Do **new** sounds and **vowel** sounds each day. Selectively review 4-5 other consonants.

Large Sound Cards

Practice sounds with the Large Sound Cards. Model these, saying the letter-keyword-sound and have the students echo.

Standard Sound Cards

Next, point to the Standard Sound Cards (in card display) with the Baby Echo pointer. You say the letter-keyword-sound and hold up Baby Echo to have the students repeat. Discuss vowels and consonants as you select letters.

Vowel Extension

Model extending the vowel sounds (example: a-/ă/...apple-/ă/). Have a student come trace the line for each of the vowels.

Storytime

Teacher Materials
- Echo the Owl and Baby Echo

BABY ECHO FLIES II

This week you will say and act out the same story, "Baby Echo Flies." Then you will perform it again, without words, and have the students retell the story as you "play it out."

Re-perform the Story

Tell and act out "Baby Echo Flies." (See Week 8, Day 5).

Perform the Story Without Words

Perform the story again, without words, and have students tell you what happened.

After a student tells you in his/her own words, restate the words from the story to clarify as needed.

Be sure to provide students positive feedback for retelling in their own words.

Put Baby Echo on your finger and tuck him into Echo's wings.

Baby Echo sat on a branch snuggled in the shelter of his mother's wings.

Move Echo's head to look at Baby Echo.

It was warm and safe there. Baby Echo was happy. Then Echo looked down at Baby Echo and said, "It is time for you to fly."

Unit 1 | Week 9

Day 5

Move Baby Echo closer to Echo.

Baby Echo snuggled closer to his mother and said, "But I don't know how to fly!"

Fly Echo to the floor.

Echo said, "Watch me, I will teach you," and she flapped her wings.

Fly Baby Echo to the floor.

Baby Echo was brave. He followed his mother and landed next to her.

"I did it!" cried Baby Echo. "Yes you did and I am proud," said Echo. "Hooray for you."

Echo/Find Letters

Students match Magnetic Letter Tiles to the letter(s) on their Letter Boards. Start with tiles off the board. Dictate sounds. Students echo sound and match the tiles. Include previous sounds and new sounds. After all sounds are matched, dictate 2-3 sounds and have students repeat the sound and point to the corresponding letter.

Sounds

/t/ - t	/b/ - b	/f/ - f
/n/ - n	/m/ - m	/ĭ/ - i
/ŭ/ - u	/c/ - c	/ŏ/ - o
/ă/ - a	/g/ - g	/d/ - d
/s/ - s	/ĕ/ - e	/r/ - r
/p/ - p	/j/ - j	**/l/ - l**
/h/ - h	**/k/ - k, c**	

Unit 1 | Week 10

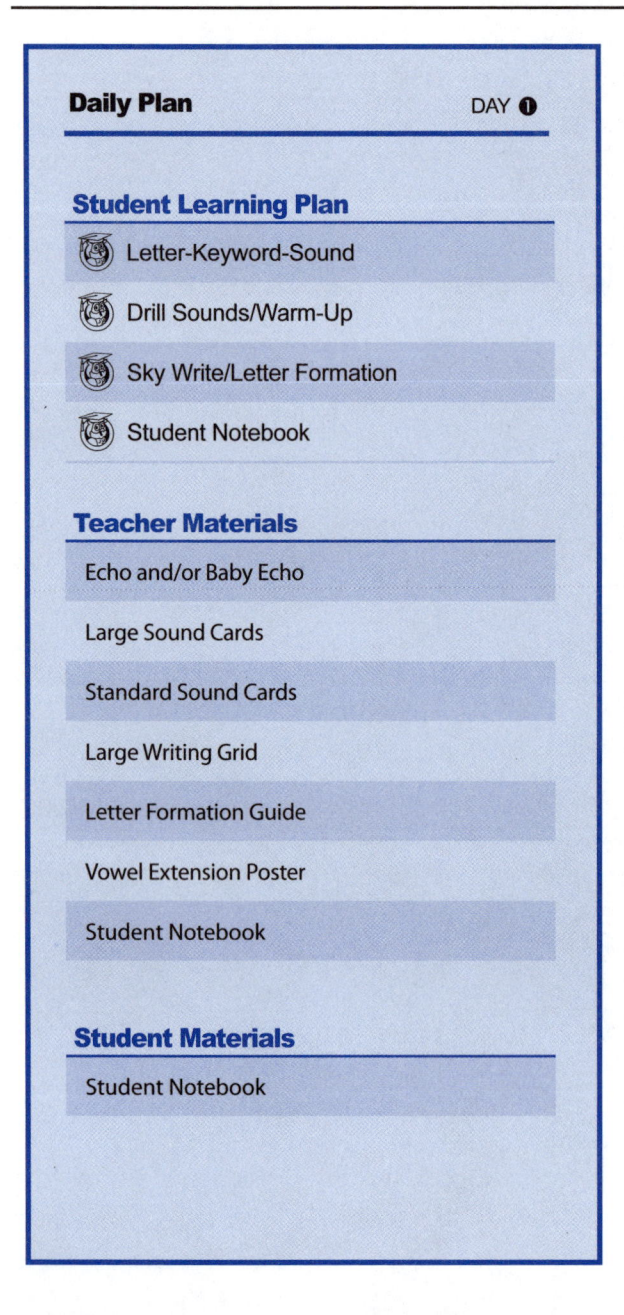

Day 1

Daily Plan — DAY 1

Student Learning Plan
- Letter-Keyword-Sound
- Drill Sounds/Warm-Up
- Sky Write/Letter Formation
- Student Notebook

Teacher Materials
- Echo and/or Baby Echo
- Large Sound Cards
- Standard Sound Cards
- Large Writing Grid
- Letter Formation Guide
- Vowel Extension Poster
- Student Notebook

Student Materials
- Student Notebook

Letter-Keyword-Sound

Introduce Letter-Keyword-Sound with Large and Standard Sound Cards. Be sure to follow procedure. First teach with Large Sound Card. Have students echo letter-keyword-sound. Then repeat with Standard Sound Card.

| v | - v - van - /v/ |

| w | - w - wind - /w/ |

These letters are plane line slide letters.

Note
As a new letter is taught, its Standard Sound Card is added to your card display to be drilled at each lesson.

Support for Spanish Speaking ELs: In Spanish, the letter **v** is pronounced /b/. Your Spanish speaking students may need additional practice with the /v/ sound.

Drill Sounds/Warm-Up

Do **new** sounds and **vowel** sounds each day. Selectively review 4-5 other consonants.

Large Sound Cards

Practice sounds with the Large Sound Cards. Model these, saying the letter-keyword-sound and have the students echo.

Standard Sound Cards

Next, point to the Standard Sound Cards (in card display) with the Baby Echo pointer. You say the letter-keyword-sound and hold up Baby Echo to have the students repeat. Discuss vowels and consonants as you select letters.

Vowel Extension

Model extending the vowel sounds (example: a-/ă/...apple-/ă/). Have a student come trace the line for each of the vowels.

Unit 1 | Week 10

Day 1

Sky Write/Letter Formation

Teach **v** and **w** formation, linking formation with letter name, keyword and sound.

Follow activity procedure and have students sky write letters.

Emphasize that these letters are plane line slide letters, so they begin on the plane line.

Letter Formation for **V**

Use the following verbalization to direct students in proper letter formation.

Say

v is a plane line slide letter.

It starts on the (plane line) and (slides).

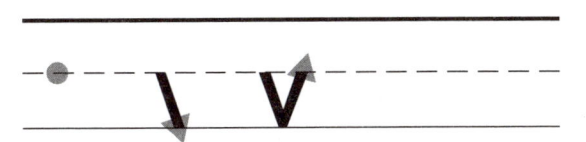

1. **Point to the plane line.**
2. **Slide down to the grass line.**
3. **Slide up to the plane line.**
4. **Say v - van - /v/, have students repeat.**

Letter Formation for **W**

Use the following verbalization to direct students in proper letter formation.

Say

w is a plane line slide letter.

It starts on the (plane line) and (slides).

1. **Point to the plane line.**
2. **Slide down to the grass line.**
3. **Slide up to the plane line.**
4. **Slide down to the grass line.**
5. **Slide up to the plane line.**
6. **Say w - wind - /w/, have students repeat.**

Student Notebook

Direct the students to find the newly introduced letters.

Use the verbalization for the letter formation to direct the students while they trace it with their finger. Do it with them to model. Have them say letter-keyword-sound.

After students trace following verbalizations, they can then color the keyword picture for the letter **v**.

© 2002, 2012 WILSON LANGUAGE TRAINING CORPORATION

TEACHER'S MANUAL **155**

Unit 1 | Week 10

Day 2

Daily Plan — DAY 2

Student Learning Plan
- Drill Sounds/Warm-Up
- Sky Write/Letter Formation
- Student Notebook
- Echo/Letter Formation

Teacher Materials
- Echo and/or Baby Echo
- Large Sound Cards
- Standard Sound Cards
- Large Writing Grid
- Letter Formation Guide
- Vowel Extension Poster
- Student Notebook

Student Materials
- Student Notebook
- Dry Erase Writing Tablet

Drill Sounds/Warm-Up

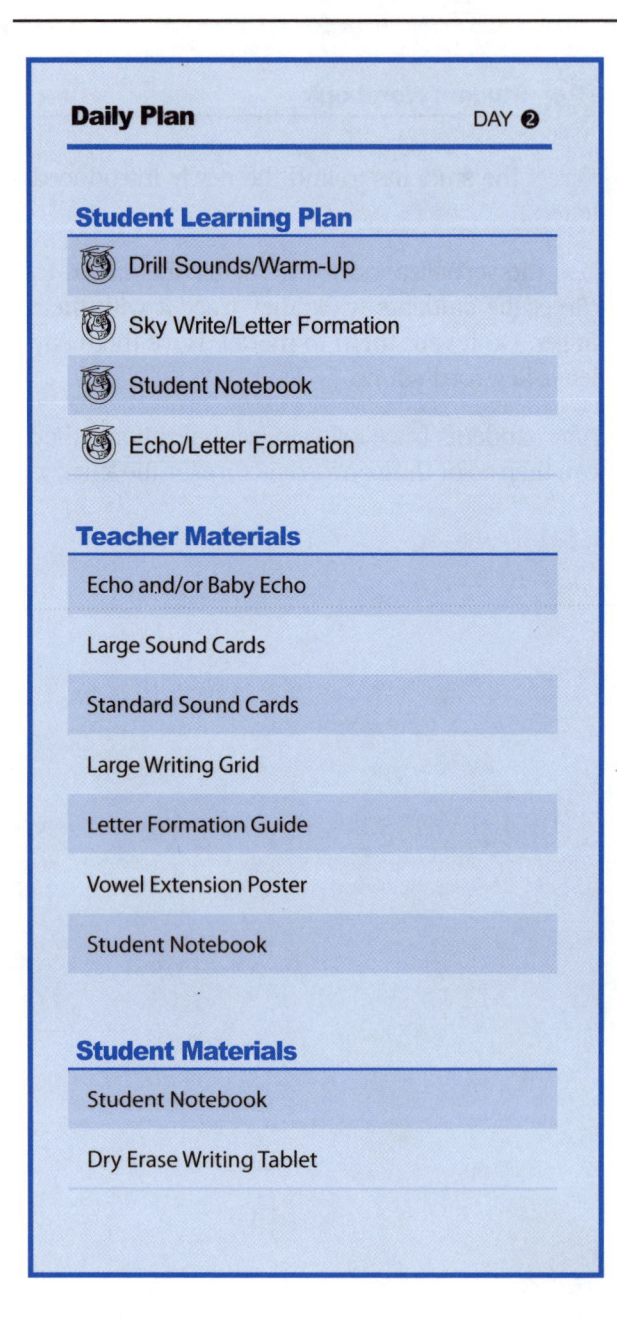

Do **new** sounds and **vowel** sounds each day. Selectively review 4-5 other consonants.

Large Sound Cards
Practice sounds with the Large Sound Cards. Model these, saying the letter-keyword-sound and have the students echo.

Standard Sound Cards
Next, point to the Standard Sound Cards (in card display) with the Baby Echo pointer. You say the letter-keyword-sound and hold up Baby Echo to have the students repeat. Discuss vowels and consonants as you select letters.

Vowel Extension
Model extending the vowel sounds (example: **a-/ă/...apple-/ă/**). Have a student come trace the line for each of the vowels.

Sky Write/Letter Formation

Review **v** and **w** formation, linking formation with letter name, keyword and sound.

Follow activity procedure and have students sky write letters.

Emphasize that these letters are plane line slide letters, so they begin on the plane line.

Select 1-2 review letters and sky write them, pointing out where they start on the Letter Formation Poster K·1.

Unit 1 | Week 10

Day 2

Student Notebook

Trace and say the letter-keyword-sound for all the previous letters introduced.

Direct the students to find the newly introduced letters.

Use the verbalization for the letter formation to direct the students while they trace it with their finger. Do it with them to model. Have them say letter-keyword-sound.

After students trace following verbalizations, they can then color the keyword picture for the letter **w**.

Echo/Letter Formation

Remind students of proper pencil grip and sitting position, and give them their Dry Erase Writing Tablets.

Sounds appear between / /. Dictate **new** sounds and a selection of previously taught sounds. You select and say the sound. Students echo the sound and say the letter.

Next have a student come up to the classroom board to make the letter on the Large Writing Grid. Direct the student with the letter formation verbalization.

Then have all students write the answer on their Dry Erase Writing Tablets as you direct them with the letter formation verbalization. Circulate to reinforce pencil grip and assist students, as needed.

Sounds

/t/ - t	/b/ - b	/f/ - f
/n/ - n	/m/ - m	/ĭ/ - i
/ŭ/ - u	/c/ - c	/ŏ/ - o
/ă/ - a	/g/ - g	/d/ - d
/s/ - s	/ĕ/ - e	/r/ - r
/p/ - p	/j/ - j	/l/ - l
/h/ - h	/k/ - k, c	**/v/ - v**
/w/ - w		

Unit 1 | Week 10

Day 3

Daily Plan — DAY 3

Student Learning Plan
- Drill Sounds/Warm-Up
- Make It Fun
- Echo/Find Letters
- Student Notebook

Teacher Materials
- Echo and/or Baby Echo
- Large Sound Cards
- Standard Sound Cards
- Letter Formation Guide
- Vowel Extension Poster
- Student Notebook

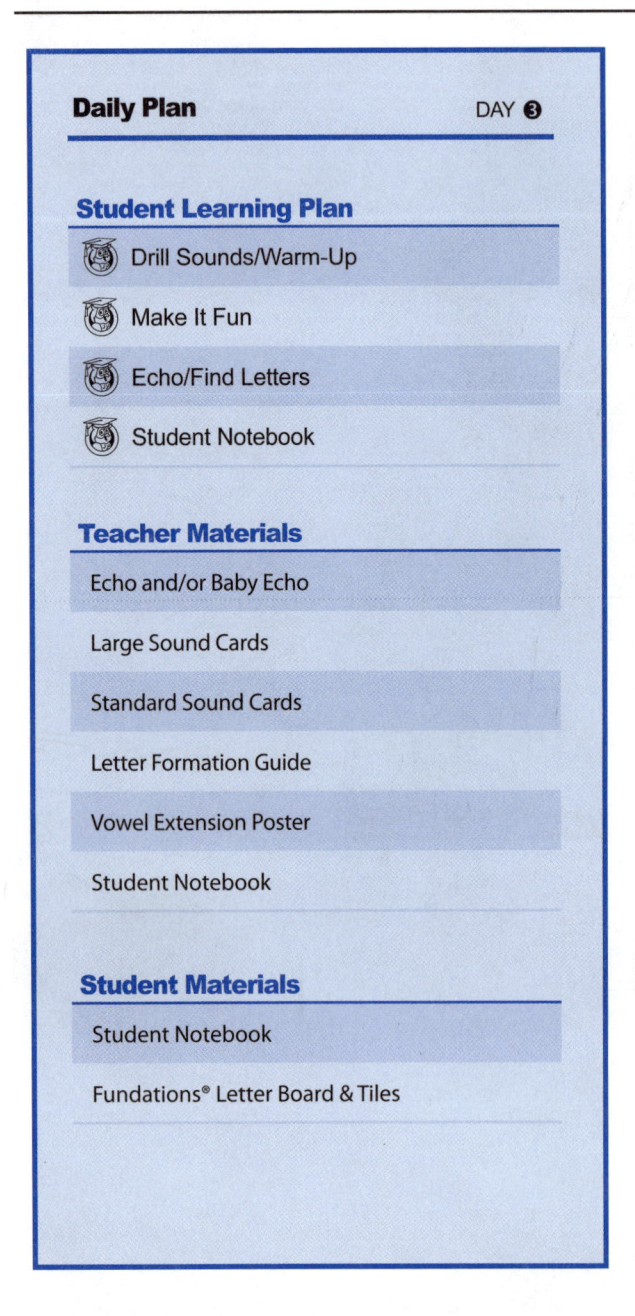

Student Materials
- Student Notebook
- Fundations® Letter Board & Tiles

Drill Sounds/Warm-Up

Do **new** sounds and **vowel** sounds each day. Selectively review 4-5 other consonants.

Large Sound Cards

Practice sounds with the Large Sound Cards. Model these, saying the letter-keyword-sound and have the students echo.

Standard Sound Cards

Next, point to the Standard Sound Cards (in card display) with the Baby Echo pointer. You say the letter-keyword-sound and hold up Baby Echo to have the students repeat. Discuss vowels and consonants as you select letters.

Vowel Extension

Model extending the vowel sounds (example: **a-/ă/...apple-/ă/**). Have a student come trace the line for each of the vowels.

a
e
i
o
u

Make It Fun

Collect objects that *end* with the letters taught so far. Put them in a big shopping bag. Call on a student to pick something out of the bag. Ask what it is (**pen**) and then have the student find the letter which *ends* the word (**n**). Have them say letter-keyword-sound and have students repeat. Then ask:

When you make this letter, where does it start?

Then provide the verbalization of the letter formation as the student sky writes it.

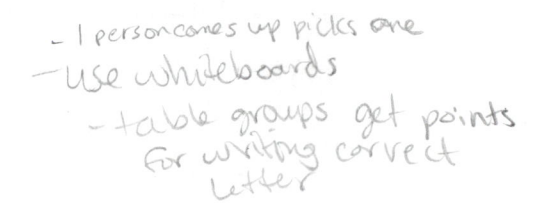

[handwritten notes:]
- 1 person comes up picks one
- use whiteboards
- table groups get points for writing correct letter

158 FUNDATIONS® LEVEL K

Unit 1 | Week 10

Day 3

Echo/Find Letters

Students match Magnetic Letter Tiles to the letter(s) on their Letter Boards. Distribute Letter Boards and the Letter Tiles **v** and **w** to each student. Start with tiles on the blank side of the board. Dictate sounds. Students echo sound and match the tiles. Include previous sounds and new sounds. After all sounds are matched, dictate 2-3 sounds and have students repeat the sound and point to the corresponding letter.

Sounds

/t/ - t	/b/ - b	/f/ - f
/n/ - n	/m/ - m	/ĭ/ - i
/ŭ/ - u	/c/ - c	/ŏ/ - o
/ă/ - a	/g/ - g	/d/ - d
/s/ - s	/ĕ/ - e	/r/ - r
/p/ - p	/j/ - j	/l/ - l
/h/ - h	/k/ - k, c	**/v/ - v**
/w/ - w		

Student Notebook

Practice Letters

Students trace previously taught letters while naming letter-keyword-sound. Do as a group saying verbalization, or circulate around the room as students do independently.

You can select a category of letters to find and practice, such as all the sky line letters or all the vowels taught thus far.

Unit 1 | Week 10

Day 4

Daily Plan — DAY 4

Student Learning Plan
- Drill Sounds/Warm-Up
- Word Play
- Sky Write/Letter Formation
- Echo/Letter Formation

Teacher Materials
- Echo and/or Baby Echo
- Large Sound Cards
- Standard Sound Cards
- Large Writing Grid
- Letter Formation Guide
- Vowel Extension Poster
- Sentence Frames

Student Materials
- Student Notebook
- Dry Erase Writing Tablet

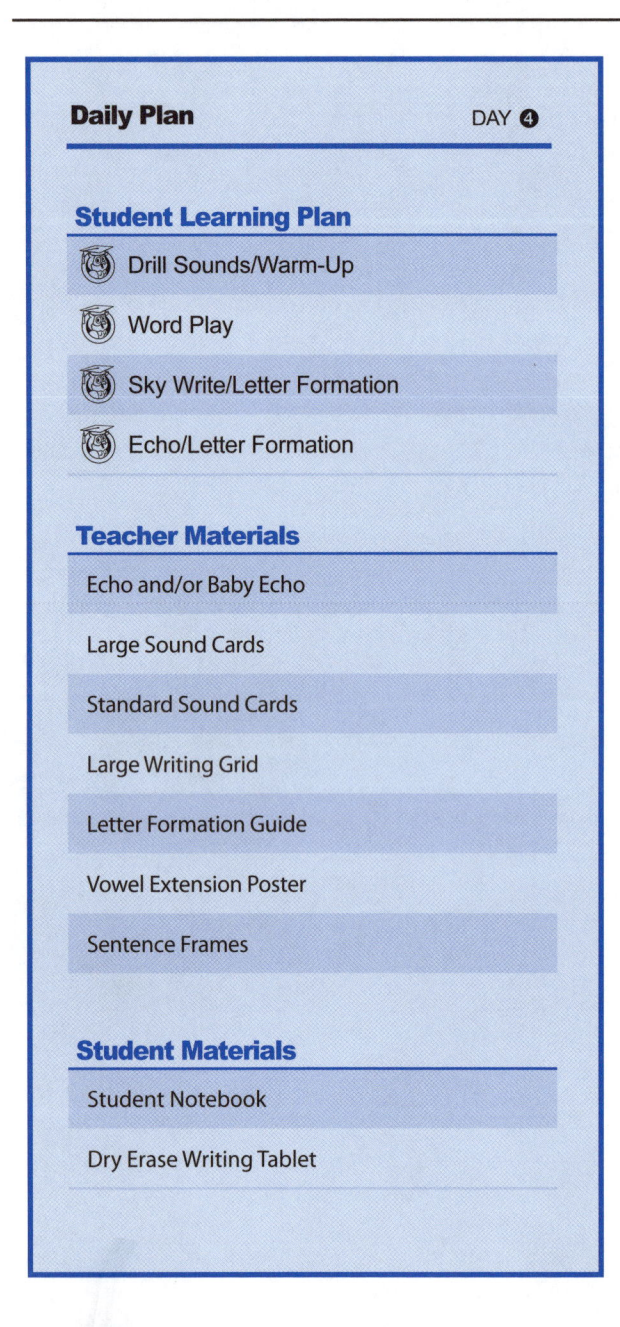

Drill Sounds/Warm-Up

Do **new** sounds and **vowel** sounds each day. Selectively review 4-5 other consonants.

Large Sound Cards

Practice sounds with the Large Sound Cards. Model these, saying the letter-keyword-sound and have the students echo.

Standard Sound Cards

Next, point to the Standard Sound Cards (in card display) with the Baby Echo pointer. You say the letter-keyword-sound and hold up Baby Echo to have the students repeat. Discuss vowels and consonants as you select letters.

Vowel Extension

Model extending the vowel sounds (example: **a-/ă/...apple-/ă/**). Have a student come trace the line for each of the vowels.

Word Play

Teacher Materials
- Sentence Frames
- Baby Echo

WORD AWARENESS

The students will again get you the frames needed so that you can write the sentence. Now they will need to get the question mark to complete asking sentences.

Display Sentence Frames in a Column

Display the word and punctuation frames in a column rather than across the board. Tell the students that you are going to have them help you get the pieces you need to write your sentence.

Demonstrate

Ask

Is it hot today?

Tell students that you need the tall frame first because every sentence must start with a capital letter. Say the words as you place the frames. Then tell them that at the end, you need to put a question mark, because it asks a question.

| Is | it | hot | today | ? |

Write the words on the frames and read it again, pointing to each word, be sure to raise your voice in a question and be dramatic (for example, put

Unit 1 | Week 10

Day 4

your finger on the side of your face in a questioning look). Have students echo.

Erase and put the frames back in a column and ask for a student volunteer. Give them a sentence.

Do you like candy?

Select a student to put the frames in order for you to write the sentence. Remind the student:

Think about what you need at the end of your sentence.

Say the sentence with them as they place the pieces. Be sure they add the question mark.

Write the sentence and ask the students if the frames are correctly placed.

| Do | you | like | candy | ? |

Erase the frames and return them to the column. Dictate other questions, emphasizing the question with your voice:

Example Sentences

Is Jimmy here today?

Where is Juan?

Can we eat lunch?

Sky Write/Letter Formation

Review **v** and **w** formation, linking formation with letter name, keyword and sound.

Follow activity procedure and have students sky write letters.

Emphasize that these letters are plane line slide letters, so they begin on the plane line.

Select 1-2 review letters and sky write them, pointing out where they start on the Letter Formation Poster K·1.

Echo/Letter Formation

Remind students of proper pencil grip and sitting position, and give them their Dry Erase Writing Tablets.

Sounds appear between / /. Dictate **new** sounds and a selection of previously taught sounds. You select and say the sound. Students echo the sound and say the letter.

Next have a student come up to the classroom board to make the letter on the Large Writing Grid. Direct the student with the letter formation verbalization.

Then have all students write the answer on their Dry Erase Writing Tablets as you direct them with the letter formation verbalization. Circulate to reinforce pencil grip and assist students, as needed.

Sounds

/t/ - t	/b/ - b	/f/ - f
/n/ - n	/m/ - m	/ĭ/ - i
/ŭ/ - u	/c/ - c	/ŏ/ - o
/ă/ - a	/g/ - g	/d/ - d
/s/ - s	/ĕ/ - e	/r/ - r
/p/ - p	/j/ - j	/l/ - l
/h/ - h	/k/ - k, c	**/v/ - v**
/w/ - w		

Unit 1 | Week 10

Day 5

Daily Plan — DAY 5

Student Learning Plan
- Drill Sounds/Warm-Up
- Storytime
- Echo/Find Letters

Teacher Materials
- Echo and/or Baby Echo
- Large Sound Cards
- Standard Sound Cards
- Vowel Extension Poster
- 4 Sheets of Large Chart Paper

Student Materials
- Student Notebook
- Fundations® Letter Board & Tiles

Drill Sounds/Warm-Up

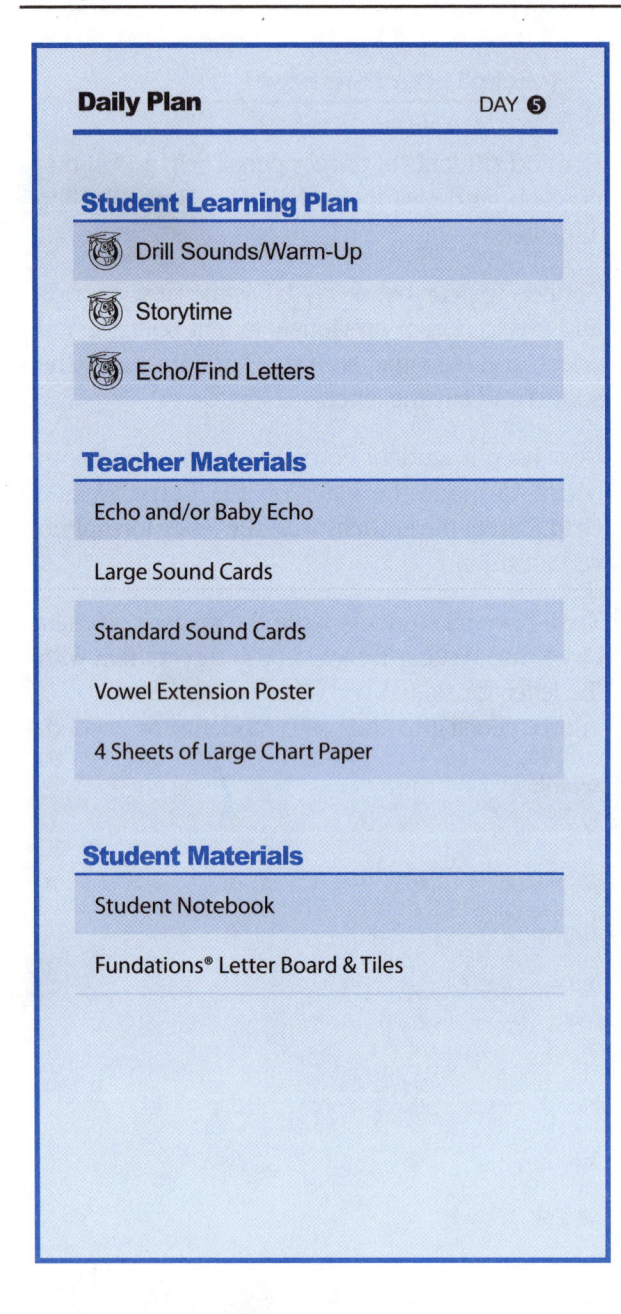

Do **new** sounds and **vowel** sounds each day. Selectively review 4-5 other consonants.

Large Sound Cards

Practice sounds with the Large Sound Cards. Model these, saying the letter-keyword-sound and have the students echo.

Standard Sound Cards

Next, point to the Standard Sound Cards (in card display) with the Baby Echo pointer. You say the letter-keyword-sound and hold up Baby Echo to have the students repeat. Discuss vowels and consonants as you select letters.

Vowel Extension

Model extending the vowel sounds (example: a-/ă/...apple-/ă/). Have a student come trace the line for each of the vowels.

Storytime

Teacher Materials
- Echo the Owl and Baby Echo
- 4 Sheets of large chart paper

BABY ECHO FLIES III

This week you will say and act out the same story, "Baby Echo Flies." Then, as the students retell the story, you will illustrate the story with four simple pictures. Leave space at the bottom of each page. You will need this space next week to write the words of the story. Keep these illustrations for next week's lesson. Remember that these illustrations can be simple. Do not worry about your artistic ability.

Perform the Story

Tell and act out "Baby Echo Flies." (See Week 9, Day 5).

Draw the Story

Next have students retell it to you as you draw it on chart paper. To assist them in retelling the story, ask:

Who was in the story? Where did the story begin?

1. Draw Baby Echo with Echo on a branch. Put a smile on Baby Echo's face.

What did Echo say to Baby Echo? How did Baby Echo feel?

2. Draw Baby Echo with Echo on a branch. Make Baby Echo look frightened.

Unit 1 | Week 10

Day 5

What happened next?

3. *Draw Echo on the ground.*

How did it end?

4. *Show Baby Echo flying, or draw Echo and Baby Echo on the ground, smiling.*

After the pictures are drawn model retelling the story. It is very important to do this in your own words. Then select a student to come tell the story, pointing to the pictures. (You can have several students do this or have them do it at another time during the day or throughout the week.)

Note

Remember to save the illustrations. You will need it for Storytime next week.

Students should draw and/or write in their My Fundations® Journal several times a week. You can have them draw pictures of Baby Echo Flies, showing the major events in the order which they occurred.

Echo/Find Letters

Students match Magnetic Letter Tiles to the letter(s) on their Letter Boards. Start with tiles off the board. Dictate sounds. Students echo sound and match the tiles. Include previous sounds and new sounds. After all sounds are matched, dictate 2-3 sounds and have students repeat the sound and point to the corresponding letter.

Sounds

/t/ - t	/b/ - b	/f/ - f
/n/ - n	/m/ - m	/ĭ/ - i
/ŭ/ - u	/c/ - c	/ŏ/ - o
/ă/ - a	/g/ - g	/d/ - d
/s/ - s	/ĕ/ - e	/r/ - r
/p/ - p	/j/ - j	/l/ - l
/h/ - h	/k/ - k, c	/v/ - v
/w/ - w		

Unit 1 | Week 11

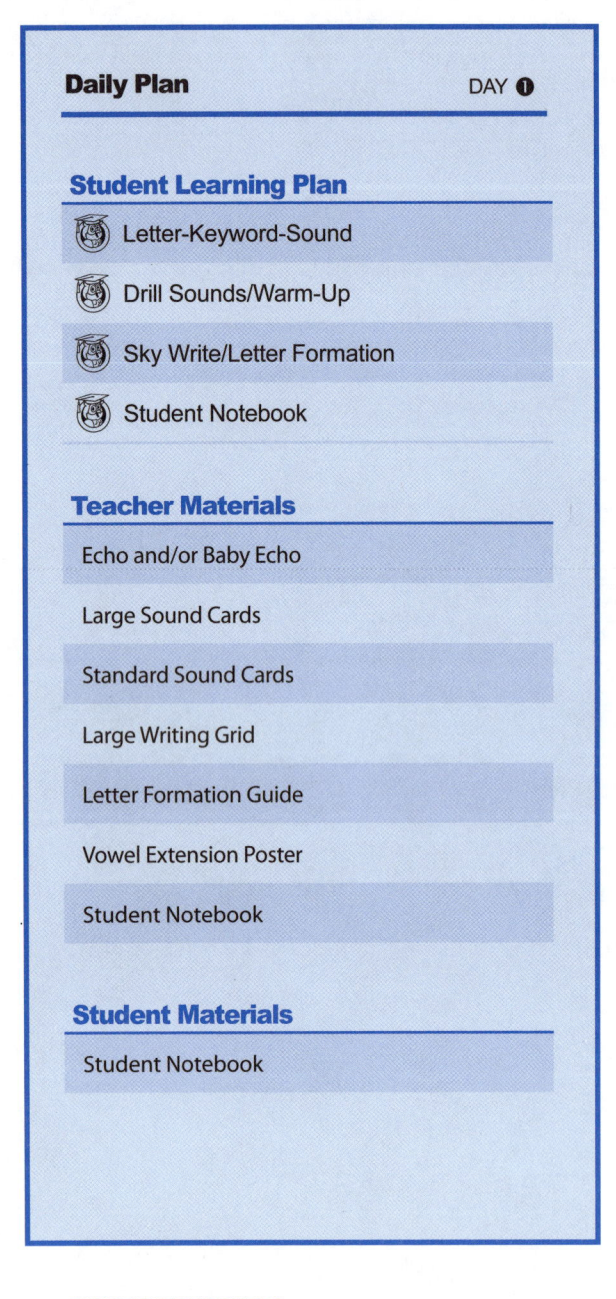

Day 1

Daily Plan — DAY 1

Student Learning Plan
- Letter-Keyword-Sound
- Drill Sounds/Warm-Up
- Sky Write/Letter Formation
- Student Notebook

Teacher Materials
- Echo and/or Baby Echo
- Large Sound Cards
- Standard Sound Cards
- Large Writing Grid
- Letter Formation Guide
- Vowel Extension Poster
- Student Notebook

Student Materials
- Student Notebook

Letter-Keyword-Sound

Introduce Letter-Keyword-Sound with Large and Standard Sound Cards. Be sure to follow procedure. First teach with Large Sound Card. Have students echo letter-keyword-sound. Then repeat with Standard Sound Card.

| y | - y - yellow - /y/ |

| x | - x - fox - /ks/ |

Note
As a new letter is taught, its Standard Sound Card is added to your card display to be drilled at each lesson.

tip
Use of keyword is critical. Students must say letter name first, keyword second, and sound last: **y - yellow - /y/**.

Drill Sounds/Warm-Up

Do **new** sounds and **vowel** sounds each day. Selectively review 4-5 other consonants.

Large Sound Cards

Practice sounds with the Large Sound Cards. Model these, saying the letter-keyword-sound and have the students echo.

Standard Sound Cards

Next, point to the Standard Sound Cards (in card display) with the Baby Echo pointer. You say the letter-keyword-sound and hold up Baby Echo to have the students repeat. Discuss vowels and consonants as you select letters.

Vowel Extension

Model extending the vowel sounds (example: a-/ă/...apple-/ă/). Have a student come trace the line for each of the vowels.

164 FUNDATIONS® LEVEL K

© 2002, 2012 WILSON LANGUAGE TRAINING CORPORATION

Unit 1 | Week 11

Day 1

Sky Write/Letter Formation

Teach **y** and **x** formation, linking formation with letter name, keyword and sound.

Follow activity procedure and have students sky write letters.

Emphasize that these letters are plane line slide, so they begin on the plane line.

Letter Formation for y

Use the following verbalization to direct students in proper letter formation.

Say

y is a plane line slide letter.

It starts on the (plane line) and (slides).

1. Point to the plane line.
2. Slide down to the grass line.
3. Pick up your pencil (finger) and leave a space and point to the plane line.
4. Slide back - all the way to the worm line.
5. Say y - yellow - /y/, have students repeat.

Letter Formation for x

Use the following verbalization to direct students in proper letter formation.

Say

x is a plane line slide letter.

It starts on the (plane line) and (slides).

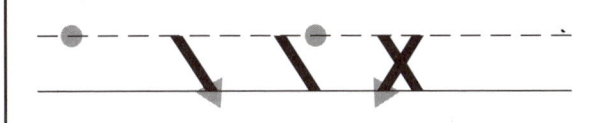

1. Point to the plane line.
2. Slide down to the grass line.
3. Leave a space and point to the plane line.
4. Slide back to the grass line.
5. Say x - fox - /ks/, have students repeat

Student Notebook

Direct the students to find the newly introduced letters.

Use the verbalization for the letter formation to direct the students while they trace it with their finger. Do it with them to model. Have them say letter-keyword-sound.

After students trace following verbalizations, they can then color the keyword picture for the letter **y**.

Unit 1 | Week 11

Day 2

Daily Plan — DAY 2

Student Learning Plan
- Drill Sounds/Warm-Up
- Sky Write/Letter Formation
- Student Notebook
- Echo/Letter Formation

Teacher Materials
- Echo and/or Baby Echo
- Large Sound Cards
- Standard Sound Cards
- Large Writing Grid
- Letter Formation Guide
- Vowel Extension Poster
- Student Notebook

Student Materials
- Student Notebook
- Dry Erase Writing Tablet

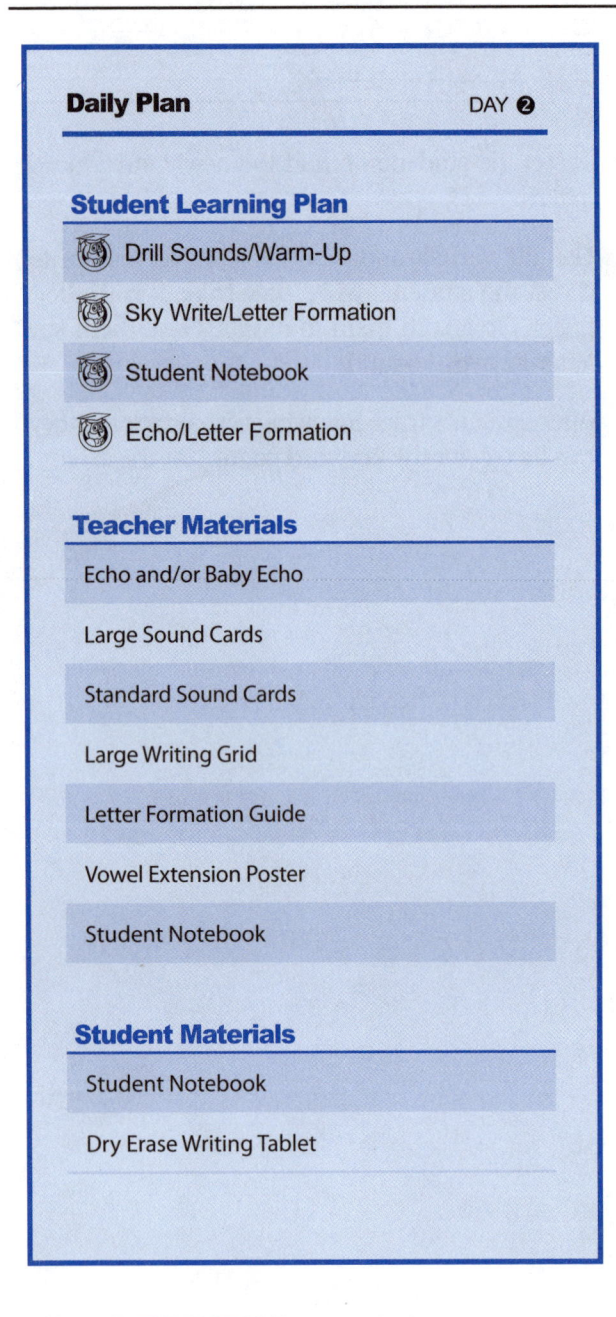

Drill Sounds/Warm-Up

Do **new** sounds and **vowel** sounds each day. Selectively review 4-5 other consonants.

Large Sound Cards

Practice sounds with the Large Sound Cards. Model these, saying the letter-keyword-sound and have the students echo.

Standard Sound Cards

Next, point to the Standard Sound Cards (in card display) with the Baby Echo pointer. You say the letter-keyword-sound and hold up Baby Echo to have the students repeat. Discuss vowels and consonants as you select letters.

Vowel Extension

Model extending the vowel sounds (example: **a-/ă/...apple-/ă/**). Have a student come trace the line for each of the vowels.

Sky Write/Letter Formation

Review **y** and **x** formation, linking formation with letter name, keyword and sound.

Follow activity procedure and have students sky write letters.

Emphasize that these letters are plane line slide, so they begin on the plane line.

Select 1-2 review letters and sky write them, pointing out where they start on the Letter Formation Poster K·1.

Unit 1 | Week 11

Day 2

Student Notebook

Trace and say the letter-keyword-sound for all the previous letters introduced.

Direct the students to find the newly introduced letters.

Use the verbalization for the letter formation to direct the students while they trace it with their finger. Do it with them to model. Have them say letter-keyword-sound.

After students trace following verbalizations, they can then color the keyword picture for the letter **x**.

Echo/Letter Formation

Remind students of proper pencil grip and sitting position, and give them their Dry Erase Writing Tablets.

Sounds appear between / /. Dictate **new** sounds and a selection of previously taught sounds. You select and say the sound. Students echo the sound and say the letter.

Next have a student come up to the classroom board to make the letter on the Large Writing Grid. Direct the student with the letter formation verbalization.

Then have all students write the answer on their Dry Erase Writing Tablets as you direct them with the letter formation verbalization. Circulate to reinforce pencil grip and assist students, as needed.

Sounds

/t/ - t	/b/ - b	/f/ - f
/n/ - n	/m/ - m	/ĭ/ - i
/ŭ/ - u	/c/ - c	/ŏ/ - o
/ă/ - a	/g/ - g	/d/ - d
/s/ - s	/ĕ/ - e	/r/ - r
/p/ - p	/j/ - j	/l/ - l
/h/ - h	/k/ - k, c	/v/ - v
/w/ - w	/y/ - y	/ks/ - x

Unit 1 | Week 11

Day 3

Daily Plan — DAY 3

Student Learning Plan
- Drill Sounds/Warm-Up
- Make It Fun
- Echo/Find Letters
- Student Notebook

Teacher Materials
- Echo and/or Baby Echo
- Large Sound Cards
- Standard Sound Cards
- Vowel Extension Poster
- Keyword Puzzle
- Student Notebook

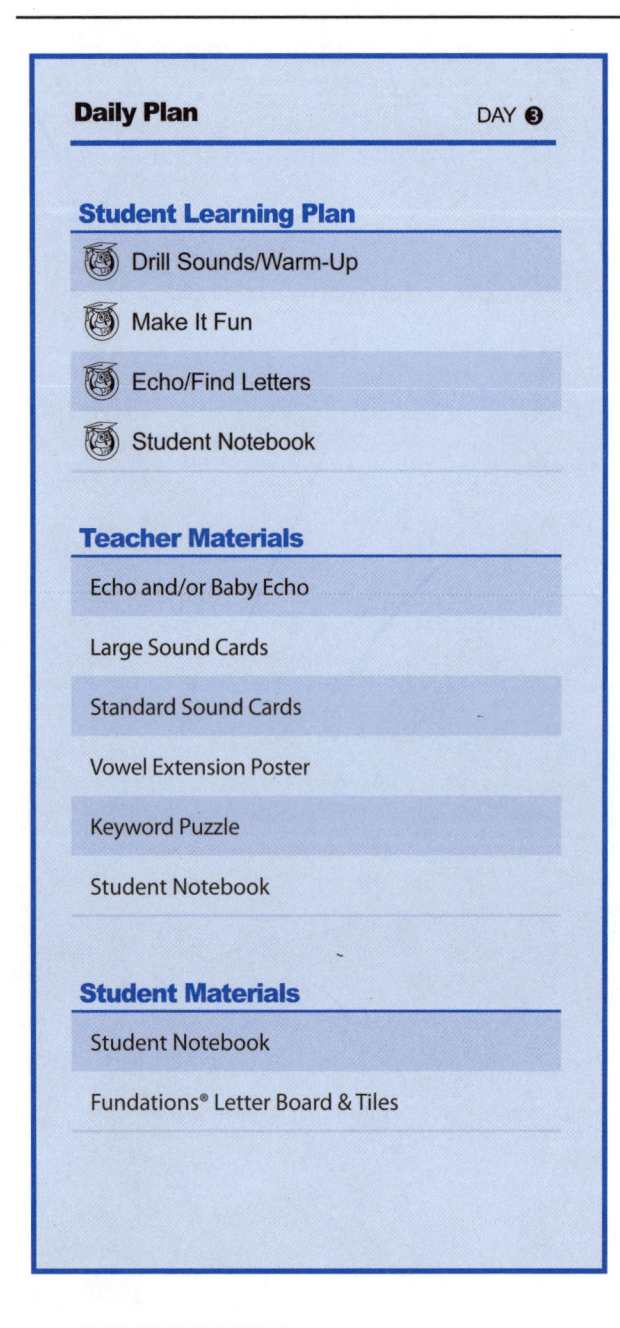

Student Materials
- Student Notebook
- Fundations® Letter Board & Tiles

Drill Sounds/Warm-Up

Do **new** sounds and **vowel** sounds each day. Selectively review 4-5 other consonants.

Large Sound Cards
Practice sounds with the Large Sound Cards. Model these, saying the letter-keyword-sound and have the students echo.

Standard Sound Cards
Next, point to the Standard Sound Cards (in card display) with the Baby Echo pointer. You say the letter-keyword-sound and hold up Baby Echo to have the students repeat. Discuss vowels and consonants as you select letters.

Vowel Extension
Model extending the vowel sounds (example: **a-/ă/...apple-/ă/**). Have a student come trace the line for each of the vowels.

Make It Fun

KEYWORD MATCH

Materials
- Keyword Puzzle

Use the puzzle pieces for the letters taught thus far. Pass out the letters (one per child) and the pictures (one per child) until they are disseminated. Then direct the students:

Stand up if you have the letter that says /b/. Stand up if you have the picture that goes with b.

Make a match!

Have the students come up front and put the cards together, then have everyone say the letter-keyword-sound.

b - bat - /b/

Unit 1 | Week 11

Day 3

Echo/Find Letters

Students match Magnetic Letter Tiles to the letter(s) on their Letter Boards. Distribute Letter Boards and the Letter Tiles **y** and **x** to each student. Start with tiles on the blank side of the board. Dictate sounds. Students echo sound and match the tiles. Include previous sounds and new sounds. After all sounds are matched, dictate 2-3 sounds and have students repeat the sound and point to the corresponding letter.

Sounds

/t/ - t	/b/ - b	/f/ - f
/n/ - n	/m/ - m	/ĭ/ - i
/ŭ/ - u	/c/ - c	/ŏ/ - o
/ă/ - a	/g/ - g	/d/ - d
/s/ - s	/ĕ/ - e	/r/ - r
/p/ - p	/j/ - j	/l/ - l
/h/ - h	/k/ - k, c	/v/ - v
/w/ - w	**/y/ - y**	**/ks/ - x**

Student Notebook

Practice Letters

Students trace previously taught letters while naming letter-keyword-sound. Do as a group saying verbalization, or circulate around the room as students do independently.

You can select a category of letters to find and practice, such as all the sky line letters or all the vowels taught thus far.

Unit 1 | Week 11

Day 4

Daily Plan — DAY 4

Student Learning Plan
- Drill Sounds/Warm-Up
- Word Play
- Sky Write/Letter Formation
- Echo/Letter Formation

Teacher Materials
- Echo and/or Baby Echo
- Large Sound Cards
- Standard Sound Cards
- Large Writing Grid
- Letter Formation Guide
- Vowel Extension Poster
- Sentence Frames

Student Materials
- Student Notebook
- Dry Erase Writing Tablet

Drill Sounds/Warm-Up

Do **new** sounds and **vowel** sounds each day. Selectively review 4-5 other consonants.

Large Sound Cards

Practice sounds with the Large Sound Cards. Model these, saying the letter-keyword-sound and have the students echo.

Standard Sound Cards

Next, point to the Standard Sound Cards (in card display) with the Baby Echo pointer. You say the letter-keyword-sound and hold up Baby Echo to have the students repeat. Discuss vowels and consonants as you select letters.

Vowel Extension

Model extending the vowel sounds (example: a-/ă/...apple-/ă/). Have a student come trace the line for each of the vowels.

Word Play

Teacher Materials
- Sentence Frames
- Baby Echo

WORD AWARENESS

The students will again get you the frames needed so that you can write the sentence. Now they will need to get the question mark or period to complete the sentences. This is just the beginning of understanding. Do not expect the students to easily do this. Provide lots of guidance and cue them by over-emphasizing questions with your voice.

Display Sentence Frames in a Column

Display the word and punctuation frames in a column rather than across the board. Tell the students that you are going to have them help you get the Sentence Frames you need to write your sentence.

Say

> Mike and Amanda have freckles.

As you place the frames, discuss your selection. Tell them that you need the tall frame first because every sentence must start with a capital letter. Tell them you need the tall frame for the name because all names begin with a capital letter. Tell them you need a small punctuation frame because this is a sentence which tells us something. It needs a period.

| Mike | and | Amanda | have | freckles | . |

Unit 1 | Week 11

Day 4

Write the words on the frames and read it again, pointing to each word. Have students echo.

Erase and put the frames back in a column and ask for a student volunteer. Give them a sentence.

> Do you like gum?

Ask a student to put the pieces in order for you to write the sentence. Remind the student,

> Don't forget which one you need to begin the sentence.

> What do you need at the end?

Say the sentence as the student places the frames. Write the sentence and ask the students if the frames are correctly placed.

| Do | you | like | gum | ? |

Echo read the sentence.

Remember to quickly weave vocabulary discussion when doing Learning Activities. For example, you can discuss apples as a fruit and brainstorm other fruit, to change the sentence.

Example Sentences

Where is the ball?

Juan has an apple.

Can we watch TV?

Sky Write/Letter Formation

Review **y** and **x** formation, linking formation with letter name, keyword and sound.

Follow activity procedure and have students sky write letters.

Emphasize that these letters are plane line slide, so they begin on the plane line.

Select 1-2 review letters and sky write them, pointing out where they start on the Letter Formation Poster K·1.

Echo/Letter Formation

Remind students of proper pencil grip and sitting position, and give them their Dry Erase Writing Tablets.

Sounds appear between //. Dictate **new** sounds and a selection of previously taught sounds. You select and say the sound. Students echo the sound and say the letter.

Next have a student come up to the classroom board to make the letter on the Large Writing Grid. Direct the student with the letter formation verbalization.

Then have all students write the answer on their Dry Erase Writing Tablets as you direct them with the letter formation verbalization. Circulate to reinforce pencil grip and assist students, as needed.

Sounds

/t/ - t	/b/ - b	/f/ - f
/n/ - n	/m/ - m	/ĭ/ - i
/ŭ/ - u	/c/ - c	/ŏ/ - o
/ā/ - a	/g/ - g	/d/ - d
/s/ - s	/ĕ/ - e	/r/ - r
/p/ - p	/j/ - j	/l/ - l
/h/ - h	/k/ - k, c	/v/ - v
/w/ - w	**/y/ - y**	/ks/ - x

Unit 1 | Week 11

Day 5

Daily Plan — DAY 5

Student Learning Plan
- Drill Sounds/Warm-Up
- Storytime
- Echo/Find Letters

Teacher Materials
- Echo and/or Baby Echo
- Large Sound Cards
- Standard Sound Cards
- Vowel Extension Poster
- Echo Story Illustrations on large chart paper
- Scooped story on large chart paper

Student Materials
- Student Notebook
- Fundations® Letter Board & Tiles

Drill Sounds/Warm-Up

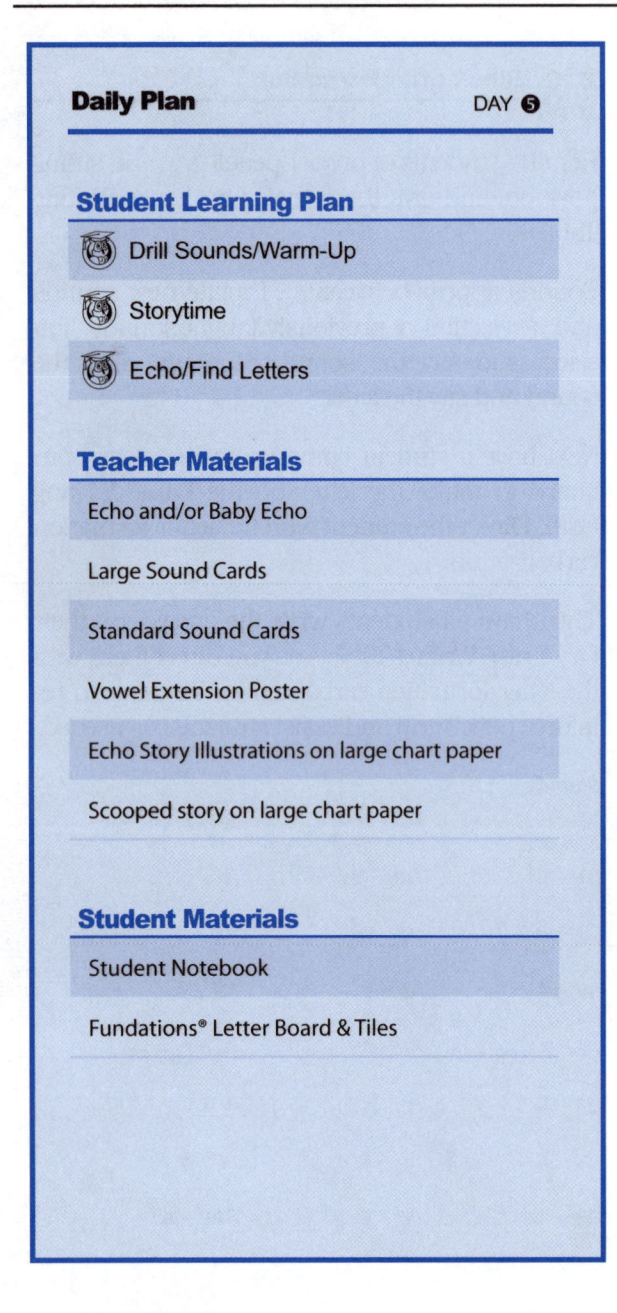

Do **new** sounds and **vowel** sounds each day. Selectively review 4-5 other consonants.

Large Sound Cards

Practice sounds with the Large Sound Cards. Model these, saying the letter-keyword-sound and have the students echo.

Standard Sound Cards

Next, point to the Standard Sound Cards (in card display) with the Baby Echo pointer. You say the letter-keyword-sound and hold up Baby Echo to have the students repeat. Discuss vowels and consonants as you select letters.

Vowel Extension

Model extending the vowel sounds (example: a-/ă/...apple-/ă/). Have a student come trace the line for each of the vowels.

Storytime

Teacher Materials
- Echo Story Illustrations on large chart paper (from Story III)
- Scooped story on large chart paper or projected to class

BABY ECHO FLIES IV

This week, use your pictures on the chart paper from "Baby Echo Flies III" (Week 10, Day 5). Have the students retell the story.

Use the Baby Echo pointer to read the story one sentence at a time and have the students echo. Be sure to scoop and read sentences in phrases.

Next, use both your pictures and the phrased story together. Look at a picture and then read the corresponding words on the phrased story chart.

Lastly, reread a sentence and ask a student to come find one of the key words in that sentence and circle it. Do several words such as: **branch**, **wings**, **happy**, **fly**, **mother**

tip

The scooped story is provided on the PLC.

Unit 1 | Week 11

Day 5

BABY ECHO FLIES IV

Baby Echo sat on a branch,

snuggled in the shelter of his mother's wings.

It was warm and safe there.

Baby Echo was happy.

Then Echo looked down at Baby Echo and said,

"It is time for you to fly."

Baby Echo snuggled closer to his mother

and said, "But I don't know how to fly!"

Echo said, "Watch me, I will teach you,"

and she flapped her wings.

Baby Echo was brave. He followed his mother

and landed next to her.

Echo/Find Letters

Students match Magnetic Letter Tiles to the letter(s) on their Letter Boards. Start with tiles off the board. Dictate sounds. Students echo sound and match the tiles. Include previous sounds and new sounds. After all sounds are matched, dictate 2-3 sounds and have students repeat the sound and point to the corresponding letter.

Sounds

/t/ - t	/b/ - b	/f/ - f
/n/ - n	/m/ - m	/ĭ/ - i
/ŭ/ - u	/c/ - c	/ŏ/ - o
/ă/ - a	/g/ - g	/d/ - d
/s/ - s	/ĕ/ - e	/r/ - r
/p/ - p	/j/ - j	/l/ - l
/h/ - h	/k/ - k, c	/v/ - v
/w/ - w	/y/ - y	/ks/ - x

tip

Be sure to write it so that you can scoop phrases. Use a different color marker to scoop the sentence into phrases.

Unit 1 | Week 12

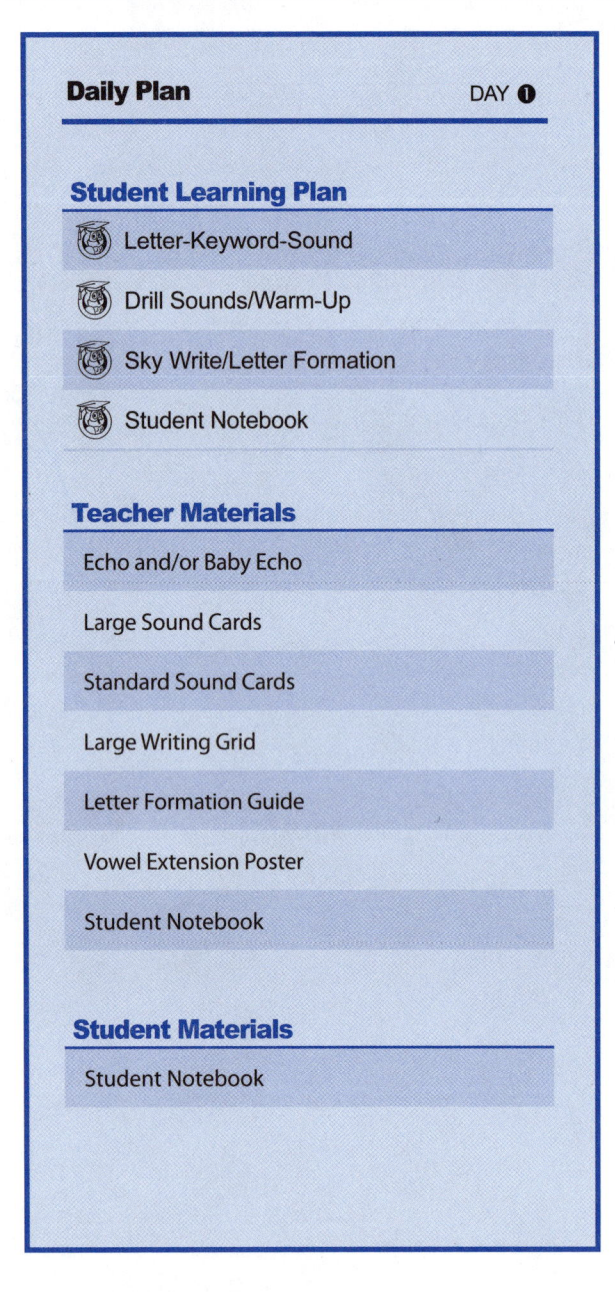

Day 1

Daily Plan — DAY 1

Student Learning Plan
- Letter-Keyword-Sound
- Drill Sounds/Warm-Up
- Sky Write/Letter Formation
- Student Notebook

Teacher Materials
- Echo and/or Baby Echo
- Large Sound Cards
- Standard Sound Cards
- Large Writing Grid
- Letter Formation Guide
- Vowel Extension Poster
- Student Notebook

Student Materials
- Student Notebook

Letter-Keyword-Sound

Introduce Letter-Keyword-Sound with Large and Standard Sound Cards. Be sure to follow procedure. First teach with Large Sound Card. Have students echo letter-keyword-sound. Then repeat with Standard Sound Card.

z - z - zebra - /z/

qu - qu - queen - /kw/

We call **q** the "buddy letter" because it will never ever go anywhere without his best buddy, **u**. Tell the students that **u** does not count as a vowel when it is with the letter **q**. It just sits there to keep **q** company.

Note
As a new letter is taught, its Standard Sound Card is added to your card display to be drilled at each lesson.

Support for Spanish Speaking ELs: In the Americas, **z** is pronounced /s/ by Spanish speakers. Be sure to reinforce the /z/ sound as needed.

Drill Sounds/Warm-Up

Do **new** sounds and **vowel** sounds each day. Selectively review 4-5 other consonants.

Large Sound Cards

Practice sounds with the Large Sound Cards. Model these, saying the letter-keyword-sound and have the students echo.

Standard Sound Cards

Next, point to the Standard Sound Cards (in card display) with the Baby Echo pointer. You say the letter-keyword-sound and hold up Baby Echo to have the students repeat. Discuss vowels and consonants as you select letters.

Vowel Extension

Model extending the vowel sounds (example: a-/ă/...apple-/ă/). Have a student come trace the line for each of the vowels.

Unit 1 | Week 12

Day 1

Sky Write/Letter Formation

Teach **z** and **q** formation, linking formation with letter name, keyword and sound.

Follow activity procedure and have students sky write letters.

The letter **z** is a plane line slide letter. The letter **q** is a plane line round letter.

Letter Formation for z

Use the following verbalization to direct students in proper letter formation.

Say

> z is a plane line slide letter, but it doesn't slide right away.
>
> Where does it start? (On the plane line).
>
> Before it slides, the z goes on the plane line.

1. Point to the plane line.
2. Go on the plane line.
3. Slide back to the grass line.
4. Then go on the grass line.
5. Say z - zebra - /z/, have students repeat.

Letter Formation for q

Use the following verbalization to direct students in proper letter formation.

Say

> q is a plane line round letter.
>
> It starts on the (plane line).
>
> Remember that q is the buddy letter so in the end it wants to point up to its "buddy," u.

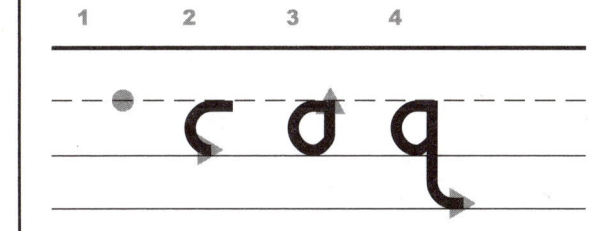

1. Point to the plane line.
2. Trace back and go down to the grass line around, back to the plane line.
3. Trace back down to the worm line,
4. and point up to his "buddy," u.
5. Say qu - queen - /kw/, have students repeat.

tip
Even though you are practicing the q letter formation, students know that q never likes to go anywhere without its buddy u. So, you can have them also add the letter u.

Student Notebook

Direct the students to find the newly introduced letters.

Use the verbalization for the letter formation to direct the students while they trace it with their finger. Do it with them to model. Have them say letter-keyword-sound.

After students trace following verbalizations, they can then color the keyword picture for the letter **z**.

Unit 1 | Week 12

Day 2

Daily Plan — DAY 2

Student Learning Plan
- Drill Sounds/Warm-Up
- Sky Write/Letter Formation
- Student Notebook
- Echo/Letter Formation

Teacher Materials
- Echo and/or Baby Echo
- Large Sound Cards
- Standard Sound Cards
- Large Writing Grid
- Letter Formation Guide
- Vowel Extension Poster
- Student Notebook

Student Materials
- Student Notebook
- Dry Erase Writing Tablet

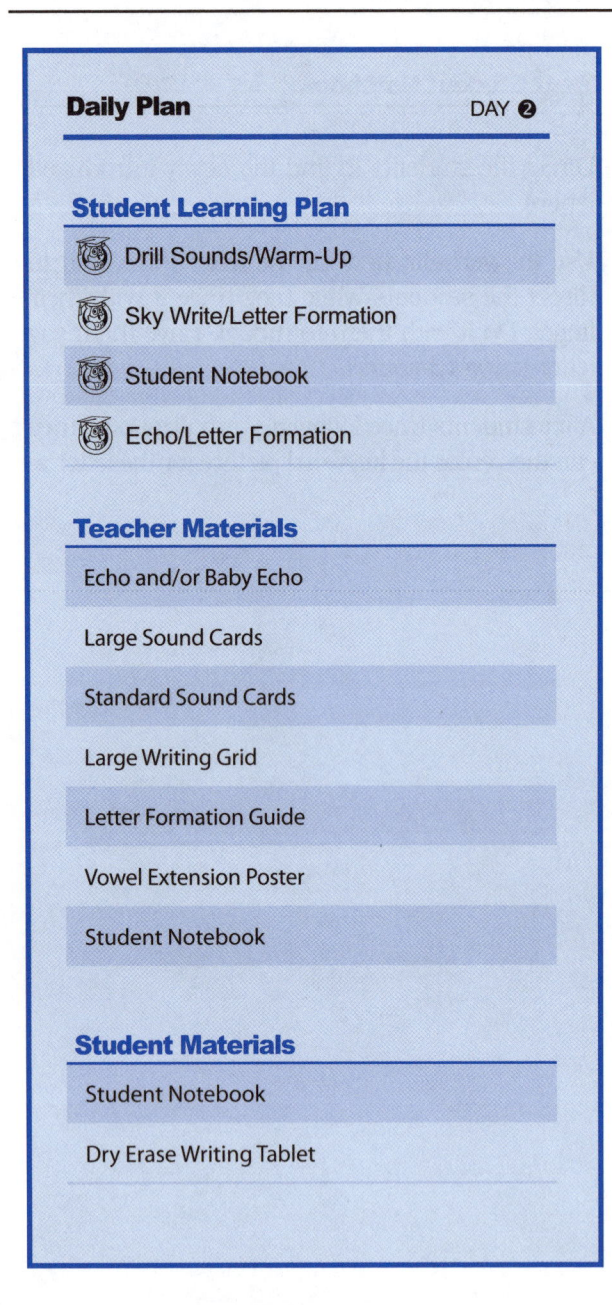

Drill Sounds/Warm-Up

Do **new** sounds and **vowel** sounds each day. Selectively review 4-5 other consonants.

Large Sound Cards

Practice sounds with the Large Sound Cards. Model these, saying the letter-keyword-sound and have the students echo.

Standard Sound Cards

Next, point to the Standard Sound Cards (in card display) with the Baby Echo pointer. You say the letter-keyword-sound and hold up Baby Echo to have the students repeat. Discuss vowels and consonants as you select letters.

Vowel Extension

Model extending the vowel sounds (example: **a-/ă/...apple-/ă/**). Have a student come trace the line for each of the vowels.

Sky Write/Letter Formation

Review **z** and **q** formation, linking formation with letter name, keyword and sound.

Follow activity procedure and have students sky write letters.

The letter **z** is a plane line slide letter. The letter **q** is a plane line round letter.

Select 1-2 review letters and sky write them, pointing out where they start on the Letter Formation Poster K·1.

176 FUNDATIONS® LEVEL K

Unit 1 | Week 12

Day 2

Student Notebook

Trace and say the letter-keyword-sound for all the previous letters introduced.

Direct the students to find the newly introduced letters.

Use the verbalization for the letter formation to direct the students while they trace it with their finger. Do it with them to model. Have them say letter-keyword-sound.

After students trace following verbalizations, they can then color the keyword picture for the letters **qu**.

Echo/Letter Formation

Remind students of proper pencil grip and sitting position, and give them their Dry Erase Writing Tablets.

Sounds appear between / /. Dictate **new** sounds and a selection of previously taught sounds. You select and say the sound. Students echo the sound and say the letter.

Next have a student come up to the classroom board to make the letter on the Large Writing Grid. Direct the student with the letter formation verbalization.

Then have all students write the answer on their Dry Erase Writing Tablets as you direct them with the letter formation verbalization. Circulate to reinforce pencil grip and assist students, as needed.

Sounds

/t/ - t	/b/ - b	/f/ - f
/n/ - n	/m/ - m	/ĭ/ - i
/ŭ/ - u	/c/ - c	/ŏ/ - o
/ă/ - a	/g/ - g	/d/ - d
/s/ - s	/ĕ/ - e	/r/ - r
/p/ - p	/j/ - j	/l/ - l
/h/ - h	/k/ - k, c	/v/ - v
/w/ - w	/y/ - y	/ks/ - x
/z/ - z	/kw/ - qu	

Unit 1 | Week 12

Day 3

Daily Plan — DAY 3

Student Learning Plan
- Drill Sounds/Warm-Up
- Make It Fun
- Echo/Find Letters
- Student Notebook

Teacher Materials
- Echo and/or Baby Echo
- Large Sound Cards
- Standard Sound Cards
- Large Writing Grid
- Vowel Extension Poster
- Student Notebook

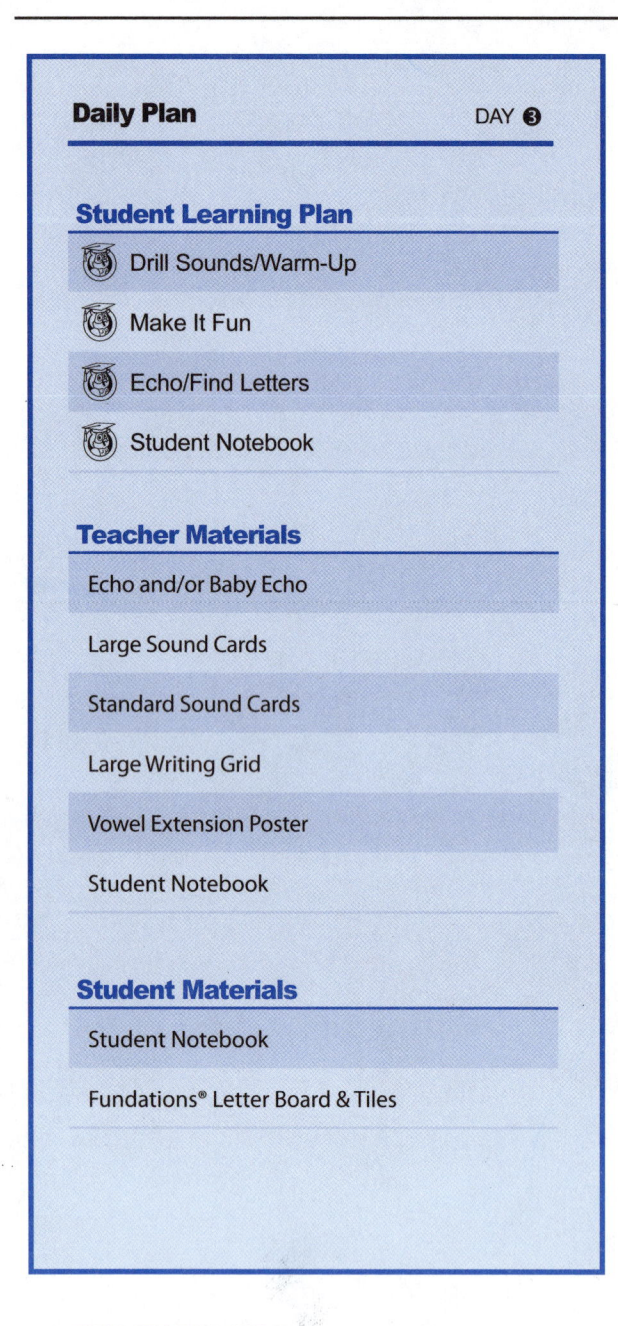

Student Materials
- Student Notebook
- Fundations® Letter Board & Tiles

Drill Sounds/Warm-Up

Do **new** sounds and **vowel** sounds each day. Selectively review 4-5 other consonants.

Large Sound Cards
Practice sounds with the Large Sound Cards. Model these, saying the letter-keyword-sound and have the students echo.

Standard Sound Cards
Next, point to the Standard Sound Cards (in card display) with the Baby Echo pointer. You say the letter-keyword-sound and hold up Baby Echo to have the students repeat. Discuss vowels and consonants as you select letters.

Vowel Extension
Model extending the vowel sounds (example: **a-/ă/...apple-/ă/**). Have a student come trace the line for each of the vowels.

Make It Fun

GUESS THE LETTER

Teacher Materials
- Large Writing Grid

Have a student come up to the front of the room. Whisper a letter name to him/her. Next have the student form the letter with their finger (not write it) on the Large Writing Grid.

The other students need to watch and decide which letter was formed. When they guess, they should say the letter-keyword-sound (**z-zebra-/z/**, etc). Whoever guesses gets to do the next one.

Unit 1 | Week 12

Day 3

Echo/Find Letters

Students match Magnetic Letter Tiles to the letter(s) on their Letter Boards. Distribute Letter Boards and the Letter Tiles **z** and **q** to each student. Start with tiles on the blank side of the board. Dictate sounds. Students echo sound and match the tiles. Include previous sounds and new sounds. After all sounds are matched, dictate 2-3 sounds and have students repeat the sound and point to the corresponding letter.

Sounds

/t/ - t	/b/ - b	/f/ - f
/n/ - n	/m/ - m	/ĭ/ - i
/ŭ/ - u	/c/ - c	/ŏ/ - o
/ă/ - a	/g/ - g	/d/ - d
/s/ - s	/ĕ/ - e	/r/ - r
/p/ - p	/j/ - j	/l/ - l
/h/ - h	/k/ - k, c	/v/ - v
/w/ - w	/y/ - y	/ks/ - x
/z/ - z	/kw/ - qu	

Student Notebook

Practice Letters

Students trace previously taught letters while naming letter-keyword-sound. Do as a group saying verbalization, or circulate around the room as students do independently.

You can select a category of letters to find and practice, such as all the sky line letters or all the vowels taught thus far.

Unit 1 | Week 12

Day 4

Daily Plan — DAY 4

Student Learning Plan
- Drill Sounds/Warm-Up
- Word Play
- Sky Write/Letter Formation
- Echo/Letter Formation

Teacher Materials
- Echo and/or Baby Echo
- Large Sound Cards
- Standard Sound Cards
- Large Writing Grid
- Letter Formation Guide
- Vowel Extension Poster
- Sentence Frames

Student Materials
- Student Notebook
- Dry Erase Writing Tablet

Drill Sounds/Warm-Up

Do **new** sounds and **vowel** sounds each day. Selectively review 4-5 other consonants.

Large Sound Cards

Practice sounds with the Large Sound Cards. Model these, saying the letter-keyword-sound and have the students echo.

Standard Sound Cards

Next, point to the Standard Sound Cards (in card display) with the Baby Echo pointer. You say the letter-keyword-sound and hold up Baby Echo to have the students repeat. Discuss vowels and consonants as you select letters.

Vowel Extension

Model extending the vowel sounds (example: **a-/ă/...apple-/ă/**). Have a student come trace the line for each of the vowels.

Word Play

Teacher Materials
- Sentence Frames
- Baby Echo

WORD AWARENESS

The students will again get you the frames needed so that you can write the sentence. Now they will need to get the question mark or period to complete the sentences. This is just the beginning of understanding. Do not expect the students to easily do this. Provide lots of guidance and cue them by over-emphasizing questions with your voice.

Display Sentence Frames in a Column

Display the word and punctuation frames in a column rather than across the board. Tell the students that you are going to have them help you get the pieces you need to write your sentence.

Demonstrate

Say

Sondra and Shana had fun.

As you place the frames, discuss your selection. Tell them that you need the tall frame first because every sentence must start with a capital letter. Tell them you need the tall frame for the name because all names begin with a capital letter. Tell them you need the square punctuation frame because this is a telling sentence.

Unit 1 | Week 12

Day 4

| Sondra | and | Shana | had | fun | . |

Write the words on the frames and read it again, pointing to each word. Have students echo.

Erase and put the frames back in a column and ask for a student volunteer. Give them a sentence.

Bert and Maria came to school.

Ask a student to put the frames in order for you to write the sentence. Remind the student,

Don't forget which one you need to begin the sentence.

What do you need at the end?

Say the sentence as the student places the frames. Write the sentence and ask the students:

Did (student name) get all the pieces I needed? Does this sentence tell us something or ask us something?

Example Sentences

Eileen has red hair.

Ed and Tom like to sing.

What did you eat for breakfast?

Sky Write/Letter Formation

Review **z** and **q** formation, linking formation with letter name, keyword and sound.

Follow activity procedure and have students sky write letters.

The letter **z** is a plane line slide letter. The letter **q** is a plane line round letter.

Select 1-2 review letters and sky write them, pointing out where they start on the Letter Formation Poster K·1.

Echo/Letter Formation

Remind students of proper pencil grip and sitting position, and give them their Dry Erase Writing Tablets.

Sounds appear between //. Dictate **new** sounds and a selection of previously taught sounds. You select and say the sound. Students echo the sound and say the letter.

Next have a student come up to the classroom board to make the letter on the Large Writing Grid. Direct the student with the letter formation verbalization.

Then have all students write the answer on their Dry Erase Writing Tablets as you direct them with the letter formation verbalization. Circulate to reinforce pencil grip and assist students, as needed.

Sounds

/t/ - t	/b/ - b	/f/ - f
/n/ - n	/m/ - m	/i/ - i
/ŭ/ - u	/c/ - c	/ŏ/ - o
/ă/ - a	/g/ - g	/d/ - d
/s/ - s	/ĕ/ - e	/r/ - r
/p/ - p	/j/ - j	/l/ - l
/h/ - h	/k/ - k, c	/v/ - v
/w/ - w	/y/ - y	/ks/ - x
/z/ - z	**/kw/ - qu**	

Unit 1 | Week 12

Day 5

Daily Plan DAY 5

Student Learning Plan
- Drill Sounds/Warm-Up
- Storytime

Teacher Materials
- Echo and/or Baby Echo
- Large Sound Cards
- Standard Sound Cards
- Vowel Extension Poster
- Large chart paper

Student Materials
- Student Notebook

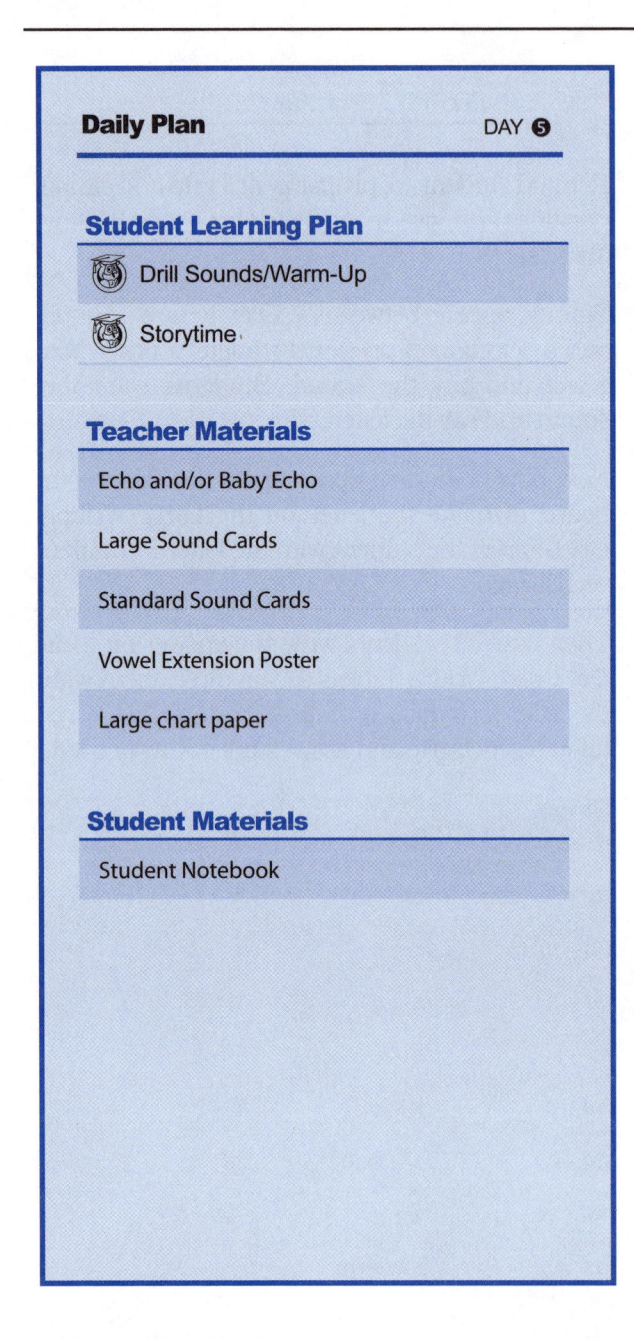

Drill Sounds/Warm-Up

Do **new** sounds and **vowel** sounds each day. Selectively review 4-5 other consonants.

Large Sound Cards
Practice sounds with the Large Sound Cards. Model these, saying the letter-keyword-sound and have the students echo.

Standard Sound Cards
Next, point to the Standard Sound Cards (in card display) with the Baby Echo pointer. You say the letter-keyword-sound and hold up Baby Echo to have the students repeat. Discuss vowels and consonants as you select letters.

Vowel Extension
Model extending the vowel sounds (example: a-/ă/...apple-/ă/). Have a student come trace the line for each of the vowels.

Storytime

Teacher Materials
- Rhyming books
- Large chart paper

Preparation
During Storytime select a rhyming picture book to read to your students. Be sure that the story has no more than 4-5 sentences per page. It should have predictable rhyming patterns. The following list provides some suggestions.

Benfanti, R. (2002). *Hide Clyde*. New York: Little Brown & Co.

Fleming, D. (1991). *In the tall, tall grass*. New York: Holt, Rinehart, & Winston.

Katz, M.J. (1990). *Ten potatoes in a pot*. New York: Harper and Row.

Lewis, K., & Kirk, D. (1999). *Chugga chugga choo choo*. New York: Hyperion Books.

Lewis, K., & Kirk, D. (2002). *My truck is stuck*. New York: Hyperion Books.

Instruct Students
Before reading, look at the front and back cover of the book with your students. Discuss the title, author and illustrator, explaining each of those terms.

Read the book once moving your finger under the words and emphasizing the rhymes. Pause 2-3 times and ask students to predict what will happen.

Unit 1 | Week 12

Day 5

Say

> Now let's do it again but this time you can help me read.

Read the book again, moving your finger under the words. This time, do not say the rhyming words and let the students say it for you. You can also provide the onset **/m/** and have students say the rime **/at/** (for the word **mat**).

Lastly, write the rhyming words from the story on chart paper or the board. Put rhyming words on the same line.

Example

bat   cat   sat

down   clown

Tell the students that these are the words they read in the story. Explain that they rhyme. Read a set of rhyming words with Baby Echo and have the students repeat. Ask them to think of other words that rhyme with each set. Add them to the list and read.

Unit 1

Unit Test

Answer Key

LOWERCASE LETTERS

a - apple - /ă/	r - rat - /r/
z - zebra - /z/	b - bat - /b/
g - game - /g/	j - jug - /j/
k - kite - /k/	e - Ed - /ĕ/
o - octopus - /ŏ/	v - van - /v/

LETTERS & SOUNDS

s	n	i	qu	f
u	h	l	p	m

LETTER FORMATION

t	c	g	n	a
p	e	d	h	f

Note
Allow students to independently reference their Student Notebooks. Count responses checked in their Notebooks as correct, but make a notation that the book was used.

Each student must be assessed individually. This will take approximately 20 minutes per student.

Copy the **Unit Test Recording Form** for each student. Use the student's durable materials, e.g., Dry Erase Writing Tablet, Letter Board and Letter Tiles, as needed.

> Print the Unit Test Recording Form from the PLC.

If a student does not score at least **8 / 10** on any given item, this student will need additional assistance with the assessed skill.

> See the Intervention Guidelines on the PLC.

tip
A Unit Test Tracker is available on Wilson Academy® / Prevention Learning Community, under My Resources. This valuable online resource will allow you to track individual student mastery as well as to evaluate readiness of your class to move on.

For any struggling students, meet with them individually to discuss errors and explain areas that need to be further practiced.

Have Student Identify Lowercase Letters and Give Sounds

Using your Standard Sound Cards, point to letters and have student name each letter. Provide an example, pointing to the letter **c**, say **c-cat-/k/**. Ask, "What is the letter, the keyword and sound?" If student is unable to **name** the letters, have student **find** letters. Say, "Find the letter **a**." Note if student can find letters but not yet name them.

a	r	z	b	g
j	k	e	o	v

Have Student Identify Letters Corresponding to Sounds

Using the student's Letter Board and Tiles, say sound and have student point to corresponding letters. Ask, "What says /s/?"

/s/	/n/	/ĭ/	/kw/	/f/
/ŭ/	/h/	/l/	/p/	/m/

Have Student Form Lowercase Letters

Using the student's Dry Erase Writing Tablet, dictate letters and have student write the lowercase letter. Say, "Write the letter **t**." Hold students accountable for correct letter formation.

t	c	g	n	a
p	e	d	h	f

tip
Be sure to give Unit Test to all students. Use scores for ongoing monitoring and planning for student trouble spots. Remind Students: We all learn by trial and error. If you make a mistake, no problem. There's always tomorrow.

Unit 1

Resources

Drill Sounds/Warm-Up

a - apple - /ă/
b - bat - /b/
c - cat - /k/
d - dog - /d/
e - Ed - /ĕ/
f - fun - /f/
g - game - /g/
h - hat - /h/
i - itch - /ĭ/
j - jug - /j/
k - kite - /k/
l - lamp - /l/
m - man - /m/
n - nut - /n/
o - octopus - /ŏ/
p - pan - /p/
qu - queen - /kw/
r - rat - /r/
s - snake - /s/
t - top - /t/
u - up - /ŭ/
v - van - /v/
w - wind - /w/
x - fox - /ks/
y - yellow - /y/
z - zebra - /z/

Echo Sounds

Sounds appear between //. You say the sound. Students echo the sound and say the letter. Depending on the activity, students then either find or make the letter corresponding to that sound.

CONSONANTS

/b/ - b	/d/ - d	/f/ - f
/g/ - g	/h/ - h	/j/ - j
/k/ - c, k	/l/ - l	/m/ - m
/n/ - n	/p/ - p	/kw/ - qu
/r/ - r	/s/ - s	/t/ - t
/v/ - v	/w/ - w	/ks/ - x
/y/ - y	/z/ - z	

VOWELS

/ă/ - a	/ĕ/ - e	/ĭ/ - i
/ŏ/ - o	/ŭ/ - u	

Unit 2 Level K

In a Nutshell

NEW CONCEPTS

- Phonemic awareness skills: blending, segmenting, and manipulation of sounds
- Blending and reading three-sound short vowel words
- Story prediction
- Alphabetical Order
- Uppercase letter formation

SAMPLE WORDS

map   sad   rat

PLANNED TIME IN UNIT

4 WEEKS

Note
Use Unit Test scores and daily classroom work to determine students' mastery. Extend the time in this Unit if needed.

Introduction

In Unit 2, you will move from beginning phoneme awareness to more advanced phoneme awareness. You will continue to tune the students into the separate sounds (or phonemes) in a word. Previously, you did this by having them identify the first or last sound in a word. Now you will have them also tune into the middle sound, and blend, segment and manipulate the sounds.

In this Unit, you will teach students how to blend and read three-sound short vowel words. These words are often called CVC words.

In Weeks 1 and 2, you will see that the CVC words begin with the consonants **f**, **l**, **m**, **n**, **r** and **s**. These consonants have sounds that can be 'held' into the vowel sound and thus are easier to blend.

In Unit 2, you will also teach students how to form capital or uppercase letters A-Z. For many students, this will be a review. The capital letters in Fundations® use simplified strokes. These will be taught in alphabetical order, since the sounds have already been linked to the letters. You will reinforce this link by also saying the letter-keyword-sound after you and your students form the letter. Remember, gross motor memory helps to imbed the letter's strokes into memory and make it automatic. Also, note that the Student Notebook presents the capital letters in alphabetical order.

Lastly, students will practice alphabetical order with their Fundations Letter Board and Tiles.

Differentiation

The uppercase letter formations are presented **very** quickly. This may be challenging for students with handwriting difficulty. They will need much more practice, over time, to master these formations.

For students who are having difficulty blending, give them additional practice with the easier initial consonants. Teach them to hold onto the consonant into the vowel sound /m..../ /a..../ /t/. Do this as you slide your finger under the cards to read the words.

For advanced students, have them tap some words, but you can also call upon them to read a word without tapping it. Be sure to challenge their understanding of the words that they decode by thinking of a word that means the opposite or another word that is similar, discussing shades of meanings.

Reminder!

Correct position and pencil grip are essential. You can refer to these pictures to guide students. You will find this page, called 1-2-3 Right / Let's Write on the PLC.

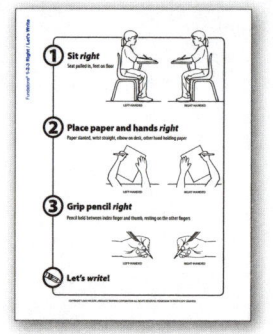

Unit 2

Arrange the sound card display in the following manner:

a	b	c	d	e	f
g	h	i	j	k	l
m	n	o	p	qu	r	s
t	u	v	w	x	y	z

Getting Ready

MATERIAL PREPARATIONS

Teacher Materials
See Storytime. You will need ABC books for this activity.

Print Lesson Plans from the PLC. See Unit Resources at the end of this Unit.

HOME SUPPORT

Copy and send home the Unit 2 Letter and Activity Packet.

STUDY THE LEARNING ACTIVITIES

Review the following activities:

- Drill Sounds/Warm-Up
- Alphabetical Order
- Word Play

Review the Learning Activity and Unit videos on the PLC.

Unit 2

Student Learning Plan

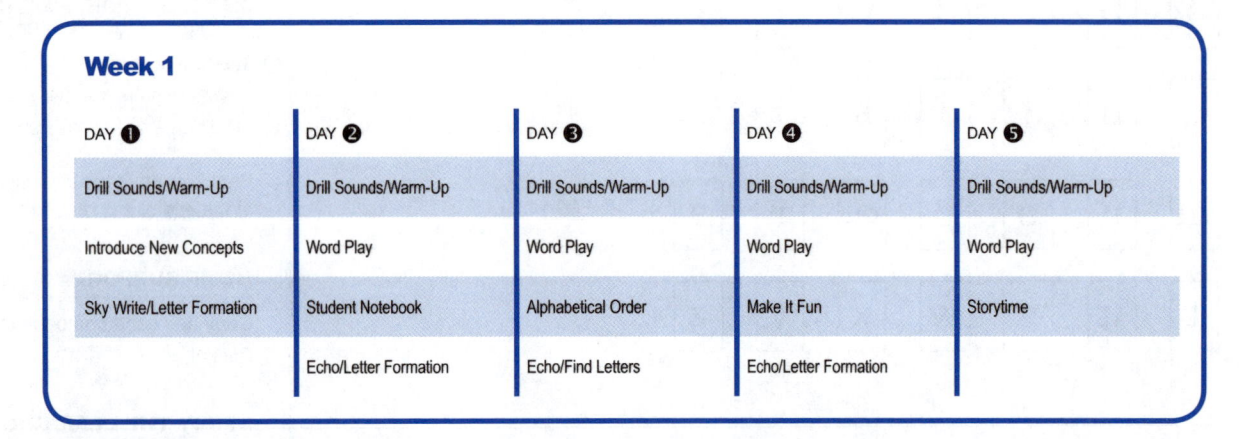

Week 1

DAY 1	DAY 2	DAY 3	DAY 4	DAY 5
Drill Sounds/Warm-Up	Drill Sounds/Warm-Up	Drill Sounds/Warm-Up	Drill Sounds/Warm-Up	Drill Sounds/Warm-Up
Introduce New Concepts	Word Play	Word Play	Word Play	Word Play
Sky Write/Letter Formation	Student Notebook	Alphabetical Order	Make It Fun	Storytime
	Echo/Letter Formation	Echo/Find Letters	Echo/Letter Formation	

Weeks 2 • 3

DAY 1	DAY 2	DAY 3	DAY 4	DAY 5
Drill Sounds/Warm-Up	Drill Sounds/Warm-Up	Drill Sounds/Warm-Up	Drill Sounds/Warm-Up	Drill Sounds/Warm-Up
Word Play	Word Play	Word Play	Make It Fun	Storytime
Sky Write/Letter Formation	Sky Write/Letter Formation	Sky Write/Letter Formation	Sky Write/Letter Formation	Alphabetical Order
Student Notebook	Student Notebook	Student Notebook	Student Notebook	Echo/Find Letters
Echo/Letter Formation	Echo/Letter Formation	Echo/Letter Formation	Echo/Letter Formation	

Unit 2

Student Learning Plan

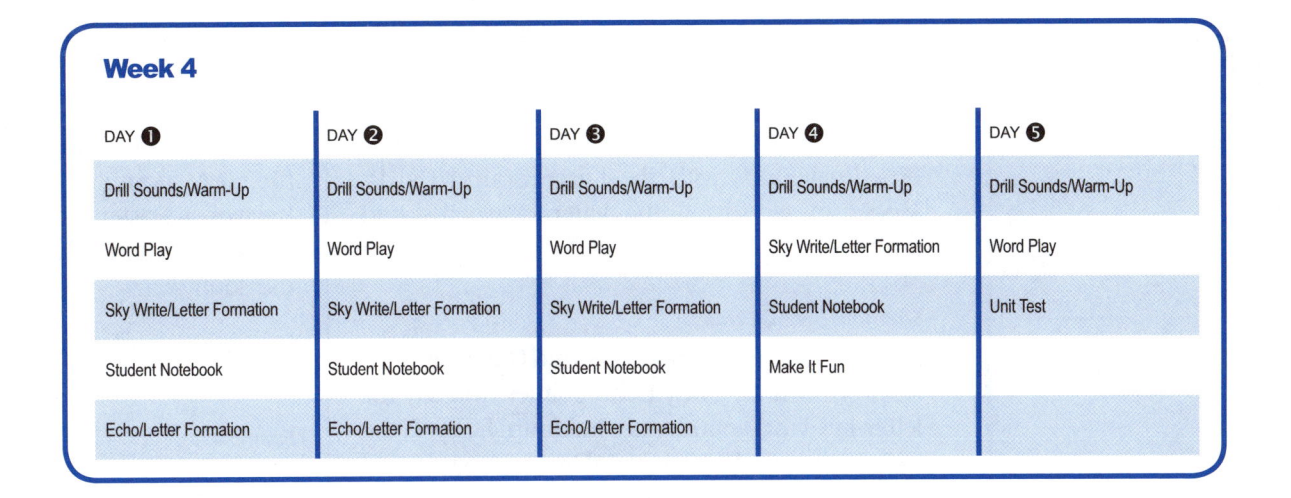

Week 4

DAY 1	DAY 2	DAY 3	DAY 4	DAY 5
Drill Sounds/Warm-Up	Drill Sounds/Warm-Up	Drill Sounds/Warm-Up	Drill Sounds/Warm-Up	Drill Sounds/Warm-Up
Word Play	Word Play	Word Play	Sky Write/Letter Formation	Word Play
Sky Write/Letter Formation	Sky Write/Letter Formation	Sky Write/Letter Formation	Student Notebook	Unit Test
Student Notebook	Student Notebook	Student Notebook	Make It Fun	
Echo/Letter Formation	Echo/Letter Formation	Echo/Letter Formation		

Unit 2 | Week 1

Day 1

Daily Plan — DAY 1

Student Learning Plan
- Drill Sounds/Warm-Up
- Introduce New Concepts
- Sky Write/Letter Formation

Teacher Materials
- Echo and/or Baby Echo
- Large Sound Cards
- Standard Sound Cards
- Large Writing Grid
- Letter Formation Guide

Student Materials
- Student Notebook

Drill Sounds/Warm-Up

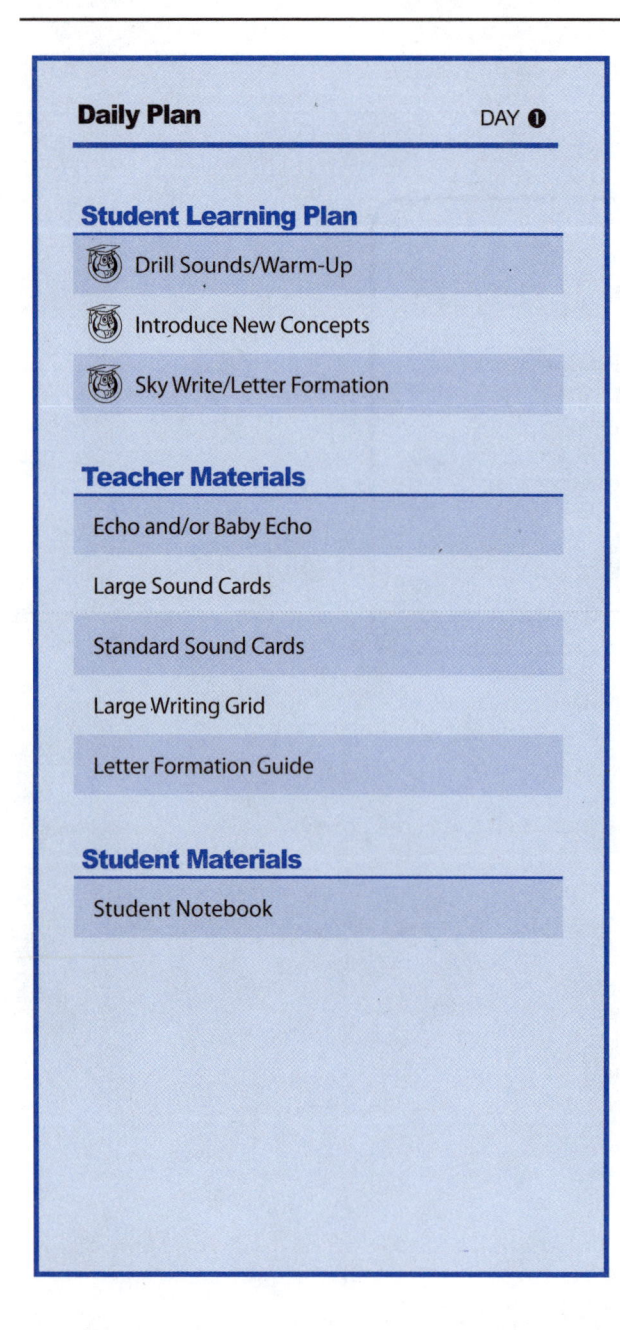

Do any new or challenging sounds and vowel sounds each day. Selectively review 4-5 other consonants.

Large Sound Cards
Practice sounds with the Large Sound Cards. Model these, saying the letter-keyword-sound and have the students echo.

Standard Sound Cards
Next, point to the Standard Sound Cards (in card display) with the Baby Echo pointer. You say the letter-keyword-sound and hold up Baby Echo to have the students repeat. Discuss vowels and consonants as you select letters.

Vowel Extension
Model extending the vowel sounds (example: a-/ă/...apple-/ă/). Have a student come trace the line for each of the vowels.

Introduce New Concepts

TEACH TAPPING TO READ WORDS

Teach students how to blend words with three sounds.

If students have trouble with any sound, point to the corresponding Large Sound Card (or Basic Keywords Poster) and ask them to say the letter-keyword-sound. Then tap out the word, using the sounds.

Use your Standard Sound Card display to make the words.

Example

| m | a | t |

Say

Say each sound separately, then blend the sounds together.

Tap a finger to your thumb over each sound card while saying the sound.

Tap your index finger to thumb while saying /m/, middle finger to thumb while saying /a/ and ring finger to thumb while saying /t/.

Then blend the sounds and say the word as you drag your thumb across your fingers beginning with the index finger.

190 FUNDATIONS® LEVEL K

© 2002, 2012 WILSON LANGUAGE TRAINING CORPORATION

Unit 2 | Week 1

Day 1

Say /m/ and tap index finger to thumb.

Say /a/ and tap middle finger to thumb.

Say /t/ and tap ring finger to thumb.

Have the students do this. Explain that they can say sounds while tapping and blending them together to make words.

Continue with other word examples. Each time, make the words with the Standard Sound Cards. Tap and blend sounds with your students.

Word Resource

mat   map   mad

sad   sat   sap

t i p

Make sure to clip sounds to avoid adding a schwa: /t/ not /tuh/

© 2002, 2012 WILSON LANGUAGE TRAINING CORPORATION

Sky Write/Letter Formation

Choose 5-6 letters to review. You can select a student to trace the letter on the Large Writing Grid at the front of the class. The other students can stand and sky write as you verbalize the directions.

whiteboards or air write

Do: capitals A, B

TEACHER'S MANUAL 191

Unit 2 | Week 1

Day 2

Daily Plan — DAY 2

Student Learning Plan
- Drill Sounds/Warm-Up
- Word Play
- Student Notebook
- Echo/Letter Formation

Teacher Materials
- Echo and/or Baby Echo
- Large Sound Cards
- Standard Sound Cards
- Large Writing Grid
- Letter Formation Guide
- Student Notebook

Student Materials
- Student Notebook
- Dry Erase Writing Tablet

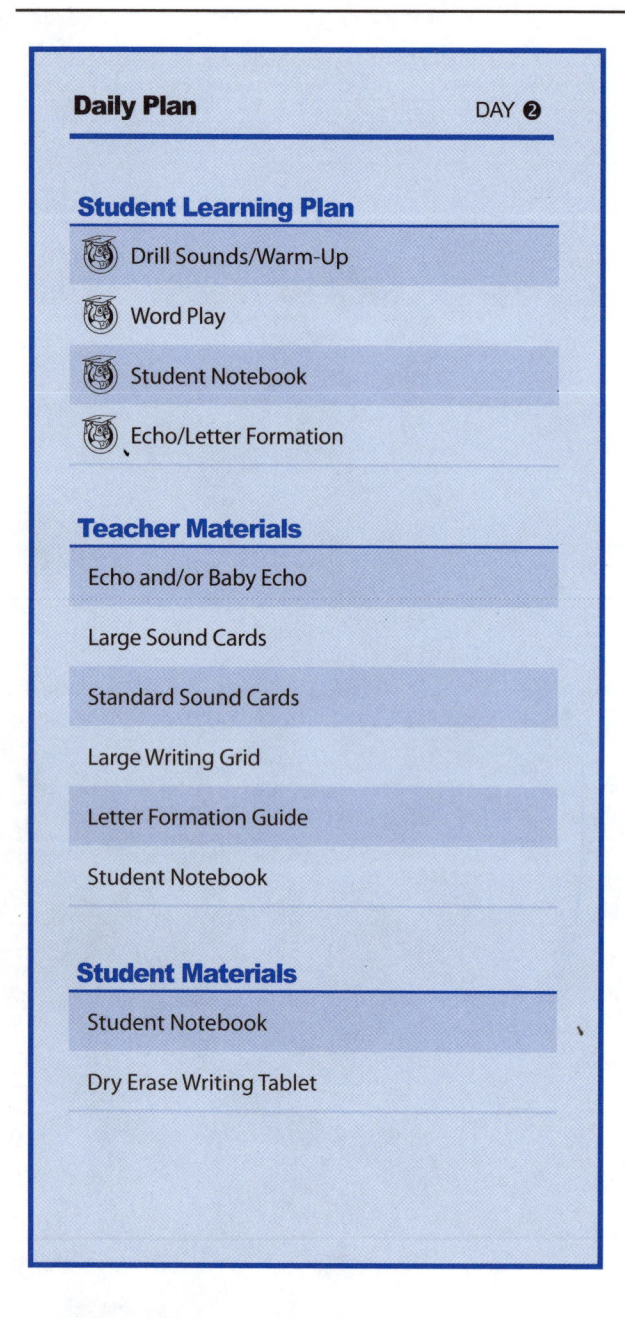

Drill Sounds/Warm-Up

Do any new or challenging sounds and vowel sounds each day. Selectively review 4-5 other consonants.

Large Sound Cards

Practice sounds with the Large Sound Cards. Model these, saying the letter-keyword-sound and have the students echo.

Standard Sound Cards

Next, point to the Standard Sound Cards (in card display) with the Baby Echo pointer. You say the letter-keyword-sound and hold up Baby Echo to have students repeat. You can have a student be the drill leader for some of the sounds.

Vowel Extension

Model extending the vowel sounds (example: a-/ă/...apple-/ă/). Have a student come trace the line for each of the vowels.

Word Play

MAKE WORDS FOR DECODING

Use your Standard Sound Card display to make Unit words. (See below.)

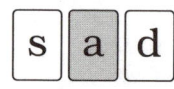

| s | a | d |

Make each word then say and tap each sound. Have students tap with you. Then blend the sounds as you drag your thumb across your fingers. Say the word.

Next, point under each card as you say each sound, then drag your finger under all three cards as you and the students blend the sounds to read the word.

Word Resources

sad   sat   sap   sip   sit

mop   map   mad   mud

Unit 2 | Week 1

Day 2

Student Notebook

PRACTICE

Also, have students find the letter-keyword Fun Match page. Explain that they have to draw a line to match the letter with its keyword picture. After students complete the matches, select someone to say the letter-keyword-sound and have students check their answers.

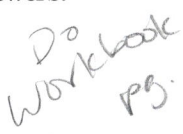

Do workbook pg.

Echo/Letter Formation

Remind students of proper pencil grip and sitting position, and give them their Dry Erase Writing Tablets.

Dictate 5-6 previously taught sounds. You select and say the sound. Students echo the sound and say the letter.

Next have a student come up to the classroom board to make the letter on the Large Writing Grid.

Then have all students write the answer on their Dry Erase Writing Tablet as you direct them with the letter formation verbalization.

(See Unit Resources.)

Do capitals CD

Unit 2 | Week 1

Day 3

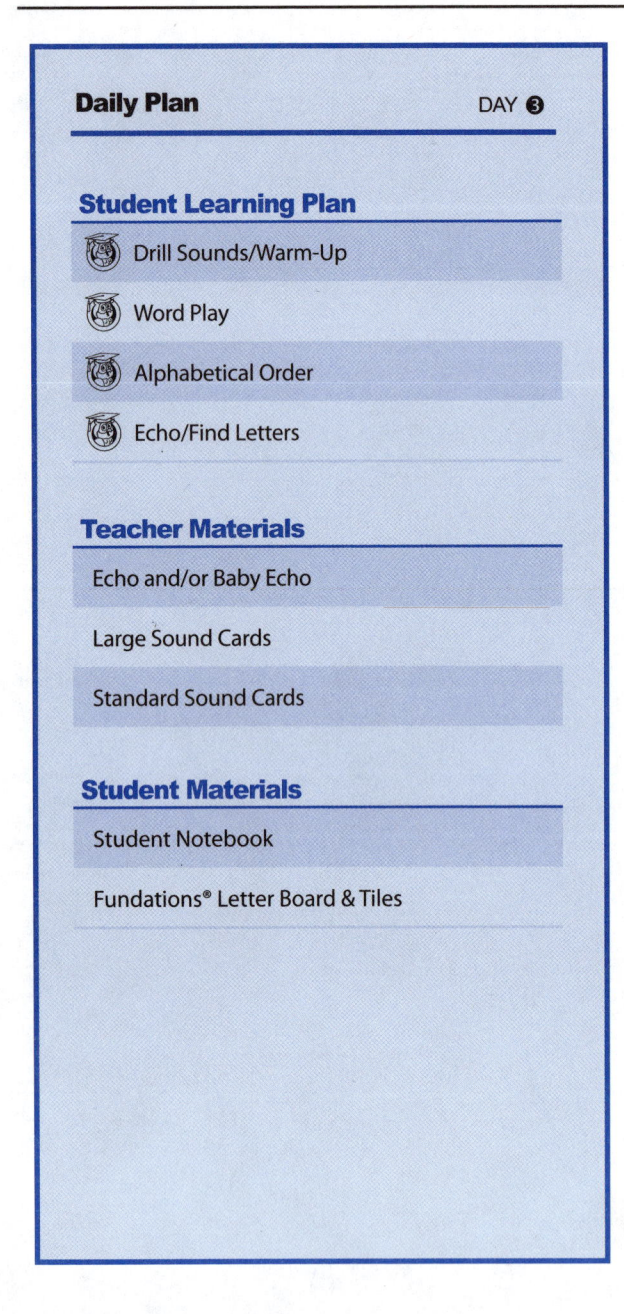

Daily Plan — DAY 3

Student Learning Plan
- Drill Sounds/Warm-Up
- Word Play
- Alphabetical Order
- Echo/Find Letters

Teacher Materials
- Echo and/or Baby Echo
- Large Sound Cards
- Standard Sound Cards

Student Materials
- Student Notebook
- Fundations® Letter Board & Tiles

Drill Sounds/Warm-Up

Do any new or challenging sounds and vowel sounds each day. Selectively review 4-5 other consonants.

Large Sound Cards
Practice sounds with the Large Sound Cards. Model these, saying the letter-keyword-sound and have the students echo.

Standard Sound Cards
Next, point to the Standard Sound Cards (in card display) with the Baby Echo pointer. You say the letter-keyword-sound and hold up Baby Echo to have students repeat. You can have a student be the drill leader for some of the sounds.

tip: You can have a student drill leader do the Standard Sound Cards. Have them do categories such as all vowels, or the plane line slide letters.

Word Play

MAKE WORDS FOR DECODING

Use your Standard Sound Card display to make Unit words. (See below.)

Make each word then say and tap each sound. Have students tap with you. Then blend the sounds as you drag your thumb across your fingers. Say the word.

Next, point under each card as you say each sound, then drag your finger under all three cards as you and the students blend the sounds to read the word.

Word Resources

rat	rap	rag
nap	nip	
fit	fig	fog

194 FUNDATIONS® LEVEL K

Unit 2 | Week 1

Day 3

Alphabetical Order

Students start with their Magnetic Letter Tiles randomly placed on the blank side of their Letter Boards. Have them sequentially match Letter Tiles on the letter squares.

After students have the tiles placed, chorally say the alphabet. Students should point to each letter as they say its name.

Echo/Find Letters

Echo/Find Letters

This activity now begins with the Letter Tiles already matched to the letter squares. Say a sound. Have students echo and point to the letter(s) on their Magnetic Letter Boards.

Ask

What says /___/? (___)

(See Echo Sounds in Unit Resources for expected student responses.)

Have students name the letter(s). Then you can have one student find the Standard Sound Card(s) as you dictate sounds. Do vowels and 3-5 other sounds.

Do capitals E, F

Unit 2 | Week 1

Day 4

Daily Plan — DAY 4

Student Learning Plan
- Drill Sounds/Warm-Up
- Word Play
- Make It Fun
- Echo/Letter Formation

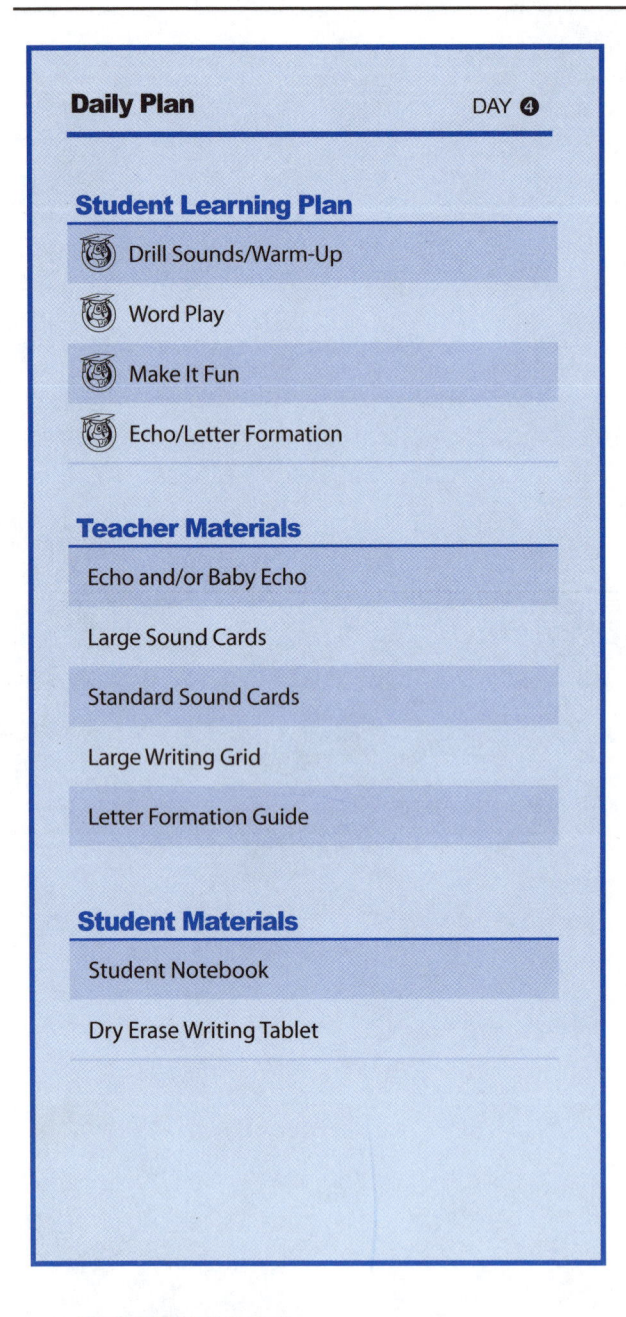

Teacher Materials
- Echo and/or Baby Echo
- Large Sound Cards
- Standard Sound Cards
- Large Writing Grid
- Letter Formation Guide

Student Materials
- Student Notebook
- Dry Erase Writing Tablet

Drill Sounds/Warm-Up

Do any new or challenging sounds and vowel sounds each day. Selectively review 4-5 other consonants.

Large Sound Cards
Practice sounds with the Large Sound Cards. Model these, saying the letter-keyword-sound and have the students echo.

Standard Sound Cards
Next, point to the Standard Sound Cards (in card display) with the Baby Echo pointer. You say the letter-keyword-sound and hold up Baby Echo to have students repeat. You can have a student be the drill leader for some of the sounds.

Word Play

MAKE WORDS FOR DECODING
Use your Standard Sound Card display to make Unit words. (See below.)

Make each word then say and tap each sound. Have students tap with you. Then blend the sounds as you drag your thumb across your fingers. Say the word.

Next, point under each card as you say each sound, then drag your finger under all three cards as you and the students blend the sounds to read the word.

Word Resources

lit	lip	lap
rap	rip	nip
sip	sit	set

Reminder!

Weave vocabulary discussion. For example, you can talk about multiple meanings of words for the words, **set** and **lap**.

Set: 1. Put something somewhere; 2. The scenery for a play; 3. To fix the time on a clock.

Lap: 1. The flat area formed by your legs when you sit; 2. The way an animal drinks water; 3. In a race, to go around the course once.

Unit 2 | Week 1

Day 4

Make It Fun

GUESS MY WORD

This activity will help students develop blending skills.

Instruct Students
Say

> I am going to say three sounds. Listen and see if you can guess the word.

Do not display letters, but tap words to assist blending. Do some all together and then call on individual students. Have a student use it in a sentence, or demonstrate the word (**sit**, **sip**, **shake**, **spin**, **bend**).

Word Resources

/s/	/ĭ/	/t/		(sit)
/s/	/ō/	/k/		(soak)
/n/	/ā/	/l/		(nail)
/f/	/ŏ/	/g/		(fog)
/sh/	/ā/	/k/		(shake)
/l/	/ī/	/t/		(light)
/s/	/ĭ/	/p/		(sip)
/n/	/ŭ/	/t/		(nut)
/s/	/p/	/ĭ/	/n/	(spin)
/b/	/ĕ/	/n/	/d/	(bend)

Echo/Letter Formation

Remind students of proper pencil grip and sitting position, and give them their Dry Erase Writing Tablets.

Dictate 5-6 previously taught sounds. You select and say the sound. Students echo the sound and say the letter.

Next have a student come up to the classroom board to make the letter on the Large Writing Grid.

Then have all students write the answer on their Dry Erase Writing Tablet as you direct them with the letter formation verbalization.

(See Unit Resources.)

[handwritten note: Add in letter formation & workbook of G, H]

Unit 2 | Week 1

Day 5

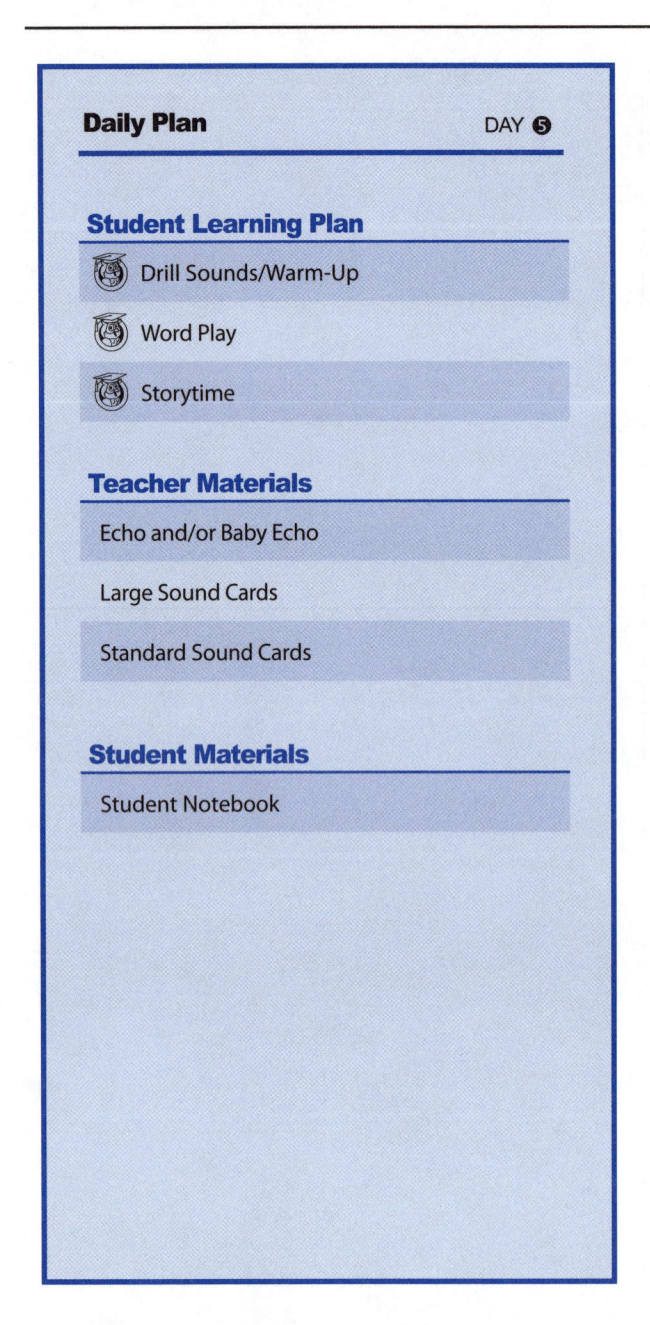

Daily Plan — DAY 5

Student Learning Plan
- Drill Sounds/Warm-Up
- Word Play
- Storytime

Teacher Materials
- Echo and/or Baby Echo
- Large Sound Cards
- Standard Sound Cards

Student Materials
- Student Notebook

Drill Sounds/Warm-Up

Do any new or challenging sounds and vowel sounds each day. Selectively review 4-5 other consonants.

Large Sound Cards
Practice sounds with the Large Sound Cards. Model these, saying the letter-keyword-sound and have the students echo.

Standard Sound Cards
Next, point to the Standard Sound Cards (in card display) with the Baby Echo pointer. You say the letter-keyword-sound and hold up Baby Echo to have students repeat. You can have a student be the drill leader for some of the sounds.

Word Play

MAKE WORDS FOR DECODING

Use your Standard Sound Card display to make Unit words. (See below.)

Make each word then say and tap each sound. Have students tap with you. Then blend the sounds as you drag your thumb across your fingers. Say the word.

Next, point under each card as you say each sound, then drag your finger under all three cards as you and the students blend the sounds to read the word.

Word Resources

sit	sip	
lip	lap	
nap	map	
rap	rat	fat

198 FUNDATIONS® LEVEL K

© 2002, 2012 WILSON LANGUAGE TRAINING CORPORATION

Unit 2 | Week 1

Day 5

Storytime

Preparation

During Storytime select an ABC Book to read to your students. There are many different ABC Books and the following list provides a small selection.

- Aylesworth, J. 1992. *Old Black Fly*. New York: Holt.
- Lobel, Arnold. 1981. *On Market Street*. New York: Greenwillow.
- MacDonald, S. 1986. *Alphabatics*. New York: Aladdin.
- Micklethwait, L. 1992. *I spy: An Alphabet in Art*. New York: Greenwillow.
- Dr. Seuss. (1991). *ABC*. New York: Random House.

Instruct Students

Before reading, look at the front and back cover of the book with your students. Discuss the title, author and illustrator, explaining each of those terms. Read the book. Periodically pause on a letter page.

Point out the letter (it is helpful to show students various letter fonts). Have a student tell you the corresponding keyword and sound. Have students find and name words that begin with the letter sound.

tip

Students should draw and/or write in their My Fundations® Journal several times a week. You can have them select a letter of the alphabet and draw pictures of words that begin with that letter.

[Handwritten note: Add in letter formation of I, J at workbook]

Unit 2 | Week 2

Day 1

Daily Plan — DAY 1

Student Learning Plan
- Drill Sounds/Warm-Up
- Word Play
- Sky Write/Letter Formation
- Student Notebook
- Echo/Letter Formation

Teacher Materials
- Echo and/or Baby Echo
- Large Sound Cards
- Standard Sound Cards
- Large Writing Grid
- Letter Formation Guide
- Student Notebook

Student Materials
- Student Notebook
- Dry Erase Writing Tablet

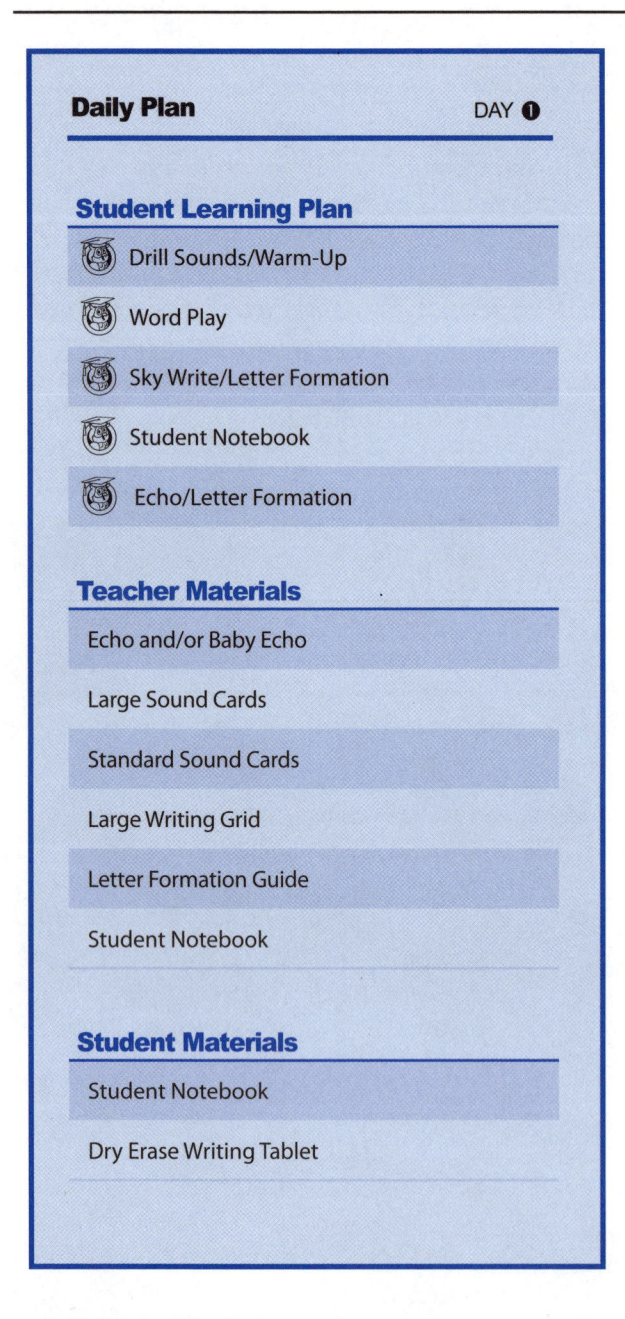

Drill Sounds/Warm-Up

Do any new or challenging sounds and vowel sounds each day. Selectively review 4-5 other consonants.

Large Sound Cards
Practice sounds with the Large Sound Cards. Model these, saying the letter-keyword-sound and have the students echo.

Standard Sound Cards
Next, point to the Standard Sound Cards (in card display) with the Baby Echo pointer. You say the letter-keyword-sound and hold up Baby Echo to have students repeat. You can have a student be the drill leader for some of the sounds.

Word Play

MAKE WORDS FOR DECODING
Use your Standard Sound Card display to make words. (See Word Resources.)

Make each word then say and tap each sound. Have students tap with you. Then blend the sounds as you drag your thumb across your fingers.

Next, point under each card as you say each sound, then drag your finger under all three cards as you and the students blend the sounds to read the word.

Word Resources

set	met	let	led
sun	run	rug	mug
fog	log	lot	rot

Unit 2 | Week 2

Day 1

Sky Write/Letter Formation

Use the following verbalizations to direct students in proper letter formation.

Letter Formation for A

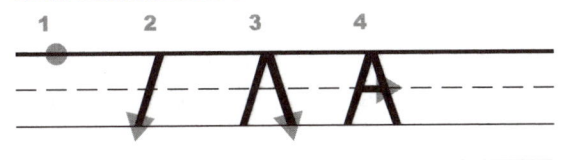

1. Point to the sky line.
2. Slide back to the grass line.
3. Start back at the sky line and slide down to the grass line.
4. Cross on the plane line.
5. Say a - apple - /ă/, have students repeat.

Letter Formation for B

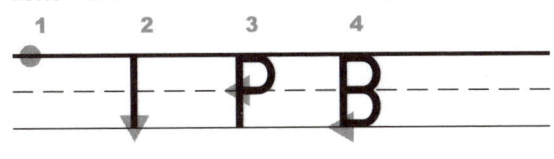

1. Point to the sky line.
2. Go down to the grass line.
3. Start back at the sky line and go around to the plane line.
4. And around again to the grass line.
5. Say b - bat - /b/, have students repeat.

Student Notebook

Direct students to find the letters corresponding to the letters introduced with sky writing.

Have students trace the large uppercase letter, then lowercase letter with their index finger while you direct them with the verbalization.

Next, have students hold their pencil. Remind them of the correct grip and be sure they are sitting with their chairs pulled in and their feet on the floor. The elbow of their writing arm should be on the desk. They should hold their Student Notebooks with their other hand.

Circulate the room and assist students with the correct position and the proper pencil grip.

Letters + workbook K, L

Echo/Letter Formation

Tell students that today you will practice capital letters on the Dry Erase Writing Tablet. Dictate sounds (see resource below). Have students repeat sound and name letter. Then use verbalization to direct them to first make the uppercase letter, then the corresponding lowercase letter. After each letter is formed say letter-keyword-sound and have students repeat.

Sound Resources   *K   L*

/a/   /b/

Unit 2 | Week 2

Day 2

Daily Plan — DAY 2

Student Learning Plan
- Drill Sounds/Warm-Up
- Word Play
- Sky Write/Letter Formation
- Student Notebook
- Echo/Letter Formation

Teacher Materials
- Echo and/or Baby Echo
- Large Sound Cards
- Standard Sound Cards
- Large Writing Grid
- Letter Formation Guide
- Student Notebook

Student Materials
- Student Notebook
- Dry Erase Writing Tablet

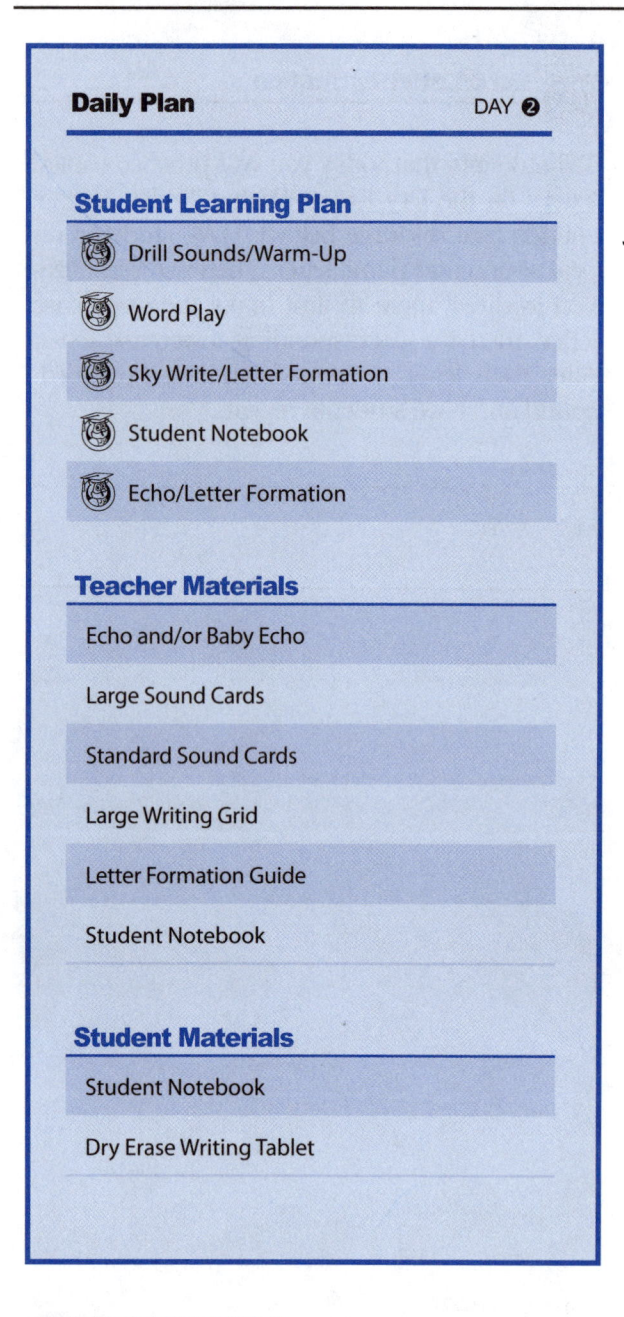

Drill Sounds/Warm-Up

Do any new or challenging sounds and vowel sounds each day. Selectively review 4-5 other consonants.

Large Sound Cards

Practice sounds with the Large Sound Cards. Model these, saying the letter-keyword-sound and have the students echo.

Standard Sound Cards

Next, point to the Standard Sound Cards (in card display) with the Baby Echo pointer. You say the letter-keyword-sound and hold up Baby Echo to have students repeat. You can have a student be the drill leader for some of the sounds.

Time
✱ HFW cards

Word Play

MAKE WORDS FOR DECODING

Use your Standard Sound Card display to make words. (See Word Resources.)

Make each word then say and tap each sound. Have students tap with you. Then blend the sounds as you drag your thumb across your fingers.

Next, point under each card as you say each sound, then drag your finger under all three cards as you and the students blend the sounds to read the word.

Word Resources

mop	map	mad	mud
fun	fin	fit	fig
rag	rug	mug	lug

Unit 2 | Week 2

Day 2

Sky Write/Letter Formation

Use the following verbalizations to direct students in proper letter formation.

Letter Formation for C

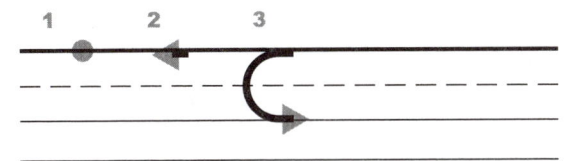

1. Point to the sky line.
2. Fly back on the sky line.
3. And down around to the grass line.
4. Say c - cat - /k/, have students repeat.

Letter Formation for D

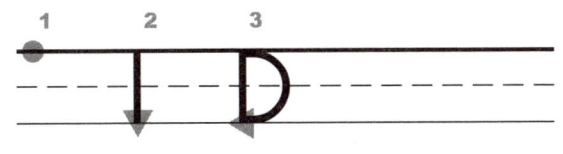

1. Point to the sky line.
2. Go down to the grass line.
3. Start back on the sky line and go all the way around to the grass line.
4. Say d - dog - /d/, have students repeat.

Student Notebook

Direct students to find the letters corresponding to the letters introduced with sky writing.

Have students trace the large uppercase letter, then lowercase letter with their index finger while you direct them with the verbalization.

Next, have students hold their pencil. Remind them of the correct grip and be sure they are sitting with their chairs pulled in and their feet on the floor. The elbow of their writing arm should be on the desk. They should hold their Student Notebooks with their other hand.

Circulate the room and assist students with the correct position and the proper pencil grip.

Letters M, N

Echo/Letter Formation

Tell students that today you will practice capital letters on the Dry Erase Writing Tablet. Dictate sounds (see resource below). Have students repeat sound and name letter. Then use verbalization to direct them to first make the uppercase letter, then the corresponding lowercase letter. After each letter is formed say letter-keyword-sound and have students repeat.

Sound Resources

/a/   /b/   /k/   /d/

Note

When you dictate /k/, have students make the uppercase and lowercase **c**, but only lowercase **k**.

Unit 2 | Week 2

Day 3

Daily Plan — DAY 3

Student Learning Plan
- Drill Sounds/Warm-Up
- Word Play
- Sky Write/Letter Formation
- Student Notebook
- Echo/Letter Formation

Teacher Materials
- Echo and/or Baby Echo
- Large Sound Cards
- Standard Sound Cards
- Large Writing Grid
- Letter Formation Guide
- Student Notebook

Student Materials
- Student Notebook
- Dry Erase Writing Tablet

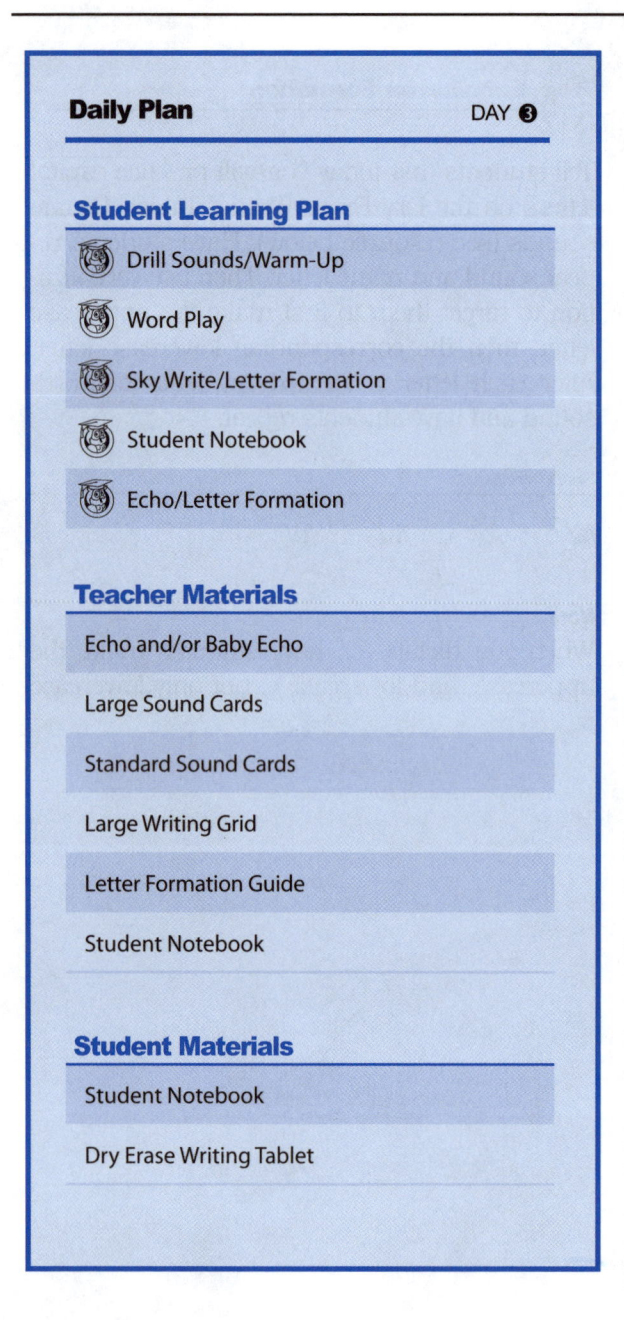

Drill Sounds/Warm-Up

Do any new or challenging sounds and vowel sounds each day. Selectively review 4-5 other consonants.

Large Sound Cards
Practice sounds with the Large Sound Cards. Model these, saying the letter-keyword-sound and have the students echo.

Standard Sound Cards
Next, point to the Standard Sound Cards (in card display) with the Baby Echo pointer. You say the letter-keyword-sound and hold up Baby Echo to have students repeat. You can have a student be the drill leader for some of the sounds.

Word Play

MAKE WORDS FOR DECODING

Use your Standard Sound Card display to make words. (See Word Resources.)

Make each word then say and tap each sound. Have students tap with you. Then blend the sounds as you drag your thumb across your fingers.

Next, point under each card as you say each sound, then drag your finger under all three cards as you and the students blend the sounds to read the word.

Word Resources

log	lag	rag	rat
fat	fit	lit	
sit	set	met	let

204 FUNDATIONS® LEVEL K

© 2002, 2012 WILSON LANGUAGE TRAINING CORPORATION

Unit 2 | Week 2

Day 3

Sky Write/Letter Formation

Use the following verbalizations to direct students in proper letter formation.

Letter Formation for E

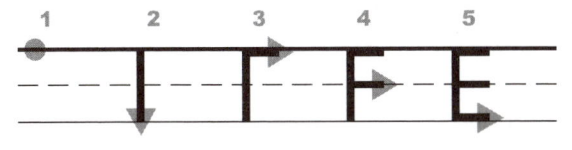

1. Point to the sky line.
2. Go down to the grass line.
3. Make a line on the sky line.
4. Make a line on the plane line.
5. And a line on the grass line.
6. Say e - Ed - /ĕ/, have students repeat.

Letter Formation for F

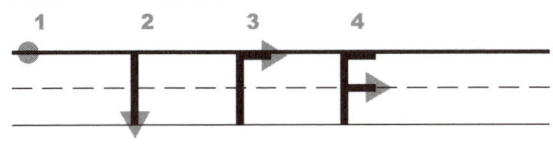

1. Point to the sky line.
2. Go down to the grass line.
3. Make a line on the sky line.
4. Make a line on the plane line.
5. Say f - fun - /f/, have students repeat.

Student Notebook

Direct students to find the letters corresponding to the letters introduced with sky writing.

Have students trace the large uppercase letter, then lowercase letter with their index finger while you direct them with the verbalization.

Next, have students hold their pencil. Remind them of the correct grip and be sure they are sitting with their chairs pulled in and their feet on the floor. The elbow of their writing arm should be on the desk. They should hold their Student Notebooks with their other hand.

Circulate the room and assist students with the correct position and the proper pencil grip.

Echo/Letter Formation

Tell students that today you will practice capital letters on the Dry Erase Writing Tablet. Dictate 2-3 sounds (see resource below). Have students repeat sound and name letter. Then use verbalization to direct them to first make the uppercase letter, then the corresponding lowercase letter. After each letter is formed say letter-keyword-sound and have students repeat.

Sound Resources

/a/   /b/   /k/   /d/   /e/   /f/

Note

When you dictate **/k/**, have students make the uppercase and lowercase **c**, but only lowercase **k**.

Unit 2 | Week 2

Day 4

Daily Plan — DAY 4

Student Learning Plan
- Drill Sounds/Warm-Up
- Make It Fun
- Sky Write/Letter Formation
- Student Notebook
- Echo/Letter Formation

Teacher Materials
- Echo and/or Baby Echo
- Large Sound Cards
- Standard Sound Cards
- Large Writing Grid
- Letter Formation Guide
- Student Notebook

Student Materials
- Student Notebook
- Dry Erase Writing Tablet

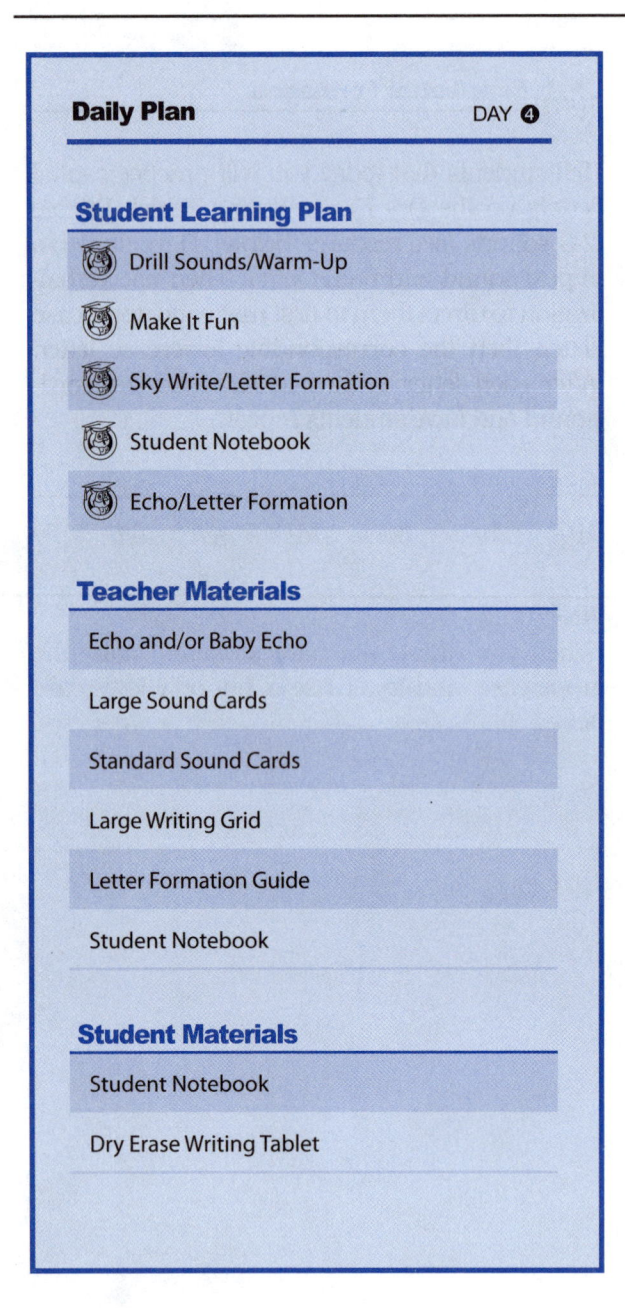

Drill Sounds/Warm-Up

Do any new or challenging sounds and vowel sounds each day. Selectively review 4-5 other consonants.

Large Sound Cards

Practice sounds with the Large Sound Cards. Model these, saying the letter-keyword-sound and have the students echo.

Standard Sound Cards

Next, point to the Standard Sound Cards (in card display) with the Baby Echo pointer. You say the letter-keyword-sound and hold up Baby Echo to have students repeat. You can have a student be the drill leader for some of the sounds.

Make It Fun

Preparation
- Your Standard Sound Card Display

LET'S RHYME

This activity will help students begin to manipulate sounds with rhyming patterns.

Instruct Students

Make the word **cat** with your Sound Cards.

| c | a | t |

Say

This word is cat. If this says cat, what is this?

Remove the **c** card and replace it with the **b**. Continue rhyming words, each time changing the first letter.

Word Resources

bat	fat	sat	rat	mat
wig	big	pig		
hop	top	mop	cop	
sap	tap	rap	lap	
kit	pit	fit	bit	sit

| t | i | p |

Remember to weave in vocabulary discussion.

Unit 2 | Week 2

Day 4

Sky Write/Letter Formation

Use the following verbalizations to direct students in proper letter formation.

Letter Formation for G

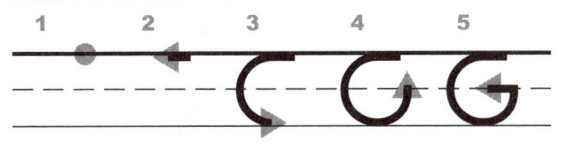

1. Point to the sky line.
2. Fly back on the sky line.
3. Around to the grass line.
4. Up to the plane line.
5. And back straight on the plane line.
6. Say g - game - /g/, have students repeat.

Letter Formation for H

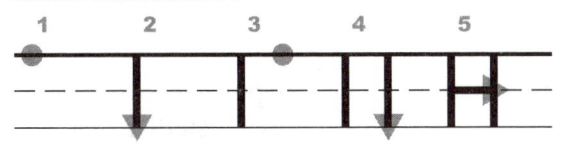

1. Point to the sky line.
2. Go down to the grass line.
3. Leave a space and point to the sky line.
4. Go down to the grass line.
5. Cross straight on the plane line.
6. Say h - hat - /h/, have students repeat.

Student Notebook

Direct students to find the letters corresponding to the letters introduced with sky writing.

Have students trace the large uppercase letter, then lowercase letter with their index finger while you direct them with the verbalization.

Next, have students hold their pencil. Remind them of the correct grip and be sure they are sitting with their chairs pulled in and their feet on the floor. The elbow of their writing arm should be on the desk. They should hold their Student Notebooks with their other hand.

Circulate the room and assist students with the correct position and the proper pencil grip.

Echo/Letter Formation

Tell students that today you will practice capital letters on the Dry Erase Writing Tablet. Dictate 2-3 sounds (see resource below). Have students repeat sound and name letter. Then use verbalization to direct them to first make the uppercase letter, then the corresponding lowercase letter. After each letter is formed say letter-keyword-sound and have students repeat.

Sound Resources

/a/   /b/   /k/   /d/   /e/   /f/

/g/   /h/

Note

When you dictate /k/, have students make the uppercase and lowercase c, but only lowercase k.

Unit 2 | Week 2

Day 5

Daily Plan — DAY 5

Student Learning Plan
- Drill Sounds/Warm-Up
- Storytime
- Alphabetical Order
- Echo/Find Letters

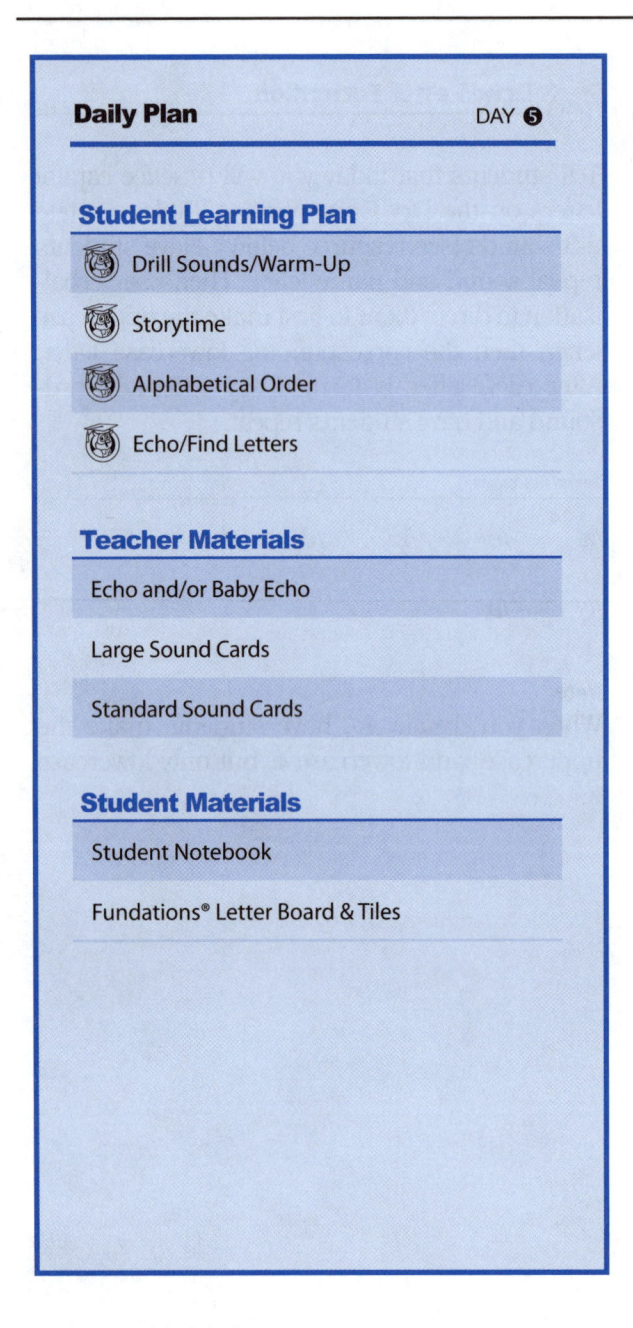

Teacher Materials
- Echo and/or Baby Echo
- Large Sound Cards
- Standard Sound Cards

Student Materials
- Student Notebook
- Fundations® Letter Board & Tiles

Drill Sounds/Warm-Up

Do any new or challenging sounds and vowel sounds each day. Selectively review 4-5 other consonants.

Large Sound Cards

Practice sounds with the Large Sound Cards. Model these, saying the letter-keyword-sound and have the students echo.

Standard Sound Cards

Next, point to the Standard Sound Cards (in card display) with the Baby Echo pointer. You say the letter-keyword-sound and hold up Baby Echo to have students repeat. You can have a student be the drill leader for some of the sounds.

Storytime

Preparation

During Storytime select an ABC Book to read to your students. There are many different ABC Books and the following list provides a small selection.

Aylesworth, J. 1992. *Old Black Fly*. New York: Holt.

Lobel, Arnold. 1981. *On Market Street*. New York: Greenwillow.

MacDonald, S. 1986. *Alphabatics*. New York: Aladdin.

Micklethwait, L. 1992. *I spy: An Alphabet in Art*. New York: Greenwillow.

Dr. Seuss. (1991). *ABC*. New York: Random House.

Instruct Students

Before reading, look at the front and back cover of the book with your students. Discuss the title, author and illustrator, explaining each of those terms. Read the book. Periodically pause on a letter page.

Point out the letter (it is helpful to show students various letter fonts). Have a student tell you the corresponding keyword and sound. Have students find and name words that begin with the letter sound.

Note

The book can be one that you have previously read to students. Young children love the repetition, and repeated exposure to text is beneficial.

Unit 2 | Week 2

Day 5

Alphabetical Order

Students start with their Magnetic Letter Tiles randomly placed on the blank side of their Letter Boards. Have them sequentially match Letter Tiles on the letter squares.

After students have the tiles placed, chorally say the alphabet. Students should point to each letter as they say its name.

Echo/Find Letters

Echo/Find Letters

Say a sound. Have students echo and point to the letter(s) on their Magnetic Letter Boards.

Ask

What says /___/? (___)

(See Echo Sounds in Unit Resources for expected student responses.)

Have students name the letter(s). Then you can have one student find the Standard Sound Card(s) as you dictate sounds. Do vowels and 3-5 other sounds.

Unit 2 | Week 3

Day 1

Daily Plan — DAY 1

Student Learning Plan
- Drill Sounds/Warm-Up
- Word Play
- Sky Write/Letter Formation
- Student Notebook
- Echo/Letter Formation

Teacher Materials
- Echo and/or Baby Echo
- Large Sound Cards
- Standard Sound Cards
- Large Writing Grid
- Letter Formation Guide
- Student Notebook

Student Materials
- Student Notebook
- Dry Erase Writing Tablet

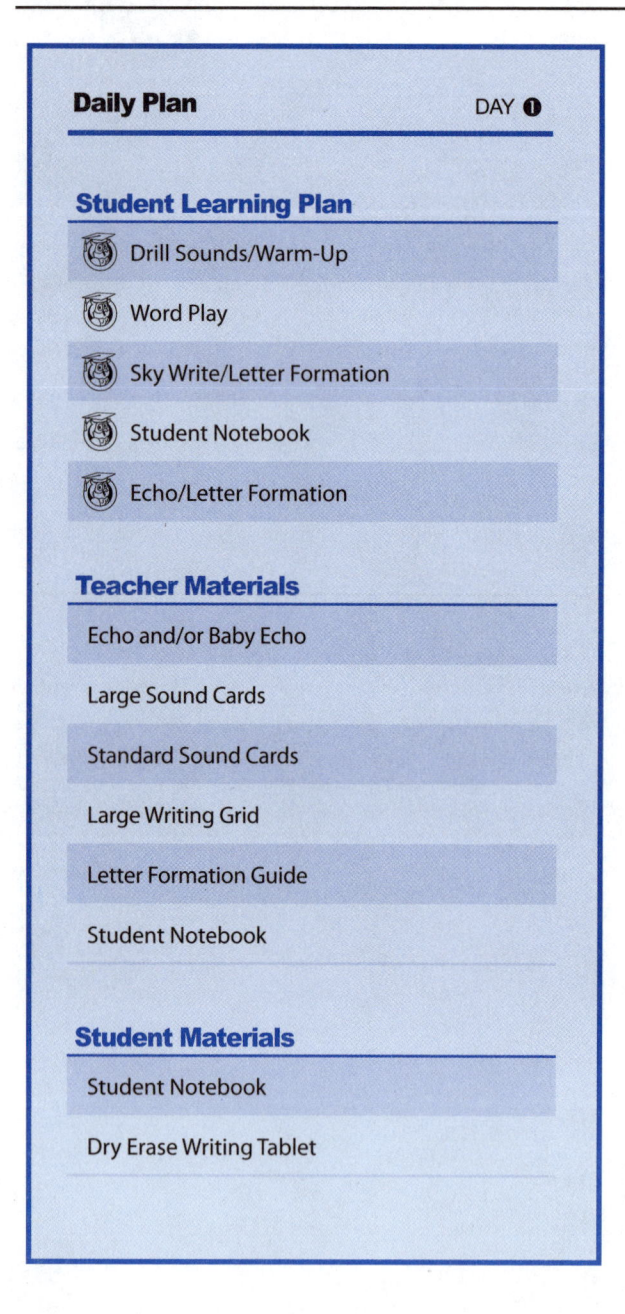

Drill Sounds/Warm-Up

Do any new or challenging sounds and vowel sounds each day. Selectively review 4-5 other consonants.

Large Sound Cards
Practice sounds with the Large Sound Cards. Model these, saying the letter-keyword-sound and have the students echo.

Standard Sound Cards
Next, point to the Standard Sound Cards (in card display) with the Baby Echo pointer. You say the letter-keyword-sound and hold up Baby Echo to have students repeat. You can have a student be the drill leader for some of the sounds.

Word Play

MAKE WORDS FOR DECODING

Use your Standard Sound Card display to make Unit words. (See Unit Resources.)

Make each word then say and tap each sound. Have students tap with you. Then blend the sounds as you drag your thumb across your fingers.

Next, point under each card as you say each sound, then drag your finger under all three cards as you and the students blend the sounds to read the word.

This week, move on to form words beginning with other consonants. Words beginning with stop consonants (such as t) may be more difficult to blend.

You can change the initial consonant to any consonant to make words. Also, change the vowel and final consonants to form new words. Make 8-10 words. Each time, tap and blend the word with your students.

Example

m a t → c a t → b a t →

b a g → b u g → m u g

sit, hit

Unit 2 | Week 3

Day 1

Sky Write/Letter Formation

Use the following verbalizations to direct students in proper letter formation.

Letter Formation for I

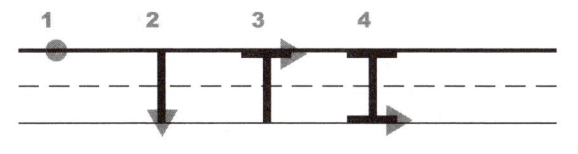

1. Point to the sky line.
2. Go down to the grass line.
3. Cross on the sky line.
4. And cross on the grass line.
5. Say i - itch - /i/, have students repeat.

Letter Formation for J

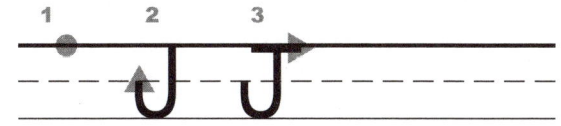

1. Point to the sky line.
2. Go down to the grass line and curve back.
3. Cross it on the sky line.
4. Say j - jug - /j/, have students repeat.

Student Notebook

Direct students to find the letters corresponding to the letters introduced with sky writing.

Have students trace the large uppercase letter, then lowercase letter with their index finger while you direct them with the verbalization.

Next, have students hold their pencil. Remind them of the correct grip and be sure they are sitting with their chairs pulled in and their feet on the floor. The elbow of their writing arm should be on the desk. They should hold their Student Notebooks with their other hand.

Circulate the room and assist students with the correct position and the proper pencil grip.

U, V

Echo/Letter Formation

Tell students that today you will practice capital letters on the Dry Erase Writing Tablet. Dictate 2-3 sounds (see resource below). Have students repeat sound and name letter. Then use verbalization to direct them to first make the uppercase letter, then the corresponding lowercase letter. After each letter is formed say letter-keyword-sound and have students repeat.

Sound Resources

| /a/ | /b/ | /k/ | /d/ | /e/ | /f/ |

| /g/ | /h/ | /i/ | /j/ |

Note

When you dictate /k/, have students make the uppercase and lowercase **c**, but only lowercase **k**.

© 2002, 2012 WILSON LANGUAGE TRAINING CORPORATION   TEACHER'S MANUAL 211

Unit 2 | Week 3

Day 2

Daily Plan — DAY 2

Student Learning Plan
- Drill Sounds/Warm-Up
- Word Play
- Sky Write/Letter Formation
- Student Notebook
- Echo/Letter Formation

Teacher Materials
- Echo and/or Baby Echo
- Large Sound Cards
- Standard Sound Cards
- Large Writing Grid
- Letter Formation Guide
- Student Notebook

Student Materials
- Student Notebook
- Dry Erase Writing Tablet

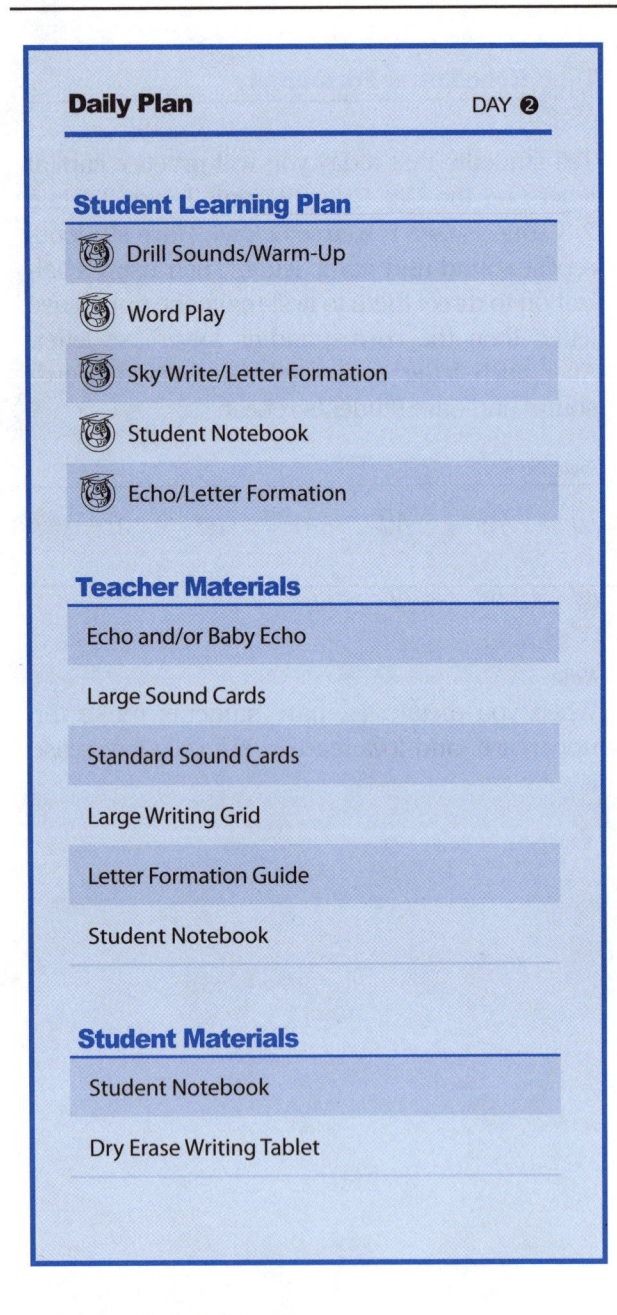

Drill Sounds/Warm-Up

Do any new or challenging sounds and vowel sounds each day. Selectively review 4-5 other consonants.

Large Sound Cards
Practice sounds with the Large Sound Cards. Model these, saying the letter-keyword-sound and have the students echo.

Standard Sound Cards
Next, point to the Standard Sound Cards (in card display) with the Baby Echo pointer. You say the letter-keyword-sound and hold up Baby Echo to have students repeat. You can have a student be the drill leader for some of the sounds.

Word Play

MAKE WORDS FOR DECODING

Use your Standard Sound Card display to make 5-6 Unit words. (See Unit Resources.)

Make each word then say and tap each sound. Have students tap with you. Then blend the sounds as you drag your thumb across your fingers.

Next, point under each card as you say each sound, then drag your finger under all three cards as you and the students blend the sounds to read the word.

tip

Remember to weave in vocabulary discussion.

Unit 2 | Week 3

Day 2

Sky Write/Letter Formation

Use the following verbalizations to direct students in proper letter formation.

Letter Formation for K

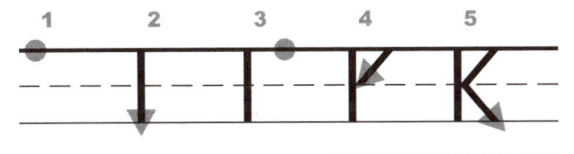

1. Point to the sky line.
2. Go down to the grass line.
3. Leave a space and point to the sky line.
4. Slide back to the plane line.
5. Slide over to the grass line.
5. Say k - kite - /k/, have students repeat.

Letter Formation for L

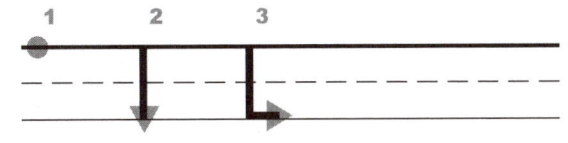

1. Point to the sky line.
2. Go down to the grass line.
3. Make a line across the grass line.
4. Say l - lamp - /l/, have students repeat.

Student Notebook

Direct students to find the letters corresponding to the letters introduced with sky writing.

Have students trace the large uppercase letter, then lowercase letter with their index finger while you direct them with the verbalization.

Next, have students hold their pencil. Remind them of the correct grip and be sure they are sitting with their chairs pulled in and their feet on the floor. The elbow of their writing arm should be on the desk. They should hold their Student Notebooks with their other hand.

Circulate the room and assist students with the correct position and the proper pencil grip.

Echo/Letter Formation

Tell students that today you will practice capital letters on the Dry Erase Writing Tablet. Dictate 2-3 sounds (see resource below). Have students repeat sound and name letter. Then use verbalization to direct them to first make the uppercase letter, then the corresponding lowercase letter. After each letter is formed say letter-keyword-sound and have students repeat.

Sound Resources

| /a/ | /b/ | /k/ | /d/ | /e/ | /f/ |
| /g/ | /h/ | /i/ | /j/ | /k/ | /l/ |

Unit 2 | Week 3

Day 3

Daily Plan — DAY 3

Student Learning Plan
- Drill Sounds/Warm-Up
- Word Play
- Sky Write/Letter Formation
- Student Notebook
- Echo/Letter Formation

Teacher Materials
- Echo and/or Baby Echo
- Large Sound Cards
- Standard Sound Cards
- Large Writing Grid
- Letter Formation Guide
- Student Notebook

Student Materials
- Student Notebook
- Dry Erase Writing Tablet

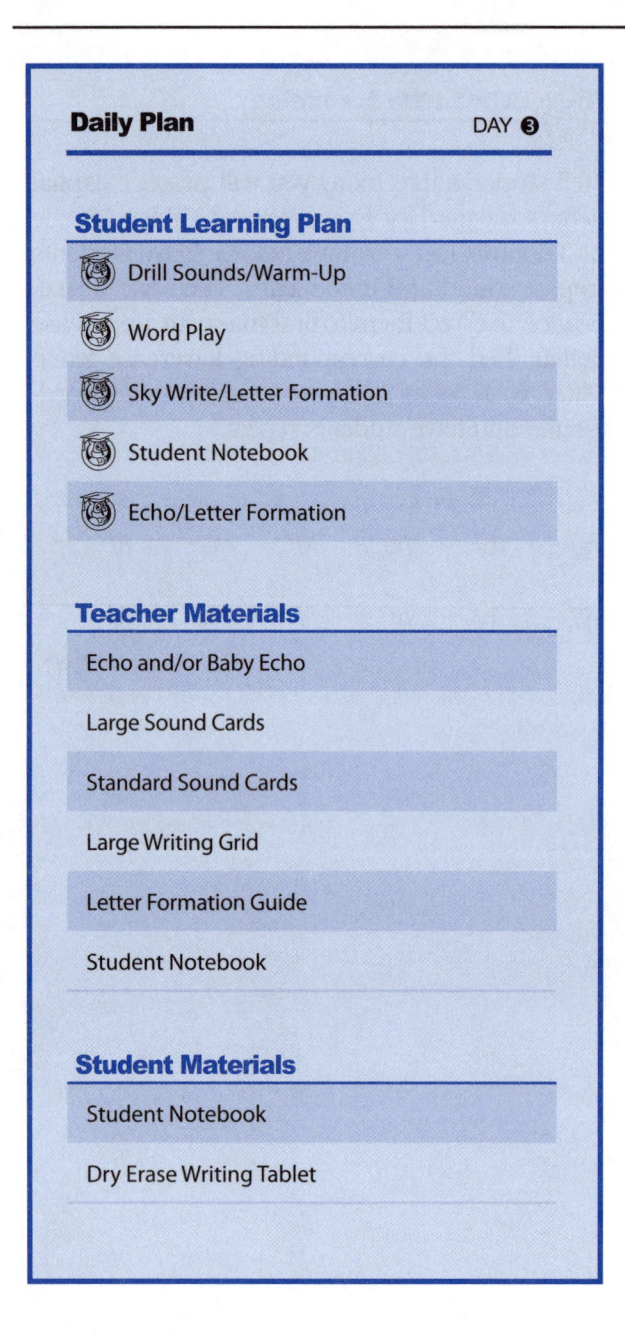

Drill Sounds/Warm-Up

Do any new or challenging sounds and vowel sounds each day. Selectively review 4-5 other consonants.

Large Sound Cards
Practice sounds with the Large Sound Cards. Model these, saying the letter-keyword-sound and have the students echo.

Standard Sound Cards
Next, point to the Standard Sound Cards (in card display) with the Baby Echo pointer. You say the letter-keyword-sound and hold up Baby Echo to have students repeat. You can have a student be the drill leader for some of the sounds.

Word Play

MAKE WORDS FOR DECODING

Use your Standard Sound Card display to make 5-6 Unit words. (See Unit Resources.)

Make each word then say and tap each sound. Have students tap with you. Then blend the sounds as you drag your thumb across your fingers.

Next, point under each card as you say each sound, then drag your finger under all three cards as you and the students blend the sounds to read the word.

Unit 2 | Week 3

Day 3

Sky Write/Letter Formation

Use the following verbalizations to direct students in proper letter formation.

Letter Formation for M

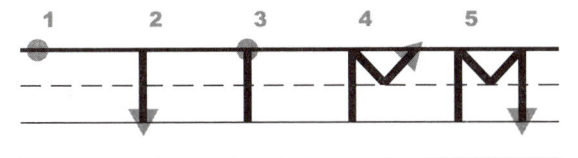

1. Point to the sky line.
2. Go down to the grass line.
3. Point to the sky line.
4. Slide down to the plane line, and slide back up to the sky line.
5. Go down to the grass line.
6. Say m - man - /m/, have students repeat.

Letter Formation for N

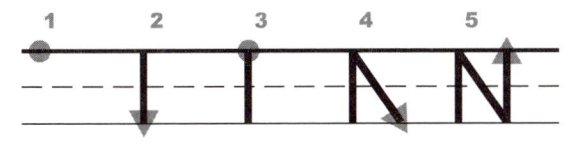

1. Point to the sky line.
2. Go down to the grass line.
3. Point to the sky line.
4. Slide down to the grass line.
5. Go straight up to the sky line.
6. Say n - nut - /n/, have students repeat.

Student Notebook

Direct students to find the letters corresponding to the letters introduced with sky writing.

Have students trace the large uppercase letter, then lowercase letter with their index finger while you direct them with the verbalization.

Next, have students hold their pencil. Remind them of the correct grip and be sure they are sitting with their chairs pulled in and their feet on the floor. The elbow of their writing arm should be on the desk. They should hold their Student Notebooks with their other hand.

Circulate the room and assist students with the correct position and the proper pencil grip.

Echo/Letter Formation

Tell students that today you will practice capital letters on the Dry Erase Writing Tablet. Dictate 2-3 sounds (see resource below). Have students repeat sound and name letter. Then use verbalization to direct them to first make the uppercase letter, then the corresponding lowercase letter. After each letter is formed say letter-keyword-sound and have students repeat.

Sound Resources

/a/	/b/	/k/	/d/	/e/	/f/
/g/	/h/	/i/	/j/	/k/	/l/
/m/	/n/				

Unit 2 | Week 3

Day 4

Daily Plan — DAY 4

Student Learning Plan
- Drill Sounds/Warm-Up
- Make It Fun
- Sky Write/Letter Formation
- Student Notebook
- Echo/Letter Formation

Teacher Materials
- Echo and/or Baby Echo
- Large Sound Cards
- Standard Sound Cards
- Large Writing Grid
- Letter Formation Guide
- Student Notebook

Student Materials
- Student Notebook
- Dry Erase Writing Tablet

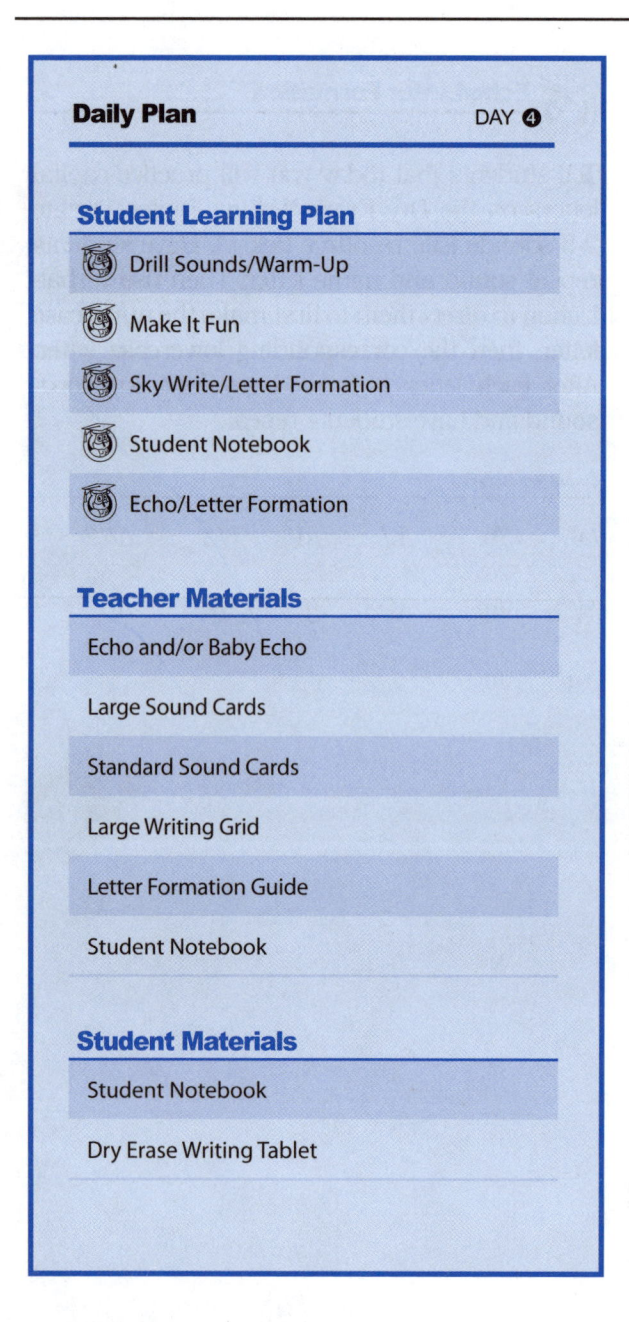

Drill Sounds/Warm-Up

Do any new or challenging sounds and vowel sounds each day. Selectively review 4-5 other consonants.

Large Sound Cards

Practice sounds with the Large Sound Cards. Model these, saying the letter-keyword-sound and have the students echo.

Standard Sound Cards

Next, point to the Standard Sound Cards (in card display) with the Baby Echo pointer. You say the letter-keyword-sound and hold up Baby Echo to have students repeat. You can have a student be the drill leader for some of the sounds.

Make It Fun

GUESS MY WORD

This activity will help students develop blending skills.

Instruct Students

Say

> I am going to say three sounds. Listen and see if you can guess the word.

Do not display letters, but tap words to assist blending. Do some all together and then call on individual students.

Word Resources

/m/	/ē/	/t/	(meat)
/s/	/ō/	/p/	(soap)
/s/	/ĭ/	/k/	(sick)
/t/	/ŭ/	/b/	(tub)
/f/	/ē/	/t/	(feet)
/sh/	/ĭ/	/p/	(ship)
/m/	/ĭ/	/ks/	(mix)
/t/	/ē/	/m/	(team)
/th/	/ĭ/	/k/	(thick)
/k/	/ă/	/p/	(cap)

Unit 2 | Week 3

Day 4

Sky Write/Letter Formation

Use the following verbalizations to direct students in proper letter formation.

Letter Formation for O

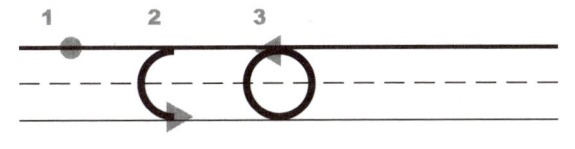

1. Point to the sky line.
2. Trace back, then down around to the grass line.
3. And around back up to the sky line.
4. Say o - octopus - /ŏ/, have students repeat.

Letter Formation for P

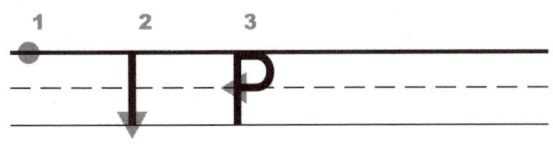

1. Point to the sky line.
2. Go down to the grass line.
3. Point to the sky line and go around to the plane line.
4. Say p - pan - /p/, have students repeat.

Student Notebook

Direct students to find the letters corresponding to the letters introduced with sky writing.

Have students trace the large uppercase letter, then lowercase letter with their index finger while you direct them with the verbalization.

Next, have students hold their pencil. Remind them of the correct grip and be sure they are sitting with their chairs pulled in and their feet on the floor. The elbow of their writing arm should be on the desk. They should hold their Student Notebooks with their other hand.

Circulate the room and assist students with the correct position and the proper pencil grip.

Echo/Letter Formation

Tell students that today you will practice capital letters on the Dry Erase Writing Tablet. Dictate 2-3 sounds (see resource below). Have students repeat sound and name letter. Then use verbalization to direct them to first make the uppercase letter, then the corresponding lowercase letter. After each letter is formed say letter-keyword-sound and have students repeat.

Sound Resources

/a/	/b/	/k/	/d/	/e/	/f/
/g/	/h/	/i/	/j/	/k/	/l/
/m/	/n/	/o/	/p/		

Unit 2 | Week 3

Day 5

Daily Plan — DAY 5

Student Learning Plan
- Drill Sounds/Warm-Up
- Storytime
- Alphabetical Order
- Echo/Find Letters

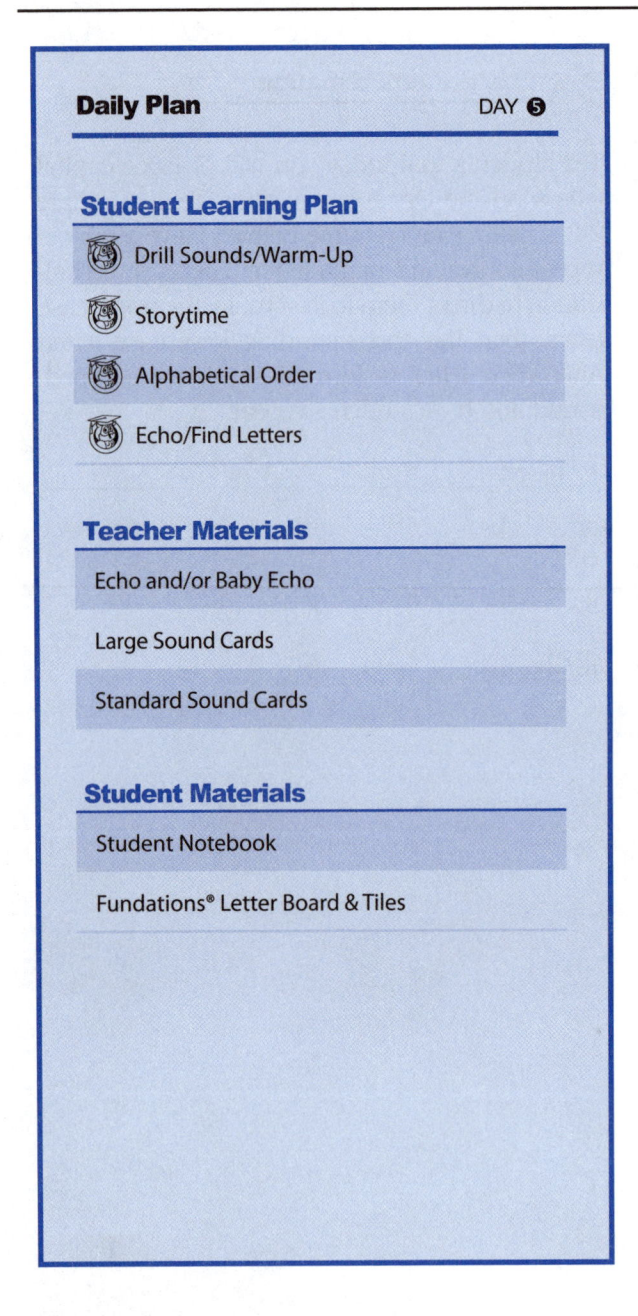

Teacher Materials
- Echo and/or Baby Echo
- Large Sound Cards
- Standard Sound Cards

Student Materials
- Student Notebook
- Fundations® Letter Board & Tiles

Drill Sounds/Warm-Up

Do any new or challenging sounds and vowel sounds each day. Selectively review 4-5 other consonants.

Large Sound Cards

Practice sounds with the Large Sound Cards. Model these, saying the letter-keyword-sound and have the students echo.

Standard Sound Cards

Next, point to the Standard Sound Cards (in card display) with the Baby Echo pointer. You say the letter-keyword-sound and hold up Baby Echo to have students repeat. You can have a student be the drill leader for some of the sounds.

Storytime

Preparation

During Storytime select an ABC Book to read to your students. There are many different ABC Books and the following list provides a small selection.

> Aylesworth, J. 1992. *Old Black Fly*. New York: Holt.
>
> Lobel, Arnold. 1981. *On Market Street*. New York: Greenwillow.
>
> MacDonald, S. 1986. *Alphabatics*. New York: Aladdin.
>
> Micklethwait, L. 1992. *I spy: An Alphabet in Art*. New York: Greenwillow.
>
> Dr. Seuss. (1991). *ABC*. New York: Random House.

Instruct Students

Before reading, look at the front and back cover of the book with your students. Discuss the title, author and illustrator, explaining each of those terms. Read the book. Periodically pause on a letter page.

Point out the letter (it is helpful to show students various letter fonts). Have a student tell you the corresponding keyword and sound. Have students find and name words that begin with the letter sound.

Note

The book can be one that you have previously read to students. Young children love the repetition, and repeated exposure to text is beneficial.

Unit 2 | Week 3

Day 5

Alphabetical Order

Students start with their Magnetic Letter Tiles randomly placed on the blank side of their Letter Boards. Have them sequentially match Letter Tiles on the letter squares.

After students have the tiles placed, chorally say the alphabet. Students should point to each letter as they say its name.

Echo/Find Letters

Echo/Find Letters

Say a sound. Have students echo and point to the letter(s) on their Magnetic Letter Boards.

Ask

What says /___/? (___)

(See Echo Sounds in Unit Resources for expected student responses.)

Have students name the letter(s). Then you can have one student find the Standard Sound Card(s) as you dictate sounds. Do vowels and 3-5 other sounds.

Unit 2 | Week 4

Day 1

Daily Plan — DAY 1

Student Learning Plan
- Drill Sounds/Warm-Up
- Word Play
- Sky Write/Letter Formation
- Student Notebook
- Echo/Letter Formation

Teacher Materials
- Echo and/or Baby Echo
- Large Sound Cards
- Standard Sound Cards
- Large Writing Grid
- Letter Formation Guide
- Student Notebook

Student Materials
- Student Notebook
- Dry Erase Writing Tablet

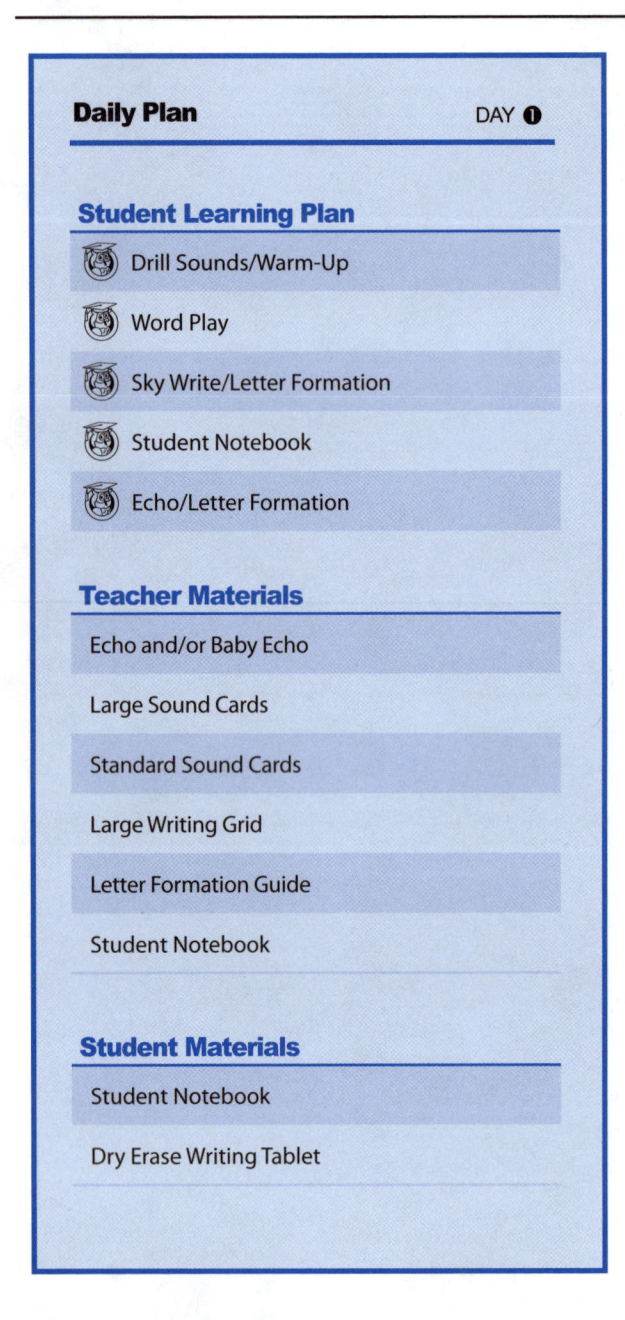

Drill Sounds/Warm-Up

Do any new or challenging sounds and vowel sounds each day. Selectively review 4-5 other consonants.

Large Sound Cards
Practice sounds with the Large Sound Cards. Model these, saying the letter-keyword-sound and have the students echo.

Standard Sound Cards
Next, point to the Standard Sound Cards (in card display) with the Baby Echo pointer. You say the letter-keyword-sound and hold up Baby Echo to have students repeat. You can have a student be the drill leader for some of the sounds.

Word Play

MAKE WORDS FOR DECODING

Use your Standard Sound Card display to make 5-6 Unit words. (See Unit Resources.)

Make each word then say and tap each sound. Have students tap with you. Then blend the sounds as you drag your thumb across your fingers.

Next, point under each card as you say each sound, then drag your finger under all three cards as you and the students blend the sounds to read the word.

red   cop   fit   bag   dug   lip

Unit 2 | Week 4

Day 1

Sky Write/Letter Formation

Use the following verbalizations to direct students in proper letter formation.

Letter Formation for Q

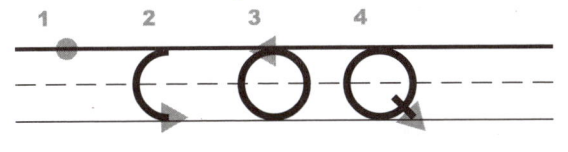

1. Point to the sky line.
2. Trace back, then down around to the grass line.
3. And around back up to the sky line.
4. Make a tail.
5. Say qu - queen - /kw/, have students repeat.

Letter Formation for R

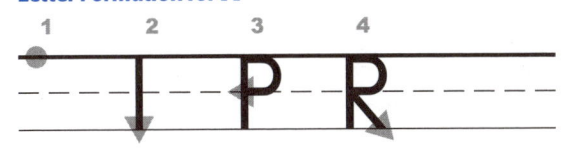

1. Point to the sky line.
2. Go down to the grass line.
3. Point to the sky line and go around to the plane line.
4. And slide down to the grass line.
5. Say r - rat - /r/, have students repeat.

Student Notebook

Direct students to find the letters corresponding to the letters introduced with sky writing.

Have students trace the large uppercase letter, then lowercase letter with their index finger while you direct them with the verbalization.

Next, have students hold their pencil. Remind them of the correct grip and be sure they are sitting with their chairs pulled in and their feet on the floor. The elbow of their writing arm should be on the desk. They should hold their Student Notebooks with their other hand.

Circulate the room and assist students with the correct position and the proper pencil grip.

Echo/Letter Formation

Tell students that today you will practice capital letters on the Dry Erase Writing Tablet. Dictate 2-3 sounds (see resource below). Have students repeat sound and name letter. Then use verbalization to direct them to first make the uppercase letter, then the corresponding lowercase letter. After each letter is formed say letter-keyword-sound and have students repeat.

Sound Resources

/a/	/b/	/k/	/d/	/e/	/f/
/g/	/h/	/i/	/j/	/k/	/l/
/m/	/n/	/o/	/p/	/q/	/r/

Unit 2 | Week 4

Day 2

Daily Plan — DAY 2

Student Learning Plan
- Drill Sounds/Warm-Up
- Word Play
- Sky Write/Letter Formation
- Student Notebook
- Echo/Letter Formation

Teacher Materials
- Echo and/or Baby Echo
- Large Sound Cards
- Standard Sound Cards
- Large Writing Grid
- Letter Formation Guide
- Student Notebook

Student Materials
- Student Notebook
- Dry Erase Writing Tablet

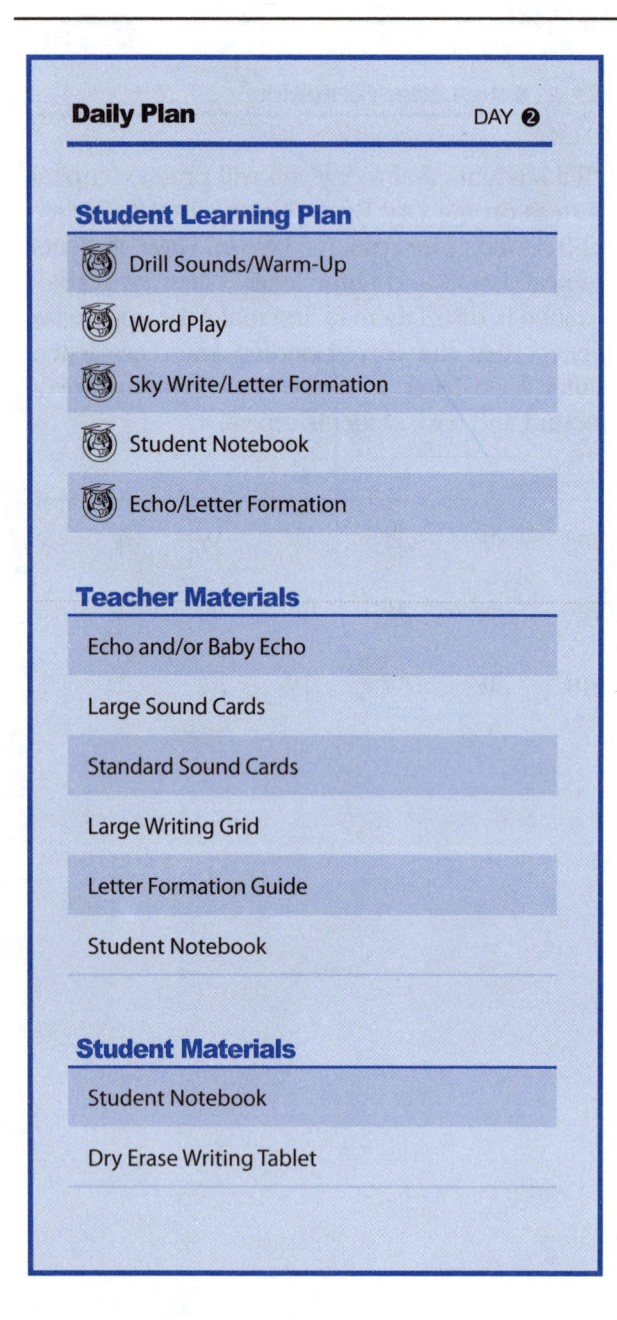

Drill Sounds/Warm-Up

Do any new or challenging sounds and vowel sounds each day. Selectively review 4-5 other consonants.

Large Sound Cards

Practice sounds with the Large Sound Cards. Model these, saying the letter-keyword-sound and have the students echo.

Standard Sound Cards

Next, point to the Standard Sound Cards (in card display) with the Baby Echo pointer. You say the letter-keyword-sound and hold up Baby Echo to have students repeat. You can have a student be the drill leader for some of the sounds.

Word Play

MAKE WORDS FOR DECODING

Use your Standard Sound Card display to make 5-6 Unit words. (See Unit Resources.)

Make each word then say and tap each sound. Have students tap with you. Then blend the sounds as you drag your thumb across your fingers.

Next, point under each card as you say each sound, then drag your finger under all three cards as you and the students blend the sounds to read the word.

jog, fun, men, rad, sick

Sky Write/Letter Formation

Use the following verbalizations to direct students in proper letter formation.

Letter Formation for S

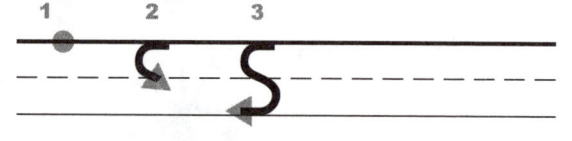

1. Point to the sky line.
2. Trace back and curve in to the plane line.
3. And curve back to the grass line.
4. Say s - snake - /s/, have students repeat.

Letter Formation for T

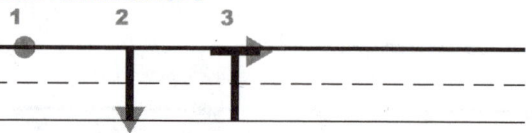

1. Point to the sky line.
2. Go down to the grass line.
3. Cross on the sky line.
4. Say t - top - /t/, have students repeat.

Unit 2 | Week 4

Day 2

Letter Formation for U

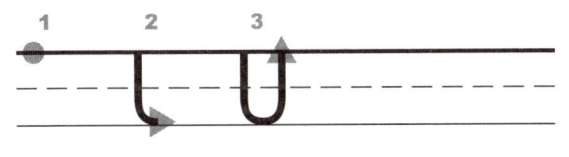

1. Point to the sky line.
2. Go to the grass line,
3. and curve up to the sky line.
4. Say u - up - /ŭ/, have students repeat.

Student Notebook

Direct students to find the letters corresponding to the letters introduced with sky writing.

Have students trace the large uppercase letter, then lowercase letter with their index finger while you direct them with the verbalization.

Next, have students hold their pencil. Remind them of the correct grip and be sure they are sitting with their chairs pulled in and their feet on the floor. The elbow of their writing arm should be on the desk. They should hold their Student Notebooks with their other hand.

Circulate the room and assist students with the correct position and the proper pencil grip.

Echo/Letter Formation

Tell students that today you will practice capital letters on the Dry Erase Writing Tablet. Dictate 2-3 sounds (see resource below). Have students repeat sound and name letter. Then use verbalization to direct them to first make the uppercase letter, then the corresponding lowercase letter. After each letter is formed say letter-keyword-sound and have students repeat.

Sound Resources

/a/	/b/	/k/	/d/	/e/	/f/
/g/	/h/	/i/	/j/	/k/	/l/
/m/	/n/	/o/	/p/	/q/	/r/
/s/	/t/	/u/			

Unit 2 | Week 4

Day 3

Daily Plan — DAY 3

Student Learning Plan
- Drill Sounds/Warm-Up
- Word Play
- Sky Write/Letter Formation
- Student Notebook
- Echo/Letter Formation

Teacher Materials
- Echo and/or Baby Echo
- Large Sound Cards
- Standard Sound Cards
- Large Writing Grid
- Letter Formation Guide
- Student Notebook

Student Materials
- Student Notebook
- Dry Erase Writing Tablet

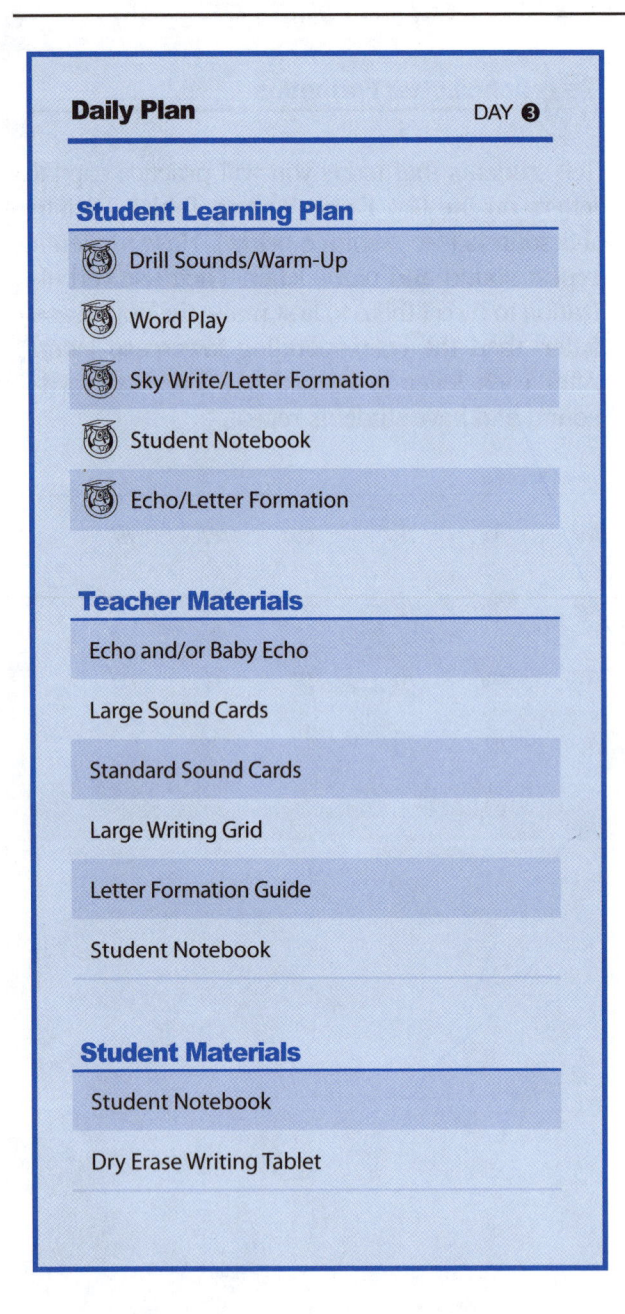

Drill Sounds/Warm-Up

Do any new or challenging sounds and vowel sounds each day. Selectively review 4-5 other consonants.

Large Sound Cards

Practice sounds with the Large Sound Cards. Model these, saying the letter-keyword-sound and have the students echo.

Standard Sound Cards

Next, point to the Standard Sound Cards (in card display) with the Baby Echo pointer. You say the letter-keyword-sound and hold up Baby Echo to have students repeat. You can have a student be the drill leader for some of the sounds.

Word Play

MAKE WORDS FOR DECODING

Use your Standard Sound Card display to make 5-6 Unit words. (See Unit Resources.)

Make each word then say and tap each sound. Have students tap with you. Then blend the sounds as you drag your thumb across your fingers.

Next, point under each card as you say each sound, then drag your finger under all three cards as you and the students blend the sounds to read the word.

Sky Write/Letter Formation

Use the following verbalizations to direct students in proper letter formation.

Letter Formation for V

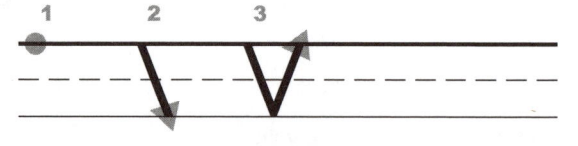

1. Point to the sky line.
2. Slide down to the grass line,
3. and slide back up to the sky line.
4. Say v - van - /v/, have students repeat.

Letter Formation for W

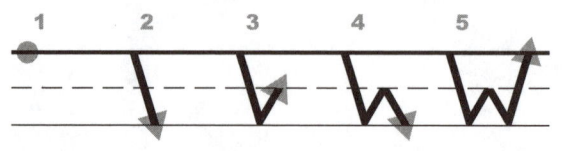

1. Point to the sky line.
2. Slide down to the grass line.
3. Slide up to the plane line.
4. Back down to the grass line.
5. And slide all the way back to the sky line.
6. Say w - wind - /w/, have students repeat.

Unit 2 | Week 4

Day 3

Letter Formation for X

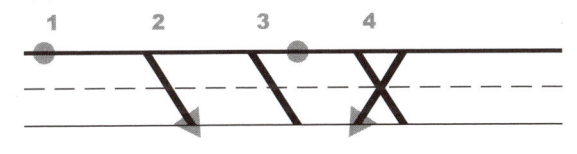

1. **Point to the sky line.**
2. **Slide down to the grass line.**
3. **Leave a space and point to the sky line.**
4. **Slide back down to the grass line.**
5. **Say x - fox - /ks/, have students repeat.**

Student Notebook

Direct students to find the letters corresponding to the letters introduced with sky writing.

Have students trace the large uppercase letter, then lowercase letter with their index finger while you direct them with the verbalization.

Next, have students hold their pencil. Remind them of the correct grip and be sure they are sitting with their chairs pulled in and their feet on the floor. The elbow of their writing arm should be on the desk. They should hold their Student Notebooks with their other hand.

Circulate the room and assist students with the correct position and the proper pencil grip.

Echo/Letter Formation

Tell students that today you will practice capital letters on the Dry Erase Writing Tablet. Dictate 2-3 sounds (see resource below). Have students repeat sound and name letter. Then use verbalization to direct them to first make the uppercase letter, then the corresponding lowercase letter. After each letter is formed say letter-keyword-sound and have students repeat.

Sound Resources

/a/	/b/	/k/	/d/	/e/	/f/
/g/	/h/	/i/	/j/	/k/	/l/
/m/	/n/	/o/	/p/	/q/	/r/
/s/	/t/	/u/	/v/	/w/	

Unit 2 | Week 4

Day 4

Daily Plan — DAY 4

Student Learning Plan
- Drill Sounds/Warm-Up
- Sky Write/Letter Formation
- Student Notebook
- Make It Fun

Teacher Materials
- Echo and/or Baby Echo
- Large Sound Cards
- Standard Sound Cards
- Large Writing Grid
- Letter Formation Guide
- Student Notebook
- Magnetic Letter Tiles

Student Materials
- Student Notebook
- Dry Erase Writing Tablet

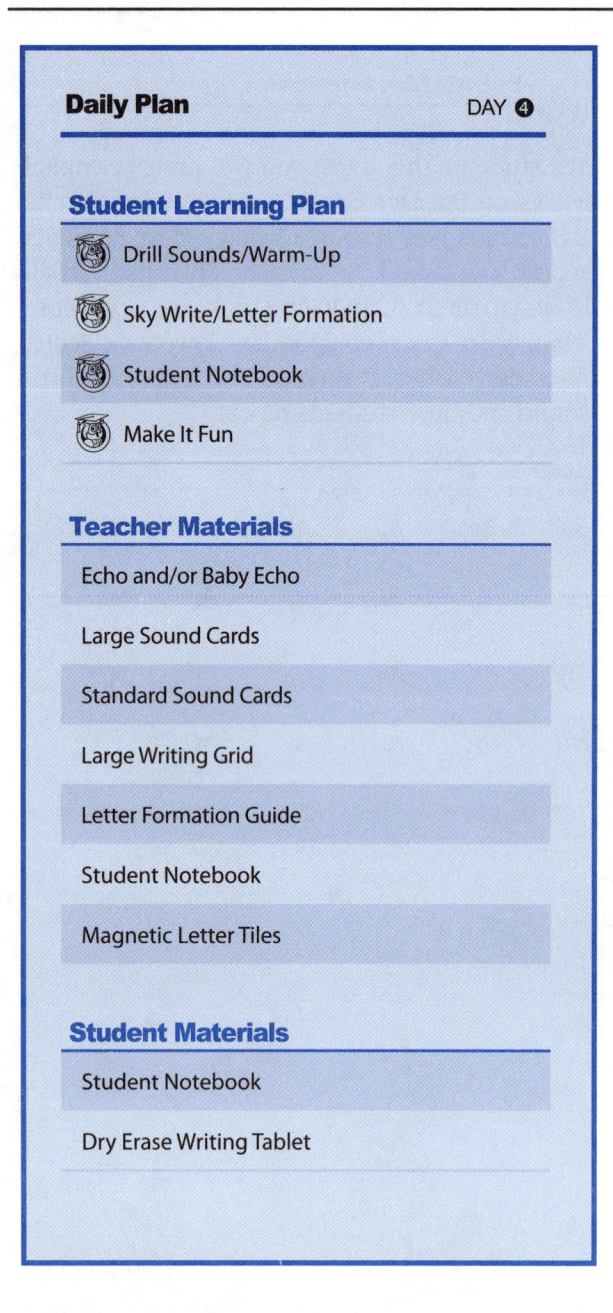

Drill Sounds/Warm-Up

Do any new or challenging sounds and vowel sounds each day. Selectively review 4-5 other consonants.

Large Sound Cards

Practice sounds with the Large Sound Cards. Model these, saying the letter-keyword-sound and have the students echo.

Standard Sound Cards

Next, point to the Standard Sound Cards (in card display) with the Baby Echo pointer. You say the letter-keyword-sound and hold up Baby Echo to have students repeat. You can have a student be the drill leader for some of the sounds.

Sky Write/Letter Formation

Use the following verbalizations to direct students in proper letter formation.

Letter Formation for Y

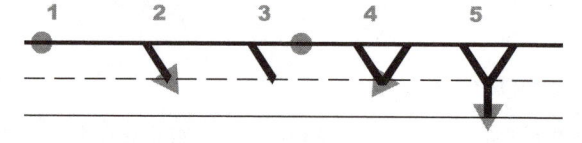

1. Point to the sky line.
2. Slide down to the plane line.
3. Leave a space and point to the sky line.
4. And then slide back to the plane line.
5. Go straight down to the grass line.
6. Say y - yellow - /y/, have students repeat.

Letter Formation for Z

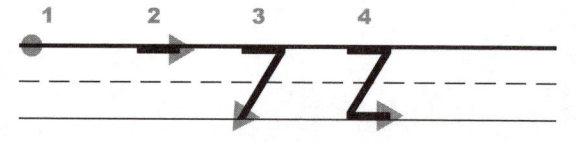

1. Point to the sky line.
2. Make a line.
3. And then slide back to the grass line.
4. And make a line.
5. Say z - zebra - /z/, have students repeat.

Day 4

Student Notebook

Direct students to find the letters corresponding to the letters introduced with sky writing.

Have students trace the large uppercase letter, then lowercase letter with their index finger while you direct them with the verbalization.

Next, have students hold their pencil. Remind them of the correct grip and be sure they are sitting with their chairs pulled in and their feet on the floor. The elbow of their writing arm should be on the desk. They should hold their Student Notebooks with their other hand.

Circulate the room and assist students with the correct position and the proper pencil grip.

Make It Fun

Preparation
- Your sample set of student Magnetic Letter Tiles (put into paper bag)
- Dry Erase Writing Tablets
- Student Notebooks (as needed for reference)

PICK-A-LETTER

This activity will enable students to practice letter formation of uppercase letters and to reinforce alphabetical order and letter-sound correspondence.

Instruct Students

Walk around and have each student select a letter from your paper bag. Have them make the uppercase letter corresponding to the selected letter tile on their Dry Erase Writing Tablets.

Tell them to look in their Student Notebooks or on their Desk Strip if needed. Walk around to assist students and help them with pencil grip and formation. When all students have their letter made, do the next part of the activity.

1. Have them arrange themselves in alphabetical order, circling around the room.
2. If there is not a student for each letter, they should leave a space.
3. When students are arranged, say the alphabet all together.
4. The student holding the spoken letter can hold it up when it is said.

Unit 2 | Week 4

Day 5

Daily Plan — DAY 5

Student Learning Plan
- Drill Sounds/Warm-Up
- Word Play

Teacher Materials
- Echo and/or Baby Echo
- Large Sound Cards
- Standard Sound Cards
- Unit Test Recording Form

Student Materials
- Student Notebook

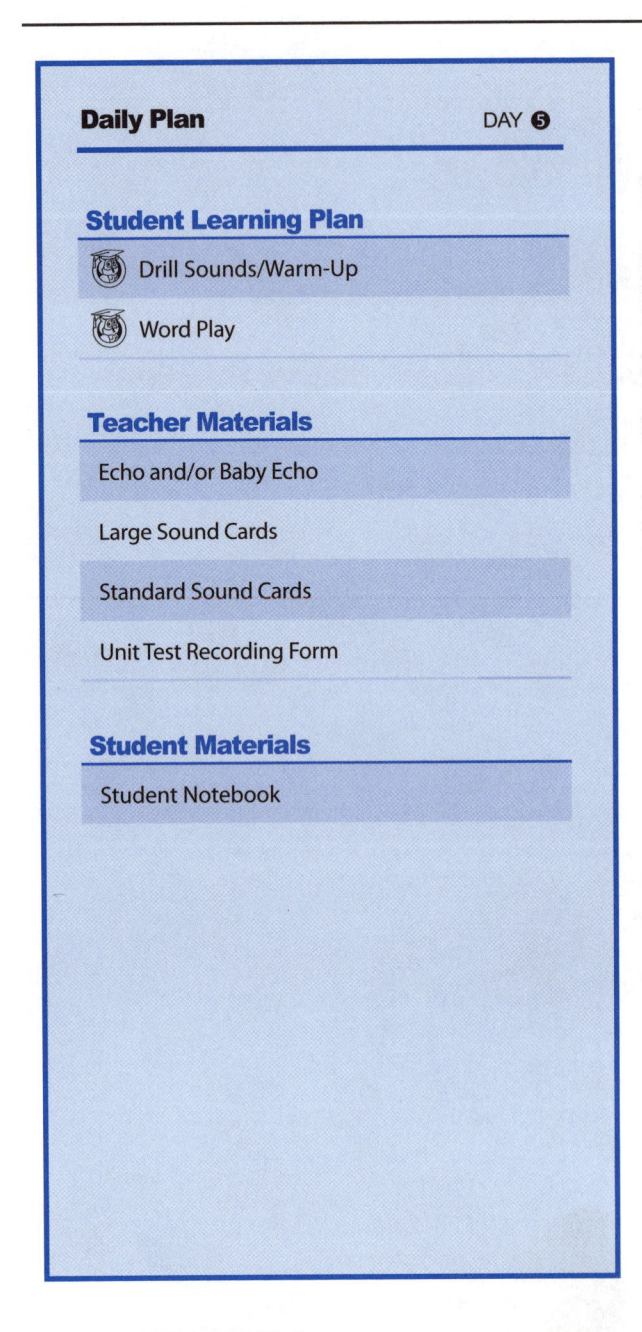

Drill Sounds/Warm-Up

Do any new or challenging sounds and vowel sounds each day. Selectively review 4-5 other consonants.

Large Sound Cards

Practice sounds with the Large Sound Cards. Model these, saying the letter-keyword-sound and have the students echo.

Standard Sound Cards

Next, point to the Standard Sound Cards (in card display) with the Baby Echo pointer. Again, select only 4-5 consonants and all of the vowels. You say the letter-keyword-sound and hold up Baby Echo to have students repeat. You can have a student be the drill leader for some of the sounds.

tip: Revisit the Vowel Extension Activity if needed.

Word Play

MAKE WORDS FOR DECODING

Use your Standard Sound Card display to make 5-6 Unit words. (See Unit Resources.)

Make each word then say and tap each sound. Have students tap with you. Then blend the sounds as you drag your thumb across your fingers.

Next, point under each card as you say each sound, then drag your finger under all three cards as you and the students blend the sounds to read the word.

Unit 2 | Week 4

Unit Test

Each student must be assessed individually. This will take approximately 15-20 minutes per student.

Copy the **Unit Test Recording Form** for each student. Use the student's durable materials, e.g., Dry Erase Writing Tablet, Letter Board and Letter Tiles, as needed.

- Print the Unit Test Recording Form from the PLC.

If a student does not score at least **80%** on any given item, this student will need additional assistance with the assessed skill.

- See the Intervention Guidelines on the PLC for information.

tip

A Unit Test Tracker is available on Wilson Academy® / Prevention Learning Community, under My Resources. This valuable online resource will allow you to track individual student mastery as well as to evaluate readiness of your class to move on.

For any struggling students, meet with them individually to discuss errors and explain areas that need to be further practiced.

© 2002, 2012 WILSON LANGUAGE TRAINING CORPORATION

Have Student Blend Sounds to Form Words

Say sounds one at a time and have student blend to form word. Say, "I will say sounds slowly. Blend them together and tell me the word."

/s/ /ă/ /t/   /f/ /ĭ/ /t/   /p/ /ō/ /k/

/m/ /ā/ /d/   /z/ /ă/ /p/

Have Student Read CVC Words

Make words below with Standard Sound Cards. Have students tap and blend to read the word.

| m a p | n a p | f u n | l i p | n e t |

| s e t | s i t | r o b | m u d | b o x |

Have Student Form Uppercase Letters

*Using the student's Dry Erase Writing Tablet, dictate letters and have student write the uppercase letter on a Large Writing Grid. Say, "Write the uppercase letter **G**."*

G   N   Z   P   H

T   F   X   B   V

Have Student Name Letters in Alphabetical Order

Ask student to place Letter Tiles onto Letter Board and to recite the alphabet in order.

Answer Key

WORDS

sat   fit   poke   made   zap

READ WORDS

map   nap   fun   lip   net
set   sit   rob   mud   box

LETTER FORMATION

G   N   Z   P   H
T   F   X   B   V

Note
Allow students to independently reference their Student Notebooks. Count responses checked in their Notebooks as correct, but make a notation that the book was used.

tip

During Unit Tests, pay attention to students who rely on Alphabet Wall Strip or classroom posters as they may need extra support.

TEACHER'S MANUAL 229

Unit 2

Resources

Drill Sounds/Warm-Up

a - apple - /ă/	b - bat - /b/
c - cat - /k/	d - dog - /d/
e - Ed - /ĕ/	f - fun - /f/
g - game - /g/	h - hat - /h/
i - itch - /ĭ/	j - jug - /j/
k - kite - /k/	l - lamp - /l/
m - man - /m/	n - nut - /n/
o - octopus - /ŏ/	p - pan - /p/
qu - queen - /kw/	r - rat - /r/
s - snake - /s/	t - top - /t/
u - up - /ŭ/	v - van - /v/
w - wind - /w/	x - fox - /ks/
y - yellow - /y/	z - zebra - /z/

Echo Sounds

Sounds appear between / /. You say the sound. Students echo the sound and say the letter. Depending on the activity, students then either find or make the letter corresponding to that sound.

CONSONANTS

/b/ - b	/d/ - d	/f/ - f
/g/ - g	/h/ - h	/j/ - j
/k/ - c, k	/l/ - l	/m/ - m
/n/ - n	/p/ - p	/kw/ - qu
/r/ - r	/s/ - s	/t/ - t
/v/ - v	/w/ - w	/ks/ - x
/y/ - y	/z/ - z	

VOWELS

/ă/ - a	/ĕ/ - e	/ĭ/ - i
/ŏ/ - o	/ŭ/ - u	

Current Unit Words

sad	sat	sap	mad	map	mat
rag	rap	rat	nag	Nat	nap
lad	lag	lap	sip	sit	rip
rig	lip	lit	fit	fig	nip
mop	not	nod	rug	rut	mud
mug	nut	lug	set	met	Meg
net	leg	let	tap	tab	tub
bad	bud	bug	dig	dip	zip
zap	tax	wet	bet	bit	job
cop	dot	Ted	web	ten	bed
at	hip	peg	had	pen	bat
hit	pet	bus	bun	bib	jab
kid	but	cup	pot	Ben	pat
tab	Jim	tin	cob	big	tip
cot	den	gum	wig	yes	cub
pup	hut	gap	dug	cab	vet
wax	pig	kit	did	pal	gas
him	tug	yet			

Unit 2

Unit 3 Level K

In a Nutshell

NEW CONCEPTS

- Phonemic awareness skills: blending, segmenting, and manipulation of sounds
- Blending sounds in nonsense CVC words
- Segmenting and spelling three-sound short vowel words
- Distinguish long and short vowel sounds
- Narrative story form: character, setting, main events
- Fluency and phrasing with echo and choral reading
- Beginning composition skills
- High frequency words (trick words)

SAMPLE WORDS

cut	tap	wet

TRICK WORDS

the	a	and	are	to
is	his	as	has	was

PLANNED TIME IN UNIT

6 WEEKS

Note
Use Unit Test scores and daily classroom work to determine students' mastery. Extend the time in this Unit if needed.

Introduction

In Unit 3, you will continue to teach students how to blend and read three-sound words. Again, these CVC words begin with any consonant. You will change the initial, final and medial sounds to create new words, and also make and blend some non-words such as **bez** for decoding mastery. In this Unit, you will teach students to listen for the vowel sound in words and to distinguish between the long and short vowel sounds in words that they segment.

You will also teach students how to segment and spell these words. Students will learn how to tap out the sounds in a word and find the letters corresponding to each tap in order to spell the word. When you begin spelling, dictate words that begin with **f**, **l**, **m**, **n**, **r** and **s**. You will then progress to words with other consonants ending with the most challenging CVC words to spell. If a word has the /k/ sound, you will teach students to use **k** if the vowel is **e** or **i** and **c** for the other words. As you progress in the Unit, you will dictate any CVC words.

You will continue to work with students to retell stories. You will introduce narrative story structure and help students re-write a short narrative story. You will also practice reading with echo and choral reading.

You will introduce high frequency words for reading. You will call these "Trick Words" and tell students that these words are not tapped out. They need to be memorized.

Nonsense words will assist with your evaluation of the application of your students' skills. The nonsense words have no meaning but they conform to the English spelling patterns and rules. A student must apply letter-sound correspondences to decode the word, versus reading a word that may be memorized from exposure. You will challenge students with nonsense words to help determine their decoding mastery.

Differentiation

In this Unit, you will gradually teach increasingly more challenging spelling of sounds. Be sure to provide additional practice for struggling students.

For advanced students, encourage them to write more extensively in their My Fundations® Journal. In the later weeks, you can also have some advanced students work in a small group for dictation and do it on Composition Paper, rather than on the Dry Erase Writing Tablet.

See Composition Paper from the PLC.

Unit 3

Arrange the sound card display in the following manner:

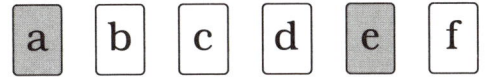

a	b	c	d	e	f
g	h	i	j	k	l
m	n	o	p	qu	r	s
t	u	v	w	x	y	z

Getting Ready

MATERIAL PREPARATIONS

Teacher Materials

Trick Word Flashcards

See Storytime. You will need to find short narrative stories to use for this activity.

Print Lesson Plans from the PLC. See Unit Resources at the end of this Unit.

HOME SUPPORT

Copy and send home the Unit 3 Letter and Activity Packet.

STUDY THE LEARNING ACTIVITIES

Review the following activities:

- Echo/Find Letters and Words
- Dictation/Sounds
- Dictation/Words
- Teach Trick Words
- Trick Word Practice

Review the Learning Activity and Unit videos on the PLC.

Unit 3

Student Learning Plan

Week 1

DAY 1	DAY 2	DAY 3	DAY 4	DAY 5
Drill Sounds/Warm-Up	Drill Sounds/Warm-Up	Drill Sounds/Warm-Up	Drill Sounds/Warm-Up	Drill Sounds/Warm-Up
Introduce New Concepts	Word Play	Word Play	Word Play	Word Play
Echo/Find Letters & Words	Alphabetical Order	Echo/Letter Formation	Dictation (Dry Erase)	Storytime
	Echo/Find Letters & Words	Introduce New Concepts	Make It Fun	

Weeks 2 - 4

DAY 1	DAY 2	DAY 3	DAY 4	DAY 5
Drill Sounds/Warm-Up	Drill Sounds/Warm-Up	Drill Sounds/Warm-Up	Drill Sounds/Warm-Up	Drill Sounds/Warm-Up
Word Play	Word Play	Teach Trick Words	Word Play	Word Play
Alphabetical Order	Echo/Find Letters & Words	Echo/Letter Formation	Make It Fun	Trick Word Practice
Echo/Find Letters & Words	Echo/Letter Formation	Dictation (Dry Erase)	Dictation (Dry Erase)	Storytime

Unit 3

Student Learning Plan

Week 5

DAY 1	DAY 2	DAY 3	DAY 4	DAY 5
Drill Sounds/Warm-Up	Drill Sounds/Warm-Up	Drill Sounds/Warm-Up	Drill Sounds/Warm-Up	Drill Sounds/Warm-Up
Word Play	Word Play	Teach Trick Words	Word Play	Word Play
Introduce New Concepts	Echo/Find Letters & Words	Echo/Letter Formation	Make It Fun	Trick Word Practice
Echo/Find Letters & Words	Echo/Letter Formation	Dictation (Dry Erase)	Dictation (Dry Erase)	Storytime

Week 6

DAY 1	DAY 2	DAY 3	DAY 4	DAY 5
Drill Sounds/Warm-Up	Drill Sounds/Warm-Up	Drill Sounds/Warm-Up	Drill Sounds/Warm-Up	Drill Sounds/Warm-Up
Word Play	Word Play	Teach Trick Words	Word Play	Word Play
Alphabetical Order	Echo/Find Letters & Words	Echo/Letter Formation	Make It Fun	Trick Word Practice
Echo/Find Letters & Words	Echo/Letter Formation	Dictation (Dry Erase)	Dictation (Dry Erase)	Storytime
				Unit Test

Unit 3 | Week 1

Day 1

Daily Plan — DAY 1

Student Learning Plan
- Drill Sounds/Warm-Up
- Introduce New Concepts
- Echo/Find Letters & Words

Teacher Materials
- Echo and/or Baby Echo
- Large Sound Cards
- Standard Sound Cards

Student Materials
- Student Notebook
- Fundations® Letter Board & Tiles

Drill Sounds/Warm-Up

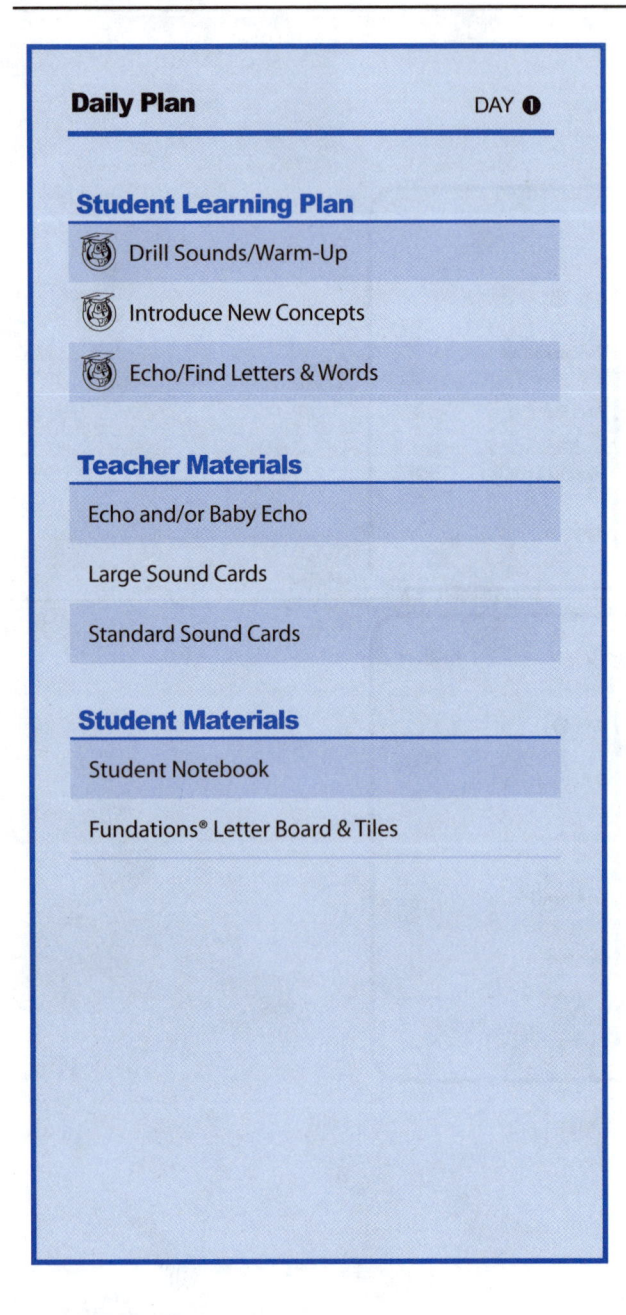

Do any new or challenging sounds and vowel sounds each day. Selectively review 4-5 other consonants.

Large Sound Cards
Practice sounds with the Large Sound Cards. Model these, saying the letter-keyword-sound and have the students echo.

Standard Sound Cards
Next, point to the Standard Sound Cards (in card display) with the Baby Echo pointer. You say the letter-keyword-sound and hold up Baby Echo to have students repeat. You can have a student be the drill leader for some of the sounds.

Vowel Extension
Model extending the vowel sounds (example: **a**-/ă/...**apple**-/ă/). Have a student come trace the line for each of the vowels.

Introduce New Concepts

REVIEW TAPPING TO READ WORDS
You can now change the initial consonant to any consonant to make words. Also, change the vowel and final consonants to form new words. Make 8-10 words. Each time, tap and blend the word with your students.

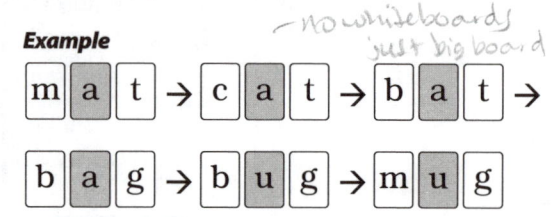

Example

[handwritten: no whiteboards just big board]

mat → cat → bat →

bag → bug → mug

TEACH TAPPING TO SPELL
Use your Standard Sound Card display to teach sound tapping for segmentation and spelling skills.

Say

> Now we are going to do something a little bit different.
>
> I'm going to say a word and we are going to tap it without seeing the letters.
>
> Are you ready to try?

[handwritten: air write 1st]

Say the word **map**, and tap out the three separate sounds without the cards. Tell the students to try to picture the three cards in their mind.

Now re-tap with fingers, but this time select the Standard Sound Cards with each tap to form the word **map**.

Unit 3 | Week 1

Day 1

Repeat this procedure dictating the word **lip**, then **mat**. Tap out sounds and have students repeat. Then find the corresponding cards and place them together to form the word.

Next, dictate the words **nap**, **mud** and **sat**. Have a student come to the front and try tapping out the sounds and finding the corresponding cards.

student helpers

Echo/Find Letters & Words

Echo/Find Letters

Magnets

Say a sound. Have students echo and point to the letter(s) on their Magnetic Letter Boards.

Ask

What says /___/? (___)

(See Echo Sounds in Unit Resources for expected student responses.)

Have students name the letter(s). Then you can have one student find the Standard Sound Card(s) as you dictate sounds. Do vowels and 3-5 other sounds.

Echo/Find Words

Dictate the word **fit**. Have students repeat the word, then tap it out with them.

Have students find Letter Tiles needed to make words on their Magnetic Letter Boards. Have one student come find your corresponding cards. After finding a word, have a student spell it orally. Have students keep the letters on the board and dictate the next word. Have students repeat and tap it out. Tell them to change one letter to make it say **fat**. After changing the letter, have students spell it orally.

Word Resources

| fit | fat | mat | map | mad | mud |

Every Activity is for teaching. Encourage students to use resources, esp. posters, Desk Strip and Student Notebook.

Unit 3 | Week 1

Day 2

Daily Plan — DAY 2

Student Learning Plan
- Drill Sounds/Warm-Up
- Word Play
- Alphabetical Order
- Echo/Find Letters & Words

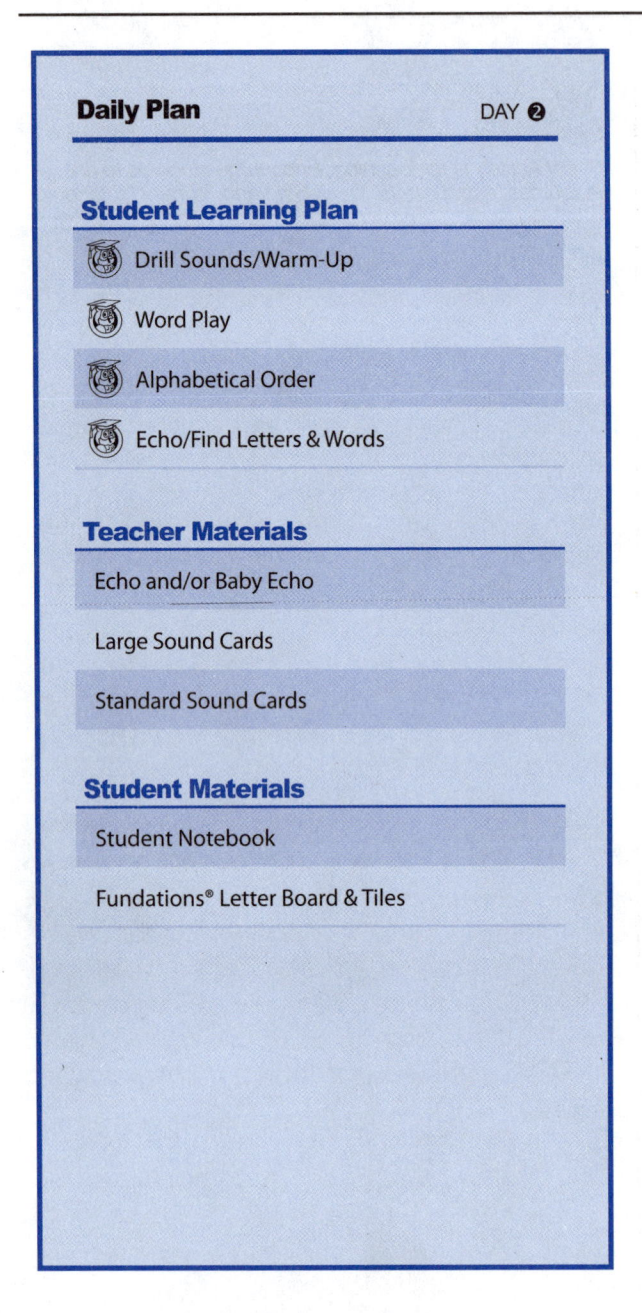

Teacher Materials
- Echo and/or Baby Echo
- Large Sound Cards
- Standard Sound Cards

Student Materials
- Student Notebook
- Fundations® Letter Board & Tiles

Drill Sounds/Warm-Up

Do any new or challenging sounds and vowel sounds each day. Selectively review 4-5 other consonants.

Large Sound Cards

Practice sounds with the Large Sound Cards. Model these, saying the letter-keyword-sound and have the students echo.

Standard Sound Cards

Next, point to the Standard Sound Cards (in card display) with the Baby Echo pointer. You say the letter-keyword-sound and hold up Baby Echo to have students repeat. You can have a student be the drill leader for some of the sounds.

Word Play

MAKE WORDS FOR DECODING

Use your Standard Sound Card display to make 5-6 Unit words. (See Unit Resources.)

Make each word then say and tap each sound. Have students tap with you. Then blend the sounds as you drag your thumb across your fingers.

Next, point under each card as you say each sound, then drag your finger under all three cards as you and the students blend the sounds to read the word.

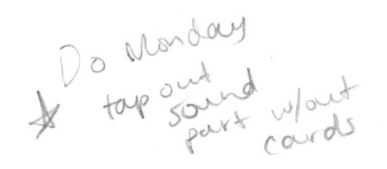

★ Do Monday tap out sound part w/out cards

tip

Remember to weave in vocabulary discussion.

Unit 3 | Week 1

Day 2

LISTEN FOR SOUNDS

This activity will help students distinguish between the long (/ā/) and short (/ă/) vowel sounds. Next say, "I am going to say a word. After I say it, you tell me all the sounds in the word. So, if I say **mad**, you would say /m/ /a/ /d/. Tell me the sounds in _____." (Use the Word Resources below.)

After students say sounds for both words that are similar with different vowel sounds (**mad**, **made**), ask which word has /ă/ sound, **mad** or **made**? Help students tap and stop at the vowel. Tell them that sometimes it will say its name /ā/, which is called a long sound, and sometimes it will say the sound /ă/, which is called a short sound. When they say the word with the short vowel sound (**mad**) say yes! and make it with the Standard Sound Cards and read it together. Tell students that we call this vowel sound a short vowel and we mark it with a breve (˘).

m ă d

Word Resources

mad	made	hope	hop
pin	pine	coat	cot

For advanced students, you can provide additional work on recognizing the long vowel sounds. See the PLC for activities.

Alphabetical Order

Students start with their Magnetic Letter Tiles randomly placed on the blank side of their Letter Boards. Have them sequentially match Letter Tiles on the letter squares.

After students have the tiles placed, chorally say the alphabet. Students should point to each letter as they say its name.

Echo/Find Letters & Words

Echo/Find Letters

Say a sound. Have students echo and point to the letter(s) on their Magnetic Letter Boards.

Ask

What says /___/? (___)

(See Echo Sounds in Unit Resources for expected student responses.)

Have students name the letter(s). Then you can have one student find the Standard Sound Card(s) as you dictate sounds. Do vowels and 3-5 other sounds.

Echo/Find Words

Dictate the word **lap**. Have students repeat the word, then tap it out with them.

Have students find Letter Tiles needed to make words on their Magnetic Letter Boards. Have one student come find your corresponding cards. After finding a word, have a student spell it orally. Have students keep the letters on the board and dictate the next word. Have students repeat and tap it out. Tell them to change one letter to make it say **lip**. After changing the letter, have students spell it orally.

Word Resources

lap	lip	rip	rap	rat	mat

Unit 3 | Week 1

Day 3

Daily Plan — DAY 3

Student Learning Plan
- Drill Sounds/Warm-Up
- Word Play
- Echo/Letter Formation
- Introduce New Concepts

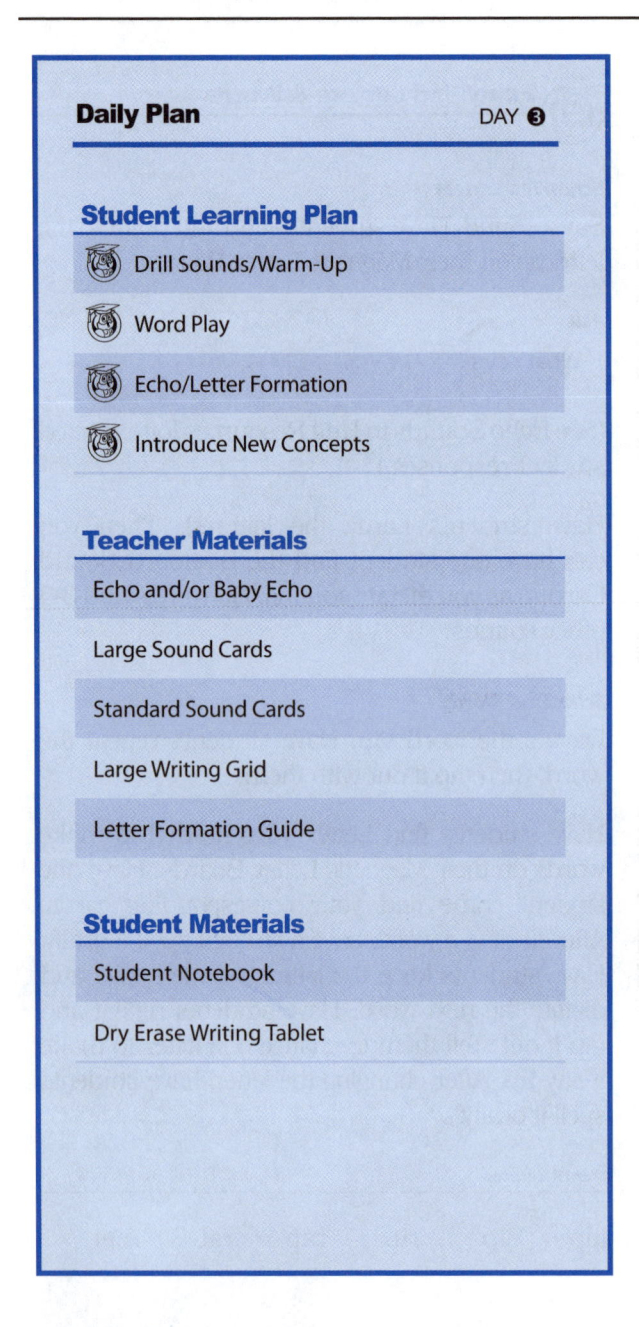

Teacher Materials
- Echo and/or Baby Echo
- Large Sound Cards
- Standard Sound Cards
- Large Writing Grid
- Letter Formation Guide

Student Materials
- Student Notebook
- Dry Erase Writing Tablet

Drill Sounds/Warm-Up

Do any new or challenging sounds and vowel sounds each day. Selectively review 4-5 other consonants.

Large Sound Cards
Practice sounds with the Large Sound Cards. Model these, saying the letter-keyword-sound and have the students echo.

Standard Sound Cards
Next, point to the Standard Sound Cards (in card display) with the Baby Echo pointer. You say the letter-keyword-sound and hold up Baby Echo to have students repeat. You can have a student be the drill leader for some of the sounds.

Word Play

MAKE WORDS FOR DECODING

Use your Standard Sound Card display to make 5-6 Unit words. (See Unit Resources.)

Make each word then say and tap each sound. Have students tap with you. Then blend the sounds as you drag your thumb across your fingers.

Next, point under each card as you say each sound, then drag your finger under all three cards as you and the students blend the sounds to read the word.

Unit 3 | Week 1

Day 3

Echo/Letter Formation

Remind students of proper pencil grip and sitting position, and give them their Dry Erase Writing Tablets.

Dictate 5-6 previously taught sounds. You select and say the sound. Students echo the sound and say the letter.

Next have a student come up to the classroom board to make the letter on the Large Writing Grid.

Then have all students write the answer on their Dry Erase Writing Tablet as you direct them with the letter formation verbalization.

(See Unit Resources.)

tip

Students can make only lowercase letters, or you can selectively do both uppercase and lowercase to reinforce certain letters. (Be sure to always do lowercase for every sound that is dictated.)

Introduce New Concepts

TEACH WORD DICTATION

Tell students that they are now ready to write words. They will need their Dry Erase Writing Tablets. Dictate a word. (See below.) Have the students echo. Next, tap the word with the students.

Say

Name the letters that go with each tap.

Tap the word again, this time naming the letters. Have a student come up and write it on the Large Writing Grid. Have all students then write it on their Dry Erase Writing Tablets. Explain that they should use lowercase letters to write the words. Tap the word again and have students check to see if they spelled the word correctly. Dictate 4-5 words.

Word Resources

mop	sad	sip	log	net	mat
lip	rap				

Unit 3 | Week 1

Day 4

Daily Plan — DAY 4

Student Learning Plan
- Drill Sounds/Warm-Up
- Word Play
- Dictation (Dry Erase)
- Make It Fun

Teacher Materials
- Echo and/or Baby Echo
- Large Sound Cards
- Standard Sound Cards
- Bingo Square Sheet (PLC)
- Scraps of Paper to cover Bingo Squares

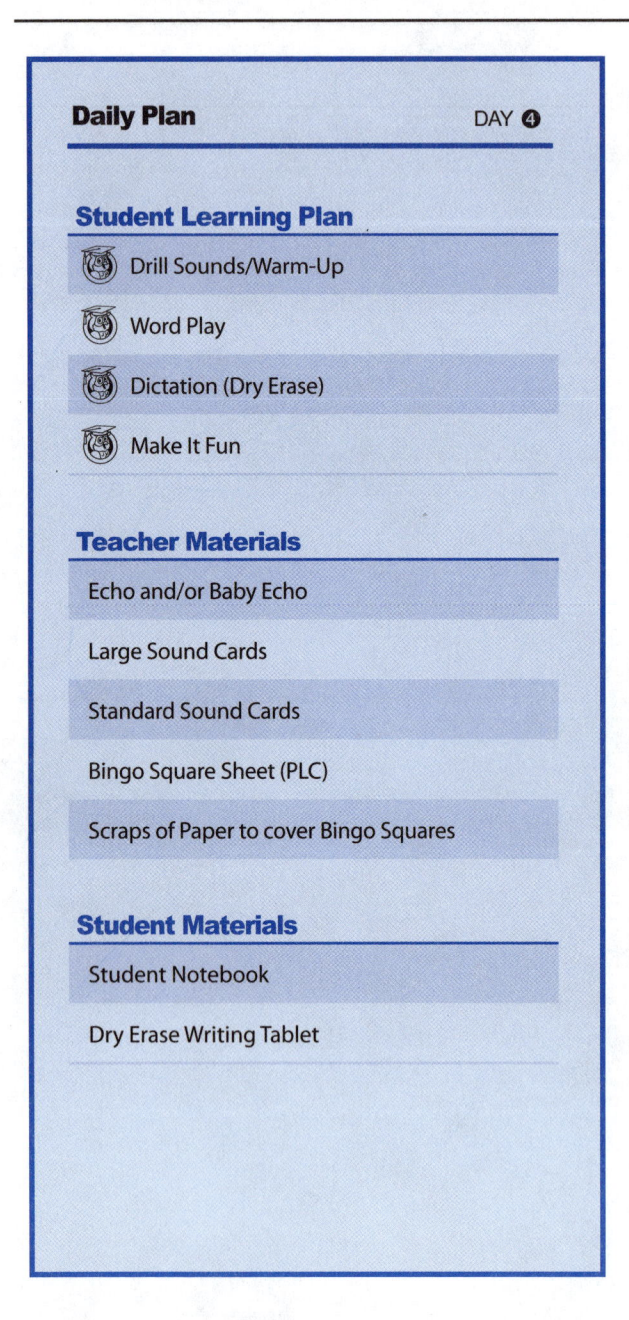

Student Materials
- Student Notebook
- Dry Erase Writing Tablet

Drill Sounds/Warm-Up

Do any new or challenging sounds and vowel sounds each day. Selectively review 4-5 other consonants.

Large Sound Cards

Practice sounds with the Large Sound Cards. Model these, saying the letter-keyword-sound and have the students echo.

Standard Sound Cards

Next, point to the Standard Sound Cards (in card display) with the Baby Echo pointer. You say the letter-keyword-sound and hold up Baby Echo to have students repeat. You can have a student be the drill leader for some of the sounds.

Word Play

MAKE WORDS FOR DECODING

Use your Standard Sound Card display to make 5-6 Unit words. (See Unit Resources.)

Make each word then say and tap each sound. Have students tap with you. Then blend the sounds as you drag your thumb across your fingers.

Next, point under each card as you say each sound, then drag your finger under all three cards as you and the students blend the sounds to read the word.

MAKE NONSENSE WORDS

Tell students that they can also blend sounds together to make silly or nonsense words. Explain that these nonsense word are not real words. They are just silly words that show that they can read sounds.

Make 3-5 nonsense words and have students tap and read them.

Nonsense Word Resources

leb   bap   sut   mig   nom

Unit 3 | Week 1

Day 4

Dictation (Dry Erase)

Proper Dictation Activity procedures are very important. Be sure to follow their demonstration on the Prevention Learning Community. This is a teaching time, not a testing time. Be sure students repeat each dictation. Dictate 3 sounds and then 3 current or review words.

Unit Sounds

Refer to this Unit's Resource List of Echo Sounds.

Unit Words

Students should tap and orally spell the Unit words before writing. Then have all spell chorally. Have one student write on the Large Writing Grid and all students write on their Dry Erase Writing Tablets.

Word Resources

nap   sit   met   mud   fat   lip

Use Activity Cue Cards – follow steps; exact wording is important.

Make It Fun

Preparation

- Word Resource List
- Copy the Bingo Square Sheet for each student (See the PLC)
- Magnetic Letter Tiles (each student selects 9 consonants)
- Chips or paper scraps to cover Bingo Squares

SOUND BINGO

This activity helps students to learn to listen for the last sound in a word.

Instruct Students

Students should select any 9 consonants from the Magnetic Letter Tiles and randomly place them onto their Bingo sheets.

Say

> I am going to say a word.
>
> Everyone will echo it and then listen for the last sound.
>
> If I say the word bug, you echo (bug) and tell me the last sound that you hear (/g/).
>
> If you have the letter that says /g/, put a chip on it.

Continue to dictate words orally and direct the students to listen for the last sound and place a chip on the corresponding consonant if they have it on their Bingo Sheet.

If no student gets Bingo after you say one-syllable words ending in different letters (**b**, **d**, **g**, **f**, **l**, **m**, **n**, **p**, **s**, **t**, **x**, **z**), have students listen for the first sound in dictated words. Dictate words beginning with the other letters (such as **h**, **j**, **r**, **w** and **y**).

Unit 3 | Week 1

Day 5

Daily Plan — DAY 5

Student Learning Plan
- Drill Sounds/Warm-Up
- Word Play
- Storytime

Teacher Materials
- Echo and/or Baby Echo
- Large Sound Cards
- Standard Sound Cards

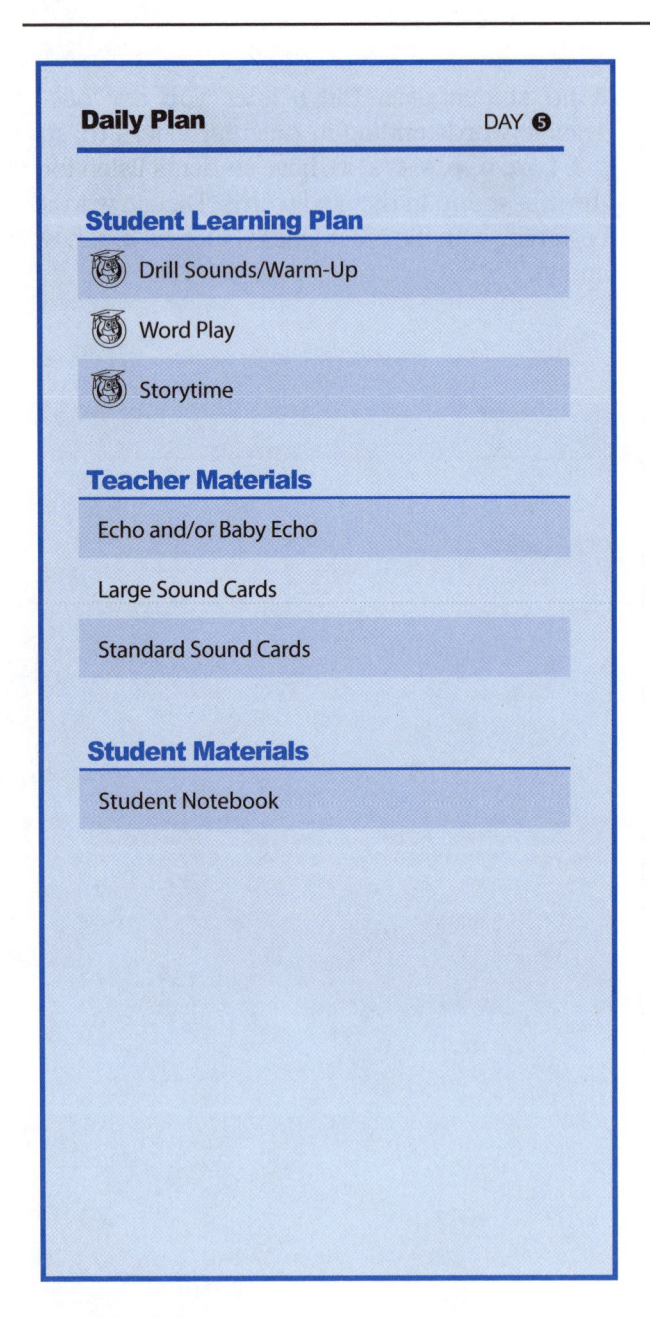

Student Materials
- Student Notebook

Drill Sounds/Warm-Up

Do any new or challenging sounds and vowel sounds each day. Selectively review 4-5 other consonants.

Large Sound Cards

Practice sounds with the Large Sound Cards. Model these, saying the letter-keyword-sound and have the students echo.

Standard Sound Cards

Next, point to the Standard Sound Cards (in card display) with the Baby Echo pointer. You say the letter-keyword-sound and hold up Baby Echo to have students repeat. You can have a student be the drill leader for some of the sounds.

Word Play

MAKE WORDS FOR DECODING

Use your Standard Sound Card display to make 5-6 Unit words. (See Unit Resources.)

Make each word then say and tap each sound. Have students tap with you. Then blend the sounds as you drag your thumb across your fingers.

Next, point under each card as you say each sound, then drag your finger under all three cards as you and the students blend the sounds to read the word.

Unit 3 | Week 1

Day 5

Storytime

Teacher Materials

- Echo the Owl (on the floor behind you)
- Baby Echo

Read through and practice the story prior to the lesson with your students.

BABY ECHO FINDS ECHO AT LAST I

Perform the Story

One day Baby Echo was looking for his mother.

Put Echo on the floor behind you. Put Baby Echo on your finger and stretch out your other arm. 'Sit' Baby Echo up at your shoulder of your out-stretched arm.

He looked and looked but he couldn't see her.

Bend him to look down at the floor.

So he hopped over to the middle of the big branch.

Hop Baby Echo to your elbow.

He looked and looked there, but he still couldn't see her.

Bend him to look at the floor.

So he hopped over to the very edge of the big long branch.

Hop him down to your fingertips.

He looked and looked there, but he still couldn't see her.

Bend him down to the floor.

He sat up and thought, "Where is my mother?"

Face him up.

Just then he heard a noise behind him. He turned around and looked down.

Turn Baby Echo around and look down.

Baby Echo saw his mother. At last he was happy.

Ask the Following Questions

Who was in this story?

Where did it take place?

What was Baby Echo's problem?

What did he do about it?

How did things turn out? What happened in the end?

How did Baby Echo feel at the beginning of the story?

How did Baby Echo feel at the end of the story?

tip

*Read a story aloud to students with the similar theme of looking for someone, such as **Are You My Mother?** Help students to compare and contrast it to Baby Echo's search.*

Unit 3 | Week 2

Day 1

Daily Plan — DAY 1

Student Learning Plan
- Drill Sounds/Warm-Up
- Word Play
- Alphabetical Order
- Echo/Find Letters & Words

Teacher Materials
- Echo and/or Baby Echo
- Large Sound Cards
- Standard Sound Cards
- Vowel Extension Poster

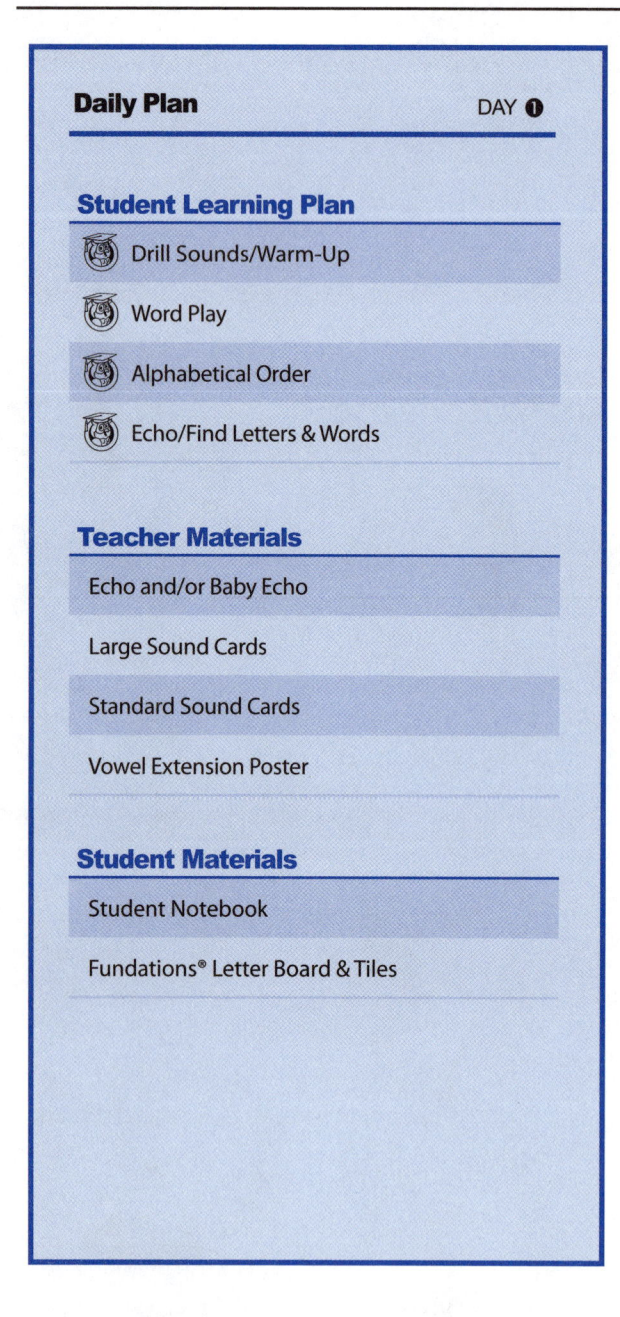

Student Materials
- Student Notebook
- Fundations® Letter Board & Tiles

Drill Sounds/Warm-Up

Do any new or challenging sounds and vowel sounds each day. Selectively review 4-5 other consonants.

Large Sound Cards
Practice sounds with the Large Sound Cards. Model these, saying the letter-keyword-sound and have the students echo.

Standard Sound Cards
Next, point to the Standard Sound Cards (in card display) with the Baby Echo pointer. You say the letter-keyword-sound and hold up Baby Echo to have students repeat. You can have a student be the drill leader for some of the sounds.

Vowel Extension
Model extending the vowel sounds (example: a-/ă/...apple-/ă/). Have a student come trace the line for each of the vowels.

Word Play

MAKE WORDS FOR DECODING

Use your Standard Sound Card display to make 5-6 Unit words. (See Unit Resources.)

Make each word then say and tap each sound. Have students tap with you. Then blend the sounds as you drag your thumb across your fingers.

Next, point under each card as you say each sound, then drag your finger under all three cards as you and the students blend the sounds to read the word.

Unit 3 | Week 2

Day 1

Alphabetical Order

Students start with their Magnetic Letter Tiles randomly placed on the blank side of their Letter Boards. Have them sequentially match Letter Tiles on the letter squares.

After students have the tiles placed, chorally say the alphabet. Students should point to each letter as they say its name.

Echo/Find Letters & Words

Echo/Find Letters

Say a sound. Have students echo and point to the letter(s) on their Magnetic Letter Boards.

Ask

What says /___/? (___)

(See Echo Sounds in Unit Resources for expected student responses.)

Have students name the letter(s). Then you can have one student find the Standard Sound Card(s) as you dictate sounds. Do vowels and 3-5 other sounds.

Echo/Find Words

Dictate the word **pot**. Have students repeat the word, then tap it out with them.

Have students find Letter Tiles needed to make words on their Magnetic Letter Boards. Have one student come find your corresponding cards. After finding a word, have a student spell it orally. Have the students replace the letters onto their letter squares and dictate another word. Do 3-5 words.

Word Resources

pot   big   pen   jab   tap   tub

| t | i | p |

Be sure to hold students accountable for correct letter formation!

Unit 3 | Week 2

Day 2

Daily Plan — DAY 2

Student Learning Plan
- Drill Sounds/Warm-Up
- Word Play
- Echo/Find Letters & Words
- Echo/Letter Formation

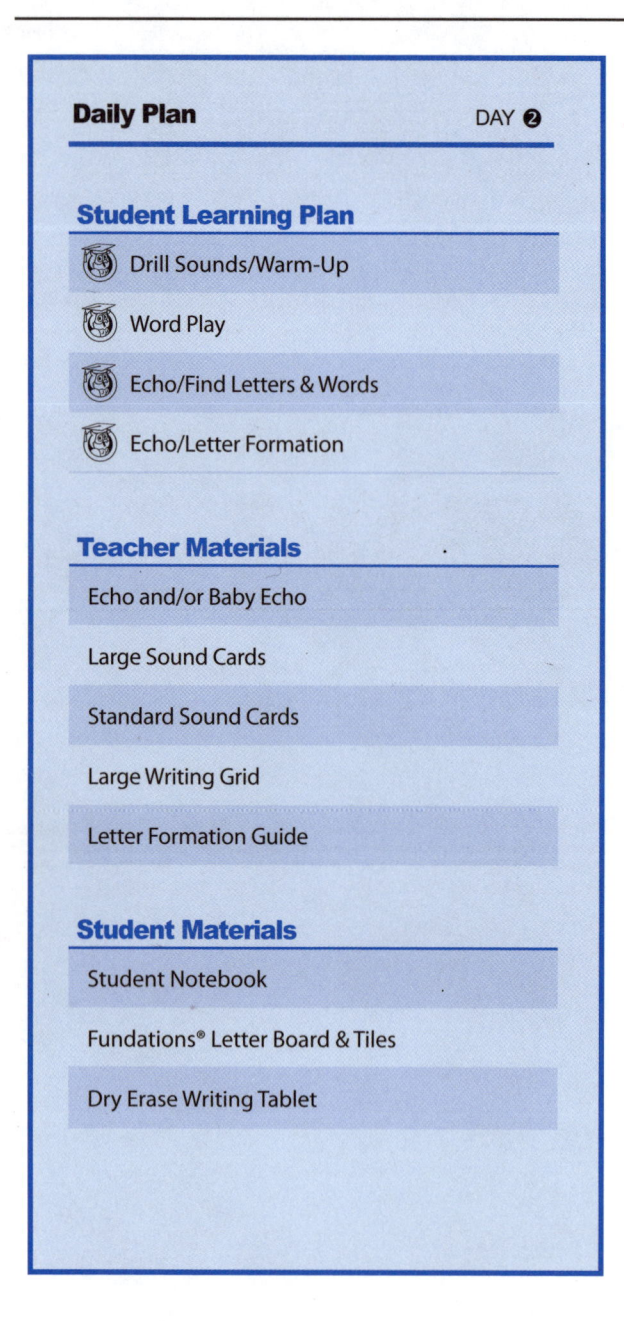

Teacher Materials
- Echo and/or Baby Echo
- Large Sound Cards
- Standard Sound Cards
- Large Writing Grid
- Letter Formation Guide

Student Materials
- Student Notebook
- Fundations® Letter Board & Tiles
- Dry Erase Writing Tablet

Drill Sounds/Warm-Up

Do any new or challenging sounds and vowel sounds each day. Selectively review 4-5 other consonants.

Large Sound Cards
Practice sounds with the Large Sound Cards. Model these, saying the letter-keyword-sound and have the students echo.

Standard Sound Cards
Next, point to the Standard Sound Cards (in card display) with the Baby Echo pointer. You say the letter-keyword-sound and hold up Baby Echo to have students repeat. You can have a student be the drill leader for some of the sounds.

Word Play

MAKE WORDS FOR DECODING

Use your Standard Sound Card display to make 5-6 Unit words. (See Unit Resources.)

Make each word then say and tap each sound. Have students tap with you. Then blend the sounds as you drag your thumb across your fingers.

Next, point under each card as you say each sound, then drag your finger under all three cards as you and the students blend the sounds to read the word.

Unit 3 | Week 2

Day 2

LISTEN FOR SOUNDS

This activity will help students distinguish between the long (/ā/) and short (/ă/) vowel sounds. Next say, "I am going to say a word. After I say it, you tell me all the sounds in the word. So, if I say **mad**, you would say /m/ /a/ /d/. Tell me the sounds in _____." (Use the Word Resources below.)

After students say sounds for both words that are similar with different vowel sounds (**mad**, **made**), ask which word has /ă/ sound, **mad** or **made**? Help students tap and stop at the vowel. Tell them that sometimes it will say its name /ā/, which is called a long sound, and sometimes it will say the sound /ă/, which is called a short sound. When they say the word with the short vowel sound (**mad**) say yes! and make it with the Standard Sound Cards and read it together. Tell students that we call this vowel sound a short vowel and we mark it with a breve (˘).

m ă d

Word Resources

bait	bat	mop	mope
sight	sit	cap	cape

For advanced students, you can provide additional work on recognizing the long vowel sounds. See the PLC for activities.

© 2002, 2012 WILSON LANGUAGE TRAINING CORPORATION

Echo/Find Letters & Words

Echo/Find Letters

Say a sound. Have students echo and point to the letter(s) on their Magnetic Letter Boards.

Ask

What says /___/? (___)

(See Echo Sounds in Unit Resources for expected student responses.)

Have students name the letter(s). Then you can have one student find the Standard Sound Card(s) as you dictate sounds. Do vowels and 3-5 other sounds.

Echo/Find Words

Dictate the word **bit**. Have students repeat the word, then tap it out with them.

Have students find Letter Tiles needed to make words on their Magnetic Letter Boards. Have one student come find your corresponding cards. After finding a word, have a student spell it orally. Have the students replace the letters onto their letter squares and dictate another word. Do 3-5 words.

Word Resources

bit	pig	dog	gap	hug	pet

Remember to weave in vocabulary discussion.

Echo/Letter Formation

Remind students of proper pencil grip and sitting position, and give them their Dry Erase Writing Tablets.

Dictate 5-6 previously taught sounds. You select and say the sound. Students echo the sound and say the letter.

Next have a student come up to the classroom board to make the letter on the Large Writing Grid.

Then have all students write the answer on their Dry Erase Writing Tablet as you direct them with the letter formation verbalization.

(See Unit Resources.)

Note

Students can make only lowercase letters, or you can selectively do both uppercase and lowercase to reinforce certain letters. (Be sure to always do lowercase for every sound that is dictated.)

TEACHER'S MANUAL **249**

Unit 3 | Week 2

Day 3

Daily Plan — DAY 3

Student Learning Plan
- Drill Sounds/Warm-Up
- Teach Trick Words
- Echo/Letter Formation
- Dictation (Dry Erase)

Teacher Materials
- Echo and/or Baby Echo
- Large Sound Cards
- Standard Sound Cards
- Large Writing Grid
- Letter Formation Guide
- Sentence Frames
- Trick Word Flashcards

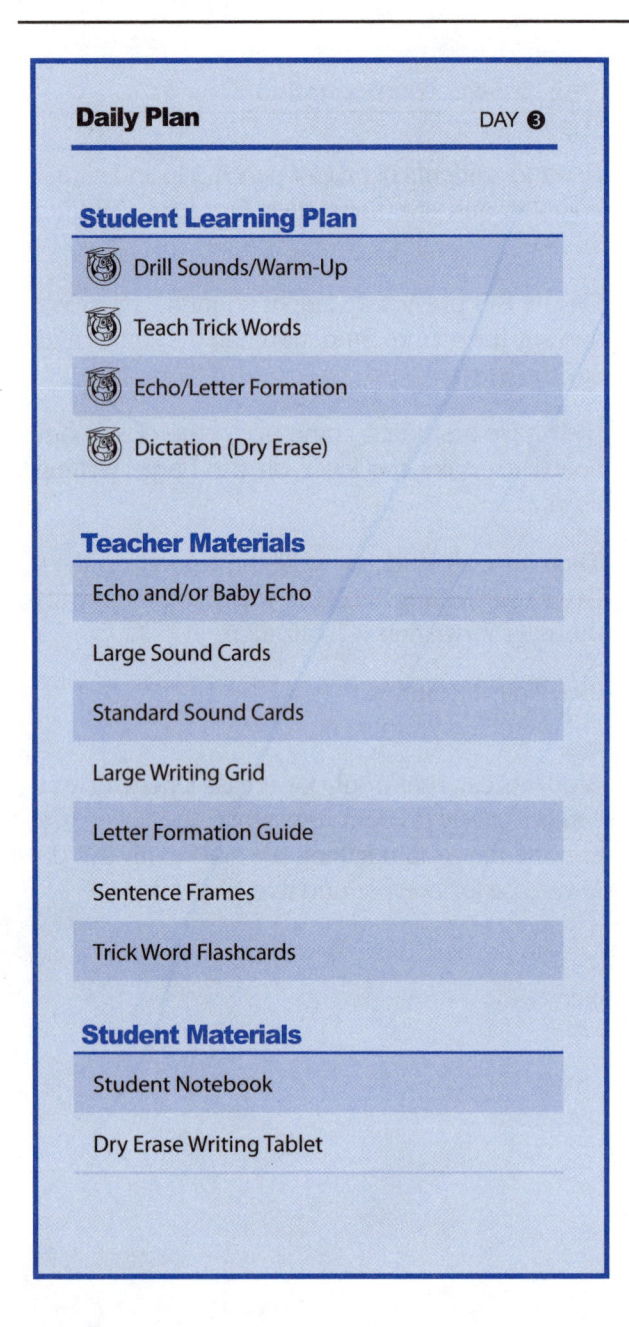

Student Materials
- Student Notebook
- Dry Erase Writing Tablet

Drill Sounds/Warm-Up

Do any new or challenging sounds and vowel sounds each day. Selectively review 4-5 other consonants.

Large Sound Cards

Practice sounds with the Large Sound Cards. Model these, saying the letter-keyword-sound and have the students echo.

Standard Sound Cards

Next, point to the Standard Sound Cards (in card display) with the Baby Echo pointer. You say the letter-keyword-sound and hold up Baby Echo to have students repeat. You can have a student be the drill leader for some of the sounds.

Teach Trick Words

Introduce the trick words **the** and **a**, and reinforce capitalization and punctuation.

Instruct Students

Say the sentence below and have students repeat. You can also use a student's name in the sentence, rather than Meg. Have a student place the Sentence Frames as needed. Write the sentence on the frames, and discuss capitalization and punctuation. Scoop the sentence into phrases, read it, and have students echo.

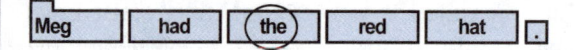

| Meg | had | (the) | red | hat | . |

Say

I am going to circle this word (circle the new trick word). Listen to the sentence and see if you can tell me the word I circled.

Let's change this sentence to: Meg had a red hat.

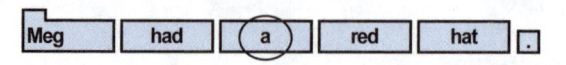

| Meg | had | (a) | red | hat | . |

(Pronounce the word a /ŭ/.)

Have a student erase **the** and then you write the word **a**.

Next, explain that the words **the** and **a** are words that you are going to practice, and that these words are called Trick Words because they can be tricky and we do not tap them out.

250 FUNDATIONS® LEVEL K

Unit 3 | Week 2

Day 3

Show students the Trick Word Flashcards **the** and **a**. Say the words and have them repeat. Tell them that the letter **a** is a letter, but sometimes it is the trick word **a**.

Echo/Letter Formation

Remind students of proper pencil grip and sitting position, and give them their Dry Erase Writing Tablets.

Dictate 5-6 previously taught sounds. You select and say the sound. Students echo the sound and say the letter.

Next have a student come up to the classroom board to make the letter on the Large Writing Grid.

Then have all students write the answer on their Dry Erase Writing Tablet as you direct them with the letter formation verbalization.

(See Unit Resources.)

Note
Students can make only lowercase letters, or you can selectively do both uppercase and lowercase to reinforce certain letters. (Be sure to always do lowercase for every sound that is dictated.)

Dictation (Dry Erase)

Proper Dictation Activity procedures are very important. Be sure to follow their demonstration on the Prevention Learning Community. This is a teaching time, not a testing time. Be sure students repeat each dictation. Dictate 3 sounds and then 3 current or review words.

Unit Sounds
Refer to this Unit's Resource List of Echo Sounds.

Unit Words
Students should tap and orally spell the Unit words before writing. Then have all spell chorally. Have one student write on the Large Writing Grid and all students write on their Dry Erase Writing Tablets.

Word Resources

nap   dug   rag   pit   fog   ten

Unit 3 | Week 2

Day 4

Daily Plan — DAY 4

Student Learning Plan
- Drill Sounds/Warm-Up
- Word Play
- Make It Fun
- Dictation (Dry Erase)

Teacher Materials
- Echo and/or Baby Echo
- Large Sound Cards
- Standard Sound Cards

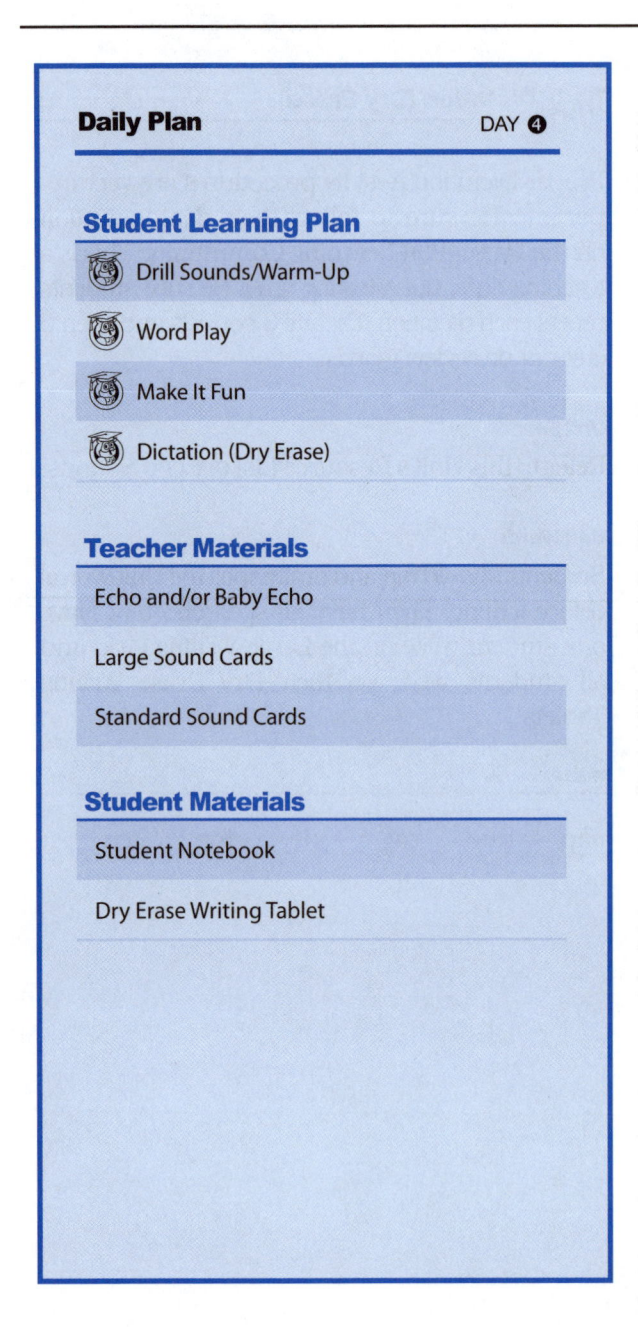

Student Materials
- Student Notebook
- Dry Erase Writing Tablet

Drill Sounds/Warm-Up

Do any new or challenging sounds and vowel sounds each day. Selectively review 4-5 other consonants.

Large Sound Cards

Practice sounds with the Large Sound Cards. Model these, saying the letter-keyword-sound and have the students echo.

Standard Sound Cards

Next, point to the Standard Sound Cards (in card display) with the Baby Echo pointer. You say the letter-keyword-sound and hold up Baby Echo to have students repeat. You can have a student be the drill leader for some of the sounds.

Word Play

MAKE WORDS FOR DECODING

Use your Standard Sound Card display to make 5-6 Unit words. (See Unit Resources.)

Make each word then say and tap each sound. Have students tap with you. Then blend the sounds as you drag your thumb across your fingers.

Next, point under each card as you say each sound, then drag your finger under all three cards as you and the students blend the sounds to read the word.

MAKE NONSENSE WORDS

Tell students that they can also blend sounds together to make silly or nonsense words. Explain that these nonsense word are not real words. They are just silly words that show that they can read sounds.

Make 3-5 nonsense words and have students tap and read them.

Nonsense Word Resources

dop   pib   gud   mag   fet

Unit 3 | Week 2

Day 4

Make It Fun

SOUND A WORD

Teacher Materials

Place approximately ten small objects (such as plastic animals, cars, pens) in a pillow case or bag. The objects should have a name that is one-syllable of varying length (such as: **pen**, **clip**, **truck**).

Directions

Select a child to pick an item from the bag, but not show it to the class, only to you. Whisper the word segmented to the student and have them repeat it, segmented to the class. For example, if it is a truck, you would say:

/t/ /r/ /ŭ/ /k/   and the student would say:

/t/ /r/ /ŭ/ /k/

Select a student to guess the object. When someone guesses, the student holding the object shows it to the class and sits down with it.

The student who correctly guessed selects the next object from the bag. When all items have been selected, have the students give the object to a student without an object. Collect objects one at a time by saying the word segmented into sounds.

Say

I'm looking for the /t/ /r/ /ŭ/ /k/. Who has the /t/ /r/ /ŭ/ /k/?

Dictation (Dry Erase)

Proper Dictation Activity procedures are very important. Be sure to follow their demonstration on the Prevention Learning Community. This is a teaching time, not a testing time. Be sure students repeat each dictation. Dictate 3 sounds and then 3 current or review words.

Unit Sounds

Refer to this Unit's Resource List of Echo Sounds.

Unit Words

Students should tap and orally spell the Unit words before writing. Then have all spell chorally. Have one student write on the Large Writing Grid and all students write on their Dry Erase Writing Tablets.

Word Resources

bib   dig   job   tap   pet   jab

Unit 3 | Week 2

Day 5

Daily Plan — DAY 5

Student Learning Plan
- Drill Sounds/Warm-Up
- Word Play
- Trick Word Practice
- Storytime

Teacher Materials
- Echo and/or Baby Echo
- Large Sound Cards
- Standard Sound Cards
- Sentence Frames
- Trick Word Flashcards

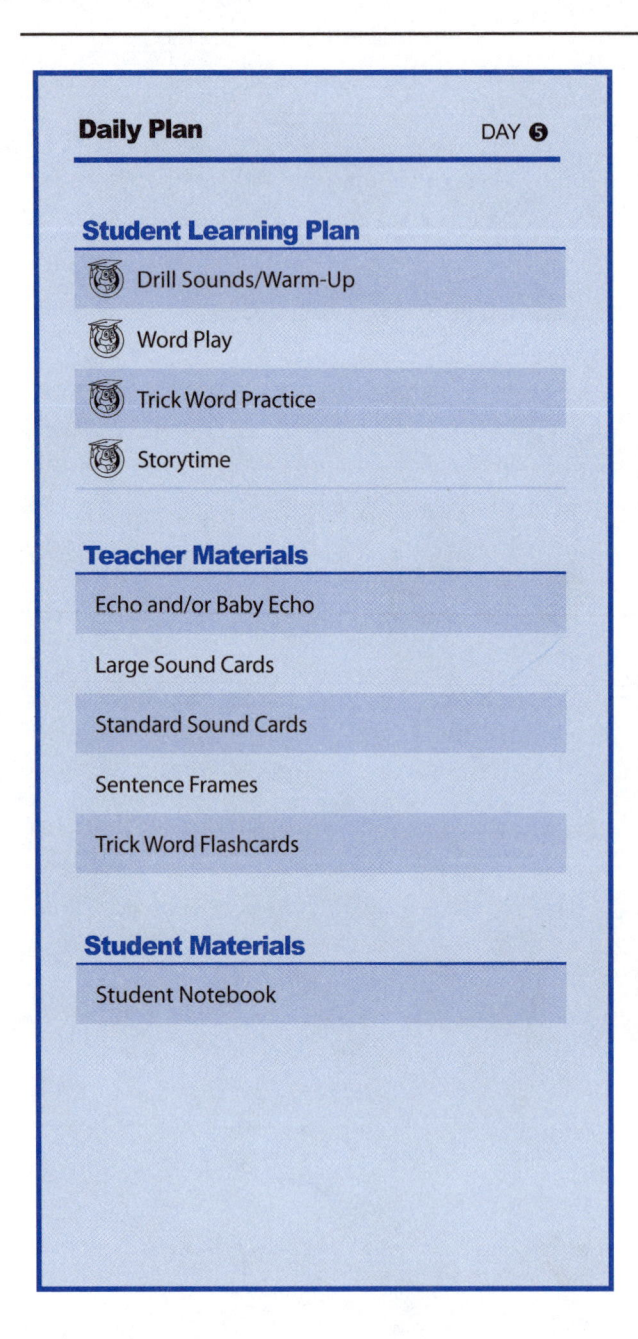

Student Materials
- Student Notebook

Drill Sounds/Warm-Up

Do any new or challenging sounds and vowel sounds each day. Selectively review 4-5 other consonants.

Large Sound Cards
Practice sounds with the Large Sound Cards. Model these, saying the letter-keyword-sound and have the students echo.

Standard Sound Cards
Next, point to the Standard Sound Cards (in card display) with the Baby Echo pointer. You say the letter-keyword-sound and hold up Baby Echo to have students repeat. You can have a student be the drill leader for some of the sounds.

Word Play

MAKE WORDS FOR DECODING

Use your Standard Sound Card display to make 5-6 Unit words. (See Unit Resources.)

Make each word then say and tap each sound. Have students tap with you. Then blend the sounds as you drag your thumb across your fingers.

Next, point under each card as you say each sound, then drag your finger under all three cards as you and the students blend the sounds to read the word.

Unit 3 | Week 2

Day 5

Trick Word Practice

Say each sentence below and have students repeat. Then write the sentence on Sentence Frames, and scoop it into phrases. Read it and have students echo. Say the trick word that is in the sentence and have a student find and circle it. After it is circled, hold up the corresponding Trick Word Flashcard and say the word and have students repeat.

Sentence Resource

Sid is a dog.

Sid is (the) best dog.

Tab is a cat.

Tab is (the) best cat.

Lastly present the Trick Word Flashcards learned thus far. Say each and have students repeat.

Storytime

Teacher Materials
- Echo the Owl (on the floor behind you)
- Baby Echo

BABY ECHO FINDS ECHO AT LAST II

This week you will say and act out the same story, "Baby Echo Finds Echo At Last." Then you will perform it again, without words, and have the students retell the story as you "play it out."

Re-perform the Story

Tell and act out "Baby Echo Finds Echo At Last." (See Week 5, Day 5).

Perform the Story Without Words

Perform the story again, without words, and have students tell you what happened.

After a student tells you in his/her own words, restate the words from the story to clarify as needed.

Be sure to provide students positive feedback for retelling in their own words.

Put Echo on the floor behind you. Put Baby Echo on your finger and stretch out your other arm. 'Sit' Baby Echo up at your shoulder of your out-stretched arm.

One day Baby Echo was looking for his mother.

Bend him to look down at the floor.

He looked and looked but he couldn't see her.

Hop Baby Echo to your elbow.

So he hopped over to the middle of the big branch.

Bend him to look at the floor.

He looked and looked there, but he still couldn't see her.

Hop him down to your fingertips.

So he hopped over to the very edge of the big long branch.

Bend him down to the floor.

He looked and looked there, but he still couldn't see her.

He sat up and thought, "Where is my mother?"

Face him up.

Just then he heard a noise behind him. He turned around and looked down.

Turn Baby Echo around and look down.

Baby Echo saw his mother. At last he was happy.

Unit 3 | Week 3

Day 1

Daily Plan — DAY 1

Student Learning Plan
- Drill Sounds/Warm-Up
- Word Play
- Alphabetical Order
- Echo/Find Letters & Words

Teacher Materials
- Echo and/or Baby Echo
- Large Sound Cards
- Standard Sound Cards
- Vowel Extension Poster

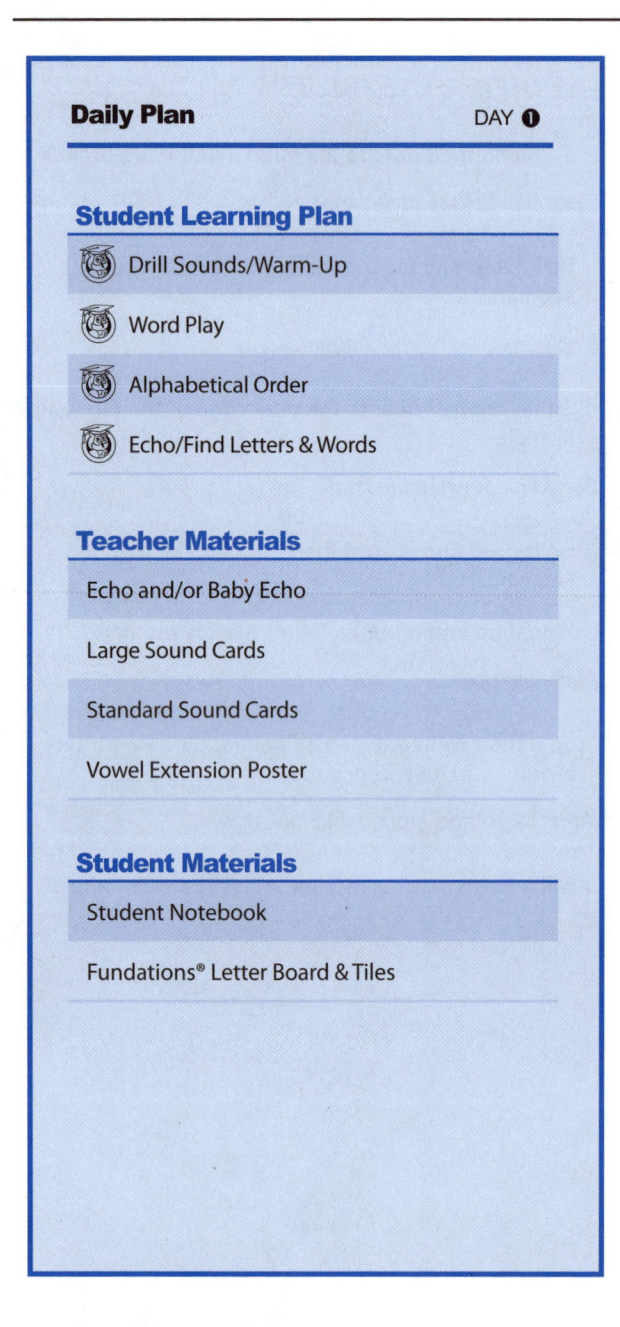

Student Materials
- Student Notebook
- Fundations® Letter Board & Tiles

Drill Sounds/Warm-Up

Do any new or challenging sounds and vowel sounds each day. Selectively review 4-5 other consonants.

Large Sound Cards
Practice sounds with the Large Sound Cards. Model these, saying the letter-keyword-sound and have the students echo.

Standard Sound Cards
Next, point to the Standard Sound Cards (in card display) with the Baby Echo pointer. You say the letter-keyword-sound and hold up Baby Echo to have students repeat. You can have a student be the drill leader for some of the sounds.

Vowel Extension
Model extending the vowel sounds (example: **a-/ă/...apple-/ă/**). Have a student come trace the line for each of the vowels.

Word Play

MAKE WORDS FOR DECODING

Use your Standard Sound Card display to make 5-6 Unit words. (See Unit Resources.)

Make each word then say and tap each sound. Have students tap with you. Then blend the sounds as you drag your thumb across your fingers.

Next, point under each card as you say each sound, then drag your finger under all three cards as you and the students blend the sounds to read the word.

Unit 3 | Week 3

Day 1

Alphabetical Order

Students start with their Magnetic Letter Tiles randomly placed on the blank side of their Letter Boards. Have them sequentially match Letter Tiles on the letter squares.

After students have the tiles placed, chorally say the alphabet. Students should point to each letter as they say its name.

Echo/Find Letters & Words

Echo/Find Letters

Say a sound. Have students echo and point to the letter(s) on their Magnetic Letter Boards.

Ask

What says /v/? (v)

What says /y/? (y)

What says /w/? (w)

What says /z/? (z)

What says /kw/? (qu)

Echo/Find Words

Explain that you will be giving them words to spell with some more sounds that might be tricky. Dictate the word **yes** and have them repeat and tap.

Ask

What is the sound at the beginning of the word? (/y/)

What letter makes that sound? (y)

Find the Letter Tiles to spell the word **yes**.

Next, dictate the word **quit**. Have students repeat the word, then tap it out with them. Have one student come find your corresponding cards.

Tell students that they will need to listen carefully to the beginning sound to spell the word.

Ask

What is the sound at the beginning of the word? (/kw/)

What letters makes that sound? (qu)

Find the Letter Tiles to spell the word **quit**.

Dictate the word **vet**. Have students repeat the word, then tap it out with them.

Have students find Letter Tiles needed to make words on their Magnetic Letter Boards. Have one student come find your corresponding cards. After finding a word, have a student spell it orally. Have the students replace the letters onto their letter squares and dictate another word. Do 3-5 words.

Word Resources

yes   quit   vet   wag   zap   quiz

Unit 3 | Week 3

Day 2

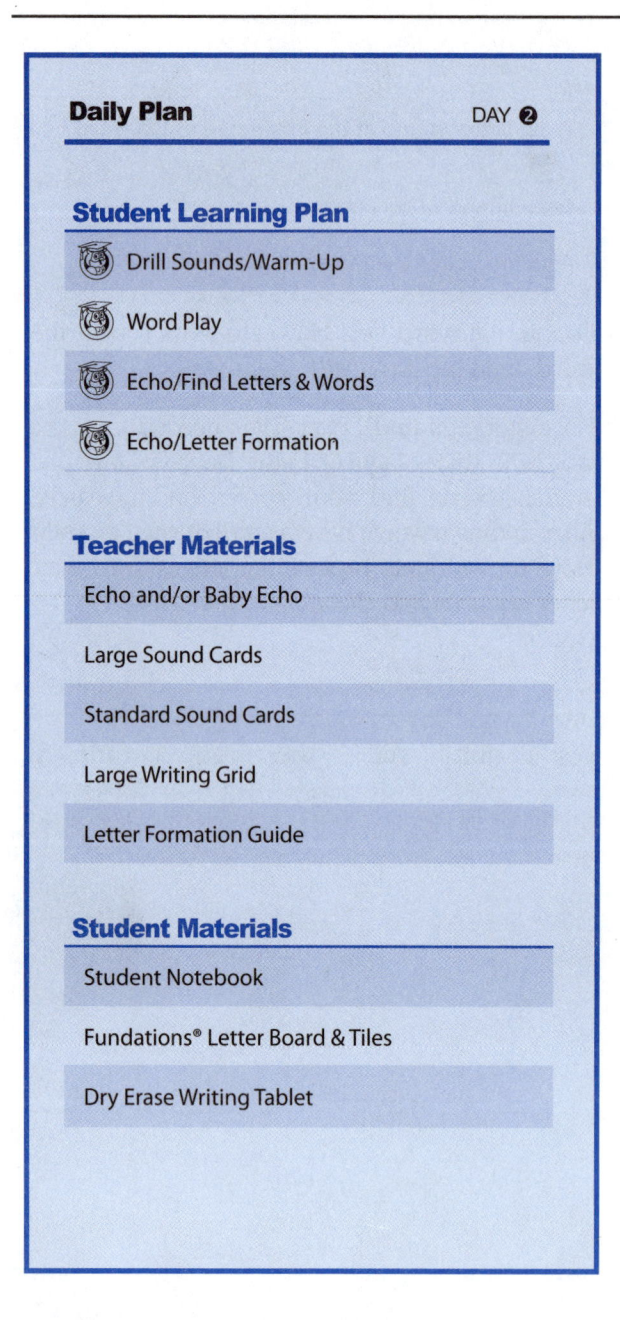

Daily Plan — DAY 2

Student Learning Plan
- Drill Sounds/Warm-Up
- Word Play
- Echo/Find Letters & Words
- Echo/Letter Formation

Teacher Materials
- Echo and/or Baby Echo
- Large Sound Cards
- Standard Sound Cards
- Large Writing Grid
- Letter Formation Guide

Student Materials
- Student Notebook
- Fundations® Letter Board & Tiles
- Dry Erase Writing Tablet

Drill Sounds/Warm-Up

Do any new or challenging sounds and vowel sounds each day. Selectively review 4-5 other consonants.

Large Sound Cards

Practice sounds with the Large Sound Cards. Model these, saying the letter-keyword-sound and have the students echo.

Standard Sound Cards

Next, point to the Standard Sound Cards (in card display) with the Baby Echo pointer. You say the letter-keyword-sound and hold up Baby Echo to have students repeat. You can have a student be the drill leader for some of the sounds.

Word Play

MAKE WORDS FOR DECODING

Use your Standard Sound Card display to make 5-6 Unit words. (See Unit Resources.)

Make each word then say and tap each sound. Have students tap with you. Then blend the sounds as you drag your thumb across your fingers.

Next, point under each card as you say each sound, then drag your finger under all three cards as you and the students blend the sounds to read the word.

Unit 3 | Week 3

Day 2

LISTEN FOR SOUNDS

This activity will help students distinguish between the long (/ā/) and short (/ă/) vowel sounds. Next say, "I am going to say a word. After I say it, you tell me all the sounds in the word. So, if I say **mad**, you would say **/m/ /a/ /d/**. Tell me the sounds in _____." (Use the Word Resources below.)

After students say sounds for both words that are similar with different vowel sounds (**mad**, **made**), ask which word has /ă/ sound, **mad** or **made**? Help students tap and stop at the vowel. Tell them that sometimes it will say its name /ā/, which is called a long sound, and sometimes it will say the sound /ă/, which is called a short sound. When they say the word with the short vowel sound (**mad**) say yes! and make it with the Standard Sound Cards and read it together. Tell students that we call this vowel sound a short vowel and we mark it with a breve (˘).

mă d   *intro. long ē little tub*

Word Resources

tap	tape	bit	bite
teen	ten	light	lit

tip

For advanced students, you can provide additional work on recognizing the long vowel sounds. See the PLC for activities.

Echo/Find Letters & Words

Echo/Find Letters

Say a sound. Have students echo and point to the letter(s) on their Magnetic Letter Board.

Ask

What says /v/? (v)   What says /y/? (y)

What says /w/? (w)   What says /z/? (z)

What says /kw/? (qu)

Echo/Find Words

Dictate the word **zip**. Have students repeat the word, then tap it out with them.

Have students find Letter Tiles needed to make words on their Magnetic Letter Boards. Have one student come find your corresponding cards. After finding a word, have a student spell it orally. Have the students replace the letters onto their letter squares and dictate another word. Do 3-5 words.

Word Resources

zip	wet	web	wig	yes
yet	vet	quit	zap	quiz

Echo/Letter Formation

Remind students of proper pencil grip and sitting position, and give them their Dry Erase Writing Tablets.

Dictate 5-6 previously taught sounds. You select and say the sound. Students echo the sound and say the letter.

Next have a student come up to the classroom board to make the letter on the Large Writing Grid.

Then have all students write the answer on their Dry Erase Writing Tablet as you direct them with the letter formation verbalization.

(See Unit Resources.)

Note

Students can make only lowercase letters, or you can selectively do both uppercase and lowercase to reinforce certain letters. (Be sure to always do lowercase for every sound that is dictated.)

Unit 3 | Week 3

Day 3

Daily Plan — DAY 3

Student Learning Plan
- Drill Sounds/Warm-Up
- Teach Trick Words
- Echo/Letter Formation
- Dictation (Dry Erase)

Teacher Materials
- Echo and/or Baby Echo
- Large Sound Cards
- Standard Sound Cards
- Large Writing Grid
- Letter Formation Guide
- Sentence Frames
- Trick Word Flashcards

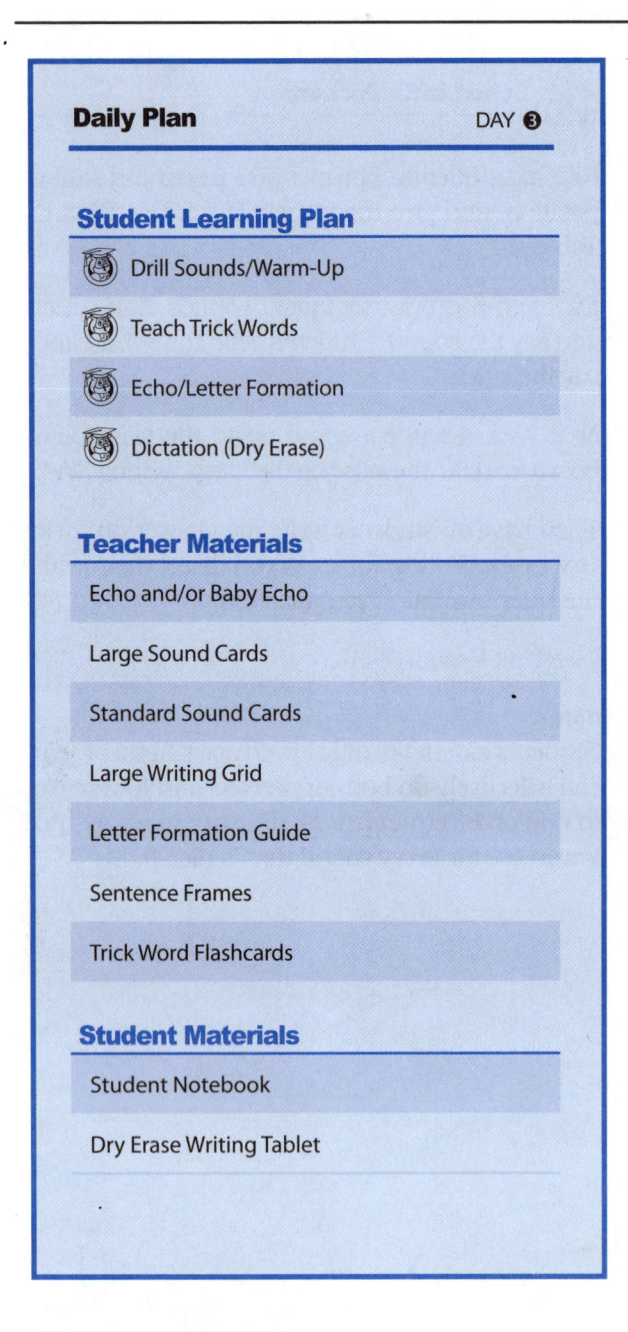

Student Materials
- Student Notebook
- Dry Erase Writing Tablet

Drill Sounds/Warm-Up

Do any new or challenging sounds and vowel sounds each day. Selectively review 4-5 other consonants.

Large Sound Cards

Practice sounds with the Large Sound Cards. Model these, saying the letter-keyword-sound and have the students echo.

Standard Sound Cards

Next, point to the Standard Sound Cards (in card display) with the Baby Echo pointer. You say the letter-keyword-sound and hold up Baby Echo to have students repeat. You can have a student be the drill leader for some of the sounds.

Teach Trick Words

Introduce the trick words **and**, **are** and **to**, and reinforce capitalization and punctuation.

Instruct Students

Say the sentence below and have students repeat. You can also use two student's names in the sentence, rather than Jack and Maria. Have a student place the Sentence Frames as needed. Write the sentence on the frames, and discuss capitalization and punctuation. Scoop the sentence into phrases, read it, and have students echo.

| Jack | and | Maria | are | friends | . |

First circle and introduce **and**, then circle and introduce **are**.

Say

> I am going to circle this word (circle the new trick word). Listen to the sentence and see if you can tell me the word I circled (point to words as you say each one).
>
> Let's change this sentence to: The friends went to a party.

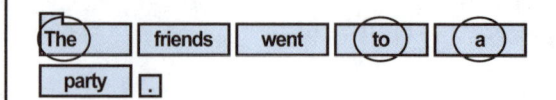

| The | friends | went | to | a |
| party | . |

First circle and review **the** and **a**. Then circle and introduce **to**.

Next, explain that the words **and**, **are** and **to** are words that you are going to practice, and that

260 FUNDATIONS® LEVEL K

© 2002, 2012 WILSON LANGUAGE TRAINING CORPORATION

Unit 3 | Week 3

Day 3

these words are called Trick Words because they can be tricky and we do not tap them out.

Show students the Trick Word Flashcards **and**, **are** and **to**. Say the words and have them repeat. Lastly, present the Trick Word Flashcards learned thus far. Say each and have students repeat.

Echo/Letter Formation

Remind students of proper pencil grip and sitting position, and give them their Dry Erase Writing Tablets.

Dictate 5-6 previously taught sounds. You select and say the sound. Students echo the sound and say the letter.

Next have a student come up to the classroom board to make the letter on the Large Writing Grid.

Then have all students write the answer on their Dry Erase Writing Tablet as you direct them with the letter formation verbalization.

(See Unit Resources.)

Note
Students can make only lowercase letters, or you can selectively do both uppercase and lowercase to reinforce certain letters. (Be sure to always do lowercase for every sound that is dictated.)

Dictation (Dry Erase)

Proper Dictation Activity procedures are very important. Be sure to follow their demonstration on the Prevention Learning Community. This is a teaching time, not a testing time. Be sure students repeat each dictation. Dictate 3 sounds and then 3 current or review words.

Unit Sounds
Refer to this Unit's Resource List of Echo Sounds.

Unit Words
Students should tap and orally spell the Unit words before writing. Then have all spell chorally. Have one student write on the Large Writing Grid and all students write on their Dry Erase Writing Tablets.

Word Resources _gas   cop   Meg   Jim   pal_

zip	wet	web	wig	yes
yet	vet	quit	zap	quiz

Unit 3 | Week 3

Day 4

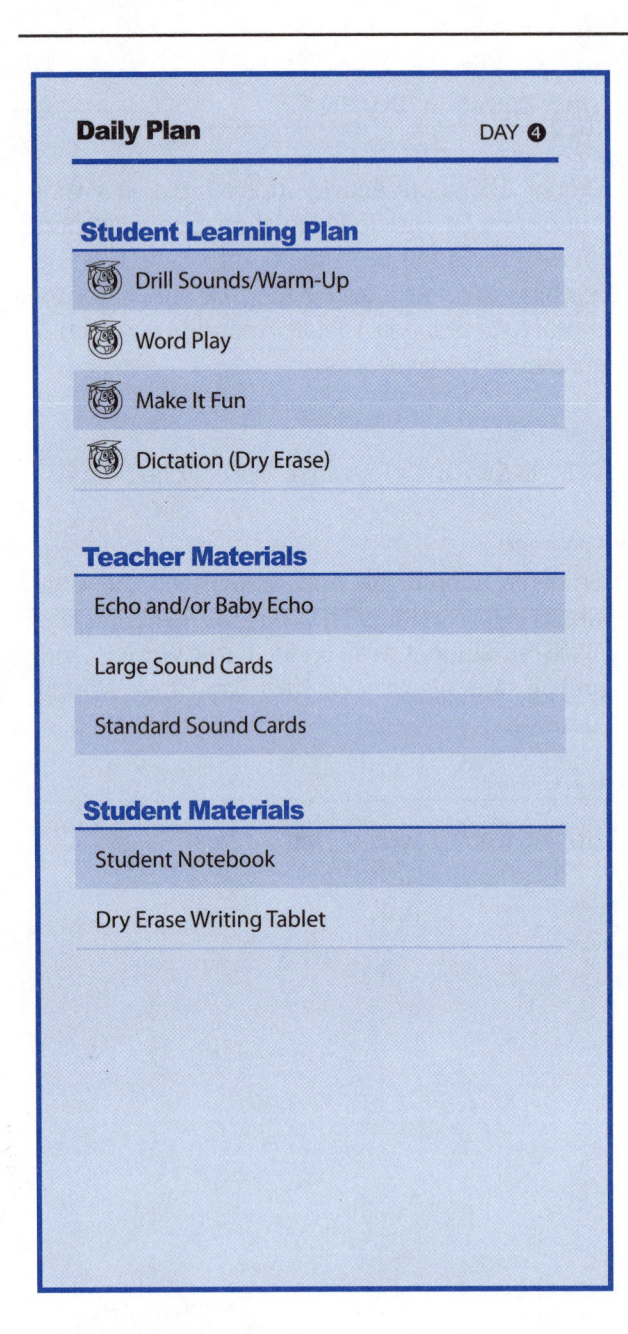

Daily Plan — DAY 4

Student Learning Plan
- Drill Sounds/Warm-Up
- Word Play
- Make It Fun
- Dictation (Dry Erase)

Teacher Materials
- Echo and/or Baby Echo
- Large Sound Cards
- Standard Sound Cards

Student Materials
- Student Notebook
- Dry Erase Writing Tablet

Drill Sounds/Warm-Up

Do any new or challenging sounds and vowel sounds each day. Selectively review 4-5 other consonants.

Large Sound Cards

Practice sounds with the Large Sound Cards. Model these, saying the letter-keyword-sound and have the students echo.

Standard Sound Cards

Next, point to the Standard Sound Cards (in card display) with the Baby Echo pointer. You say the letter-keyword-sound and hold up Baby Echo to have students repeat. You can have a student be the drill leader for some of the sounds.

Word Play

MAKE WORDS FOR DECODING

Use your Standard Sound Card display to make 5-6 Unit words. (See Unit Resources.)

Make each word then say and tap each sound. Have students tap with you. Then blend the sounds as you drag your thumb across your fingers.

Next, point under each card as you say each sound, then drag your finger under all three cards as you and the students blend the sounds to read the word.

MAKE NONSENSE WORDS

Tell students that they can also blend sounds together to make silly or nonsense words. Explain that these nonsense word are not real words. They are just silly words that show that they can read sounds.

Make 3-5 nonsense words and have students tap and read them.

Nonsense Word Resources

zeb   wog   quib   vum   zat

Unit 3 | Week 3

Day 4

Make It Fun

Preparation

- Standard Sound Cards
- Word Resource List

KID SPELLING

This activity helps students to spell.

Instruct Students

Disseminate your Standard Sound Cards, giving one card per student. Avoid the letters **x**, **c** and **k**.

Tell the students that you need them to help you spell and that they will come up to the front if they have a letter that will help to spell a word.

Dictate a word such as **map**. Have students echo and tap it out.

Say

What is the first sound in map?

(Hold your index finger to your thumb.)

I need that letter.

Have the student come up to the front of the room. Proceed with the other sounds until the word is spelled with the three students holding the cards. Have the students spell the word before they sit down. Dictate several words.

Dictation (Dry Erase)

Proper Dictation Activity procedures are very important. Be sure to follow their demonstration on the Prevention Learning Community. This is a teaching time, not a testing time. Be sure students repeat each dictation. Dictate 3 sounds and then 3 current or review words.

Unit Sounds

Refer to this Unit's Resource List of Echo Sounds.

Unit Words

Students should tap and orally spell the Unit words before writing. Then have all spell chorally. Have one student write on the Large Writing Grid and all students write on their Dry Erase Writing Tablets.

Word Resources

zip	wet	web	wig	yes
yet	vet	quit	zap	quiz

Remember to weave in vocabulary discussion.

Unit 3 | Week 3

Day 5

Daily Plan — DAY 5

Student Learning Plan
- Drill Sounds/Warm-Up
- Word Play
- Trick Word Practice
- Storytime

Teacher Materials
- Echo and/or Baby Echo
- Large Sound Cards
- Standard Sound Cards
- Sentence Frames
- Trick Word Flashcards
- 4 Sheets of large chart paper

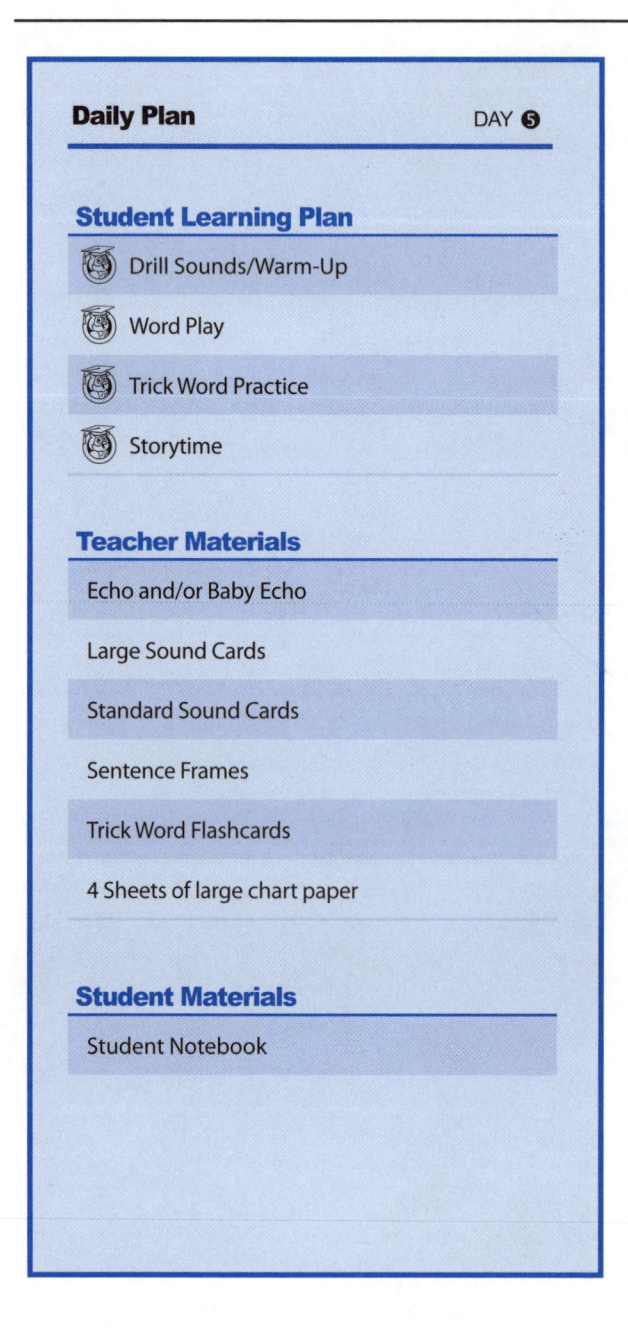

Student Materials
- Student Notebook

Drill Sounds/Warm-Up

Do any new or challenging sounds and vowel sounds each day. Selectively review 4-5 other consonants.

Large Sound Cards

Practice sounds with the Large Sound Cards. Model these, saying the letter-keyword-sound and have the students echo.

Standard Sound Cards

Next, point to the Standard Sound Cards (in card display) with the Baby Echo pointer. You say the letter-keyword-sound and hold up Baby Echo to have students repeat. You can have a student be the drill leader for some of the sounds.

Word Play

MAKE WORDS FOR DECODING

Use your Standard Sound Card display to make 5-6 Unit words. (See Unit Resources.)

Make each word then say and tap each sound. Have students tap with you. Then blend the sounds as you drag your thumb across your fingers.

Next, point under each card as you say each sound, then drag your finger under all three cards as you and the students blend the sounds to read the word.

Unit 3 | Week 3

Day 5

Trick Word Practice

Say each sentence below and have students repeat. Then write the sentence, and scoop it into phrases. Read it and have students echo. Say the trick word that is in the sentence and have a student find and circle it. After it is circled, hold up the corresponding Trick Word Flashcard and say the word and have students repeat.

Sentence Resource

Sid (and) Tab (are) friends.

(The) man went (to) (the) shop.

Lastly present the Trick Word Flashcards, say each and have student repeat.

Storytime

Teacher Materials

- Echo the Owl
- 4 Sheets of large chart paper

BABY ECHO FINDS ECHO AT LAST III

This week you will say and act out the same story, "Baby Echo Finds Echo At Last." Then, as the students retell the story, you will illustrate the story with four simple pictures. Leave space at the bottom of each page. You will need this space next week to write the words of the story. Keep these illustrations for next week's lesson. Remember that these illustrations can be simple. Do not worry about your artistic ability.

Perform the Story

Tell and act out "Baby Echo Finds Echo At Last." (See Week 6, Day 5).

Draw the Story

Next have students retell it to you as you draw it on chart paper. To assist them in retelling the story, ask:

> Who was in the story? Where did the story begin? What was Echo's problem?

1. Draw Baby Echo at one end of the branch. Draw Echo on the ground.

> What did she do about it next?

2. Draw Baby Echo in the middle of the branch looking down.

> Then what did he do?

3. Draw Baby Echo at the other end of the branch, looking down.

> How did it end?

4. Draw Baby Echo looking at Echo with a smile.

After the pictures are drawn, model retelling the story. It is very important to do this in your own words. Then select a student to come tell the story, pointing to the pictures. (You can have several students do this or have them do it at another time during the day or throughout the week.)

Reminder!

Students should draw and/or write in their My Fundations Journal several times a week. You can have them draw pictures of Baby Echo Finds Echo at Last III.

Unit 3 | Week 4

Day 1

Daily Plan — DAY 1

Student Learning Plan
- Drill Sounds/Warm-Up
- Word Play
- Alphabetical Order
- Echo/Find Letters & Words

Teacher Materials
- Echo and/or Baby Echo
- Large Sound Cards
- Standard Sound Cards
- Vowel Extension Poster

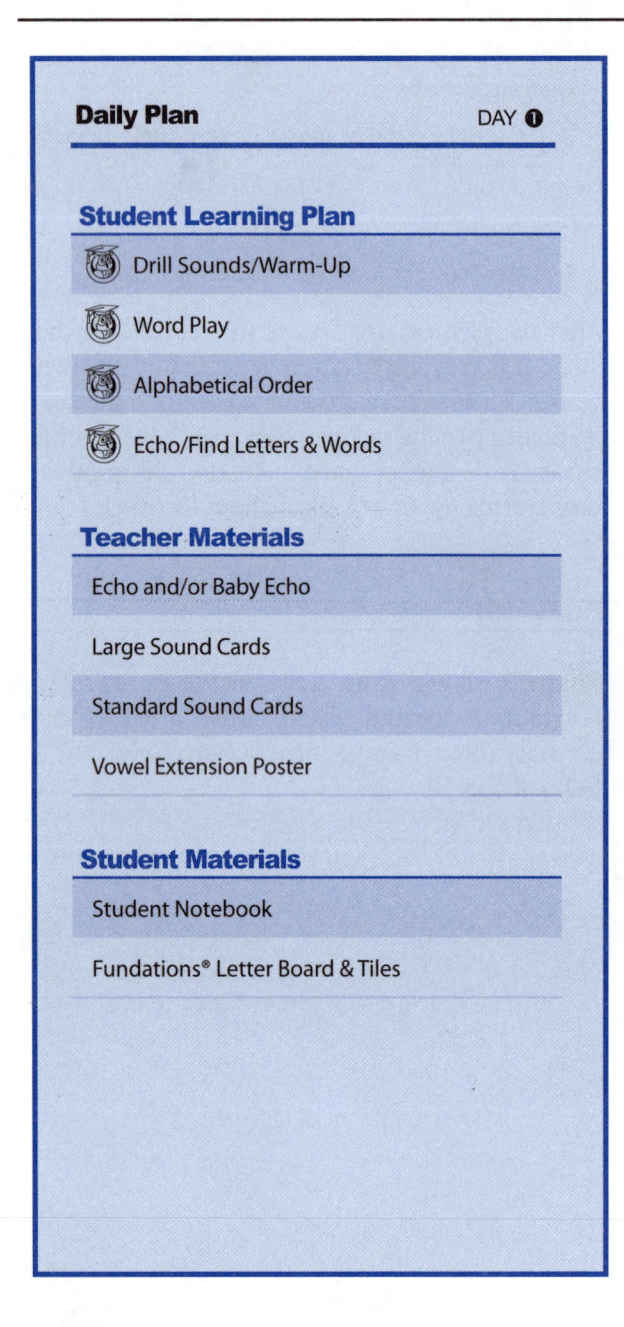

Student Materials
- Student Notebook
- Fundations® Letter Board & Tiles

Drill Sounds/Warm-Up

Do any new or challenging sounds and vowel sounds each day. Selectively review 4-5 other consonants.

Large Sound Cards

Practice sounds with the Large Sound Cards. Model these, saying the letter-keyword-sound and have the students echo.

Standard Sound Cards

Next, point to the Standard Sound Cards (in card display) with the Baby Echo pointer. You say the letter-keyword-sound and hold up Baby Echo to have students repeat. You can have a student be the drill leader for some of the sounds.

Vowel Extension

Model extending the vowel sounds (example: **a-/ă/...apple-/ă/**). Have a student come trace the line for each of the vowels.

Word Play

MAKE WORDS FOR DECODING

Use your Standard Sound Card display to make 5-6 Unit words. (See Unit Resources.)

Make each word then say and tap each sound. Have students tap with you. Then blend the sounds as you drag your thumb across your fingers.

Next, point under each card as you say each sound, then drag your finger under all three cards as you and the students blend the sounds to read the word.

Unit 3 | Week 4

Day 1

Alphabetical Order

Students start with their Magnetic Letter Tiles randomly placed on the blank side of their Letter Boards. Have them sequentially match Letter Tiles on the letter squares.

After students have the tiles placed, chorally say the alphabet. Students should point to each letter as they say its name.

Echo/Find Letters & Words

Echo/Find Letters

Say a sound. Have students echo and point to the letter(s) on their Magnetic Letter Boards.

Ask

What says /ks/? (x)

What says /___/? (___)

(See Echo Sounds in Unit Resources for expected student responses.)

Have students name the letter(s). Then you can have one student find the Standard Sound Card(s) as you dictate sounds. Do vowels and 3-5 other sounds.

Echo/Find Words

Words with X

Make the word **wax** with Standard Sound Cards.

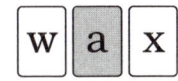

| w | a | x |

Tap it out with students. Point to the letter **x** and

Ask

What does this letter say? (/ks/)

Explain that it might be tricky to spell because it sounds like a **k** and an **s**, but it is spelled with the letter **x**. Take the letters off the board and dictate the word **wax**, and have students repeat and tap it.

Then have a student find the letters to spell it again.

Dictate the word **fix**. Have students repeat the word, then tap it out with them.

Have students find Letter Tiles needed to make words on their Magnetic Letter Boards. Have one student come find your corresponding cards. After finding a word, have a student spell it orally. Have the students replace the letters onto their letter squares and dictate another word. Do 3-5 words.

Word Resources

| wax | fix | yet | jug |
| dot | pal | gum | fox |

Unit 3 | Week 4

Day 2

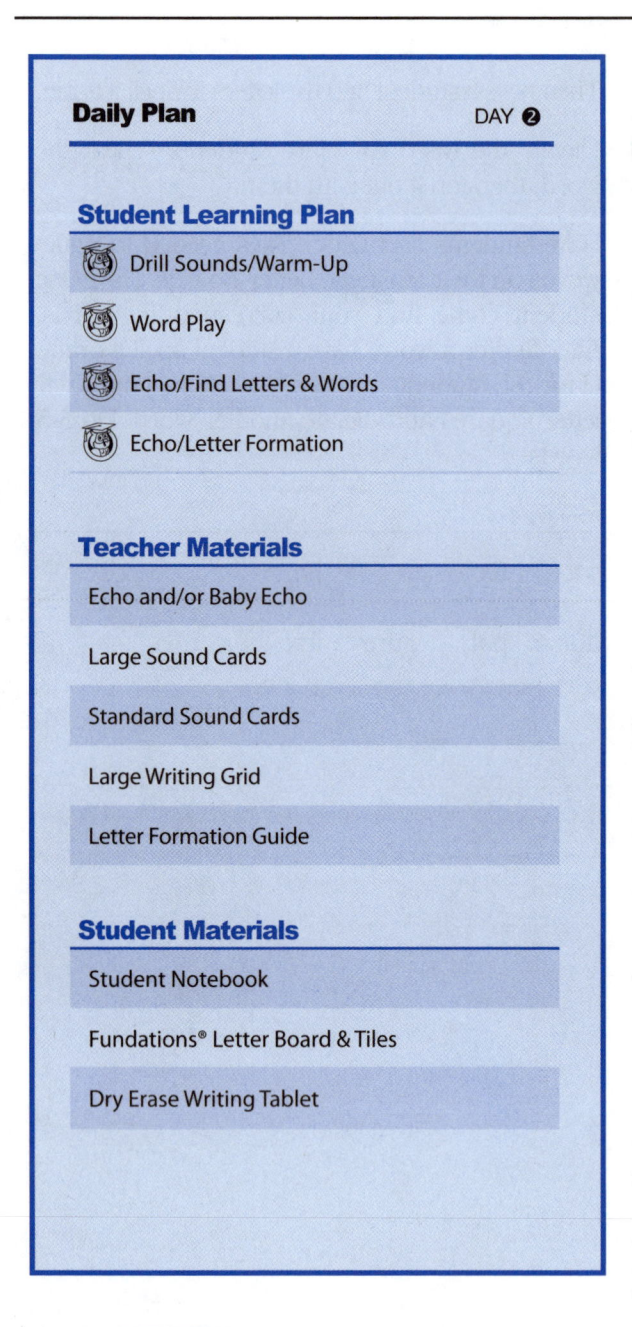

Daily Plan — DAY 2

Student Learning Plan
- Drill Sounds/Warm-Up
- Word Play
- Echo/Find Letters & Words
- Echo/Letter Formation

Teacher Materials
- Echo and/or Baby Echo
- Large Sound Cards
- Standard Sound Cards
- Large Writing Grid
- Letter Formation Guide

Student Materials
- Student Notebook
- Fundations® Letter Board & Tiles
- Dry Erase Writing Tablet

Drill Sounds/Warm-Up

Do any new or challenging sounds and vowel sounds each day. Selectively review 4-5 other consonants.

Large Sound Cards
Practice sounds with the Large Sound Cards. Model these, saying the letter-keyword-sound and have the students echo.

Standard Sound Cards
Next, point to the Standard Sound Cards (in card display) with the Baby Echo pointer. You say the letter-keyword-sound and hold up Baby Echo to have students repeat. You can have a student be the drill leader for some of the sounds.

Word Play

MAKE WORDS FOR DECODING

Use your Standard Sound Card display to make 5-6 Unit words. (See Unit Resources.)

Make each word then say and tap each sound. Have students tap with you. Then blend the sounds as you drag your thumb across your fingers.

Next, point under each card as you say each sound, then drag your finger under all three cards as you and the students blend the sounds to read the word.

Unit 3 | Week 4

Day 2

LISTEN FOR SOUNDS

This activity will help students distinguish between the long (/ā/) and short (/ă/) vowel sounds. Next say, "I am going to say a word. After I say it, you tell me all the sounds in the word. So, if I say **mad**, you would say **/m/ /a/ /d/**. Tell me the sounds in _____." (Use the Word Resources below.)

After students say sounds for both words that are similar with different vowel sounds (**mad**, **made**), ask which word has /ă/ sound, **mad** or **made**? Help students tap and stop at the vowel. Tell them that sometimes it will say its name /ā/, which is called a long sound, and sometimes it will say the sound /ă/, which is called a short sound. When they say the word with the short vowel sound (**mad**) say yes! and make it with the Standard Sound Cards and read it together. Tell students that we call this vowel sound a short vowel and we mark it with a breve (˘).

mă d

Word Resources

lead	led	lit	light
fit	fight	cop	cope

tip

For advanced students, you can provide additional work on recognizing the long vowel sounds. See the PLC for activities.

Echo/Find Letters & Words

Echo/Find Letters

Say a sound. Have students echo and point to the letter(s) on their Magnetic Letter Boards.

Ask

What says /___/? (___)

(See Echo Sounds in Unit Resources for expected student responses.)

Have students name the letter(s). Then you can have one student find the Standard Sound Card(s) as you dictate sounds. Do vowels and 3-5 other sounds.

Echo/Find Words

Dictate the word **wax**. Have students repeat the word, then tap it out with them.

Have students find Letter Tiles needed to make words on their Magnetic Letter Boards. Have one student come find your corresponding cards. After finding a word, have a student spell it orally. Have the students replace the letters onto their letter squares and dictate another word. Do 3-5 words.

Word Resources

wax	led	fox	yes
fix	rug	tax	nap

Echo/Letter Formation

Remind students of proper pencil grip and sitting position, and give them their Dry Erase Writing Tablets.

Dictate 5-6 previously taught sounds. You select and say the sound. Students echo the sound and say the letter.

Next have a student come up to the classroom board to make the letter on the Large Writing Grid.

Then have all students write the answer on their Dry Erase Writing Tablet as you direct them with the letter formation verbalization.

(See Unit Resources.)

Note

Students can make only lowercase letters, or you can selectively do both uppercase and lowercase to reinforce certain letters. (Be sure to always do lowercase for every sound that is dictated.)

Unit 3 | Week 4

Day 3

Daily Plan — DAY 3

Student Learning Plan
- Drill Sounds/Warm-Up
- Teach Trick Words
- Echo/Letter Formation
- Dictation (Dry Erase)

Teacher Materials
- Echo and/or Baby Echo
- Large Sound Cards
- Standard Sound Cards
- Large Writing Grid
- Letter Formation Guide
- Sentence Frames
- Trick Word Flashcards

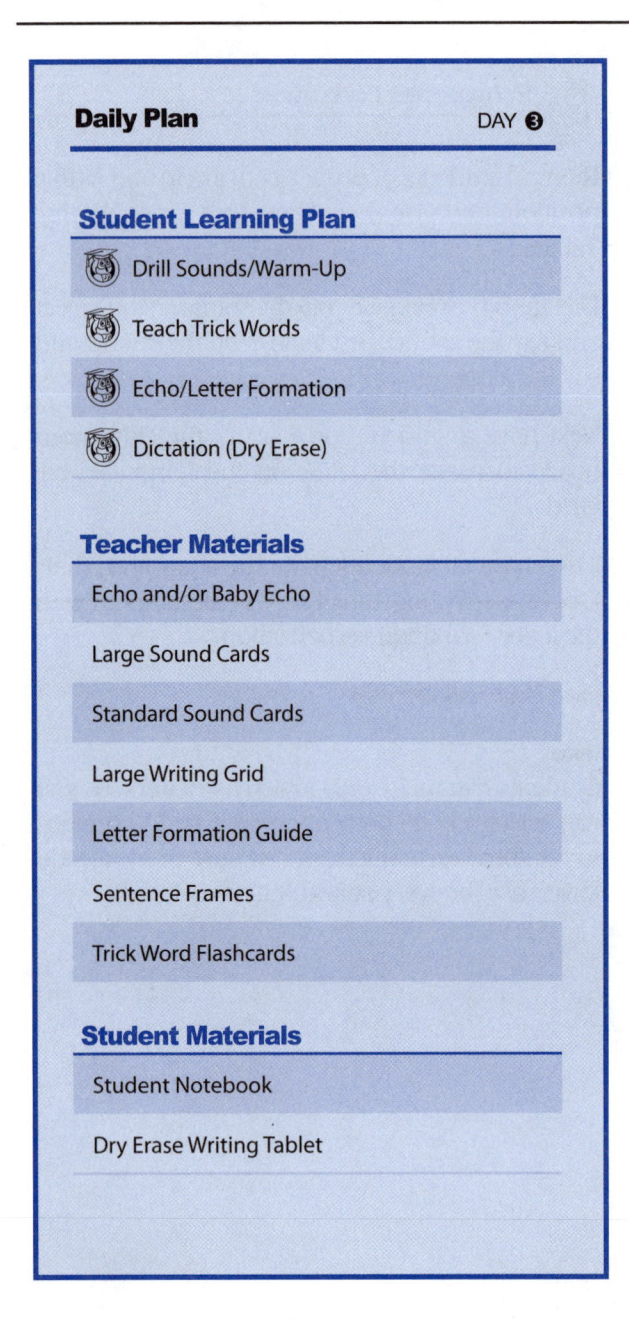

Student Materials
- Student Notebook
- Dry Erase Writing Tablet

Drill Sounds/Warm-Up

Do any new or challenging sounds and vowel sounds each day. Selectively review 4-5 other consonants.

Large Sound Cards

Practice sounds with the Large Sound Cards. Model these, saying the letter-keyword-sound and have the students echo.

Standard Sound Cards

Next, point to the Standard Sound Cards (in card display) with the Baby Echo pointer. You say the letter-keyword-sound and hold up Baby Echo to have students repeat. You can have a student be the drill leader for some of the sounds.

Teach Trick Words

Introduce the trick words **is** and **his**, and reinforce capitalization and punctuation.

Instruct Students

Say the sentence below and have students repeat. Have a student place the Sentence Frames as needed. Write the sentence on the frames, and discuss capitalization and punctuation. Scoop the sentence into phrases, read it, and have students echo.

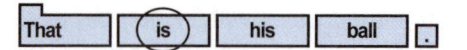

| That | (is) | his | ball | . |

Say

> I am going to circle this word (circle the new trick word). Listen to the sentence and see if you can tell me the word I circled (point to words as you say each one).
>
> Let's change this sentence to: Is that his ball?

| Is | that | (his) | ball | ? |

Next, explain that the words **is** and **his** are words that you are going to practice, and that these words are called Trick Words because they can be tricky and we do not tap them out.

Show students the Trick Word Flashcard with **is** and **his**. Point to **is**. Say the words and have them repeat. Lastly, present the Trick Word Flashcards learned thus far. Say each and have students repeat.

Day 3

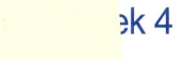

Echo/Letter Formation

Remind students of proper pencil grip and sitting position, and give them their Dry Erase Writing Tablets.

Dictate 5-6 previously taught sounds. You select and say the sound. Students echo the sound and say the letter.

Next have a student come up to the classroom board to make the letter on the Large Writing Grid.

Then have all students write the answer on their Dry Erase Writing Tablet as you direct them with the letter formation verbalization.

(See Unit Resources.)

Note
Students can make only lowercase letters, or you can selectively do both uppercase and lowercase to reinforce certain letters. (Be sure to always do lowercase for every sound that is dictated.)

Dictation (Dry Erase)

Proper Dictation Activity procedures are very important. Be sure to follow their demonstration on the Prevention Learning Community. This is a teaching time, not a testing time. Be sure students repeat each dictation. Dictate 3 sounds and then 3 current or review words.

Unit Sounds
Refer to this Unit's Resource List of Echo Sounds.

Unit Words
Students should tap and orally spell the Unit words before writing. Then have all spell chorally. Have one student write on the Large Writing Grid and all students write on their Dry Erase Writing Tablets.

Word Resources

| wax | bib | tug | vet |
| nod | mud | pen | jab |

Handwritten note:

is / his

That (is) his ball.
- place sent. frames
- then write
- circle trick word

Is that (his) ball?

Write to sounds
wax, bib, tug, vet

Unit 3 | Week 4

Day 4

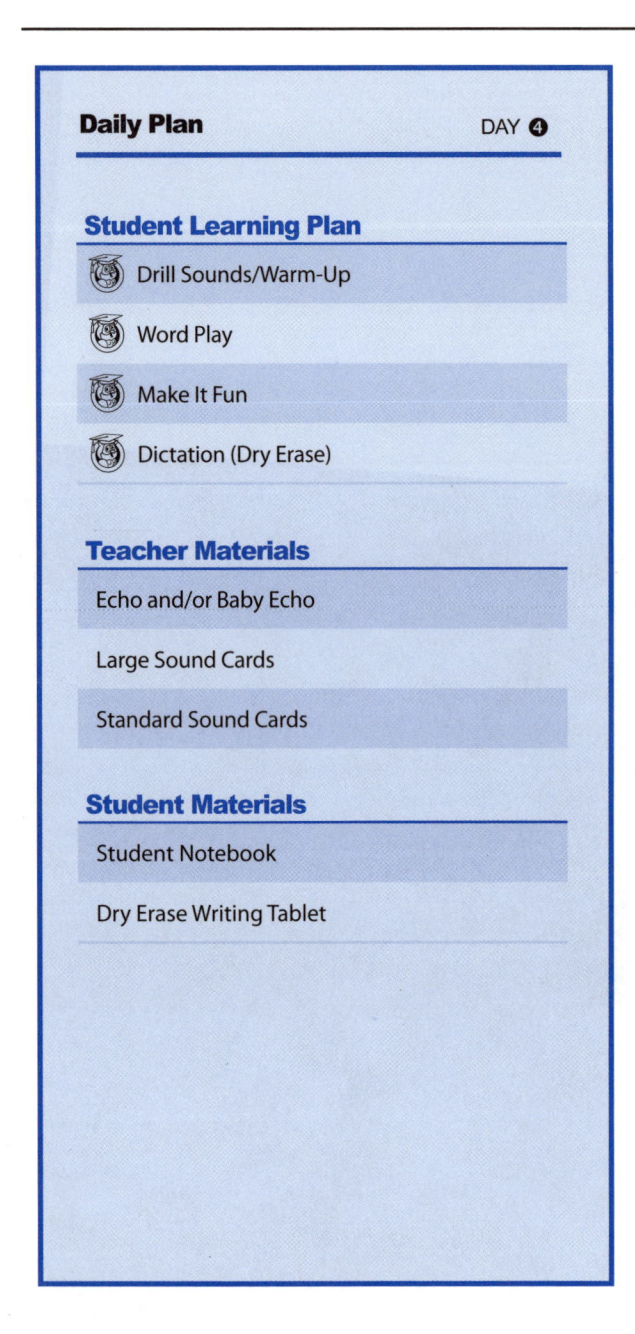

Daily Plan — DAY 4

Student Learning Plan
- Drill Sounds/Warm-Up
- Word Play
- Make It Fun
- Dictation (Dry Erase)

Teacher Materials
- Echo and/or Baby Echo
- Large Sound Cards
- Standard Sound Cards

Student Materials
- Student Notebook
- Dry Erase Writing Tablet

Drill Sounds/Warm-Up

Do any new or challenging sounds and vowel sounds each day. Selectively review 4-5 other consonants.

Large Sound Cards
Practice sounds with the Large Sound Cards. Model these, saying the letter-keyword-sound and have the students echo.

Standard Sound Cards
Next, point to the Standard Sound Cards (in card display) with the Baby Echo pointer. You say the letter-keyword-sound and hold up Baby Echo to have students repeat. You can have a student be the drill leader for some of the sounds.

Word Play

MAKE WORDS FOR DECODING

Use your Standard Sound Card display to make 5-6 Unit words. (See Unit Resources.)

Make each word then say and tap each sound. Have students tap with you. Then blend the sounds as you drag your thumb across your fingers.

Next, point under each card as you say each sound, then drag your finger under all three cards as you and the students blend the sounds to read the word.

MAKE NONSENSE WORDS

Tell students that they can also blend sounds together to make silly or nonsense words. Explain that these nonsense word are not real words. They are just silly words that show that they can read sounds.

Make 3-5 nonsense words and have students tap and read them.

Nonsense Word Resources

nex   vit   pix   boz   tup

272 FUNDATIONS® LEVEL K

© 2002, 2012 WILSON LANGUAGE TRAINING CORPORATION

Unit 3 | Week 4

Day 4

Make It Fun

Preparation
- Standard Sound Cards
- Word Resource List

KID SPELLING

This activity helps students to spell.

Instruct Students

Disseminate your Standard Sound Cards, giving one card per student. Avoid letters **c** and **k**.

Tell the students that you need them to help you spell and that they will come up to the front if they have a letter that will help to spell a word.

Dictate a word such as **map**. Have students echo and tap it out.

Say

> What is the first sound in map?

(Hold your index finger to your thumb.)

> I need that letter.

Have the student come up to the front of the room. Proceed with the other sounds until the word is spelled with the three students holding the cards. Have the students spell the word before they sit down. Dictate several words.

Dictation (Dry Erase)

Proper Dictation Activity procedures are very important. Be sure to follow their demonstration on the Prevention Learning Community. This is a teaching time, not a testing time. Be sure students repeat each dictation. Dictate 3 sounds and then 3 current or review words.

Unit Sounds

Refer to this Unit's Resource List of Echo Sounds.

Unit Words

Students should tap and orally spell the Unit words before writing. Then have all spell chorally. Have one student write on the Large Writing Grid and all students write on their Dry Erase Writing Tablets.

Word Resources

| fox | quit | sip | nut |
| pup | led | vet | map |

Unit 3 | Week 4

Day 5

Daily Plan — DAY 5

Student Learning Plan
- Drill Sounds/Warm-Up
- Word Play
- Trick Word Practice
- Storytime

Teacher Materials
- Echo and/or Baby Echo
- Large Sound Cards
- Standard Sound Cards
- Sentence Frames
- Trick Word Flashcards
- Echo Story Illustrations on large chart paper
- Scooped story on large chart paper

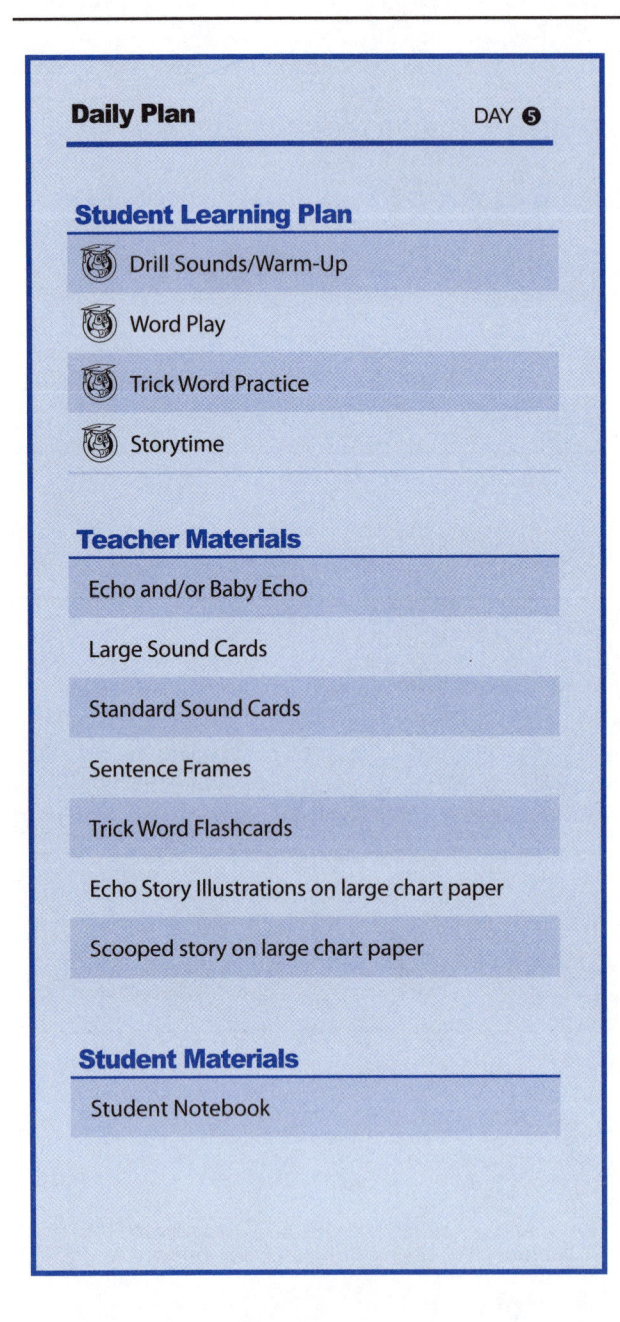

Student Materials
- Student Notebook

Drill Sounds/Warm-Up

Do any new or challenging sounds and vowel sounds each day. Selectively review 4-5 other consonants.

Large Sound Cards

Practice sounds with the Large Sound Cards. Model these, saying the letter-keyword-sound and have the students echo.

Standard Sound Cards

Next, point to the Standard Sound Cards (in card display) with the Baby Echo pointer. You say the letter-keyword-sound and hold up Baby Echo to have students repeat. You can have a student be the drill leader for some of the sounds.

Word Play

MAKE WORDS FOR DECODING

Use your Standard Sound Card display to make 5-6 Unit words. (See Unit Resources.)

Make each word then say and tap each sound. Have students tap with you. Then blend the sounds as you drag your thumb across your fingers.

Next, point under each card as you say each sound, then drag your finger under all three cards as you and the students blend the sounds to read the word.

274 FUNDATIONS® LEVEL K

© 2002, 2012 WILSON LANGUAGE TRAINING CORPORATION

Unit 3 | Week 4

Day 5

Trick Word Practice

Say each sentence below and have students repeat. Then write the sentence on Sentence Frames, and scoop it into phrases. Read it and have students echo. Say the trick word that is in the sentence and have a student find and circle it. After it is circled, hold up the corresponding Trick Word Flashcard and say the word and have students repeat.

Sentence Resource

This (is) John's pencil.

(Is) it (his) eraser?

Lastly present the Trick Word Flashcards, say each and have student repeat.

Storytime

Teacher Materials

- Echo Story Illustrations on large chart paper (from Story III)
- Scooped story on large chart paper or projected to class

BABY ECHO FINDS ECHO AT LAST

This week, use your pictures on the chart paper from "Baby Echo Finds Echo At Last" (Week 3, Day 5). Have the students retell the story.

Use the Baby Echo pointer to read the story one sentence at a time and have the students echo. Be sure to scoop and read sentences in phrases.

Next, use both your pictures and the phrased story together. Look at a picture and then read the corresponding words on the phrased story chart.

Lastly, reread a sentence and ask a student to come find one of the key words in that sentence and circle it. Do several words such as: **Echo, mother, hopped, looked, down**

tip
The phrased story is provided on the PLC.

Baby Echo Finds Echo at Last

One day Baby Echo was looking for his mother.

He looked and looked but he couldn't see her.

So he hopped over to the middle of the big branch. He looked and looked there, but he still couldn't see her.

So he hopped over to the very edge of the big long branch. He looked and looked there, but he still couldn't see her.

He sat up and thought, "Where is my mother?"

Just then he heard a noise behind him.

He turned around and looked down.

Baby Echo saw his mother. At last he was happy.

tip
Be sure to write it so that you can scoop phrases. Use a different color marker to scoop the sentence into phrases.

Unit 3 | Week 5

Day 1

Daily Plan — DAY 1

Student Learning Plan
- Drill Sounds/Warm-Up
- Word Play
- Introduce New Concepts
- Echo/Find Letters & Words

Teacher Materials
- Echo and/or Baby Echo
- Large Sound Cards
- Standard Sound Cards

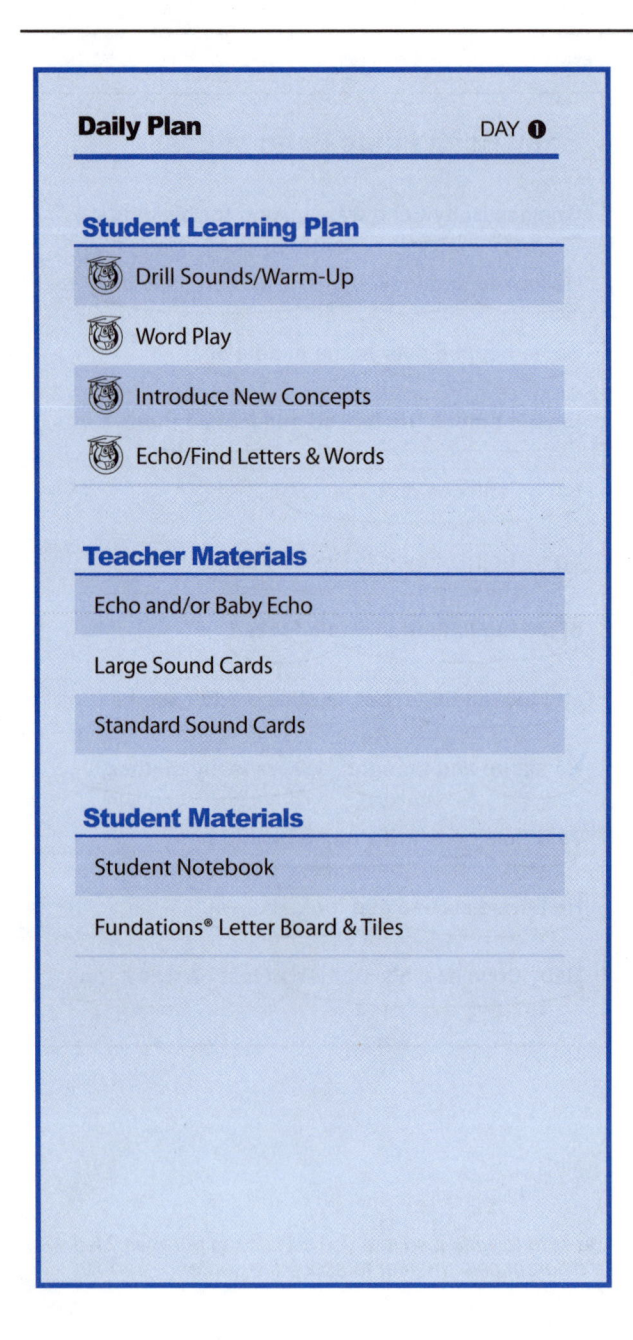

Student Materials
- Student Notebook
- Fundations® Letter Board & Tiles

Drill Sounds/Warm-Up

Do any new or challenging sounds and vowel sounds each day. Selectively review 4-5 other consonants.

Large Sound Cards
Practice sounds with the Large Sound Cards. Model these, saying the letter-keyword-sound and have the students echo.

Standard Sound Cards
Next, point to the Standard Sound Cards (in card display) with the Baby Echo pointer. You say the letter-keyword-sound and hold up Baby Echo to have students repeat. You can have a student be the drill leader for some of the sounds.

Vowel Extension
Model extending the vowel sounds (example: **a-/ă/...apple-/ă/**). Have a student come trace the line for each of the vowels.

Word Play

MAKE WORDS FOR DECODING
Use your Standard Sound Card display to make 5-6 Unit words. (See Unit Resources.)

Make each word then say and tap each sound. Have students tap with you. Then blend the sounds as you drag your thumb across your fingers.

Next, point under each card as you say each sound, then drag your finger under all three cards as you and the students blend the sounds to read the word.

Unit 3 | Week 5

Day 1

Introduce New Concepts

Ask

What says /**k**/? (k, c)

Tell students that they are going to learn something special about when to use **k** or when to use **c** at the beginning of a word, because they both say /**k**/. Put the following Standard Sound Cards on the board:

| c | a | o | u |
| k | e | i | |

Explain that when the /**k**/ sound is followed by the letters **a**, **o**, or **u**, the letter **c** is used. Demonstrate with the words **cat**, **cot** and **cut**. Tell students that whenever /**k**/ has an **e** or **i** after it, the word is spelled with a **k**. Show them the word **kit** and **kid**.

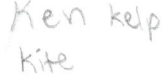

[handwritten: Ken kelp kite]

tip

*For your information, The **k** is used for the /**k**/ sound because **c** followed by **e**, **i**, **y**, says /**s**/. You do not teach this in Kindergarten, however, reinforce the /**k**/ spelling as described above.*

Echo/Find Letters & Words

Echo/Find Letters

Say a sound. Have students echo and point to the letter(s) on their Magnetic Letter Boards.

Ask

What says /___/? (___)

(See Echo Sounds in Unit Resources for expected student responses.)

Have students name the letter(s). Then you can have one student find the Standard Sound Card(s) as you dictate sounds. Do vowels and 3-5 other sounds.

Echo/Find Words

Dictate the word **nut**. Have students repeat the word, then tap it out with them.

Have students find Letter Tiles needed to make words on their Magnetic Letter Boards. Have one student come find your corresponding cards. After finding a word, have a student spell it orally. Have the students replace the letters onto their letter squares and dictate another word. Do 3-5 words.

Word Resources

| nut | cat | rag | kid |
| fix | cub | mix | cap |

Unit 3 | Week 5

Day 2

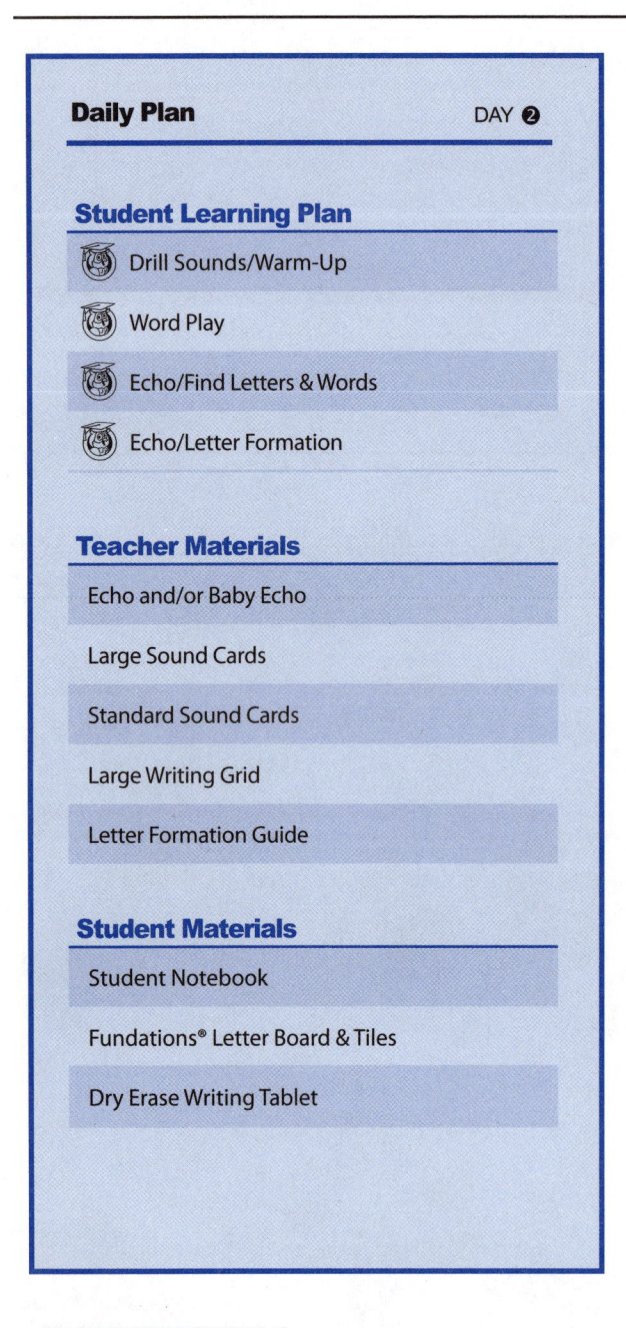

Daily Plan — DAY 2

Student Learning Plan
- Drill Sounds/Warm-Up
- Word Play
- Echo/Find Letters & Words
- Echo/Letter Formation

Teacher Materials
- Echo and/or Baby Echo
- Large Sound Cards
- Standard Sound Cards
- Large Writing Grid
- Letter Formation Guide

Student Materials
- Student Notebook
- Fundations® Letter Board & Tiles
- Dry Erase Writing Tablet

Drill Sounds/Warm-Up

Do any new or challenging sounds and vowel sounds each day. Selectively review 4-5 other consonants.

Large Sound Cards
Practice sounds with the Large Sound Cards. Model these, saying the letter-keyword-sound and have the students echo.

Standard Sound Cards
Next, point to the Standard Sound Cards (in card display) with the Baby Echo pointer. You say the letter-keyword-sound and hold up Baby Echo to have students repeat. You can have a student be the drill leader for some of the sounds.

Word Play

MAKE WORDS FOR DECODING

Use your Standard Sound Card display to make 5-6 Unit words. (See Unit Resources.)

Make each word then say and tap each sound. Have students tap with you. Then blend the sounds as you drag your thumb across your fingers.

Next, point under each card as you say each sound, then drag your finger under all three cards as you and the students blend the sounds to read the word.

Unit 3 | Week 5

Day 2

LISTEN FOR SOUNDS

This activity will help students distinguish between the long (/ā/) and short (/ă/) vowel sounds. Next say, "I am going to say a word. After I say it, you tell me all the sounds in the word. So, if I say **mad**, you would say /m/ /a/ /d/. Tell me the sounds in _____." (Use the Word Resources below.)

After students say sounds for both words that are similar with different vowel sounds (**mad**, **made**), ask which word has /ă/ sound, **mad** or **made**? Help students tap and stop at the vowel. Tell them that sometimes it will say its name /ā/, which is called a long sound, and sometimes it will say the sound /ă/, which is called a short sound. When they say the word with the short vowel sound (**mad**) say yes! and make it with the Standard Sound Cards and read it together. Tell students that we call this vowel sound a short vowel and we mark it with a breve (˘).

m ă d

Word Resources

note	not	tap	tape
mad	maid	robe	rob

tip

For advanced students, you can provide additional work on recognizing the long vowel sounds. See the PLC for activities.

© 2002, 2012 WILSON LANGUAGE TRAINING CORPORATION

Echo/Find Letters & Words

Echo/Find Letters

Say a sound. Have students echo and point to the letter(s) on their Magnetic Letter Boards.

Ask

What says /k/? (c, k)

What says /___/? (___)

(See Echo Sounds in Unit Resources for expected student responses.) Have students name the letter(s). Then you can have one student find the Standard Sound Card(s) as you dictate sounds. Do vowels and 3-5 other sounds.

Echo/Find Words

Review /k/ spelling at beginning of the word. Make the words **cat** and **kit** with Standard Sound Cards:

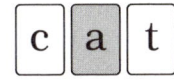

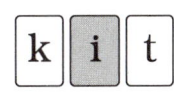

c a t   **k i t**

Dictate the word **kid**. Have students repeat the word, then tap it out with them. Have students find Letter Tiles needed to make words on their Magnetic Letter Boards. Have one student come find your corresponding cards. After finding a word, have a student spell it orally. Have the students replace the letters onto their letter squares and dictate another word. Do 3-5 words.

Word Resources

| kid | cap | cot | yet | fix | zap |

Echo/Letter Formation

Remind students of proper pencil grip and sitting position, and give them their Dry Erase Writing Tablets.

Dictate 5-6 previously taught sounds. You select and say the sound. Students echo the sound and say the letter.

Next have a student come up to the classroom board to make the letter on the Large Writing Grid.

Then have all students write the answer on their Dry Erase Writing Tablet as you direct them with the letter formation verbalization.

(See Unit Resources.)

Note

Students can make only lowercase letters, or you can selectively do both uppercase and lowercase to reinforce certain letters. (Be sure to always do lowercase for every sound that is dictated.)

TEACHER'S MANUAL 279

Unit 3 | Week 5

Day 3

Daily Plan — DAY 3

Student Learning Plan
- Drill Sounds/Warm-Up
- Teach Trick Words
- Echo/Letter Formation
- Dictation (Dry Erase)

Teacher Materials
- Echo and/or Baby Echo
- Large Sound Cards
- Standard Sound Cards
- Large Writing Grid
- Letter Formation Guide
- Sentence Frames
- Trick Word Flashcards

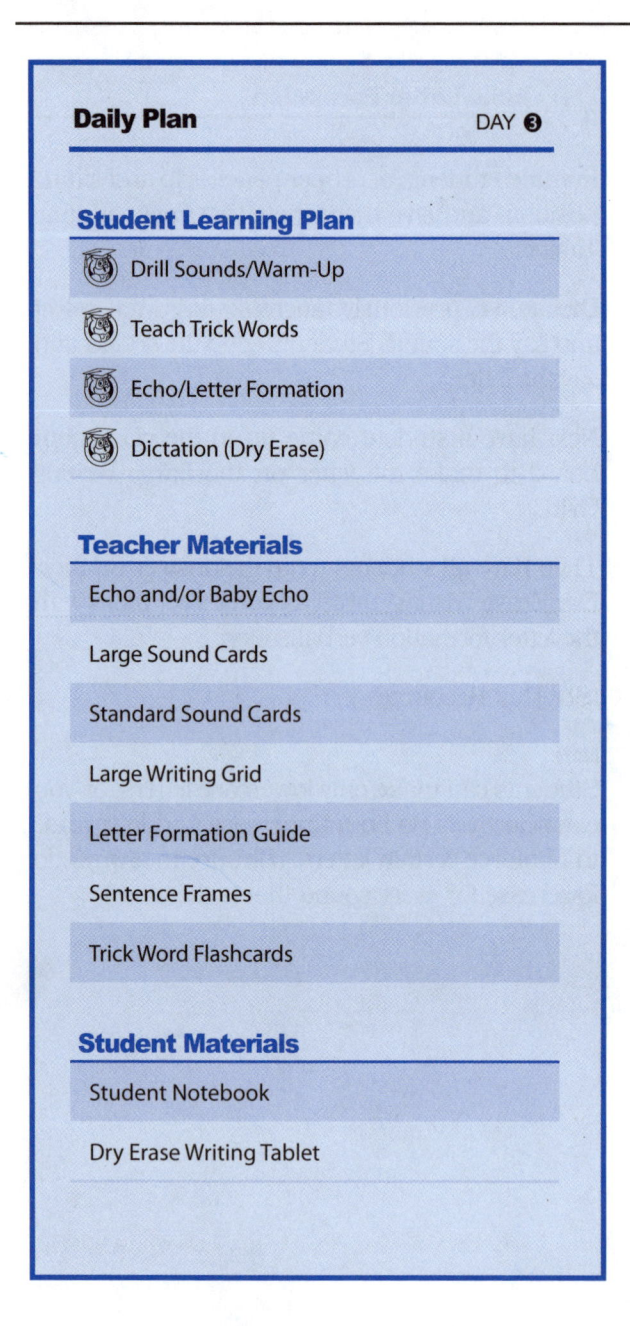

Student Materials
- Student Notebook
- Dry Erase Writing Tablet

Drill Sounds/Warm-Up

Do any new or challenging sounds and vowel sounds each day. Selectively review 4-5 other consonants.

Large Sound Cards

Practice sounds with the Large Sound Cards. Model these, saying the letter-keyword-sound and have the students echo.

Standard Sound Cards

Next, point to the Standard Sound Cards (in card display) with the Baby Echo pointer. You say the letter-keyword-sound and hold up Baby Echo to have students repeat. You can have a student be the drill leader for some of the sounds.

Teach Trick Words

Introduce the trick words **as** and **has**, and reinforce capitalization and punctuation.

Instruct Students

Say the sentence below and have students repeat. You can also use two student's names in the sentence, rather than Meg and Tom. Have a student place the Sentence Frames as needed. Write the sentence on the frames, and discuss capitalization and punctuation. Scoop the sentence into phrases, read it, and have students echo.

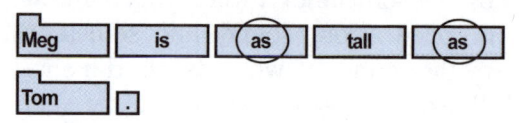

| Meg | is | (as) | tall | (as) |
| Tom | . |

Say

I am going to circle this word (circle the new trick word). Listen to the sentence and see if you can tell me the word I circled (point to words as you say each one). Let's change this sentence to: Tom has five pennies.

| Tom | (has) | five | pennies | . |

Next, explain that the words **as** and **has** are words that you are going to practice, and that these words are called Trick Words because they can be tricky and we do not tap them out.

Show students the Trick Word Flashcard with **as** and **has**. Point to **as**. Say the words and have them repeat. Lastly, present the Trick Word Flashcards learned thus far. Say each and have students repeat.

Unit 3 | Week 5

Day 3

Echo/Letter Formation

Remind students of proper pencil grip and sitting position, and give them their Dry Erase Writing Tablets.

Dictate 5-6 previously taught sounds. You select and say the sound. Students echo the sound and say the letter.

Next have a student come up to the classroom board to make the letter on the Large Writing Grid.

Then have all students write the answer on their Dry Erase Writing Tablet as you direct them with the letter formation verbalization.

(See Unit Resources.)

Note
Students can make only lowercase letters, or you can selectively do both uppercase and lowercase to reinforce certain letters. (Be sure to always do lowercase for every sound that is dictated.)

Dictation (Dry Erase)

Proper Dictation Activity procedures are very important. Be sure to follow their demonstration on the Prevention Learning Community. This is a teaching time, not a testing time. Be sure students repeat each dictation. Dictate 3 sounds and then 3 current or review words.

Unit Sounds
Refer to this Unit's Resource List of Echo Sounds.

Unit Words
Students should tap and orally spell the Unit words before writing. Then have all spell chorally. Have one student write on the Large Writing Grid and all students write on their Dry Erase Writing Tablets. (See Current and Review Words in Unit Resources.)

Unit 3 | Week 5

Day 4

Daily Plan — DAY 4

Student Learning Plan
- Drill Sounds/Warm-Up
- Word Play
- Make It Fun
- Dictation (Dry Erase)

Teacher Materials
- Echo and/or Baby Echo
- Large Sound Cards
- Standard Sound Cards

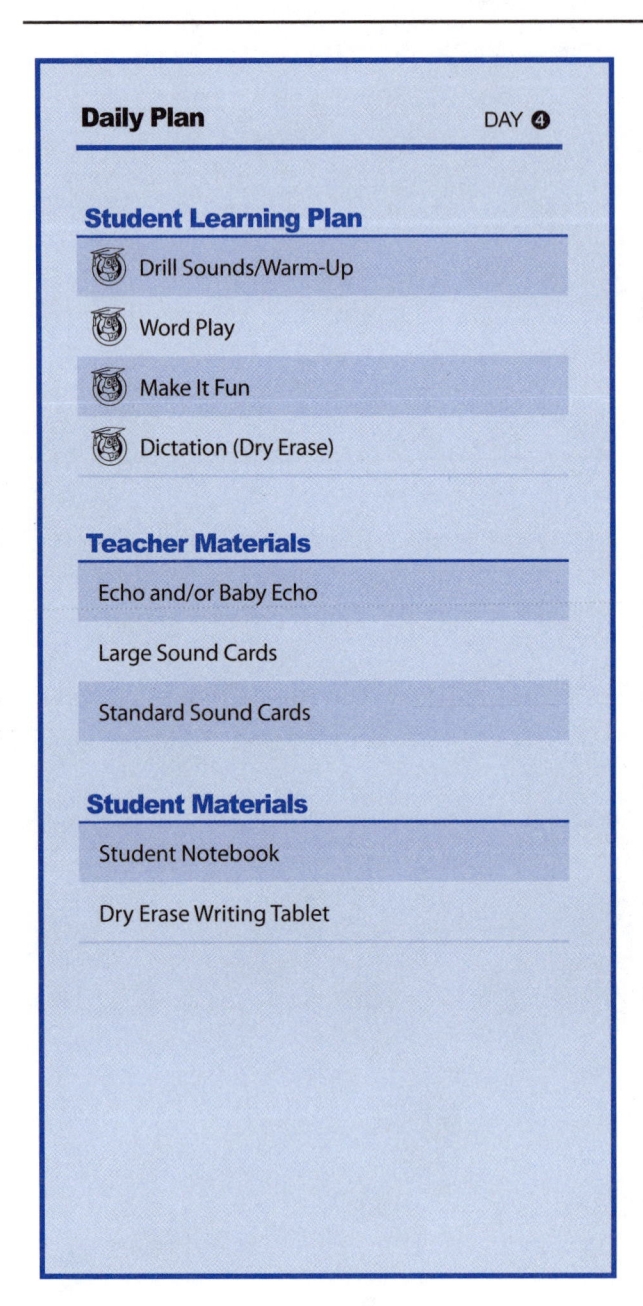

Student Materials
- Student Notebook
- Dry Erase Writing Tablet

Drill Sounds/Warm-Up

Do any new or challenging sounds and vowel sounds each day. Selectively review 4-5 other consonants.

Large Sound Cards

Practice sounds with the Large Sound Cards. Model these, saying the letter-keyword-sound and have the students echo.

Standard Sound Cards

Next, point to the Standard Sound Cards (in card display) with the Baby Echo pointer. You say the letter-keyword-sound and hold up Baby Echo to have students repeat. You can have a student be the drill leader for some of the sounds.

Word Play

MAKE WORDS FOR DECODING

Use your Standard Sound Card display to make 5-6 Unit words. (See Unit Resources.)

Make each word then say and tap each sound. Have students tap with you. Then blend the sounds as you drag your thumb across your fingers.

Next, point under each card as you say each sound, then drag your finger under all three cards as you and the students blend the sounds to read the word.

MAKE NONSENSE WORDS

Tell students that they can also blend sounds together to make silly or nonsense words. Explain that these nonsense word are not real words. They are just silly words that show that they can read sounds.

Make 3-5 nonsense words and have students tap and read them.

Nonsense Word Resources

kiz   kep   cag   zot   vum

Unit 3 | Week 5

Day 4

Make It Fun

SOUND A WORD

Teacher Materials

Place approximately ten small objects (such as plastic animals, cars, pens) in a pillow case or bag. The objects should have a name that is one-syllable of varying length (such as: **pen**, **clip**, **truck**).

Directions

Select a child to pick an item from the bag, but not show it to the class, only to you. Whisper the word segmented to the student and have them repeat it, segmented to the class. For example, if it is a truck, you would say:

/t/ /r/ /ŭ/ /k/ and the student would say:

/t/ /r/ /ŭ/ /k/

Select a student to guess the object. When someone guesses, the student holding the object shows it to the class and sits down with it.

The student who correctly guessed selects the next object from the bag. When all items have been selected, have the students give the object to a student without an object. Collect objects one at a time by saying the word segmented into sounds.

Say

I'm looking for the /t/ /r/ /ŭ/ /k/. Who has the /t/ /r/ /ŭ/ /k/?

Dictation (Dry Erase)

Proper Dictation Activity procedures are very important. Be sure to follow their demonstration on the Prevention Learning Community. This is a teaching time, not a testing time. Be sure students repeat each dictation. Dictate 3 sounds and then 3 current or review words.

Unit Sounds

Refer to this Unit's Resource List of Echo Sounds.

Unit Words

Students should tap and orally spell the Unit words before writing. Then have all spell chorally. Have one student write on the Large Writing Grid and all students write on their Dry Erase Writing Tablets. (See Current and Review Words in Unit Resources.)

Unit 3 | Week 5

Day 5

Daily Plan — DAY 5

Student Learning Plan
- Drill Sounds/Warm-Up
- Word Play
- Trick Word Practice
- Storytime

Teacher Materials
- Echo and/or Baby Echo
- Large Sound Cards
- Standard Sound Cards
- Sentence Frames
- Trick Word Flashcards
- Large chart paper

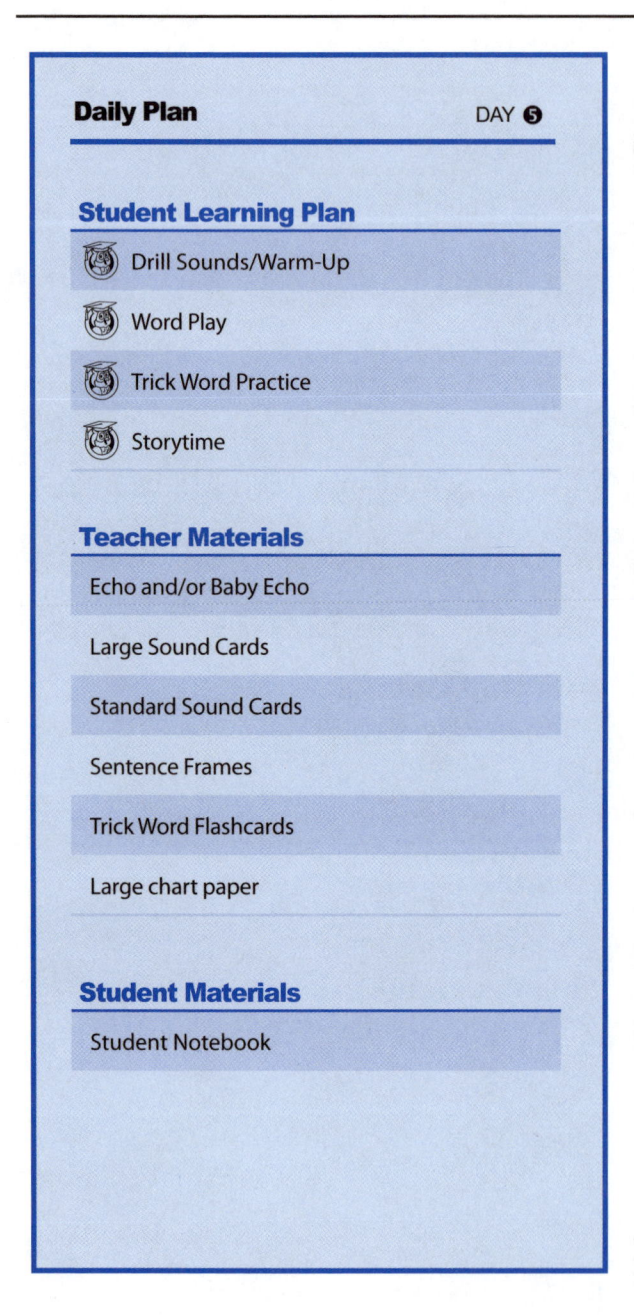

Student Materials
- Student Notebook

Drill Sounds/Warm-Up

Do any new or challenging sounds and vowel sounds each day. Selectively review 4-5 other consonants.

Large Sound Cards
Practice sounds with the Large Sound Cards. Model these, saying the letter-keyword-sound and have the students echo.

Standard Sound Cards
Next, point to the Standard Sound Cards (in card display) with the Baby Echo pointer. You say the letter-keyword-sound and hold up Baby Echo to have students repeat. You can have a student be the drill leader for some of the sounds.

Word Play

MAKE WORDS FOR DECODING

Use your Standard Sound Card display to make 5-6 Unit words. (See Unit Resources.)

Make each word then say and tap each sound. Have students tap with you. Then blend the sounds as you drag your thumb across your fingers.

Next, point under each card as you say each sound, then drag your finger under all three cards as you and the students blend the sounds to read the word.

Unit 3 | Week 5

Day 5

Trick Word Practice

Say each sentence below and have students repeat. Then write the sentence on Sentence Frames, and scoop it into phrases. Read it and have students echo. Say the trick word that is in the sentence and have a student find and circle it. After it is circled, hold up the corresponding Trick Word Flashcard and say the word and have students repeat.

Sentence Resource

Meg is as fast as a rabbit!

Tom is as slow as a turtle!

Meg has a bad cut.

Lastly present the Trick Word Flashcards, say each and have student repeat.

Storytime

Preparation

During Storytime, select a picture book that tells a narrative story. Be sure that there are no more than 5-6 sentences per page.

The story can include predictable language patterns. It is important that it presents sequential events. The following list provides some suggestions.

> Allard, Harry. 1977. *Miss Nelson Is Missing.* Houghton Mifflin.
>
> Hoban, Russell. 1964,1992. *A Baby Sister for Frances.* Harper Trophy.
>
> Hutchins, P. 1972. *Good-Night Owl.* New York: Macmillan.
>
> McCloskey, Robert. 1941, 1969. *Make Way for Ducklings.* Viking Press, Penguin.
>
> Rey, H. A. 1941, 1969. *Curious George.* Houghton Mifflin.
>
> Rice, E. 1977. *Sam Who Never Forgets.* New York: Greenwillow.
>
> Rosen, M. 1989. *We're Going On a Bear Hunt.* New York: McElderry.

Instruct Students

Before reading, look at the front and back cover of the book with your students. Discuss the title, author and illustrator, explaining each of those terms.

Read the title, look at the cover and discuss what the story might be about. Read the book to the students. Pause to have students predict what might happen next. After you read the book, write the following on chart paper:

Characters	Setting	Main Events

When you ask the questions below, draw a quick sketch to answer the questions. Explain that characters are "Who was in the story," the setting is "Where it took place," and the Main Events are "What important things happened in the story."

Ask

Who was in this story?

Where did the story take place?

What happened first?

Then what happened?

What happened next?

What happened at the end?

Unit 3 | Week 6

Day 1

Daily Plan — DAY 1

Student Learning Plan
- Drill Sounds/Warm-Up
- Word Play
- Alphabetical Order
- Echo/Find Letters & Words

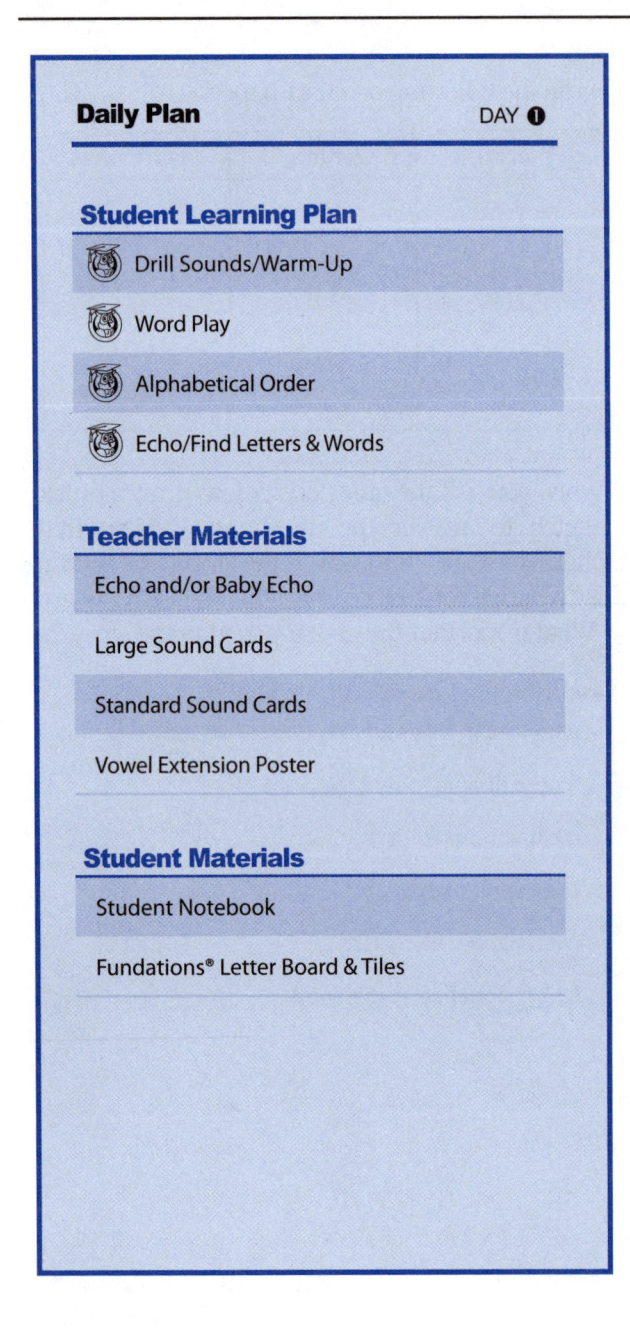

Teacher Materials
- Echo and/or Baby Echo
- Large Sound Cards
- Standard Sound Cards
- Vowel Extension Poster

Student Materials
- Student Notebook
- Fundations® Letter Board & Tiles

Drill Sounds/Warm-Up

Do any new or challenging sounds and vowel sounds each day. Selectively review 4-5 other consonants.

Large Sound Cards
Practice sounds with the Large Sound Cards. Model these, saying the letter-keyword-sound and have the students echo.

Standard Sound Cards
Next, point to the Standard Sound Cards (in card display) with the Baby Echo pointer. You say the letter-keyword-sound and hold up Baby Echo to have students repeat. You can have a student be the drill leader for some of the sounds.

Vowel Extension
Model extending the vowel sounds (example: **a-/ă/...apple-/ă/**). Have a student come trace the line for each of the vowels.

Word Play

MAKE WORDS FOR DECODING

Use your Standard Sound Card display to make 5-6 Unit words. (See Unit Resources.)

Make each word then say and tap each sound. Have students tap with you. Then blend the sounds as you drag your thumb across your fingers.

Next, point under each card as you say each sound, then drag your finger under all three cards as you and the students blend the sounds to read the word.

Unit 3 | Week 6

Day 1

Alphabetical Order

Students start with their Magnetic Letter Tiles randomly placed on the blank side of their Letter Boards. Have them sequentially match Letter Tiles on the letter squares.

After students have the tiles placed, chorally say the alphabet. Students should point to each letter as they say its name.

Echo/Find Letters & Words

Echo/Find Letters

Say a sound. Have students echo and point to the letter(s) on their Magnetic Letter Boards.

Ask

What says /___/? (___)

(See Echo Sounds in Unit Resources for expected student responses.)

Have students name the letter(s). Then you can have one student find the Standard Sound Card(s) as you dictate sounds. Do vowels and 3-5 other sounds.

Echo/Find Words

Dictate a Unit word. Do 3-5 words. (See Current Unit Words in Unit Resources.)

Have students find Letter Tiles needed to make words on their Magnetic Letter Boards. Have one student come find your corresponding cards. After finding a word, have students spell it orally and replace the tiles on the letter squares.

Unit 3 | Week 6

Day 2

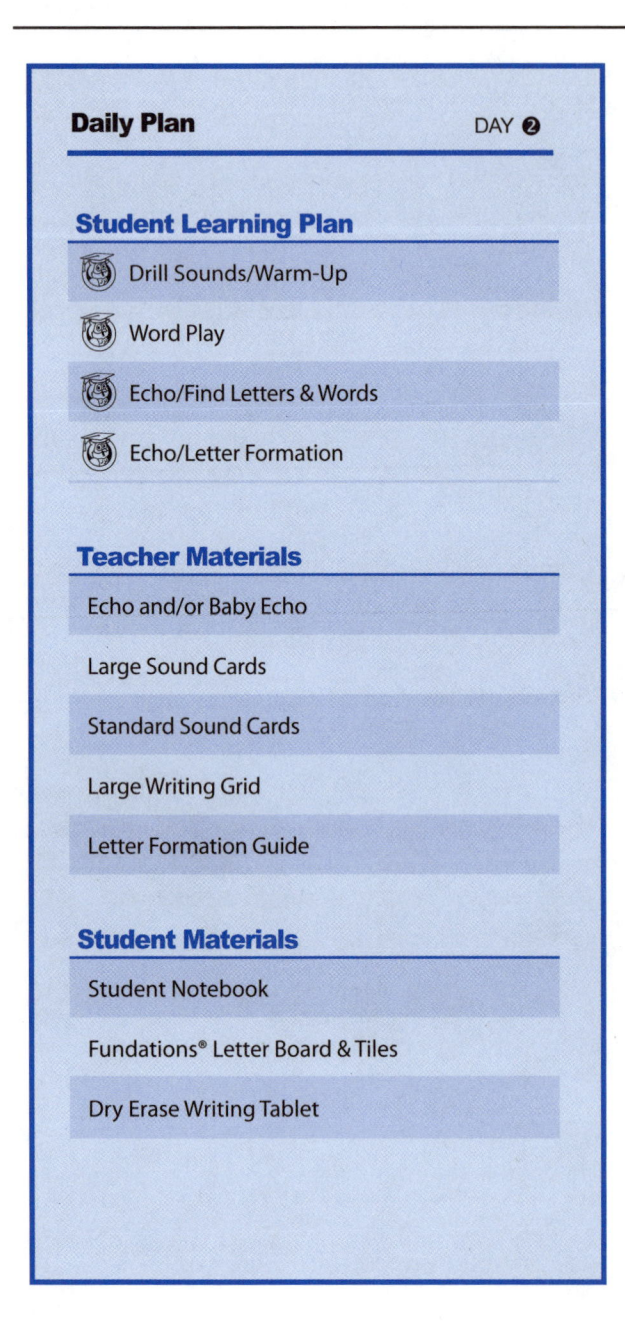

Daily Plan — DAY 2

Student Learning Plan
- Drill Sounds/Warm-Up
- Word Play
- Echo/Find Letters & Words
- Echo/Letter Formation

Teacher Materials
- Echo and/or Baby Echo
- Large Sound Cards
- Standard Sound Cards
- Large Writing Grid
- Letter Formation Guide

Student Materials
- Student Notebook
- Fundations® Letter Board & Tiles
- Dry Erase Writing Tablet

Drill Sounds/Warm-Up

Do any new or challenging sounds and vowel sounds each day. Selectively review 4-5 other consonants.

Large Sound Cards
Practice sounds with the Large Sound Cards. Model these, saying the letter-keyword-sound and have the students echo.

Standard Sound Cards
Next, point to the Standard Sound Cards (in card display) with the Baby Echo pointer. You say the letter-keyword-sound and hold up Baby Echo to have students repeat. You can have a student be the drill leader for some of the sounds.

Word Play

MAKE WORDS FOR DECODING
Use your Standard Sound Card display to make 5-6 Unit words. (See Unit Resources.)

Make each word then say and tap each sound. Have students tap with you. Then blend the sounds as you drag your thumb across your fingers.

Next, point under each card as you say each sound, then drag your finger under all three cards as you and the students blend the sounds to read the word.

Unit 3 | Week 6

Day 2

LISTEN FOR SOUNDS

This activity will help students distinguish between the long (/ā/) and short (/ă/) vowel sounds. Next say, "I am going to say a word. After I say it, you tell me all the sounds in the word. So, if I say **mad**, you would say /m/ /a/ /d/. Tell me the sounds in _____." (Use the Word Resources below.)

After students say sounds for both words that are similar with different vowel sounds (**mad**, **made**), ask which word has /ă/ sound, **mad** or **made**? Help students tap and stop at the vowel. Tell them that sometimes it will say its name /ā/, which is called a long sound, and sometimes it will say the sound /ă/, which is called a short sound. When they say the word with the short vowel sound (**mad**) say yes! and make it with the Standard Sound Cards and read it together. Tell students that we call this vowel sound a short vowel and we mark it with a breve (˘).

mă d

Word Resources

kit	kite	quit	quite
rate	rat	lead	led

For advanced students, you can provide additional work on recognizing the long vowel sounds. See the PLC for activities.

Echo/Find Letters & Words

Echo/Find Letters

Say a sound. Have students echo and point to the letter(s) on their Magnetic Letter Boards.

Ask

What says /___/? (___)   *[handwritten: What is ending sound in bed, lit, man, fog?]*

(See Echo Sounds in Unit Resources for expected student responses.)

Have students name the letter(s). Then you can have one student find the Standard Sound Card(s) as you dictate sounds. Do vowels and 3-5 other sounds.

Echo/Find Words

[handwritten: Do ending sounds of words like big sat mad hum]

Dictate a Unit word. Do 3-5 words. (See Current Unit Words in Unit Resources.)

Have students find Letter Tiles needed to make words on their Magnetic Letter Boards. Have one student come find your corresponding cards. After finding a word, have students spell it orally and replace the tiles on the letter squares.

This week you will practice all CVC words, so select any word from the Unit Resources. Target challenging or "trouble spot" sounds.

Echo/Letter Formation

Remind students of proper pencil grip and sitting position, and give them their Dry Erase Writing Tablets.

Dictate 5-6 previously taught sounds. You select and say the sound. Students echo the sound and say the letter.

Next have a student come up to the classroom board to make the letter on the Large Writing Grid.

Then have all students write the answer on their Dry Erase Writing Tablet as you direct them with the letter formation verbalization.

(See Unit Resources.)

Note

Students can make only lowercase letters, or you can selectively do both uppercase and lowercase to reinforce certain letters. (Be sure to always do lowercase for every sound that is dictated.)

Unit 3 | Week 6

Day 3

Daily Plan — DAY 3

Student Learning Plan
- Drill Sounds/Warm-Up
- Teach Trick Words
- Echo/Letter Formation
- Dictation (Dry Erase)

Teacher Materials
- Echo and/or Baby Echo
- Large Sound Cards
- Standard Sound Cards
- Large Writing Grid
- Letter Formation Guide
- Sentence Frames
- Trick Word Flashcards

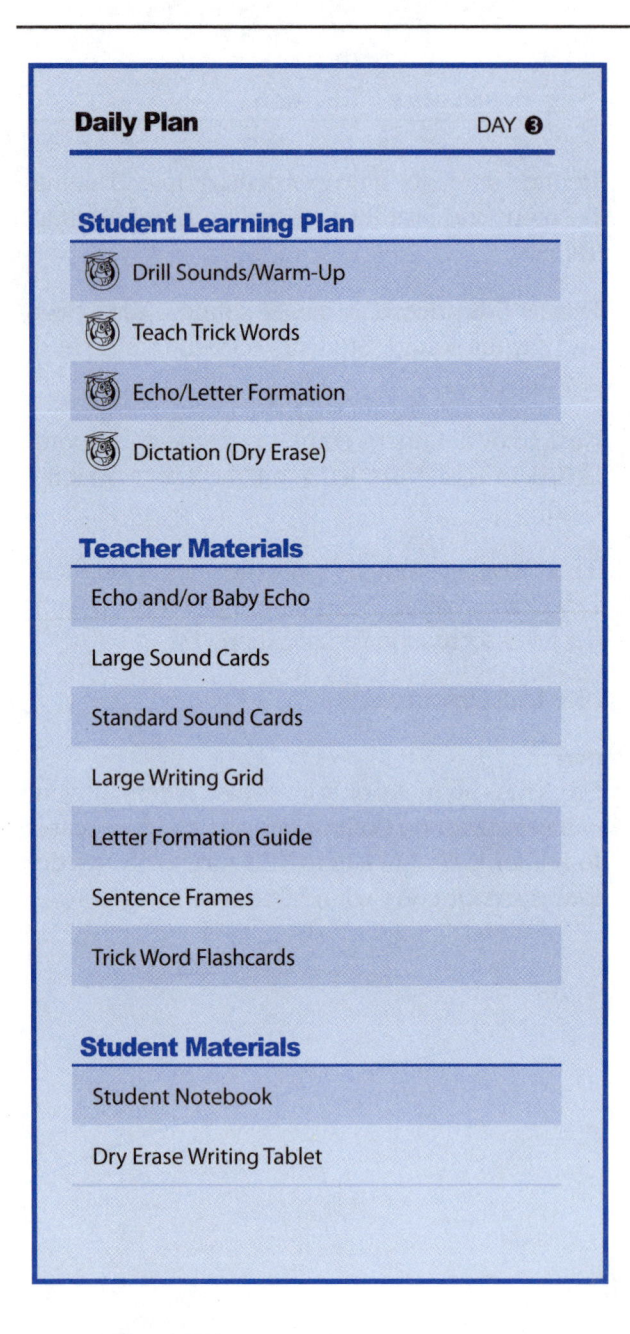

Student Materials
- Student Notebook
- Dry Erase Writing Tablet

Drill Sounds/Warm-Up

Do any new or challenging sounds and vowel sounds each day. Selectively review 4-5 other consonants.

Large Sound Cards

Practice sounds with the Large Sound Cards. Model these, saying the letter-keyword-sound and have the students echo.

Standard Sound Cards

Next, point to the Standard Sound Cards (in card display) with the Baby Echo pointer. You say the letter-keyword-sound and hold up Baby Echo to have students repeat. You can have a student be the drill leader for some of the sounds.

Teach Trick Words

Introduce the trick word **was**, and reinforce capitalization and punctuation.

Instruct Students

Say the sentence below and have students repeat. You can also use a student's name in the sentence, rather than Meg. Have a student place the Sentence Frames as needed. Write the sentence on the frames, and discuss capitalization and punctuation. Scoop the sentence into phrases, read it, and have students echo.

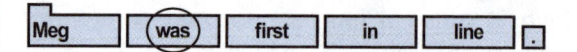

| Meg | (was) | first | in | line | . |

Say

I am going to circle this word (circle the new trick word). Listen to the sentence and see if you can tell me the word I circled (point to words as you say each one).

Next, explain that the word **was** is a word that you are going to practice, and this word is called a Trick Word because it can be tricky and we do not tap it out.

Show students the Trick Word Flashcard **was**. Say the word and have them repeat. Lastly, present the Trick Word Flashcards learned thus far. Say each and have students repeat.

Day 3

Echo/Letter Formation

Remind students of proper pencil grip and sitting position, and give them their Dry Erase Writing Tablets.

Dictate 5-6 previously taught sounds. You select and say the sound. Students echo the sound and say the letter.

Next have a student come up to the classroom board to make the letter on the Large Writing Grid.

Then have all students write the answer on their Dry Erase Writing Tablet as you direct them with the letter formation verbalization.

(See Unit Resources.)

Note
Students can make only lowercase letters, or you can selectively do both uppercase and lowercase to reinforce certain letters. (Be sure to always do lowercase for every sound that is dictated.)

Dictation (Dry Erase)

Proper Dictation Activity procedures are very important. Be sure to follow their demonstration on the Prevention Learning Community. This is a teaching time, not a testing time. Be sure students repeat each dictation. Dictate 3 sounds and then 3 current or review words.

Unit Sounds
Refer to this Unit's Resource List of Echo Sounds.

Unit Words
Students should tap and orally spell the Unit words before writing. Then have all spell chorally. Have one student write on the Large Writing Grid and all students write on their Dry Erase Writing Tablets. (See Current and Review Words in Unit Resources.)

Unit 3 | Week 6

Day 4

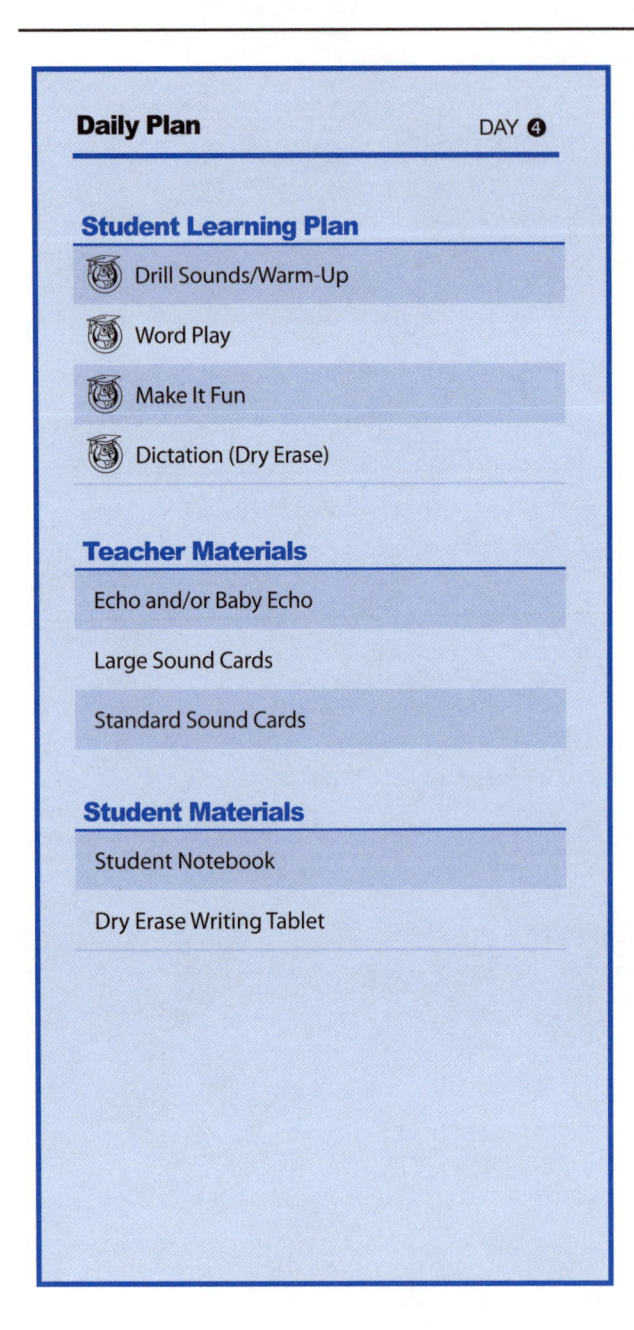

Daily Plan — DAY 4

Student Learning Plan
- Drill Sounds/Warm-Up
- Word Play
- Make It Fun
- Dictation (Dry Erase)

Teacher Materials
- Echo and/or Baby Echo
- Large Sound Cards
- Standard Sound Cards

Student Materials
- Student Notebook
- Dry Erase Writing Tablet

Drill Sounds/Warm-Up

Do any new or challenging sounds and vowel sounds each day. Selectively review 4-5 other consonants.

Large Sound Cards

Practice sounds with the Large Sound Cards. Model these, saying the letter-keyword-sound and have the students echo.

Standard Sound Cards

Next, point to the Standard Sound Cards (in card display) with the Baby Echo pointer. You say the letter-keyword-sound and hold up Baby Echo to have students repeat. You can have a student be the drill leader for some of the sounds.

Word Play

MAKE WORDS FOR DECODING

Use your Standard Sound Card display to make 5-6 Unit words. (See Unit Resources.)

Make each word then say and tap each sound. Have students tap with you. Then blend the sounds as you drag your thumb across your fingers.

Next, point under each card as you say each sound, then drag your finger under all three cards as you and the students blend the sounds to read the word.

MAKE NONSENSE WORDS

Tell students that they can also blend sounds together to make silly or nonsense words. Explain that these nonsense word are not real words. They are just silly words that show that they can read sounds.

Make 3-5 nonsense words and have students tap and read them.

Nonsense Word Resources

bep   bip   guz   kig   quet

Unit 3 | Week 6

Day 4

Make It Fun

Preparation

- Standard Sound Cards
- Word Resource List

KID SPELLING

This activity helps students to spell.

Instruct Students

Disseminate your Standard Sound Cards, giving one card per student. Avoid uncommon letters (such as **y**) unless you plan to dictate words with that sound to practice them.

Tell the students that you need them to help you spell and that they will come up to the front if they have a letter that will help to spell a word.

Dictate a word such as **map**. Have students echo and tap it out.

Say

> What is the first sound in map?

(Hold your index finger to your thumb.)

> I need that letter.

Have the student come up to the front of the room. Proceed with the other sounds until the word is spelled with the three students holding the cards. Have the students spell the word before they sit down. Dictate several words.

Dictation (Dry Erase)

Proper Dictation Activity procedures are very important. Be sure to follow their demonstration on the Prevention Learning Community. This is a teaching time, not a testing time. Be sure students repeat each dictation. Dictate 3 sounds and then 3 current or review words.

Unit Sounds

Refer to this Unit's Resource List of Echo Sounds.

Unit Words

Students should tap and orally spell the Unit words before writing. Then have all spell chorally. Have one student write on the Large Writing Grid and all students write on their Dry Erase Writing Tablets. (See Current and Review Words in Unit Resources.)

Unit 3 | Week 6

Day 5

Daily Plan — DAY 5

Student Learning Plan
- Drill Sounds/Warm-Up
- Word Play
- Trick Word Practice
- Storytime

Teacher Materials
- Echo and/or Baby Echo
- Large Sound Cards
- Standard Sound Cards
- Sentence Frames
- Trick Word Flashcards
- Unit Test Recording Form

Student Materials
- Student Notebook

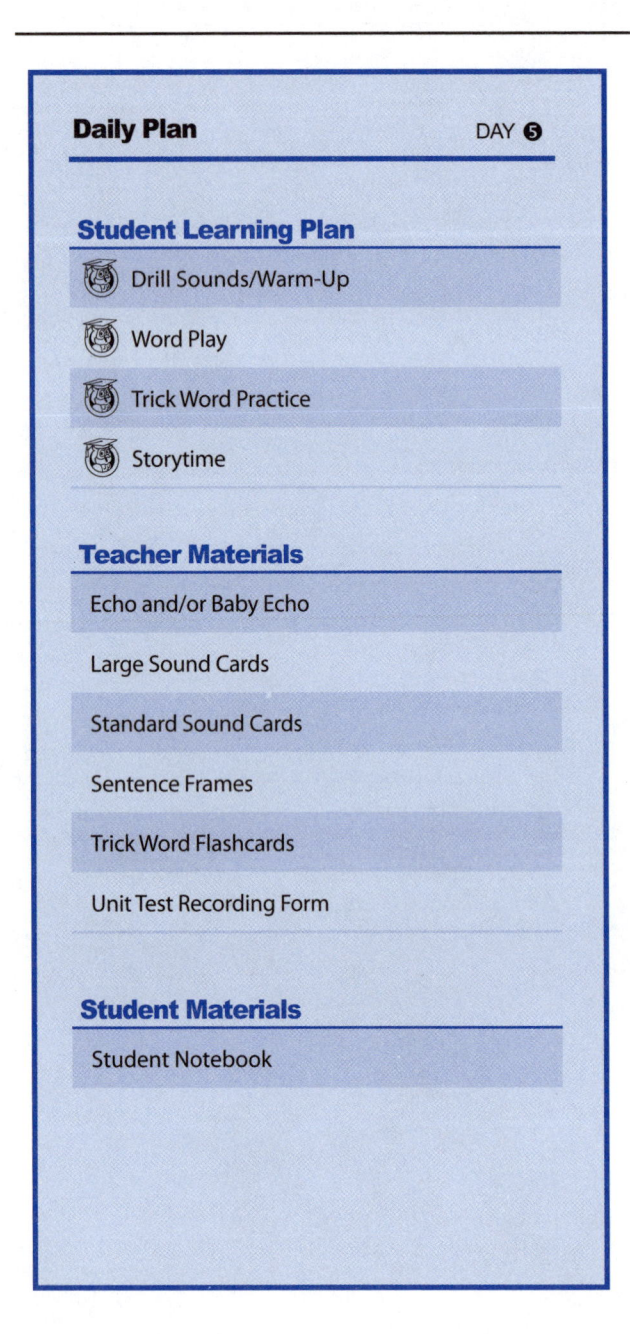

Drill Sounds/Warm-Up

Do any new or challenging sounds and vowel sounds each day. Selectively review 4-5 other consonants.

Large Sound Cards
Practice sounds with the Large Sound Cards. Model these, saying the letter-keyword-sound and have the students echo.

Standard Sound Cards
Next, point to the Standard Sound Cards (in card display) with the Baby Echo pointer. You say the letter-keyword-sound and hold up Baby Echo to have students repeat. You can have a student be the drill leader for some of the sounds.

Word Play

MAKE WORDS FOR DECODING
Use your Standard Sound Card display to make 5-6 Unit words. (See Unit Resources.)

Make each word then say and tap each sound. Have students tap with you. Then blend the sounds as you drag your thumb across your fingers.

Next, point under each card as you say each sound, then drag your finger under all three cards as you and the students blend the sounds to read the word.

Unit 3 | Week 6

Day 5

Trick Word Practice

Say each sentence below and have students repeat. Then write the sentence on Sentence Frames, and scoop it into phrases. Read it and have students echo. Say the trick word that is in the sentence and have a student find and circle it. After it is circled, hold up the corresponding Trick Word Flashcard and say the word and have students repeat.

Sentence Resource

That boy (was) here yesterday.

We (are) all done.

(The) kids went (to) (the) playground.

Lastly present the Trick Word Flashcards, say each and have student repeat.

Storytime

Preparation
Use the storybook selected in previous week. You will use this book to help develop the students' retelling ability.

Instruct Students

Last week I read this story to you.

Today, I am going to see if you can tell it to me.

Let's see if you remember the story.

Tell the students the story's title. Next go through the book, page by page and show the students the pictures. Have them tell you what happened on each page. Go through the whole book, without reading.

Ask

Let's see if you remember it.

I'll read it to see if you were right.

(Read the story.)

Who were the characters?

What was the setting for this story?

What happened first?

Then what happened?

What happened next?

What happened at the end?

Unit 3

Unit Test

Answer Key

SEGMENTED WORDS

/t/ /ă/ /p/	/sh/ /ē/ /p/
/j/ /ŏ/ /b/	/d/ /ĭ/ /g/
/n/ /ō/ /t/	/b/ /ā/ /t/
/b/ /ĭ/ /b/	/p/ /ĕ/ /t/
/k/ /ō/ /t/	/l/ /ē/ /d/

Note
Allow students to independently reference their Student Notebooks. Count responses checked in their Notebooks as correct but make a notation that the book was used.

Each student must be assessed individually. This will take approximately 10-15 minutes per student and can be done by a paraprofessional or volunteer if one is available to assist you.

Copy the **Unit Test Recording Form** for each student (see Appendix). Use the student's durable materials, e.g., Dry Erase Writing Tablet, Letter Board and Letter Tiles, as needed.

If a student does not score at least **8 / 10** or **4 / 5** on any given item, this student will need additional assistance with the assessed skill.

See the Intervention Guidelines on the PLC for information.

A Unit Test Tracker is available on Wilson Academy® / Prevention Learning Community, under My Resources. This valuable online resource will allow you to track individual student mastery as well as to evaluate readiness of your class to move on.

For any struggling students, meet with them individually to discuss errors and explain areas that need to be further practiced.

Have Student Segment a Word into Its Sounds

*I am going to say a word. After I say it, you tell me all the sounds in the word. So, if I say '**mop**', you would say /**m**/ /**ŏ**/ /**p**/. "Tell me the sounds in '**tap**'."*

tap	sheep	job	dig	note
bait	bib	pet	coat	lead

Have Student Tap and Read Words

Form words using the student's Letter Board and Letter Tiles and have student tap and read the words. Say, "Tap these sounds and tell me the word that I made."

top	gum	dip	bet	wax

Have Student Tap and Spell Words

Say a word and have student repeat the word, tap it and then find corresponding Letter Tiles to spell the word on the student's Letter Board.

quit	job	yes	mad	bug

Have Student Retell a Story

Using one of the stories from a Storytime activity, see if student can retell the story with the pictures as a guide.

Unit 3

Resources

Drill Sounds/Warm-Up

a - apple - /ă/	b - bat - /b/
c - cat - /k/	d - dog - /d/
e - Ed - /ĕ/	f - fun - /f/
g - game - /g/	h - hat - /h/
i - itch - /ĭ/	j - jug - /j/
k - kite - /k/	l - lamp - /l/
m - man - /m/	n - nut - /n/
o - octopus - /ŏ/	p - pan - /p/
qu - queen - /kw/	r - rat - /r/
s - snake - /s/	t - top - /t/
u - up - /ŭ/	v - van - /v/
w - wind - /w/	x - fox - /ks/
y - yellow - /y/	z - zebra - /z/

Echo Sounds

Sounds appear between / /. You say the sound. Students echo the sound and say the letter. Depending on the activity, students then either find or make the letter corresponding to that sound.

CONSONANTS

/b/ - b	/d/ - d	/f/ - f
/g/ - g	/h/ - h	/j/ - j
/k/ - c, k	/l/ - l	/m/ - m
/n/ - n	/p/ - p	/kw/ - qu
/r/ - r	/s/ - s	/t/ - t
/v/ - v	/w/ - w	/ks/ - x
/y/ - y	/z/ - z	

VOWELS

/ă/ - a	/ĕ/ - e	/ĭ/ - i
/ŏ/ - o	/ŭ/ - u	

Current Trick Words

the	a	and	are	to	is
his	as	has	was		

Current Unit Words

WEEKS 1 • 2

mop	map	tap	tab	tub	rub
led	lad	bad	bud	bug	rug
dig	dip	bet	bit	fit	fig
fog	rib	sob	job	dot	lid
mud	Ted	lap	not	ten	bed
at	hip	peg	had	pen	bat
hit	pet	bus	bun	bib	red
jab	nod	but	pot	Ben	pat
tab	Jim	tin	rat	big	tip
mad	den	gum	mug	sub	fun
pup	lot	hut	sit	let	gap
sip	dug	Sid	mat	lit	pig
nap	did	pal	nut	gas	him
tug					

WEEK 3

vet	yes	yet	wet	web	wig
zip	zap	quit	quiz		

WEEK 4

tax	fix	mix	fox	wax

WEEK 5

cop	cup	cob	cot	cub	cab
kid	kit				

Unit 4 Level K

In a Nutshell

NEW CONCEPTS

- Phoneme segmentation
- Concept of consonant digraph, keywords and sounds: **wh**, **ch**, **sh**, **th**, **ck**
- Decoding three-sound words with digraphs
- Spelling three-sound words with digraphs
- Spelling of **ck** at end of words
- Narrative story form: character, setting, main events

SAMPLE WORDS

bath   chop   thick

TRICK WORDS

we   she   he   be   me
I   you   they

PLANNED TIME IN UNIT

4 WEEKS

Note
Use Unit Test scores and daily classroom work to determine students' mastery. Extend the time in this Unit if needed.

Introduction

In Unit 4, you will teach that the digraphs **wh**, **ch**, **sh**, **th**, and **ck** 'stick together' to form one sound, even though there are two letters. That is why they are on one card.

When tapping to segment words with digraphs, the digraph will get only one tap. Thus the word **math** will be segmented /m/ /ă/ /th/ with 3 taps.

The digraph **th** says both /th/ as in **thumb** and /th/ as in **this**. You will teach the keyword **thumb** and sound /th/. This is the unvoiced **th** and is most common. The distinction between the two sounds is very subtle and many people can't hear the difference. Since the same digraph is used to spell both, by teaching the **th-thumb-/th/** sound, students will be able to read and spell words with **th**, even if the sound is the voiced /th/. Most of the words students will learn in early grades with /th/ are high frequency words such as **this**, **that**, **those** and **them**. Explain that the **th** sound is just a little different in these words, but it is still spelled with the letters **th**.

You will also explain that **wh** is only used at the beginning of a word and **ck** is only used at the end of a word or syllable right after a short vowel. Point out that you have the **wh** card first on your sound card display, and the **ck** card last.

| wh | ch | sh | th | ck |

This will help them remember where these sounds are found in words.

In Unit 4, you will teach additional high frequency words and continue to review previously taught words.

You will emphasize the fluent reading of sentences, using phrasing. Explain to students that when they read a sentence, it should sound like they are talking rather than reading one word at a time. You will model reading with phrasing and expression, and will scoop under phrases to help guide students.

The dog and cat sat on the deck.

You will also continue to teach narrative story form and retelling of stories.

Be sure to have students write in their My Fundations Journal. Encourage them to attempt to spell words, but do not hold them accountable for patterns not yet taught.

Differentiation

Struggling students will likely need assistance tapping each word in sentences. Advanced students can be challenged with additional sentences and can independently read them with fluency. Help with tapping and phrasing as needed.

Unit 4

Arrange the sound card display in the following manner:

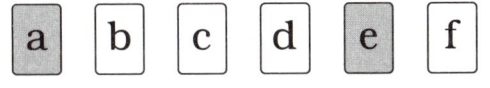

a	b	c	d	e	f
g	h	i	j	k	l
m	n	o	p	qu	r	s
t	u	v	w	x	y	z
wh	ch	sh	th	ck

Getting Ready

MATERIAL PREPARATIONS

Teacher Materials

Add the digraphs (wh, ch, sh, th, and ck) to your Standard Sound Card display.

You will also need the digraphs from your Large Sound Cards pack.

Print Lesson Plans from the PLC. See Unit Resources at the end of this Unit.

Student Materials

Students should have the magnetic Letter Tiles on the letter squares on their Letter Boards.

Students will need to add digraphs (wh, ch, sh, th, and ck) to their Letter Boards.

HOME SUPPORT

Copy and send home the Unit 4 Letter and Activity Packet.

STUDY THE LEARNING ACTIVITIES

There are no new Learning Activities to learn this Unit. Continue to review and master the procedures for the following activities:

- Echo/Find Letters and Words
- Teach Trick Words
- Dictation/ Sounds
- Trick Word Practice

tip

Review the Learning Activity and Unit videos on the PLC.

Unit 4

Student Learning Plan

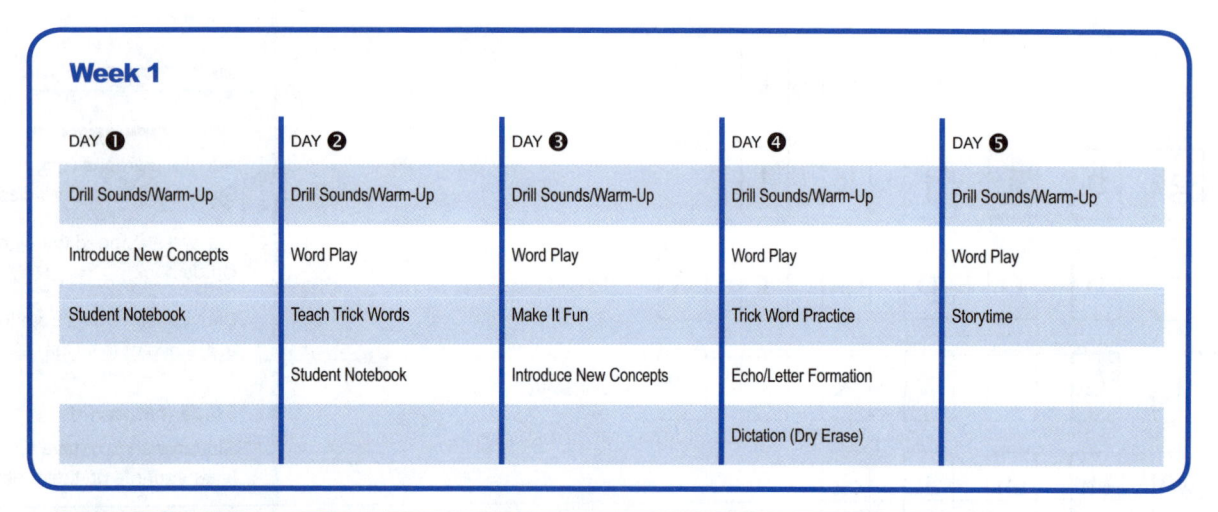

Week 1

DAY 1	DAY 2	DAY 3	DAY 4	DAY 5
Drill Sounds/Warm-Up	Drill Sounds/Warm-Up	Drill Sounds/Warm-Up	Drill Sounds/Warm-Up	Drill Sounds/Warm-Up
Introduce New Concepts	Word Play	Word Play	Word Play	Word Play
Student Notebook	Teach Trick Words	Make It Fun	Trick Word Practice	Storytime
	Student Notebook	Introduce New Concepts	Echo/Letter Formation	
			Dictation (Dry Erase)	

Week 2

DAY 1	DAY 2	DAY 3	DAY 4	DAY 5
Drill Sounds/Warm-Up	Drill Sounds/Warm-Up	Drill Sounds/Warm-Up	Drill Sounds/Warm-Up	Drill Sounds/Warm-Up
Word Play	Word Play	Word Play	Word Play	Word Play
Echo/Find Letters & Words	Teach Trick Words	Make It Fun	Trick Word Practice	Storytime
	Echo/Find Letters & Words	Dictation (Dry Erase)	Echo/Letter Formation	
			Dictation (Dry Erase)	

Unit 4

Student Learning Plan

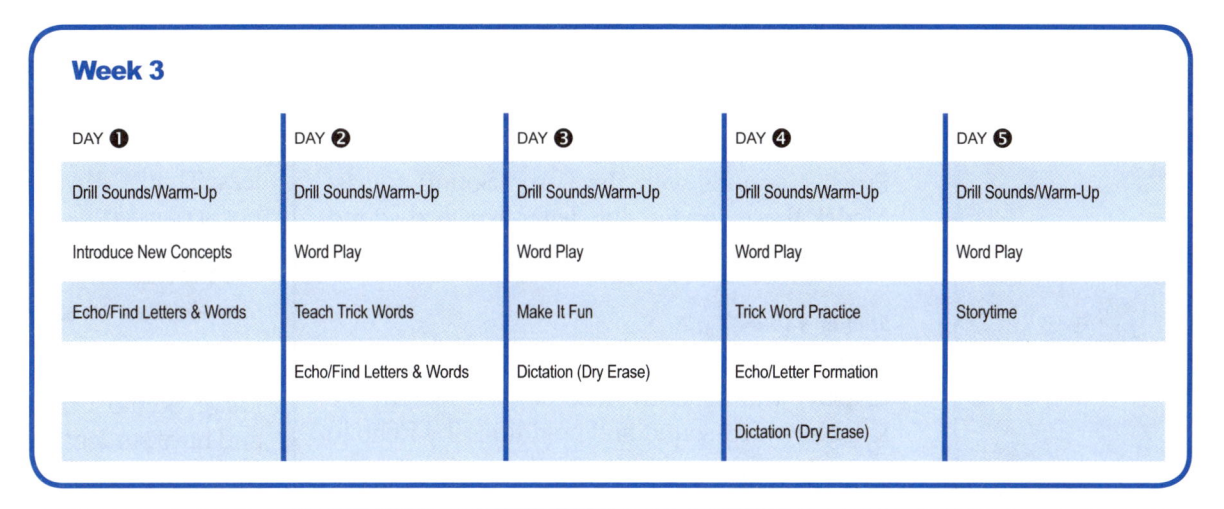

Week 3

DAY 1	DAY 2	DAY 3	DAY 4	DAY 5
Drill Sounds/Warm-Up	Drill Sounds/Warm-Up	Drill Sounds/Warm-Up	Drill Sounds/Warm-Up	Drill Sounds/Warm-Up
Introduce New Concepts	Word Play	Word Play	Word Play	Word Play
Echo/Find Letters & Words	Teach Trick Words	Make It Fun	Trick Word Practice	Storytime
	Echo/Find Letters & Words	Dictation (Dry Erase)	Echo/Letter Formation	
			Dictation (Dry Erase)	

Week 4

DAY 1	DAY 2	DAY 3	DAY 4	DAY 5
Drill Sounds/Warm-Up	Drill Sounds/Warm-Up	Drill Sounds/Warm-Up	Drill Sounds/Warm-Up	Drill Sounds/Warm-Up
Introduce New Concepts	Word Play	Word Play	Word Play	Word Play
Echo/Find Letters & Words	Teach Trick Words	Make It Fun	Trick Word Practice	Storytime
	Echo/Find Letters & Words	Dictation (Dry Erase)	Echo/Letter Formation	Unit Test
			Dictation (Dry Erase)	

Unit 4 | Week 1

Day 1

Daily Plan — DAY 1

Student Learning Plan
- Drill Sounds/Warm-Up
- Introduce New Concepts
- Student Notebook

Teacher Materials
- Echo and/or Baby Echo
- Large Sound Cards
- Standard Sound Cards
- Vowel Extension Poster
- Student Notebook

Student Materials
- Student Notebook

Drill Sounds/Warm-Up

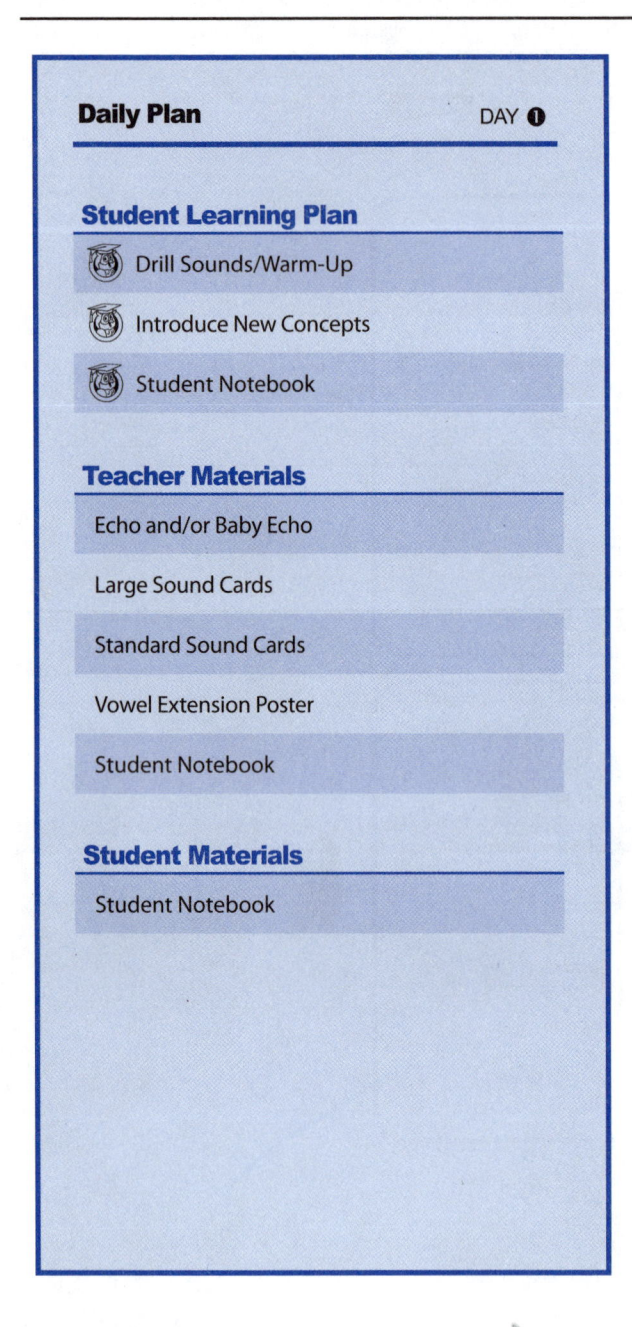

Do any new or challenging sounds and vowel sounds each day. Selectively review 4-5 other consonants.

Large Sound Cards

Practice sounds with the Large Sound Cards. Model these, saying the letter-keyword-sound and have the students echo.

Standard Sound Cards

Next, point to the Standard Sound Cards (in card display) with the Baby Echo pointer. You say the letter-keyword-sound and hold up Baby Echo to have students repeat. You can have a student be the drill leader for some of the sounds.

Vowel Extension

Model extending the vowel sounds (example: a-/ă/...apple-/ă/). Have a student come trace the line for each of the vowels.

Introduce New Concepts

TEACH DIGRAPHS

wh, ch, sh, th, ck — *plays song*

Explain that these consonants 'stick together' to form one sound, even though there are two letters. That is why they are on one card. They are not separated.

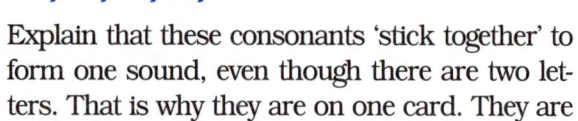

Sh, for example, will not say /s/, /h/. These letters stay together to say /sh/.

Teach the digraphs **wh**, **ch**, **sh**, **th**, **ck** with the Large Sound Cards. Say, letter-keyword-sound and have students repeat. Then do the same with the Standard Sound Cards.

Digraphs Get One Tap, With One Finger

Make the word **mash**.

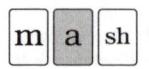

| m | a | sh |

Say the sounds separately, and then blend them together.

Tap a finger to your thumb over each sound card while saying the sound.

Tap your index finger to your thumb while saying /m/, middle finger to thumb while saying /ă/, and ring finger to thumb while saying /sh/.

Unit 4 | Week 1

Day 1

left hand for me

Say /**m**/ and tap index finger to thumb.

Say /**a**/ and tap middle finger to thumb.

Say /**sh**/ and tap ring finger to thumb.

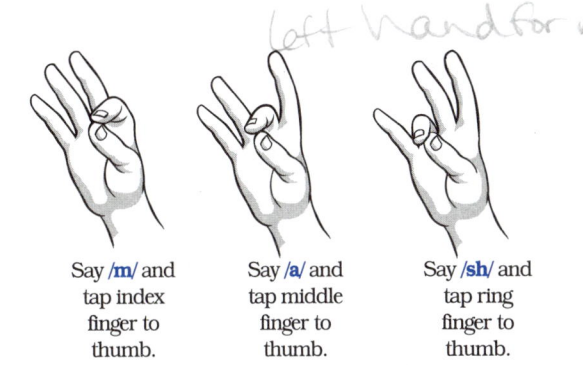

Then blend the sounds and say the word while dragging your thumb across your fingers, starting with the index finger.

Next, form three-sound words (short vowels with digraphs) with the Standard Sound Cards. Use only the letters and sounds taught thus far. (See Current Unit Words in Unit Resources.) *chip, deck, this*

Have students practice this with 5-6 words. *when*

TEACH HOW TO MARK WORDS

Whenever a digraph is in a word, you can identify it by underlining it.

In the word **ship**, the letters **sh** are a digraph. To show that these letters stay together, you can underline them in the word: **ship**.

Examples *write on board*

chop   duck   ship

Student Notebook *Notebooks today*

Direct the students to find the newly introduced digraphs.

Have students trace the letters and say the letter names, keyword and sound. After you do this the students can then color the keyword pictures. Do 3 digraphs today.

Support for Spanish Speaking ELs: The **sh** digraph doesn't exist in Spanish, therefore, Spanish speaking students may say /**s**/ when they see **sh**. Provide additional practice with the keyword to master the sound.

Unit 4 | Week 1

Day 2

Daily Plan — DAY 2

Student Learning Plan
- Drill Sounds/Warm-Up
- Word Play
- Teach Trick Words
- Student Notebook

Teacher Materials
- Echo and/or Baby Echo
- Large Sound Cards
- Standard Sound Cards
- Student Notebook
- Sentence Frames
- Trick Word Flashcards

Student Materials
- Student Notebook

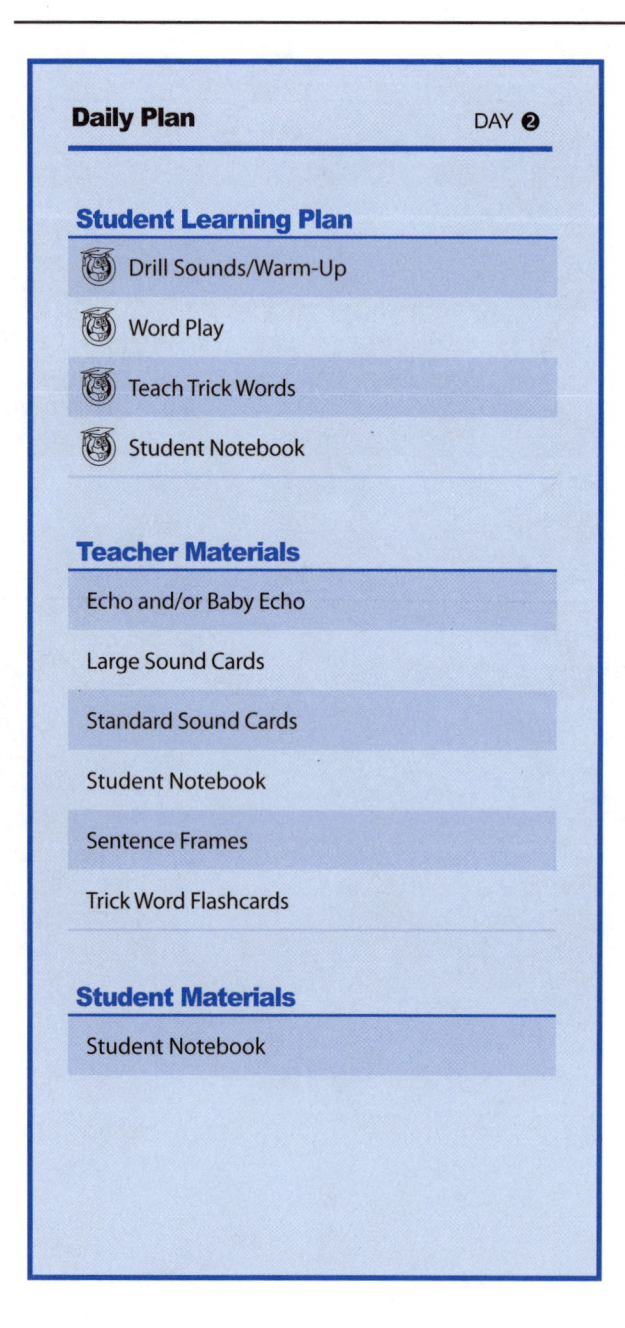

Drill Sounds/Warm-Up

Do any new or challenging sounds and vowel sounds each day. Selectively review 4-5 other consonants.

Large Sound Cards
Practice sounds with the Large Sound Cards. Model these, saying the letter-keyword-sound and have the students echo.

Standard Sound Cards
Next, point to the Standard Sound Cards (in card display) with the Baby Echo pointer. You say the letter-keyword-sound and hold up Baby Echo to have students repeat. You can have a student be the drill leader for some of the sounds.

Word Play

[handwritten: rash math chop whip rich]

MAKE WORDS FOR DECODING
Use your Standard Sound Card display to make 5-6 Unit words. (See Unit Resources.)

Make each word then say and tap each sound. Have students tap with you. Then blend the sounds as you drag your thumb across your fingers.

Next, point under each card as you say each sound, then drag your finger under all three cards as you and the students blend the sounds to read the word.

Have students find and underline digraphs.

Unit 4 | Week 1

Day 2

Teach Trick Words

(handwritten: write on chart)

Introduce the trick words **we**, **she** and **he**, and reinforce capitalization and punctuation.

Instruct Students

Say the sentence below and have students repeat. Have a student place the Sentence Frames as needed. Write the sentence on the frames, and discuss capitalization and punctuation. Scoop the sentence into phrases, read it, and have students echo.

| We | went | home | . |

Say

> I am going to circle this word (circle the new trick word). Listen to the sentence and see if you can tell me the word I circled (point to words as you say each one).
>
> Let's change this sentence to: She went home.

| She | went | home | . |

> Let's change this sentence to: He went home.

| He | went | home | . |

Next, explain that the words **we**, **she** and **he** are words that you are going to practice, and that these words are called Trick Words because they can be tricky and we do not tap them out.

Show students the Trick Word Flashcards **we**, **she** and **he**. Say the words and have them repeat. Lastly, present the Trick Word Flashcards learned thus far. Say each and have students repeat.

Student Notebook

Direct the students to find the newly introduced digraphs.

Have students trace the letters and say the letter names, keyword and sound. After you do this the students can then color the Keyword pictures. Do the last 2 digraphs today.

(handwritten: whiteboard game ck th ch sh wh)

Unit 4 | Week 1

Day 3

Daily Plan — DAY 3

Student Learning Plan
- Drill Sounds/Warm-Up
- Word Play
- Make It Fun
- Introduce New Concepts

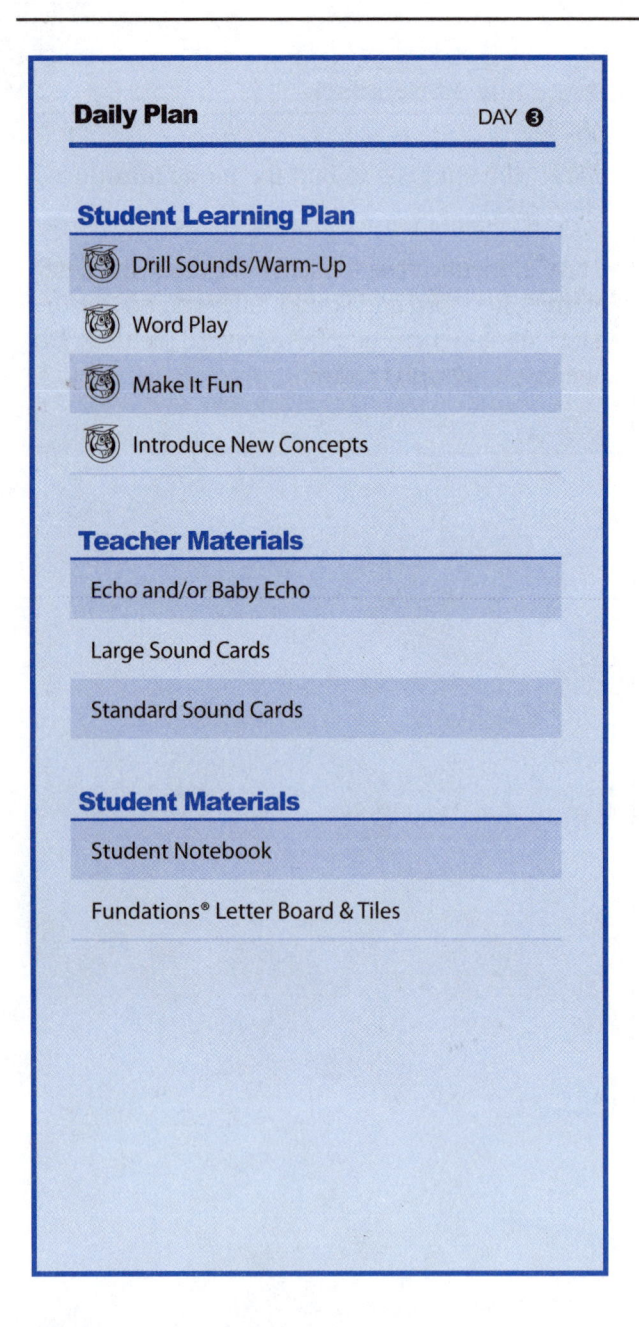

Teacher Materials
- Echo and/or Baby Echo
- Large Sound Cards
- Standard Sound Cards

Student Materials
- Student Notebook
- Fundations® Letter Board & Tiles

Drill Sounds/Warm-Up

Do any new or challenging sounds and vowel sounds each day. Selectively review 4-5 other consonants.

Large Sound Cards
Practice sounds with the Large Sound Cards. Model these, saying the letter-keyword-sound and have the students echo.

Standard Sound Cards
Next, point to the Standard Sound Cards (in card display) with the Baby Echo pointer. You say the letter-keyword-sound and hold up Baby Echo to have students repeat. You can have a student be the drill leader for some of the sounds.

Word Play

MAKE WORDS FOR DECODING
Use your Standard Sound Card display to make 5-6 Unit words. (See Unit Resources.)

Make each word then say and tap each sound. Have students tap with you. Then blend the sounds as you drag your thumb across your fingers.

Next, point under each card as you say each sound, then drag your finger under all three cards as you and the students blend the sounds to read the word.

Have students find and underline digraphs.

Unit 4 | Week 1

Day 3

Make It Fun

Preparation
- Resource List of Current and Review Words

DIGRAPH DETECTIVES

This activity will help students learn to find digraphs.

Instruct Students

Write 10-15 words on the classroom board, some with digraphs and some without. Tell the students they are **digraph detectives** and they need to find all the digraphs and underline them. Read the list of words together with the class.

Variation

Break the class into groups of 3 students and assign each group a digraph to look for. Have the students copy the words with their digraph onto their Dry Erase Writing Tablets. Then call on a student from each group to come and underline the digraph in the words with their designated digraph.

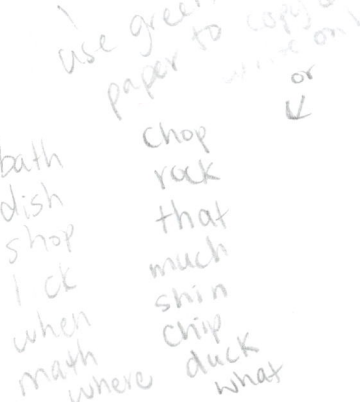

[Handwritten notes: use green paper to copy & write on board or L; bath, dish, shop, lck, when, math, where, chop, rock, that, much, shin, chip, duck, what]

Introduce New Concepts

TEACH SPELLING

Have students use their Magnetic Tiles and Letter Boards. (See Resources for Echo Sounds and Words.)

Echo/Find Letters

Say a sound. Have students echo and point to the letter(s) on their Magnetic Letter Boards.

Ask

What says /sh/? (sh)

Sound Resources

/sh/ - sh	/ch/ - ch
/th/ - th	/wh/ - wh, w
/k/ - c, k, ck	

Echo/Find Words

Dictate a word with a digraph, such as **shop**, without first getting the corresponding sound cards. Tap out sounds and have students repeat. Then find the corresponding sound cards and place them together to form the word.

Next, dictate a word and have the students try tapping out the sounds. Call a student up to find the corresponding sound cards. Have the students tap out sounds and then name the corresponding letters.

Dictate several words, including words with digraphs such as **path**. These words will get three taps: **/p/ - /ă/ - /th/**.

Have students find Letter Tiles needed to make words on their Magnetic Letter Boards. Have one student come find your corresponding cards. After finding a word, have a student spell it orally. Have the students replace the letters onto their letter squares and dictate another word. Do 3-5 words.

Word Resources

shop   ship   chin   chat   thud   thin

Unit 4 | Week 1

Day 4

Daily Plan — DAY 4

Student Learning Plan
- Drill Sounds/Warm-Up
- Word Play
- Trick Word Practice
- Echo/Letter Formation
- Dictation (Dry Erase)

Teacher Materials
- Echo and/or Baby Echo
- Large Sound Cards
- Standard Sound Cards
- Sentence Frames
- Trick Word Flashcards

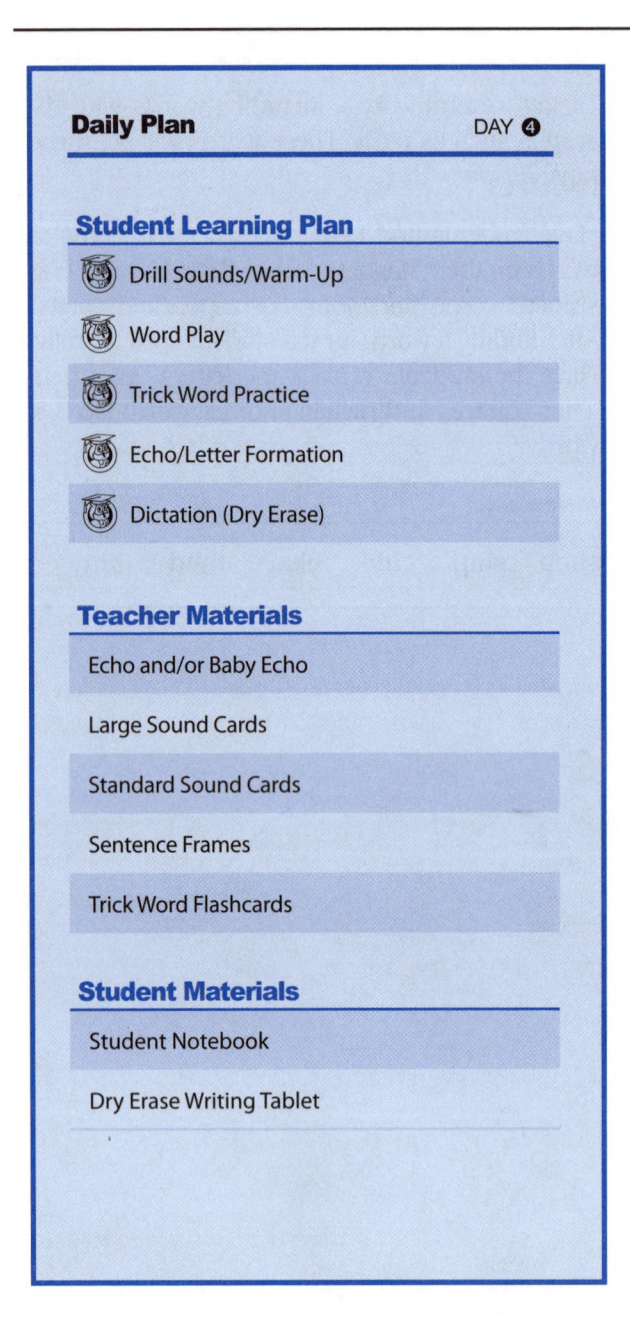

Student Materials
- Student Notebook
- Dry Erase Writing Tablet

Drill Sounds/Warm-Up

Do any new or challenging sounds and vowel sounds each day. Selectively review 4-5 other consonants.

Large Sound Cards

Practice sounds with the Large Sound Cards. Model these, saying the letter-keyword-sound and have the students echo.

Standard Sound Cards

Next, point to the Standard Sound Cards (in card display) with the Baby Echo pointer. You say the letter-keyword-sound and hold up Baby Echo to have students repeat. You can have a student be the drill leader for some of the sounds.

Word Play

MAKE WORDS FOR DECODING

Use your Standard Sound Card display to make 5-6 Unit words. (See Unit Resources.)

Make each word then say and tap each sound. Have students tap with you. Then blend the sounds as you drag your thumb across your fingers.

Next, point under each card as you say each sound, then drag your finger under all three cards as you and the students blend the sounds to read the word.

Have students find and underline digraphs.

MAKE NONSENSE WORDS

Tell students that they can also blend sounds together to make silly or nonsense words. Explain that these nonsense word are not real words. They are just silly words that show that they can read sounds.

Make 3-5 nonsense words and have students tap and read them (see Unit Resources).

Unit 4 | Week 1

Day 4

Trick Word Practice

Say each sentence below and have students repeat. Then write the sentence on Sentence Frames, and scoop it into phrases. Read it and have students echo. Say the trick word that is in the sentence and have a student find and circle it. After it is circled, hold up the corresponding Trick Word Flashcard and say the word and have students repeat.

Sentence Resource

(We) went (to) (the) shop.

(She) (has) (a) pony.

(He) (was) not sad.

Lastly present the Trick Word Flashcards, say each and have student repeat.

Echo/Letter Formation

Remind students of proper pencil grip and sitting position, and give them their Dry Erase Writing Tablets.

Dictate 5-6 previously taught sounds. You select and say the sound. Students echo the sound and say the letter.

Next have a student come up to the classroom board to make the letter on the Large Writing Grid.

Then have all students write the answer on their Dry Erase Writing Tablet as you direct them with the letter formation verbalization.

(See Unit Resources.)

Note
Students can make only lowercase letters, or you can selectively do both uppercase and lowercase to reinforce certain letters. (Be sure to always do lowercase for every sound that is dictated.)

Dictation (Dry Erase)

Proper Dictation Activity procedures are very important. Be sure to follow their demonstration on the Prevention Learning Community. This is a teaching time, not a testing time. Be sure students repeat each dictation. Dictate 3 sounds and then 3 current or review words.

Unit Sounds

Refer to this Unit's Resource List of Echo Sounds.

Unit Words

Students should tap and orally spell the Unit words before writing. Then have all spell chorally. Have one student write on the Large Writing Grid and all students write on their Dry Erase Writing Tablets. (See Current and Review Words in Unit Resources.)

Unit 4 | Week 1

Day 5

Daily Plan — DAY 5

Student Learning Plan
- Drill Sounds/Warm-Up
- Word Play
- Storytime

Teacher Materials
- Echo and/or Baby Echo
- Large Sound Cards
- Standard Sound Cards
- Large chart paper

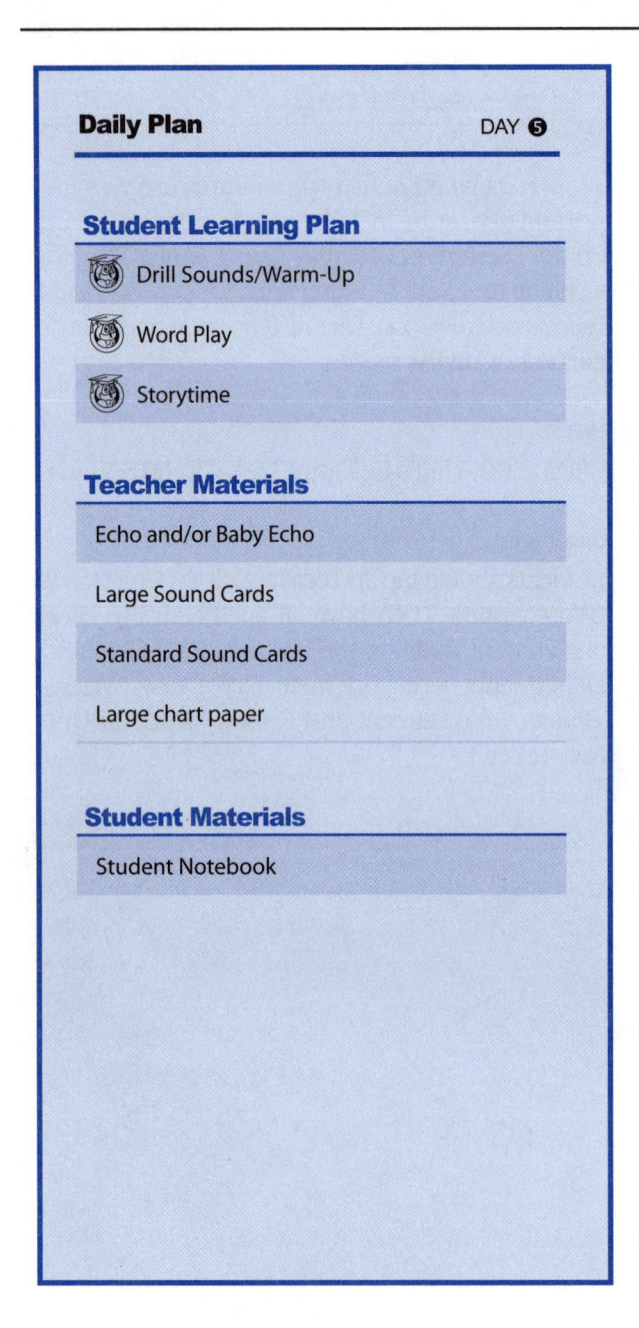

Student Materials
- Student Notebook

Drill Sounds/Warm-Up

Do any new or challenging sounds and vowel sounds each day. Selectively review 4-5 other consonants.

Large Sound Cards

Practice sounds with the Large Sound Cards. Model these, saying the letter-keyword-sound and have the students echo.

Standard Sound Cards

Next, point to the Standard Sound Cards (in card display) with the Baby Echo pointer. You say the letter-keyword-sound and hold up Baby Echo to have students repeat. You can have a student be the drill leader for some of the sounds.

Word Play

MAKE WORDS FOR DECODING

Use your Standard Sound Card display to make 5-6 Unit words. (See Unit Resources.)

Make each word then say and tap each sound. Have students tap with you. Then blend the sounds as you drag your thumb across your fingers.

Next, point under each card as you say each sound, then drag your finger under all three cards as you and the students blend the sounds to read the word.

Have students find and underline digraphs.

Unit 4 | Week 1

Day 5

🦉 Storytime

Preparation

During Storytime, select a picture book that tells a narrative story. Be sure that there are no more than 5-6 sentences per page.

The story can include predictable language patterns. It is important that it presents sequential events. The following list provides some suggestions.

Allard, Harry. 1977. *Miss Nelson Is Missing.* Houghton Mifflin.

Hoban, Russell. 1964,1992. *A Baby Sister for Frances.* Harper Trophy.

Hutchins, P. 1972. *Good-Night Owl.* New York: Macmillan.

McCloskey, Robert. 1941, 1969. *Make Way for Ducklings.* Viking Press, Penguin.

Rey, H. A. 1941, 1969. *Curious George.* Houghton Mifflin.

Rice, E. 1977. *Sam Who Never Forgets.* New York: Greenwillow.

Rosen, M. 1989. *We're Going On a Bear Hunt.* New York: McElderry.

Instruct Students

Before reading, look at the front and back cover of the book with your students. Discuss the title, author and illustrator, explaining each of those terms.

Discuss what the story might be about. Read the book to the students. Pause to have students predict what might happen next. After you read the book, write the following on chart paper:

Characters	Setting	Main Events

When you ask the questions below, draw a quick sketch to answer the questions. Explain that characters are "Who was in the story," the setting is "Where it took place," and the Main Events are "What important things happened in the story."

Using the chart as a guide, have a student retell each category.

Ask

Let's see if you remember it.

I'll read it to see if you were right.

(Read the story.)

Who were the characters?

What was the setting for this story?

What happened first?

Then what happened?

What happened next?

What happened at the end?

Unit 4 | Week 2

Day 1

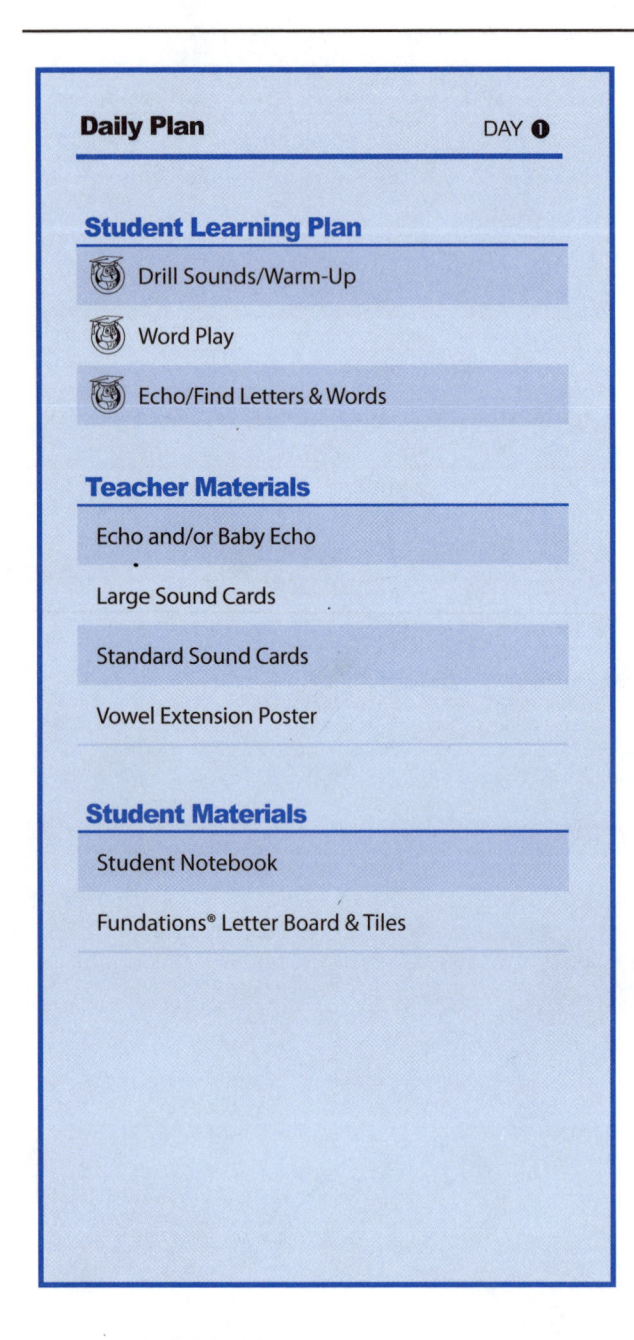

Daily Plan — DAY 1

Student Learning Plan
- Drill Sounds/Warm-Up
- Word Play
- Echo/Find Letters & Words

Teacher Materials
- Echo and/or Baby Echo
- Large Sound Cards
- Standard Sound Cards
- Vowel Extension Poster

Student Materials
- Student Notebook
- Fundations® Letter Board & Tiles

Drill Sounds/Warm-Up

Do any new or challenging sounds and vowel sounds each day. Selectively review 4-5 other consonants.

Large Sound Cards
Practice sounds with the Large Sound Cards. Model these, saying the letter-keyword-sound and have the students echo.

Standard Sound Cards
Next, point to the Standard Sound Cards (in card display) with the Baby Echo pointer. You say the letter-keyword-sound and hold up Baby Echo to have students repeat. You can have a student be the drill leader for some of the sounds.

Vowel Extension
Model extending the vowel sounds (example: **a-/ă/...apple-/ă/**). Have a student come trace the line for each of the vowels.

Word Play

MAKE WORDS FOR DECODING
Use your Standard Sound Card display to make 5-6 Unit words. (See Unit Resources.)

Make each word then say and tap each sound. Have students tap with you. Then blend the sounds as you drag your thumb across your fingers.

Next, point under each card as you say each sound, then drag your finger under all three cards as you and the students blend the sounds to read the word.

Have students find and underline digraphs.

Unit 4 | Week 2

Day 1

Echo/Find Letters & Words

Echo/Find Letters

Say a sound. Have students echo and point to the letter(s) on their Magnetic Letter Boards.

Ask

What says /___/? (___)

(See Echo Sounds in Unit Resources for expected student responses.)

Have students name the letter(s). Then you can have one student find the Standard Sound Card(s) as you dictate sounds. Do vowels and 3-5 other sounds.

(handwritten note: j g, sh ch, th)

Echo/Find Words

Dictate the word **shop**. Have students repeat the word, then tap it out with them.

Have students find Letter Tiles needed to make words on their Magnetic Letter Boards. Have one student come find your corresponding cards. After finding a word, have a student spell it orally. Have the students replace the letters onto their letter squares and dictate another word. Do 3-5 words.

Word Resources

shop   ship   chin   chat   thud   thin

Unit 4 | Week 2

Day 2

Daily Plan — DAY 2

Student Learning Plan
- Drill Sounds/Warm-Up
- Word Play
- Teach Trick Words
- Echo/Find Letters & Words

Teacher Materials
- Echo and/or Baby Echo
- Large Sound Cards
- Standard Sound Cards
- Sentence Frames
- Trick Word Flashcards

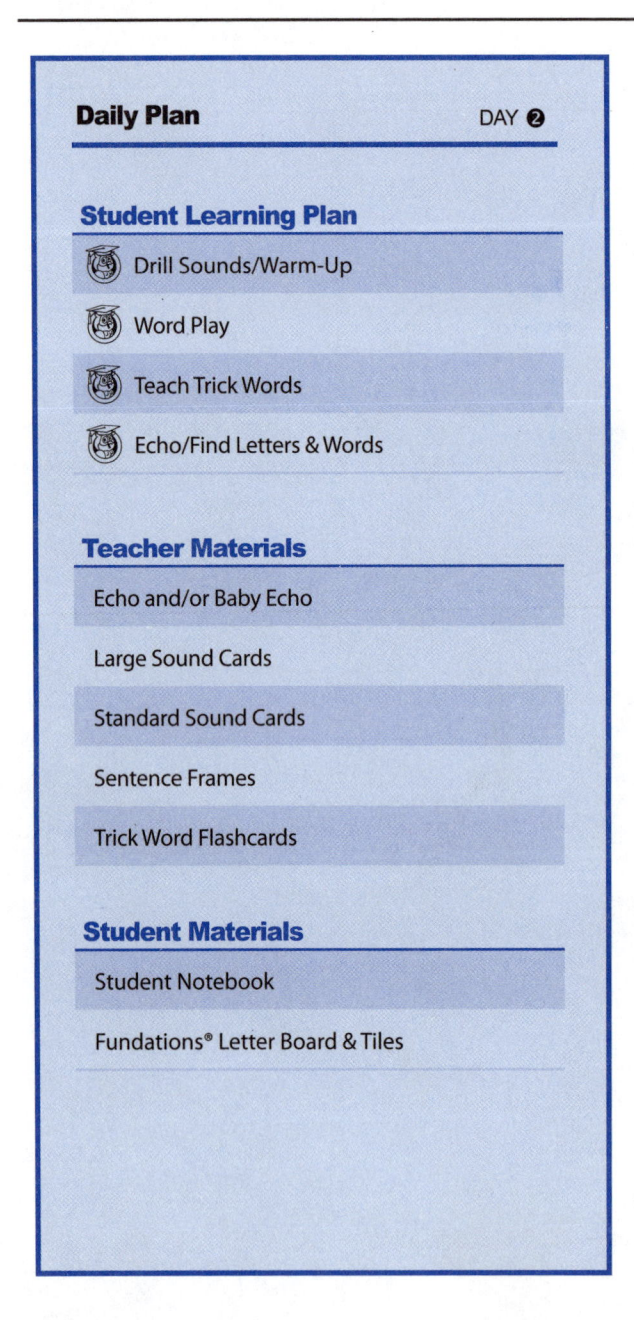

Student Materials
- Student Notebook
- Fundations® Letter Board & Tiles

Drill Sounds/Warm-Up

Do any new or challenging sounds and vowel sounds each day. Selectively review 4-5 other consonants.

Large Sound Cards

Practice sounds with the Large Sound Cards. Model these, saying the letter-keyword-sound and have the students echo.

Standard Sound Cards

Next, point to the Standard Sound Cards (in card display) with the Baby Echo pointer. You say the letter-keyword-sound and hold up Baby Echo to have students repeat. You can have a student be the drill leader for some of the sounds.

Word Play

MAKE WORDS FOR DECODING

Use your Standard Sound Card display to make 5-6 Unit words. (See Unit Resources.)

Make each word then say and tap each sound. Have students tap with you. Then blend the sounds as you drag your thumb across your fingers.

Next, point under each card as you say each sound, then drag your finger under all three cards as you and the students blend the sounds to read the word.

Have students find and underline digraphs.

path
wish
chip
fish
whip

Unit 4 | Week 2

Day 2

Teach Trick Words

Introduce the trick words **be** and **me**, and reinforce capitalization and punctuation.

Instruct Students

Say the sentence below and have students repeat. Have a student place the Sentence Frames as needed. Write the sentence on the frames, and discuss capitalization and punctuation. Scoop the sentence into phrases, read it, and have students echo.

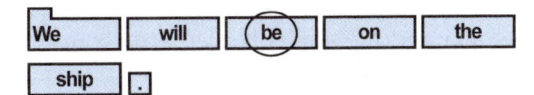

| We | will | (be) | on | the |
| ship | . |

Say

> I am going to circle this word (circle the new trick word). Listen to the sentence and see if you can tell me the word I circled (point to words as you say each one).
>
> Let's change this sentence to: Can you help me?

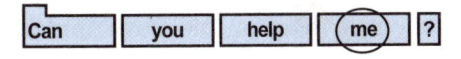

| Can | you | help | (me) | ? |

Next, explain that the words **be** and **me** are words that you are going to practice, and that these words are called Trick Words because they can be tricky and we do not tap them out.

Show students the Trick Word Flashcards **be** and **me**. Say the words and have them repeat. Lastly, present the Trick Word Flashcards learned thus far. Say each and have students repeat.

Echo/Find Letters & Words

Echo/Find Letters

Say a sound. Have students echo and point to the letter(s) on their Magnetic Letter Boards.

Ask

> Which letters say /k/? (k, c, ck)
>
> Which letters say /w/? (w, wh)
>
> What says /___/? (___)

(See Echo Sounds in Unit Resources for expected student responses.)

Have students name the letter(s). Then you can have one student find the Standard Sound Card(s) as you dictate sounds. Do vowels and 3-5 other sounds.

Echo/Find Words

Dictate a Unit word. Do 3-5 words. (See Current Unit Words in Unit Resources.)

Have students find Letter Tiles needed to make words on their Magnetic Letter Boards. Have one student come find your corresponding cards. After finding a word, have students spell it orally and replace the tiles on the letter squares.

Unit 4 | Week 2

Day 3

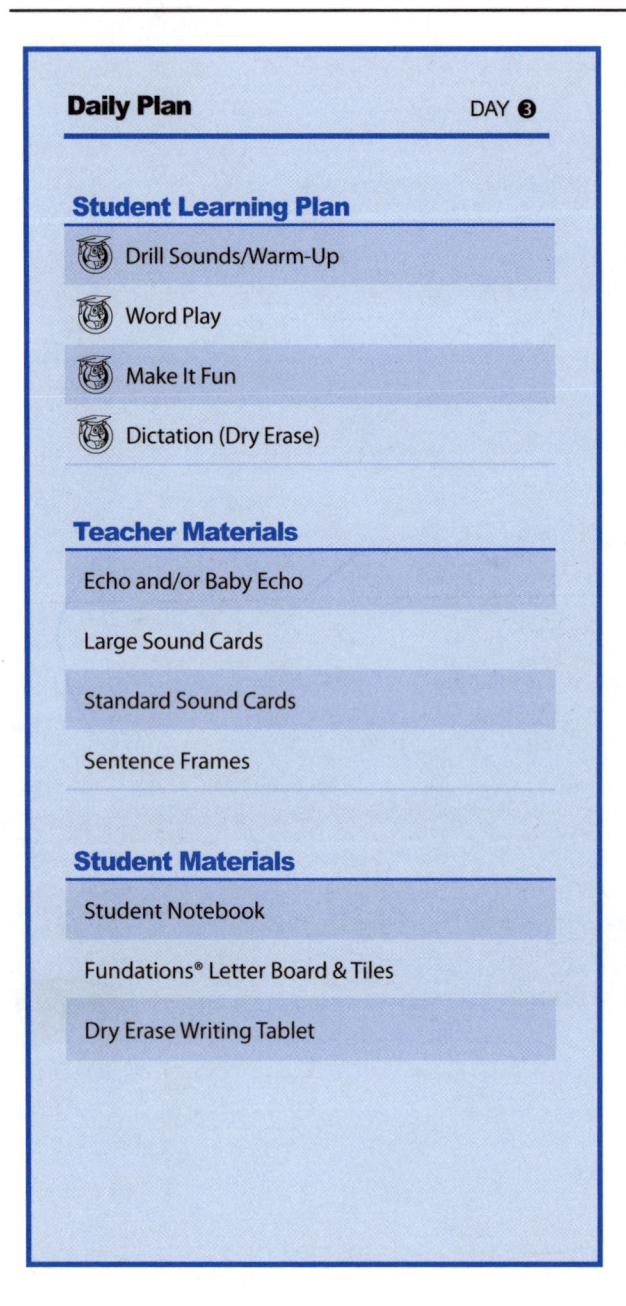

Daily Plan — DAY 3

Student Learning Plan
- Drill Sounds/Warm-Up
- Word Play
- Make It Fun
- Dictation (Dry Erase)

Teacher Materials
- Echo and/or Baby Echo
- Large Sound Cards
- Standard Sound Cards
- Sentence Frames

Student Materials
- Student Notebook
- Fundations® Letter Board & Tiles
- Dry Erase Writing Tablet

Drill Sounds/Warm-Up

Do any new or challenging sounds and vowel sounds each day. Selectively review 4-5 other consonants.

Large Sound Cards

Practice sounds with the Large Sound Cards. Model these, saying the letter-keyword-sound and have the students echo.

Standard Sound Cards

Next, point to the Standard Sound Cards (in card display) with the Baby Echo pointer. You say the letter-keyword-sound and hold up Baby Echo to have students repeat. You can have a student be the drill leader for some of the sounds.

Word Play

MAKE WORDS FOR DECODING

Use your Standard Sound Card display to make 5-6 Unit words. (See Unit Resources.)

Make each word then say and tap each sound. Have students tap with you. Then blend the sounds as you drag your thumb across your fingers.

Next, point under each card as you say each sound, then drag your finger under all three cards as you and the students blend the sounds to read the word.

Have students find and underline digraphs.

READ SENTENCES

Write sentences on Sentence Frames and scoop into phrases. Have student circle trick words and tap out other words. Read the sentence together, modeling fluency as you scoop into phrases. Select a student to read it, and have students repeat.

Sentence Resources

That (is) (a) big fish.

Beth had (a) bad rash.

Unit 4 | Week 2

Day 3

Make It Fun

Preparation

- Resource List of Current and Review Words

DIGRAPH DETECTIVES

This activity will help students learn to find digraphs.

Instruct Students

Write 10-15 words on the classroom board, some with digraphs and some without. Tell the students they are **digraph detectives** and they need to find all the digraphs and underline them. Read the list of words together with the class.

Variation

Break the class into groups of 3 students and assign each group a digraph to look for. Have the students copy the words with their digraph onto their Dry Erase Writing Tablets. Then call on a student from each group to come and underline the digraph in the words with their designated digraph.

Dictation (Dry Erase)

Proper Dictation Activity procedures are very important. Be sure to follow their demonstration on the Prevention Learning Community. This is a teaching time, not a testing time. Be sure students repeat each dictation. Dictate 3 sounds and then 3 current or review words.

Unit Sounds

Refer to this Unit's Resource List of Echo Sounds.

Unit Words

Students should tap and orally spell the Unit words before writing. Then have all spell chorally. Have one student write on the Large Writing Grid and all students write on their Dry Erase Writing Tablets. (See Current and Review Words in Unit Resources.)

Unit 4 | Week 2

Day 4

Daily Plan — DAY 4

Student Learning Plan
- Drill Sounds/Warm-Up
- Word Play
- Trick Word Practice
- Echo/Letter Formation
- Dictation (Dry Erase)

Teacher Materials
- Echo and/or Baby Echo
- Large Sound Cards
- Standard Sound Cards
- Sentence Frames
- Trick Word Flashcards

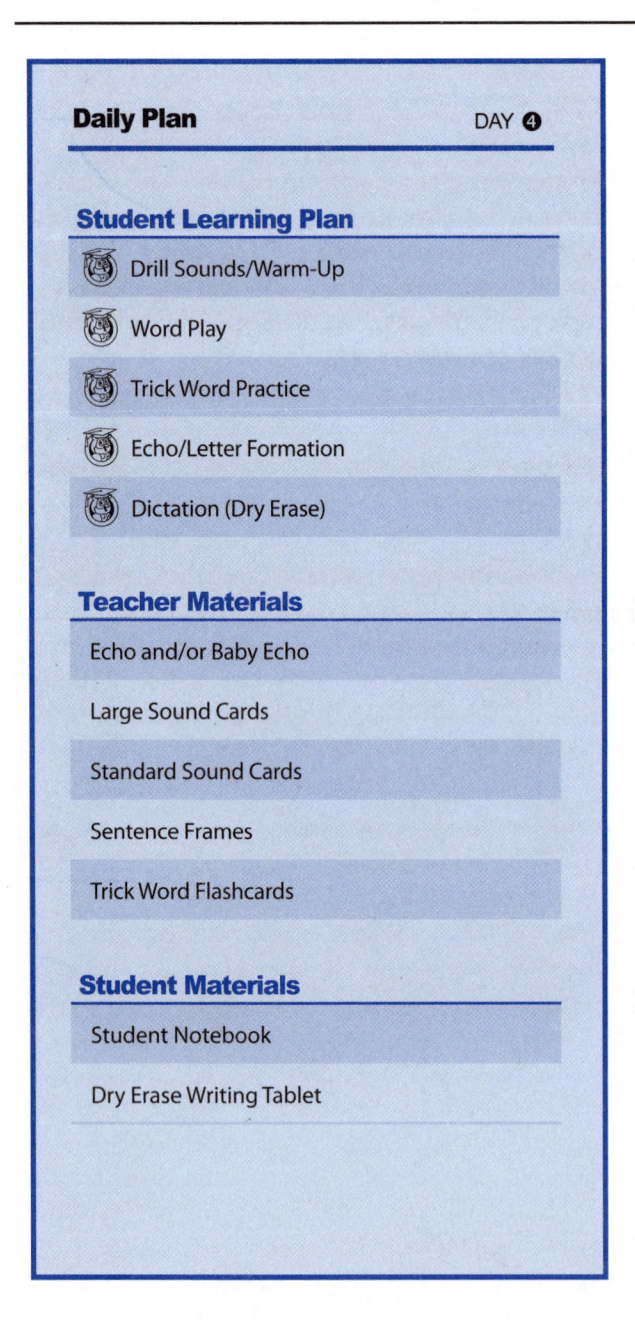

Student Materials
- Student Notebook
- Dry Erase Writing Tablet

Drill Sounds/Warm-Up

Do any new or challenging sounds and vowel sounds each day. Selectively review 4-5 other consonants.

Large Sound Cards

Practice sounds with the Large Sound Cards. Model these, saying the letter-keyword-sound and have the students echo.

Standard Sound Cards

Next, point to the Standard Sound Cards (in card display) with the Baby Echo pointer. You say the letter-keyword-sound and hold up Baby Echo to have students repeat. You can have a student be the drill leader for some of the sounds.

Instruct Students

Name the digraphs.

Which letters say /k/? (k, c, ck)

Which letters say /w/? (w, wh)

Word Play

MAKE WORDS FOR DECODING

Use your Standard Sound Card display to make 5-6 Unit words. (See Unit Resources.)

Make each word then say and tap each sound. Have students tap with you. Then blend the sounds as you drag your thumb across your fingers.

Next, point under each card as you say each sound, then drag your finger under all three cards as you and the students blend the sounds to read the word.

Have students find and underline digraphs.

MAKE NONSENSE WORDS

Tell students that they can also blend sounds together to make silly or nonsense words. Explain that these nonsense word are not real words. They are just silly words that show that they can read sounds.

Make 3-5 nonsense words and have students tap and read them (see Unit Resources).

Unit 4 | Week 2

Day 4

Trick Word Practice

Say each sentence below and have students repeat. Then write the sentence on Sentence Frames, and scoop it into phrases. Read it and have students echo. Say the trick word that is in the sentence and have a student find and circle it. After it is circled, hold up the corresponding Trick Word Flashcard and say the word and have students repeat.

Sentence Resource

(He) would like (to) (be) (a) clown.

(She) will go with (me) now.

Lastly present the Trick Word Flashcards, say each and have student repeat.

Echo/Letter Formation

Remind students of proper pencil grip and sitting position, and give them their Dry Erase Writing Tablets.

Dictate 5-6 previously taught sounds. You select and say the sound. Students echo the sound and say the letter.

Next have a student come up to the classroom board to make the letter on the Large Writing Grid.

Then have all students write the answer on their Dry Erase Writing Tablet as you direct them with the letter formation verbalization.

(See Unit Resources.)

Note
Students can make only lowercase letters, or you can selectively do both uppercase and lowercase to reinforce certain letters. (Be sure to always do lowercase for every sound that is dictated.)

Dictation (Dry Erase)

Proper Dictation Activity procedures are very important. Be sure to follow their demonstration on the Prevention Learning Community. This is a teaching time, not a testing time. Be sure students repeat each dictation. Dictate 3 sounds and then 3 current or review words.

Unit Sounds

Refer to this Unit's Resource List of Echo Sounds.

Unit Words

Students should tap and orally spell the Unit words before writing. Then have all spell chorally. Have one student write on the Large Writing Grid and all students write on their Dry Erase Writing Tablets. (See Current and Review Words in Unit Resources.)

Unit 4 | Week 2

Day 5

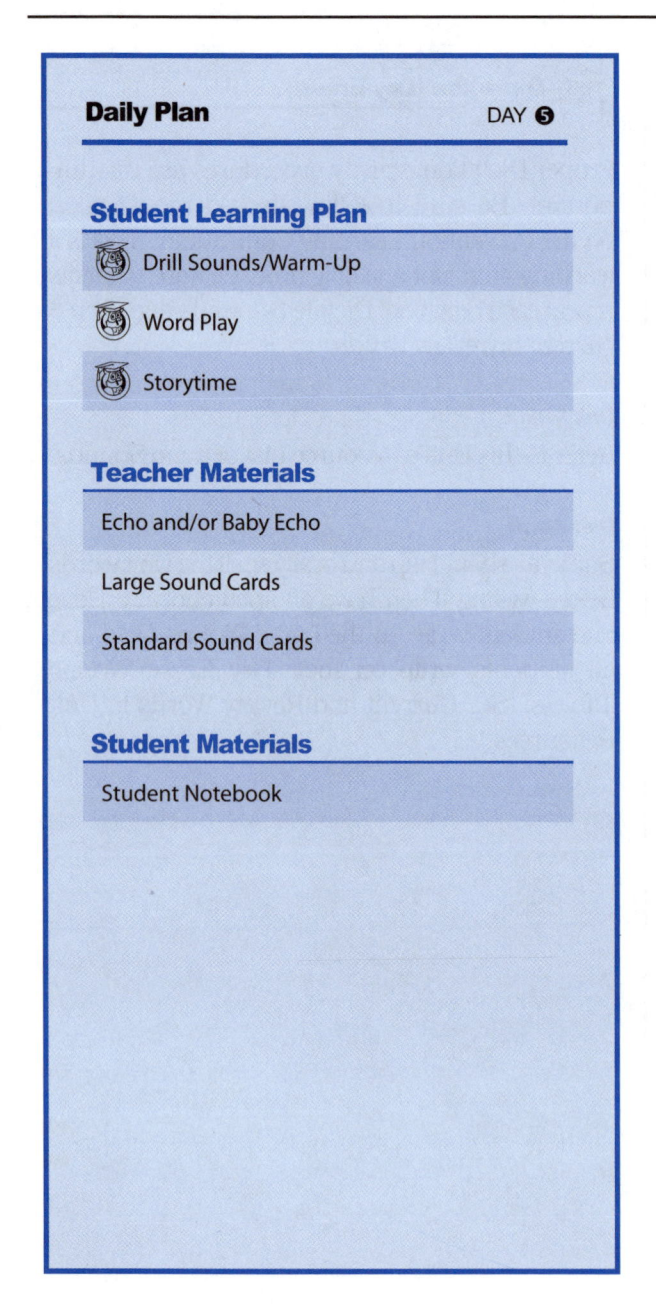

Daily Plan — DAY 5

Student Learning Plan
- Drill Sounds/Warm-Up
- Word Play
- Storytime

Teacher Materials
- Echo and/or Baby Echo
- Large Sound Cards
- Standard Sound Cards

Student Materials
- Student Notebook

Drill Sounds/Warm-Up

Do any new or challenging sounds and vowel sounds each day. Selectively review 4-5 other consonants.

Large Sound Cards
Practice sounds with the Large Sound Cards. Model these, saying the letter-keyword-sound and have the students echo.

Standard Sound Cards
Next, point to the Standard Sound Cards (in card display) with the Baby Echo pointer. You say the letter-keyword-sound and hold up Baby Echo to have students repeat. You can have a student be the drill leader for some of the sounds.

Word Play

MAKE WORDS FOR DECODING
Use your Standard Sound Card display to make 5-6 Unit words. (See Unit Resources.)

Make each word then say and tap each sound. Have students tap with you. Then blend the sounds as you drag your thumb across your fingers.

Next, point under each card as you say each sound, then drag your finger under all three cards as you and the students blend the sounds to read the word.

Have students find and underline digraphs.

320 FUNDATIONS® LEVEL K

© 2002, 2012 WILSON LANGUAGE TRAINING CORPORATION

Unit 4 | Week 2

Day 5

Storytime

Preparation

Use the storybook selected in the previous week. You will use this book to help develop the students' retelling ability. Before reading, look at the front and back cover of the book with your students. Discuss the title, author and illustrator, explaining each of those terms.

Ask

> Who were the characters?
>
> What was the setting for this story?

Instruct Students

> Last week I read this story to you.
>
> Today, I am going to see if you can tell it to me.
>
> Let's see if you remember the story.

Next go through the book, page by page and show the students the pictures. Have them tell you what happened on each page. Go through the whole book, without reading.

Ask

> Let's see if you remember it.
>
> I'll read it to see if you were right.
>
> (Read the story.)
>
> What happened first?
>
> Then what happened?
>
> What happened next?
>
> What happened at the end?

Unit 4 | Week 3

Day 1

Daily Plan — DAY 1

Student Learning Plan
- Drill Sounds/Warm-Up
- Introduce New Concepts
- Echo/Find Letters & Words

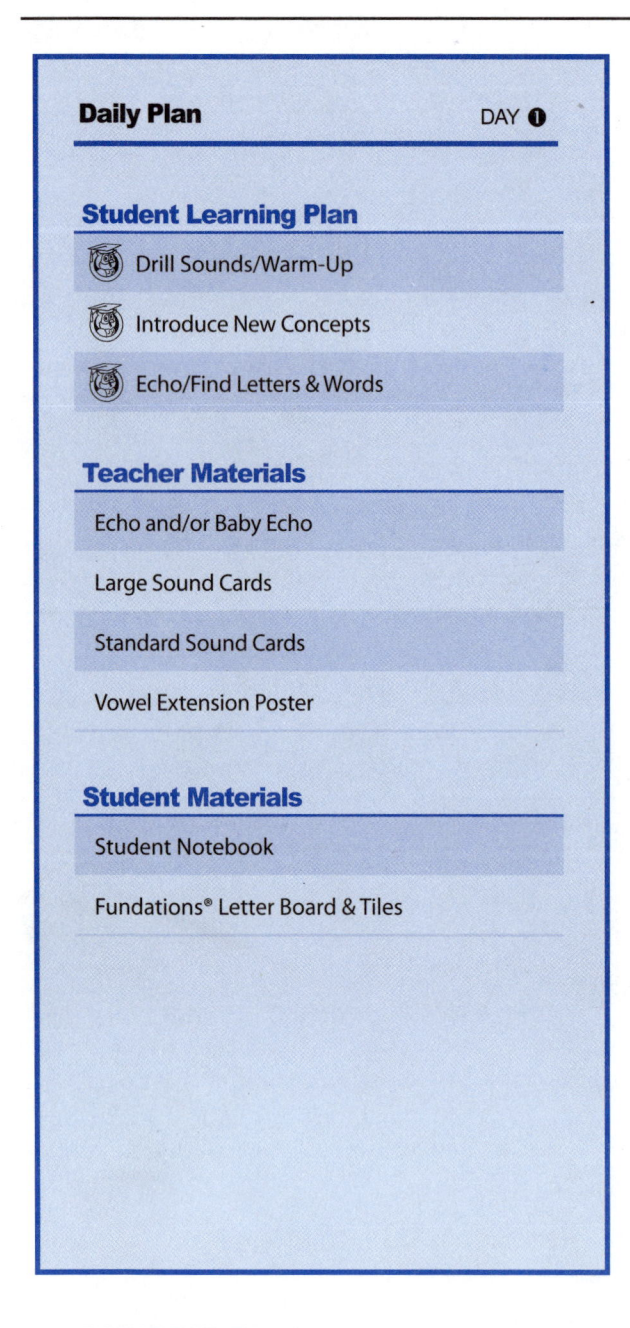

Teacher Materials
- Echo and/or Baby Echo
- Large Sound Cards
- Standard Sound Cards
- Vowel Extension Poster

Student Materials
- Student Notebook
- Fundations® Letter Board & Tiles

Drill Sounds/Warm-Up

Do any new or challenging sounds and vowel sounds each day. Selectively review 4-5 other consonants.

Large Sound Cards
Practice sounds with the Large Sound Cards. Model these, saying the letter-keyword-sound and have the students echo.

Standard Sound Cards
Next, point to the Standard Sound Cards (in card display) with the Baby Echo pointer. You say the letter-keyword-sound and hold up Baby Echo to have students repeat. You can have a student be the drill leader for some of the sounds.

Vowel Extension
Model extending the vowel sounds (example: a-/ă/...apple-/ă/). Have a student come trace the line for each of the vowels.

Introduce New Concepts

TEACH SPELLING OF CK

Echo/Find Letters
Ask the students, "**What says /k/?**" Now they should answer **k**, **c**, and **ck**.

Echo/Find Words
Explain to the students that **ck** is used only at the **end of words** right **after the short vowel**.

Example
Make the word **duck**. Tell students that the /ŭ/ is the short vowel sound for **u** and mark it with a breve.

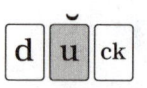

Cover the **ck** with the letter **c**. Tell them that **c** says /k/ but does not end words. Cover the **ck** with the letter **k**. Tell them that **k** says /k/ but does not end words right after a short vowel.

Tell students that even though **c** and **k** both say /k/, right after a short vowel they should always use **ck**.

Dictate other **ck** words and have a student come spell the word with Standard Sound Cards (see Unit Resources).

[handwritten: lick, Jack, rock, neck]

Unit 4 | Week 3

Day 1

Echo/Find Letters & Words

Tell students to arrange their digraph Letter Tiles with **ck** last to remind them that **ck** is only found at the end of words.

Echo/Find Letters

Say a sound. Have students echo and point to the letter(s) on their Magnetic Letter Boards.

Ask

What says /___/? (___)

(See Echo Sounds in Unit Resources for expected student responses.)

Have students name the letter(s). Then you can have one student find the Standard Sound Card(s) as you dictate sounds. Do vowels and 3-5 other sounds.

Echo/Find Words

Dictate a Unit word. Do 3-5 words. (See Current Unit Words in Unit Resources.)

Have students find Letter Tiles needed to make words on their Magnetic Letter Boards. Have one student come find your corresponding cards. After finding a word, have students spell it orally and replace the tiles on the letter squares.

sack   fish
this
chop

Unit 4 | Week 3

Day 2

Daily Plan — DAY 2

Student Learning Plan
- Drill Sounds/Warm-Up
- Word Play
- Teach Trick Words
- Echo/Find Letters & Words

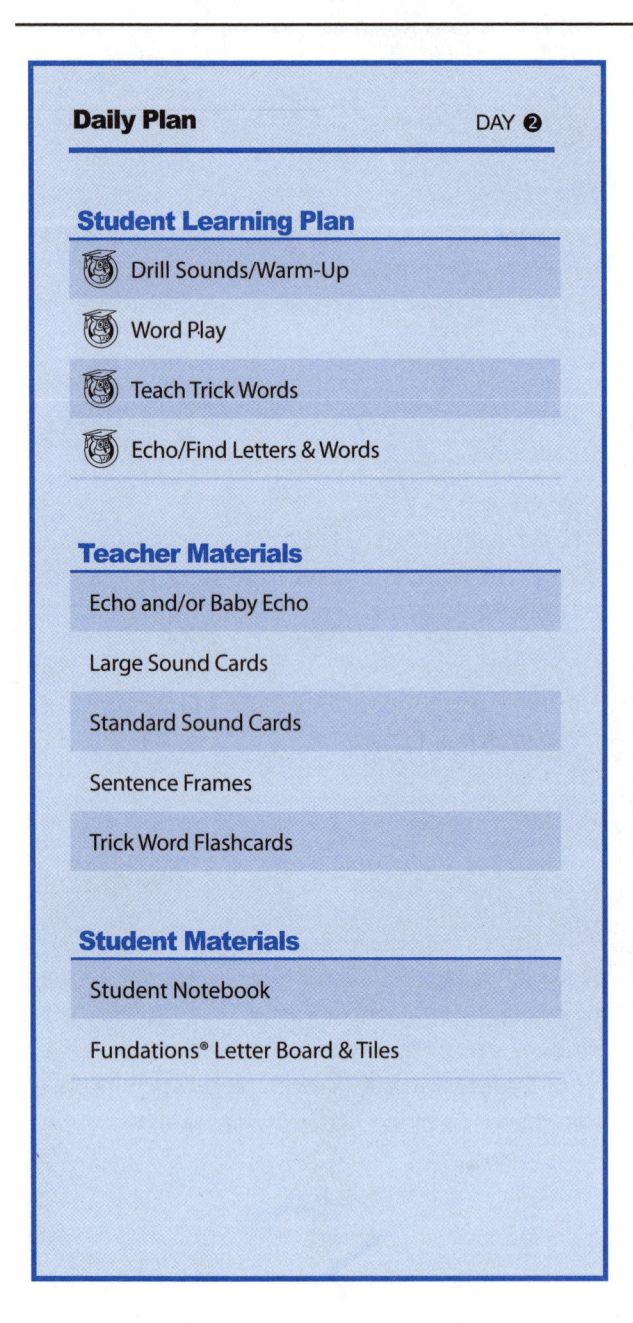

Teacher Materials
- Echo and/or Baby Echo
- Large Sound Cards
- Standard Sound Cards
- Sentence Frames
- Trick Word Flashcards

Student Materials
- Student Notebook
- Fundations® Letter Board & Tiles

Drill Sounds/Warm-Up

Do any new or challenging sounds and vowel sounds each day. Selectively review 4-5 other consonants.

Large Sound Cards
Practice sounds with the Large Sound Cards. Model these, saying the letter-keyword-sound and have the students echo.

Standard Sound Cards
Next, point to the Standard Sound Cards (in card display) with the Baby Echo pointer. You say the letter-keyword-sound and hold up Baby Echo to have students repeat. You can have a student be the drill leader for some of the sounds.

Word Play

MAKE WORDS FOR DECODING

Use your Standard Sound Card display to make 5-6 Unit words. (See Unit Resources.)

Make each word then say and tap each sound. Have students tap with you. Then blend the sounds as you drag your thumb across your fingers.

Next, point under each card as you say each sound, then drag your finger under all three cards as you and the students blend the sounds to read the word.

Have students find and underline digraphs.

324 FUNDATIONS® LEVEL K

© 2002, 2012 WILSON LANGUAGE TRAINING CORPORATION

Unit 4 | Week 3

Day 2

LISTEN FOR SOUNDS

This activity will help students distinguish between the long (/ā/) and short (/ă/) vowel sounds. Next say, "I am going to say a word. After I say it, you tell me all the sounds in the word. So, if I say **mad**, you would say **/m/ /a/ /d/**. Tell me the sounds in _____." (Use the Word Resources below.)

After students say sounds for both words that are similar with different vowel sounds (**mad**, **made**), ask which word has /ă/ sound, **mad** or **made**? Help students tap and stop at the vowel. Tell them that sometimes it will say its name /ā/, which is called a long sound, and sometimes it will say the sound /ă/, which is called a short sound. When they say the word with the short vowel sound (**mad**) say yes! and make it with the Standard Sound Cards and read it together. Tell students that we call this vowel sound a short vowel and we mark it with a breve (˘).

m ă d

Word Resources

lick   like   soak   sock   back   bake

shin   shine   peek   peck

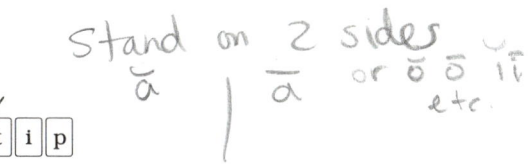

[handwritten: Stand on 2 sides ă | ā or ō ō ĭĭ etc.]

tip

For advanced students, you can provide additional work on recognizing the long vowel sounds. See the PLC for activities.

Teach Trick Words

Introduce the trick words **I** and **you**, and reinforce capitalization and punctuation.

Instruct Students

Say the sentence below and have students repeat. Have a student place the Sentence Frames as needed. Write the sentence on the frames, and discuss capitalization and punctuation. Scoop the sentence into phrases, read it, and have students echo.

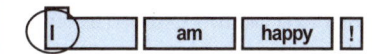

| ⓘ | am | happy | ! |

Say

I am going to circle this word (circle the new trick word). Listen to the sentence and see if you can tell me the word I circled (point to words as you say each one).

Let's change this sentence to: Can you come play with me?

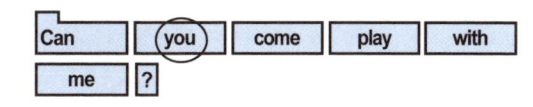

| Can | ⓨou | come | play | with |
| me | ? |

Next, explain that the words **I** and **you** are words that you are going to practice, and that these words are called Trick Words because they can be tricky and we do not tap them out.

Show students the Trick Word Flashcards **I** and **you**. Say the words and have them repeat. Lastly, present the Trick Word Flashcards learned thus far. Say each and have students repeat.

Echo/Find Letters & Words

Echo/Find Letters

Say a sound. Have students echo and point to the letter(s) on their Magnetic Letter Boards.

Ask

Which letters say /k/? (k, c, ck)

Which one do you use at the end of a word after a short vowel? (ck)

What says /___/? (___)

(See Echo Sounds in Unit Resources for expected student responses.)

Have students name the letter(s). Then you can have one student find the Standard Sound Card(s) as you dictate sounds. Do vowels and 3-5 other sounds.

Echo/Find Words

Dictate a Unit word. Do 3-5 words. (See Current Unit Words in Unit Resources.)

Have students find Letter Tiles needed to make words on their Magnetic Letter Boards. Have one student come find your corresponding cards. After finding a word, have students spell it orally and replace the tiles on the letter squares.

Unit 4 | Week 3

Day 3

Daily Plan — DAY 3

Student Learning Plan
- Drill Sounds/Warm-Up
- Word Play
- Make It Fun
- Dictation (Dry Erase)

Teacher Materials
- Echo and/or Baby Echo
- Large Sound Cards
- Standard Sound Cards

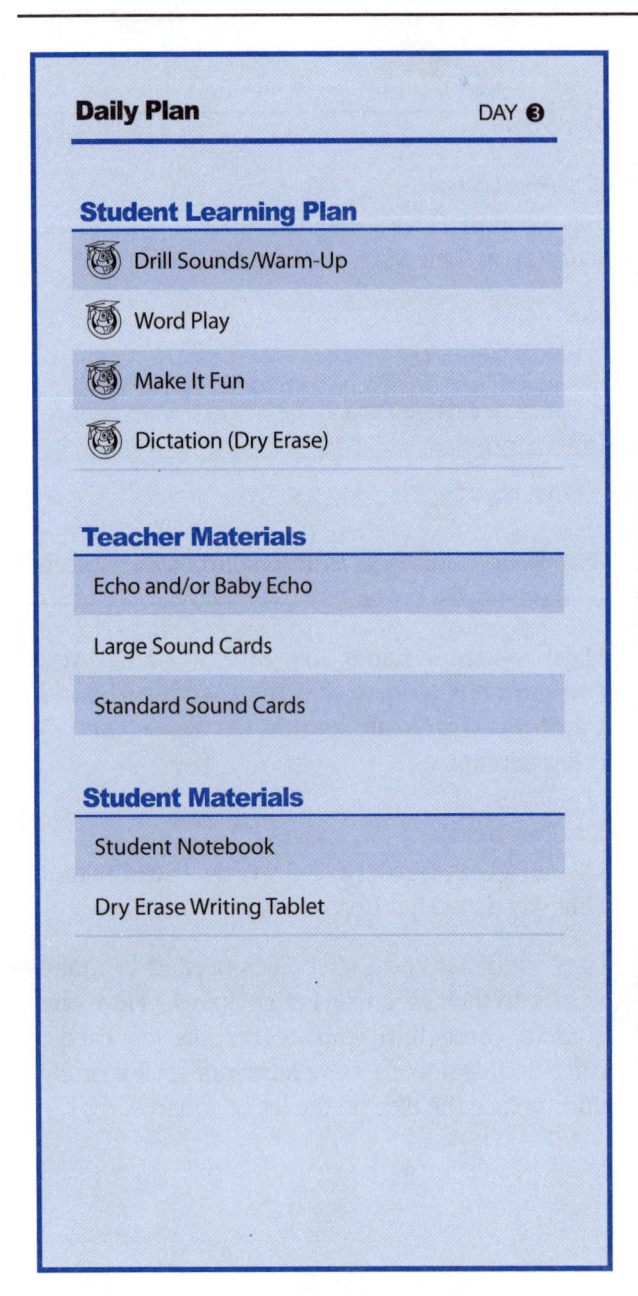

Student Materials
- Student Notebook
- Dry Erase Writing Tablet

Drill Sounds/Warm-Up

Do any new or challenging sounds and vowel sounds each day. Selectively review 4-5 other consonants.

Large Sound Cards

Practice sounds with the Large Sound Cards. Model these, saying the letter-keyword-sound and have the students echo.

Standard Sound Cards

Next, point to the Standard Sound Cards (in card display) with the Baby Echo pointer. You say the letter-keyword-sound and hold up Baby Echo to have students repeat. You can have a student be the drill leader for some of the sounds.

Word Play

MAKE WORDS FOR DECODING

Use your Standard Sound Card display to make 5-6 Unit words. (See Unit Resources.)

Make each word then say and tap each sound. Have students tap with you. Then blend the sounds as you drag your thumb across your fingers.

Next, point under each card as you say each sound, then drag your finger under all three cards as you and the students blend the sounds to read the word.

Have students find and underline digraphs.

READ SENTENCES

Write sentences on Sentence Frames and scoop into phrases. Have student circle trick words and tap out other words. Read the sentence together, modeling fluency as you scoop into phrases. Select a student to read it, and have students repeat.

Sentence Resources

Jack sat on (the) dock.

The cat (is) quick.

Unit 4 | Week 3

Day 3

Make It Fun

SOUND A WORD

Teacher Materials

Place approximately ten small objects (such as plastic animals, cars, pens) in a pillow case or bag. The objects should have a name that is one-syllable of varying length (such as: **pen**, **clip**, **truck**).

Directions

Select a child to pick an item from the bag, but not show it to the class, only to you. Whisper the word segmented to the student and have them repeat it, segmented to the class. For example, if it is a truck, you would say:

/t/ /r/ /ŭ/ /k/   and the student would say:

/t/ /r/ /ŭ/ /k/

Select a student to guess the object. When someone guesses, the student holding the object shows it to the class and sits down with it.

The student who correctly guessed selects the next object from the bag. When all items have been selected, have the students give the object to a student without an object. Collect objects one at a time by saying the word segmented into sounds.

Say

I'm looking for the /t/ /r/ /ŭ/ /k/. Who has the /t/ /r/ /ŭ/ /k/?

Dictation (Dry Erase)

Proper Dictation Activity procedures are very important. Be sure to follow their demonstration on the Prevention Learning Community. This is a teaching time, not a testing time. Be sure students repeat each dictation. Dictate 3 sounds and then 3 current or review words.

Unit Sounds

Refer to this Unit's Resource List of Echo Sounds.

Unit Words

Students should tap and orally spell the Unit words before writing. Then have all spell chorally. Have one student write on the Large Writing Grid and all students write on their Dry Erase Writing Tablets. (See Current and Review Words in Unit Resources.)

Sid did
zip vet

Unit 4 | Week 3

Day 4

Daily Plan — DAY 4

Student Learning Plan
- Drill Sounds/Warm-Up
- Word Play
- Trick Word Practice
- Echo/Letter Formation
- Dictation (Dry Erase)

Teacher Materials
- Echo and/or Baby Echo
- Large Sound Cards
- Standard Sound Cards
- Sentence Frames
- Trick Word Flashcards

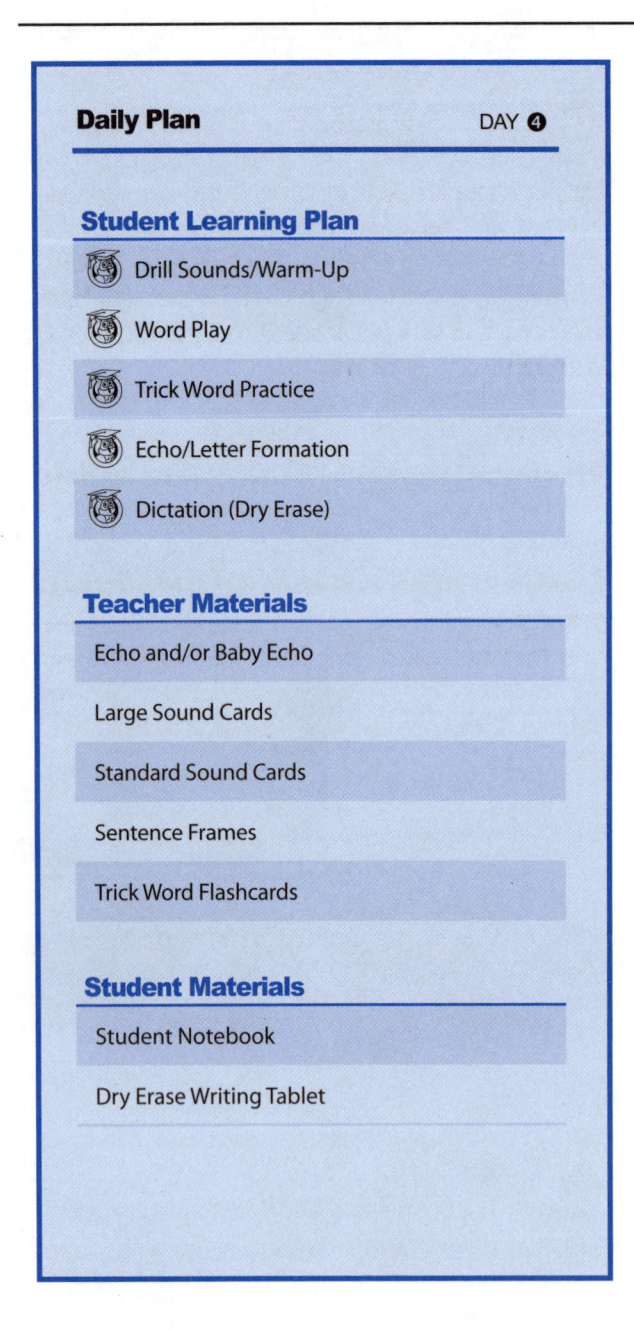

Student Materials
- Student Notebook
- Dry Erase Writing Tablet

Drill Sounds/Warm-Up

Do any new or challenging sounds and vowel sounds each day. Selectively review 4-5 other consonants.

Large Sound Cards

Practice sounds with the Large Sound Cards. Model these, saying the letter-keyword-sound and have the students echo.

Standard Sound Cards

Next, point to the Standard Sound Cards (in card display) with the Baby Echo pointer. You say the letter-keyword-sound and hold up Baby Echo to have students repeat. You can have a student be the drill leader for some of the sounds.

Word Play

MAKE WORDS FOR DECODING

Use your Standard Sound Card display to make 5-6 Unit words. (See Unit Resources.)

Make each word then say and tap each sound. Have students tap with you. Then blend the sounds as you drag your thumb across your fingers.

Next, point under each card as you say each sound, then drag your finger under all three cards as you and the students blend the sounds to read the word.

Have students find and underline digraphs.

MAKE NONSENSE WORDS

Tell students that they can also blend sounds together to make silly or nonsense words. Explain that these nonsense words are not real words. They are just silly words that show that they can read sounds.

Make 3-5 nonsense words and have students tap and read them (see Unit Resources).

Unit 4 | Week 3

Day 4

Trick Word Practice

Say each sentence below and have students repeat. Then write the sentence on Sentence Frames, and scoop it into phrases. Read it and have students echo. Say the trick word that is in the sentence and have a student find and circle it. After it is circled, hold up the corresponding Trick Word Flashcard and say the word and have students repeat.

Sentence Resource

(Are)(you) okay?

(I) had an apple (and) an orange.

Lastly present the Trick Word Flashcards, say each and have student repeat.

Echo/Letter Formation

Remind students of proper pencil grip and sitting position, and give them their Dry Erase Writing Tablets.

Dictate 5-6 previously taught sounds. You select and say the sound. Students echo the sound and say the letter.

Next have a student come up to the classroom board to make the letter on the Large Writing Grid.

Then have all students write the answer on their Dry Erase Writing Tablet as you direct them with the letter formation verbalization.

(See Unit Resources.)

Note
Students can make only lowercase letters, or you can selectively do both uppercase and lowercase to reinforce certain letters. (Be sure to always do lowercase for every sound that is dictated.)

Dictation (Dry Erase)

Proper Dictation Activity procedures are very important. Be sure to follow their demonstration on the Prevention Learning Community. This is a teaching time, not a testing time. Be sure students repeat each dictation. Dictate 3 sounds and then 3 current or review words.

Unit Sounds

Refer to this Unit's Resource List of Echo Sounds.

Unit Words

Students should tap and orally spell the Unit words before writing. Then have all spell chorally. Have one student write on the Large Writing Grid and all students write on their Dry Erase Writing Tablets. (See Current and Review Words in Unit Resources.)

Unit 4 | Week 3

Day 5

Daily Plan — DAY 5

Student Learning Plan
- Drill Sounds/Warm-Up
- Word Play
- Storytime

Teacher Materials
- Echo and/or Baby Echo
- Large Sound Cards
- Standard Sound Cards
- Large chart paper with Cod Fish story

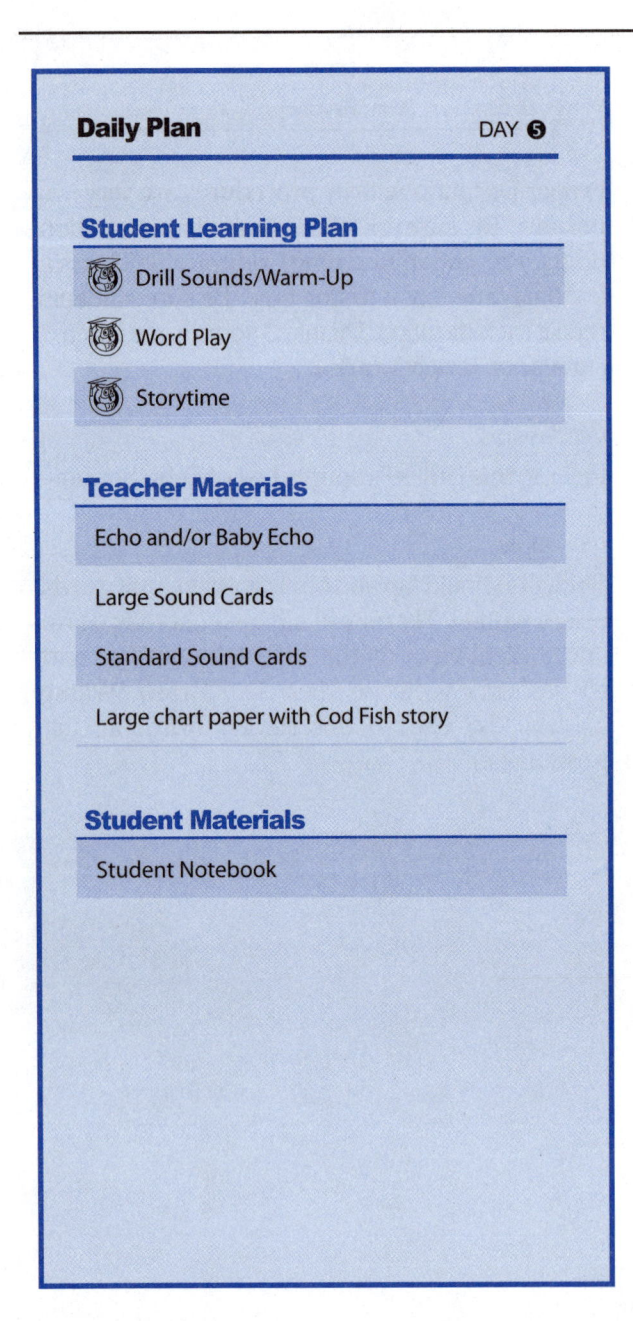

Student Materials
- Student Notebook

Drill Sounds/Warm-Up

Do any new or challenging sounds and vowel sounds each day. Selectively review 4-5 other consonants.

Large Sound Cards

Practice sounds with the Large Sound Cards. Model these, saying the letter-keyword-sound and have the students echo.

Standard Sound Cards

Next, point to the Standard Sound Cards (in card display) with the Baby Echo pointer. You say the letter-keyword-sound and hold up Baby Echo to have students repeat. You can have a student be the drill leader for some of the sounds.

Instruct Students

Name the digraphs.

Which letters say /k/? (k, c, ck)

Word Play

MAKE WORDS FOR DECODING

Use your Standard Sound Card display to make 5-6 Unit words. (See Unit Resources.)

Make each word then say and tap each sound. Have students tap with you. Then blend the sounds as you drag your thumb across your fingers.

Next, point under each card as you say each sound, then drag your finger under all three cards as you and the students blend the sounds to read the word.

Have students find and underline digraphs.

Unit 4 | Week 3

Day 5

Storytime

Preparation

- Baby Echo (on a pointer or ruler)
- Scooped story on large chart paper or projected to class

COD FISH I

Write the following story, with the phrases scooped, on chart paper.

Cod Fish

Beth got Rick

a red net at the shop.

Then Rick got a big fish

in the net. It was a cod fish.

Rick fed the fish

to his pet cat, Chip.

Chip had the dish of cod fish.

Yum! Yum!

Instruct Students

Ask the students to read the title silently. (Tell students to tap words when reading silently, if necessary.) Discuss the title and predict what the story might be about.

Read Sentences

Continue reading one sentence at a time.

- Have students read a sentence silently. (Tell students to tap words when reading silently, if necessary.)
- Select a student to come read the sentence with the Baby Echo pointer. Be sure the student uses proper expression and phrasing. If not, model.
- Have the whole class repeat the sentence.

After the story has been read once in this manner, read it all together with choral reading as you scoop the phrases with Baby Echo.

Make a Movie

Have students "make a movie" in their heads. Tell them to close their eyes and picture the story.

Ask someone to describe what they see in their movie, discussing each sentence.

Continue with the whole story. Then model retelling the story in your own words and ask a student to retell it in their own words.

Mark Words

Lastly, select students to come mark words as directed.

- Make a capital letter frame around words that have a capital letter and discuss why (at the beginning of a sentence or a person's name).
- Highlight the exclamation marks (briefly discuss).
- Underline digraphs.

Unit 4 | Week 4

Day 1

Daily Plan — DAY 1

Student Learning Plan
- Drill Sounds/Warm-Up
- Introduce New Concepts
- Echo/Find Letters & Words

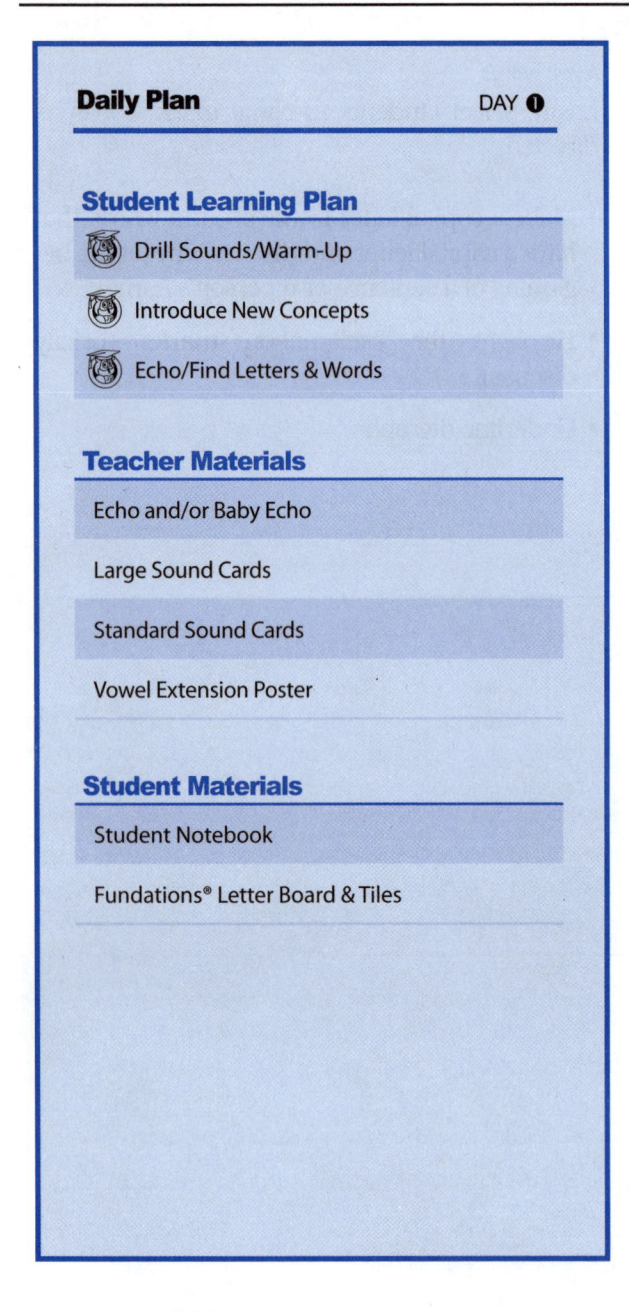

Teacher Materials
- Echo and/or Baby Echo
- Large Sound Cards
- Standard Sound Cards
- Vowel Extension Poster

Student Materials
- Student Notebook
- Fundations® Letter Board & Tiles

Drill Sounds/Warm-Up

Do any new or challenging sounds and vowel sounds each day. Selectively review 4-5 other consonants.

Large Sound Cards
Practice sounds with the Large Sound Cards. Model these, saying the letter-keyword-sound and have the students echo.

Standard Sound Cards
Next, point to the Standard Sound Cards (in card display) with the Baby Echo pointer. You say the letter-keyword-sound and hold up Baby Echo to have students repeat. You can have a student be the drill leader for some of the sounds.

Vowel Extension
Model extending the vowel sounds (example: a-/ă/...apple-/ă/). Have a student come trace the line for each of the vowels.

Introduce New Concepts

REVIEW SPELLING
Dictate several words, including words with digraphs such as **path**. These words will get three taps: /p/ - /ă/ - /th/.

Have one student spell the word for the class, by tapping the sounds, building the word at the Standard Sound Card display, and naming the letters.

Ask the students, "**What says /k/?**" Now they should answer **k**, **c**, and **ck**.

Ask students what says /k/ at the **end of words** right **after the short vowel**? (**ck**) Make the word **back**, and reteach **ck** spelling.

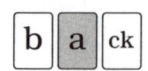

| b | a | ck |

Cover the **ck** with the letter **c**. Tell them that **c** says /k/ but does not end words. Cover the **ck** with the letter **k**. Tell them that **k** says /k/ but does not end words right after a short vowel.

Tell students that even though **c** and **k** both say /k/, right after a short vowel they should always use **ck**.

Dictate several words that end in **ck** selecting a student to spell them with Standard Sound Cards. (See Unit Resources.)

Unit 4 | Week 4

Day 1

🦉 Echo/Find Letters & Words

Echo/Find Letters

Say a sound. Have students echo and point to the letter(s) on their Magnetic Letter Boards.

Ask

What says /___/? (___)

(See Echo Sounds in Unit Resources for expected student responses.)

Have students name the letter(s). Then you can have one student find the Standard Sound Card(s) as you dictate sounds. Do vowels and 3-5 other sounds.

Echo/Find Words

Dictate a Unit word. Do 3-5 words. (See Current Unit Words in Unit Resources.)

Have students find Letter Tiles needed to make words on their Magnetic Letter Boards. Have one student come find your corresponding cards. After finding a word, have students spell it orally and replace the tiles on the letter squares.

Handwritten notes:
Benchmark teach
fork form
fort
make like
choke cute
show core more
soar

Unit 4 | Week 4

Day 2

Daily Plan — DAY 2

Student Learning Plan
- Drill Sounds/Warm-Up
- Word Play
- Teach Trick Words
- Echo/Find Letters & Words

Teacher Materials
- Echo and/or Baby Echo
- Large Sound Cards
- Standard Sound Cards
- Sentence Frames
- Trick Word Flashcards

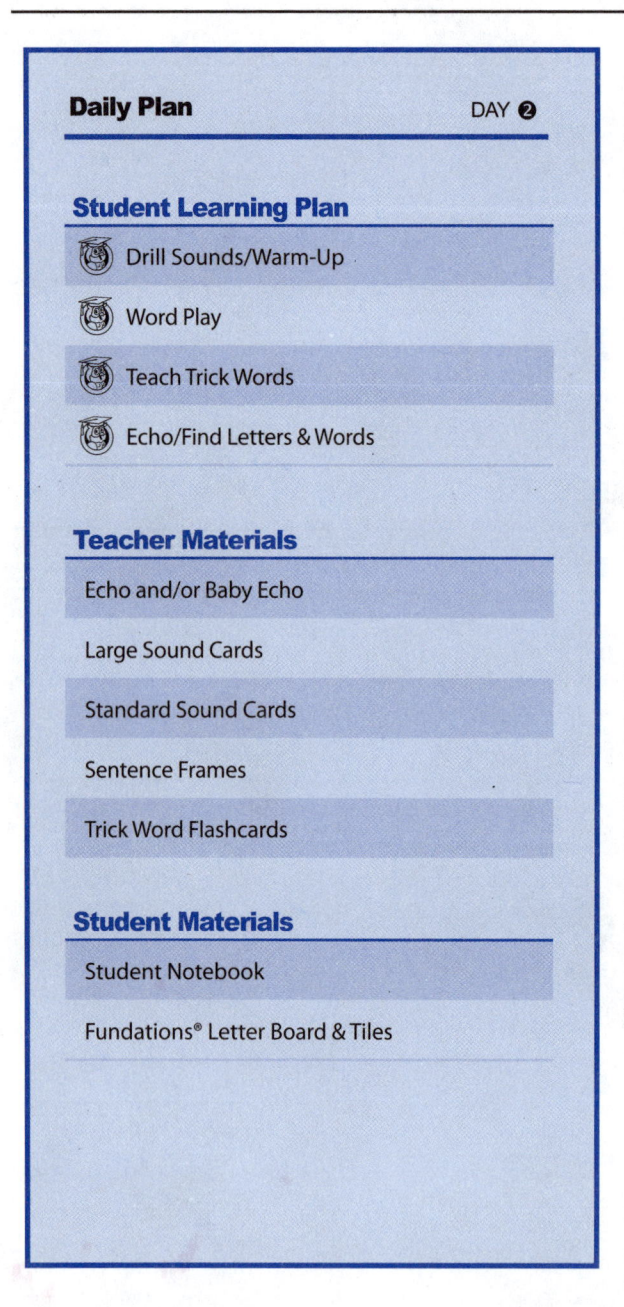

Student Materials
- Student Notebook
- Fundations® Letter Board & Tiles

Drill Sounds/Warm-Up

Do any new or challenging sounds and vowel sounds each day. Selectively review 4-5 other consonants.

Large Sound Cards
Practice sounds with the Large Sound Cards. Model these, saying the letter-keyword-sound and have the students echo.

Standard Sound Cards
Next, point to the Standard Sound Cards (in card display) with the Baby Echo pointer. You say the letter-keyword-sound and hold up Baby Echo to have students repeat. You can have a student be the drill leader for some of the sounds.

Instruct Students

Name the digraphs.

Which letters say /k/? (k, c, ck)

Which digraph is only used after a short vowel? (ck)

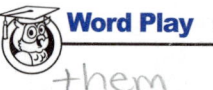

Word Play   *chat*   *them*   *wish*

MAKE WORDS FOR DECODING

Use your Standard Sound Card display to make 5-6 Unit words. (See Unit Resources.)

Make each word then say and tap each sound. Have students tap with you. Then blend the sounds as you drag your thumb across your fingers.

Next, point under each card as you say each sound, then drag your finger under all three cards as you and the students blend the sounds to read the word.

Have students find and underline digraphs.

Unit 4 | Week 4

Day 2

Teach Trick Words

Introduce the trick words **they**, and reinforce capitalization and punctuation.

Instruct Students

Say the sentence below and have students repeat. Have a student place the Sentence Frames as needed. Write the sentence on the frames, and discuss capitalization and punctuation. Scoop the sentence into phrases, read it, and have students echo.

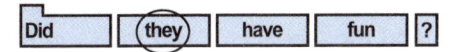

| Did | (they) | have | fun | ? |

Say

> I am going to circle this word (circle the new trick word). Listen to the sentence and see if you can tell me the word I circled (point to words as you say each one).

Next, explain that the word **they** is a word that you are going to practice, and that this word is called a Trick Word because it can be tricky and we do not tap it out.

Show students the Trick Word Flashcard with **they**. Say the word and have them repeat.

Lastly, present the Trick Word Flashcards learned thus far. Say each and have students repeat.

Echo/Find Letters & Words

Echo/Find Letters

Say a sound. Have students echo and point to the letter(s) on their Magnetic Letter Boards.

Ask

> What says /___/? (___)

(See Echo Sounds in Unit Resources for expected student responses.)

Have students name the letter(s). Then you can have one student find the Standard Sound Card(s) as you dictate sounds. Do vowels and 3-5 other sounds.

Echo/Find Words

Dictate a Unit word. Do 3-5 words. (See Current Unit Words in Unit Resources.) *long vowels*

Have students find Letter Tiles needed to make words on their Magnetic Letter Boards. Have one student come find your corresponding cards. After finding a word, have students spell it orally and replace the tiles on the letter squares.

gate   bike   + chick
rude   quick

Unit 4 | Week 4

Day 3

Daily Plan — DAY 3

Student Learning Plan
- Drill Sounds/Warm-Up
- Word Play
- Make It Fun
- Dictation (Dry Erase)

Teacher Materials
- Echo and/or Baby Echo
- Large Sound Cards
- Standard Sound Cards

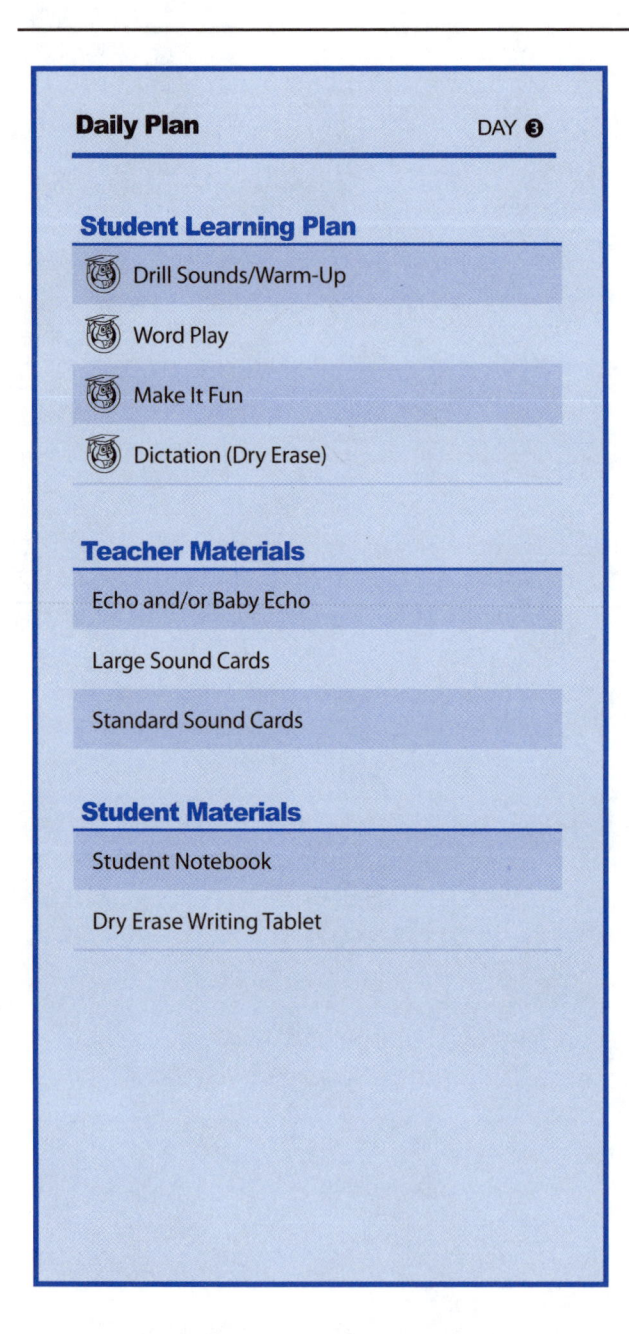

Student Materials
- Student Notebook
- Dry Erase Writing Tablet

Drill Sounds/Warm-Up

Do any new or challenging sounds and vowel sounds each day. Selectively review 4-5 other consonants.

Large Sound Cards
Practice sounds with the Large Sound Cards. Model these, saying the letter-keyword-sound and have the students echo.

Standard Sound Cards
Next, point to the Standard Sound Cards (in card display) with the Baby Echo pointer. You say the letter-keyword-sound and hold up Baby Echo to have students repeat. You can have a student be the drill leader for some of the sounds.

Word Play

MAKE WORDS FOR DECODING

Use your Standard Sound Card display to make 5-6 Unit words. (See Unit Resources.)

Make each word then say and tap each sound. Have students tap with you. Then blend the sounds as you drag your thumb across your fingers.

Next, point under each card as you say each sound, then drag your finger under all three cards as you and the students blend the sounds to read the word.

Have students find and underline digraphs.

READ SENTENCES

Write sentences on Sentence Frames and scoop into phrases. Have student circle trick words and tap out other words. Read the sentence together, modeling fluency as you scoop into phrases. Select a student to read it, and have students repeat.

Sentence Resources

The dog had a bath.

Did the duck quack?

Unit 4 | Week 4

Day 3

Make It Fun

SOUND A WORD

Teacher Materials

Place approximately ten small objects (such as plastic animals, cars, pens) in a pillow case or bag. The objects should have a name that is one-syllable of varying length (such as: **pen**, **clip**, **truck**).

Directions

Select a child to pick an item from the bag, but not show it to the class, only to you. Whisper the word segmented to the student and have them repeat it, segmented to the class. For example, if it is a truck, you would say:

/t/ /r/ /ŭ/ /k/   and the student would say:

/t/ /r/ /ŭ/ /k/

Select a student to guess the object. When someone guesses, the student holding the object shows it to the class and sits down with it.

The student who correctly guessed selects the next object from the bag. When all items have been selected, have the students give the object to a student without an object. Collect objects one at a time by saying the word segmented into sounds.

Say

I'm looking for the /t/ /r/ /ŭ/ /k/. Who has the /t/ /r/ /ŭ/ /k/?

Dictation (Dry Erase)

Proper Dictation Activity procedures are very important. Be sure to follow their demonstration on the Prevention Learning Community. This is a teaching time, not a testing time. Be sure students repeat each dictation. Dictate 3 sounds and then 3 current or review words.

Unit Sounds

Refer to this Unit's Resource List of Echo Sounds.

Unit Words

Students should tap and orally spell the Unit words before writing. Then have all spell chorally. Have one student write on the Large Writing Grid and all students write on their Dry Erase Writing Tablets. (See Current and Review Words in Unit Resources.)

Unit 4 | Week 4

Day 4

Daily Plan — DAY 4

Student Learning Plan
- Drill Sounds/Warm-Up
- Word Play
- Trick Word Practice
- Echo/Letter Formation
- Dictation (Dry Erase)

Teacher Materials
- Echo and/or Baby Echo
- Large Sound Cards
- Standard Sound Cards
- Sentence Frames
- Trick Word Flashcards

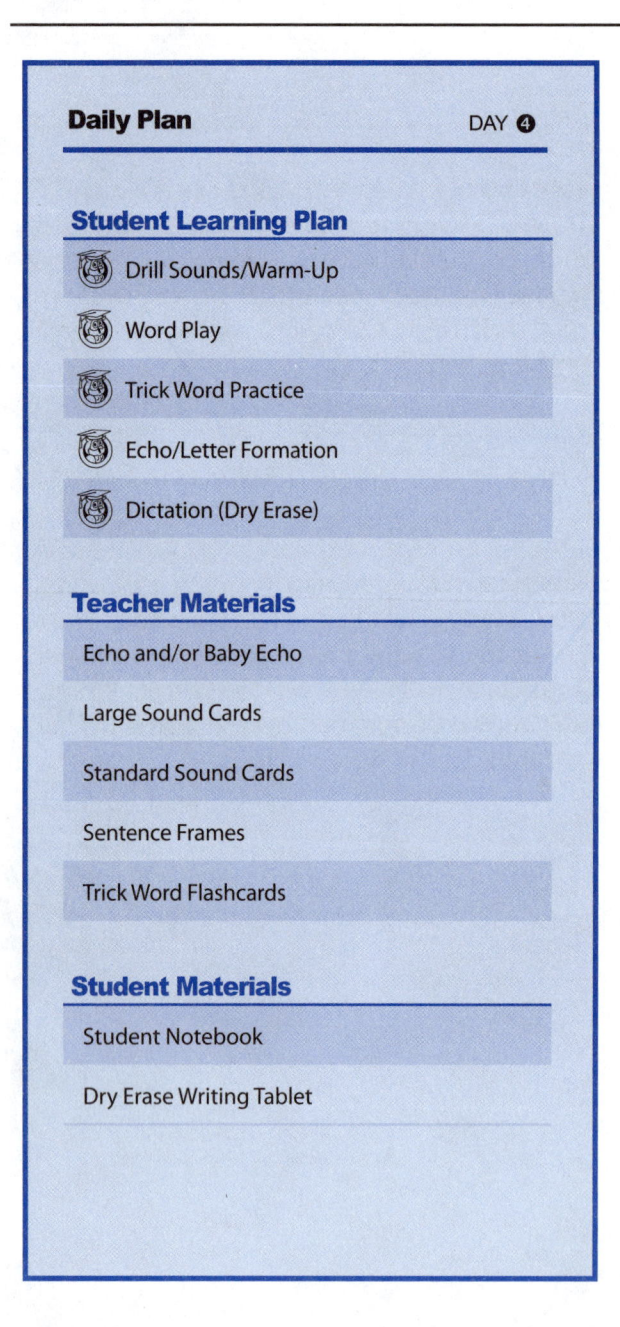

Student Materials
- Student Notebook
- Dry Erase Writing Tablet

Drill Sounds/Warm-Up

Do any new or challenging sounds and vowel sounds each day. Selectively review 4-5 other consonants.

Large Sound Cards
Practice sounds with the Large Sound Cards. Model these, saying the letter-keyword-sound and have the students echo.

Standard Sound Cards
Next, point to the Standard Sound Cards (in card display) with the Baby Echo pointer. You say the letter-keyword-sound and hold up Baby Echo to have students repeat. You can have a student be the drill leader for some of the sounds.

Instruct Students

Name the digraphs.

Which letters say /k/? (k, c, ck)

Which letter do you use to spell /k/ at the beginning of a word if it is followed by an a, o, or u? (c)

Word Play

MAKE WORDS FOR DECODING

Use your Standard Sound Card display to make 5-6 Unit words. (See Unit Resources.)

Make each word then say and tap each sound. Have students tap with you. Then blend the sounds as you drag your thumb across your fingers.

Next, point under each card as you say each sound, then drag your finger under all three cards as you and the students blend the sounds to read the word.

Have students find and underline digraphs.

MAKE NONSENSE WORDS

Tell students that they can also blend sounds together to make silly or nonsense words. Explain that these nonsense word are not real words. They are just silly words that show that they can read sounds.

Make 3-5 nonsense words and have students tap and read them (see Unit Resources).

Unit 4 | Week 4

Day 4

Trick Word Practice

Say each sentence below and have students repeat. Then write the sentence on Sentence Frames, and scoop it into phrases. Read it and have students echo. Say the trick word that is in the sentence and have a student find and circle it. After it is circled, hold up the corresponding Trick Word Flashcard and say the word and have students repeat.

Sentence Resource

(I) wish (they) could come here.

(We) hope (they) had fun.

Lastly present the Trick Word Flashcards, say each and have student repeat.

Echo/Letter Formation

Remind students of proper pencil grip and sitting position, and give them their Dry Erase Writing Tablets.

Dictate 5-6 previously taught sounds. You select and say the sound. Students echo the sound and say the letter.

Next have a student come up to the classroom board to make the letter on the Large Writing Grid.

Then have all students write the answer on their Dry Erase Writing Tablet as you direct them with the letter formation verbalization.

(See Unit Resources.)

Note
Students can make only lowercase letters, or you can selectively do both uppercase and lowercase to reinforce certain letters. (Be sure to always do lowercase for every sound that is dictated.)

Dictation (Dry Erase)

Proper Dictation Activity procedures are very important. Be sure to follow their demonstration on the Prevention Learning Community. This is a teaching time, not a testing time. Be sure students repeat each dictation. Dictate 3 sounds and then 3 current or review words.

Unit Sounds

Refer to this Unit's Resource List of Echo Sounds.

Unit Words

Students should tap and orally spell the Unit words before writing. Then have all spell chorally. Have one student write on the Large Writing Grid and all students write on their Dry Erase Writing Tablets. (See Current and Review Words in Unit Resources.)

Unit 4 | Week 4

Day 5

Daily Plan — DAY 5

Student Learning Plan
- Drill Sounds/Warm-Up
- Word Play
- Storytime

Teacher Materials
- Echo and/or Baby Echo
- Large Sound Cards
- Standard Sound Cards
- Large chart paper with the Cod Fish story
- Unit Test Recording Form

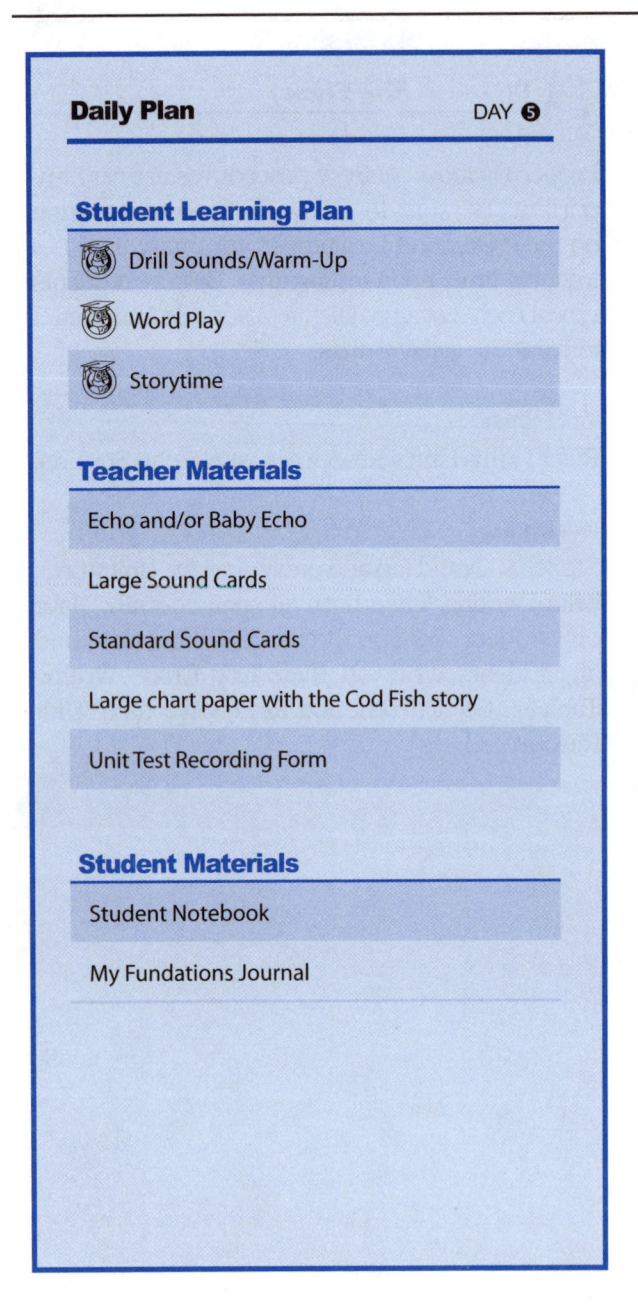

Student Materials
- Student Notebook
- My Fundations Journal

Drill Sounds/Warm-Up

Do any new or challenging sounds and vowel sounds each day. Selectively review 4-5 other consonants.

Large Sound Cards

Practice sounds with the Large Sound Cards. Model these, saying the letter-keyword-sound and have the students echo.

Standard Sound Cards

Next, point to the Standard Sound Cards (in card display) with the Baby Echo pointer. You say the letter-keyword-sound and hold up Baby Echo to have students repeat. You can have a student be the drill leader for some of the sounds.

Instruct Students

Name the digraphs.

Which letters say /k/? (k, c, ck)

Word Play

MAKE WORDS FOR DECODING

Use your Standard Sound Card display to make 5-6 Unit words. (See Unit Resources.)

Make each word then say and tap each sound. Have students tap with you. Then blend the sounds as you drag your thumb across your fingers.

Next, point under each card as you say each sound, then drag your finger under all three cards as you and the students blend the sounds to read the word.

Have students find and underline digraphs.

Unit 4 | Week 4

Day 5

🦉 Storytime

Preparation

- Baby Echo (on a pointer or ruler)
- Large chart paper with the story from Week 3

COD FISH II

Instruct Students

Ask the students to read the title silently. Have them try to remember the "movie" in their mind. Have someone describe the story by retelling it. Read chorally as you point with Baby Echo and determine if the retelling was accurate.

---

tip

You can also have students draw a picture for the Cod Fish story on a page in their Journal and have them write a sentence about the Cod Fish story.

Unit 4

Unit Test

Answer Key

SOUNDS

a - apple - /ă/	o - octopus - /ŏ/
e - Ed - /ĕ/	u - up - /ŭ/
i - itch - /ĭ/	ch - chin - /ch/
th - thumb - /th/	wh - whistle - /wh/
sh - ship - /sh/	ck - sock - /k/

READ WORDS

1. shop   2. lash   3. much
4. whiz   5. peck

READ TRICK WORDS

1. the   2. and   3. to
4. she   5. he   6. a
7. they   8. we   9. I
10. you

Note
Allow students to independently reference their Student Notebooks. Count responses checked in their Notebooks as correct but make a notation that the book was used.

Each student must be assessed individually. This will take approximately 10-15 minutes per student and can be done by a paraprofessional or volunteer if one is available to assist you.

Copy the **Unit Test Recording Form** for each student. Use the student's durable materials, e.g., Dry Erase Writing Tablet, Letter Board and Letter Tiles, as needed.

Print the Unit Test Recording Form from the PLC.

If a student does not score at least **8 / 10** or **4 / 5** on any given item, this student will need additional assistance with the assessed skill.

See the Intervention Guidelines on the PLC.

tip
A Unit Test Tracker is available on Wilson Academy® / Prevention Learning Community, under My Resources. This valuable online resource will allow you to track individual student mastery as well as to evaluate readiness of your class to move on.

For any struggling students, meet with them individually to discuss errors and explain areas that need to be further practiced.

Have Student Give Sounds for Vowels and Digraphs

Using your Standard Sound Cards, Ask, "What is the letter-keyword-sound?"

a	o	e	u	i

ch	th	wh	sh	ck

Have Student Tap and Read Words

Form words using the student's Letter Board and Letter Tiles and have student tap and read the words. Say, "Tap these sounds and tell me the word that I made."

shop   lash   much   whiz   peck

Have Student Identify Trick Words

Spread out all Trick Word Flashcards taught thus far and have student find the trick word that you dictate. Say, "Find the trick word _____."

the   and   to   she   he
a   they   we   I   you

Have Student Tap and Spell Words

Say a word and have student repeat the word, tap it and then find corresponding Letter Tiles to spell the word on the student's Letter Board.

moth   sick   mash   chin   luck

tip
During Unit Tests, pay attention to students who rely on Alphabet Wall Strip or classroom posters as they may need extra support.

Unit 4

Resources

Drill Sounds/Warm-Up

a - apple - /ă/	b - bat - /b/
c - cat - /k/	d - dog - /d/
e - Ed - /ĕ/	f - fun - /f/
g - game - /g/	h - hat - /h/
i - itch - /ĭ/	j - jug - /j/
k - kite - /k/	l - lamp - /l/
m - man - /m/	n - nut - /n/
o - octopus - /ŏ/	p - pan - /p/
qu - queen - /kw/	r - rat - /r/
s - snake - /s/	t - top - /t/
u - up - /ŭ/	v - van - /v/
w - wind - /w/	x - fox - /ks/
y - yellow - /y/	z - zebra - /z/

DIGRAPHS

sh - ship - /sh/	ck - sock - /k/
wh - whistle - /w/	th - thumb - /th/
ch - chin - /ch/	

Echo Sounds

Sounds appear between / /. You say the sound. Students echo the sound and say the letter. Depending on the activity, students then either find or make the letter corresponding to that sound.

CONSONANTS / CONSONANTS DIGRAPHS

/b/ - b	/d/ - d	/f/ - f
/g/ - g	/h/ - h	/j/ - j
/k/ - c, k, ck	/l/ - l	/m/ - m
/n/ - n	/p/ - p	/kw/ - qu
/r/ - r	/s/ - s	/t/ - t
/v/ - v	/w/ - w, wh	/ks/ - x
/y/ - y	/z/ - z	/ch/ - ch
/sh/ - sh	/th/ - th	

VOWELS

/ă/ - a	/ĕ/ - e	/ĭ/ - i
/ŏ/ - o	/ŭ/ - u	

Review Trick Words

the	a	and	are	to	is
his	as	has	was		

Current Trick Words

we	she	he	be	me	I
you	they				

Review Words

dip	fox	nut	gas	him	mob
nab	fib	lab	rob	lob	lug
rut	sun	yet	zip	quiz	box

Current Unit Words

WEEKS 1 • 4

rash	such	chip	much	shot	moth
rich	lash	path	dash	whip	math
dish	shut	rush	shop	wish	fish
shed	chin	chop	chat	Beth	with
bath	Seth	thin	thud	ship	mash

WEEKS 3 • 4

shock	Rick	neck	back	pack	chick
Jack	sock	quick	dock	deck	sick
thick	luck	puck	rack	duck	tuck
lick	sack	lock	peck	quick	quack

Current & Review Nonsense Words

thub	zeth	theg	yit	shob	muth
chep	sish	whep	chuz	nish	wob
tiz	fesh	leck	bez	fom	vop

Unit 5 Level K

In a Nutshell

NEW CONCEPTS

- Sentence structure
- Sentence dictation
- Narrative fiction vs. informational books

TRICK WORDS

| or | for | of | have | from |
| by | my | do | one | |

PLANNED TIME IN UNIT

6 WEEKS

Note
Use Unit Test scores and daily classroom work to determine students' mastery. Extend the time in this Unit if needed.

Introduction

In this Unit, you will reinforce sentence structure. The students will not only read short sentences, they will begin to write sentences from dictation.

You will continue to emphasize the fluent reading of sentences, using phrasing. Explain to students that when they read a sentence, it should sound like they are talking rather than reading one word at a time. You will model reading with phrasing and expression, and will scoop under phrases to help guide students.

The dog and cat sat on the deck.

You will teach students how to proofread to check for capitalization, punctuation and spelling. You will also teach students additional high frequency, non-phonetic Trick Words.

Lastly, you will discuss the differences between narrative vs. informational text. You will explain to your students that some books that they read are "make-believe" (fiction) whereas other books present them with true facts.

Differentiation

Be sure to provide guidance for students who are just emerging with their skills so that they can successfully write the sentence. If some students have not yet developed enough automaticity with sound/letter association and/or letter formation, they will not be ready to independently write the whole sentence as quickly as others.

You can select some students who are having difficulty to write the sentence on the frames with you. You can support and guide them as others write it independently.

You will also have some students who can more easily write the sentence independently. If you have someone in class to assist during Dictation, they can work with a small group and do the Dictation on Composition Paper. Dictate more challenging Unit words and sentences. Be sure to emphasize proofreading and using their Notebook to reference the Trick Words, as needed.

Print Composition Paper from the PLC.

Unit 5

Arrange the sound card display in the following manner:

a	b	c	d	e	f
g	h	i	j	k	l
m	n	o	p	qu	r	s
t	u	v	w	x	y	z
wh	ch	sh	th	ck		

Getting Ready

MATERIAL PREPARATIONS

Teacher Materials
Trick Word Flashcards for the Drill Sounds/Warm-Up Activity.

See Storytime. You will need two narrative and informational books which feature the same kind of animal.

Print Lesson Plans from the PLC. See Unit Resources at the end of this Unit.

HOME SUPPORT

Copy and send home the Unit 5 Letter and Activity Packet.

STUDY THE LEARNING ACTIVITIES

Review the following activities:

- Dictation/Sentences

Review the Learning Activity and Unit videos on the PLC.

Unit 5

Student Learning Plan

Week 1

DAY 1	DAY 2	DAY 3	DAY 4	DAY 5
Drill Sounds/Warm-Up	Drill Sounds/Warm-Up	Drill Sounds/Warm-Up	Drill Sounds/Warm-Up	Drill Sounds/Warm-Up
Word Play	Word Play	Word Play	Trick Word Practice	Storytime
Introduce New Concepts	Teach Trick Words	Echo/Letter Formation	Make It Fun	
Echo/Find Letters & Words	Introduce New Concepts	Dictation (Dry Erase)	Dictation (Dry Erase)	

Week 2

DAY 1	DAY 2	DAY 3	DAY 4	DAY 5
Drill Sounds/Warm-Up	Drill Sounds/Warm-Up	Drill Sounds/Warm-Up	Drill Sounds/Warm-Up	Drill Sounds/Warm-Up
Word Play	Word Play	Word Play	Trick Word Practice	Storytime
Echo/Find Letters & Words	Teach Trick Words	Echo/Letter Formation	Make It Fun	
	Echo/Find Letters & Words	Dictation (Dry Erase)	Dictation (Dry Erase)	

Week 3

DAY 1	DAY 2	DAY 3	DAY 4	DAY 5
Drill Sounds/Warm-Up	Drill Sounds/Warm-Up	Drill Sounds/Warm-Up	Drill Sounds/Warm-Up	Drill Sounds/Warm-Up
Word Play	Word Play	Word Play	Trick Word Practice	Storytime
Echo/Find Letters & Words	Teach Trick Words	Echo/Letter Formation	Make It Fun	
		Dictation (Dry Erase)	Dictation (Dry Erase)	

Unit 5

Student Learning Plan

Week 4

DAY 1	DAY 2	DAY 3	DAY 4	DAY 5
Drill Sounds/Warm-Up	Drill Sounds/Warm-Up	Drill Sounds/Warm-Up	Drill Sounds/Warm-Up	Drill Sounds/Warm-Up
Word Play	Word Play	Word Play	Word Play	Storytime
Dictation (Dry Erase)	Teach Trick Words	Echo/Letter Formation	Trick Word Practice	
Introduce New Concepts		Dictation (Dry Erase)	Make It Fun	

Week 5

DAY 1	DAY 2	DAY 3	DAY 4	DAY 5
Drill Sounds/Warm-Up	Drill Sounds/Warm-Up	Drill Sounds/Warm-Up	Drill Sounds/Warm-Up	Drill Sounds/Warm-Up
Word Play	Word Play	Word Play	Trick Word Practice	Storytime
Dictation (Dry Erase)	Teach Trick Words	Echo/Letter Formation	Make It Fun	
	Echo/Find Letters & Words	Dictation (Dry Erase)	Dictation (Dry Erase)	

Week 6

DAY 1	DAY 2	DAY 3	DAY 4	DAY 5
Drill Sounds/Warm-Up	Drill Sounds/Warm-Up	Drill Sounds/Warm-Up	Drill Sounds/Warm-Up	Drill Sounds/Warm-Up
Word Play	Word Play	Word Play	Trick Word Practice	Storytime
Dictation (Dry Erase)	Teach Trick Words	Echo/Letter Formation	Make It Fun	Unit Test
	Echo/Find Letters & Words	Dictation (Dry Erase)	Dictation (Dry Erase)	

Unit 5 | Week 1

Day 1

Daily Plan — DAY 1

Student Learning Plan
- Drill Sounds/Warm-Up
- Word Play
- Introduce New Concepts
- Echo/Find Letters & Words

Teacher Materials
- Echo and/or Baby Echo
- Large Sound Cards
- Standard Sound Cards
- Trick Word Flashcards

Student Materials
- Student Notebook
- Fundations® Letter Board & Tiles

Drill Sounds/Warm-Up

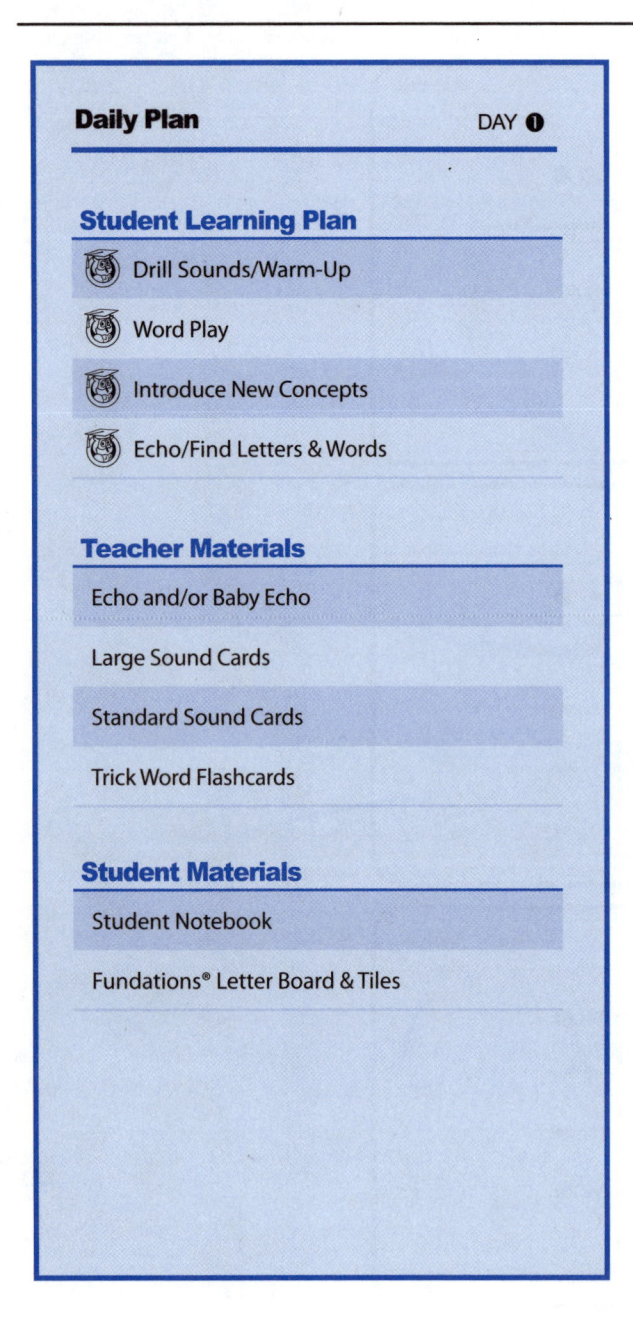

Do any new or challenging sounds and vowel sounds each day. Selectively review 4-5 other consonants.

Large Sound Cards
Practice sounds with the Large Sound Cards. Model these, saying the letter-keyword-sound and have the students echo.

Standard Sound Cards
Next, point to the Standard Sound Cards (in card display) with the Baby Echo pointer. You say the letter-keyword-sound and hold up Baby Echo to have students repeat. You can have a student be the drill leader for some of the sounds.

Drill Trick Word Flashcards
Present the Trick Word Flashcards. Have students quickly read the packet. You will eliminate some of the mastered trick words as you add new Level K words to the packet.

Word Play

MAKE WORDS FOR DECODING
Use your Standard Sound Card display to make 3-5 Unit words. (See Unit Resources.)

Make each word then say and tap each sound. Have students tap with you. Then blend the sounds as you drag your thumb across your fingers.

Next, point under each card as you say each sound, then drag your finger under all three cards as you and the students blend the sounds to read the word.

rash
whip
fish
with

Unit 5 | Week 1

Day 1

Introduce New Concepts

REVIEW SENTENCE READING

Write the following sentence on the board:

Meg is sad.

Help students tap out the words **Meg** and **sad**. Tell them the word **is** (do not tap it out).

Use Baby Echo to point to the words and read the sentence. Have students echo. Discuss the capital letter at the beginning of the sentence and the period at the end.

Do the same with the following sentences. (Circle the word **the**. It is a trick word and is not tapped out.)

Rob sat in the sun.

The rat sat in the mud.

Next, demonstrate how to read these sentences with fluency. Draw the scoops under the sentences. Read it in phrases as you scoop with Baby Echo.

Rob sat in the sun.

The rat sat in the mud.

That is a big dog!

Discuss the exclamation point and model reading with expression.

Echo/Find Letters & Words

Echo/Find Letters

Say a sound. Have students echo and point to the letter(s) on their Magnetic Letter Boards.

Ask

What says /___/? (___)

(See Echo Sounds in Unit Resources for expected student responses.)

Have students name the letter(s). Then you can have one student find the Standard Sound Card(s) as you dictate sounds. Do vowels and 3-5 other sounds.

Echo/Find Words

Dictate a Unit word. Do 3-5 words. (See Current Unit Words in Unit Resources.)

Have students find Letter Tiles needed to make words on their Magnetic Letter Boards. Have one student come find your corresponding cards. After finding a word, have students spell it orally and replace the tiles on the letter squares.

such
shop
math

tip

Be sure to weave discussion of vocabulary with words that you dictate. Challenge more advanced students to provide a sentence that illustrates the word's meaning.

Unit 5 | Week 1

Day 2

Daily Plan — DAY 2

Student Learning Plan
- Drill Sounds/Warm-Up
- Word Play
- Teach Trick Words
- Introduce New Concepts

Teacher Materials
- Echo and/or Baby Echo
- Large Sound Cards
- Standard Sound Cards
- Sentence Frames
- Trick Word Flashcards

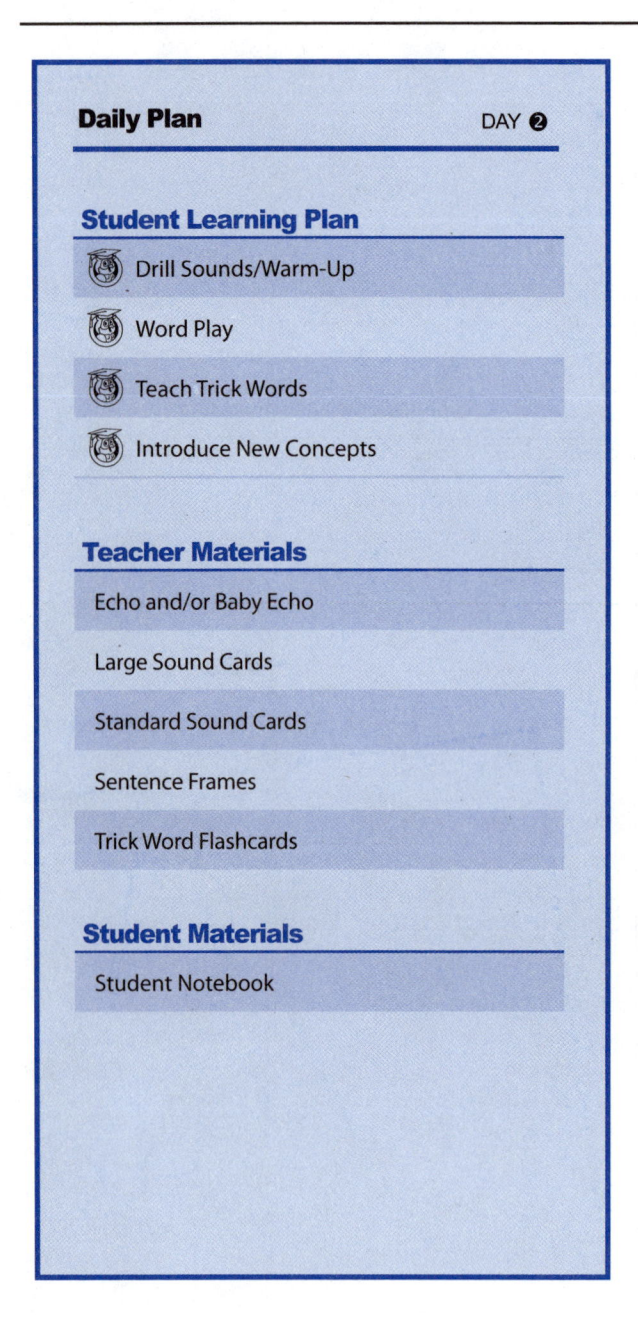

Student Materials
- Student Notebook

Drill Sounds/Warm-Up

Do any new or challenging sounds and vowel sounds each day. Selectively review 4-5 other consonants.

Large Sound Cards
Practice sounds with the Large Sound Cards. Model these, saying the letter-keyword-sound and have the students echo.

Standard Sound Cards
Next, point to the Standard Sound Cards (in card display) with the Baby Echo pointer. You say the letter-keyword-sound and hold up Baby Echo to have students repeat. You can have a student be the drill leader for some of the sounds.

Word Play

MAKE WORDS FOR DECODING

Use your Standard Sound Card display to make 3-5 Unit words. (See Unit Resources.)

Make each word then say and tap each sound. Have students tap with you. Then blend the sounds as you drag your thumb across your fingers.

Next, point under each card as you say each sound, then drag your finger under all three cards as you and the students blend the sounds to read the word.

Unit 5 | Week 1

Day 2

Teach Trick Words

Introduce the trick words **or** and **for**, and reinforce capitalization and punctuation.

Instruct Students

Say the sentence below and have students repeat. Have a student place the Sentence Frames as needed. Write the sentence on the frames, and discuss capitalization and punctuation. Scoop the sentence into phrases, read it, and have students echo.

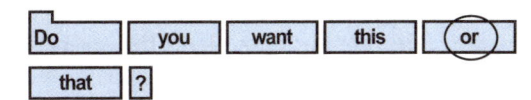

| Do | you | want | this | (or) |
| that | ? |

Say

> I am going to circle this word (circle the new trick word). Listen to the sentence and see if you can tell me the word I circled (point to words as you say each one).
>
> Let's change this sentence to: This book is for you.

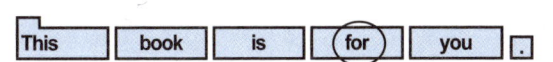

| This | book | is | (for) | you | . |

Next, explain that the words **or** and **for** are words that you are going to practice, and that these words are called Trick Words because they can be tricky and we do not tap them out.

Show students the Trick Word Flashcard with **or** and **for**. Point to **or**. Say the word and have them repeat. Next point to **for**. Say the words and have them repeat. Lastly, present the Trick Word Flashcards learned thus far. Say each and have students repeat.

Introduce New Concepts

BEGIN SENTENCE DICTATION

Say a sentence and have students repeat. Have a student place the Sentence Frames as needed. Write the sentence on the frames, scoop it and read it with phrasing.

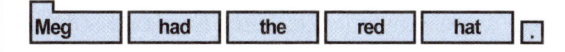

| Meg | had | the | red | hat | . |

Say

> Let's change this sentence to: Pat had the red hat.

Have a student erase **Meg** and change the word to **Pat**.

Tap out the word to check the student's spelling.

Continue dictating changes, reading the entire sentence and have a student make the necessary change. If you change a trick word do not tap it out, tell students to open their Student Notebooks to the Trick Word page and find the word to check its spelling.

Sentence Resource

Meg had the red hat.

Pat had the red hat.

Pat had the red mug.

Jim had the red mug.

Unit 5 | Week 1

Day 3

Daily Plan — DAY 3

Student Learning Plan
- Drill Sounds/Warm-Up
- Word Play
- Echo/Letter Formation
- Dictation (Dry Erase)

Teacher Materials
- Echo and/or Baby Echo
- Large Sound Cards
- Standard Sound Cards
- Large Writing Grid
- Letter Formation Guide
- Trick Word Flashcards

Student Materials
- Student Notebook
- Dry Erase Writing Tablet

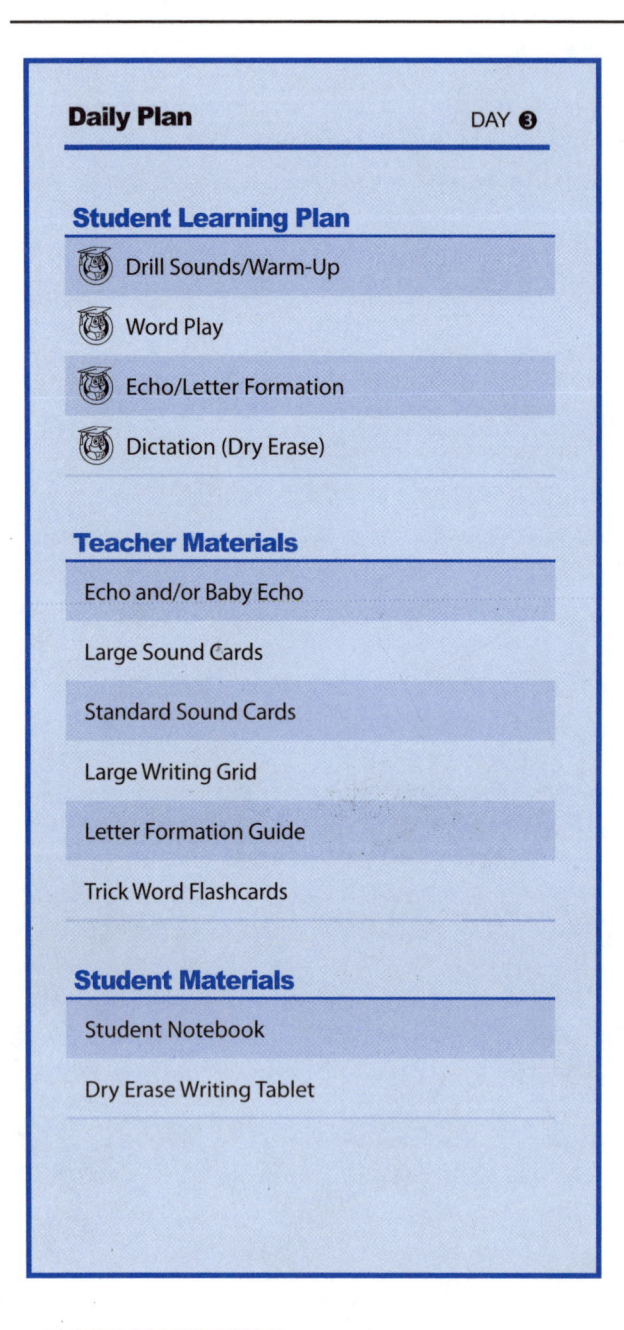

Drill Sounds/Warm-Up

Do any new or challenging sounds and vowel sounds each day. Selectively review 4-5 other consonants.

Large Sound Cards

Practice sounds with the Large Sound Cards. Model these, saying the letter-keyword-sound and have the students echo.

Standard Sound Cards

Next, point to the Standard Sound Cards (in card display) with the Baby Echo pointer. You say the letter-keyword-sound and hold up Baby Echo to have students repeat. You can have a student be the drill leader for some of the sounds.

Drill Trick Word Flashcards

Present the Trick Word Flashcards. Have students quickly read the packet. You will eliminate some of the mastered trick words as you add new Level K words to the packet.

Word Play

MAKE WORDS FOR DECODING

Use your Standard Sound Card display to make 3-5 Unit words. (See Unit Resources.)

Make each word then say and tap each sound. Have students tap with you. Then blend the sounds as you drag your thumb across your fingers.

Next, point under each card as you say each sound, then drag your finger under all three cards as you and the students blend the sounds to read the word.

READ SENTENCES

Write a sentence on the board and scoop it into phrases. Have the students try to read each word to themselves and then call on a student. After each word is decoded, chorally read the sentence with fluency. Do 2-3 sentences. (See Unit Resources.)

Unit 5 | Week 1

Day 3

Echo/Letter Formation

Remind students of proper pencil grip and sitting position, and give them their Dry Erase Writing Tablets.

Dictate 5-6 previously taught sounds. You select and say the sound. Students echo the sound and say the letter.

Next have a student come up to the classroom board to make the letter on the Large Writing Grid.

Then have all students write the answer on their Dry Erase Writing Tablets as you direct them with the letter formation verbalization.

(See Unit Resources.)

Note
Students can make only lowercase letters, or you can selectively do both uppercase and lowercase to reinforce certain letters. (Be sure to always do lowercase for every sound that is dictated.)

Dictation (Dry Erase)

Proper Dictation Activity procedures are very important. Be sure to follow their demonstration on the Prevention Learning Community. This is a teaching time, not a testing time. Be sure students repeat each dictation. Dictate 3 current or review words.

Unit Words

Students should tap and orally spell the Unit words before writing. Then have all spell chorally. Have one student write on the Large Writing Grid and all students write on their Dry Erase Writing Tablets. (See Current and Review Words in Unit Resources.)

[handwritten: lug, lob, with, whip, shut]

Unit 5 | Week 1

Day 4

Daily Plan — DAY 4

Student Learning Plan
- Drill Sounds/Warm-Up
- Trick Word Practice
- Make It Fun
- Dictation (Dry Erase)

Teacher Materials
- Echo and/or Baby Echo
- Large Sound Cards
- Standard Sound Cards
- Sentence Frames
- Trick Word Flashcards

Student Materials
- Student Notebook
- Dry Erase Writing Tablet

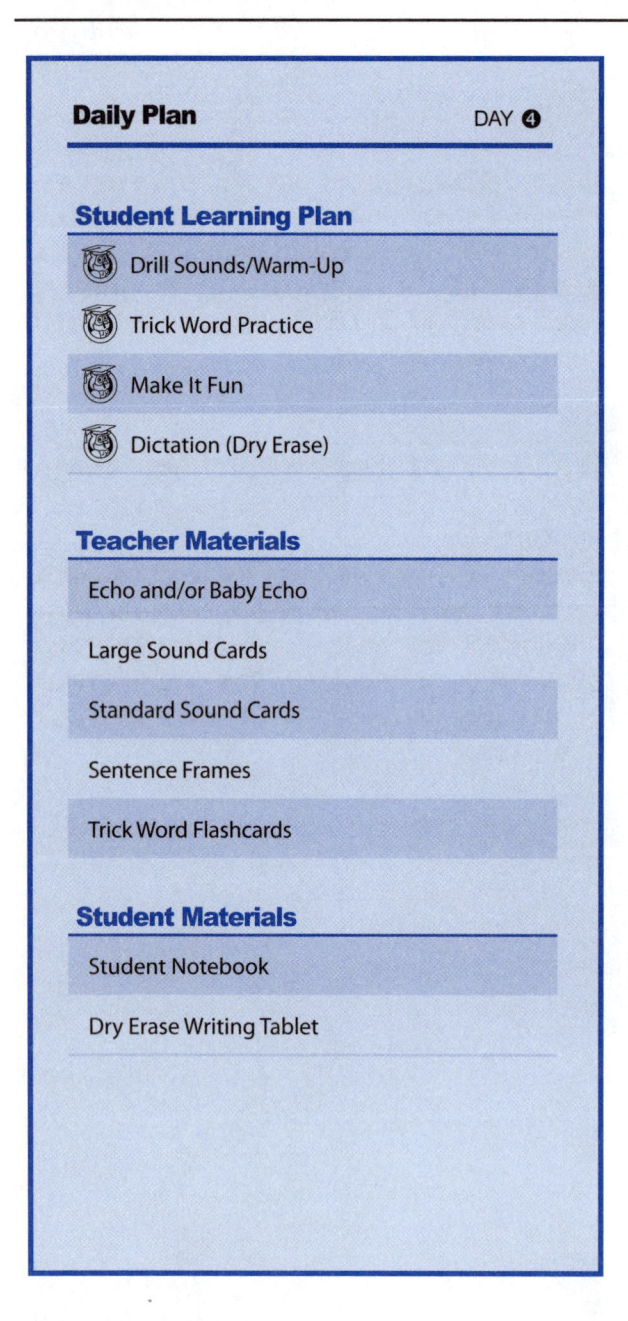

Drill Sounds/Warm-Up

Do any new or challenging sounds and vowel sounds each day. Selectively review 4-5 other consonants.

Large Sound Cards

Practice sounds with the Large Sound Cards. Model these, saying the letter-keyword-sound and have the students echo.

Standard Sound Cards

Next, point to the Standard Sound Cards (in card display) with the Baby Echo pointer. You say the letter-keyword-sound and hold up Baby Echo to have students repeat. You can have a student be the drill leader for some of the sounds.

Trick Word Practice

Say each sentence below and have students repeat. Then write the sentence on Sentence Frames, and scoop it into phrases. Read it and have students echo. Say the trick word that is in the sentence and have a student find and circle it. After it is circled, hold up the corresponding Trick Word Flashcard and say the word and have students repeat.

Sentence Resource

Is this (for) John (or) Meg?

It (was) (for) John.

Lastly present the Trick Word Flashcards, say each and have student repeat.

Unit 5 | Week 1

Day 4

Make It Fun

Preparation
- Sentence Frames

CHANGE THE SENTENCE

The purpose of this activity is to reinforce sentence structure and spelling.

Instruct Students

Say a sentence and have students repeat. Have a student place the Sentence Frames as needed. Next, distribute the Sentence Frames to individual students, saying the word that they are to write. Have each student write their word. When they have the words on the Sentence Frames, dictate the sentence again and have them come up and stand in order to form the sentence. Read it together.

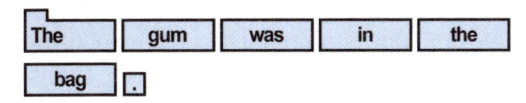

| The | gum | was | in | the |
| bag | . |

Say

Let's change this sentence to: The gum was in the box.

Select a student to erase **bag** and change the word to **box**. They can then hold the Sentence Frame and have the other student sit down.

Tap out the word to check the student's spelling.

Continue dictating changes, reading the entire sentence and have a student make the necessary change. If you change a trick word do not tap it out.

Sentence Resource

The gum was in the bag.

The gum was in the <u>box</u>.

The <u>nut</u> was in the box.

The nut <u>is</u> in the box. (Help students spell this without tapping.)

The <u>sock</u> is in the box.

Dictation (Dry Erase)

Proper Dictation Activity procedures are very important. Be sure to follow their demonstration on the Prevention Learning Community. This is a teaching time, not a testing time. Be sure students repeat each dictation. Dictate 3 sounds and then 3 current or review words.

Unit Sounds

Refer to this Unit's Resource List of Echo Sounds.

Unit Words

Students should tap and orally spell the Unit words before writing. Then have all spell chorally. Have one student write on the Large Writing Grid and all students write on their Dry Erase Writing Tablets. (See Current and Review Words in Unit Resources.)

Unit 5 | Week 1

Day 5

Daily Plan — DAY 5

Student Learning Plan
- Drill Sounds/Warm-Up
- Storytime

Teacher Materials
- Echo and/or Baby Echo
- Large Sound Cards
- Standard Sound Cards
- Trick Word Flashcards
- An informational book about fish

Student Materials
- Student Notebook

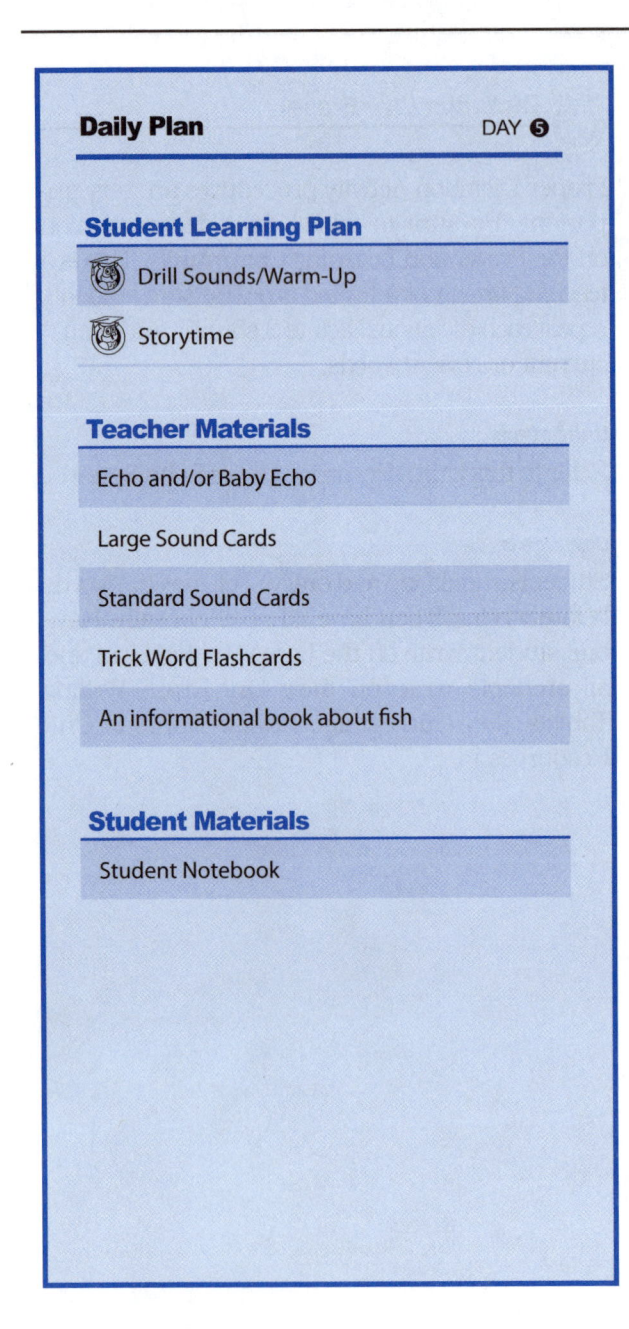

Drill Sounds/Warm-Up

Do any new or challenging sounds and vowel sounds each day. Selectively review 4-5 other consonants.

Large Sound Cards

Practice sounds with the Large Sound Cards. Model these, saying the letter-keyword-sound and have the students echo.

Standard Sound Cards

Next, point to the Standard Sound Cards (in card display) with the Baby Echo pointer. You say the letter-keyword-sound and hold up Baby Echo to have students repeat. You can have a student be the drill leader for some of the sounds.

Drill Trick Word Flashcards

Present the Trick Word Flashcards. Have students quickly read the packet. You will eliminate some of the mastered trick words as you add new Level K words to the packet.

Storytime

Preparation

- Find an informational book about fish, such as **Hello Fish! Visiting the Coral Reef**, by Earle, Silvia A., Washington, DC: National Geographic Society, 1999

Instruct Students

Tell students that some books have stories that are pretend or make-believe. The story can be about people or animals, but it is make-believe. The story that you read, Cod Fish, was a make-believe story.

Explain that other books tell us facts about things. They teach us things that are true. Show them your informational book and tell the students that it is a book that teaches them true things about fish.

Before reading, look at the front and back cover of the book with your students. Discuss the title, author and illustrator, explaining each of those terms.

Read the book (or part of the book) to your students. After each page, ask them to name one true fact that they have learned.

Note

When reading other books with your students, be sure to discuss whether they are pretend stories or if they teach true facts.

Unit 5 | Week 2

Day 1

Daily Plan — DAY 1

Student Learning Plan
- Drill Sounds/Warm-Up
- Word Play
- Echo/Find Letters & Words

Teacher Materials
- Echo and/or Baby Echo
- Large Sound Cards
- Standard Sound Cards
- Sentence Frames
- Trick Word Flashcards

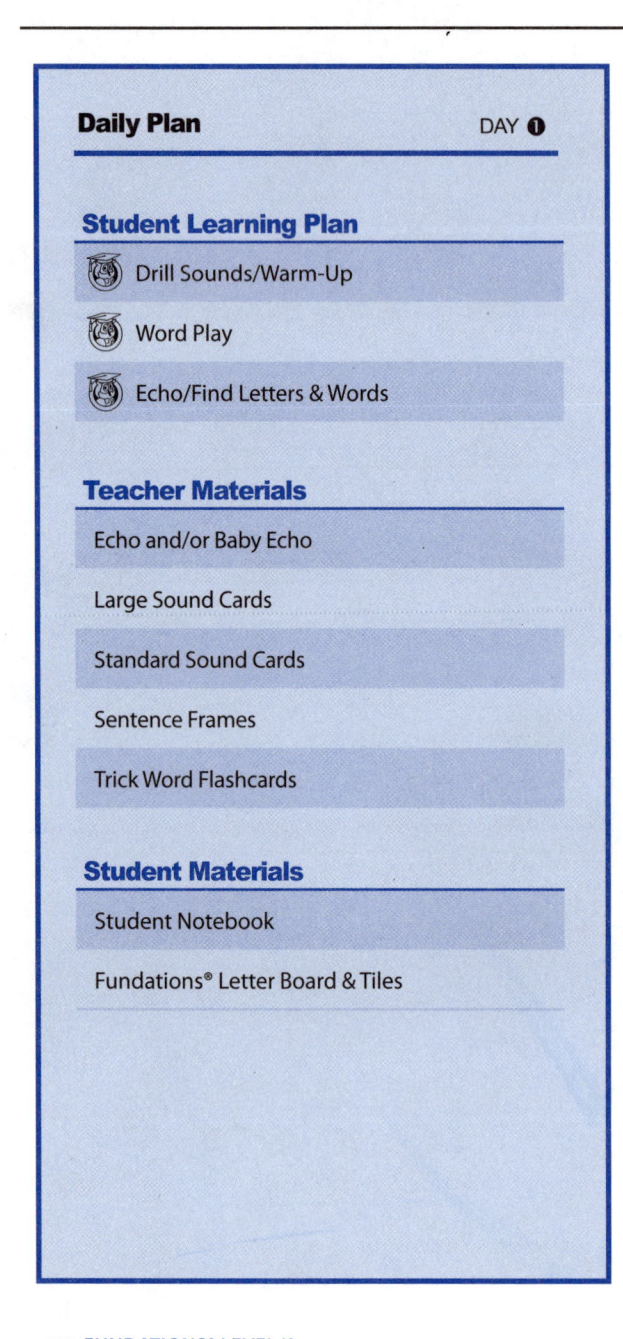

Student Materials
- Student Notebook
- Fundations® Letter Board & Tiles

Drill Sounds/Warm-Up

Do any new or challenging sounds and vowel sounds each day. Selectively review 4-5 other consonants.

Large Sound Cards
Practice sounds with the Large Sound Cards. Model these, saying the letter-keyword-sound and have the students echo.

Standard Sound Cards
Next, point to the Standard Sound Cards (in card display) with the Baby Echo pointer. You say the letter-keyword-sound and hold up Baby Echo to have students repeat. You can have a student be the drill leader for some of the sounds.

Drill Trick Word Flashcards
Present the Trick Word Flashcards. Have students quickly read the packet. You will eliminate some of the mastered trick words as you add new Level K words to the packet.

Word Play

MAKE WORDS FOR DECODING
Use your Standard Sound Card display to make 3-5 Unit words. (See Unit Resources.)

Make each word then say and tap each sound. Have students tap with you. Then blend the sounds as you drag your thumb across your fingers.

Next, point under each card as you say each sound, then drag your finger under all three cards as you and the students blend the sounds to read the word.

READ SENTENCES
Write a sentence on the board and scoop it into phrases. Have the students try to read each word to themselves and then call on a student. Tell them untaught Trick Words. After each word is decoded, chorally read the sentence with fluency. Do 2-3 sentences. (See Unit Resources.)

REVIEW SENTENCE DICTATION
Say a sentence and have students repeat. Have a student place the Sentence Frames as needed. Write the sentence on the frames.

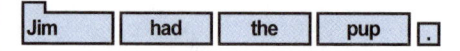

| Jim | had | the | pup | . |

Say

Let's change this sentence to: Jim had the mop.

Unit 5 | Week 2

Day 1

Have a student erase **pup** and change the word to **mop**.

Tap out the word to check the student's spelling.

Continue dictating changes, reading the entire sentence and have a student make the necessary change. If you change a trick word do not tap it out.

Sentence Resource

Jim had the mo<u>p</u>.

Jim had the <u>m</u>ap.

<u>Tom</u> had the map.

Tom <u>hid</u> the map.

Echo/Find Letters & Words

Echo/Find Letters

Say a sound. Have students echo and point to the letter(s) on their Magnetic Letter Boards.

Ask

What says /___/? (___)

(See Echo Sounds in Unit Resources for expected student responses.)

Have students name the letter(s). Then you can have one student find the Standard Sound Card(s) as you dictate sounds. Do vowels and 3-5 other sounds.

Echo/Find Words

Dictate a Unit word. Do 3-5 words. (See Current Unit Words in Unit Resources.)

Have students find Letter Tiles needed to make words on their Magnetic Letter Boards. Have one student come find your corresponding cards. After finding a word, have students spell it orally and replace the tiles on the letter squares.

[handwritten: thud, wish, chip, moth]

Unit 5 | Week 2

Day 2

Daily Plan — DAY 2

Student Learning Plan
- Drill Sounds/Warm-Up
- Word Play
- Teach Trick Words
- Echo/Find Letters & Words

Teacher Materials
- Echo and/or Baby Echo
- Large Sound Cards
- Standard Sound Cards
- Sentence Frames
- Trick Word Flashcards

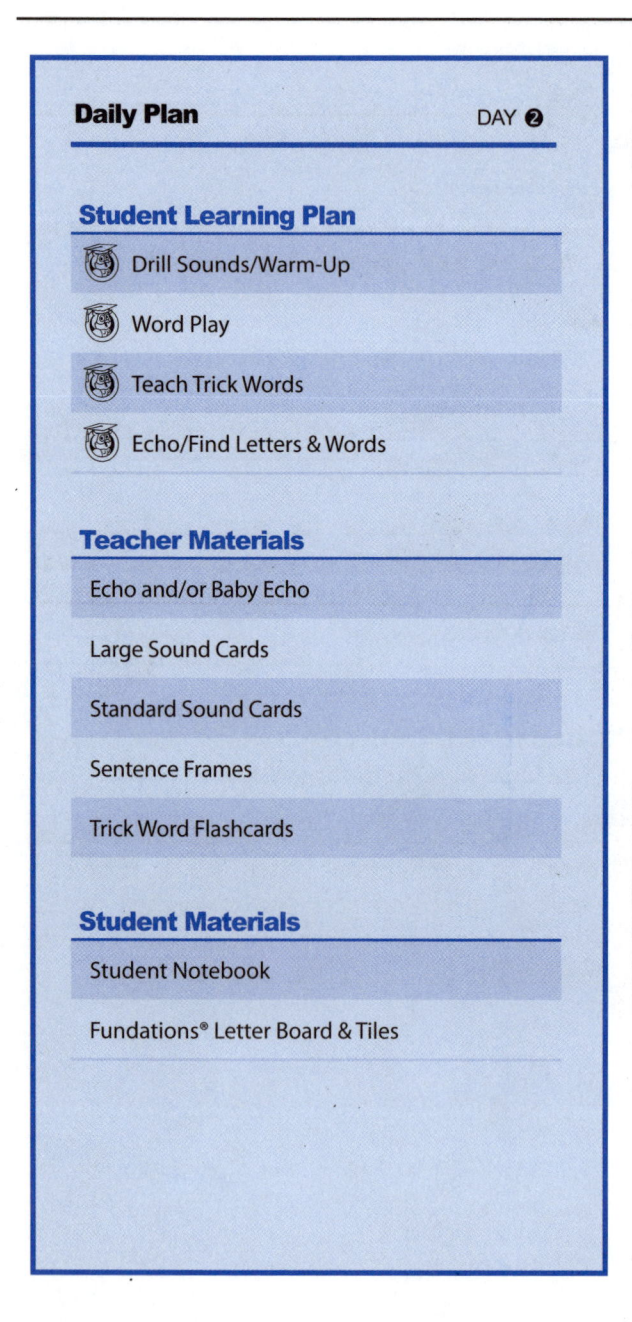

Student Materials
- Student Notebook
- Fundations® Letter Board & Tiles

Drill Sounds/Warm-Up

Do any new or challenging sounds and vowel sounds each day. Selectively review 4-5 other consonants.

Large Sound Cards
Practice sounds with the Large Sound Cards. Model these, saying the letter-keyword-sound and have the students echo.

Standard Sound Cards
Next, point to the Standard Sound Cards (in card display) with the Baby Echo pointer. You say the letter-keyword-sound and hold up Baby Echo to have students repeat. You can have a student be the drill leader for some of the sounds.

Word Play

MAKE WORDS FOR DECODING

Use your Standard Sound Card display to make 3-5 Unit words. (See Unit Resources.)

Make each word then say and tap each sound. Have students tap with you. Then blend the sounds as you drag your thumb across your fingers.

Next, point under each card as you say each sound, then drag your finger under all three cards as you and the students blend the sounds to read the word.

MAKE NONSENSE WORDS

Tell students that they can also blend sounds together to make silly or nonsense words. Explain that these nonsense words are not real words. They are just silly words that show that they can read sounds.

Make 3-5 nonsense words and have students tap and read them (see Unit Resources).

REVIEW SENTENCE DICTATION

Say a sentence and have students repeat. Have a student place the Sentence Frames as needed. Write the sentence on the frames.

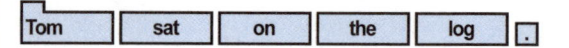

| Tom | sat | on | the | log | . |

Say

Let's change this sentence to: Tom sat on the mat.

Unit 5 | Week 2

Day 2

Have a student erase **log** and change the word to **mat**.

Tap out the word to check the student's spelling.

Continue dictating changes, reading the entire sentence and have a student make the necessary change. If you change a trick word do not tap it out.

Sentence Resource

Tom sat on the mat.

<u>Beth</u> sat on the mat.

Beth sat on the <u>box</u>.

<u>Dad</u> sat on the box.

Teach Trick Words

Introduce the trick words **of** and **have**, and reinforce capitalization and punctuation.

Instruct Students

Say the sentence below and have students repeat. Have a student place the Sentence Frames as needed. Write the sentence on the frames, and discuss capitalization and punctuation. Scoop the sentence into phrases, read it, and have students echo.

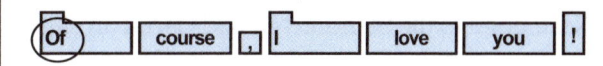

[Of] [course] , [I] [love] [you] !

Say

> I am going to circle this word (circle the new trick word). Listen to the sentence and see if you can tell me the word I circled (point to words as you say each one).
>
> Let's change this sentence to: I have a new puppy.

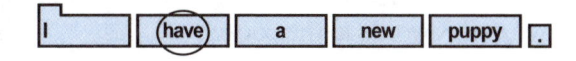

[I] [have] [a] [new] [puppy] .

Next, explain that the words **of** and **have** are words that you are going to practice, and that these words are called Trick Words because they can be tricky and we do not tap them out.

Show students the Trick Word Flashcards **of** and **have**. Say the words and have them repeat. Lastly, present the Trick Word Flashcards learned thus far. Say each and have students repeat.

Echo/Find Letters & Words

Echo/Find Letters

Say a sound. Have students echo and point to the letter(s) on their Magnetic Letter Boards.

Ask

> What says /___/? (___)

(See Echo Sounds in Unit Resources for expected student responses.)

Have students name the letter(s). Then you can have one student find the Standard Sound Card(s) as you dictate sounds. Do vowels and 3-5 other sounds.

Echo/Find Words

Dictate a Unit word. Do 3-5 words. (See Current Unit Words in Unit Resources.)

Have students find Letter Tiles needed to make words on their Magnetic Letter Boards. Have one student come find your corresponding cards. After finding a word, have students spell it orally and replace the tiles on the letter squares.

Unit 5 | Week 2

Day 3

Daily Plan — DAY 3

Student Learning Plan
- Drill Sounds/Warm-Up
- Word Play
- Echo/Letter Formation
- Dictation (Dry Erase)

Teacher Materials
- Echo and/or Baby Echo
- Large Sound Cards
- Standard Sound Cards
- Large Writing Grid
- Letter Formation Guide
- Trick Word Flashcards

Student Materials
- Student Notebook
- Dry Erase Writing Tablet

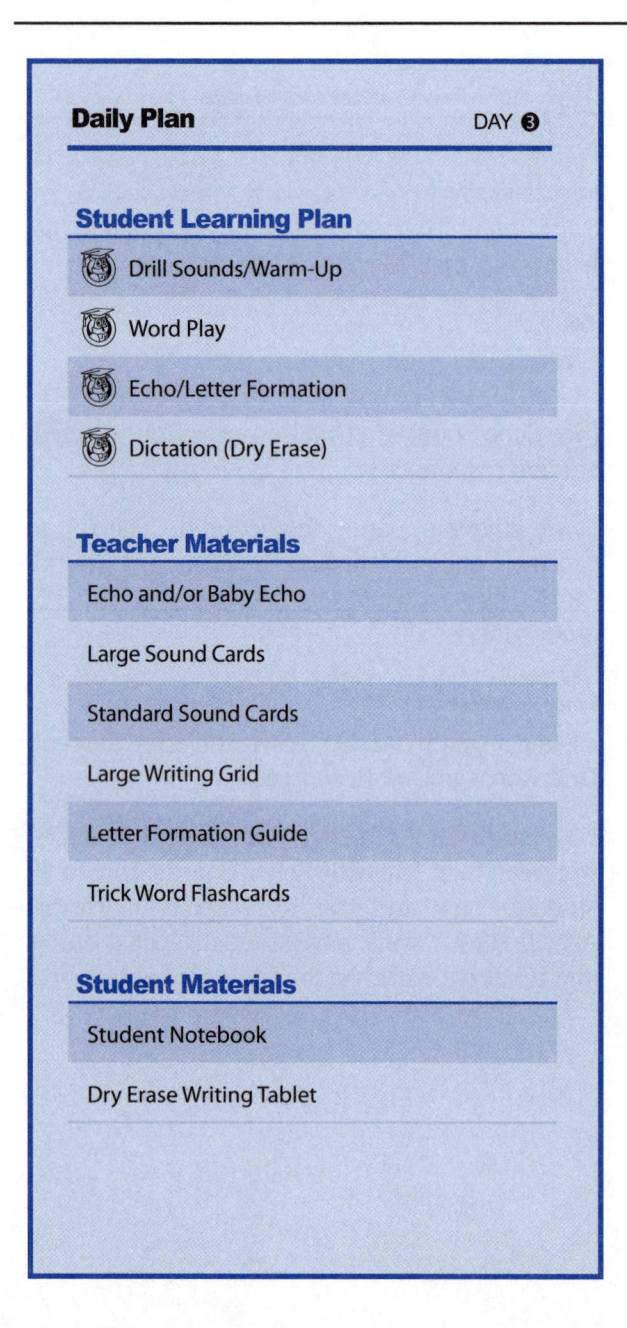

Drill Sounds/Warm-Up

Do any new or challenging sounds and vowel sounds each day. Selectively review 4-5 other consonants.

Large Sound Cards
Practice sounds with the Large Sound Cards. Model these, saying the letter-keyword-sound and have the students echo.

Standard Sound Cards
Next, point to the Standard Sound Cards (in card display) with the Baby Echo pointer. You say the letter-keyword-sound and hold up Baby Echo to have students repeat. You can have a student be the drill leader for some of the sounds.

Drill Trick Word Flashcards
Present the Trick Word Flashcards. Have students quickly read the packet. You will eliminate some of the mastered trick words as you add new Level K words to the packet.

Word Play

MAKE WORDS FOR DECODING
Use your Standard Sound Card display to make 3-5 Unit words. (See Unit Resources.)

Make each word then say and tap each sound. Have students tap with you. Then blend the sounds as you drag your thumb across your fingers.

Next, point under each card as you say each sound, then drag your finger under all three cards as you and the students blend the sounds to read the word.

READ SENTENCES
Write a sentence on the board and scoop it into phrases. Have the students try to read each word to themselves and then call on a student. Tell them untaught Trick Words. After each word is decoded, chorally read the sentence with fluency. Do 2-3 sentences. (See Unit Resources.)

Unit 5 | Week 2

Day 3

Echo/Letter Formation

Remind students of proper pencil grip and sitting position, and give them their Dry Erase Writing Tablets.

Dictate 5-6 previously taught sounds. You select and say the sound. Students echo the sound and say the letter.

Next have a student come up to the classroom board to make the letter on the Large Writing Grid.

Then have all students write the answer on their Dry Erase Writing Tablets as you direct them with the letter formation verbalization.

(See Unit Resources.)

Note
Students can make only lowercase letters, or you can selectively do both uppercase and lowercase to reinforce certain letters. (Be sure to always do lowercase for every sound that is dictated.)

Dictation (Dry Erase)

Proper Dictation Activity procedures are very important. Be sure to follow their demonstration on the Prevention Learning Community. This is a teaching time, not a testing time. Be sure students repeat each dictation. Dictate 3 current or review words.

Unit Words

Students should tap and orally spell the Unit words before writing. Then have all spell chorally. Have one student write on the Large Writing Grid and all students write on their Dry Erase Writing Tablets. (See Current and Review Words in Unit Resources.)

Unit 5 | Week 2

Day 4

Daily Plan — DAY 4

Student Learning Plan
- Drill Sounds/Warm-Up
- Trick Word Practice
- Make It Fun
- Dictation (Dry Erase)

Teacher Materials
- Echo and/or Baby Echo
- Large Sound Cards
- Standard Sound Cards
- Sentence Frames
- Trick Word Flashcards

Student Materials
- Student Notebook
- Dry Erase Writing Tablet

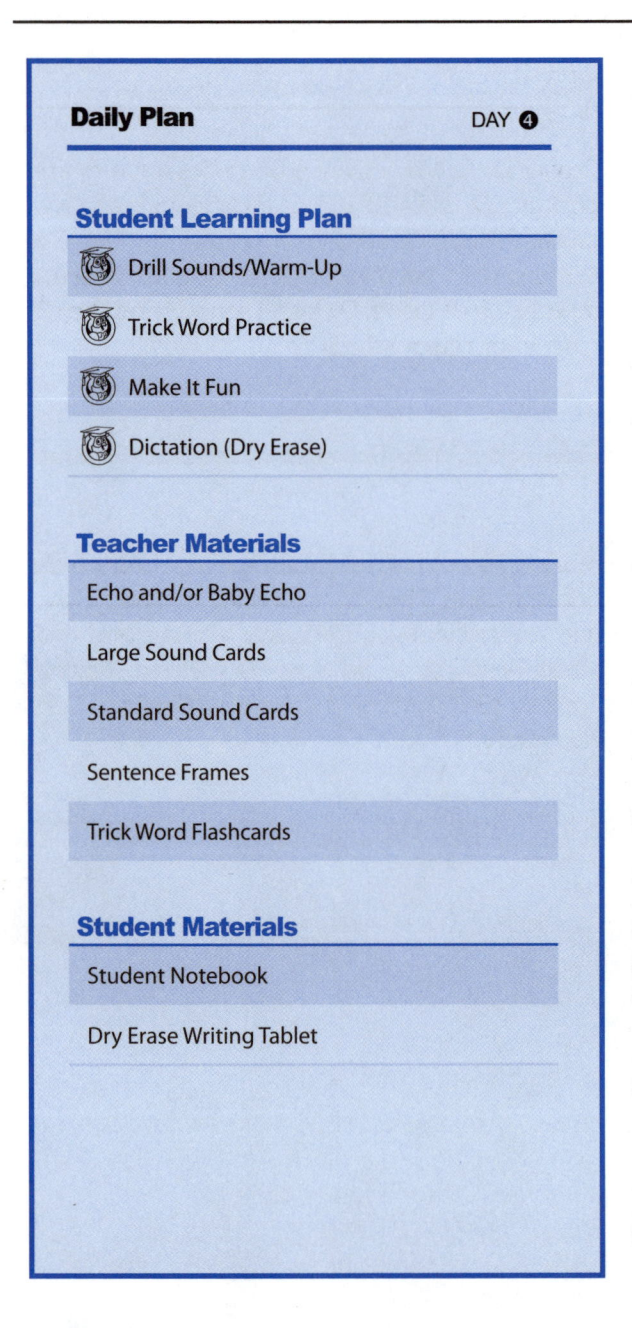

Drill Sounds/Warm-Up

Do any new or challenging sounds and vowel sounds each day. Selectively review 4-5 other consonants.

Large Sound Cards

Practice sounds with the Large Sound Cards. Model these, saying the letter-keyword-sound and have the students echo.

Standard Sound Cards

Next, point to the Standard Sound Cards (in card display) with the Baby Echo pointer. You say the letter-keyword-sound and hold up Baby Echo to have students repeat. You can have a student be the drill leader for some of the sounds.

Trick Word Practice

Say each sentence below and have students repeat. Then write the sentence on Sentence Frames, and scoop it into phrases. Read it and have students echo. Say the trick word that is in the sentence and have a student find and circle it. After it is circled, hold up the corresponding Trick Word Flashcard and say the word and have students repeat.

Sentence Resource

Can (he) (have) this candy?

(She) thought (of) everything!

Lastly present the Trick Word Flashcards, say each and have student repeat.

Unit 5 | Week 2

Day 4

Make It Fun

Preparation
- Sentence Frames

CHANGE THE SENTENCE

The purpose of this activity is to reinforce sentence structure and spelling.

Instruct Students

Say a sentence and have students repeat. Have a student place the Sentence Frames as needed. Next, distribute the Sentence Frames to individual students, saying the word that they are to write. Have each student write their word. When they have the words on the Sentence Frames, dictate the sentence again and have them come up and stand in order to form the sentence. Read it together.

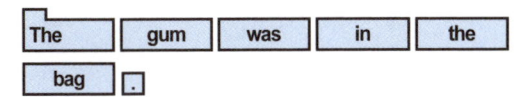

| The | gum | was | in | the |
| bag | . |

Say

> Let's change this sentence to: The gum was in the box.

Select a student to erase **bag** and change the word to **box**. They can then hold the Sentence Frame and have the other students sit down.

Tap out the word to check the student's spelling.

Continue dictating changes, reading the entire sentence and have a student make the necessary change. If you change a trick word do not tap it out.

Sentence Resource

Did the duck sit on the dock?

Did the duck sit on the <u>deck</u>?

Did the <u>kid</u> sit on the deck?

Did the kid <u>run</u> on the deck?

Did the <u>dog</u> run on the deck?

Dictation (Dry Erase)

Proper Dictation Activity procedures are very important. Be sure to follow their demonstration on the Prevention Learning Community. This is a teaching time, not a testing time. Be sure students repeat each dictation. Dictate 3 sounds and then 3 current or review words.

Unit Sounds

Refer to this Unit's Resource List of Echo Sounds.

Unit Words

Students should tap and orally spell the Unit words before writing. Then have all spell chorally. Have one student write on the Large Writing Grid and all students write on their Dry Erase Writing Tablets. (See Current and Review Words in Unit Resources.)

Unit 5 | Week 2

Day 5

Daily Plan — DAY 5

Student Learning Plan
- Drill Sounds/Warm-Up
- Storytime

Teacher Materials
- Echo and/or Baby Echo
- Large Sound Cards
- Standard Sound Cards
- Trick Word Flashcards
- Narrative and informational stories

Student Materials
- Student Notebook

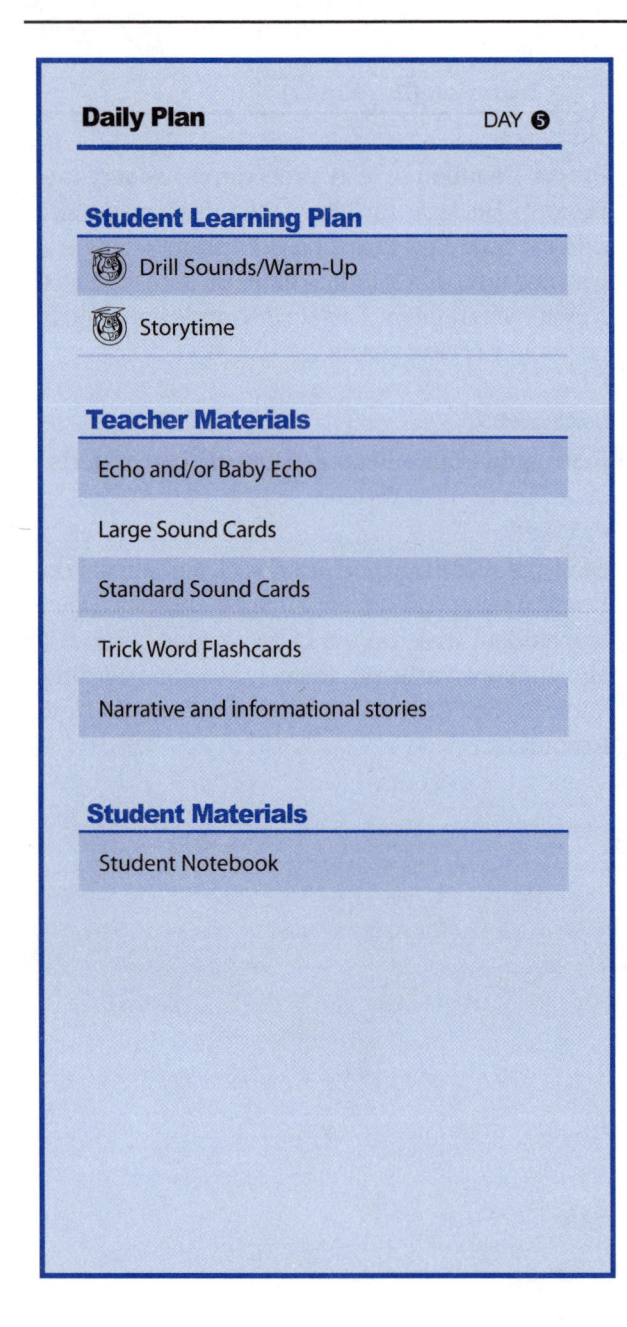

Drill Sounds/Warm-Up

Do any new or challenging sounds and vowel sounds each day. Selectively review 4-5 other consonants.

Large Sound Cards

Practice sounds with the Large Sound Cards. Model these, saying the letter-keyword-sound and have the students echo.

Standard Sound Cards

Next, point to the Standard Sound Cards (in card display) with the Baby Echo pointer. You say the letter-keyword-sound and hold up Baby Echo to have students repeat. You can have a student be the drill leader for some of the sounds.

Drill Trick Word Flashcards

Present the Trick Word Flashcards. Have students quickly read the packet. You will eliminate some of the mastered trick words as you add new Level K words to the packet.

Storytime

Preparation

You will select additional books to demonstrate narrative fiction versus informational text. Do this by finding another narrative story with an animal in it and a corresponding informational book about that animal. For example, you can select a story with an owl in it and then a book about owls.

Narrative

Yolen, Jane. 1987. **Owl Moon.** New York: Philonel Books.

Informational

Arnosky, Jim. 1995. **All About Owls.** New York, New York: Scholastic Inc.

Jarvis, Kila and Holt, Denver. 1996. **Owls: Whoo Are They?** Missoula, MT: Mountain Press Publishing Company.

Instruct Students

Show the students the two books. Tell them that some books tell make-believe stories and other books tell us facts that are true. Read the narrative book.

Before reading, look at the front and back cover of the book with your students. Discuss the title, author and illustrator, explaining each of those terms.

Ask

Who are the characters in the story?

What is the setting?

Unit 5 | Week 2

Day 5

What are the main events of the story?

What happened first?

Then what happened?

What happened next?

What happened at the end?

Tell the students that stories which are make-believe have something happen in them, and they have an ending like the one you just read.

Then show them the informational book and explain that this book has true facts. Tell them that during Storytime next week, you will read them this book and they will learn some true facts about owls (or the animal that you have chosen).

Have students draw major events from the story in their My Fundations® Journal. More advanced students can add words or sentences.

Unit 5 | Week 3

Day 1

Daily Plan — DAY 1

Student Learning Plan
- Drill Sounds/Warm-Up
- Word Play
- Echo/Find Letters & Words

Teacher Materials
- Echo and/or Baby Echo
- Large Sound Cards
- Standard Sound Cards
- Sentence Frames
- Trick Word Flashcards

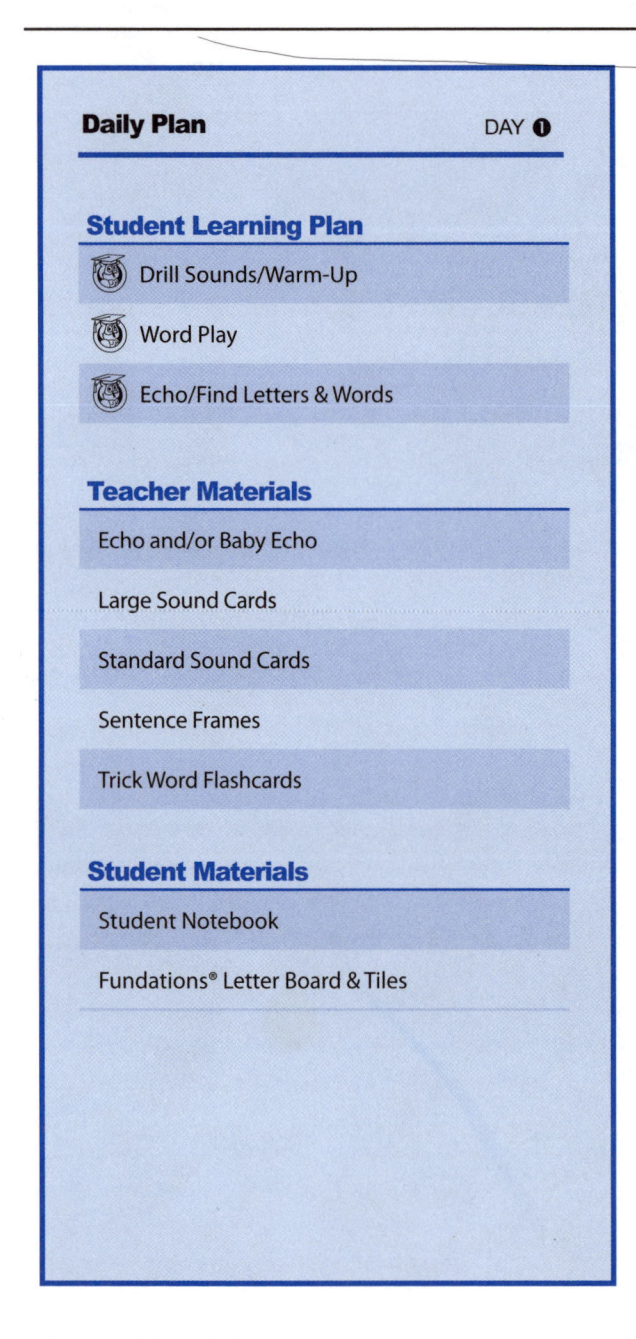

Student Materials
- Student Notebook
- Fundations® Letter Board & Tiles

Drill Sounds/Warm-Up

Do any new or challenging sounds and vowel sounds each day. Selectively review 4-5 other consonants.

Large Sound Cards
Practice sounds with the Large Sound Cards. Model these, saying the letter-keyword-sound and have the students echo.

Standard Sound Cards
Next, point to the Standard Sound Cards (in card display) with the Baby Echo pointer. You say the letter-keyword-sound and hold up Baby Echo to have students repeat. You can have a student be the drill leader for some of the sounds.

Drill Trick Word Flashcards
Present the Trick Word Flashcards. Have students quickly read the packet. You will eliminate some of the mastered trick words as you add new Level K words to the packet.

Word Play

MAKE WORDS FOR DECODING
Use your Standard Sound Card display to make 3-5 Unit words. (See Unit Resources.)

Make each word then say and tap each sound. Have students tap with you. Then blend the sounds as you drag your thumb across your fingers.

Next, point under each card as you say each sound, then drag your finger under all three cards as you and the students blend the sounds to read the word.

READ SENTENCES
Write a sentence on the board and scoop it into phrases. Have the students try to read each word to themselves and then call on a student. Tell them untaught Trick Words. After each word is decoded, chorally read the sentence with fluency. Do 2-3 sentences. (See Unit Resources.)

REVIEW SENTENCE DICTATION
Review sentence dictation using the Sentence Frames on the classroom board.

Say the sentence and have students echo. Then write the sentence on the Sentence Frames.

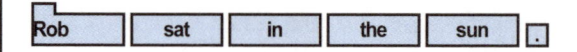

| Rob | sat | in | the | sun | . |

Unit 5 | Week 3

Day 1

Explain that at the beginning of a sentence, the word must begin with a capital letter. That is why the frame at the beginning is tall.

Discuss period used to end the sentence. Have a student circle the trick word. Scoop the sentence into phrases, read it, and have students echo.

Erase the Sentence Frames and place them in a column. Next dictate another sentence.

Say

Tom had a dog.

Have the students echo. Select a student to come forward and find the Sentence Frames needed for the sentence. Have a student circle the Sentence Frame with the trick word. Next, tap out the first word and have a student come up and write the word on the Sentence Frame. Continue with each word, calling on a different student. Tap each word before the student writes it. Write the word **a** for the student. (Do not tap it - it is a Trick Word.) Be sure to discuss capital letters and punctuation.

Proofread the sentence with students. First tell them to check the capital letters and punctuation to be sure these are correct. Next, have them check spelling by tapping each word. Show students how to find and check the spelling of the trick word in their Student Notebooks on the Trick Word page. Do 1-2 other sentences (see Unit Resources).

Echo/Find Letters & Words

Echo/Find Letters

Say a sound. Have students echo and point to the letter(s) on their Magnetic Letter Boards.

Ask

What says /___/? (___)

(See Echo Sounds in Unit Resources for expected student responses.)

Have students name the letter(s). Then you can have one student find the Standard Sound Card(s) as you dictate sounds. Do vowels and 3-5 other sounds.

Echo/Find Words

Dictate a Unit word. Do 3-5 words. (See Current Unit Words in Unit Resources.)

Have students find Letter Tiles needed to make words on their Magnetic Letter Boards. Have one student come find your corresponding cards. After finding a word, have students spell it orally and replace the tiles on the letter squares.

Unit 5 | Week 3

Day 2

Daily Plan — DAY 2

Student Learning Plan
- Drill Sounds/Warm-Up
- Word Play
- Teach Trick Words

Teacher Materials
- Echo and/or Baby Echo
- Large Sound Cards
- Standard Sound Cards
- Sentence Frames
- Trick Word Flashcards

Student Materials
- Student Notebook

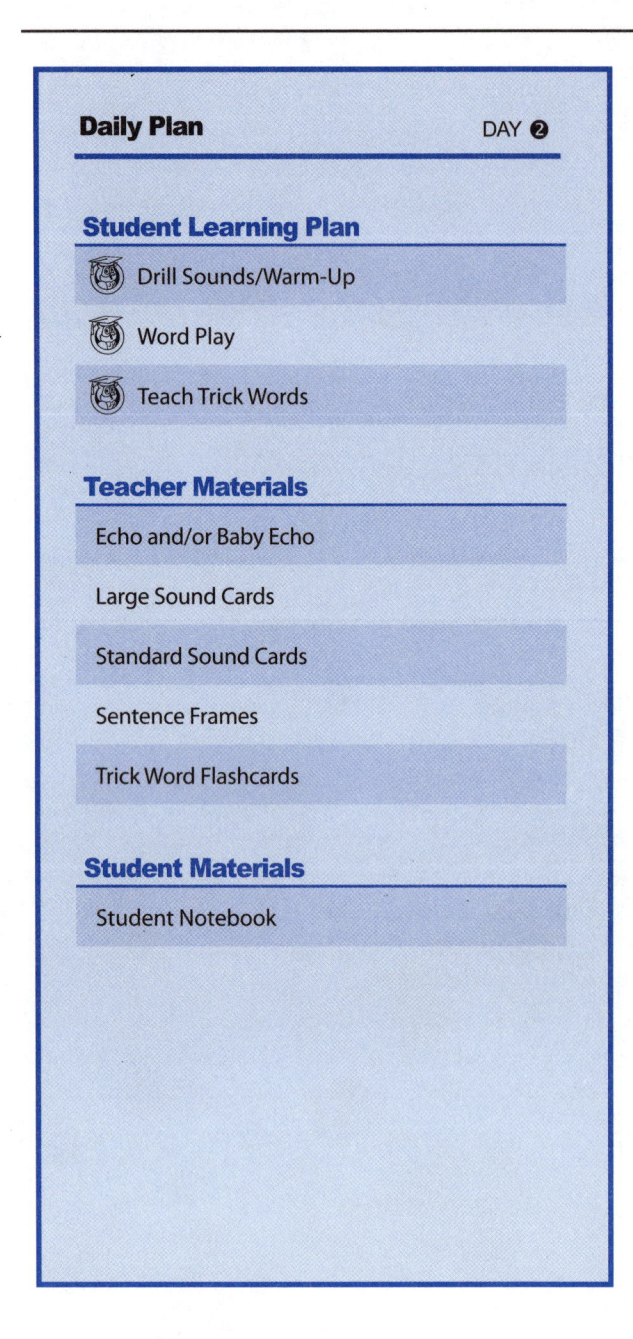

Drill Sounds/Warm-Up

Do any new or challenging sounds and vowel sounds each day. Selectively review 4-5 other consonants.

Large Sound Cards
Practice sounds with the Large Sound Cards. Model these, saying the letter-keyword-sound and have the students echo.

Standard Sound Cards
Next, point to the Standard Sound Cards (in card display) with the Baby Echo pointer. You say the letter-keyword-sound and hold up Baby Echo to have students repeat. You can have a student be the drill leader for some of the sounds.

Word Play

MAKE WORDS FOR DECODING

Use your Standard Sound Card display to make 3-5 Unit words. (See Unit Resources.)

Make each word then say and tap each sound. Have students tap with you. Then blend the sounds as you drag your thumb across your fingers.

Next, point under each card as you say each sound, then drag your finger under all three cards as you and the students blend the sounds to read the word.

MAKE NONSENSE WORDS

Tell students that they can also blend sounds together to make silly or nonsense words. Explain that these nonsense words are not real words. They are just silly words that show that they can read sounds.

Make 3-5 nonsense words and have students tap and read them (see Unit Resources).

REVIEW SENTENCE DICTATION

Review sentence dictation using the Sentence Frames on the classroom board.

Say the sentence and have students echo. Then write the sentence on the Sentence Frames.

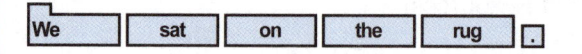

| We | sat | on | the | rug | . |

Unit 5 | Week 3

Day 2

Explain that at the beginning of a sentence, the word must begin with a capital letter. That is why the frame at the beginning is tall.

Discuss period used to end the sentence. Have a student circle the Sentence Frame with the trick word.

Erase the Sentence Frames and place them in a column. Next dictate another sentence.

Say

> I did that big job.

Have the students echo. Select a student to come forward and find the Sentence Frames needed for the sentence. Have a student circle the Sentence Frame with the trick word. Next, tap out the first word and have a student come up and write the word on the Sentence Frame. Continue with each word, calling on a different student. Tap each word before the student writes it. Write the word **I** for the student. (Do not tap it - it is a Trick Word.) Be sure to discuss capital letters and punctuation.

Proofread the sentence with students. First tell them to check the capital letters and punctuation to be sure these are correct. Next, have them check spelling by tapping each word. Show students how to find and check the spelling of the trick word in their Student Notebooks on the Trick Word page. Do 1-2 other sentences (see Unit Resources).

Teach Trick Words

Introduce the trick word **from**, and reinforce capitalization and punctuation.

Instruct Students

Say the sentence below and have students repeat. Have a student place the Sentence Frames as needed. Write the sentence on the frames, and discuss capitalization and punctuation. Scoop the sentence into phrases, read it, and have students echo.

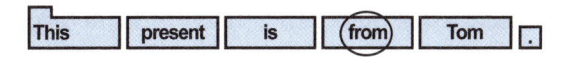

| This | present | is | (from) | Tom | . |

Say

> I am going to circle this word (circle the new trick word). Listen to the sentence and see if you can tell me the word I circled (point to words as you say each one).

Next, explain that the word **from** is a word that you are going to practice, and that this word is called a Trick Word because it can be tricky and we do not tap it out.

Show students the Trick Word Flashcard **from**. Say the word and have them repeat. Lastly, present the Trick Word Flashcards learned thus far. Say each and have students repeat.

Unit 5 | Week 3

Day 3

Daily Plan — DAY 3

Student Learning Plan
- Drill Sounds/Warm-Up
- Word Play
- Echo/Letter Formation
- Dictation (Dry Erase)

Teacher Materials
- Echo and/or Baby Echo
- Large Sound Cards
- Standard Sound Cards
- Large Writing Grid
- Letter Formation Guide
- Sentence Frames
- Trick Word Flashcards

Student Materials
- Student Notebook
- Dry Erase Writing Tablet

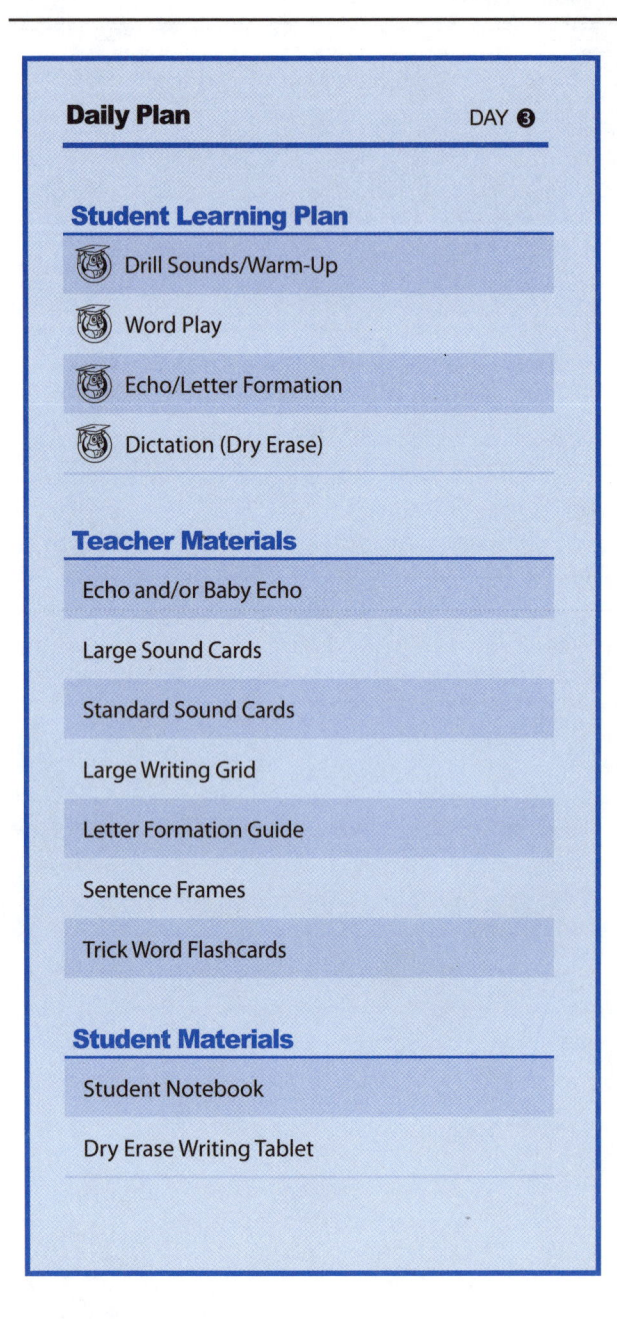

Drill Sounds/Warm-Up

Do any new or challenging sounds and vowel sounds each day. Selectively review 4-5 other consonants.

Large Sound Cards
Practice sounds with the Large Sound Cards. Model these, saying the letter-keyword-sound and have the students echo.

Standard Sound Cards
Next, point to the Standard Sound Cards (in card display) with the Baby Echo pointer. You say the letter-keyword-sound and hold up Baby Echo to have students repeat. You can have a student be the drill leader for some of the sounds.

Drill Trick Word Flashcards
Present the Trick Word Flashcards. Have students quickly read the packet. You will eliminate some of the mastered trick words as you add new Level K words to the packet.

Word Play

MAKE WORDS FOR DECODING
Use your Standard Sound Card display to make 3-5 Unit words. (See Unit Resources.)

Make each word then say and tap each sound. Have students tap with you. Then blend the sounds as you drag your thumb across your fingers.

Next, point under each card as you say each sound, then drag your finger under all three cards as you and the students blend the sounds to read the word.

READ SENTENCES
[handwritten: Rick has to go home. Beth and I like the plant.]

Write a sentence on the board and scoop it into phrases. Have the students try to read each word to themselves and then call on a student. Tell them untaught Trick Words. After each word is decoded, chorally read the sentence with fluency. Do 2-3 sentences. (See Unit Resources.)

WRITE SENTENCES
Use the Sentence Frames and dictate 2-3 sentences. (See Unit Resources.) Follow the procedure for sentence dictation described in Introduce New Concepts.

[handwritten: They write on board. He can not swim. We are in the lake.]

Unit 5 | Week 3

Day 3

Echo/Letter Formation

Remind students of proper pencil grip and sitting position, and give them their Dry Erase Writing Tablets.

Dictate 5-6 previously taught sounds. You select and say the sound. Students echo the sound and say the letter.

Next have a student come up to the classroom board to make the letter on the Large Writing Grid.

Then have all students write the answer on their Dry Erase Writing Tablets as you direct them with the letter formation verbalization.

(See Unit Resources.)

Note
Students can make only lowercase letters, or you can selectively do both uppercase and lowercase to reinforce certain letters. (Be sure to always do lowercase for every sound that is dictated.)

Dictation (Dry Erase)

Proper Dictation Activity procedures are very important. Be sure to follow their demonstration on the Prevention Learning Community. This is a teaching time, not a testing time. Be sure students repeat each dictation. Dictate 3 current or review words.

Unit Words

Students should tap and orally spell the Unit words before writing. Then have all spell chorally. Have one student write on the Large Writing Grid and all students write on their Dry Erase Writing Tablets. (See Current and Review Words in Unit Resources.)

Unit 5 | Week 3

Day 4

Daily Plan — DAY 4

Student Learning Plan
- Drill Sounds/Warm-Up
- Trick Word Practice
- Make It Fun
- Dictation (Dry Erase)

Teacher Materials
- Echo and/or Baby Echo
- Large Sound Cards
- Standard Sound Cards
- Sentence Frames
- Trick Word Flashcards

Student Materials
- Student Notebook
- Dry Erase Writing Tablet

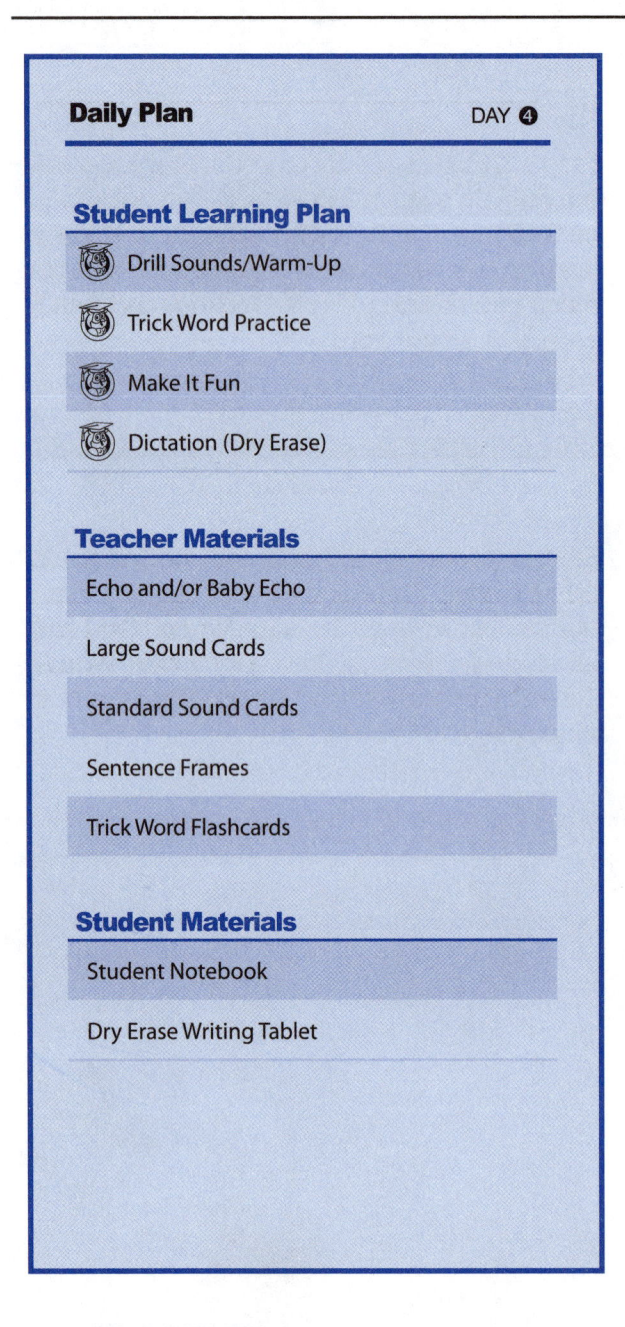

Drill Sounds/Warm-Up

Do any new or challenging sounds and vowel sounds each day. Selectively review 4-5 other consonants.

Large Sound Cards
Practice sounds with the Large Sound Cards. Model these, saying the letter-keyword-sound and have the students echo.

Standard Sound Cards
Next, point to the Standard Sound Cards (in card display) with the Baby Echo pointer. You say the letter-keyword-sound and hold up Baby Echo to have students repeat. You can have a student be the drill leader for some of the sounds.

Trick Word Practice

Say each sentence below and have students repeat. Then write the sentence on Sentence Frames, and scoop it into phrases. Read it and have students echo. Say the trick word that is in the sentence and have a student find and circle it. After it is circled, hold up the corresponding Trick Word Flashcard and say the word and have students repeat.

Sentence Resource

The book (is) (from) Meg.

(Was) this (from) (you)?

Lastly present the Trick Word Flashcards, say each and have student repeat.

Unit 5 | Week 3

Day 4

🦉 Make It Fun

Preparation
- Sentence Frames

CHANGE THE SENTENCE

The purpose of this activity is to reinforce sentence structure and spelling.

Instruct Students

Say a sentence and have students repeat. Have a student place the Sentence Frames as needed. Next, distribute the Sentence Frames to individual students, saying the word that they are to write. Have each student write their word. When they have the words on the Sentence Frames, dictate the sentence again and have them come up and stand in order to form the sentence. Read it together.

| Tom | met | Beth | at | the |
| shop | . |

Say

> Let's change this sentence to: Tim met Beth at the shop.

Select a student to erase **Tom** and change the word to **Tim**. They can then hold the Sentence Frame and have the other student sit down.

Tap out the word to check the student's spelling.

Continue dictating changes, reading the entire sentence and have a student make the necessary change.

Sentence Resource

Tom met Beth at the shop.

<u>Tim</u> met Beth at the shop.

Tim met Beth at the <u>dock</u>.

Tim met <u>Bob</u> at the dock.

<u>Jack</u> met Bob at the dock.

🦉 Dictation (Dry Erase)

Proper Dictation Activity procedures are very important. Be sure to follow their demonstration on the Prevention Learning Community. This is a teaching time, not a testing time. Be sure students repeat each dictation. Dictate 3 sounds and then 3 current or review words.

Unit Sounds

Refer to this Unit's Resource List of Echo Sounds.

Unit Words

Students should tap and orally spell the Unit words before writing. Then have all spell chorally. Have one student write on the Large Writing Grid and all students write on their Dry Erase Writing Tablets. (See Current and Review Words in Unit Resources.)

Unit 5 | Week 3

Day 5

Daily Plan — DAY 5

Student Learning Plan
- Drill Sounds/Warm-Up
- Storytime

Teacher Materials
- Echo and/or Baby Echo
- Large Sound Cards
- Standard Sound Cards
- Trick Word Flashcards
- Narrative and informational stories

Student Materials
- Student Notebook

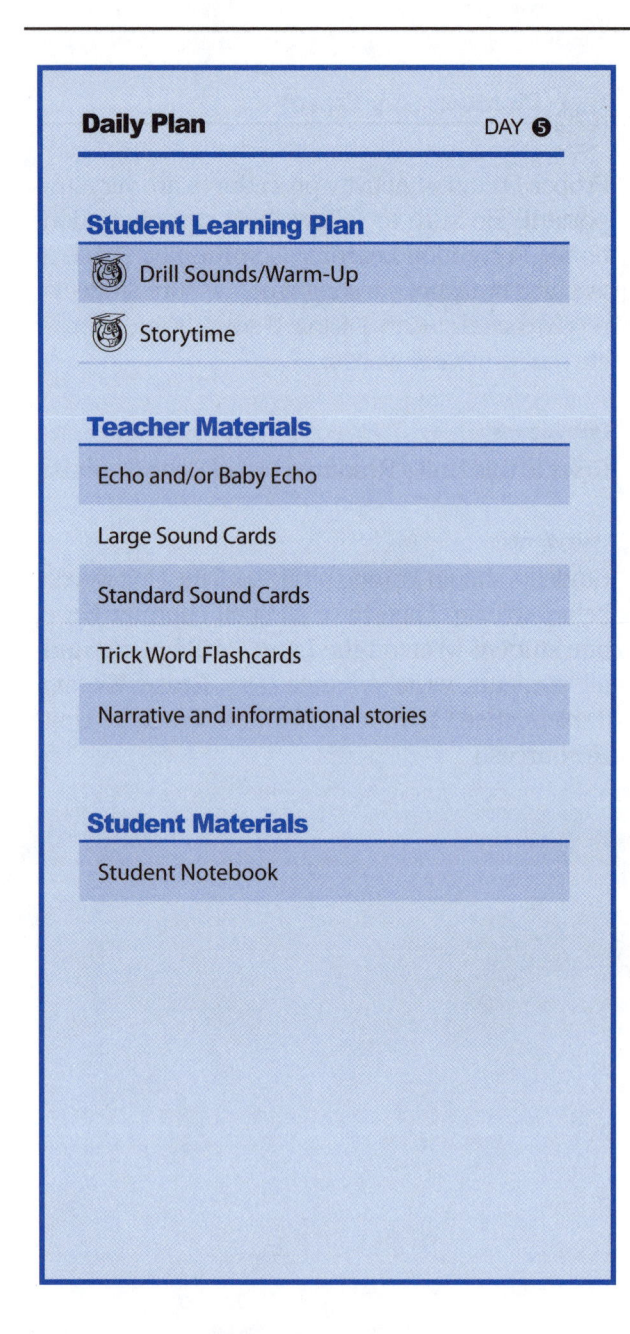

Drill Sounds/Warm-Up

Do any new or challenging sounds and vowel sounds each day. Selectively review 4-5 other consonants.

Large Sound Cards

Practice sounds with the Large Sound Cards. Model these, saying the letter-keyword-sound and have the students echo.

Standard Sound Cards

Next, point to the Standard Sound Cards (in card display) with the Baby Echo pointer. You say the letter-keyword-sound and hold up Baby Echo to have students repeat. You can have a student be the drill leader for some of the sounds.

Drill Trick Word Flashcards

Present the Trick Word Flashcards. Have students quickly read the packet. You will eliminate some of the mastered trick words as you add new Level K words to the packet.

Storytime

Preparation

Use the same narrative book and informational book that you had in Week 2. For example, you can select a story with an owl in it and then a book about owls.

Narrative

Yolen, Jane. 1987. **Owl Moon.** New York: Philonel Books.

Informational

Arnosky, Jim. 1995. **All About Owls.** New York, New York: Scholastic Inc.

Jarvis, Kila and Holt, Denver. 1996. **Owls: Whoo Are They?** Missoula, MT: Mountain Press Publishing Company.

Instruct Students

Show the students the two books. Tell them that some books tell make-believe stories and other books tell us facts that are true. Read the informational book.

Before reading, look at the front and back cover of the book with your students. Discuss the title, author and illustrator, explaining each of those terms.

Read the book (or part of the book) to your students. After each page, ask them to name one true fact that they have learned.

tip

Have students draw pictures to represent some of the facts in their My Fundations® Journal. More advanced students can write some facts as well.

Unit 5 | Week 3

Unit 5 | Week 4

Day 1

Daily Plan — DAY 1

Student Learning Plan
- Drill Sounds/Warm-Up
- Word Play
- Dictation (Dry Erase)
- Introduce New Concepts

Teacher Materials
- Echo and/or Baby Echo
- Large Sound Cards
- Standard Sound Cards
- Sentence Frames
- Trick Word Flashcards

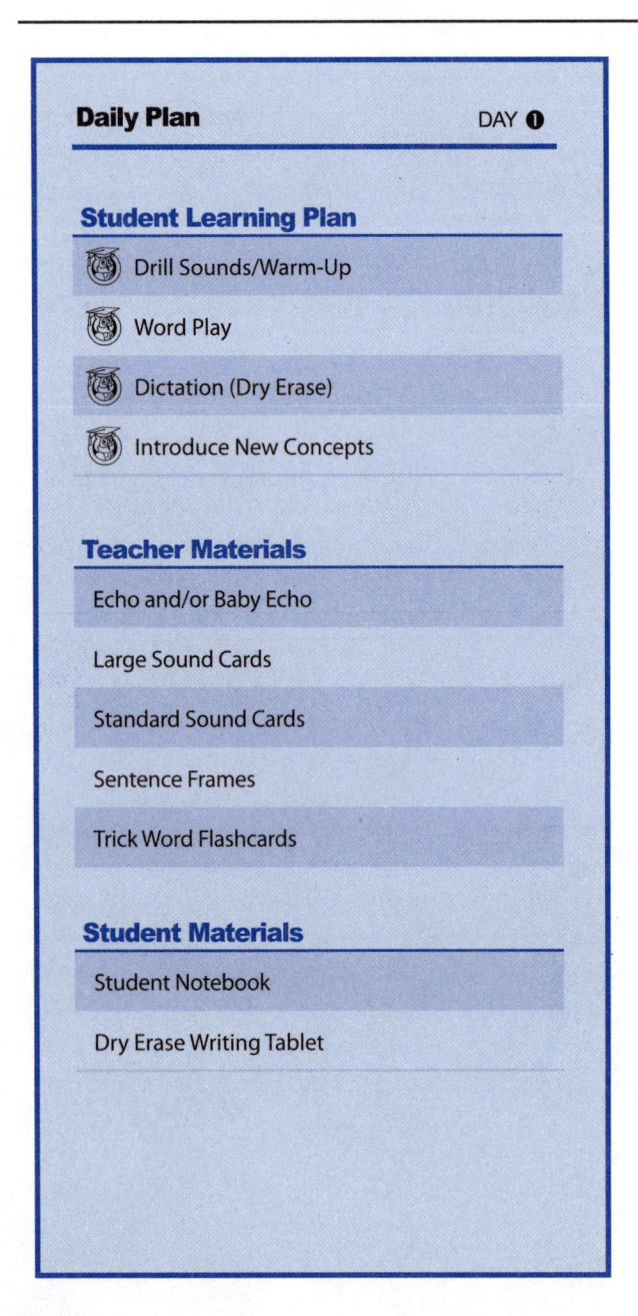

Student Materials
- Student Notebook
- Dry Erase Writing Tablet

Drill Sounds/Warm-Up

Do any new or challenging sounds and vowel sounds each day. Selectively review 4-5 other consonants.

Large Sound Cards
Practice sounds with the Large Sound Cards. Model these, saying the letter-keyword-sound and have the students echo.

Standard Sound Cards
Next, point to the Standard Sound Cards (in card display) with the Baby Echo pointer. You say the letter-keyword-sound and hold up Baby Echo to have students repeat. You can have a student be the drill leader for some of the sounds.

Drill Trick Word Flashcards
Present the Trick Word Flashcards. Have students quickly read the packet. You will eliminate some of the mastered trick words as you add new Level K words to the packet.

Word Play

MAKE WORDS FOR DECODING
Use your Standard Sound Card display to make 3-5 Unit words. (See Unit Resources.)

Make each word then say and tap each sound. Have students tap with you. Then blend the sounds as you drag your thumb across your fingers.

Next, point under each card as you say each sound, then drag your finger under all three cards as you and the students blend the sounds to read the word.

READ SENTENCES
Write a sentence on the board and scoop it into phrases. Have the students try to read each word to themselves and then call on a student. Tell them untaught Trick Words. After each word is decoded, chorally read the sentence with fluency. Do 2-3 sentences. (See Unit Resources.)

Unit 5 | Week 4

Day 1

Dictation (Dry Erase)

Proper Dictation Activity procedures are very important. Be sure to follow their demonstration on the Prevention Learning Community. This is a teaching time, not a testing time. Be sure students repeat each dictation. Dictate 3 sounds and then 3 current or review words.

Unit Sounds
Refer to this Unit's Resource List of Echo Sounds.

Unit Words
Students should tap and orally spell the Unit words before writing. Then have all spell chorally. Have one student write on the Large Writing Grid and all students write on their Dry Erase Writing Tablets. (See Current and Review Words in Unit Resources.)

Be sure to hold students accountable for correct letter formation!

Introduce New Concepts

TEACH SENTENCE DICTATION - DRY ERASE

Do sentence dictation as a group using the Sentence Frames on your magnetic board. Have students also do the sentences on their Dry Erase Writing Tablets.

Say the sentence and have students echo. Then write the sentence on the Sentence Frames.

Example

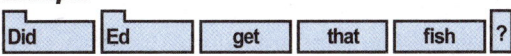

| Did | Ed | get | that | fish | ? |

Explain that at the beginning of a sentence, the word must begin with a capital letter. That is why the frame at the beginning is tall. Next explain why the frame with Ed is also tall. Tell students that people's names always begin with a capital letter. Show students the tall punctuation frame and explain the question mark. Tell them that they will need to think about whether the sentences needs a period or a question mark. Have a student circle the trick word (**the**). Tap out other words to proofread.

Next, dictate a sentence, and tell students that they will write it on the Dry Erase Writing Tablets.

Sentence Resources

Tim had a rash.

Did Jack hit his chin?

Have the students echo. Have a student place Sentence Frames on the board and circle the trick word. Select a student to come forward and write each word on the Sentence Frames, while other students write it on their Dry Erase Writing Tablets. Remind them that trick words cannot be tapped out and that they can look them up in their Student Notebooks to check spelling. Be sure to discuss capital letters and punctuation.

Proofread the sentence with students. First tell them to check the capital letters and punctuation to be sure these are correct. Next, have them check spelling by tapping each word. Show students how to find and check the spelling of the trick word in their Student Notebooks on the Trick Word page. Do 1-2 other sentences (see Unit Resources).

Unit 5 | Week 4

Day 2

Daily Plan — DAY 2

Student Learning Plan
- Drill Sounds/Warm-Up
- Word Play
- Teach Trick Words

Teacher Materials
- Echo and/or Baby Echo
- Large Sound Cards
- Standard Sound Cards
- Sentence Frames
- Trick Word Flashcards

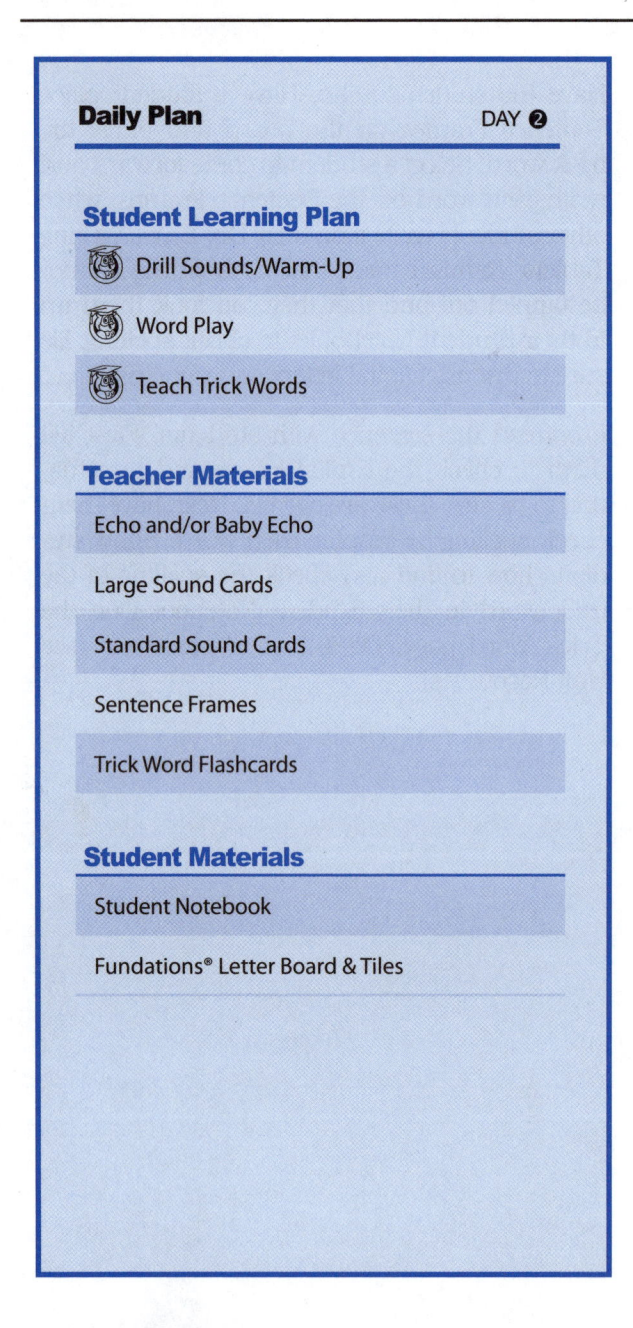

Student Materials
- Student Notebook
- Fundations® Letter Board & Tiles

Drill Sounds/Warm-Up

Do any new or challenging sounds and vowel sounds each day. Selectively review 4-5 other consonants.

Large Sound Cards
Practice sounds with the Large Sound Cards. Model these, saying the letter-keyword-sound and have the students echo.

Standard Sound Cards
Next, point to the Standard Sound Cards (in card display) with the Baby Echo pointer. You say the letter-keyword-sound and hold up Baby Echo to have students repeat. You can have a student be the drill leader for some of the sounds.

Word Play

MAKE WORDS FOR DECODING
Use your Standard Sound Card display to make 3-5 Unit words. (See Unit Resources.)

Make each word then say and tap each sound. Have students tap with you. Then blend the sounds as you drag your thumb across your fingers.

Next, point under each card as you say each sound, then drag your finger under all three cards as you and the students blend the sounds to read the word.

MAKE NONSENSE WORDS
Tell students that they can also blend sounds together to make silly or nonsense words. Explain that these nonsense words are not real words. They are just silly words that show that they can read sounds.

Make 3-5 nonsense words and have students tap and read them (see Unit Resources).

REVIEW SENTENCE DICTATION
Review sentence dictation using the Sentence Frames on the classroom board.

Say the sentence and have students echo. Then write the sentence on the Sentence Frames.

Example

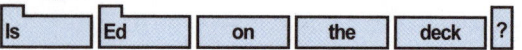

| Is | Ed | on | the | deck | ? |

Explain that at the beginning of a sentence, the word must begin with a capital letter. That is why the frame at the beginning is tall. Next explain

Unit 5 | Week 4

Day 2

why the frame with Ed is also tall. Tell students that people's names always begin with a capital letter. Show students the tall punctuation frame and explain the question mark. Tell them that they will need to think about whether the sentences needs a period or a question mark. Have a student circle the trick words (**is**, **the**). Tap out other words to show students how to proofread.

Next, dictate the following sentences. Have a student find and place Sentence Frames and circle the frame with a trick word.

Sentence Resources

Beth had a pet.

Did Jim sit on the log?

Have the students echo. Have a student place Sentence Frames on the board and circle the trick word. Select a student to come forward and write each word on the Sentence Frames, while other students write it on their Dry Erase Writing Tablets. Remind them that trick words cannot be tapped out and that they can look them up in their Student Notebooks to check spelling. Be sure to discuss capital letters and punctuation.

Proofread the sentence with students. First tell them to check the capital letters and punctuation to be sure these are correct. Next, have them check spelling by tapping each word. Show students how to find and check the spelling of the trick word in their Student Notebooks on the Trick Word page. Do 1-2 other sentences (see Unit Resources).

Teach Trick Words

Introduce the trick words **by** and **my**, and reinforce capitalization and punctuation.

Instruct Students

Say the sentence below and have students repeat. Have a student place the Sentence Frames as needed. Write the sentence on the frames, and discuss capitalization and punctuation. Scoop the sentence into phrases, read it, and have students echo.

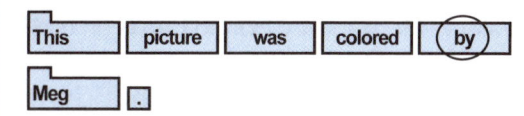

| This | picture | was | colored | (by) |
| Meg | . |

Say

I am going to circle this word (circle the new trick word). Listen to the sentence and see if you can tell me the word I circled (point to words as you say each one).

Let's change this sentence to: That is my jacket.

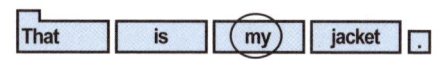

| That | is | (my) | jacket | . |

Next, explain that the words **by** and **my** are words that you are going to practice, and that these words are called Trick Words because they can be tricky and we do not tap them out.

Show students the Trick Word Flashcards **by** and **my**. Say the words and have them repeat. Lastly, present the Trick Word Flashcards learned thus far. Say each and have students repeat.

Unit 5 | Week 4

Day 3

Daily Plan — DAY 3

Student Learning Plan
- Drill Sounds/Warm-Up
- Word Play
- Echo/Letter Formation
- Dictation (Dry Erase)

Teacher Materials
- Echo and/or Baby Echo
- Large Sound Cards
- Standard Sound Cards
- Large Writing Grid
- Letter Formation Guide
- Sentence Frames
- Trick Word Flashcards

Student Materials
- Student Notebook
- Dry Erase Writing Tablet

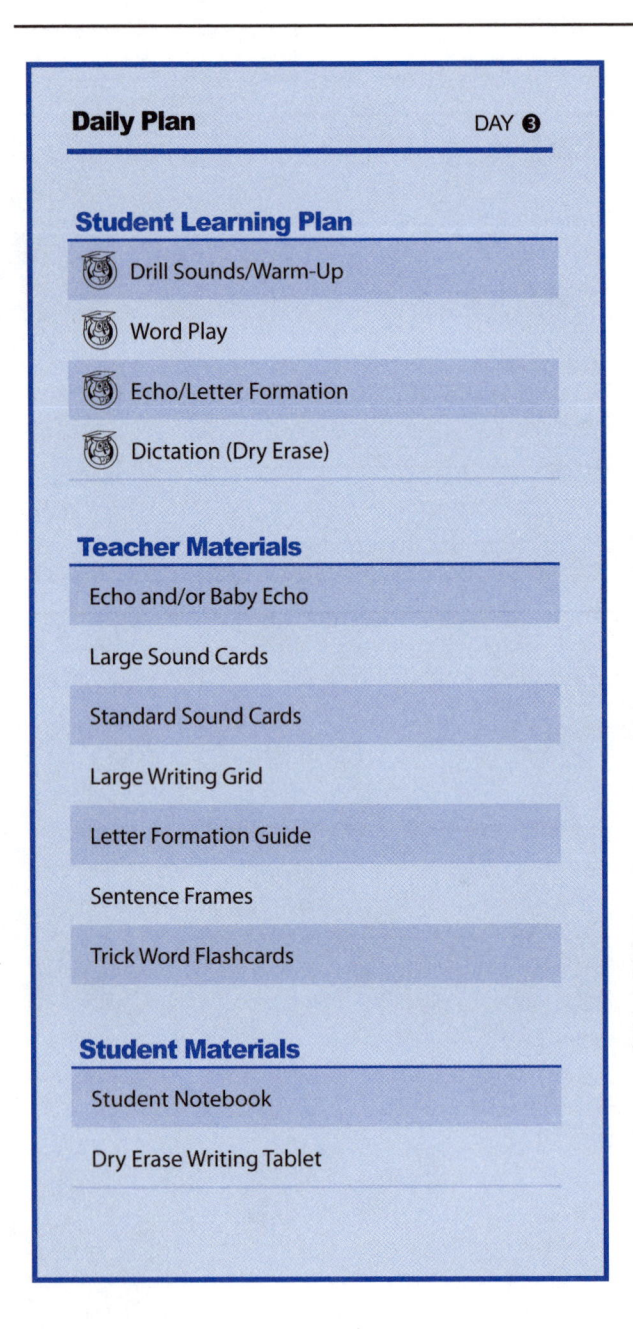

Drill Sounds/Warm-Up

Do any new or challenging sounds and vowel sounds each day. Selectively review 4-5 other consonants.

Large Sound Cards

Practice sounds with the Large Sound Cards. Model these, saying the letter-keyword-sound and have the students echo.

Standard Sound Cards

Next, point to the Standard Sound Cards (in card display) with the Baby Echo pointer. You say the letter-keyword-sound and hold up Baby Echo to have students repeat. You can have a student be the drill leader for some of the sounds.

Drill Trick Word Flashcards

Present the Trick Word Flashcards. Have students quickly read the packet. You will eliminate some of the mastered trick words as you add new Level K words to the packet.

Word Play

MAKE WORDS FOR DECODING

Use your Standard Sound Card display to make 3-5 Unit words. (See Unit Resources.)

Make each word then say and tap each sound. Have students tap with you. Then blend the sounds as you drag your thumb across your fingers.

Next, point under each card as you say each sound, then drag your finger under all three cards as you and the students blend the sounds to read the word.

READ SENTENCES

Write a sentence on the board and scoop it into phrases. Have the students try to read each word to themselves and then call on a student. Tell them untaught Trick Words. After each word is decoded, chorally read the sentence with fluency. Do 2-3 sentences. (See Unit Resources.)

Unit 5 | Week 4

Day 3

Echo/Letter Formation

Remind students of proper pencil grip and sitting position, and give them their Dry Erase Writing Tablets.

Dictate 5-6 previously taught sounds. You select and say the sound. Students echo the sound and say the letter.

Next have a student come up to the classroom board to make the letter on the Large Writing Grid.

Then have all students write the answer on their Dry Erase Writing Tablets as you direct them with the letter formation verbalization.

(See Unit Resources.)

Note
Students can make only lowercase letters, or you can selectively do both uppercase and lowercase to reinforce certain letters. (Be sure to always do lowercase for every sound that is dictated.)

Dictation (Dry Erase)

Proper Dictation Activity procedures are very important. Be sure to follow their demonstration on the Prevention Learning Community. This is a teaching time, not a testing time. Be sure students repeat each dictation. Dictate 3 current or review words and 1 sentence.

Unit Words
Students should tap and orally spell the Unit words before writing. Then have all spell chorally. Have one student write on the Large Writing Grid and all students write on their Dry Erase Writing Tablets. (See Current and Review Words in Unit Resources.)

Sentence
Use the Sentence Frames and dictate one sentence. (See Unit Resources.) Have students echo and have one student place Sentence Frames and circle the frame with a trick word. Have all students write it on their Dry Erase Writing Tablets. Have one student write it on the Sentence Frame. Next, have students scoop their sentence, and read it with fluency. Proofread it together.

tip

Use questioning technique to help students discover an error, don't just provide the answer.

Unit 5 | Week 4

Day 4

Daily Plan — DAY 4

Student Learning Plan
- Drill Sounds/Warm-Up
- Word Play
- Trick Word Practice
- Make It Fun

Teacher Materials
- Echo and/or Baby Echo
- Large Sound Cards
- Standard Sound Cards
- Sentence Frames
- Trick Word Flashcards

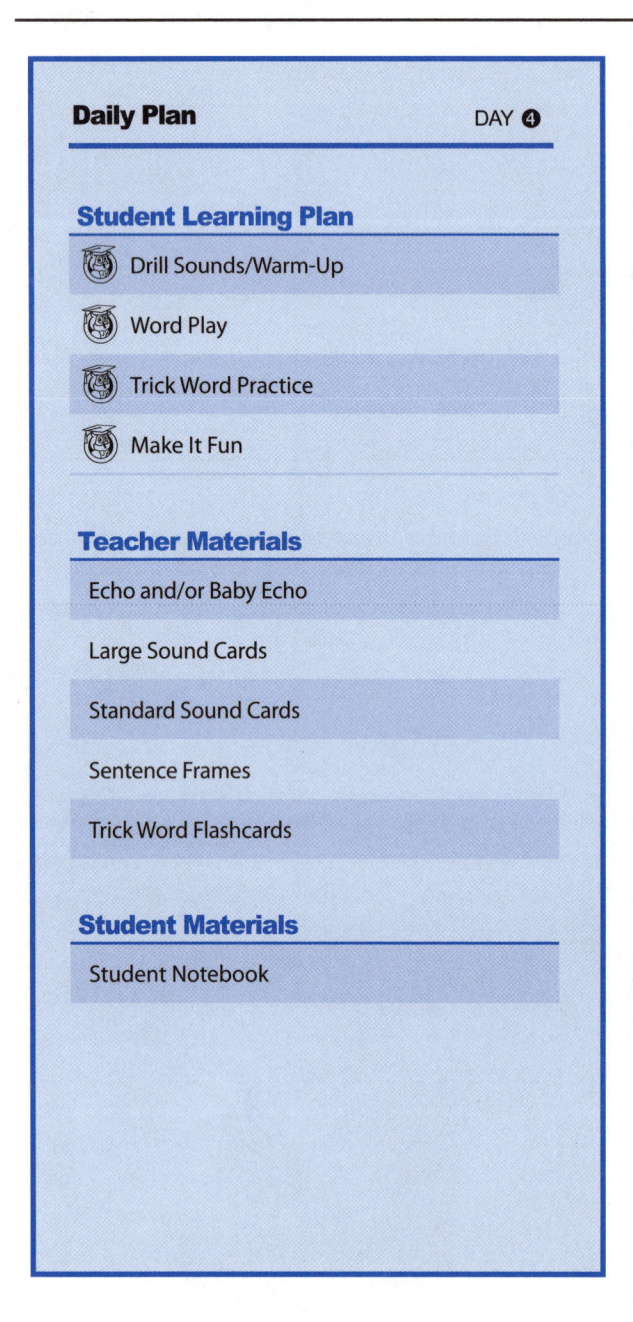

Student Materials
- Student Notebook

Drill Sounds/Warm-Up

Do any new or challenging sounds and vowel sounds each day. Selectively review 4-5 other consonants.

Large Sound Cards
Practice sounds with the Large Sound Cards. Model these, saying the letter-keyword-sound and have the students echo.

Standard Sound Cards
Next, point to the Standard Sound Cards (in card display) with the Baby Echo pointer. You say the letter-keyword-sound and hold up Baby Echo to have students repeat. You can have a student be the drill leader for some of the sounds.

Word Play

MAKE WORDS FOR DECODING
Use your Standard Sound Card display to make 3-5 Unit words. (See Unit Resources.)

Make each word then say and tap each sound. Have students tap with you. Then blend the sounds as you drag your thumb across your fingers.

Next, point under each card as you say each sound, then drag your finger under all three cards as you and the students blend the sounds to read the word.

READ SENTENCES
Write a sentence on the board and scoop it into phrases. Have the students try to read each word to themselves and then call on a student. Tell them untaught Trick Words. After each word is decoded, chorally read the sentence with fluency. Do 2-3 sentences. (See Unit Resources.)

Unit 5 | Week 4

Day 4

Trick Word Practice

Say each sentence below and have students repeat. Then write the sentence on Sentence Frames, and scoop it into phrases. Read it and have students echo. Say the trick word that is in the sentence and have a student find and circle it. After it is circled, hold up the corresponding Trick Word Flashcard and say the word and have students repeat.

Sentence Resource

This book (is) written (by) (me).

(She) (has) (my) doll.

Lastly present the Trick Word Flashcards, say each and have student repeat.

Make It Fun

GUESS WHERE

Preparation
You will need the narrative stories previously read during Storytime in Units 4 and 5.

Instruct Students
Show books to the students one a time. Read the title, the author and the illustrator's name. Have students recall the main events in each story. Then tell them that you are going to play a guessing game. Say, I am going to describe a place and see if you can guess in which story that setting belongs.

Say

I'm thinking of a story setting that is…(add description).

Unit 5 | Week 4

Day 5

Daily Plan — DAY 5

Student Learning Plan
- Drill Sounds/Warm-Up
- Storytime

Teacher Materials
- Echo and/or Baby Echo
- Large Sound Cards
- Standard Sound Cards
- Narrative and informational book
- Trick Word Flashcards

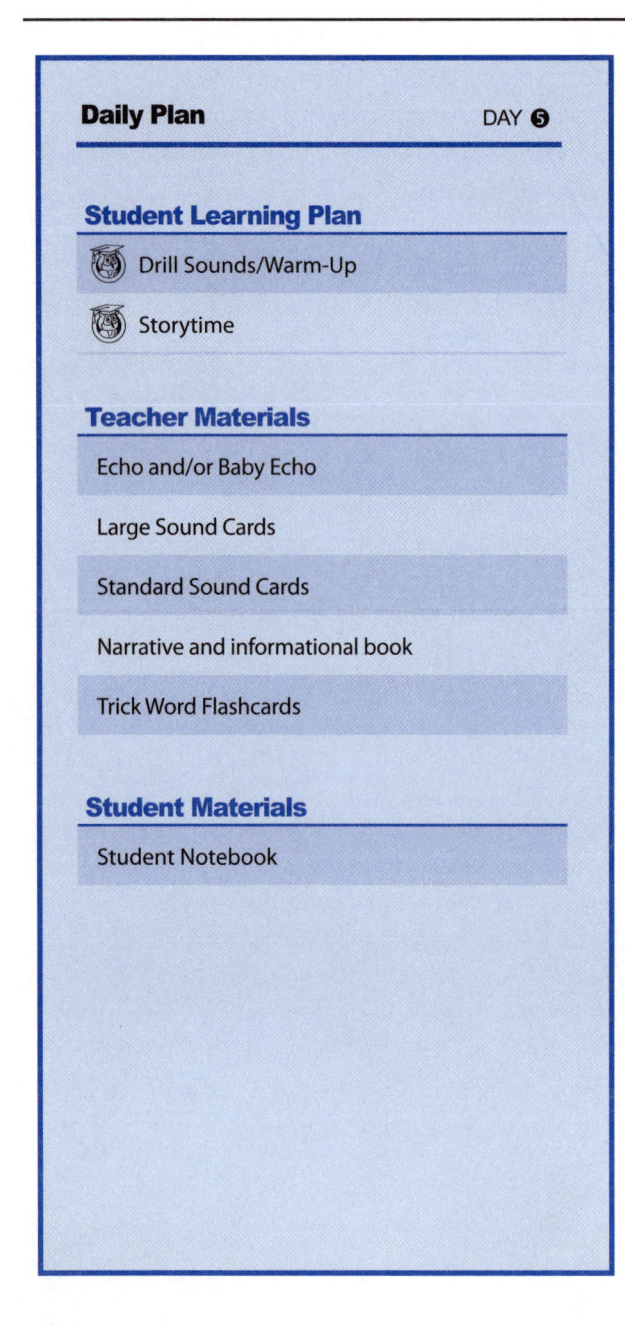

Student Materials
- Student Notebook

Drill Sounds/Warm-Up

Do any new or challenging sounds and vowel sounds each day. Selectively review 4-5 other consonants.

Large Sound Cards
Practice sounds with the Large Sound Cards. Model these, saying the letter-keyword-sound and have the students echo.

Standard Sound Cards
Next, point to the Standard Sound Cards (in card display) with the Baby Echo pointer. You say the letter-keyword-sound and hold up Baby Echo to have students repeat. You can have a student be the drill leader for some of the sounds.

Drill Trick Word Flashcards
Present the Trick Word Flashcards. Have students quickly read the packet. You will eliminate some of the mastered trick words as you add new Level K words to the packet.

Storytime

Preparation

You will select 2 more books to demonstrate narrative fiction versus informational text. Do this by finding a narrative story with an animal in it and a corresponding informational book about that animal. For example, you can select a story about a ladybug in it and then a book about bugs.

Narrative

Carle, E. (1996). *The Grouchy Ladybug*. HarperCollins.

Carle, E. (1994). *The Very Hungry Caterpillar*. Philomel Books.

Informational

Coughlan, C (2006). *Ladybugs*. Capstone Press, MN.

Marsh, L. (2012) *Caterpillar to Butterfly*. National Geographic Society.

Instruct Students

Show the students the two books. Tell them that some books tell make-believe stories and other books tell us facts that are true. Read the narrative book.

Before reading, look at the front and back cover of the book with your students. Discuss the title, author and illustrator, explaining each of those terms.

Ask

Who are the characters in the story?

What is the setting?

Unit 5 | Week 4

Day 5

What are the main events of the story?

What happened first?

Then what happened?

What happened next?

What happened at the end?

Tell the students that stories which are make-believe have something happen in them, and they have an ending like the one you just read.

Then show them the informational book and explain that this book has true facts. Tell them that during Storytime next week, you will read them this book and they will learn some true facts about bugs (or the animal that you have chosen).

tip

Have students draw major events from the story in their My Fundations® Journal. More advanced students can add words or sentences.

Unit 5 | Week 5

Day 1

Daily Plan — DAY 1

Student Learning Plan
- Drill Sounds/Warm-Up
- Word Play
- Dictation (Dry Erase)

Teacher Materials
- Echo and/or Baby Echo
- Large Sound Cards
- Standard Sound Cards
- Sentence Frames
- Trick Word Flashcards

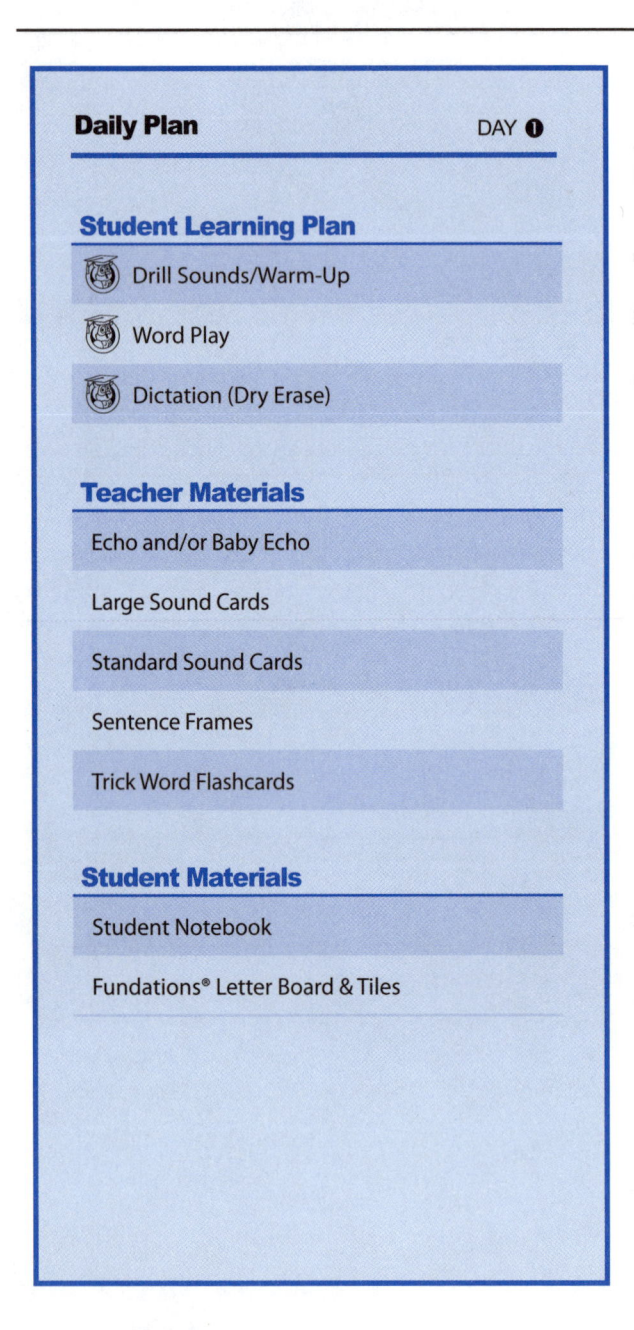

Student Materials
- Student Notebook
- Fundations® Letter Board & Tiles

Drill Sounds/Warm-Up

Do any new or challenging sounds and vowel sounds each day. Selectively review 4-5 other consonants.

Large Sound Cards

Practice sounds with the Large Sound Cards. Model these, saying the letter-keyword-sound and have the students echo.

Standard Sound Cards

Next, point to the Standard Sound Cards (in card display) with the Baby Echo pointer. You say the letter-keyword-sound and hold up Baby Echo to have students repeat. You can have a student be the drill leader for some of the sounds.

Drill Trick Word Flashcards

Present the Trick Word Flashcards. Have students quickly read the packet. You will eliminate some of the mastered trick words as you add new Level K words to the packet.

Word Play

MAKE WORDS FOR DECODING

Use your Standard Sound Card display to make 3-5 Unit words. (See Unit Resources.)

Make each word then say and tap each sound. Have students tap with you. Then blend the sounds as you drag your thumb across your fingers.

Next, point under each card as you say each sound, then drag your finger under all three cards as you and the students blend the sounds to read the word.

READ SENTENCES

Write a sentence on the board and scoop it into phrases. Have the students try to read each word to themselves and then call on a student. Tell them untaught Trick Words. After each word is decoded, chorally read the sentence with fluency. Do 2-3 sentences. (See Unit Resources.)

Unit 5 | Week 5

Day 1

🦉 Dictation (Dry Erase)

Proper Dictation Activity procedures are very important. Be sure to follow their demonstration on the Prevention Learning Community. This is a teaching time, not a testing time. Be sure students repeat each dictation. Dictate 3 sounds and then 3 current or review words and 1 sentence

Unit Sounds
Refer to this Unit's Resource List of Echo Sounds.

Unit Words
Students should tap and orally spell the Unit words before writing. Then have all spell chorally. Have one student write on the Large Writing Grid and all students write on their Dry Erase Writing Tablets. (See Current and Review Words in Unit Resources.)

Sentence
Use the Sentence Frames and dictate one sentence. (See Unit Resources.) Have students echo and have one student place Sentence Frames and circle the frame with a trick word. Have all students write it on their Dry Erase Writing Tablets. Have one student write it on the Sentence Frame. Next, have students scoop their sentence, and read it with fluency. Proofread it together.

Unit 5 | Week 5

Day 2

Daily Plan — DAY 2

Student Learning Plan
- Drill Sounds/Warm-Up
- Word Play
- Teach Trick Words
- Echo/Find Letters & Words

Teacher Materials
- Echo and/or Baby Echo
- Large Sound Cards
- Standard Sound Cards
- Sentence Frames
- Trick Word Flashcards

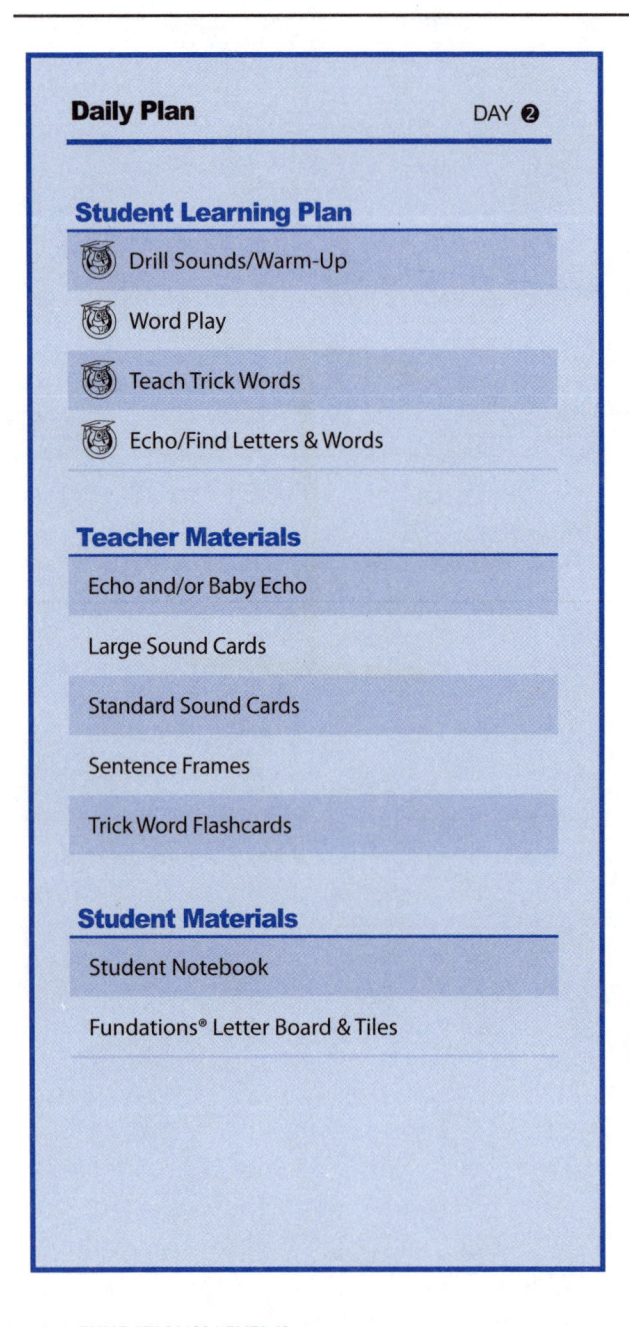

Student Materials
- Student Notebook
- Fundations® Letter Board & Tiles

Drill Sounds/Warm-Up

Do any new or challenging sounds and vowel sounds each day. Selectively review 4-5 other consonants.

Large Sound Cards
Practice sounds with the Large Sound Cards. Model these, saying the letter-keyword-sound and have the students echo.

Standard Sound Cards
Next, point to the Standard Sound Cards (in card display) with the Baby Echo pointer. You say the letter-keyword-sound and hold up Baby Echo to have students repeat. You can have a student be the drill leader for some of the sounds.

Word Play

MAKE WORDS FOR DECODING
Use your Standard Sound Card display to make 3-5 Unit words. (See Unit Resources.)

Make each word then say and tap each sound. Have students tap with you. Then blend the sounds as you drag your thumb across your fingers.

Next, point under each card as you say each sound, then drag your finger under all three cards as you and the students blend the sounds to read the word.

MAKE NONSENSE WORDS
Tell students that they can also blend sounds together to make silly or nonsense words. Explain that these nonsense words are not real words. They are just silly words that show that they can read sounds.

Make 3-5 nonsense words and have students tap and read them (see Unit Resources).

zeth
yit
whep

Unit 5 | Week 5

Day 2

Teach Trick Words

Introduce the trick word **do**, and reinforce capitalization and punctuation.

Instruct Students

Say the sentence below and have students repeat. Have a student place the Sentence Frames as needed. Write the sentence on the frames, and discuss capitalization and punctuation. Scoop the sentence into phrases, read it, and have students echo.

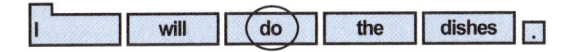

| I | will | (do) | the | dishes | . |

Say

> I am going to circle this word (circle the new trick word). Listen to the sentence and see if you can tell me the word I circled (point to words as you say each one).

Next, explain that the word **do** is a word that you are going to practice, and that this word is called a Trick Word because it can be tricky and we do not tap it out.

Show students the Trick Word Flashcard with **do** Say the word and have them repeat. Lastly, present the Trick Word Flashcards learned thus far. Say each and have students repeat.

Echo/Find Letters & Words

Echo/Find Letters

Say a sound. Have students echo and point to the letter(s) on their Magnetic Letter Boards.

Ask

> What says /___/? (___)

(See Echo Sounds in Unit Resources for expected student responses.)

Have students name the letter(s). Then you can have one student find the Standard Sound Card(s) as you dictate sounds. Do vowels and 3-5 other sounds.

Echo/Find Words

Dictate a Unit word. Do 3-5 words. (See Current Unit Words in Unit Resources.)

Have students find Letter Tiles needed to make words on their Magnetic Letter Boards. Have one student come find your corresponding cards. After finding a word, have students spell it orally and replace the tiles on the letter squares.

lick
puck
chick

Unit 5 | Week 5

Day 3

Daily Plan — DAY 3

Student Learning Plan
- Drill Sounds/Warm-Up
- Word Play
- Echo/Letter Formation
- Dictation (Dry Erase)

Teacher Materials
- Echo and/or Baby Echo
- Large Sound Cards
- Standard Sound Cards
- Large Writing Grid
- Letter Formation Guide
- Sentence Frames
- Trick Word Flashcards

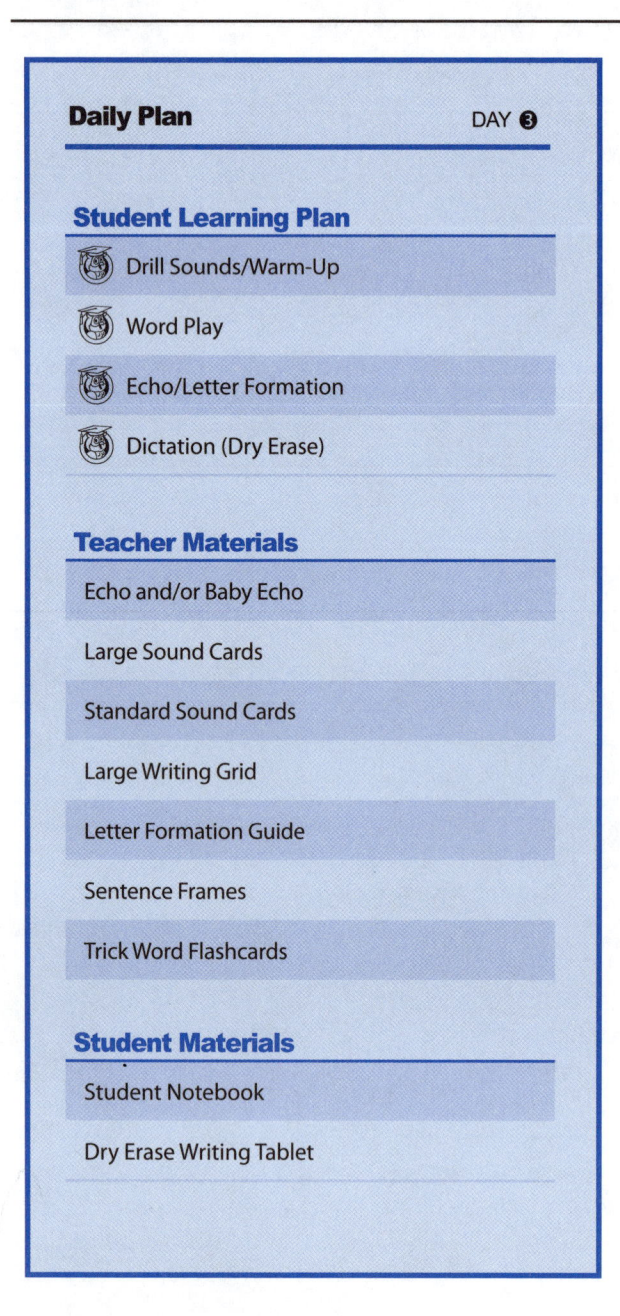

Student Materials
- Student Notebook
- Dry Erase Writing Tablet

Drill Sounds/Warm-Up

Do any new or challenging sounds and vowel sounds each day. Selectively review 4-5 other consonants.

Large Sound Cards
Practice sounds with the Large Sound Cards. Model these, saying the letter-keyword-sound and have the students echo.

Standard Sound Cards
Next, point to the Standard Sound Cards (in card display) with the Baby Echo pointer. You say the letter-keyword-sound and hold up Baby Echo to have students repeat. You can have a student be the drill leader for some of the sounds.

Drill Trick Word Flashcards
Present the Trick Word Flashcards. Have students quickly read the packet. You will eliminate some of the mastered trick words as you add new Level K words to the packet.

Word Play

MAKE WORDS FOR DECODING
Use your Standard Sound Card display to make 3-5 Unit words. (See Unit Resources.)

Make each word then say and tap each sound. Have students tap with you. Then blend the sounds as you drag your thumb across your fingers.

Next, point under each card as you say each sound, then drag your finger under all three cards as you and the students blend the sounds to read the word.

READ SENTENCES
Write a sentence on the board and scoop it into phrases. Have the students try to read each word to themselves and then call on a student. Tell them untaught Trick Words. After each word is decoded, chorally read the sentence with fluency. Do 2-3 sentences. (See Unit Resources.)

[Handwritten notes:]
We can wash and dry our hands.
She likes to eat apples and bananas.

Unit 5 | Week 5

Day 3

Echo/Letter Formation

Remind students of proper pencil grip and sitting position, and give them their Dry Erase Writing Tablets.

Dictate 5-6 previously taught sounds. You select and say the sound. Students echo the sound and say the letter.

Next have a student come up to the classroom board to make the letter on the Large Writing Grid.

Then have all students write the answer on their Dry Erase Writing Tablet as you direct them with the letter formation verbalization.

(See Unit Resources.)

Note
Students can make only lowercase letters, or you can selectively do both uppercase and lowercase to reinforce certain letters. (Be sure to always do lowercase for every sound that is dictated.)

Dictation (Dry Erase)

Proper Dictation Activity procedures are very important. Be sure to follow their demonstration on the Prevention Learning Community. This is a teaching time, not a testing time. Be sure students repeat each dictation. Dictate 3 current or review words and 1 sentence.

Unit Words
Students should tap and orally spell the Unit words before writing. Then have all spell chorally. Have one student write on the Large Writing Grid and all students write on their Dry Erase Writing Tablets. (See Current and Review Words in Unit Resources.)

Sentence
Use the Sentence Frames and dictate one sentence. (See Unit Resources.) Have students echo and have one student place Sentence Frames and circle the frame with a trick word. Have all students write it on their Dry Erase Writing Tablets. Have one student write it on the Sentence Frame. Next, have students scoop their sentence, and read it with fluency. Proofread it together.

[handwritten: rich, with, quick]

[handwritten: I see a red moth.]

Unit 5 | Week 5

Day 4

Daily Plan — DAY 4

Student Learning Plan
- Drill Sounds/Warm-Up
- Trick Word Practice
- Make It Fun
- Dictation (Dry Erase)

Teacher Materials
- Echo and/or Baby Echo
- Large Sound Cards
- Standard Sound Cards
- Sentence Frames
- Trick Word Flashcards

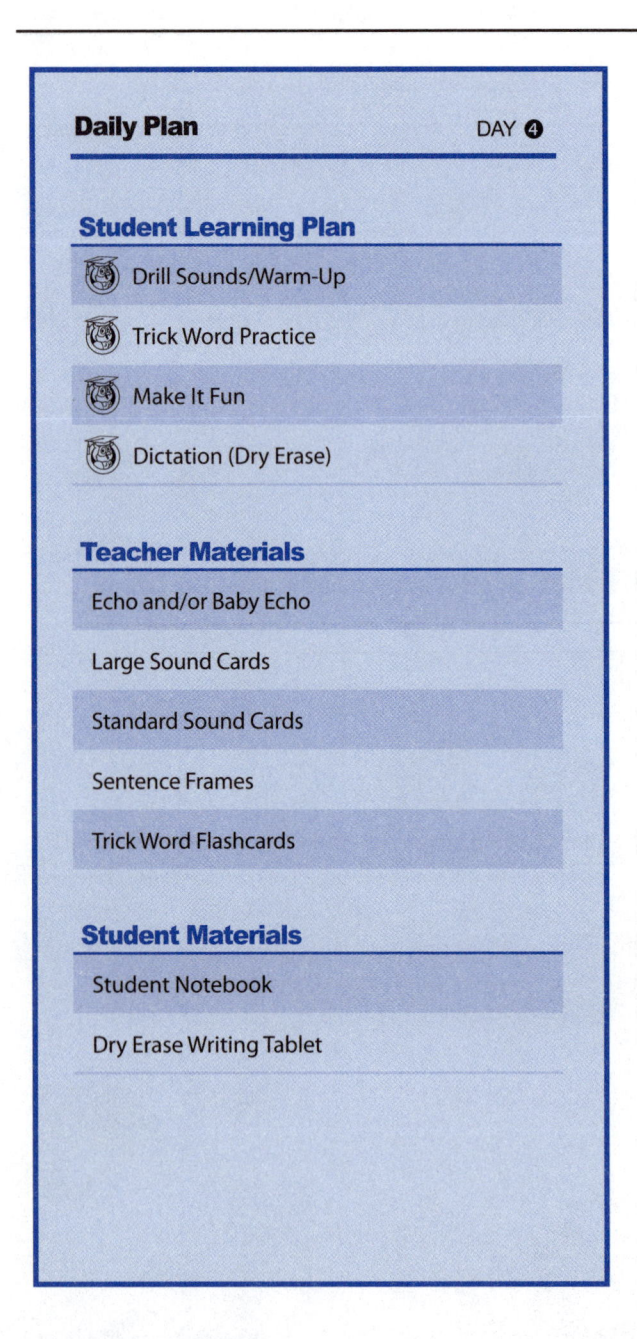

Student Materials
- Student Notebook
- Dry Erase Writing Tablet

Drill Sounds/Warm-Up

Do any new or challenging sounds and vowel sounds each day. Selectively review 4-5 other consonants.

Large Sound Cards

Practice sounds with the Large Sound Cards. Model these, saying the letter-keyword-sound and have the students echo.

Standard Sound Cards

Next, point to the Standard Sound Cards (in card display) with the Baby Echo pointer. You say the letter-keyword-sound and hold up Baby Echo to have students repeat. You can have a student be the drill leader for some of the sounds.

Trick Word Practice

Say each sentence below and have students repeat. Then write the sentence on Sentence Frames, and scoop it into phrases. Read it and have students echo. Say the trick word that is in the sentence and have a student find and circle it. After it is circled, hold up the corresponding Trick Word Flashcard and say the word and have students repeat.

Sentence Resource

Did (you) (do) (my) puzzle yet?

(Are) (they) (my) friends?

This toy (is) (from) (my) dad.

Lastly present the Trick Word Flashcards, say each and have student repeat.

Unit 5 | Week 5

Day 4

Make It Fun

GUESS WHO

Preparation

You will need the narrative stories previously read during Storytime in Unit 4 and 5.

Instruct Students

Show books to the students one a time. Read the title, the author and the illustrator's name. Have students recall the main events in each story. Then tell them that you are going to play another guessing game. Say, I am going to describe a character and see if you can guess in which story that character belongs.

Say

I'm thinking of someone who…(add description).

Dictation (Dry Erase)

Proper Dictation Activity procedures are very important. Be sure to follow their demonstration on the Prevention Learning Community. This is a teaching time, not a testing time. Be sure students repeat each dictation. Dictate 3 sounds, 3 current or review words, and 1 sentence.

Unit Sounds

Refer to this Unit's Resource List of Echo Sounds.

Unit Words

Students should tap and orally spell the Unit words before writing. Then have all spell chorally. Have one student write on the Large Writing Grid and all students write on their Dry Erase Writing Tablets. (See Current and Review Words in Unit Resources.)

Sentence

Use the Sentence Frames and dictate one sentence. (See Unit Resources.) Have students echo and have one student place Sentence Frames and circle the frame with a trick word. Have all students write it on their Dry Erase Writing Tablets. Have one student write it on the Sentence Frame. Next, have students scoop their sentence, and read it with fluency. Proofread it together.

Unit 5 | Week 5

Day 5

Daily Plan — DAY 5

Student Learning Plan
- Drill Sounds/Warm-Up
- Storytime

Teacher Materials
- Echo and/or Baby Echo
- Large Sound Cards
- Standard Sound Cards
- Narrative and informational stories
- Trick Word Flashcards

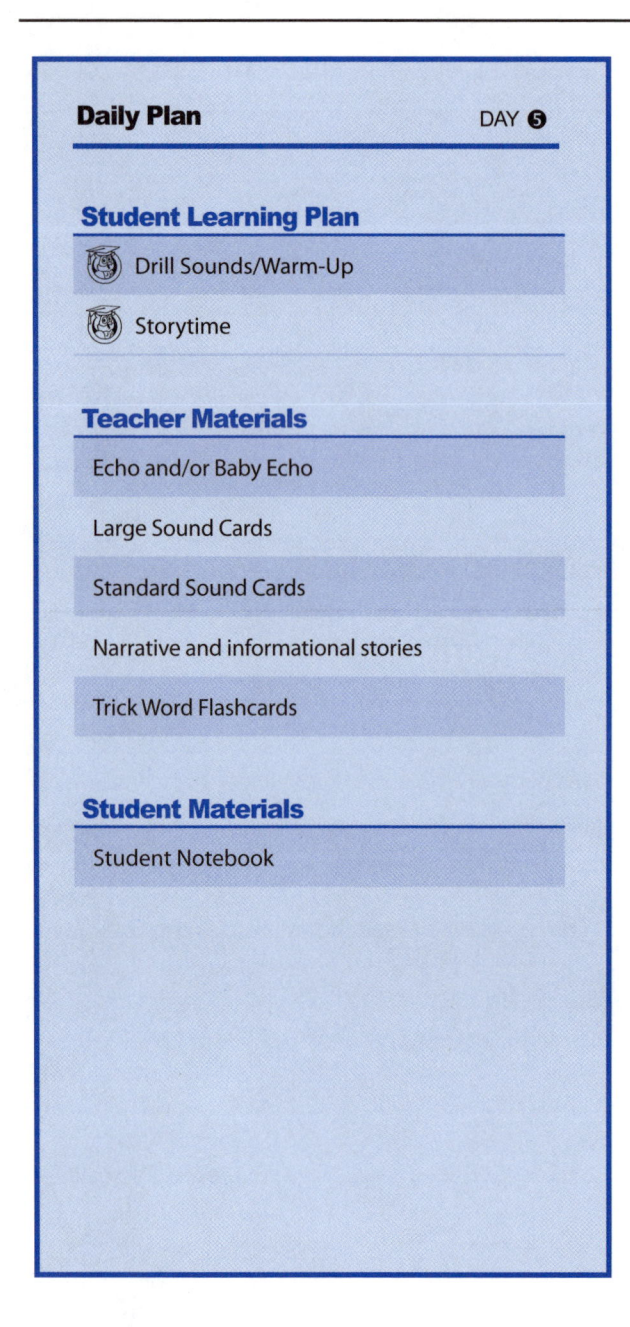

Student Materials
- Student Notebook

Drill Sounds/Warm-Up

Do any new or challenging sounds and vowel sounds each day. Selectively review 4-5 other consonants.

Large Sound Cards

Practice sounds with the Large Sound Cards. Model these, saying the letter-keyword-sound and have the students echo.

Standard Sound Cards

Next, point to the Standard Sound Cards (in card display) with the Baby Echo pointer. You say the letter-keyword-sound and hold up Baby Echo to have students repeat. You can have a student be the drill leader for some of the sounds.

Drill Trick Word Flashcards

Present the Trick Word Flashcards. Have students quickly read the packet. You will eliminate some of the mastered trick words as you add new Level K words to the packet.

Storytime

Preparation

Use the same narrative book and informational book that you had in Week 4.

Narrative

Carle, E. (1996). *The Grouchy Ladybug*. HarperCollins.

Carle, E. (1994). *The Very Hungry Caterpillar*. Philomel Books.

Informational

Coughlan, C (2006). *Ladybugs*. Capstone Press, MN.

Marsh, L. (2012) *Caterpillar to Butterfly*. National Geographic Society.

Instruct Students

Show the students the two books. Tell them that some books tell make-believe stories and other books tell us facts that are true. Read the informational book.

Before reading, look at the front and back cover of the book with your students. Discuss the title, author and illustrator, explaining each of those terms.

Read the book (or part of the book) to your students. After each page, ask them to name one true fact that they have learned.

tip

Have students draw pictures to represent some of the facts in their My Fundations® Journal. More advanced students can write some facts as well.

Unit 5 | Week 5

Unit 5 | Week 6

Day 1

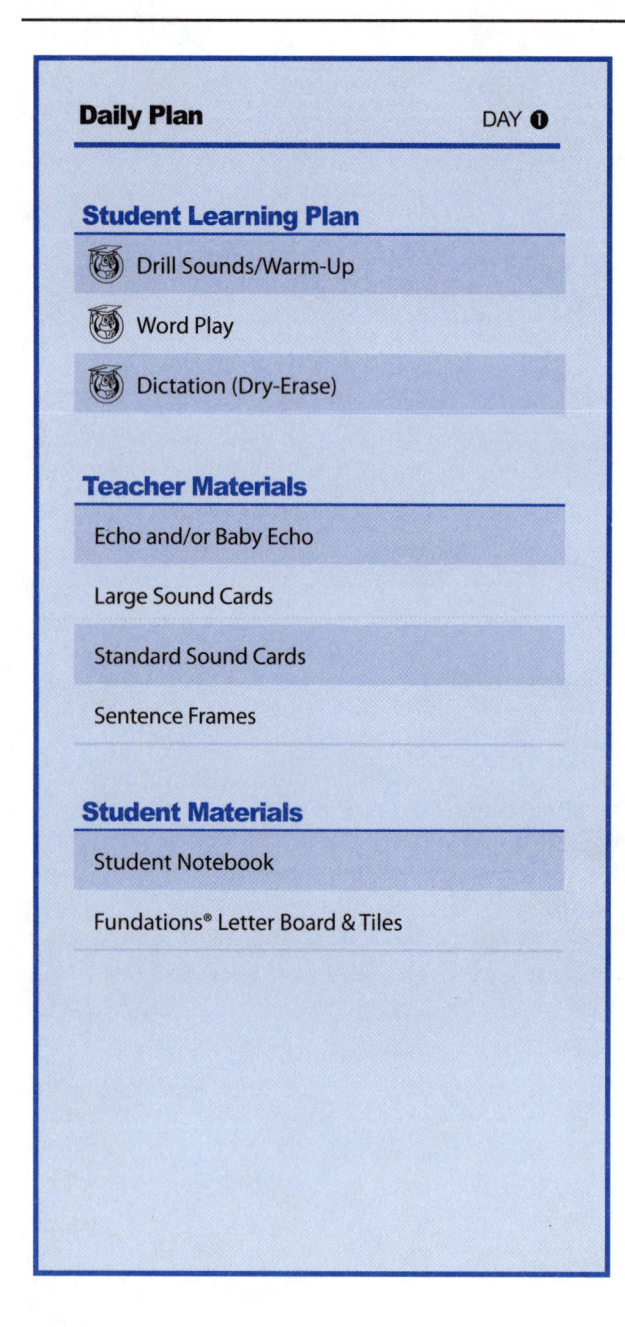

Daily Plan — DAY 1

Student Learning Plan
- Drill Sounds/Warm-Up
- Word Play
- Dictation (Dry-Erase)

Teacher Materials
- Echo and/or Baby Echo
- Large Sound Cards
- Standard Sound Cards
- Sentence Frames

Student Materials
- Student Notebook
- Fundations® Letter Board & Tiles

Drill Sounds/Warm-Up

Do any new or challenging sounds and vowel sounds each day. Selectively review 4-5 other consonants.

Large Sound Cards
Practice sounds with the Large Sound Cards. Model these, saying the letter-keyword-sound and have the students echo.

Standard Sound Cards
Next, point to the Standard Sound Cards (in card display) with the Baby Echo pointer. You say the letter-keyword-sound and hold up Baby Echo to have students repeat. You can have a student be the drill leader for some of the sounds.

Drill Trick Word Flashcards
Present the Trick Word Flashcards. Have students quickly read the packet. You will eliminate some of the mastered trick words as you add new Level K words to the packet.

Word Play

MAKE WORDS FOR DECODING
Use your Standard Sound Card display to make 3-5 Unit words. (See Unit Resources.)

Make each word then say and tap each sound. Have students tap with you. Then blend the sounds as you drag your thumb across your fingers.

Next, point under each card as you say each sound, then drag your finger under all three cards as you and the students blend the sounds to read the word.

READ SENTENCES
Write a sentence on the board and scoop it into phrases. Have the students try to read each word to themselves and then call on a student. Tell them untaught Trick Words. After each word is decoded, chorally read the sentence with fluency. Do 2-3 sentences. (See Unit Resources.)

[Handwritten:] The dog had a big wish to get a bone.

[Handwritten:] My mom has brown hair and green eyes.

Unit 5 | Week 6

Day 1

Dictation (Dry Erase)

Proper Dictation Activity procedures are very important. Be sure to follow their demonstration on the Prevention Learning Community. This is a teaching time, not a testing time. Be sure students repeat each dictation. Dictate 3 sounds, 3 current or review words, and 1 sentence.

Unit Sounds

Refer to this Unit's Resource List of Echo Sounds.

Unit Words

Students should tap and orally spell the Unit words before writing. Then have all spell chorally. Have one student write on the Large Writing Grid and all students write on their Dry Erase Writing Tablets. (See Current and Review Words in Unit Resources.)

Sentence

Use the Sentence Frames and dictate one sentence. (See Unit Resources.) Have students echo and have one student place Sentence Frames and circle the frame with a trick word. Have all students write it on their Dry Erase Writing Tablets. Have one student write it on the Sentence Frame. Next, have students scoop their sentence, and read it with fluency. Proofread it together.

---

thick
rush
whip

My cat can see the sky.

Unit 5 | Week 6

Day 2

Daily Plan — DAY 2

Student Learning Plan
- Drill Sounds/Warm-Up
- Word Play
- Teach Trick Words
- Echo/Find Letters & Words

Teacher Materials
- Echo and/or Baby Echo
- Large Sound Cards
- Standard Sound Cards
- Sentence Frames
- Trick Word Flashcards

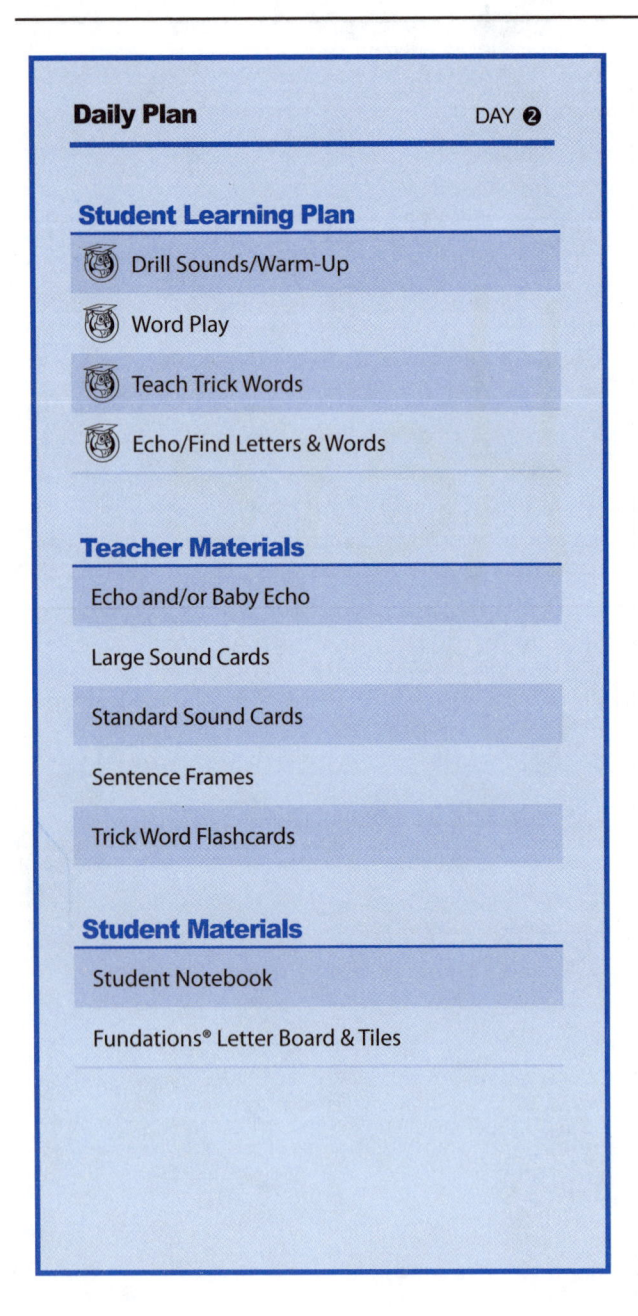

Student Materials
- Student Notebook
- Fundations® Letter Board & Tiles

Drill Sounds/Warm-Up

Do any new or challenging sounds and vowel sounds each day. Selectively review 4-5 other consonants.

Large Sound Cards
Practice sounds with the Large Sound Cards. Model these, saying the letter-keyword-sound and have the students echo.

Standard Sound Cards
Next, point to the Standard Sound Cards (in card display) with the Baby Echo pointer. You say the letter-keyword-sound and hold up Baby Echo to have students repeat. You can have a student be the drill leader for some of the sounds.

Word Play

MAKE WORDS FOR DECODING

Use your Standard Sound Card display to make 3-5 Unit words. (See Unit Resources.)

Make each word then say and tap each sound. Have students tap with you. Then blend the sounds as you drag your thumb across your fingers.

Next, point under each card as you say each sound, then drag your finger under all three cards as you and the students blend the sounds to read the word.

MAKE NONSENSE WORDS

Tell students that they can also blend sounds together to make silly or nonsense words. Explain that these nonsense words are not real words. They are just silly words that show that they can read sounds.

Make 3-5 nonsense words and have students tap and read them (see Unit Resources).

Unit 5 | Week 6

Day 2

Teach Trick Words

Introduce the trick word **one**, and reinforce capitalization and punctuation.

Instruct Students

Say the sentence below and have students repeat. Have a student place the Sentence Frames as needed. Write the sentence on the frames, and discuss capitalization and punctuation. Scoop the sentence into phrases, read it, and have students echo.

| Here | is | (one) | pencil | . |

Say

> I am going to circle this word (circle the new trick word). Listen to the sentence and see if you can tell me the word I circled (point to words as you say each one).

Next, explain that the word **one** is a word that you are going to practice, and that this word is called a Trick Word because it can be tricky and we do not tap it out.

Show students the Trick Word Flashcard with **one**. Say the word and have them repeat. Lastly, present the Trick Word Flashcards learned thus far. Say each and have students repeat.

Echo/Find Letters & Words

Echo/Find Letters

Say a sound. Have students echo and point to the letter(s) on their Magnetic Letter Boards.

Ask

> What says /___/? (___)

(See Echo Sounds in Unit Resources for expected student responses.)

Have students name the letter(s). Then you can have one student find the Standard Sound Card(s) as you dictate sounds. Do vowels and 3-5 other sounds.

Echo/Find Words

Dictate a Unit word. Do 3-5 words. (See Current Unit Words in Unit Resources.)

Have students find Letter Tiles needed to make words on their Magnetic Letter Boards. Have one student come find your corresponding cards. After finding a word, have students spell it orally and replace the tiles on the letter squares.

Unit 5 | Week 6

Day 3

Daily Plan — DAY 3

Student Learning Plan
- Drill Sounds/Warm-Up
- Word Play
- Echo/Letter Formation
- Dictation (Dry Erase)

Teacher Materials
- Echo and/or Baby Echo
- Large Sound Cards
- Standard Sound Cards
- Large Writing Grid
- Letter Formation Guide
- Sentence Frames

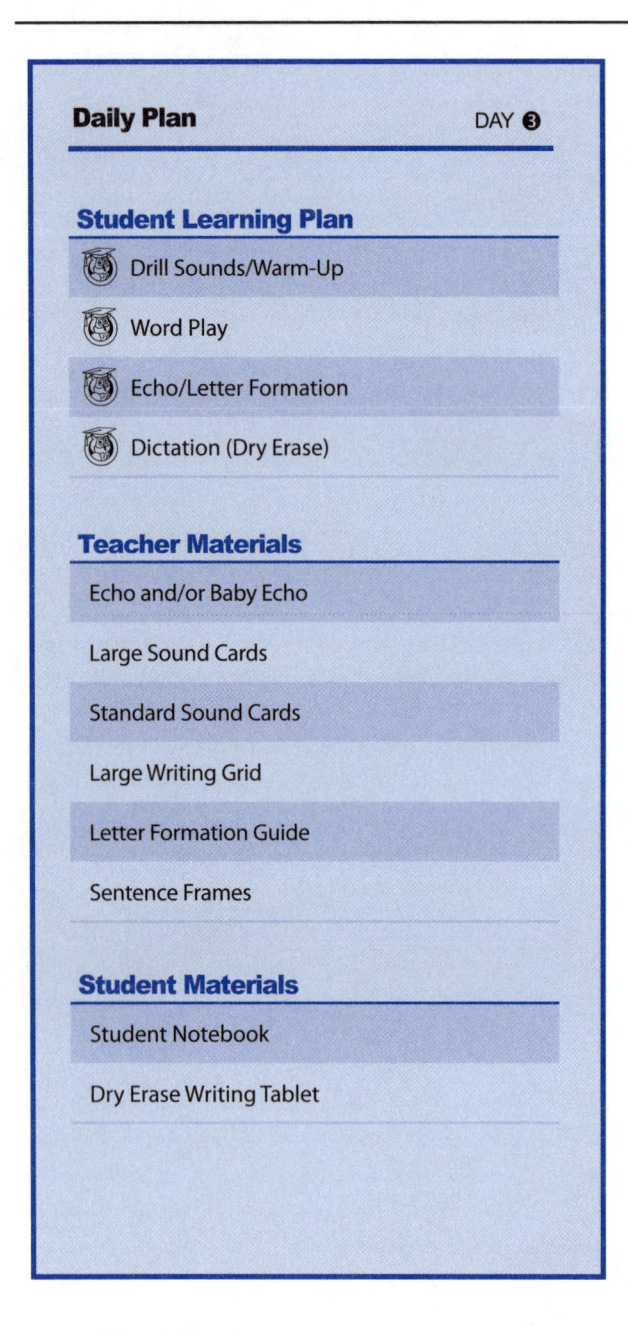

Student Materials
- Student Notebook
- Dry Erase Writing Tablet

Drill Sounds/Warm-Up

Do any new or challenging sounds and vowel sounds each day. Selectively review 4-5 other consonants.

Large Sound Cards
Practice sounds with the Large Sound Cards. Model these, saying the letter-keyword-sound and have the students echo.

Standard Sound Cards
Next, point to the Standard Sound Cards (in card display) with the Baby Echo pointer. You say the letter-keyword-sound and hold up Baby Echo to have students repeat. You can have a student be the drill leader for some of the sounds.

Word Play

MAKE WORDS FOR DECODING
Use your Standard Sound Card display to make 3-5 Unit words. (See Unit Resources.)

Make each word then say and tap each sound. Have students tap with you. Then blend the sounds as you drag your thumb across your fingers.

Next, point under each card as you say each sound, then drag your finger under all three cards as you and the students blend the sounds to read the word.

READ SENTENCES
Write a sentence on the board and scoop it into phrases. Have the students try to read each word to themselves and then call on a student. Tell them untaught Trick Words. After each word is decoded, chorally read the sentence with fluency. Do 2-3 sentences. (See Unit Resources.)

Unit 5 | Week 6

Day 3

Echo/Letter Formation

Remind students of proper pencil grip and sitting position, and give them their Dry Erase Writing Tablets.

Dictate 5-6 previously taught sounds. You select and say the sound. Students echo the sound and say the letter.

Next have a student come up to the classroom board to make the letter on the Large Writing Grid.

Then have all students write the answer on their Dry Erase Writing Tablet as you direct them with the letter formation verbalization.

(See Unit Resources.)

Note
Students can make only lowercase letters, or you can selectively do both uppercase and lowercase to reinforce certain letters. (Be sure to always do lowercase for every sound that is dictated.)

Dictation (Dry Erase)

Proper Dictation Activity procedures are very important. Be sure to follow their demonstration on the Prevention Learning Community. This is a teaching time, not a testing time. Be sure students repeat each dictation. Dictate 3 current or review words and 1 sentence.

Unit Words

Students should tap and orally spell the Unit words before writing. Then have all spell chorally. Have one student write on the Large Writing Grid and all students write on their Dry Erase Writing Tablets. (See Current and Review Words in Unit Resources.)

Sentence

Use the Sentence Frames and dictate one sentence. (See Unit Resources.) Have students echo and have one student place Sentence Frames and circle the frame with a trick word. Have all students write it on their Dry Erase Writing Tablets. Have one student write it on the Sentence Frame. Next, have students scoop their sentence, and read it with fluency. Proofread it together.

Be sure to hold students accountable for correct letter formation!

Unit 5 | Week 6

Day 4

Daily Plan — DAY 4

Student Learning Plan
- Drill Sounds/Warm-Up
- Trick Word Practice
- Make It Fun
- Dictation (Dry Erase)

Teacher Materials
- Echo and/or Baby Echo
- Large Sound Cards
- Standard Sound Cards
- Sentence Frames
- Trick Word Flashcards

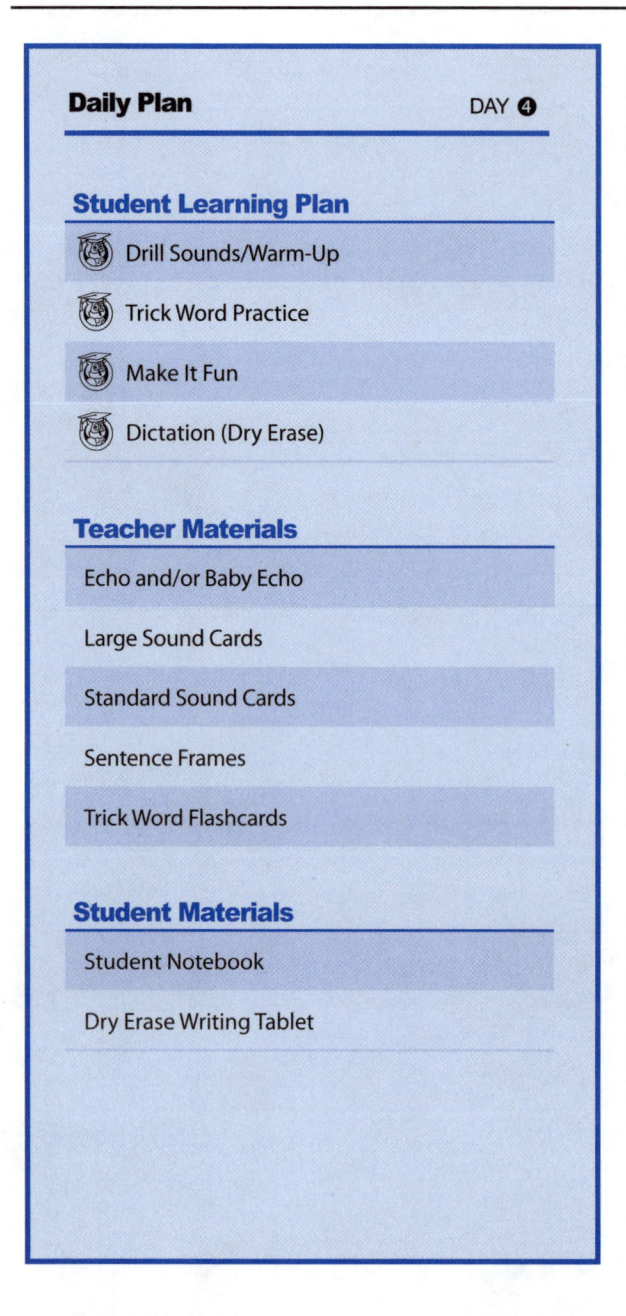

Student Materials
- Student Notebook
- Dry Erase Writing Tablet

Drill Sounds/Warm-Up

Do any new or challenging sounds and vowel sounds each day. Selectively review 4-5 other consonants.

Large Sound Cards

Practice sounds with the Large Sound Cards. Model these, saying the letter-keyword-sound and have the students echo.

Standard Sound Cards

Next, point to the Standard Sound Cards (in card display) with the Baby Echo pointer. You say the letter-keyword-sound and hold up Baby Echo to have students repeat. You can have a student be the drill leader for some of the sounds.

Trick Word Practice

Say each sentence below and have students repeat. Then write the sentence on Sentence Frames, and scoop it into phrases. Read it and have students echo. Say the trick word that is in the sentence and have a student find and circle it. After it is circled, hold up the corresponding Trick Word Flashcard and say the word and have students repeat.

Sentence Resource

(We) can (have) (one) candy.

Bring (one) bone (to) (the) puppy.

(I) have (a) toy (for) (you).

Lastly present the Trick Word Flashcards, say each and have student repeat.

Unit 5 | Week 6

Day 4

Make It Fun

GUESS WHO

Preparation

You will need the narrative stories previously read during Storytime in Unit 4 and 5.

Instruct Students

Show books to the students one a time. Read the title, the author and the illustrator's name. Have students recall the main events in each story. Tell students that you will do another guessing game this week but this time the students will give the hints.

Say

> This week instead of me describing the characters in the stories, I am going to have you describe a character without saying that character's name. You will give hints about the character so the other students can guess who it is.

Select a student and prompt them to describe a character, providing support with questions as needed. Do several characters.

Dictation (Dry Erase)

Proper Dictation Activity procedures are very important. Be sure to follow their demonstration on the Prevention Learning Community. This is a teaching time, not a testing time. Be sure students repeat each dictation. Dictate 3 sounds, 3 current or review words, and 1 sentence.

Unit Sounds

Refer to this Unit's Resource List of Echo Sounds.

Unit Words

Students should tap and orally spell the Unit words before writing. Then have all spell chorally. Have one student write on the Large Writing Grid and all students write on their Dry Erase Writing Tablets. (See Current and Review Words in Unit Resources.)

Sentence

Use the Sentence Frames and dictate one sentence. (See Unit Resources.) Have students echo and have one student place Sentence Frames and circle the frame with a trick word. Have all students write it on their Dry Erase Writing Tablets. Have one student write it on the Sentence Frame. Next, have students scoop their sentence, and read it with fluency. Proofread it together.

Unit 5 | Week 6

Day 5

Daily Plan — DAY 5

Student Learning Plan
- Drill Sounds/Warm-Up
- Storytime

Teacher Materials
- Echo and/or Baby Echo
- Large Sound Cards
- Standard Sound Cards
- Narrative and informational stories
- Unit Test Recording Form

Student Materials
- Student Notebook

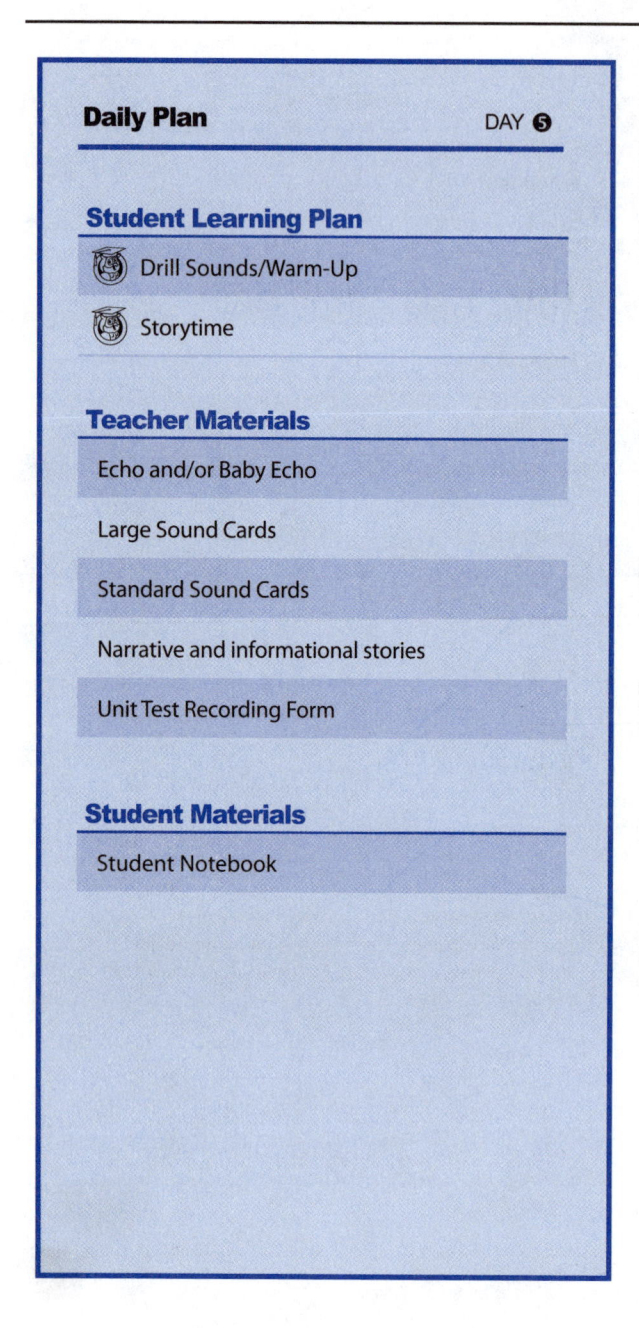

Drill Sounds/Warm-Up

Do any new or challenging sounds and vowel sounds each day. Selectively review 4-5 other consonants.

Large Sound Cards

Practice sounds with the Large Sound Cards. Model these, saying the letter-keyword-sound and have the students echo.

Standard Sound Cards

Next, point to the Standard Sound Cards (in card display) with the Baby Echo pointer. You say the letter-keyword-sound and hold up Baby Echo to have students repeat. You can have a student be the drill leader for some of the sounds.

Drill Trick Word Flashcards

Present the Trick Word Flashcards. Have students quickly read the packet. You will eliminate some of the mastered trick words as you add new Level K words to the packet.

Storytime

Preparation

You will need the narrative and informational books from all previous Storytimes in this Unit.

Instruct Students

Tell students that you want their help to put these books into two piles. In one pile, you are going to put the books that are narrative fiction, or make-believe stories. In the other pile, you are going to put the informational non-fiction books that teach each true facts.

Hold up each book one at a time. Read the title.

Ask

> Does this tell a make-believe story or true facts?

Put all the books in two piles; one for narrative fiction and one for informational non-fiction. Lastly, select each of the informational non-fiction books.

Ask

> Can you tell me some true facts about (topic)?

Unit 5 | Week 6

Unit Test

The first three parts of the Unit 5 test can be given to the whole class for students who are ready to do this on Composition Paper. For students who require more support, do in small groups on their Dry Erase Tablets.

Copy the **Unit Test Recording Form** for each student. Distribute the Dictation Page.

Print the Unit Test Recording Form from the PLC.

If a student does not score at least **4 / 5** correct on any given item, this student will need additional assistance with the assessed skill.

Dictate Sounds

Say a sound, have students repeat and write letter(s) on their Dry Erase Writing Tablets, or on Composition Paper (see PLC).

/m/   /sh/   /ŭ/   /ch/   /k/

Dictate Words

Dictate a word, have students repeat it, tap it out and write it on their Dry Erase Writing Tablet, or on Composition Paper (see PLC).

fox   deck   pit   pack   thud

Dictate Sentence

Dictate a sentence. Have students repeat and write it on their Dry Erase Writing Tablet, or on Composition Paper (see PLC).

The rat had a nap.

Note

Give students one point each for the correct spelling of **rat**, **had** and **nap**. Also give them one point for capitalization and one point for the period. Encourage them to refer to their Student Notebook for the spelling of the Trick Words in the sentence.

Have Student Identify Trick Words

Present trick words on flashcards and have student read them. (Do not tap trick words.)

by   my   or   for   have

Have Student Read a Sentence

Using your Sentence Frames, write the following sentence and have student read it: **Ted had a red bug.** Note which words student reads correctly.

Ted had a red bug.

A Unit Test Tracker is available on Wilson Academy® / Prevention Learning Community, under My Resources. This valuable online resource will allow you to track individual student mastery as well as to evaluate readiness of your class to move on.

For any struggling students, meet with them individually to discuss errors and explain areas that need to be further practiced.

Answer Key

SOUNDS

1. m   2. sh   3. u
4. ch   5. k, c, ck

WORDS

1. fox   2. deck   3. pit
4. pack   5. thud

SENTENCE

The rat had a nap.

TRICK WORDS

1. by   2. my   3. or
4. for   5. have

Note

Allow students to independently reference their Student Notebooks. Count responses checked in their Notebooks as correct but make a notation that the book was used.

Unit 5

Resources

Drill Sounds/Warm-Up

a - apple - /ă/	b - bat - /b/
c - cat - /k/	d - dog - /d/
e - Ed - /ĕ/	f - fun - /f/
g - game - /g/	h - hat - /h/
i - itch - /ĭ/	j - jug - /j/
k - kite - /k/	l - lamp - /l/
m - man - /m/	n - nut - /n/
o - octopus - /ŏ/	p - pan - /p/
qu - queen - /kw/	r - rat - /r/
s - snake - /s/	t - top - /t/
u - up - /ŭ/	v - van - /v/
w - wind - /w/	x - fox - /ks/
y - yellow - /y/	z - zebra - /z/

Echo Sounds

Sounds appear between / /. You say the sound. Students echo the sound and say the letter. Depending on the activity, students then either find or make the letter corresponding to that sound.

CONSONANTS / CONSONANTS DIGRAPHS

/b/ - b	/d/ - d	/f/ - f
/g/ - g	/h/ - h	/j/ - j
/k/ - c, k, ck	/l/ - l	/m/ - m
/n/ - n	/p/ - p	/kw/ - qu
/r/ - r	/s/ - s	/t/ - t
/v/ - v	/w/ - w, wh	/ks/ - x
/y/ - y	/z/ - z	/ch/ - ch
/sh/ - sh	/th/ - th	

VOWELS

/ă/ - a	/ĕ/ - e	/ĭ/ - i
/ŏ/ - o	/ŭ/ - u	

Review Trick Words

the	a	and	are	to	is
his	as	has	was	we	she
he	be	me	I	you	they

Current Trick Words

or	for	of	have	from
by	my	do	one	

Current Unit Words

mop	map	tap	tab	tub	rub
led	lad	bad	bud	bug	rug
dig	dip	zip	zap	wet	bet
bit	fit	fig	fog	rib	sob
job	cop	dot	lid	mud	Ted
fix	lap	web	not	ten	bed
at	hip	peg	had	pen	bat
hit	pet	bus	bun	bib	red
jab	kid	nod	but	cup	mix
pot	Ben	pat	Jim	tin	cob
rat	big	tip	cot	mad	den
gum	mug	sub	wig	yes	fun

Unit 5

Resources

cub	pup	lot	hut	sit	let
gap	sip	dug	cab	Sid	vet
wax	mat	lit	pig	nap	kit
did	pal	fox	nut	gas	him
tug	yet				

DIGRAPHS

rash	such	chip	much	shot	moth
rich	lash	path	dash	whip	math
dish	shut	rush	shop	wish	fish
shed	chin	chop	chat	Beth	with
bath	Seth	thin	thud	ship	mash
whiz	rush	shock	Rick	neck	back
pack	chick	Jack	sock	quick	dock
deck	sick	thick	luck	puck	rack
duck	tuck	lick	sack	lock	peck
quick	quack				

Current Nonsense Words

hig	lon	pem	mub	teb	jep
leck	shob	chig	thup	kiz	mub
thez	nop	vem	fip	kev	rik
mup	niz	wup	faz	thim	sheb

Sentences

*Words in **bold** are trick words. Write trick words on Sentence Frames for students or have them check the spelling in their Student Notebooks.*

Nat **is** sad.

The rag **is** on **the** mat.

The rat had **a** nap.

Mom had **a** map.

Rob **is** on **the** mat.

The rat sat in **the** mud.

Rob sat in **the** sun.

Meg **is** not sad.

Mom sat on **the** log.

The bug **is** in **the** pot.

The gum **is** in **the** bag.

Rob bit **the** fig.

Mom had **a** sip **of** pop.

Deb met Tom.

Deb had **a** bad cut.

Meg had **a** red hat.

The cat hid in **the** box.

The wax **is** hot.

The pup had fun.

Max had **a** dog.

The wig **is** on Viv.

The fox **is** in **the** pen.

Tom had **a** quiz.

Appendix

Appendix

PLC Resources

Obtain these resources on the Prevention/Early Intervention Learning Community

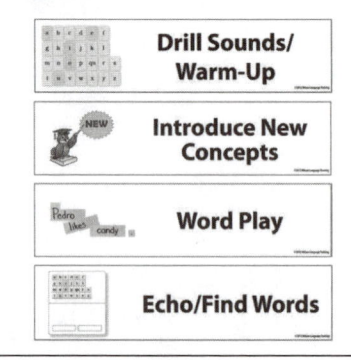

ACTIVITY STRIPS

Post the Activity Strips to introduce the day's Fundations® Activities to students as well as to help the teacher keep organized.

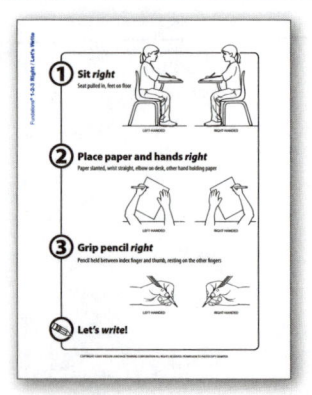

- Drill Sounds/Warm-Up
- Introduce New Concepts
- Word Play
- Echo/Find Words

1-2-3 RIGHT/ LET'S WRITE

Post this picture in the classroom to guide students on correct position and pencil grip for writing.

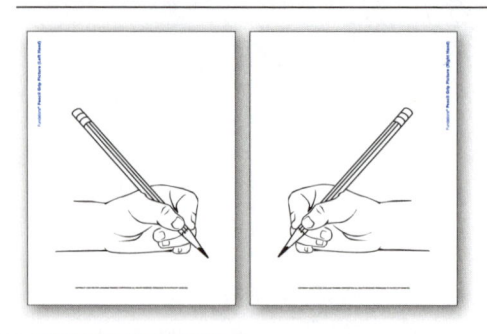

FUNDATIONS PENCIL GRIP (RIGHT HAND AND LEFT HAND)

This picture can be used as a reference for students learning correct pencil grip for writing.

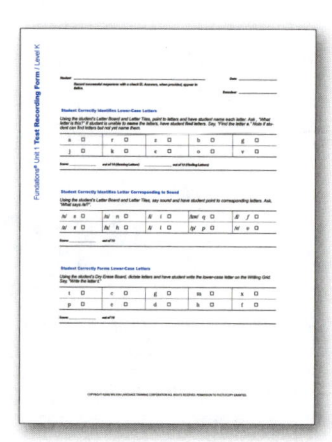

FUNDATIONS UNITS 1- 5 TEST RECORDING FORM/LEVEL K

Copy for each student to use during Unit Tests.

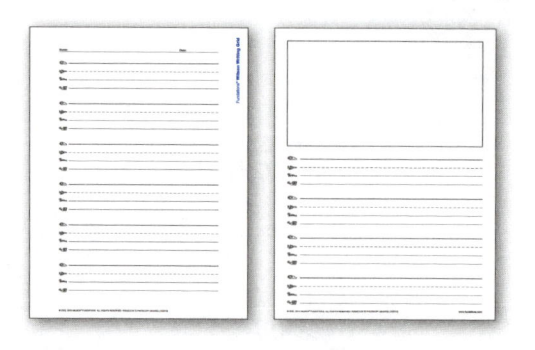

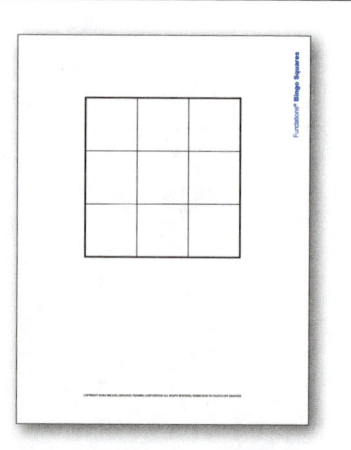

FUNDATIONS COMPOSITION PAPER

Use paper for writing activities.

FUNDATIONS BINGO SQUARES

Copy this page and provide to students for the activity, as directed.

412 FUNDATIONS® LEVEL K

© 2002, 2012 WILSON LANGUAGE TRAINING CORPORATION

Appendix

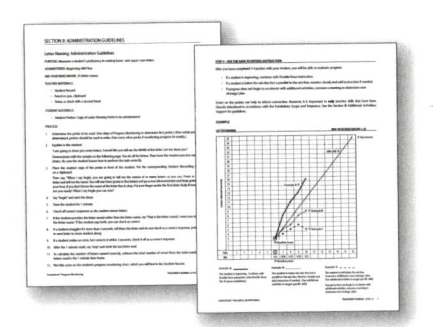

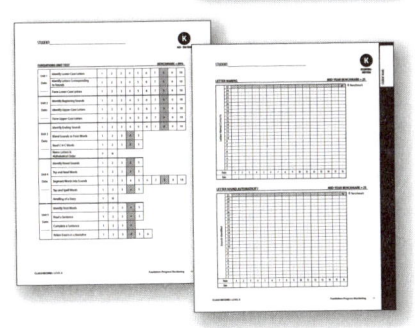

FUNDATIONS® PROGRESS MONITORING TOOL

Use for Tier 2 students to measure progress compared to the skills taught in the curriculum.

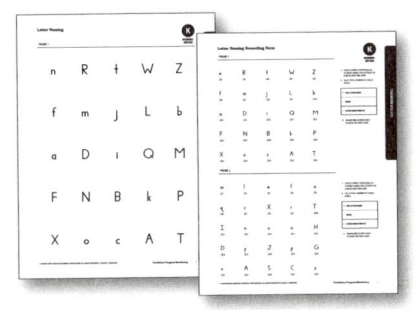

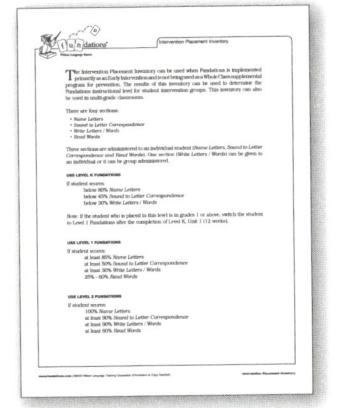

FUNDATIONS INTERVENTION INVENTORY

Use this inventory tool to help place students in the appropriate Fundations Level.

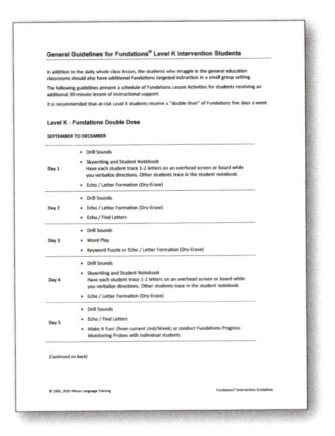

FUNDATIONS INTERVENTION GUIDELINES

Provides guidance and specific recommendations for intervention lessons.

© 2002, 2012 WILSON LANGUAGE TRAINING CORPORATION

TEACHER'S MANUAL 413

NOTES

NOTES

NOTES

NOTES

NOTES